¡Ven conmigo! Adelante

¡Ven conmigo! En camino

Your passport to proficiency

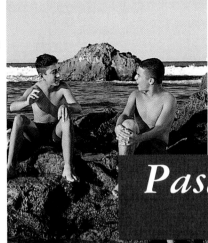

Pasaporte al mundo

Plan your itinerary for success

What's your **Destination?**

Communication!

Adelante and En camino

take your classroom there.

It's even possible that

"What's next?"

becomes your

students' favorite

question!

Communication
and culture in context

The clear structure of each chapter makes it easy to present, practice, and apply language skills—all in the context of the location where the chapter takes place!

Grammar support and
practice in
every lesson

Adelante and *En camino* build a proven communicative approach on a solid foundation of grammar and vocabulary so students become proficient readers, writers, and speakers of Spanish. With the Grammar and Vocabulary Workbook, Grammar Tutor, and the **CD-ROM Tutor,** students can practice the way they learn best.

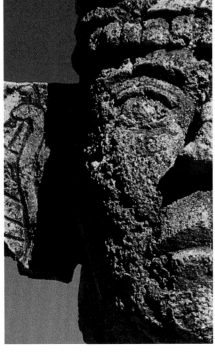

Technology that takes you there

Bring the world into your classroom with integrated audio, video, CD-ROM, and Internet resources that immerse students in authentic language and culture.

Assessment for state and national standards

To help you incorporate standardized test practice, the Standardized Assessment Tutor provides reading, writing, and math tests in Spanish that target the skills students need. The ¡Lee conmigo! Reader and Reading Strategies and Skills Handbook offer additional reading practice and reading skills development.

Easy lesson planning for all learning styles

Planning lessons has never been easier with a Lesson Planner with Substitute Teacher Lesson Plans and a One-Stop Planner® with all resources on CD-ROM.

Travel a balanced program that's easy to navigate.

¡El mundo a su alcance!

The ¡Ven conmigo!® family

or

Program components
Adelante and *En camino*

Texts
- Pupil's Edition
- Teacher's Edition

Planning and Presenting
- One-Stop Planner CD-ROM with Test Generator
- Exploratory Guide
- Lesson Planner with Substitute Teacher Lesson Plans
- Teaching Transparencies

Native Speakers
- Cuaderno para hispanohablantes

Grammar
- Grammar and Vocabulary Workbook
- Grammar Tutor for Students of Spanish

Reading and Writing
- Reading Strategies and Skills Handbook
- ¡Lee conmigo! Reader
- Practice and Activity Book

Listening and Speaking
- Audio CD Program
- Listening Activities
- Activities for Communication
- TPR Storytelling Book

Assessment
- Testing Program
- Grammar and Vocabulary Quizzes
- Alternative Assessment Guide
- Standardized Assessment Tutor

Technology
- One-Stop Planner CD-ROM with Test Generator
- Audio CD Program
- Interactive CD-ROM Tutor
- Video Program
- Video Guide

Internet
- go.hrw.com
- www.hrw.com
- www.hrw.com/passport

HOLT WORLD LANGUAGES
DESTINATION: COMMUNICATION

ANNOTATED TEACHER'S EDITION

¡Ven conmigo!
Adelante
HOLT SPANISH

LEVEL 1A

T 72861

HOLT, RINEHART AND WINSTON

A Harcourt Classroom Education Company

Austin • New York • Orlando • Atlanta • San Francisco • Boston • Dallas • Toronto • London

In the *Annotated Teacher's Edition:*

Photography Credits

Abbreviations used: (t) top, (b) bottom, (c) center, (l)left, (r) right, (i) inset, (bkgd) background.
All pre-Columbian symbols by EclectiCollections/HRW.
All photos by Marty Granger/Edge Video Productions/HRW except:
Front Cover: (bl), Townsend P. Dickinson/Comstock; (br), Dallas and John Heaton/Westlight; (bkgd), © Robert Fried; (c), Joe Viesti/Viesti Associates, Inc. **Front Matter:** Page T1, (cr); T2, (bl), (cr); T3 (bl); T4, (bl), (tr), Sam Dudgeon/HRW Photo; T22 (tc), Stuart Cohen/Comstock; T23 (tl), Christine Galida/HRW Photo; (bc), Peter Van Steen/HRW Photo; T24 (cl), Richard Hutchings/HRW Photo; T32 (br), T43 (c), Michelle Bridwell/Frontera Fotos; T51 (b), Michelle Bridwell/HRW Photo; T55 (bc), Michelle Bridwell/ Frontera Fotos; T61 (b), Sam Dudgeon/HRW Photo. **Preliminary Chapter:** Page T66 (bl), S. Howell/Gamma Liaison, (br) Culver Pictures, Inc. **Location Opener—Spain:** Page15D (c), David R. Frazier Photolibrary. **Chapter Two:** Page 57J (br), Sam Dudgeon/HRW Photo. **Location Opener—Mexico:** Page 97D (b), Jorge Nuñez/Latin Focus. **Location Opener—Florida:** Page 183B (br), Latin Focus; 183C (cl), Tony Arruza; 183D (b), Steve Ferry/P & F Communications.

Illustration Credits

All art, unless otherwise noted, by Holt, Rinehart & Winston.
Preliminary Chapter: Page T71, Deborah Haley Melmon/Sharon Morris Associates.
Chapter One: Page 15C, MapQuest.com. **Chapter Two:** Page 57F, Eldon Doty/Pat Hackett. **Chapter Three:** Page 97C, MapQuest.com; 101F, Elizabeth Brandt; 101I, Michael Morrow; 101J, Deborah Haley Melmon/Sharon Morris Associates. **Chapter Four:** 141E, Edson Campos; 141F, Deborah Haley Melmon/Sharon Morris Associates, 141K, Eva Vagretti Cockrille. **Chapter Five:** 183C, MapQuest.com; 187J, Deborah Haley Melmon/Sharon Morris Associates. **Chapter Six:** 227F, Edson Campos; 227H, Lori Osiecki; 227J, Fian Arroyo/ Dick Washington.

In the *Pupil's Edition:*

Acknowledgments

For permission to reprint copyrighted material, grateful acknowledgment is made to the following sources:

Banco Central de Cuenca: Excerpts and illustrations from "Calendario de Eventos" from *60 Aniversario de la Fundación del Banco Central de Cuenca, Antiguo Hospital San Vicente de Paul,* June–July 1988.

Bayard Revistas-Súper Júnior: Excerpts and illustrations from "¡Anímate a escribir!" from *Súper Júnior,* no. 22–23, July–August, 1996. Copyright © 1996 by Súper Júnior Bayard Revistas, Hispano Francesa de Ediciones, S.A.

Cines Lumiere: Advertisement for "Cines Lumiere" from *Guía El País,* no. 57, December 27, 1990.

Club de Tenis Las Lomas: Advertisement for "Club de Tenis Las Lomas" from *Guía El País,* no. 57, December 27, 1990.

Editorial Atlántida, S.A.: Videocassette cover from *Billiken presenta: Mundo Marino.* Jacket cover from *La isla del terror* by Tony Koltz, illustrations by Ron Wing. Photograph from "Empezar con todo" from *Billiken: Diccionario Escolar,* primera entrega, no. 3765, March 9, 1992. Copyright © 1992 by Editorial Atlántida, S.A. Illustration on page 34 from *Billiken de Regalo: Almanaque 1997,* no. 4016, December 30, 1996. From "Deportes en el agua" by Alejandra Becco from *Billiken,* February 17, 1992. Copyright © 1992 by Editorial Atlántida, S.A.

Editorial Eres: Illustration "Regresa a clases" from *Eres,* December 16, 1993. Copyright © 1993 by Editorial Eres.

Editorial Everest, S.A.: Front cover and text from *Everest enciclopedia ilustrada de los animales, Tomo I: Mamíferos* by Dr. Philip Whitfield. Copyright © by Editorial Everest, S.A.

Editorial Televisa, S.A.: Adapted from *Tele*Guía,* año 42, no. 2159, December 25–31, 1993. Copyright ©1993 by Editorial Television, S.A. From "La Chica Sándwich" from *Tú internacional,* año 14, no. 1, January 1993. Copyright ©1993 by Editorial América, S.A. Header and adapted excerpts from "línea directa" from *Tú internacional,* año 14, no. 6, June 1993. Copyright ©1993 by Editorial América, S.A.

Emecé Editores España, S.A.: Illustration and text from jacket cover for *50 cosas que los niños pueden hacer para salvar la tierra* by The Earth Works Group.

Gativideo S.A.: Videocassette cover from *Las nuevas aventuras de Mofli* by Gativideo.

Hotel Agua Escondida: Advertisement for Hotel Agua Escondida.

Instituto Municipal de Deportes, Ayuntamiento de Madrid: Advertisement for "Piscina Municipal Aluche" from the "En Forma" section from *Guía El País,* no. 57, December 27, 1990.

Metro Vídeo Española, S.L.: Videocassette cover from *Los dinosaurios. Su descubrimiento.*

The Quintus Communications Group: Excerpts from "Diez cosas curiosas para hacer en la Pequeña Habana" from *Miami Mensual,* año 13, no. 3, March 1993. Copyright © 1993 by The Quintus Communications Group.

ANNOTATED TEACHER'S EDITION CREDITS

Contributing Writers

Dr. Marjorie E. Artzer
Northern Kentucky University
Highland Heights, KY

Jackie Moase-Burke
Language Arts Oakland Schools
Clinton Township, MI

Elizabeth Coscio
Houston, TX

Pablo Muirhead Montesinos
Shorewood Intermediate School
Milwaukee, WI

Jacqueline Hall-Muirhead
Pius XI High School
Milwaukee, WI

Lois Seijo
Churchville Middle School
Elmhurst, IL

Paula Camardella Twomey
Ithaca High School
Ithaca, NY

*The following people researched and wrote
culture features:*

Mildred Cancel-García
Austin, TX

Mary Nichols
Austin, TX

Mariángeles LaPointe
Austin, TX

Amy Propps
Austin, TX

Field Test Participants

Bill Braden
South Junior High School
Boise, ID

Paula Critchlow
Indian Hills Middle School
Sandy, UT

Frances Cutter
Convent of the Visitation School
St. Paul, MN

Carlos Fernández
Sandy Creek High School
Tyrone, GA

Maureen Fischer
Marian Catholic High School
Chicago Heights, IL

Jan Holland
Lovejoy High School
Lovejoy, GA

Nancy Holmes
Marian Catholic High School
Chicago Heights, IL

Gloria Holmstrom
Emerson Junior High School
Yonkers, NY

K. A. Lagana
Ponus Ridge Middle School
Norwalk, CT

Michelle Mistric
Iowa High School
Iowa, LA

Rubén Moreno
Aycock Middle School
Greensboro, NC

Fred Pratt
San Marcos High School
San Marcos, TX

Regina Salvi
Museum Junior High School
Yonkers, NY

Lorraine Walsh
Lincoln Southeast High School
Lincoln, NE

Reviewers

Dr. Edward D. Allen
Ohio State University
Columbus, OH

Daniel J. Bender
Adlai Stevenson High School
Lincolnshire, IL

Marie Carrera Lambert
Iona College
New Rochelle, NY

Dr. June Carter
The University of Texas
Austin, TX

Myrtress G. Eddleman
Carver High School
Birmingham, AL

Rubén Garza
James Bowie High School
Austin, TX

Joseph N. Harris
Poudre School District
Fort Collins, CO

Stephen L. Levy
Roslyn Public Schools
Roslyn, NY

Laura Olson
Austin Waldorf School
Austin, TX

Carmen Reyes
Jonesboro High School
Jonesboro, GA

Dr. Yolanda Russinovich Solé
The University of Texas
Austin, TX

Brian A. Souza
Plymouth South High School
Plymouth, MA

Elena Steele
Clark County School District
Las Vegas, NV

Dora Villani
John F. Kennedy High School
Bronx, NY

Jo Anne S. Wilson
J. Wilson Associates
Glen Arbor, MI

Professional Essays

*Technology in the Foreign
Language Classroom*
Cindy A. Kendall
Williamston High School
Williamston, MI

*Standards for Foreign
Language Learning*
Robert LaBouve
Board of National Standards in
Foreign Language Education
Austin, TX

Teaching Culture
Nancy A. Humbach
Miami University
Oxford, OH

Dorothea Bruschke
Parkway School District
Chesterfield, MO

*Using Portfolios in the Foreign
Language Classroom*
Jo Anne S. Wilson
J. Wilson Associates
Glen Arbor, MI

*Learning Styles and
Multi-Modality Teaching*
Mary B. McGehee
Louisiana State University
Baton Rouge, LA

New Perspectives for Native Speakers
Cecilia Rodríguez-Pino
New Mexico State University
Las Cruces, NM

AUTHORS

Nancy A. Humbach
Miami University
Ms. Humbach collaborated in the development of the scope and sequence and video material, and created activities and culture features.

Dr. Oscar Ozete
University of Southern Indiana
Dr. Ozete collaborated in the development of the scope and sequence, reviewed all Pupil's Edition material, and wrote grammar explanations.

CONTRIBUTING WRITERS

Dr. Pennie Nichols-Alem
Baton Rouge, LA
Dr. Nichols-Alem wrote the
Enlaces.

Susan Peterson
The Ohio State University
Columbus, OH
Mrs. Peterson selected realia for readings and developed reading activities.

CONSULTANTS

John DeMado
John DeMado Language Seminars
Washington, CT

Dr. Ingeborg R. McCoy
Southwest Texas State University
San Marcos, TX

Jo Anne S. Wilson
J. Wilson Associates
Glen Arbor, MI

REVIEWERS

Susan Campbell
Lisha Kill Middle School
Albany, New York

Rocco Fuschetto
Northside Middle School
Muncie, Indiana

Gabriela Gándara
Austin, TX

Ester García
Coral Gables Senior High
Coral Gables, FL

Francisco González-Soldevilla
Mast Academy
Miami, FL

Gretchen Hatcher
Foley Senior High School
Foley, AL

Sheila D. Landre
Turlock Junior High School
Turlock, CA

Steve Lucero
Arrowview Middle School
San Bernardino, CA

Mary Luzzi
Lisha Kill Middle School
Albany, NY

Marta Meacham
Bethlehem Central High School
Delmar, NY

Joanne Micale
Lisha Kill Middle School
Albany, NY

Linda Nass
Farnsworth Middle School
Guilderland, NY

Francisco Perea
Austin, TX

Gail Saucedo
Coronado Middle School
Coronado, CA

Barbara Sawhill
The Noble and Greenough School
Dedham, MA

Lois Seijo
Churchville Middle School
Elmhurst, IL

Teresa Shu
Austin, TX

Paula Twomey
Ithaca High School
Ithaca, NY

Cristina Villarreal
Houston, TX

FIELD TEST PARTICIPANTS

We express our appreciation to the teachers and students who participated in the field test. Their comments were instrumental in the development of this program.

Bill Braden
South Junior High School
Boise, ID

Paula Critchlow
Indian Hills Middle School
Sandy, UT

Gloria Holmstrom
Emerson Junior High School
Yonkers, NY

K.A. Lagana
Ponus Ridge Middle School
Norwalk, CT

Rubén Moreno
Aycock Middle School
Greensboro, NC

Regina Salvi
Museum Junior High School
Yonkers, NY

iii

T8

TO THE STUDENT

Some people have the opportunity to learn a new language by living in another country. Most of us, however, begin learning another language and getting acquainted with another culture in a classroom with the help of a teacher, classmates, and a book. To use your book effectively, you need to know how it works.

Adelante *(Let's get started)* is the first book in a series called *¡Ven conmigo!* It's organized to help you learn about the Spanish language and about the cultures of people who speak Spanish. A Preliminary Chapter presents some basic concepts in Spanish and offers some strategies for learning a new language. This is followed by six chapters and three Location Openers. Each of these six chapters and each Location Opener follow the same pattern.

Adelante takes you to three different Spanish-speaking locations. Each location you visit is introduced with photos and information on four special pages called the Location Openers. You can also see these locations on video and on CD-ROM.

The two Chapter Opener pages at the beginning of each chapter tell you about the chapter theme and goals. These goals outline what you learn to do in each section of the chapter.

De antemano *(Getting started)* This part of the chapter is an illustrated story that shows you Spanish-speaking people in real-life situations, using the language you'll learn in the chapter. You also might watch this story on video.

Primer, Segundo, and **Tercer paso** *(First, Second, Third Part)* After **De antemano,** the chapter is divided into three sections called **pasos.** At the beginning of each **paso,** there is a reminder of the goals you'll aim for in this part. Within the **paso,** you will find boxes called **Así se dice** *(Here's how to say it)* that give the Spanish expressions you'll need to communicate. You'll also find boxes called **Vocabulario** that list new vocabulary you'll need to know and that you'll be responsible for on the Chapter Test. Along with the new expressions and vocabulary words, you'll need to learn certain structures. These structures are provided in the **Gramática** and **Nota gramatical** boxes. To learn all the new expressions, vocabulary, and grammar,

there are several fun activities to practice what you're learning. These activities help you develop your listening, speaking, reading, and writing skills. By the end of each **paso,** you'll have met your goal.

Panorama cultural *(Cultural Panorama)* On this page of the chapter, you'll read interviews with Spanish-speaking people around the world. They'll talk about themselves and their lives, and you can compare their culture to yours. You can watch these interviews on video or listen to them on CD. You can also watch them on a computer using the CD-ROM program, then check to see if you've understood by answering some questions.

Nota cultural *(Culture Note)* Within each chapter, there are culture notes to give you more information about the culture of Spanish-speaking people. These notes might tell you interesting facts, describe common customs, or offer other information that will help you understand what's expected of you if you visit a Spanish-speaking area.

Encuentro cultural *(Cultural Encounter)* This culture section is found in every even-numbered chapter. A native Spanish-speaker will host a first-hand encounter with some aspect of Spanish-speaking culture. You can also watch this section on the video.

Enlaces *(Links)* These pages link the study of Spanish-speaking culture with other subjects you might be studying at school, such as social studies, science, or math.

Vamos a leer *(Let's read)* You'll find the reading section after the three **pasos**. The readings, which are related to the chapter theme, will help you develop your reading skills in Spanish. The **Estrategia** in each chapter will give you helpful strategies to improve your reading comprehension.

iv

Repaso *(Review)* These review pages give you the chance to practice what you've learned in the chapter. You'll improve your listening and reading skills and practice communicating with others. You'll also practice what you've learned about culture.

A ver si puedo *(Let's see if I can . . .)* This page will help you check what you've learned without your teacher's help. A series of questions, followed by short activities, will help you decide how well you can do on your own. Page numbers beside each section will tell you where to go for help if you need it.

Throughout each chapter, certain special features provide extra tips and reminders. **Sugerencia** *(Suggestion)* offers helpful study hints to help you succeed in a foreign language class. **¿Te acuerdas?** *(Do you remember?)* reminds you of grammar and vocabulary you may have forgotten. **Vocabulario extra** *(Extra Vocabulary)* gives you some extra words to use when talking about yourself and your own special interests.

Vocabulario *(Vocabulary)* You'll find a Spanish-English vocabulary list on the last page of the chapter. The words are grouped by the **paso** they're in. These are the words that will be required on the quizzes and tests.

You'll also find Spanish-English and English-Spanish vocabulary lists at the end of the book. The words you'll need to know for the quizzes and tests will be in bold face type.

Also, at the end of your book, you'll find more helpful material, such as:
- a summary of the expressions you'll learn in the **Así se dice** boxes
- a summary of the grammar you'll study
- additional vocabulary words you might want to use
- a grammar index to help you find where grammar structures are introduced

Adelante Let's get started on an exciting trip to new cultures and a new language!

¡Buen viaje!

EXPLANATION OF ICONS IN ADELANTE

Throughout *Adelante* you'll see these symbols, or icons, next to activities. They'll tell you what you'll probably do with that activity. Here's a key to help you understand the icons.

Listening Activities
This icon means that this is a listening activity. You'll need to listen to the CD or your teacher in order to complete the activity.

CD-ROM Activities
Whenever this icon appears, it lets you know that there's a related activity on the *Interactive CD-ROM Program.*

Internet Activities
This icon will remind you to check the **¡Ven conmigo!** Internet site for additional activities and games to practice what you are learning. Enter the keyword under the icon and click on "Go."

Writing Activities
When you see this icon, it means that the activity is a writing activity. The directions may ask you to write words, sentences, paragraphs, or a whole composition.

Pair Work Activities
Activities with this icon are designed to be completed with a partner. Both you and your partner are responsible for completing the activity.

Group Work Activities
If an activity has this icon next to it, you can expect to complete it with two or three of your classmates. Each person in the group is responsible for a share of the work.

PARA MEJOR APRENDER EL ESPAÑOL

How best to learn Spanish

LISTEN

It's important to listen carefully in class. Take notes and ask questions if you don't understand, even if you think your question seems a little silly. Other people are probably wondering the same thing you are. You won't be able to understand everything you hear at first, but don't feel frustrated. You're actually absorbing a lot even when you don't realize it.

ORGANIZE

Your memory is going to get a workout, so it's important to get organized. Throughout the textbook you'll see learning tips (**Sugerencias**) that can improve your study skills. For starters, here's a hint: see things with your mind. Associate each new word, sentence, or phrase with an exaggerated or unusual mental picture. For example, if you're learning the word **regla** *(ruler),* visualize an enormous ruler on an enormous desk as you practice saying a sentence with the word.

EXPAND

Increase your contact with Spanish outside of class in every way you can. You may be able to find someone living near you who speaks Spanish. It's easy to find Spanish-language programs on TV, on the radio, or at the video store. Many magazines and newspapers in Spanish are published or sold in the United States. Don't be afraid to read, watch, or listen. You won't understand every word, but that's okay. You can get a lot out of a story or an article by concentrating on the words you do recognize and doing a little intelligent guesswork.

SPEAK

Practice speaking Spanish aloud every day. Talking with your teachers and classmates is an easy and fun way to learn. Don't be afraid to experiment. Your mistakes will help identify problems, and they'll show you important differences in the way English and Spanish "work" as languages.

PRACTICE

Learning a foreign language is like learning to ride a bicycle or play an instrument. You can't spend one night cramming and then expect instantly to be able to ride or play the next morning. You didn't learn English that way either! Short, daily practice sessions are more effective than long, once-a-week sessions. Also, try to practice with a friend or a classmate. After all, language is about communication, and it takes two to communicate.

CONNECT

Some English and Spanish words have common roots in Latin, and the two languages have influenced each other, so your knowledge of English can give you clues about the meaning of many Spanish words. Look for an English connection when you need to guess at unfamiliar words. You may also find that learning Spanish will help you in English class!

HAVE FUN!

Above all, remember to have fun! The more you try, the more you'll learn. Besides, having fun will help you relax, and relaxed people learn better and faster. **¡Buena suerte!** *(Good luck!)*

ANNOTATED TEACHER'S EDITION

Contents

Adelante *Contents*

Come along—to a world of new experiences!

Adelante offers you the opportunity to learn the language spoken by millions of people in the many Spanish-speaking countries around the world. Let's find out about the countries, the people, and the Spanish language.

vii

¡Ven conmigo a España!

VISIT THE EXCITING CITY OF MADRID WITH FOUR SPANISH-SPEAKING TEENAGERS AND—

Introduce yourself to some
Spanish-speaking students • CAPÍTULO 1

Talk about what you need
and want to do • CAPÍTULO 2

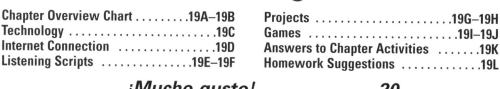

CAPÍTULO 1

¡Mucho gusto! 20

Capítulo 2

¡Organízate! 58

¡Ven conmigo a México!

CAPÍTULO ③

Nuevas clases, nuevos amigos 102

x

T16

CAPÍTULO 4

¿Qué haces esta tarde?. 142

xi

T17

¡Ven conmigo a la Florida!

VISIT THE LIVELY CITY OF MIAMI WITH
FIVE HISPANIC TEENAGERS AND—

Talk about what you do during a
typical week • CAPÍTULO 5

Describe a family • CAPÍTULO 6

CAPÍTULO 5

El ritmo de la vida *188*

CAPÍTULO ⑥

Entre familia............ 228

Page numbers referring to material in the Pupil's Edition *appear in regular type. Page numbers for material located in the Annotated Teacher's Edition appear in boldface type.*

Telephone

Transportation

Vacation

Variation in the Spanish Language

Sayings and Expressions

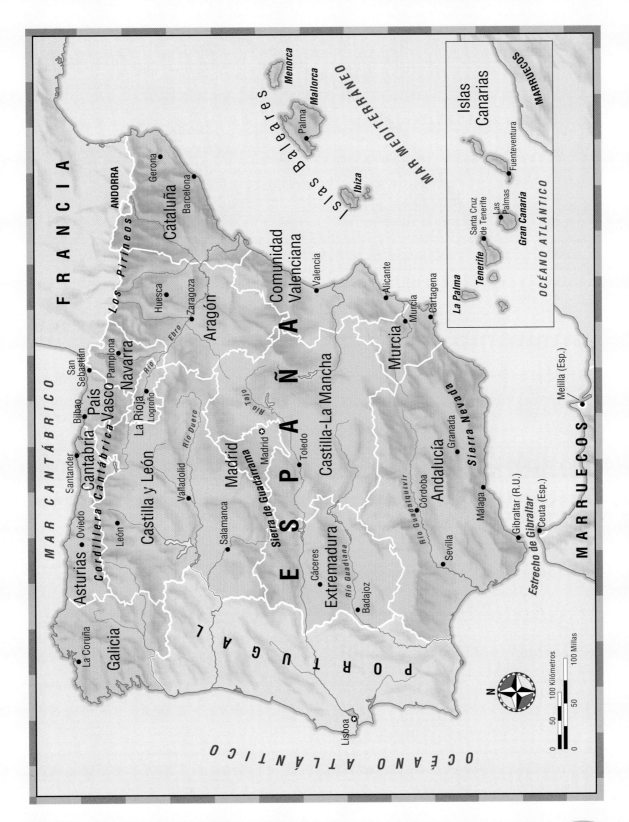

LA PENÍNSULA IBÉRICA

FRANCIA

ANDORRA

Los Pirineos

Gerona

Cataluña

Barcelona

Menorca

Mallorca

Palma

Ibiza

Islas Baleares

MAR MEDITERRÁNEO

Huesca

Zaragoza

Aragón

Ebro

Comunidad
Valenciana

Valencia

Alicante

San
Sebastián

Bilbao

País
Vasco

Navarra

Pamplona

La Rioja

Logroño

Río

Río Tajo

Murcia

Murcia

Cartagena

MAR CANTÁBRICO

Santander

Cantabria

Cordillera Cantábrica

Asturias

Oviedo

Castilla y León

León

Valladolid

Río Duero

Madrid

Madrid

Sierra de Guadarrama

Toledo

Castilla-La Mancha

Granada

Sierra Nevada

Andalucía

La Coruña

Galicia

Salamanca

Cáceres

Extremadura

Río Guadiana

Badajoz

Río Guadalquivir

Córdoba

Sevilla

Málaga

Gibraltar (R.U.)

Estrecho de Gibraltar

Ceuta (Esp.)

MARRUECOS

Melilla (Esp.)

E S P A Ñ A

P O R T U G A L

Lisboa

O C É A N O   A T L Á N T I C O

N

100 Kilómetros

100 Millas

50

50

0

0

Islas Canarias

MARRUECOS

Fuenteventura

Las
Palmas

Gran Canaria

Santa Cruz
de Tenerife

Tenerife

La Palma

OCÉANO ATLÁNTICO

xvii

T25

OCÉANO
ÁRTICO

GROENLANDIA
(DINAMARCA)

ALASKA
(EE.UU.)

CANADÁ

AMÉRICA
DEL NORTE

OCÉANO
ATLÁNTICO

Ottawa

Nueva York

ESTADOS UNIDOS
DE AMÉRICA

Washington, D.C.

BERMUDA
(R.U.)

Islas Canarias
(Esp.)

MARRUECOS

SAHARA
OCCIDENTAL

ISLAS HAWAII
(EE.UU.)

La Habana

BAHAMAS

MÉXICO

CUBA

REP. DOMINICANA

CABO VERDE

MAURITANIA

Ciudad de México

JAMAICA

PUERTO RICO (EE.UU.)

SENEGAL

BELICE

HAITÍ

San Juan

GAMBIA

BURK
FAS

GUATEMALA
EL SALVADOR

HONDURAS
NICARAGUA

GUINEA BISSAU

OCÉANO PACÍFICO

COSTA RICA

Caracas

TRINIDAD Y TOBAGO

SIERRA LEONA

COSTA
DE
MARFIL

PANAMÁ

VENEZUELA

GUYANA
SURINAM

LIBERIA

GUYANA FRANCESA

GUINEA EQUATO

Bogotá

Ecuador

Islas Galápagos
(Ecuador)

COLOMBIA

SANTO TOMÉ Y PRÍNCIPE

ECUADOR

KIRIBATI

AMÉRICA
DEL SUR

BRASIL

PERÚ

Lima

OCÉANO
ATLÁNTICO

BOLIVIA

PARAGUAY

Río de Janeiro

ARGENTINA

CHILE

URUGUAY

Santiago

Buenos
Aires

N

Islas Malvinas
(R.U.)

| 0 | 1,000 | 2,000 Kilómetros |
| 0 | 1,000 | 2,000 Millas |

A N

RUSIA

KAZAJSTÁN
MONGOLIA
ASIA
Pekín
COREA DEL NORTE
JAPÓN
Seúl
Tokio
COREA DEL SUR
CHINA
OCÉANO PACÍFICO

GEORGIA
ARMENIA
UZBEKISTÁN
TURKMENISTÁN
KIRGUIZISTÁN
TAJIKISTÁN
AFGANISTÁN
Teherán
Ankara
TURQUÍA
LÍBANO SIRIA IRAQ
Damasco
ISRAEL
El Cairo
Bagdad
IRÁN
JORDANIA
KUWAIT
ARABIA SAUDITA
BAHREIN
QATAR
UNIÓN DE EMIRATOS ÁRABES
OMÁN
EGIPTO
PAQUISTÁN
Nueva Delhi
NEPAL
BHUTÁN
INDIA
MYANMAR
BANGLADESH
LAOS
TAILANDIA
VIETNAM
CAMBOYA
Taipeh
TAIWÁN
Manila
FILIPINAS
GUAM (EE.UU.)

SUDÁN
ERITREA
YEMEN
YIBUTI
ETIOPÍA
SOMALIA
SRI LANKA
REPÚBLICA CENTROAFRICANA
Ecuador
MALASIA

UGANDA
KENIA
RUANDA
BURUNDI
Nairobi
SEYCHELLES
OCÉANO ÍNDICO
INDONESIA
PAPÚA NUEVA GUINEA
KIRIBATI
NAURÚ
ISLAS SALOMÓN
ISLAS TUVALU
REPÚBLICA DEL CONGO
TANZANIA
COMORES
MALAWI
ZAMBIA
ZIMBABWE
MADAGASCAR
MAURICIO
VANUATU
NUEVA CALEDONIA (Fr.)
ISLAS FIDJI
BOTSWANA
MOZAMBIQUE
AUSTRALIA
SWAZILANDIA
LESOTHO
Pretoria
ÁFRICA
Canberra
Wellington
NUEVA ZELANDIA

TIDA

	PAÍS	CAPITAL
1	REPÚBLICA CHECA	Praga
2	REPÚBLICA ESLOVACA	Bratislava
3	ESLOVENIA	Liubliana
4	CROACIA	Zagreb
5	BOSNIA Y HERZEGOVINA	Sarajevo
6	MACEDONIA	Skopje
7	YUGOSLAVIA	Belgrado
8	LITUANIA	Vilna
9	LETONIA	Riga
10	ESTONIA	Tallin
11	LIECHTENSTEIN	Vaduz
12	LUXEMBURGO	Luxemburgo

Europa

OCÉANO ÁRTICO
ISLANDIA
Reikiavik
NORUEGA
SUECIA
FINLANDIA
Helsinki
Oslo
Estocolmo
San Petersburgo
RUSIA
10
Moscú
REINO UNIDO
DINAMARCA
Copenhague
9
8
Minsk
Dublín
HOLANDA
Amsterdam
Berlín
Varsovia
BIELORRUSIA
IRLANDA
Londres
BÉLGICA
Bruselas
ALEMANIA
POLONIA
Kiev
UCRANIA
OCÉANO ATLÁNTICO
París
FRANCIA
SUIZA
Berna
12
Viena
AUSTRIA HUNGRÍA
11
1
2
Kishinev
MOLDAVIA
3
4
5
7
RUMANIA
Bucarest
Roma
6
Sofía
MAR NEGRO
PORTUGAL
Madrid
ANDORRA
ITALIA
Tirana
BULGARIA
Lisboa
ESPAÑA
ALBANIA
Atenas
TURQUÍA
GRECIA
MAR MEDITERRÁNEO
MALTA
CHIPRE

xix

T27

AMÉRICA DEL SUR

MAR DE LAS ANTILLAS

OCÉANO ATLÁNTICO

América Central

Cartagena
Maracaibo
Caracas
VENEZUELA
Río Orinoco
Ciudad Bolívar
GUYANA
SURINAM
Georgetown
Paramaribo
Cayena
GUYANA FRANCESA

Medellín
COLOMBIA
Bogotá

Islas Galápagos (Ecuador)

Quito
ECUADOR
Guayaquil
Cuenca

Río Putumayo
Cordillera

Río Amazonas
Manaus

Ecuador

Belén

B R A S I L

Recife

PERÚ
Andes
de los
Lima
Cuzco

Lago Titicaca
La Paz
BOLIVIA
Sucre

Brasilia

Salvador

OCÉANO

Cordillera de los

Río Paraná
PARAGUAY
Asunción
San Pablo
Río de Janeiro

Trópico de Capricornio

CHILE
Tucumán
Río
ARGENTINA
Córdoba

PACÍFICO

Andes
Valparaíso
Mendoza
Santiago
Buenos Aires
URUGUAY
Montevideo
Río de la Plata

N

Bariloche

OCÉANO

ATLÁNTICO

Cordillera de los

0   500   1.000 Kilómetros
0   500   1.000 Millas

Andes

Estrecho de Magallanes
Islas Malvinas (R.U.)

Punta Arenas
Tierra del Fuego

Cabo de Hornos

XX

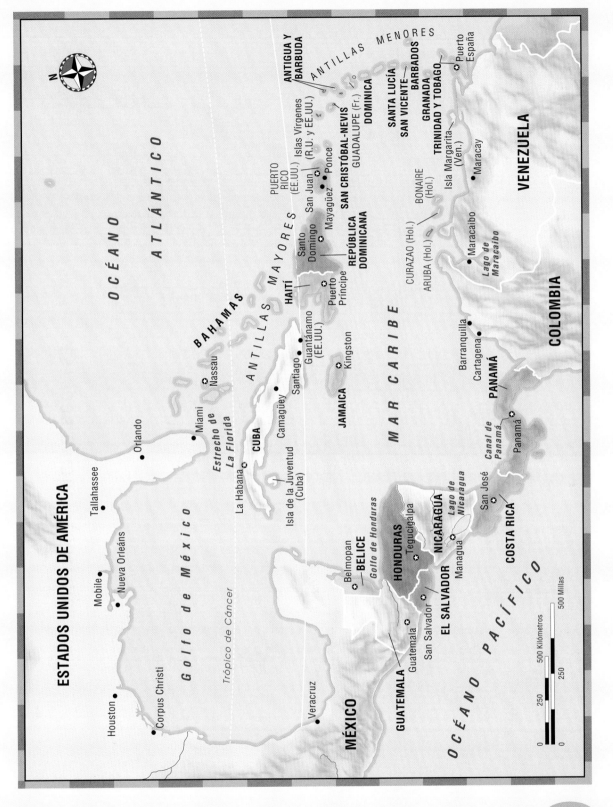

AMÉRICA CENTRAL Y LAS ANTILLAS

ESTADOS UNIDOS DE AMÉRICA

OCÉANO ATLÁNTICO

Houston •
Corpus Christi •
Mobile •
Nueva Orleáns •
Tallahassee •
Orlando •
Miami •

MÉXICO

Veracruz •

Golfo de México

Trópico de Cáncer

Estrecho de La Florida

La Habana •

CUBA

Isla de la Juventud (Cuba)

Camagüey •
Santiago •

BAHAMAS

Nassau ✪

ANTILLAS MAYORES

ANTILLAS MENORES

ANTIGUA Y BARBUDA

Puerto España ✪

PUERTO RICO (EE.UU.)
Islas Vírgenes (R.U. y EE.UU.)
San Juan ●
Ponce ●
Mayagüez •

SAN CRISTÓBAL-NEVIS
GUADALUPE (Fr.)
DOMINICA
SANTA LUCÍA
SAN VICENTE
BARBADOS
GRANADA
TRINIDAD Y TOBAGO

Santo Domingo ✪

REPÚBLICA DOMINICANA

HAITÍ

Puerto Príncipe ✪

Guantánamo (EE.UU.) •

Kingston ✪

JAMAICA

MAR CARIBE

BONAIRE (Hol.)
Isla Margarita (Ven.)
Maracay •

VENEZUELA

CURAZAO (Hol.)
ARUBA (Hol.)

Maracaibo •
Lago de Maracaibo

COLOMBIA

Barranquilla •
Cartagena •

PANAMÁ

Canal de Panamá
Panamá ✪

San José ✪

COSTA RICA

Lago de Nicaragua

NICARAGUA

Managua ✪

Lago de Honduras

Tegucigalpa ✪

HONDURAS

Golfo de Honduras

Belmopan ✪

BELICE

EL SALVADOR

San Salvador ✪

GUATEMALA

Guatemala ✪

OCÉANO PACÍFICO

500 Kilómetros
250
250
0
500 Millas
250
250
0

ESTADOS UNIDOS DE AMÉRICA

CLAVE DE ESTADOS

1. NAYARIT
2. COLIMA
3. AGUASCALIENTES
4. GUANAJUATO
5. QUERÉTARO
6. HIDALGO
7. MÉXICO
8. DISTRITO FEDERAL
9. MORELOS
10. PUEBLA
11. TLAXCALA
12. NUEVO LEÓN
13. SAN LUIS POTOSÍ
14. TABASCO

Trópico de Cáncer

OCÉANO

PACÍFICO

Tijuana
Mexicali
San Diego

BAJA CALIFORNIA

BAJA CALIFORNIA SUR

La Paz

Nogales
Nogales
Tucson

SONORA

Hermosillo

Ciudad Juárez
El Paso

CHIHUAHUA

Chihuahua

Río Conchos

Sierra Madre Occidental

MÉXICO

Culiacán

SINALOA

Mazatlán

Puerto Vallarta

Tepic

Colima

JALISCO

Aguascalientes

Guadalajara

Río Lerma

Morelia

MICHOACÁN

Toluca

Taxco

Río Balsas

Acapulco

GUERRERO

Oaxaca

OAXACA

San Cristóbal
de Las Casas

CHIAPAS

Golfo de Tehuantepec

Río Usumacinta

Villahermosa

DURANGO

Durango

ZACATECAS

Zacatecas

San Luis
Potosí

Guanajuato

Querétaro

Pachuca

México, D.F.

Tlaxcala

Puebla

VERACRUZ

Veracruz

Torreón

COAHUILA

Río Bravo del Norte

Sierra Madre Oriental

Ciudad
Victoria

TAMAULIPAS

Del Río

Nuevo
Laredo
Laredo

Reynosa
Monterrey

Matamoros
Brownsville

San Antonio

McAllen

Houston

Galveston

Puerto
Arturo

Baton
Rouge

Nueva Orleáns

Golfo de México

Campeche

CAMPECHE

YUCATÁN

Mérida

QUINTANA
ROO

Chetumal

Cozumel

GUATEMALA

BELICE

HONDURAS

N

0
125
125
250 Kilómetros
0
125
125
250 Millas

T30

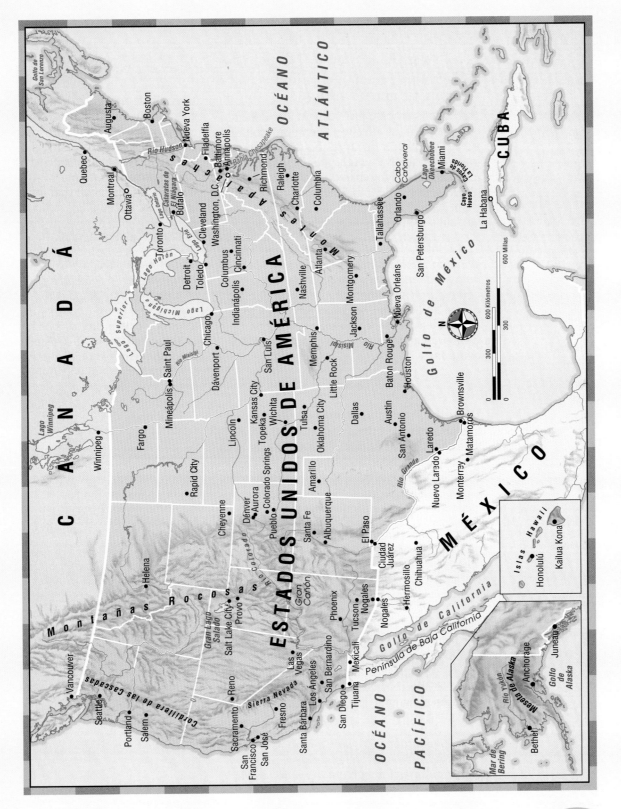

Golfo de San Lorenzo

CANADÁ

OCÉANO ATLÁNTICO

CUBA

Quebec
Montreal
Ottawa
Augusta
Boston
Nueva York
Filadelfia
Baltimore
Annápolis
Washington, D.C.
Richmond
Raleigh
Charlotte
Columbia

Lago Winnipeg
Winnipeg

Toronto
Buffalo
Cleveland
Detroit
Toledo
Columbus
Cincinnati
Indianápolis
Chicago

Lago Ontario
Lago Erie
Lago Hurón
Lago Michigan
Lago Superior

Cataratas de El Niágara
Río Hudson
Bahía Chesapeake

Montes Apalaches

ESTADOS UNIDOS DE AMÉRICA

Atlanta
Nashville
Tallahassee
Orlando
San Petersburgo
Miami
La Habana

Cabo Cañaveral
Lago Okeechobee
Cayos de la Florida
Cayo Hueso

Golfo de México

Fargo
Mineápolis
Saint Paul
Dávenport
Rapid City
Lincoln
Kansas City
Topeka
Wichita
Tulsa
Oklahoma City
Little Rock
Memphis
San Luis
Jackson
Montgomery
Nueva Orleáns
Baton Rouge
Houston
Dallas
Austin
San Antonio
Laredo
Brownsville
Matamoros

Río Misisipi
Río Misisipi

N
600 Kilómetros
600 Millas
300
300
0
0

Helena
Cheyenne
Dénver
Aurora
Colorado Springs
Pueblo
Santa Fe
Amarillo
Albuquerque
El Paso
Ciudad Juárez

Montañas Rocosas

Río Colorado

Nuevo Laredo
Monterrey

MÉXICO

Vancouver
Seattle
Portland
Salem
Sacramento
Reno
Salt Lake City
Provo
Las Vegas
San Bernardino
Los Ángeles
San Diego
Tijuana
Mexicali
Nogales
Nogales
Tucson
Phoenix
Hermosillo
Chihuahua

Gran Lago Salado
Gran Cañón
Sierra Nevada
Cordillera de las Cascadas

San Francisco
San José
Fresno
Santa Bárbara

OCÉANO PACÍFICO

Golfo de California
Península de Baja California

Islas Hawaii
Honolulú
Kailua Kona

Río Yukón
Meseta de Alaska
Anchorage
Juneau
Golfo de Alaska
Bethel
Mar de Bering

xxiii

TO THE TEACHER

In recent years, we have seen significant advances in modern foreign language curriculum practices:

1 *a redefinition of the objectives of foreign language study involving a commitment to the development of proficiency in the four skills and in cultural awareness;*

2 *a recognition of the need for longer sequences of study;*

3 *a new student-centered approach that redefines the role of the teacher as facilitator and encourages students to take a more active role in their learning;*

4 *the inclusion of students of all learning abilities.*

The new Holt, Rinehart and Winston foreign language programs take into account not only these advances in the field of foreign language education, but also the input of teachers and students from around the country. ◆

Principles and Practices

As nations become increasingly interdependent, the need for effective communication and sensitivity to other cultures becomes more important. Today's youth must be culturally and linguistically prepared to participate in a global society. At Holt, Rinehart and Winston, we believe that proficiency in more than one language is essential to meeting this need.

The primary goal of the Holt, Rinehart and Winston foreign language programs is to help students develop linguistic proficiency and cultural sensitivity. By interweaving language and culture, our programs seek to broaden students' communication skills while deepening their appreciation of other cultures.

◆◆◆

We believe that all students can benefit from foreign language instruction. We recognize that not everyone learns at the same rate or in the same way; nevertheless, we believe that all students should have the opportunity to acquire language proficiency to a degree commensurate with their individual abilities.

Holt, Rinehart and Winston's foreign language programs are designed to accommodate all students by appealing to a variety of learning styles.

◆◆◆

We believe that effective language programs should motivate students. Students deserve an answer to a question they often ask: "Why are we doing this?" They need to have goals that are interesting, practical, clearly stated, and attainable.

Holt, Rinehart and Winston's foreign language programs promote success. They present interesting content in manageable increments that encourage students to achieve the functional objectives.

We believe that proficiency in a foreign language is best nurtured by programs that encourage students to think critically and to take risks when expressing themselves in the language. We also recognize that students should strive for accuracy in communication. While it is imperative that students have a knowledge of the basic structures of the language, it is also important that they go beyond the simple manipulation of forms.

Holt, Rinehart and Winston's foreign language program reflects a careful progression of activities that guides students from comprehensible input of authentic language through structured practice to creative, personalized expression. This progression, accompanied by consistent re-entry and spiraling of functions, vocabulary, and structures, provides students with the tools and the confidence to express themselves in their new language.

◆◆◆

Finally, we believe that a complete program of language instruction should take into account the needs of teachers in today's increasingly demanding classrooms.

At Holt, Rinehart and Winston, we have designed programs that offer practical teacher support and provide resources to meet individual learning and teaching styles.

USING THE PUPIL'S EDITION

¡Ven conmigo!
Adelante

Adelante *offers an integrated approach to language learning. Presentation and practice of functional expressions, vocabulary, and grammar structures are interwoven with cultural information, language-learning tips, and realia to facilitate both learning and teaching. The technology, audiovisual materials, and additional print resources integrated into each chapter allow instruction to be adapted to a variety of teaching and learning styles.* ◆

¡Ven conmigo! Adelante Level 1A

Adelante consists of a preliminary chapter that introduces students to Spanish and the Spanish-speaking world, followed by six instructional chapters. Below is a description of the various features in *Adelante* and suggestions on how to use them in the classroom. While it is not crucial for students to cover all material and do all activities to achieve the goals listed at the beginning of each chapter, the material within each chapter has been carefully sequenced to enable students to progress steadily at a realistic pace to the ultimate goal of linguistic and cultural proficiency. As presenter, facilitator, and guide, you will determine the precise depth of coverage, taking into account the individual needs of each class and the amount and type of alternative instructional material to be used from the *Adelante* program.

Setting the Scene . . .

In *Adelante* chapters are arranged in groups of two, with each pair of chapters set in a different Spanish-speaking location. Each new location is introduced by a **Location Opener**, four pages of colorful photos and background information that can be used to introduce the region and help motivate students.

The two-page **Chapter Opener** is intended to pique students' interest and focus their attention on the task at hand. It is a visual introduction to the theme of the chapter and includes a list of objectives they will be expected to achieve.

Starting Out . . .

Language instruction begins with **De antemano**, comprehensible input that models language in a culturally authentic setting. Whether presented on video or as a reading accompanied by the compact disc recording, the highly visual presentation—in **fotonovela** format—ensures success as students practice their receptive skills and begin to recognize some of the new functions and vocabulary they will encounter in the chapter. Following **De antemano** is a series of activities that can be used to help guide students through the story and to check comprehension.

Building Proficiency Step by Step . . .

Primer, Segundo, and **Tercer paso** are the three core instructional sections where the greater part of language acquisition will take place. The communicative goals in each chapter center on the functional expressions presented in **Así se dice** boxes. These expressions are supported and expanded by material in the **Vocabulario, Gramática,** and **Nota gramatical** sections. Activities immediately following these features are designed to practice recognition or to provide closed-ended practice with the new material. Activities then progress from controlled to open-ended practice where students are able to express themselves in meaningful communication. Depending on class size, general ability level, and class dynamics, you may wish to proceed sequentially through all activities in a chapter, supplementing presentation or practice at various points with additional materials from *Adelante,* or you may proceed more quickly to open-ended pair and group work.

Discovering the Culture . . .

Cultural information has been incorporated throughout the chapter wherever possible. There are also three types of culture features to help students develop an appreciation and understanding of the cultures of Spanish-speaking countries.

Panorama cultural presents spontaneous interviews conducted in various countries in the Spanish-speaking world on a topic related to the chapter theme. The interviews may be presented on video or done as a reading supplemented by the compact disc recording. Culminating activities on this page may be used to verify comprehension and encourage students to think critically about the target culture as well as their own.

Encuentro cultural introduces students to people, places, and customs throughout the Spanish-speaking world and invites them to compare and contrast the target culture with their own. The presentation may be done through the use of video or as a reading.

Nota cultural provides short presentations of both "big C" and "little c" culture that can be used to enrich and enliven activities and presentations at various places throughout each chapter.

Understanding Authentic Documents . . .

Vamos a leer presents reading strategies that help students understand authentic Spanish-language documents and literature. The reading selections vary from advertisements to letters to short stories or poems in order to accommodate different interests and familiarize the students with different styles and formats. The accompanying activities progress from prereading to reading and postreading tasks and are designed to develop students' overall reading skills and challenge their critical thinking abilities.

Targeting Students' Needs . . .

In each **paso** these special features may be used to enhance language learning and cultural appreciation.

Sugerencia suggests effective ways for students to learn a foreign language.

Vocabulario extra presents optional vocabulary related to the chapter theme. These words are provided to help students personalize activities; students will not be required to produce this vocabulary on the Chapter Quizzes and Test.

Letra y sonido

At the end of each **Tercer paso** is **Letra y sonido**, a recorded pronunciation feature that explains sounds and spelling rules. Pronunciation is practiced using vocabulary words that contain the targeted sounds. In a dictation exercise that follows, students hear and write sentences using the targeted sounds and letters. The last part of this feature, the **trabalenguas**, gives students an additional opportunity to practice the targeted sounds in amusing and challenging tongue twisters.

Interdisciplinary Connections

Enlaces is an interdisciplinary feature that links the learning of Spanish to other subjects students might be studying. Each **Enlaces** presents further aspects of Spanish-speaking culture and relates them to an academic subject. It encourages students to apply what they learn in other classes to the acquisition of a second language and culture.

Wrapping it All Up . . .

Repaso, at the end of each chapter, gives students the opportunity to review what they have learned and to apply their skills in new communicative contexts. Beginning in Chapter 3, **Repaso** contains **Vamos a escribir**, a process-writing feature that provides students with guided writing activities as well as strategies to further develop their writing skills. Focusing on all four language skills as well as cultural awareness, **Repaso** can help you determine whether students are ready for the Chapter Test.

A ver si puedo... follows **Repaso** and is a checklist that students can use on their own to see if they have achieved the goals stated in the Chapter Opener. Each communicative function is paired with one or more activities for students to use as a self-check. Page references are given for students who need to return to the chapter for review.

Vocabulario presents the chapter vocabulary grouped by **paso** and arranged according to communicative function or theme. This list represents the active words and expressions that students will be expected to know for the **Paso** Quizzes and Chapter Test.

ANCILLARIES

The **Adelante** *Spanish program offers a state-of-the-art ancillary package that addresses the concerns of today's teachers. Because foreign language teachers work with all types of students, the activities in our ancillaries accommodate all learning styles. The variety of activities provided in the* ¡Ven conmigo! *ancillary materials are both innovative and relevant to students' experiences.* ◆

Technology Resources

Adelante and *En camino* are the first Spanish programs to offer technology resources specifically designed for students in the middle grades. Interviews with young adolescent native speakers and an **Encuentro cultural** feature enhance a highly effective video program. The cultural interviews are incorporated in the middle school *Interactive CD-ROM Tutor* with appropriate activities and with vocabulary support in the online reference section. For a detailed description of all the technology resources available with *Adelante*, see pages T40–T41.

Grammar and Vocabulary Workbook

The *Grammar and Vocabulary Workbook* re-presents all major grammar points and offers additional focused practice with the structures, words, and phrases targeted in each **paso**. Instruction lines and exercise items have been revised to ensure that students in Grades 6–9 will be able to follow directions and succeed at these important practice activities whether they are done in class or at home. Suggestions for using these activities as homework can be found in the Chapter Interleaf pages of the *Annotated Teacher's Edition*. The *Grammar and Vocabulary Workbook Teacher's Edition* contains the same pages as the workbook with overprinted answers.

Practice and Activity Book

The *Practice and Activity Book* is filled with a variety of activities that provide further practice with the functions, grammar, and vocabulary presented in each **paso**. Additional reading, culture, and journal activities for each chapter give students the opportunity to apply the reading and writing strategies they've learned in relevant, personalized contexts. The Practice and Activity Book reinforces many of the same concepts practiced in the Grammar and Vocabulary Workbook and provides opportunities to use them in more open-ended, creative contexts. *The Practice and Activity Book Teacher's Edition* contains the same pages as the student edition plus overprinted answers for convenient use.

Listening Activities

This component contains all print material associated with the *Audio Program*. Student Response Forms for Textbook Listening Activities and scripts and answers appear here for convenient use.

Additional Listening Activities provide students with a unique opportunity to actively develop their listening skills in a variety of authentic contexts. They appear here as activity masters with scripts and answers.

Each chapter contains a song culturally or thematically related to the chapter or location. The lyrics for each of these songs are provided with each chapter's listening material.

Audio Assessment Items are integrated into the **Paso** Quizzes and Chapter Tests, and the scripts and answers for these items complete the *Listening Activities* component.

Activities for Communication

Oral communication is the most challenging language skill to develop and test. The *Adelante Activities for Communication* book is designed to help facilitate students' development of listening and speaking skills through pair activities in which students communicate in a variety of life-like situations and contexts. The Communicative Activities offer information-gap tasks in which students rely on a partner to fill in the gaps, and the Situation Cards offer opportunities for interviews and role-playing.

This component also contains **Realia** pages, which reproduce real documents to provide students with additional reading and language practice. Included with the **Realia** are teacher suggestions and student activities.

Testing Program

The *Testing Program* encourages students to work toward realistic, communicative goals.

• Three **Quizzes** per chapter (one per **paso**); each **Quiz** includes a listening, reading, and writing section, and very often a culture section

• Each **Chapter Test** includes listening, reading, writing, and culture sections and a score sheet for easy grading. Selected sections of each Chapter Test can be corrected on ScanTron®

• One **Speaking Test** per chapter

• One **Midterm** and one **Final Exam**

Also included in the *Testing Program* are scripts and answers to the **Paso Quizzes, Chapter Tests, Midterm,** and **Final Exam.**

Additional quizzes targeting specific grammar points and vocabulary are available in the *Grammar and Vocabulary Quizzes*.

Alternative Assessment Guide

The *Alternative Assessment Guide* describes various testing and scoring methods. This guide also includes **Portfolio Assessment** suggestions and rubrics as well as suggestions for **Performance Assessment.**

Exploratory Guide

The *Exploratory Guide* provides suggestions and techniques for teaching an exploratory class using *Adelante* and *En camino*'s wealth of materials, such as the *Video and Audio Programs,* the *Interactive CD-ROM Program,* the *Teaching Transparencies,* and a host of workbook materials.

Teaching Transparencies

Colorful teaching transparencies benefit all students, and the visual learner in particular, by adding variety and focus to your daily lesson plans. Situations, Vocabulary, and Maps allow you to present and practice vocabulary, culture, and a variety of communicative functions. Each transparency in the *Teaching Transparencies* package comes with a copying master as well as suggestions to practice four skills and culture. In addition to the teaching suggestions that accompany the transparencies, numerous other activities, projects, and games using the maps can be found throughout the *Annotated Teacher's Edition.* Answer transparencies for the *Grammar and Vocabulary Workbook* are also found in the *Teaching Transparencies.*

Lesson Planner

The *Lesson Planner* contains chapter-by-chapter suggestions on how to structure the daily lesson for optimal pacing and effectiveness. Each chapter's Lesson Plan guides the teacher through the program's cycle of presentation, practice, and assessment. Specific suggestions for block scheduling give the teacher the option of expanding the material as needed. In addition, all lesson material is correlated to the Standards for Foreign Language Learning and can readily be adapted to document weekly or monthly progress.

Cuaderno para hispanohablantes

The *¡Ven conmigo!* Level 1 *Cuaderno para hispanohablantes* includes suggestions and activities designed to address the needs of the native speakers in your Spanish class. It includes reading, writing, and speaking tasks for native speakers to complete, rounding out their Spanish language learning. *The Teacher's Edition* contains an answer key at the back.

Test Generator

The *¡Ven conmigo!* Level 1 *Test Generator's* user-friendly software, which enables you to create customized practice sheets, quizzes, and tests for each chapter in *¡Ven conmigo!,* is available for Macintosh® computers and Windows®.

TECHNOLOGY

Adelante Video and *Audio Programs* bring the textbook to life and introduce your students to people they will encounter in every chapter of the Pupil's Edition. *The video and audio programs feature native speakers of Spanish in realistic, interesting situations.* ◆

VIDEO TECHNOLOGY

Adelante *Video Program*

Video is an ideal medium for providing authentic input needed to increase proficiency in Spanish. Both informative and entertaining, the episodes of the *Video Program* provide rich visual clues to aid comprehension and motivate students to learn more.

The *Video Program* is fully integrated and correlates directly with the *Adelante Pupil's Edition:*

Location Opener A narrated collage of images from regions of the Spanish-speaking world expands students' acquaintance with the geography and people presented in each Location Opener.

De antemano The introductory dialogue or story in each chapter is a videotaped dramatic episode based on the chapter theme. It introduces the targeted functions, vocabulary, and grammar of the chapter, in addition to re-entering material from previous chapters in new contexts. Since this video episode corresponds directly with the **De antemano** and the chapter, it can be used as a general introduction to the chapter, as a chapter review, and as a visual support for presenting the elements of the lesson.

A continuación These continuations of the dramatic episodes provide high-interest input that helps motivate students and offers additional opportunities to expand on what they have learned. **A continuación** continues the story and resolves the dramatic conflict that was created in **De antemano.** Designed to facilitate proficiency by providing additional comprehensible input, this episode offers an extended presentation of the chapter material and re-enters functions, vocabulary, and structures from previous chapters.

Panorama cultural Authentic interviews with native speakers of Spanish bring the Spanish-speaking world to life as real people talk about themselves, their country, and their way of life. Each interview topic is thematically related to the chapter.

Encuentro cultural A tour guide from one of the many Spanish-speaking locations of *Adelante* introduces students to people, places, and customs.

Videoclips Students will enjoy the authentic footage from Spanish and Latin American television: music videos, commercials, and more. These short segments of video give students confidence as they realize that they can understand and enjoy material that was produced for native speakers of Spanish!

Adelante *Video Guide*

Adelante Video Guide provides background information together with suggestions for presentation and pre- and postviewing activities for all portions of the *Video Program*. In addition, the *Video Guide* contains reproducible student activity sheets as well as a transcript and synopsis of each episode and supplementary vocabulary lists.

AUDIO TECHNOLOGY

Adelante *Audio Program*

Audio is another ideal medium for providing authentic input needed to increase language proficiency. The activities in the **Audio Program** allow students to focus their attention on the sound of the language while at the same time accomplishing authentic real-life linguistic tasks.

The *Audio Program,* available in compact disc format, is fully integrated and correlates directly with the following sections of *Adelante Pupil's Edition:*

De antemano The **De antemano** as it appears in the *Pupil's Edition* is an abridged version of the video episode. The *Audio Program* contains the soundtrack of the video episode edited to match **De antemano** to bring the page to life and to give students an opportunity to practice pronunciation.

DVD/VIDEO

The *¡Ven conmigo!* DVD Tutor may also be used with *Adelante.* It contains all the **De antemano/ A continuación** dramatic videos, the **Location Openers,** and the *¡Ven conmigo!* **Panorama cultural** interviews with interactive comprehension questions. It also contains all the **Videoclips** as well as the *¡Ven conmigo!* CD-ROM Tutor in DVD-ROM format.

Textbook Listening Activities Each chapter contains various listening activities that give students aural practice with the chapter's linguistic functions and communicative goals. These listening activities integrate previous chapter material with new structures being taught in the chapter.

Panorama cultural Audio recordings of these authentic interviews are contained in the *Audio Program.* The interviews are on separate tracks on the Audio CDs for convenient random access.

Adelante *Listening Activities*

Adelante Listening Activities contains all print material related the *Audio Program* including Student Response Forms, scripts and answers for the Textbook Listening Activities, copying masters for the Additional Listening Activities, and song lyrics.

CD-ROM TECHNOLOGY

Adelante *and* En camino *Interactive CD-ROM Tutor*

CD-ROM technology offers students an opportunity to interact with the target language and culture in new and exciting ways. This medium brings together print, graphics, video, and audio to provide a language-learning experience that is both enjoyable and challenging. Simulated real-life tasks provide a realistic context for language learning and will appeal to students with a variety of learning styles.

The **Interactive CD-ROM Tutor** is correlated to both *Adelante* and *En camino* to offer students a complete interactive language-learning experience.

Location Opener

The ¡Ven conmigo a... ! presentations include a travelogue movie about specific locations around the Spanish-speaking world. The map on the right-hand side of the screen contains a map of the featured country and buttons that control the

different portions of the travelogue. After students have watched the travelogue presentation, they use what they have learned to complete a related activity.

En contexto

Students complete a lifelike conversation with a video character that targets the chapter functions, vocabulary, and grammar in meaningful, realistic contexts. Students choose the best response based on a series of audio and visual prompts. When students choose the correct response, the conversation continues. If students answer incorrectly, feedback will then help guide them.

¡A escoger! This multiple-choice activity practices vocabulary, grammar concepts, functional expressions, or culture. Students respond to each item based on what they see or hear.

¿Cuál es? In this game students organize words and phrases according to two or more categories.

Imagen y sonido In the presentation mode of this activity, students identify and pronounce vocabulary and/or functional expressions by exploring an image. The test mode evaluates students' aural recognition of vocabulary words and expressions.

Patas arriba In this activity, students will sequence words into sentences or sentences into paragraphs or dialogues.

¿Qué falta? This activity makes use of a familiar game, Tic Tac Toe, to practice vocabulary or grammar. Students can play with each other or against the computer.

¡Super memoria! This activity gives students an opportunity to practice vocabulary, grammar concepts, functional expressions, or culture by matching sound or text with images.

Panorama cultural

Each **Panorama cultural** screen includes six QuickTime™ movies with interviews of students from around the Spanish-

speaking world as well as multiple-choice comprehension questions.

Speaking and Writing

¡A hablar! and ¡A escribir! provide both guided and open-ended speaking and writing tasks that combine the functions, vocabulary, grammar, and culture of each chapter. These sections can be used for self evaluation, for peer evaluation, or assessment by the teacher.

En voz alta and **¡Exprésate!** These features allow students to record and write original assignments. Suggestions for assignments are included in every chapter of the *CD-ROM Teacher's Guide.*

Reference Sections

Vocabulary The vocabulary reference section provides a glossary of Spanish-English and English-Spanish words and expressions. Students can access this online reference at any time.

Grammar The grammar reference section provides a summary of the grammar concepts presented in *¡Ven conmigo!* Students can access this online reference at any time.

Help This section guides users through the mechanics of the program. Students may access this online reference at any time to find information about navigation, control panels, directions for activities, and file storage and retrieval.

INTERACTIVE CD-ROM TUTOR

 The *Interactive CD-ROM Tutor* offers a Teacher Management System that allows teachers to view and assess students' work, manage passwords and records, track students' progress as they complete the activities, and activate English translations if desired.

THE ANNOTATED TEACHER'S EDITION

The **Adelante** *Annotated Teacher's Edition is designed to help you meet the increasingly varied needs of today's students by providing an abundance of suggestions and strategies. The* **Annotated Teacher's Edition** *includes the pages of the* **Pupil's Edition** *with teacher annotation, side column teacher text with video references, notes, suggestions, answers, and additional activities, as well as icon annotations that correlate each presentation to a corresponding ancillary. The* **Annotated Teacher's Edition** *also includes interleafed pages with scripts, suggestions for use of technology, projects, games, and homework suggestions before each chapter.* ◆

Using the Location Opener and Location Opener Interleaf

In the interleaf and side column extension of each student page you will find background information about the photographs and settings. In addition, teaching suggestions help you motivate students to learn more about the history, geography, and culture of Spanish-speaking countries.

Using the Chapter Interleaf

The chapter interleaf includes a chapter overview correlation chart for teaching resources, *Pupil's Edition* listening scripts, and suggestions for homework, the use of technology, projects, and games.

The **Chapter Overview** chart outlines at a glance the functions, grammar, vocabulary, culture, and re-entry items featured in each **paso**. A list of corresponding print and audiovisual resource materials for each section of the chapter is provided to help integrate media and print ancillaries into your lessons. The pronunciation, reading, interdisciplinary, and review features for each chapter are also referenced,

as are a variety of assessment and portfolio options.

The **Technology** pages provide a variety of suggestions on how to effectively implement the various technology components that accompany *Adelante.*

Textbook Listening Activities Scripts provide the scripts of the chapter listening activities for reference or for use in class. The answers to each activity are provided below each script for easy reference.

Projects propose extended four-skills activities based on the chapter theme and content. **Projects** suggestions are provided to give students the opportunity to personalize the information they've learned in the chapter. Individual projects offer students the chance to explore topics related to the chapter theme that are of interest to them. Group and cooperative learning projects encourage students to work together to apply what they've learned in the chapter by creating a poster, brochure, or report, often accompanied by an oral presentation.

Games provide students with informal, entertaining activities in which they can apply and reinforce the functions, structures, vocabulary, and culture of the chapter. Games appeal to a variety of learners and encourage teamwork and cooperation among students of different levels and learning styles.

Answers to Chapter Activities contains answers to selected activities from the chapter.

Homework Suggestions provide a list of assignments from the *Pupil's Edition, Grammar and Vocabulary Workbook, Practice and Activity Book,* and *Interactive CD-ROM Tutor* that would be appropriate for students to do as homework. Each suggestion is correlated to a specific presentation from the chapter.

Using the Side-Column Teacher Text

Side-column teacher text gives point-of-use suggestions and information to help you make the most of class time. The side-column style of the *Annotated Teacher's Edition* also conveniently presents video references and activity answers together on the same page with the *Pupil's Edition* page.

Teaching Cycle

For each **paso**, a logical instructional sequence includes the following steps:

- **Bell Work** gives your students an individual writing activity that focuses their attention on previously learned material while they wait for class to begin.

- **Motivate** introduces students to the topic in a personalized and contextualized way.

- **Teach** provides suggestions for presenting and practicing the functions, vocabulary, structures, and culture.

- **Close** suggests activities that review and practice the goals of each **paso**.

- **Assess** indicates materials that allow you to evaluate students' progress. **Performance Assessment** suggestions provide an alternative to pen and paper tests and give you the option of evaluating students' progress by having them perform communicative, competency-based tasks. These may include teacher-student interviews, conversations, dialogues, or skits that students perform for the entire class. These tasks can also be recorded or videotaped for evaluation at a later time.

Portfolio icons signal activities that are appropriate for students' oral or written portfolios. They may include lists, posters, letters, journal entries, or taped conversations or skits. A variety of suggestions are provided within each chapter so that you can work with your students to select the activities that would best document their strengths and progress in the language. Portfolio information, including checklists and suggestions for evaluation, are provided in the *Alternative Assessment Guide,* which also contains suggestions for the expansion of the designated portfolio activities from the *Pupil's Edition.* For a discussion of portfolio creation and use, see *Using Portfolios in the Foreign Language Classroom,* pages T52–T53.

For Individual Needs

Suggestions under the following categories provide alternative approaches to help you address students' diverse learning styles.

- **Visual, Auditory, Tactile, and Kinesthetic Learners** benefit from activities that accommodate their unique learning styles.
- **Slower Pace** provides ideas for presenting material in smaller steps to facilitate comprehension.
- **Challenge** extends activities into more challenging tasks that encourage students to expand their communicative skills.

Native Speakers

Native speakers benefit from the various projects and activities that validate their individual culture and language. They are encouraged to share their knowledge of Spanish regionalisms and culture with non-native Spanish-speaking students. Native-speaker activities are designed to highlight the skills and culture of native speakers and channel their input to the advantage of the entire class. The in-class activities and out-of-class assignments for native speakers often integrate family and community into the students' learning experience. Native speaker work lends authenticity to Spanish-language instruction and guides students toward a comprehensive understanding of the Spanish-speaking world. For more information on native speakers, see the essay *New Perspectives for Native Speakers* by Cecilia Rodríguez-Pino on pages T56–T57.

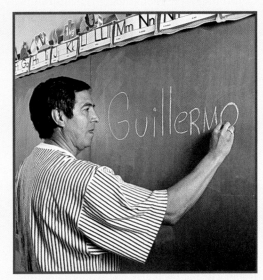

Making Connections

To help students appreciate their membership in a global society, suggestions for linking Spanish with other disciplines, their community, and other cultures appear under several categories:

- **Math... Geography... Health... Science... History... Language** and **Arts Links** relate the chapter topic to other subject areas, and make Spanish relevant to the students' overall academic experience.
- **Multicultural Links** provide students the opportunity to compare and contrast their language and culture with those of Spanish-speaking countries and other parts of the world.
- **Community... Family Links** encourage students to seek opportunities for learning outside of the classroom by interacting with neighbors and family members. These suggestions also call on students to share their learning with their family and community.

Developing Thinking Skills

Critical Thinking helps students develop their higher-order thinking skills with suggestions to extend activities beyond an informational level. It increases comprehension of language and cultures and helps students exercise and develop higher-order thinking skills.

Establishing Collaborative Learning

Cooperative Learning allows students to work together in small groups to attain common goals by sharing responsibilities. Students are accountable for setting group objectives, completing the assignment, and ensuring that all group members master the material. Working together in cooperative groups allows students to take an active role in the classroom, to develop more confidence as they contribute to the success of the group, and to experience less anxiety by working in small groups. Cooperative learning enables students to improve interpersonal communication skills by encouraging them to listen to and respect other opinions.

Total Physical Response (TPR) techniques reinforce structures and vocabulary visually and kinesthetically. They are active-learning exercises that encourage students to focus on class interaction while learning Spanish.

Teaching Vamos a leer

Teacher's notes and suggestions in **Vamos a leer** offer prereading, reading, and postreading skills. Background information and useful terms related to the reading are provided as well.

ADELANTE AND EN CAMINO IN THE MIDDLE GRADES

Middle-grade teachers can readily describe the excitement they feel when students are able to make complex connections for the first time, and are so fired up about what they are learning that sparks fly. Teachers at these grade levels delight in their students' wonderful curiosity about and openness to others. They can also describe the challenges of teaching students who can't seem to sit still, who want to hang out with friends all the time, and who are painfully self-conscious.

Increased understanding of this exciting age group, a well-designed curriculum and textbook, and appropriate classroom management approaches can maximize teaching fun and effectiveness, greatly decrease teacher frustration, and enhance the students' experiences in a multitude of ways.

Characteristics of the Middle-Grades Learner

Young adolescents undergo tremendous physical and mental growth. This is a time when they undertake the important tasks of forming a personal identity, acquiring social skills, establishing personal autonomy, and developing discipline.

This is also a time of rapid cognitive growth. Around the age of twelve, most students begin a gradual transition from concrete operations (the ability to think logically about real experiences) to formal operations (the ability to think reflectively, to reason, and to consider complex issues). For the majority of students, this highly unique and individual process may continue until age 15. An integrated curriculum that involves students in global thinking and interdisciplinary learning furthers the higher-order thinking skills that the students are beginning to develop. A task-focused curriculum that organizes content around themes or issues increases student engagement in learning and leads to increased skill and understanding. It recognizes effort and progress, utilizing portfolios and other authentic assessment tools.

As formal thinking skills develop, the middle-grades student is able to consider the thoughts of others and to perceive him or herself as the object of others' attention. While this means the student now lives in a broader and more interesting world, the student can also feel alone, unsure, and self-conscious. These feelings can manifest themselves as intense egocentrism and self-consciousness, qualities that the teacher needs to understand and work with creatively. It is generally more effective with young adolescent learners to provide cooperative group learning opportunities while avoiding singling out students. This helps maintain an atmosphere of emotional safety and high motivation while facilitating the development of autonomy and self-confidence.

The middle-grades teacher needs to assist students in increasing their concentration span, improving self discipline, and beginning to think about long-term goals. Because young adolescents have a relatively short attention span, an ideal curriculum should provide for diversity in both presentation and practice. It should also provide opportunities for students to move around in non-disruptive ways and work in a variety of groups.

Increased understanding of this exciting age group, a well-designed curriculum and textbook, and appropriate classroom management approaches can maximize teaching fun and effectiveness and enhance students' learning experiences.

Curriculum Materials in the Middle-Grades

A well-constructed set of curriculum materials should take advantage of students' thirst for peer interactions and their willingness to learn. The ideal program builds on students' strengths with concrete, contextualized learning activities, gradually offering more opportunities to challenge students and stretch their skills into new areas of development. This can be accomplished in a variety of ways: by strategically introducing abstract topics that require creativity and flexibility, by making connections with other disciplines, and by providing as many opportunities as possible to apply new learning in authentic, life-like settings. The well-designed curriculum should also address the special characteristics of the middle-grade learner and allow the teacher to turn students' preoccupations into assets.

Using Adelante in the Middle Grades

Levels 1A and 1B of the Holt Spanish program have been designed to accomplish two major goals. First, *Adelante* and *En camino* were specifically created to address the unique needs and interests of young adolescents with a rich and highly diverse program that engages students' interest and promotes enthusiasm for learning at various stages of development. Second, *Adelante* and *En camino* teach the full scope and sequence of *¡Ven conmigo!* Level 1, allowing students who have completed Levels 1A and 1B to continue successfully with *¡Ven conmigo!* Level 2.

Adelante and *En camino* capitalize on young adolescents' interest in peer interaction and physical activity by building in a wide selection of projects, games, and pair and group activities. A variety of TPR (Total Physical Response) suggestions are included in the *Annotated Teacher's Edition.*

High-interest themes (such as sports, food, shopping, and friendships) and geographic locations integrate the audio, video, and text, and workbook content. Short learning units called **pasos** allow for frequent assessment. The testing program, oriented to the specific needs of the middle grades learner, includes **paso** quizzes, chapter tests, speaking tests, and authentic assessment tools such as portfolios and performance-based activities. A structured approach to peer assessment is included to further profit from students' interest in peer interaction.

Each proficiency-oriented learning unit flows from concrete, closed-ended activities to more abstract, open-ended activities.
These offer opportunities for students to interact with a variety of realia and other multisensory input. This progression solidifies the active use of language and generates opportunities to employ newly emerging cognitive skills.

Global thinking is inspired through a variety of program features. **Enlaces** tie the theme or location of the chapter to other disciplines, encouraging students to draw together thoughts and ideas from different sources and to use their background knowledge. **Encuentro cultural** and **Panorama cultural** furnish an opportunity for students to relate to the interests, thoughts, and priorities of young adolescents in the Spanish-speaking world. Students are encouraged to think reflectively about their own lives and interests in comparison to their counterparts in other parts of the world. **Notas culturales** present high-interest cultural information and again invite students to make connections and comparisons.

References

Irvin, Judith L. *Cognitive Growth During Early Adolescence: The Regulator of Developmental Tasks.* Middle School Journal. September 1995.

Irvin, Judith, L. *Developmental Tasks of Early Adolescence: How Adult Awareness Can Reduce At-Risk Behavior.* The Clearing House Vol. 69 (4). March/April 1996.

Raven, Patrick T. and Wilson, Jo Anne S. *Focus on Teaching Foreign Languages in the Middle Grades: A Summary Statement from the Central States Conference.* Central States Conference on the Teaching of Foreign Languages. April, 1997.

ADELANTE

Adelante supports the middle-grades teacher in the following ways:

◆ Engages students with Spanish-speaking adolescents through new video, audio, and CD-ROM programs.

◆ Promotes skill development with both print and technology resources.

◆ Provides appealing, age-appropriate reading selections.

◆ Instructs students on the process of writing.

◆ Relates language learning to other disciplines.

Adelante also builds on young adolescents' growing social skills by

◆ Providing diverse pair, group, and cooperative learning experiences.

◆ Offering a wide variety of games, projects, and activities.

◆ Including peer assessment of writing.

◆ Building connections with the lives of young adolescents in Spanish-speaking countries.

Adelante supports appropriate classroom management strategies in the following ways:

◆ Provides suggestions for how to modify activities for different types of learners.

◆ Includes portfolio management.

◆ Offers lesson-planning suggestion for traditional or block-scheduling.

◆ Provides materials and suggestions for building an exploratory Spanish course.

TECHNOLOGY IN THE FOREIGN LANGUAGE CLASSROOM

By Cindy A. Kendall

Many remember when overhead projectors and audiocassettes were on the cutting edge. Today's foreign language teachers and their students are discovering new technological applications that make teaching and learning more exciting and effective. Teachers are integrating these technologies into their classes and fundamentally changing the way students learn languages.

The wealth of technological possibilities available to foreign language teachers, such as multimedia computer software, and the Internet, is more sophisticated than ever. This wider range of technological possibilities offers new challenges. In order to use technology effectively, teachers must become familiar with the resources available and understand how the use of technology can enhance language learning.

What role does technology play in the foreign language classroom?

Technology is a powerful tool in the foreign language classroom because it combines visual, auditory, and cultural input and allows for the simultaneous practice of listening, speaking, reading, and writing skills. It can help the instructor reach the five goals of the Standards for Foreign Language Learning: Communication, Culture, Connections, Comparisons, and Community.

The versatility, immediacy, and interactive nature of technology make studying a foreign language more relevant and meaningful to students. Through technology, students can "visit" countries where the target language is spoken and listen to and interact with native speakers. On the Internet, students can perform tasks in the target language at World Wide Web sites created in target-language countries. Technology makes the notion of the global village a reality for today's foreign language students.

In addition, technology helps the teacher work with students of differing skills and learning styles. Technology-based instruction offers teachers and students the flexibility of working as a class, in small groups, or as individuals.

What technological resources are available?

Overhead Projection

The overhead projector, a long-time companion in the classroom, provides a way to effectively combine visual and auditory practice. Transparencies can be an alternative to writing on the chalkboard, and have the added advantage of permitting the teacher to write presentations in advance that can be used over and over.

Audio

Foreign language instructors are familiar with the use of audiocassettes as part of students' listening comprehension practice, and know all too well some common problems with this format: the loss of time in cueing the appropriate segment and wear and tear on the audiocassette. Audio compact discs enable the teacher to cue the desired track quickly and deliver the same content with much greater ease. Other benefits of compact discs include higher-quality recordings and longer product shelf life.

Video

Video technology offers multiple benefits to teachers and is increasingly becoming a standard part of the curriculum system. Videos that are shot on location and feature native speakers in real settings can supply linguistically and culturally authentic input and facilitate comprehension with richer contexts, while at the same time reinforcing new language and structures. The use of video has progressed beyond simply watching. Videos and the print-matter guides that often accompany them give teachers ideas to motivate students, to provide comprehensible input, and to review material. By watching videoclips of interviews, ads, music performances, and other authentic target-language programming, students get a taste of the "real" foreign language.

Multimedia Software

Interactive CD-ROM programs are easy-to-use computer software programs that deliver large amounts of sound and images along with text. In the most effective CD-ROM programs, students not only hear and see language in action, but interact with it as well. This powerful learning tool weaves listening, reading, speaking, writing, and culture into a tapestry of realistic situations that motivates students to practice and communicate in the foreign language. As an added benefit for busy teachers, CD-ROM technology requires little or no training and is virtually foolproof. No matter how many students use the disk, it is impossible to erase the program or write over it.

CD-ROM technology gives teachers flexibility in several areas. They can work with students as a whole class, in small groups, or individually; they can use the program at any phase of the lesson cycle; and they can easily help students with varied learning strengths and styles.

Internet

The Internet is an electronic resource that offers unmatched potential for connecting the foreign language classroom to the outside world. The World Wide Web (WWW) is a treasure trove of authentic materials that can bring target-language cultures into the classroom on a daily basis. By connecting to the Internet and using WWW resources, teachers can overcome the difficulties inherent in teaching a foreign language in an English-speaking country and provide students with experiences they would otherwise not have. Students can find out what is playing at the movies in Buenos Aires or what the hours of operation are at the Prado Museum; they might read the latest headlines in Santiago de Chile or get information about the Spanish royal family; or they can scan weather reports in Puerto Rico or soccer scores in Mexico. They can also download audio; thanks to this new resource, accessing international music and broadcasts is easier than ever.

What implications does increased use of technology have for teachers and students?

Both teachers and students benefit in many ways from the growing variety of technological tools available for use in and out of the classroom. Students are more motivated to learn, and motivated students are easier to teach. The variety of formats the teacher can now offer makes it much easier to address individual learning styles

in classrooms that have grown increasingly diverse.

New technologies also facilitate classroom management in many ways. Software programs can help the teacher build more effective presentations using less time and energy. Multimedia programs can often give students immediate feedback, track their progress through different types of assignments, and make accurate records management much easier for the teacher.

Along with their many benefits, teachers will find that new technologies also bring new responsibilities. Teachers who have used magazine articles and books understand the need to review such materials to be sure content is appropriate and will naturally apply similar standards to CD-ROM programs and to Internet activities. In addition, activities that put students in contact with the public on the Internet make it imperative that teachers set standards and communicate clearly with both parents and students about what is acceptable and safe.

As students move into working more independently with creative technologies both as individuals and in groups, teachers may also need to modify their strategies for monitoring students' work to maintain accountability and to make sure students are getting the most out of their time with each medium. Teachers may want to reexamine how they assess students; performance assessment and portfolio assessment offer opportunities for students to demonstrate their increasing skill in the language and can help prepare them for the kinds of proficiency tests that are becoming more common at checkpoints or as exit requirements.

Properly used, new technology tools can bring the language to life for students and make teachers' work easier and more effective. Teachers are learning new skills and adapting their approaches to classroom management and assessment. Students are also learning "how to learn" with these new resources, and the rewards can be great.

ADELANTE

Adelante's *technology package facilitates presentation, practice, review, and assessment in the following ways:*

Video
◆ Provides high-interest stories, interviews, and travelogues shot on location.

◆ Is fully integrated into each corresponding section of the *Pupil's Edition*.

Audio Program
◆ Allows students ample practice in every chapter listening to native speakers.

◆ Is available on audio CDs for ease of use.

Interactive CD-ROM Tutor
◆ Provides interactive, authentic, multisensory practice with corrective feedback.

◆ Practices each chapter's functions, grammar, vocabulary, and culture.

◆ Offers an online teacher management system to insure student accountability.

Teaching Transparencies
◆ Present situations, vocabulary, and maps that practice key concepts and skills.

Test Generator
◆ Allows teachers to create and print alternate tests and make short practice tests.

Adelante's *planning tools facilitate the integration of technology in the following ways:*

Pupil's Edition
◆ Indicates for both teacher and student when CD-ROM activities are available.

Annotated Teacher's Edition
◆ Includes a quick guide to technology resources for each chapter.

Ancillaries
◆ Include a *Lesson Planner* that suggests appropriate places to integrate technology.

STANDARDS FOR FOREIGN LANGUAGE LEARNING

BY PAUL SANDROCK, FOREIGN LANGUAGE CONSULTANT, WISCONSIN DEPARTMENT OF PUBLIC EDUCATION

Bringing Standards into the Classroom

The core question that guided the development of the National Standards and their accompanying goals was simply: what matters in instruction?

Each proposed standard was evaluated. Did the standard target material that will have application beyond the classroom? Was the standard too specific or not specific enough? Teachers should be able to teach the standard and assess it in multiple ways. A standard needs to provide a target for instruction and learning throughout a student's K–12 education.

In the development of standards, foreign languages faced other unique challenges. The writers could not assume a K–12 sequence available to all students. In fact, unlike other disciplines, they could not guarantee that all students would experience even any common sequence.

From this context, the National Standards in Foreign Language Education Project's task force generated the five C's, five goals for learning languages: communication, cultures, connections, comparisons, and communities. First presented in 1995, the standards quickly became familiar to foreign language educators across the US, representing our professional consensus and capturing a broad view of the purposes for learning another language.

To implement the standards, however, requires a shift from emphasizing the means to focusing on the ends. It isn't a matter of grammar versus communication, but rather how much grammar is needed to communicate. Instead of teaching to a grammatical sequence, teaching decisions become based on what students need to know to achieve the communicative goal.

The Focus on Communication

The first standard redefined communication, making its purpose **interpersonal, interpretive,** and **presentational** communication. Teaching to the purpose of interpersonal communication takes us away from memorized dialogues to spontaneous, interactive conversation, where the message is most important and where meaning needs to be negotiated between the speakers. Interpretive communication is not an exercise in translation, but asks beginners to tell the gist of an authentic selection that is heard, read, or viewed, while increasingly advanced learners tell deeper and

STANDARDS FOR FOREIGN LANGUAGE LEARNING

Communication Communicate in Languages Other than English	**Standard 1.1**	Students engage in conversations, provide and obtain information, express feelings and emotions, and exchange opinions.
	Standard 1.2	Students understand and interpret written and spoken language on a variety of topics.
	Standard 1.3	Students present information, concepts, and ideas to an audience of listeners or readers on a variety of topics.
Cultures Gain knowledge and understanding of Other Cultures	**Standard 2.1**	Students demonstrate an understanding of the relationship between the practices and perspectives of the culture studied.
	Standard 2.2	Students demonstrate an understanding of the relationship between the products and perspectives of the culture studied.
Connections Connect with other disciplines and Acquire Information	**Standard 3.1**	Students reinforce and further their knowledge of other disciplines through the foreign language.
	Standard 3.2	Students acquire information and recognize the distinctive viewpoints that are only available through the foreign language and its cultures.
Comparisons Develop Insight into the Nature of Language and Culture	**Standard 4.1**	Students demonstrate understanding of the nature of language through comparisons of the language studied and their own.
	Standard 4.2	Students demonstrate understanding of the concept of culture through comparisons of the cultures studied and their own.
Communities Participate in Multilingual Communities at Home and Around the World	**Standard 5.1**	Students use the language both within and beyond the school setting.
	Standard 5.2	Students show evidence of becoming life-long learners by using the language for personal enjoyment and enrichment.

deeper levels of detail and can interpret based on their knowledge of the target culture. In the presentational mode of communication, the emphasis is on the audience, requiring the speaker or writer to adapt language to fit the situation and to allow for comprehension without any interactive negotiation of the meaning.

Standards challenge us to refocus many of the things we've been doing all along. The requirements of speaking and our expectation of how well students need to speak change when speaking is for a different purpose. This focus on the purpose of the communication changes the way we teach and test the skills of listening, speaking, reading, and writing.

Standards help us think about how to help students put the pieces of language to work in meaningful ways. Our standards answer *why* we are teaching various components of language, and we select *what* we teach in order to achieve those very standards.

The 5 C's

Originally the five C's were presented as five equal circles. During the years since the national standards were printed, teachers implementing and using the standards to write curriculum, texts, and lesson plans have come to see that communication is at the core, surrounded by four C's that influence the context for teaching and assessing.

The four C's surrounding our core goal of **Communication** change our classrooms by bringing in real-life applications for the language learned:

- **Cultures:** Beyond art and literature, learning occurs in the context of the way of life, patterns of behavior, and contributions of the people speaking the language being taught.
- **Connections:** Beyond content limited to the culture of the people speaking the target language, teachers go out to other disciplines to find topics and ideas to form the context for language learning.
- **Comparisons:** Foreign language study is a great way for students to learn more about native language and universal principles of language and culture by comparing and contrasting their own to the target language and culture.

- **Communities:** This goal of the standards adds a broader motivation to the context for language learning. The teacher makes sure students use their new language beyond the class hour, seeking ways to experience the target culture.

Implementation at the Classroom Level: Assessment and Instruction

Standards provide the organizing principle for teaching and assessing. Textbook writers and materials providers are responding to this shift. Standards provide our goals; the useful textbooks and materials give us an organization and a context.

To really know that standards are the focus of teaching materials, look at the assessment. If standards are the target, assessment won't consist only of evaluation of the means (grammatical structures and vocabulary) in isolation. If standards are the focus, teachers will assess students' use of the second language in context. The summative assessment of our target needs to go beyond the specific and include open-ended, personalized tasks. Regardless of how the students show what they can do, the teacher will be able to gauge each student's progress toward the goal.

Assessment is like a jigsaw puzzle. If we test students only on the means, we just keep collecting random puzzle pieces. We have to test, and students have to practice, putting the pieces together in meaningful and purposeful ways. In order to learn vocabulary that will help students "describe themselves," for example, students may have a quiz on Friday with an expectation of close to 100% accuracy. But if that is all we ever do with those ten words, they will quickly be gone from students' memory, and we will only have collected a puzzle piece from each student. It is absolutely essential to have students use those puzzle pieces to complete the puzzle to provide evidence of what they "can do" with the language.

During this period of implementing our standards, we've learned that the standards provide a global picture, the essence of our goals. But they are not curriculum, nor are they lesson plans. The standards influence how we teach, but do not dictate one content nor one methodology. How can we

implement the standards in our classrooms? Think about the targets; think about how students will show achievement of those targets through our evaluation measures; then think about what we need to teach and how that will occur in our classrooms. Make it happen in your classroom to get the results we've always wanted: students who can communicate in a language other than English.

TEACHING CULTURE

By Nancy A. Humbach and
Dorothea Bruschke

Ask students what they like best about studying a foreign language. Chances are that learning about culture, the way people live, is one of their favorite aspects. Years after language study has ended, adults remember with fondness the customs of the target culture, even pictures in their language texts. It is this interest in the people and their way of life that is the great motivator and helps us sustain students' interest in language study.

We must integrate culture and language in a way that encourages curiosity, stimulates analysis, and teaches students to hypothesize and seek answers to questions about the people whose language they are studying. Teaching isolated facts about how people in other cultures live is not enough. This information is soon dated and quickly forgotten. We must go a step beyond and teach students that all behavior, values, and traditions exist because of certain aspects of history, geography, and socio-economic conditions.

There are many ways to help students become culturally knowledgeable and to assist them in developing an awareness of differences and similarities between the target culture and their own. Two of these approaches involve critical thinking, that is, trying to find reasons for a certain behavior through observation and analysis, and putting individual observations into larger cultural patterns. ◆

First Approach: Questioning

The first approach involves questioning as the key strategy. At the earliest stages of language learning, students begin to learn ways to greet peers, elders, and strangers, as well as the use of **tú** and **usted**. Students need to consider questions such as: "How do Spanish-speaking people greet each other? Are there different levels of formality? Who initiates a handshake? What's considered a good handshake?" Each of these questions leads students to think about the values that are expressed through word and gesture. They start to "feel" the other culture and, at the same time, understand how much of their own behavior is rooted in their cultural background.

Magazines, newspapers, advertisements, and television commercials are all excellent sources of cultural material. For example, browsing through a Spanish magazine, one finds an extraordinary number of advertisements for health-related products. Could this indicate a great interest in staying healthy? Reading advertisements can be followed up with viewing videos and films, or with interviewing native speakers or people who have lived in Spanish-speaking countries to learn about customs involving health. Students might want to find answers to questions such as: "How do Spanish speakers treat a cold? What is their attitude toward fresh air? toward exercise?" This type of questioning might lead students to discover that we view health matters and the curative properties of food and exercise differently. As in this country, many of the concepts have their roots in the traditions of the past.

An advertisement for a refrigerator or a picture of a Spanish or Latin American kitchen can provide an insight into practices of shopping for food. Students first need to think about the refrigerator at home, take an inventory of what is kept in it, and consider when and where their family shops. Next, students should look closely at a Spanish or Latin American refrigerator. Is it smaller? What could that mean? (Shopping takes place more often, stores are within walking distance, and people eat more fresh foods.)

Food wrappers and containers also provide good clues to cultural insight. For example, laundry detergent is packaged in small plastic bags in many Spanish-speaking countries. Further, instead of "blue-white" cleaning properties, a "red-white" is preferred and considered the epitome of clean. Because of the lack of paper board for boxes, the humidity in many areas, the use for hand laundry, and shopping habits, plastic bags are a more practical form of packaging.

> We must integrate culture and language in a way that encourages curiosity, stimulates analysis, and teaches students to hypothesize.

Second Approach: Associating Words with Images

The second approach for developing cultural understanding involves forming associations of words with the cultural images they suggest. Language and culture are so closely related that one might actually say that language is culture. Most words, especially nouns, carry a cultural connotation. Knowing the literal equivalent of a word in another language is of little use to students in understanding this connotation. For example, **relación** cannot be translated simply as relationship, **comida** as food, or **paseo** as walk. The Spanish phrase **dar un paseo,** for instance, carries with it such social images as people out walking with

T50

friends or family, sitting in a sidewalk café, seeing people and being seen by others. In Spanish-speaking countries, "to go for a walk" often means something entirely different than it does for North Americans.

When students have acquired some sense of the cultural connotation of words—not only through teachers' explanations but, more importantly, through observation of visual images—they start to discover the larger underlying cultural themes, or what is often called "deep culture."

These larger cultural themes serve as organizing categories into which individual cultural phenomena fit to form a pattern. Students might discover, for example, that Spanish speakers, because they live in much more crowded conditions, have a great need for privacy (cultural theme), as reflected in such phenomena as fences or walls around property, and curtains on windows. Students might also discover that love of nature and the outdoors is an important cultural theme, as indicated by such phenomena as flower boxes and planters in public places—even on small traffic islands—well-kept public parks in every town, and people going for a walk or going hiking.

As we teach culture, students learn to recognize elements not only of the target culture but also of their American cultural heritage. They see how elements of culture reflect larger themes or patterns. Learning what constitutes American culture and how that information relates to other people throughout the world can be an exciting journey for a young person.

As language teachers, we are able to facilitate that journey into another culture and into our own, to find our similarities as well as our differences from others. We do not encourage value judgments about others and their culture, nor do we recommend adopting other ways. We simply say to students, "Other ways exist. They exist for many reasons, just as our ways exist due to what our ancestors have bequeathed us through history, traditions, values, and geography."

USING PORTFOLIOS IN THE FOREIGN LANGUAGE CLASSROOM

BY JO ANNE S. WILSON

The communicative, whole-language approach of today's foreign language instruction requires assessment methods that parallel the teaching and learning strategies in the proficiency-oriented classroom. We know that language acquisition is a process. Portfolios are designed to assess the steps in that process. ◆

What Is a Portfolio?

A portfolio is a purposeful, systematic collection of a student's work. A useful tool in developing a student profile, the portfolio shows the student's efforts, progress, and achievements for a given period of time. It may be used for periodic evaluation, as the basis for overall evaluation, or for placement. It may also be used to enhance or provide alternatives to traditional assessment measures, such as formal tests, quizzes, class participation, and homework.

Why Use Portfolios?

Portfolios benefit both students and teachers because they

- **Are ongoing and systematic.** A portfolio reflects the real-world process of production, assessment, revision, and reassessment. It parallels the natural rhythm of learning.

- **Offer an incentive to learn.** Students have a vested interest in creating the portfolios, through which they can showcase their ongoing efforts and tangible achievements. Students select the works to be included and have a chance to revise, improve, evaluate, and explain the contents.

- **Are sensitive to individual needs.** Language learners bring varied abilities to the classroom and do not acquire skills in a uniformly neat and orderly fashion. The personalized, individualized assessment offered by portfolios responds to this diversity.

- **Provide documentation of language development.** The material in a portfolio is evidence of student progress in the language learning process. The contents of the portfolio make it easier to discuss their progress with the students as well as with parents and others.

- **Offer multiple sources of information.** A portfolio presents a way to collect and analyze information from multiple sources that reflects a student's efforts, progress, and achievements in the language.

Portfolio Components

The foreign language portfolio should include both oral and written work, student self-evaluation, and teacher observation, usually in the form of brief, non-evaluative comments about various aspects of the student's performance.

Portfolios offer a more realistic and accurate way to assess the process of language teaching and learning.

The Oral Component

The oral component of a portfolio might be an audio- or videocassette. It may contain both rehearsed and extemporaneous monologues and conversations. For a rehearsed speaking activity, give a specific communicative task that students can personalize according to their individual interests (for example, ordering a favorite meal in a restaurant). If the speaking activity is extemporaneous, first acquaint students with possible topics for discussion or even the specific task they will be expected to perform. (For example, tell them they will be asked to discuss a picture showing a sports activity or a restaurant scene.)

The Written Component

Portfolios are excellent tools for incorporating process writing strategies into the foreign language classroom. Documentation of various stages of the writing process—brainstorming, multiple drafts, and peer comments—may be included with the finished product.

Involve students in selecting writing tasks for the portfolio. At the beginning levels, the tasks might include some structured writing, such as labeling or listing. As students become more proficient, journals, letters, and other more complicated writing tasks are valuable ways for them to monitor their progress in using the written language.

Student Self-Evaluation

Students should be actively involved in critiquing and evaluating their portfolios and monitoring their own progress. The process and procedure for student self-evaluation should be considered in planning the contents of the portfolio. Students should work with you and their peers to design the exact format. Self-evaluation encourages them to think about what they are learning (content), how they learn (process), why they are learning (purpose), and where they are going in their learning (goals).

Teacher Observation

Systematic, regular, and ongoing observations should be placed in the portfolio after they have been discussed with the student. These observations provide feedback on the student's progress in the language learning process.

Teacher observations should be based on an established set of criteria that has been developed earlier with input from the student. Observation techniques may include the following:
• Jotting notes in a journal to be discussed with the student and then placed in the portfolio
• Using a checklist of observable behaviors, such as the willingness to take risks when using the target language or staying on task during the lesson
• Making observations on adhesive notes that can be placed in folders
• Recording anecdotal comments, during or after class, using a cassette recorder.

Knowledge of the criteria you use in your observations gives students a framework for their performance.

How Are Portfolios Evaluated?

The portfolio should reflect the process of student learning over a specific period of time. At the beginning of that time period, determine the criteria by which you will assess the final product and convey them to the students. Make this evaluation a collaborative effort by seeking students' input as you formulate these criteria and your instructional goals.

Students need to understand that evaluation based on a predetermined standard is but one phase of the assessment process; demonstrated effort and growth are just as important. As you consider correctness and accuracy in both oral and written work, also consider the organization, creativity, and improvement revealed by the student's portfolio over the time period. The portfolio provides a way to monitor the growth of a student's knowledge, skills, and attitudes and shows the student's efforts, progress, and achievements.

How to Implement Portfolios

Teacher-teacher collaboration is as important to the implementation of portfolios as teacher-student collaboration. Confer with your colleagues to determine, for example, what kinds of information you want to see in the student portfolio, how the information will be presented, the purpose of the portfolio, the intended purposes (grading, placement, or a combination of the two), and criteria for evaluating the portfolio. Conferring among colleagues helps foster a departmental cohesiveness and consistency that will ultimately benefit the students.

The Promise of Portfolios

The high degree of student involvement in developing portfolios and deciding how they will be used generally results in renewed student enthusiasm for learning and improved achievement. As students

compare portfolio pieces done early in the year with work produced later, they can take pride in their progress as well as reassess their motivation and work habits.

Portfolios also provide a framework for periodic assessment of teaching strategies, programs, and instruction. They offer schools a tool to help solve the problem of vertical articulation and accurate student placement. The more realistic and accurate assessment of the language learning process that is provided by portfolios is congruent with the strategies that should be used in the proficiency-oriented classroom.

ADELANTE

Adelante *supports the use of portfolios in the following ways:*

The Pupil's Edition
◆ Includes numerous oral and written activities that can be easily adapted for student portfolios, such as **En mi cuaderno** and the more global review activities in Repaso.

◆ Includes a process writing strategy in Chapters 3–6 that progressively develops students' skills at drafting, revising, and evaluating assignments suitable for their portfolios.

The Interactive CD-ROM Program
◆ Includes word-processing and sound-recording capabilities that allow students to create original or guided work for their portfolios.

The Annotated Teacher's Edition
◆ Suggests activities in the Portfolio and Performance Assessment features that may serve as portfolio items.

The Ancillary Program
◆ Includes criteria in the *Alternative Assessment Guide* for evaluating portfolios, as well as Speaking Tests in the *Testing Program* for each chapter that can be adapted for use as portfolio assessment items.

LEARNING STYLES AND MULTI-MODALITY TEACHING

BY MARY B. MCGEHEE

The larger and broader population of students who are enrolling in foreign language classes brings a new challenge to foreign language educators, calling forth an evolution in teaching methods to enhance learning for all our students. Educational experts now recognize that every student has a preferred sense for learning and retrieving information: visual, auditory, or kinesthetic. Incorporating a greater variety of activities to accommodate the learning styles of all students can make the difference between struggle and pleasure in the foreign language classroom. ◆

Accommodating Different Learning Styles

A modified arrangement of the classroom is one way to provide more effective and enjoyable learning for all students. Rows of chairs and desks must give way at times to circles, semicircles, or small clusters. Students may be grouped in fours or in pairs for cooperative work or peer teaching. It is important to find a balance of arrangements, thereby providing the most comfort in varied situations.

Since visual, auditory, and kinesthetic learners will be in the class, and because every student's learning will be enhanced by a multisensory approach, lessons must be directed toward all three learning styles. Any language lesson content may be presented visually, aurally, or kinesthetically.

Visual presentations and practice may include the chalkboard, charts, posters, television, overhead projectors, books, magazines, picture diagrams, flash cards, bulletin boards, films, slides, or videos. Visual learners need to see what they are to learn. Lest the teacher think he or she will never have the time to prepare all those visuals, Dickel and Slak (1983) found that visual aids generated by students are more effective than ready-made ones.

Auditory presentations and practice may include stating aloud the requirements of the lesson, oral questions and answers, paired or group work on a progression of oral exercises from repetition to communication, CDs, computer sound recordings, dialogues, and role-playing. Jingles, catchy stories, and memory devices using songs and rhymes are good learning aids. Having students record themselves and then listen as they play back the recording allows them to practice in the auditory mode.

Kinesthetic presentations entail the students' use of manipulatives, chart materials, gestures, signals, typing, songs, games, and role-playing. These lead the students to associate sentence constructions with meaningful movements.

A Sample Lesson Using Multi-Modality Teaching

A multi-sensory presentation on greetings might proceed as follows.

For Visual Learners
As the teacher begins oral presentation of greetings and introductions, he or she simultaneously shows the written forms on transparencies, with the formal expressions marked with an adult's hat, and the informal expressions marked with a baseball cap.

The teacher then distributes cards with the hat and cap symbols representing the formal and informal expressions. As the students hear taped mini-dialogues, they hold up the appropriate card to indicate whether the dialogues are formal or informal. On the next listening, the students repeat the sentences they hear.

> Incorporating a greater variety of activities to accommodate the learning styles of all students can make the difference between struggle and pleasure in the foreign language classroom.

For Auditory Learners
A longer recorded dialogue follows, allowing the students to hear the new expressions a number of times. They write from dictation several sentences containing the new expressions. They may work in pairs, correcting each other's work as they "test" their own understanding of the lesson at hand. Finally, students respond to simple questions using the appropriate formal and informal responses cued by the cards they hold.

For Kinesthetic Learners

For additional kinesthetic input, members of the class come to the front of the room, each holding a hat or cap symbol. As the teacher calls out situations, the students play the roles, using gestures and props appropriate to the age group they are portraying. Non-cued, communicative role-playing with props further enables the students to "feel" the differences between formal and informal expressions.

Helping Students Learn How to Use Their Preferred Mode

Since we require all students to perform in all language skills, part of the assistance we must render is to help them develop strategies within their preferred learning modes to carry out an assignment in another mode. For example, visual students hear the teacher assign an oral exercise and visualize what they must do. They must see themselves carrying out the assignment, in effect watching themselves as if there were a movie going on in their heads. Only then can they also hear themselves saying the right things. Thus, this assignment will be much easier for the visual learners who have been taught this process, if they have not already figured it out for themselves. Likewise, true auditory students, confronted with a reading/ writing assignment, must talk themselves through it, converting the entire process into sound as they plan and prepare their work. Kinesthetic students presented with a visual or auditory task must first break the assignment into tasks and then work their way through them.

Students who experience difficulty because of a strong preference for one mode of learning are often unaware of the degree of preference. In working with these students, I prefer the simple and direct assessment of learning styles offered by Richard Bandler and John Grinder in their book *Frogs into Princes,* which allows the teacher and student to quickly determine how the student learns. In an interview with the student, I follow the assessment with certain specific recommendations of techniques to make the student's study time more effective.

It is important to note here that teaching students to maximize their study does not require that the teacher give each student an individualized assignment. It does require that each student who needs it be taught how to prepare the assignment using his or her own talents and strengths. This communication between teacher and student, combined with teaching techniques that reinforce learning in all modes,

can only maximize pleasure and success in learning a foreign language.

References

Dickel, M.J. and S. Slak. "Imaging Vividness and Memory for Verbal Material." *Journal of Mental Imagery* 7, i (1983):121–126.

Bandler, Richard, and John Grinder. *Frogs into Princes.* Real People Press, Moab, UT. 1978.

ADELANTE

Adelante *accommodates different learning styles in the following ways:*

The Pupil's Edition

◆ Presents basic material in audio, video, and print formats.

◆ Includes role-playing activities and a variety of multi-modal activities, including an extensive listening strand and many art-based activities.

The Annotated Teacher's Edition

◆ Provides suggested activities for visual, auditory, and kinesthetic learners as well as suggestions for slower-paced learning and challenge activities.

◆ Includes Total Physical Response activities.

The Ancillary Program

◆ Provides additional reinforcement activities for a variety of learning styles.

◆ Presents a rich blend of audiovisual input through the video, audio, and CD-ROM programs, and through transparencies and copying masters.

NEW PERSPECTIVES FOR NATIVE SPEAKERS

By Cecilia Rodríguez-Pino

Spanish teachers often simultaneously teach two groups of students whose learning needs are markedly different. The first group, the majority, for whom most curricula are developed, are English-proficient but at a beginner's level in Spanish. The second group consists of students whose proficiency in English varies but who already speak Spanish, often quite proficiently. From their own experience they already understand a great deal about the Spanish language and the cultures of Spanish speakers. Many schools have not yet set up Spanish for Native Speakers (SNS) sections with specialized curricula that would build on these students' linguistic and cultural strengths. As a result, in some schools native speakers who want to study Spanish are enrolled in courses where Spanish is taught as a foreign language. Addressing their learning needs thus becomes the particular challenge of the teacher, who must create and implement supplemental classroom materials. ◆

Types of Native Spanish Speakers

The greatest number of native Spanish speakers in the classroom are Spanish-speaking immigrants and American students of Hispanic descent. Many immigrants have been uprooted from their native countries and find themselves in a new and foreign environment without the skills to communicate. Often they must struggle to adapt to mainstream sociocultural norms and values. Psychological adjustment, cultural integration, and the acquisition of new communicative skills are daily concerns for them. Building teacher-student and peer-peer learning relationships may be harder for such students.

American students of Hispanic descent are often bilingual. Some are highly proficient in both written and oral Spanish, but many are proficient to varying degrees, depending on the circumstances, topics, tasks, and informal situations. These students reflect the various socio-economic classes of society and speak a wide range of Spanish dialects. Research indicates that the dialect they speak affects how they are viewed at school. When they speak a "standard" variety of Spanish or are from an educated class, as are many Cuban Americans in Florida, reactions to them are usually positive. But when Spanish speakers are from a rural background, speak a "non-standard" dialect, or come from a non-literate background, reactions in school are often negative. Attempting to modify their dialect can be detrimental to their linguistic and social development.

Linguistic Needs

Native Spanish speakers need to retrieve any Spanish they may have lost, maintain the competency they already have, and expand their knowledge and skills in Spanish.

The problem of native language loss is receiving much attention in the profession. Children appear to lose production skills more quickly than they lose comprehension ability. Thus retrieval efforts should focus on production. Rapid changes in society and in the patterns by which Spanish is transmitted from one generation to the next account for much of students' language loss. Word borrowing and code switching to English may also account for language loss. These practices are not unique to bilingual students in the United States; they are common linguistic phenomena, observed wherever languages are in contact. A native speaker may switch from Spanish to English when referring to activities generally associated with the dominant culture—even when the speaker is perfectly familiar with the relevant Spanish vocabulary. Efforts to eradicate code switching may harm students' linguistic and social development.

Affective Needs

Native Spanish-speaking students bring to class much valuable cultural and linguistic experience. Cultural opportunities need to be provided for them through which they can express their knowledge of their own particular Spanish-speaking culture and gain a greater overview of other Spanish-speaking communities and countries. They need to understand that their heritage, language, culture, dialect, and individual abilities are valuable to society. As teachers we must respect and value the different languages and dialects our students speak, and we must create an instructional context in which students will develop positive attitudes toward their own ethnic group and their own ethnic identity.

An SNS Program Approach

A task-based, whole-language approach is recommended. Receptive and productive skills can be developed through culturally meaningful activities whose contexts are community, school, home, and self. These activities can be carried out in conjunction with textbook thematic units. Such an approach creates a student-centered classroom in which the teacher acts as a facilitator connecting students to the bilingual community.

Expanding Receptive Skills

Students should perform activities in which they listen to their native language in a broad range of formal and informal contexts, from simple topics to complex ones. Audio- or videotaped versions of stories, songs, documentaries, speeches, or debates can be adapted for class assignments. Guest speakers from the community are extremely valuable resources for presentations or interviews on the chapter topic.

Students should have access to diverse, authentic reading materials from the popular culture as well as from more formal subject areas. Chicano, Cuban, Dominican, Colombian, Nicaraguan, Honduran, Panamanian, and Puerto Rican writings—which are underrepresented in the mainstream literary canon—can play an important role in instilling in students a sense of pride and awareness of their cultural heritage. Students relate well to literature written by contemporary Hispanic authors who have had experiences similar to the students' in the United States. For example, they might read the short story "Desde que se fue," from the collection *Madreselvas en flor* by literary prize-winning Chicano author Ricardo Aguilar-Melantzón, about growing up in a bilingual setting.

Developing Productive Skills

Oral history projects, ethnographic interviews, sociolinguistic surveys, dialogue journals, letter writing, and other purposeful authentic activities are effective techniques that focus on interactions among students, teacher, and community. These kinds of activities give students the opportunity to develop individual strengths and to explore their language and culture in a community context.

Classroom Environment

We can change the classroom space itself to create an environment that recognizes the prestige of the students' language and cultural heritage. Using a brief questionnaire, the teacher can find out the students' backgrounds and then display relevant posters, travel brochures, art, literature, or historical information. Students can contribute captioned photographs depicting cultural events and family traditions, so that the bulletin board reflects their personal view of the Spanish-speaking world rather than just the teacher's perspective.

Individual Assessment and Evaluation

Individual assessment at the beginning of the year should be based primarily on content so that students' errors are not the main focus. Use content, organization, and language as criteria for evaluating speaking and writing. In evaluating students' work for the year, take into account how students have broadened their functional range. This requires students to be responsible for the concepts that are essential to comprehension and production. A writing portfolio is a valuable component of the evaluation process. Oral presentations of ethnographic and sociolinguistic projects are contextualized activities for evaluating speaking.

PROFESSIONAL REFERENCES

*T*his section provides information about resources that can enrich your Spanish class. Included are addresses of Spanish and Latin American government offices, pen pal organizations, subscription agencies, and many others. Since addresses change frequently, you may want to verify them before you send your requests. ◆

Pen pal organizations

For the names of pen pal groups other than those listed below, contact your local chapter of AATSP. There are fees involved, so be sure to write for information.

Student Letter Exchange
(League of Friendship)
211 Broadway, Suite 201
Lynbrook, NY 11563
(516) 887-8628

World Pen Pals
1694 Como Avenue
St. Paul, MN 55108
(612) 647-0191

Embassies and consulates

Addresses and phone numbers of embassies and consulates for Spanish-speaking countries are available in most U.S. city telephone directories. All are available in the directory for Washington, D.C.

Periodicals

Subscriptions to the following cultural materials are available through jobbers or directly from the publishers. See also the section on Subscription Services.

- **Blanco y negro,** a general interest weekly magazine in Spain
- **Eres,** a Mexican magazine for teens
- **El País,** a major daily newspaper in Spain

- **Hispanic,** an English-language magazine about Hispanics in the U.S.
- **La Prensa,** a major daily paper in Argentina
- **Tú internacional,** a magazine for teens published in several Spanish-speaking countries
- **México desconocido,** a cultural and environmental magazine about Mexico

Cultural agencies

For historical and tourist information about Spanish-speaking countries, contact:

Tourist Office of Spain
666 Fifth Avenue
New York, NY 10022
(212) 265-8822

Intercultural exchange

CIEE Student Travel Services
205 East 42nd St.
New York, NY 10017
(888) 268-6245

American Field Service
198 Madison, 8th Floor
New York, NY 10016
(212) 299-9000

Professional organizations

The American Council on the Teaching of Foreign Languages (ACTFL)
6 Executive Plaza
Yonkers, NY 10701
(914) 963-8830

American Association of Teachers of Spanish and Portuguese (AATSP)
Butter-Hancock Hall #210
University of Northern Colorado
Greeley, CO 80639
(970) 351-1090

Subscription services

Spanish-language magazines can be obtained through subscription agencies in the United States. The following companies are among the many which can provide your school with subscriptions:

EBSCO Subscription Services
P.O. Box 1943
Birmingham, AL 35201-1943
(205) 991-6600

Continental Book Company
8000 Cooper Ave., Bldg. 29
Glendale, NY 11385
(718) 326-0560

Miscellaneous

Educational Resources Information Center (ERIC)
2277 Research Blvd.
Rockville, MD 20852
(800) 538-3742
- Foreign language periodicals

The International Film Bureau
332 South Michigan Ave.
Chicago, IL 60604-4382
(312) 427-4545
- Foreign language videos for sale and/or rent

Américas
Organization of American States
17th and Constitution Ave. NW
Room #307
Washington, D.C. 20006
(202) 458-3000
- Magazine available in English or Spanish text

A BIBLIOGRAPHY FOR THE SPANISH TEACHER

¡Ven conmigo!
Adelante

This bibliography is a compilation of resources available for professional enrichment. ◆

Selected and annotated list of readings

I. Methods and Approaches

Cohen, Andrew D. *Assessing Language Ability in the Classroom, 2/e.* Boston, MA: Heinle, 1994.

- Assessment processes, oral interviews, role-playing situations, dictation, and portfolio assessment.

Hadley, Alice Omaggio. *Teaching Language in Context, 2/e.* Boston, MA: Heinle, 1993.

- Language acquisition theories and models and adult second language proficiency.

Krashen, Stephen, and Tracy D. Terrell. *The Natural Approach: Language Acquisition in the Classroom.* New York: Pergamon, 1983.

- Optimal Input Theory: listening, oral communication development, and testing.

Oller, John W., Jr. *Methods That Work: Ideas for Language Teachers, 2/e.* Boston, MA: Heinle, 1993.

- Literacy in multicultural settings, co-operative learning, peer teaching, and computer-assisted instruction.

Shrum, Judith L., and Eileen W. Glisan. *Teacher's Handbook: Contextualized Language Instruction.* Boston, MA: Heinle, 1993.

- Grammar, testing, using video texts, microteaching, case studies and daily plans.

II. Second-Language Theory

Krashen, Stephen. *The Power of Reading.* New York: McGraw-Hill, 1994.

- Updates Optimal Input Theory by incorporating the reading of authentic texts.

Liskin-Gasparro, Judith. *A Guide to Testing and Teaching for Oral Proficiency.* Boston, MA: Heinle, 1990.

- Oral proficiency through interview techniques and speech samples.

Rubin, Joan, and Irene Thompson. *How To Be a More Successful Language Learner, 2/e.* Boston, MA: Heinle, 1993.

- Psychological, linguistic, and practical matters of second-language learning.

III. Video and computer-assisted instruction

Altmann, Rick. *The Video Connection: Integrating Video into Language Teaching.* Boston, MA: Houghton Mifflin, 1989.

- Diverse strategies for using video texts to support second- language learning.

Dunkel, Patricia A. *Computer-Assisted Language Learning and Testing.* Boston, MA: Heinle, 1992.

- CAI and computer-assisted language learning (CALL) in the foreign language classroom.

Kenning, M. J., and M. M. Kenning. *Computers and Language Learning: Current Theory and Practice.* New York, NY: E. Horwood, 1990.

- Theoretical discussions and practical suggestions for CAI in second-language development.

IV. Teaching Native Speakers

Aguilar-Melantzón, Ricardo. "Desde que se fue."

- Produced for Teaching Spanish to Southwest Hispanic Students, National Endowment for the Humanities Summer Conference, Cecilia Rodríguez-Pino, project director. Las Cruces: New Mexico State University, 1993. Available through Spanish for Native Speakers Program, New Mexico State University. Audiotape of short story narrated by author.

Merino, Barbara J., Henry T. Trueba, and Fabián A. Samaniego. *Language and Culture in Learning: Teaching Spanish to Native Speakers of Spanish.* London, England: Falmer Press, 1993.

Rodríguez-Pino, Cecilia, and Daniel Villa. "A Student-Centered Spanish for Native Speakers Program: Theory, Curriculum Design and Outcome Assessment." *In Faces in a Crowd: The Individual Learner in Multisection Courses.* Edited by Carol A. Klee. American Association of University Supervisors Series. Boston, MA: Heinle, 1994.

Valdés, Guadalupe. "The Role of the Foreign Language Teaching Profession in Maintaining Non-English Languages in the United States." In *Northeast Conference Reports: Languages for a Multicultural World in Transition.* Edited by Heidi Byrnes. Lincolnwood, IL: National Textbook, 1992.

SCOPE AND SEQUENCE: SPANISH LEVEL 1A

FUNCTIONS	GRAMMAR	VOCABULARY	CULTURE	RE-ENTRY
CAPÍTULO PRELIMINAR ¡Adelante!				
• Map of the Spanish-speaking world	• ¿Cómo te llamas?, Los acentos • El alfabeto, Los cognados • Frases útiles	• Los colores • El calendario	• El español—¿Por qué? • ¿Sabías? • ¿Los conoces?	• Los números

España

FUNCTIONS	GRAMMAR	VOCABULARY	CULTURE	RE-ENTRY
CAPÍTULO 1 ¡Mucho gusto!				
• Saying hello and goodbye • Introducing people and responding to an introduction • Asking how someone is and saying how you are • Asking and saying how old someone is • Asking where someone is from and saying where you're from • Talking about likes and dislikes	• Punctuation marks • Pronouns **tú** and **yo** • **Soy, eres** and **es** • Asking questions • Nouns and definite articles	• Numbers 0–30, p. 36 • Sports, p. 44 • Classes at school, p. 44 • Musical genres, p. 45 • Foods, p. 45	• First and last names in Spanish • First names and Catholicism • Saint's Days • Greetings • Handwriting in Spanish-speaking countries • Snack foods in Spain • **¿De dónde eres?**	• Accents (from **Capítulo preliminar**) • Numbers 0–30 (from **Capítulo preliminar**)

España

FUNCTIONS	GRAMMAR	VOCABULARY	CULTURE	RE-ENTRY
CAPÍTULO 2 ¡Organízate!				
• Talking about what you want or need • Telling what's in your room • Talking about what you need and want to do	• Indefinite articles **un** and **una** • Noun plurals • Plural indefinite articles • Subject pronouns **él** and **ella** • Plurals of **¿cuánto?** and **mucho** • Identifying infinitives	• School supplies, p. 65 • The contents of your room, p. 75 • Things you do, p. 86 • Numbers 31–199, p. 88	• Extended family • School uniforms • Apartment in Spain/Sharing TV set • Exclamations • **Los saludos** • **¿Qué necesitas para el colegio?**	• Subject pronouns: **tú** and **yo** (from **Capítulo 1**) • Definite articles: **el** and **la** (from **Capítulo 1**) • Numbers 0–30 (from **Capítulo preliminar**) • Using cognates (from **Capítulo preliminar**)

México

FUNCTIONS	GRAMMAR	VOCABULARY	CULTURE	RE-ENTRY
CAPÍTULO 3 Nuevas clases, nuevos amigos				
• Talking about classes and sequencing events • Telling time • Telling at what time something happens • Talking about being late or in a hurry • Describing people and things • Talking about things you like and explaining why	• Plural definite articles **los** and **las** • Telling time with **ser** • The preposition **de** • The verb **ser** for descriptions • Adjective agreement • Tag questions	• School subjects, p. 109 • Time expressions, p. 119 • Words that describe people and things, p. 125 • Free-time activities and things you like, p. 130	• Class schedules in Spanish-speaking countries • Grades in Spanish-speaking countries • The **siesta** • Titles of respect • **¿Cómo es un día escolar típico?**	• Present tense of **tener** • Numbers 0–99 • School supplies • Forming questions • Present tense of **tener** • Noun-adjective agreement • **necesitar** and **querer** • Talking about likes and dislikes • Question formation

México

CAPÍTULO 4 ¿Qué haces esta tarde?

FUNCTIONS	GRAMMAR	VOCABULARY	CULTURE	RE-ENTRY
• Talking about what you and others like to do • Talking about what you and others do during free time • Telling where people and things are • Talking about where you and others go during free time	• Present tense of regular -**ar** verbs • **con, conmigo, contigo** • Relative pronoun **que** • The verb **estar** • Subject pronouns • The verb **ir** • Days of the week	• Things you like to do, p. 154 • Places in town and their location, p. 163 • The days of the week, p. 174	• Hispanic athletes • Referring to or greeting friends • Sights and activities in Cuernavaca • **tú** and **usted** • **Un recorrido de la Plaza de las Armas** • **¿Te gusta pasear con tus amigos?**	• Present tense of **tener** • Present tense of **gustar** • Subject pronouns **yo, tú, él, ella** • Describing with **ser** • Telling time • Days of the week

Florida

CAPÍTULO 5 El ritmo de la vida

FUNCTIONS	GRAMMAR	VOCABULARY	CULTURE	RE-ENTRY
• Discussing how often you do things • Talking about what you do and your friends like to do together • Talking about what you do during a typical week • Giving today's date • Talking about the weather	• Negation • The question words **¿quién?** and **¿quiénes?** • The pronoun **les** • -**er** and -**ir** verbs • The formula for giving today's date	• Weekend activities, p. 204 • Frequency terms, p. 208 • The seasons and the months, p. 214 • Weather expressions, p. 216	• Leisure time activities • Meeting places • The seasons of the year in South America • **¿Cómo es una semana típica?**	• Present tense of regular -**ar** verbs • Negation with **no** • **¿quién?** • **gustar** • Subject pronouns • Days of the week

Florida

CAPÍTULO 6 Entre familia

FUNCTIONS	GRAMMAR	VOCABULARY	CULTURE	RE-ENTRY
• Describing a family • Describing people • Discussing things a family does together • Discussing problems and giving advice	• Possessive adjectives • the verbs **hacer** and **salir** • The personal **a** • The verb **deber** • The verb **poner** • Present tense of **decir: dice**	• Members of the family, p. 235 • Pets and the words to describe them, p. 241 • Words that describe people, pp. 245, 248 • Household chores, p. 256	• Diminutive names • El Compadrazgo • **La importancia de la familia hispana** • **¿Cuántos son en tu familia?**	• **hay** • Possessive adjectives • Demonstrative adjectives • Use of **de** • Colors • Descriptions of people • Pastimes/hobbies • **¿con qué frecuencia?** • Adjective agreement • Forming questions with **¿cómo?** and **¿cuántos?**

SCOPE AND SEQUENCE: SPANISH LEVEL 1B

FUNCTIONS	GRAMMAR	VOCABULARY	CULTURE	RE-ENTRY

CAPÍTULO PUENTE   En camino | *Bridge Chapter*

• Greeting others; saying what you have • Talking about what you do and when; describing people and places • Talking about how often you do things; talking about your family	• The verbs **estar, ser,** and **tener** • Indirect object pronouns • Using **hay** • Possessive adjectives • Telling time • Present tense of regular **-ar, -er,** and **-ir** verbs • Adjective agreement • The verbs **hacer, salir, poner, deber,** and **ir**	• Pastimes • Family members • Weather expressions • Place names • Time expressions	• The **Capítulo puente** reviews material presented in chapters 1–6 of *Adelante*.

Ecuador — CAPÍTULO 7   ¿Qué te gustaría hacer?

• Talking on the telephone • Extending and accepting invitations • Making plans • Talking about getting ready • Turning down an invitation and explaining why	• **e** to **ie** stem-changing verbs • **pensar** + infinitive and **ir** + **a** + infinitive • Reflexive verbs (infinitives only) • Expressions with **tener**	• Places and events, p. 55 • Transportation, p. 62 • Personal items, p. 63 • Expression of apology, p. 69	• Telephone greetings • Modes of transportation • **¿Qué haces para conocer a un nuevo estudiante?**	• Invitations: **gustar** • Days of the week • Future expressions: **hoy, mañana,** etc. • Expressions of frequency • The verb **tener**

Ecuador — CAPÍTULO 8   ¡A comer!

• Talking about meals and food • Commenting on food • Making polite requests • Ordering dinner in a restaurant • Asking for and paying the bill in a restaurant	• The verb **encantar** and indirect object pronouns • **o** to **ue** stem-changing verbs • **Ser** and **estar** with food • Expressions with **tener** • **Así se dice:** Indirect object pronouns **nos** and **me** • **otro** • **Así se dice:** Indirect object pronoun **le; quisiera**	• Breakfast foods, p. 88 • Lunch foods, p. 90 • Foods, p. 100 • Tableware, p. 105 • Dinner foods, p. 107 • Numbers 200–100,000, p. 110	• Names of fruits and vegetables • Main meal of the day • Eating out in Ecuador • Table manners • Dinner and snacks • Types of foods • **La comida en el mundo hispanohablante** • **¿Cuál es un plato típico de tu país o región?**	• Expressing likes and dislikes • Present tense of regular and **e** to **ie** stem-changing verbs • Times of day • **estar** versus **ser** • Expressions with **tener** • Numbers 200–100,000 • Question words **¿qué?** and **¿cuánto?**

	FUNCTIONS	GRAMMAR	VOCABULARY	CULTURE	RE-ENTRY

Texas

CAPÍTULO 9 ¡Vamos de compras!

FUNCTIONS	GRAMMAR	VOCABULARY	CULTURE	RE-ENTRY
• Talking about giving gifts • Asking for and giving directions downtown • Commenting on clothes • Making comparisons • Expressing preferences • Asking about prices and paying	• Indirect object pronouns **le** and **les** • Use of **ser** to tell what something is made of • Making comparisons: **más... que, menos... que, tan... como** • Using the demonstrative adjectives **este** and **ese**	• Gift items, p.132 • Store names, p.135 • Clothing, pp. 140,143 • Expressions related to cost, p. 151	• Specialty stores in Spain • Personal care and dress in Spanish-speaking countries • Currencies in Spanish-speaking countries • **¿Estás a la moda?**	• **ir** + **a** + infinitive for planning • Describing family • Talking about locations • Talking about where things are • Present tense of **ser** for description • Numbers 0–100,000

Texas

CAPÍTULO 10 Celebraciones

FUNCTIONS	GRAMMAR	VOCABULARY	CULTURE	RE-ENTRY
• Talking about what you're doing right now • Asking for and giving an opinion • Asking for help and responding to requests • Telling a friend what to do • Talking about past events	• Present progressive • Informal commands • Preterite tense of regular **-ar** verbs • Direct object pronouns **lo** and **la**	• Holidays, p. 169 • Party expressions, p. 180 • Time expressions, p. 188	• **Día del santo** • **La quinceañera** • Traditional holiday foods • **El Paseo del Río** • **¿Qué hacen ustedes para celebrar?**	• **estar** • Dates, months, seasons • Extending, accepting, turning down invitations • **tú** versus **usted** • Household chores • Days of the week • Question words **¿quién?** and **¿quiénes?** • Free-time activities

Puerto Rico

CAPÍTULO 11 Para vivir bien

FUNCTIONS	GRAMMAR	VOCABULARY	CULTURE	RE-ENTRY
• Making suggestions and expressing feelings • Talking about moods and physical condition • Saying what you did • Talking about where you went and when	• **¿Te acuerdas?:** the verb **dormir** • Present tense of **sentirse** • The verb **doler** with **me, te, le** • The verb **jugar** in the preterite • The verb **ir** in the preterite	• Keeping fit, p. 215 • Physical conditions, p. 221 • Parts of the body, p. 223 • Different sports fields, p. 232	• Body parts in common expressions • Baseball in Spanish-speaking countries • Sports in Spanish-speaking countries • **¿Qué deporte practicas?**	• **e** to **ie** stem-changing verbs • Food vocabulary • Expressions of frequency • Definite articles • **estar** + condition • **o** to **ue** stem-changing verbs • Use of preterite tense to discuss past events

Puerto Rico

CAPÍTULO 12 Las vacaciones ideales   *Review Chapter*

FUNCTIONS	GRAMMAR	VOCABULARY	CULTURE	RE-ENTRY
• Talking about what you do and like to do every day; making future plans • Discussing what you would like to do on vacation • Saying where you went and what you did on vacation	• **e** to **ie** and **o** to **ue** stem-changing verbs • Verbs followed by an infinitive • Uses of **ser** and **estar** • Uses of the preterite	• Vacation items, p. 254 • Vacation activities, p. 261 • Countries, p. 272	• **¿Adónde vas y qué haces en las vacaciones?**	• Chapter 12 reviews material presented in chapters 7–12 of *En camino*.

SCOPE AND SEQUENCE: SPANISH LEVEL 2

	FUNCTIONS	GRAMMAR	VOCABULARY	CULTURE	RE-ENTRY

Andalucía — **CAPÍTULO 1** **Mis amigos y yo,** *Pages 4–33* — *Review Chapter*

FUNCTIONS	GRAMMAR	VOCABULARY	CULTURE	RE-ENTRY
• Introducing yourself and others • Describing people • Talking about what you and others do • Saying what you like and don't like	• Present tense of **tener** • Adjective agreement • Present tense of regular verbs • Indirect object pronouns with verbs like **gustar**	• Nationalities • Numbers • Colors • Family members	• Description of appearance of Hispanics • **¿Qué es americano?** • Planning evening activities in Spain • **¿Qué es un buen amigo?** • **cafeterías**	• Chapter 1 reviews Spanish taught in *Adelante, Level 1A* and *En camino, Level 1B.*

Andalucía — **CAPÍTULO 2** **Un viaje al estranjero,** *Pages 34–61* — *Review Chapter*

FUNCTIONS	GRAMMAR	VOCABULARY	CULTURE	RE-ENTRY
• Talking about how you're feeling • Making suggestions and responding to them • Saying if something has already been done • Asking for and offering help • Describing your city or town	• The verb **estar** • Preterite of **-ar** verbs • Present tense of **querer** and **poder**	• Calendar expressions • Places around town • Weather expressions • Clothing	• Extended family living together • **¿En dónde te gustaría vivir?** • Celsius vs. Fahrenheit	• Chapter 2 reviews Spanish taught in *Adelante, Level 1A* and *En camino, Level 1B.*

Valle de México — **CAPÍTULO 3** **La vida cotidiana,** *Pages 66–93*

FUNCTIONS	GRAMMAR	VOCABULARY	CULTURE	RE-ENTRY
• Talking about your daily routine • Talking about responsibilities • Complaining • Talking about hobbies and pastimes • Saying how long something has been going on	• Reflexive verbs and pronouns • **e** to **i** stem change in **vestirse** • Adverbs ending in **-mente** • Direct object pronouns **lo, la, los, las** • **hace** + quantity of time + **que** + present tense	• Daily activities • Chores • Hobbies and pastimes	• **¿Cuál es tu profesión?** • Household chores • Expressions of agreement • Popular free-time activities among teenagers	• Verbs of personal grooming • Adverbs of time and place • Vocabulary of hobbies and pastimes • making excuses • Question formation

FUNCTIONS	GRAMMAR	VOCABULARY	CULTURE	RE-ENTRY

Valle de México

CAPÍTULO 4 ¡Adelante con los estudios *Pages 94–123*

FUNCTIONS	GRAMMAR	VOCABULARY	CULTURE	RE-ENTRY
• Asking for and giving opinions • Giving advice • Talking about things and people you know • Making comparisons • Making plans	• **deberías** vs. **debes** • **ser** + adjective to describe people • **estar** + adjective to describe location • Present tense of the verb **conocer** • Direct object pronouns	• Classroom activities • School and computer terms • Describing people • Activities around town	• School levels in Mexico • Cost of university education in Latin America • **¿Qué haces después del colegio?** • **¿Cuándo asistes a clases?**	• School subjects • **para** (in order to) + infinitive • **ser** vs. **estar** • Comparisons: **más... que** • **ir** + **a** + infinitive

Texas

CAPÍTULO 5 ¡Ponte en forma!, *Pages 128–157*

FUNCTIONS	GRAMMAR	VOCABULARY	CULTURE	RE-ENTRY
• Talking about staying fit and healthy • Telling someone what to do and not to do • Making excuses	• Preterite of the verb **dormir** • Preterite of regular **-er** and **-ir** verbs • Informal commands • Irregular informal commands • Preterite of **poder** • Reflexives with verbs of emotion	• Sports • Fitness activities • Health and fitness terms • Body parts • Injuries and explanations	• Student responses about health habits in Spanish-speaking countries • Vending machines in high schools • Snack foods in Spanish-speaking countries • **Garnachas, antojitos y bocadillos** • **Qué haces para mantenerte en forma?**	• Preterite of regular **-ar** verbs • Informal commands • Spelling changes in verbs that end in **-car, -gar, -zar** • Reflexive verbs

Texas

CAPÍTULO 6 De visita en la ciudad, *Pages 158–185*

FUNCTIONS	GRAMMAR	VOCABULARY	CULTURE	RE-ENTRY
• Asking for and giving information • Relating a series of events • Ordering in a restaurant	• Present tense of **saber** • **saber** vs. **conocer** • Preterite forms of **pedir, servir, traer**	• In the city • Places in the city • In the train station • In a restaurant	• San Antonio • **¿Cómo llegas al colegio?** • Birthday celebrations	• Direct object pronouns • **poder** • The preterite for listing events • Food vocabulary

T65

SCOPE AND SEQUENCE: SPANISH LEVEL 2

	FUNCTIONS	GRAMMAR	VOCABULARY	CULTURE	RE-ENTRY
El Caribe	**CAPÍTULO 7** ¿Conoces bien tu pasado?, *Pages 190–219*				
	• Talking about what you used to do • Saying what you used to like and dislike • Describing what people and things were like • Using comparisons to describe people	• The imperfect tense of **-ar, -er, -ir** verbs • The imperfect tense of **ir** and **ver** • Spelling change of **o** to **u** and **y** to **e** to avoid vowel repetition • Imperfect of **ser** to describe people and things • The imperfect of **hay** • **tan** + adjective/ adverb + **como**	• Childhood activities • Describing peole • Describing places • Conveniences	• **Lo mejor de lo antiguo** • Public services in Latin American cities • **dichos** • **¿De quién es esta estatua?**	• The preterite • Talking about likes and dislikes using the preterite • Comparisons: **más/menos** + adjective + **que** • Complaining • Descriptive adjectives
El Caribe	**CAPÍTULO 8** Diversiones, *Pages 220–247*				
	• Describing a past event • Saying why you couldn't do something • Reporting what someone said	• Adjectives with **-ísimo/a** • Superlatives • Verbs with prepositions • Using **mientras** in the past • Preterite of **decir**	• In the zoo, the amusement park, and movie theater • Running errands • At a festival	• **El Yunque** and **el coquí** • **¿Cuáles son las fiestas más importantes de tu ciudad o país?** • Holidays and festivals in Spanish-speaking countries	• Describing things • Describing what you did • The imperfect tense • The preterite
Los Andes	**CAPÍTULO 9** ¡Día de mercado!, *Pages 252–281*				
	• Asking for and giving directions • Asking for help in a store • Talking about how clothes look and fit • Bargaining in a market	• Formal commands with **usted, ustedes**	• Giving directions • In a clothing store • In a market	• **En la ventanilla tres, por favor** • Clothing and shoe sizes • **¿Dónde compras tu comida?** • Expressions for shopping • Mural art	• Numbers • **ser** + **de** + material • Comparisons • Clothing material and pattern • Direct and indirect objects

FUNCTIONS	GRAMMAR	VOCABULARY	CULTURE	RE-ENTRY

Los Andes

CAPÍTULO 10 ¡Cuéntame!, *Pages 282–311*

FUNCTIONS	GRAMMAR	VOCABULARY	CULTURE	RE-ENTRY
• Setting the scene for a story • Continuing and ending a story • Talking about the latest news • Reacting to news	• The preterite vs. the imperfect • Preterite of **oír, creer, leer, caerse** • The preterite and the imperfect to tell a story	• Weather • Accidents, mishaps, and daily events • Science fiction and fairy tales • The latest news	• **¿Te sabes algún cuento?** • A Chilean folk tale • An Ecuadorean legend • **Mafalda** comic strip • **La Llorona**	• Reflexive verbs • Preterite of **ser** • Weather expressions

California

CAPÍTULO 11 Nuestro medio ambiente, *Pages 316–345*

FUNCTIONS	GRAMMAR	VOCABULARY	CULTURE	RE-ENTRY
• Describing a problem • Talking about consequences • Expressing agreement and disagreement • Talking about obligations and solutions	• Negative words • **si** clauses in present tense • **nosotros** commands	• Environmental problems • Animals • Protecting the environment • Materials and resources	• The rain forest • **¿Qué haces para el medio ambiente?** • Environmental programs • **el medio ambiente** • San Diego and Tijuana	• Affirmative and negative words • Giving an opinion • Cognates • Informal commands

California

CAPÍTULO 12 Veranos pasados, veranos por venir, *Pages 346–371*   *Review Chapter*

FUNCTIONS	GRAMMAR	VOCABULARY	CULTURE	RE-ENTRY
• Exchanging the latest news • Talking about where you went and what you did • Telling when something happened • Saying how you feel about people • Describing places • Saying when you're going to do something	• The subjunctive mood	• Writing a letter • Vacation activities • Describing places	• Baja California • **¿Cómo celebran el fin de cursos?** • **viaje de curso**	• Chapter 12 is a global review of Chapters 1–11, *Level 2.*

¡Adelante! pp. T74–15
CHAPTER OVERVIEW

The following material introduced in the **Capítulo preliminar** is presented again for testing in the chapters cited.

TEXTBOOK LISTENING ACTIVITIES SCRIPTS

¿CÓMO TE LLAMAS?   pp. 6–7

The script is the same as the list of names in the *Pupil's Edition*, pp. 6–7

3 Nombres en español   p. 7

Marta	Miguel	Cristóbal
Claudia	Luisa	Gregorio
Margarita	Isabel	Antonio
Andrés		

EL ALFABETO   pp. 8–9

A	a de águila	N	ene de naranja
B	be de bandera	Ñ	eñe de castañuelas
C	ce de ciclismo	O	o de oso
CH	che de chaleco	P	pe de piñata
D	de de dinero	Q	cu de quetzal
E	e de ensalada	R	ere de toro
F	efe de fruta	RR	erre de burro
G	ge de geografía	S	ese de salvavidas
H	hache de helicóptero	T	te de teléfono
I	i de iguana	U	u de uvas
J	jota de jabón	V	ve de violín
K	ka de karate	W	doble ve de Walter
L	ele de lámpara	X	equis de examen
LL	elle de llanta	Y	i griega de yate
M	eme de máscara	Z	zeta de zapatos

6 Por teléfono   p. 9

1. Pe, a, u, ele, a; Paula
2. I, ge, ene, a, ce, i, o; Ignacio
3. Jota, o, ere, ge, e; Jorge
4. Eme, a, ere, te, a; Marta
5. A, de, ere, i, a, ene, a; Adriana
6. Che, a, ere, o; Charo

FRASES ÚTILES PARA ESCUCHAR   p. 10

Abran el libro (en la página 20), por favor.
Levántense, por favor.
Siéntense, por favor.
Levanten la mano.
Bajen la mano.
Escuchen con atención.
Repitan.
Saquen una hoja de papel.
Silencio, por favor.
Miren la pizarra.

8 Simón dice   p. 10

1. Simón dice, "levántense, por favor".
2. Simón dice, "siéntense".
3. Simón dice, "saquen una hoja de papel".
4. Simón dice, "levanten la mano".
5. Bajen la mano.
6. Simón dice, "bajen la mano".
7. Miren la pizarra.
8. Simón dice, "repitan después de mí: ¡Gracias!"

PARA DECIR   p. 11

Buenos días.	¿Puedo ir por mi libro?
Buenas tardes.	No entiendo.
¿Cómo se dice... en español?	No sé.
	¿Puede repitir, por favor?
¿Cómo se escribe?	Perdón.
Más despacio, por favor.	Tengo una pregunta.

17 Números de teléfono   p. 14

1. Me llamo Nicolás Guillén y mi número de teléfono es el 4-7-3-0-0-1-6.
2. Me llamo Juana Gómez Berea. Mi número de teléfono es el 3-9-1-2-3-4-6.
3. Soy Miguel Campos Romero. Mi número de teléfono es el 7-4-5-0-8-1-2.
4. Soy Cristina García. Mi número de teléfono es el 5-1-0-5-7-2-4.

¡Adelante!
PROJECTS

LAS INTENCIONES CUENTAN

Students will consider their reasons for studying Spanish and set personal goals for the year. Students will share their ideas with the class through creative poster or brochure presentations. You may wish to have students make a brochure to include in their individual Portfolios. (See pages T52–T53.) This project should be completed in English unless you have fluent native speakers. It may be assigned as either an individual or small-group assignment.

Materials students may need

- Poster board
- Scissors
- Tape
- Travel brochures
- Construction paper
- Glue
- Magazines

Introduction

Have students address the following questions:

- **Motivation**—Why are you learning Spanish? Where could you use the Spanish you will learn? To be able to talk to Spanish speakers you know? Where could you travel to speak Spanish? What country would you like to visit?

- **Objectives**—What would you like to learn in Spanish this semester? (For example, to write a postcard to a Spanish-speaking pen pal.) What words would you like to learn to say?

- **Long-term Application**—Would you like to be able to converse with friends or relatives in Spanish? to write a letter or make a phone call in Spanish?

Sequence

1 Discuss the importance of being clear about personal objectives and goals for language learning. Mention that their perceptions are likely to change throughout the learning process. You may want to share with students your own learning experience. Explain what inspired you to study another language. Recount how your motivation, objectives, and the ways you used your second language unfolded over the years.

2 Describe the project and assign dates for oral presentations. Write project questions on the board, or distribute a project assignment sheet. Be sure to set a firm time limit for presentations.

3 Go over project questions and elicit a few sample answers from the class. If no one has any ideas at first, you might suggest a few of these examples.

   a. Motivation—need to learn a language for high school or college; have Spanish-speaking friends or relatives

   b. Objectives—carry on simple conversations in Spanish; write letters to a Spanish-speaking pen pal; get a good grade in this class

   c. Long-Term Application—talk to Spanish-speaking friends or relatives; travel in Spanish-speaking countries

4 Emphasize that students should be specific about motivation, objectives, and goals. Give students time in class to brainstorm and organize their thoughts.

5 Students create posters based on personal motivations, objectives, and goals. Suggest that they include information on culture, food, work opportunities, and so forth. Encourage students to be as expressive as they wish, using words, photos, and drawings. This can be done in class or at home. Students present their posters or brochures to the class, explaining their reasons for studying Spanish. Students may then select some of the personal goals as class goals.

Grading the project

Because of the personal nature of this project, grading should focus on completion, presentation, and effort.

Suggested point distribution (total = 100 points):

Completion of assignment	**30**
Poster/Brochure	**40**
Effort	**10**
Presentation	**10**
Teamwork (if done as a group)	**10**

EL MUNDO HISPANOHABLANTE

Making a map of the Spanish-speaking world is a great way to learn the names of the countries and capitals in Spanish. Students identify a Spanish-speaking country by its shape, then find information concerning principal cities and geographical features. They can then relate these locations to the people they will see and hear in the video. A variety of items can be attached to this map as the semester goes by, including pictures of the characters from the fotonovela, or small symbols for the items reported about each country in the second half of this project.

Materials students may need

- ◆ Large roll of paper
- ◆ Library Resources
- ◆ Scissors
- ◆ Markers
- ◆ Glue or tape

Sequence

Part 1: Create a **World Map** highlighting Spanish-speaking countries

1 Enlarge a blank, outline map of the countries where Spanish is spoken to make individual maps of each country on standard or legal size paper. You may want to use the Copying Masters of the maps from the *Teaching Transparencies.* Include all the Spanish-speaking countries in South and Central America, the Caribbean, Mexico, and Spain. (You may also include Equatorial Guinea and the Philippines). Do not identify the countries. Pass out the outline maps to pairs of students.

2 Students must identify their individual country, locate its capital, and label both in Spanish on their map. They can use the maps on pages xvii–xxiii. Then have them indicate the capital with a star, draw in mountains, major rivers, and write the names of other cities in Spanish.

TEACHER NOTE

You may wish to assign step two as homework, if students work individually. Set a date for students to bring in their country maps and attach them to the world map in the classroom.

Part 2: **Country Report**

3 Allow pairs or small groups to choose a country for a class report. The project should be flexible enough to allow for individual differences, as well as creative abilities. Stress hands-on action in this activity.

4 Students could make a travel video with two students playing travel guide and tourist respectively. This can be done outside of class, during school with the school's video equipment, or as a class skit. The guide should point out major points of interest and special cultural customs, songs, dances, history, or traditional foods. Students may want to consult travel books for information.

5 Native speakers may choose to demonstrate a dance, teach a song, or bring in traditional foods and explain their importance. One student could explain while the others demonstrate. It is important that the native speakers have the choice whether or not to play this informational role so that they feel comfortable sharing with the class.

6 Other possibilities: students perform skits about the history of the country they have chosen, create a commercial for a Spanish-speaking country, or present cultural customs or other features of the countries to the class. If your school has the technology, have your class design a web page about Latin America using the information they have researched. Allow students to be creative in how they present their country report and have them submit their topics to you for approval.

7 In conjunction with student reports, offer each group suggestions for research. Suggest they call the local consulate or a travel agent to request posters or ask for any free information. Also, they might ask local folklore groups to perform for the class. Check with these contacts beforehand to make sure they are willing to interact with students.

8 Allow library research time. Remind students to check all resources for information, including the Internet.

Grading the project

Suggested Point Distribution (total = 100 points):

Map Identifications **35**
Appearance. **15**
Originality **25**
Oral presentation **25**

CAPÍTULO PRELIMINAR

¡Adelante!

GAMES

TEACHER NOTE

Simulations and playful learning activities can be effective teaching tools, lowering students' anxieties and aiding language acquisition. For games to be most beneficial, the atmosphere needs to be fun and relaxed—the students should look forward to doing the activity. Games can be cooperative rather than competitive. Here are some suggestions to help you incorporate games in your lesson plan:

- Games should be played in Spanish as much as possible. Ground rules may be explained in English, as necessary.
- Keep games simple so that a minimum of class time is spent explaining the rules.
- Involve students as scorekeepers or referees, to help with classroom management.
- Choose games that practice comprehension or production in meaningful contexts.
- Identify your teaching objective. Is the game for recognition only? Is it to improve student production, to recycle previously presented material, to practice a particular skill, or to develop higher-order thinking skills?
- Always set a time limit. If you stick to announced time limits, students will help each other stay on task.
- When you find a game that both you and your students respond to well, recycle it in new contexts throughout the year. This will give students a sense of security and continuity and reduce set-up time.

ALFABETO

This game helps students recognize and produce letters in Spanish.

Procedure

1 Write some randomly chosen letters on the board or on a transparency.

2 Ask students recognition questions, such as **¿Es una "ere"?**

3 Students respond with thumbs up or thumbs down, or by holding up a **sí** or **no** card. Board races are appropriate at this level of recognition as well.

4 Dictate words letter by letter. Try including names of famous people, students' first or last names, your school mascot, or local sports stars. Have students write the words on the board or on paper. Write the words on a transparency so students can check their answers.

¿DERECHA O IZQUIERDA?

This is a game to practice the alphabet, as well as introduce words for left and right. It may be played in small or large groups.

Procedure

1 A group leader stands in the middle of the circle of chairs.

2 The leader says **a la izquierda,** points to a person, and begins counting to 10 in Spanish. That person must say the name of the person to the left and spell it using the Spanish alphabet before the leader counts to 10.

3 If the leader points to a person and says **a la derecha,** that person must say the name of the person to his or her right and spell it.

4 If the person fails to say the letters correctly, he or she takes the role of leader and goes to the center of the circle. The former leader takes the empty chair.

5 You may decide to allow the game to continue until all students have had a turn to be the leader, or you may limit it to only five different leaders.

COLORES

This game is good for visual and tactile learners.

Materials students may need
◆ Colored construction paper
◆ Scissors

Preparation
1 Have students cut colored construction paper into 16 squares by folding it in half three times, unfolding it, and cutting along the folds.
2 Students pass out one square of the color to each student.

Procedure
1 Have students begin by pointing out the colors in Spanish to his or her partner.
2 Then have students arrange the papers left to right or top to bottom on their desks in the order you name the colors.
3 Finally, at the end of the game, students write the Spanish word for the color on their pieces of construction paper to use them as flash cards.

 NÚMEROS

This game is good to help students practice recognizing numbers.

Procedure
1 Have students listen as you say various combinations of numbers.
2 Then ask comprehension questions such as: "**Uno-tres-cinco-siete,** even or odd?" "**Nueve-ocho-siete-seis,** forward or backward?"
3 Dictate a series of numbers and have students say or write the next number in the series.

CHALLENGE
Have students solve simple arithmetic problems using numerals as you read the problems to them in Spanish. They will need to know **más** (+), **menos** (−), **por** (×), **dividido por** (÷), and **es/son** (=).

 NÚMEROS EN LÍNEA

This game gives students practice understanding and saying numbers in Spanish.

Preparation
Have students prepare index cards with numbers written out as words.

Procedure
1 Randomly pass out cards to students.

2 Instruct students to line up in numerical order in complete silence, then read off their numbers.
3 Repeat the lineup with even numbers (**pares**) on one side of the room and odd numbers (**nones, impares**) on the other or (**del 30 al uno**), or (**por dos**) reading off their cards again after the lineup.

¡Adelante!

VIDEO INTEGRATION

Adelante LEVEL 1A
Video Program
Videocassette 1, 1:15–4:49

¡Ven conmigo! LEVEL 1
DVD Tutor, Disc 1

The video for the Preliminary Chapter introduces your students to some of the people they will view in the rest of the program. Some are the actors in the **fotonovelas** found in **De antemano**, and others are people interviewed on the street for the **Panorama cultural.** Play the video now to give your students an introduction to the Spanish language.

MOTIVATING ACTIVITIES

• Ask students: What comes to mind when you think of the Spanish-speaking world? Which states have Spanish names? (Colorado, Florida, Montana, Nevada, California) Can you think of cities with Spanish names? (San Francisco, San Antonio, Boca Raton)

• Ask students to name any movies or TV shows in which Spanish is spoken. Ask if they know of celebrities who have a Hispanic heritage. (Selena, Rosie Perez, Emilio Estevez)

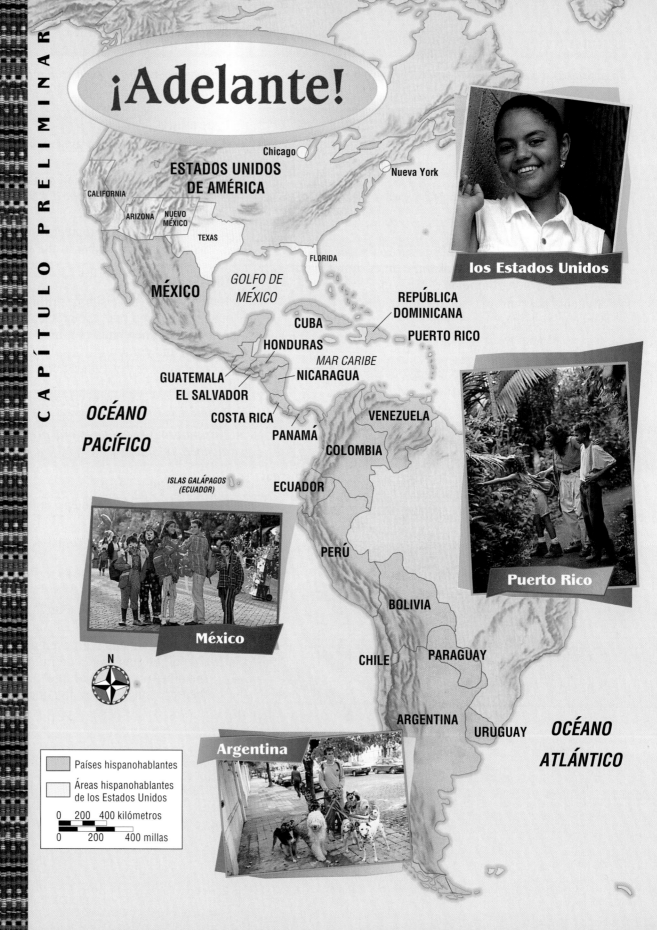

¡Adelante!

los Estados Unidos

Puerto Rico

México

Argentina

Chicago
ESTADOS UNIDOS DE AMÉRICA
Nueva York
CALIFORNIA
ARIZONA
NUEVO MÉXICO
TEXAS
FLORIDA
MÉXICO
GOLFO DE MÉXICO
REPÚBLICA DOMINICANA
CUBA
PUERTO RICO
HONDURAS
MAR CARIBE
GUATEMALA
EL SALVADOR
NICARAGUA
OCÉANO PACÍFICO
COSTA RICA
PANAMÁ
VENEZUELA
COLOMBIA
ISLAS GALÁPAGOS (ECUADOR)
ECUADOR
PERÚ
BOLIVIA
CHILE
PARAGUAY
ARGENTINA
URUGUAY
OCÉANO ATLÁNTICO

Países hispanohablantes
Áreas hispanohablantes de los Estados Unidos
0   200   400 kilómetros
0   200   400 millas

ESPAÑA

ISLAS BALEARES
(ESPAÑA)

Argentina

MAR MEDITERRÁNEO

ISLAS CANARIAS
(ESPAÑA)

Venezuela

OCÉANO
ÍNDICO

España

GUINEA
ECUATORIAL

OCÉANO
ATLÁNTICO

Costa Rica

Ecuador

¡Bienvenido al mundo hispanohablante!

Spanish, one of the five official languages of the United Nations, is spoken by over 340 million people in the world today. Spanish is spoken in Spain (where it originated), in 19 Latin American countries, and in parts of Africa and the Philippines. It's also spoken in the United States, where about one out of ten residents is a Spanish speaker. Can you find the countries where the Spanish speakers on these pages live?

PHOTO FLASH!

Some photos on this page are of people that your students will view in the videos. Some are actors who play characters in the **fotonovelas**, and others are people interviewed on the street in numerous Spanish-speaking countries.

HISTORY LINK

Guinea Ecuatorial *(Equatorial Guinea)* is a country on the west coast of Africa. The territory that the country now occupies was ceded to Spain by Portugal in 1778. Spanish is its official language and is spoken mainly in schools and government offices. In Equatorial Guinea each ethnic group also speaks its own language, such as Fang or Bubi.

HISTORY LINK

The Spanish began colonizing the Philippines in 1565 and ruled the islands until 1898, when they lost control to the United States in the Spanish-American War. They named the islands after King Philip II (**Felipe II**). The Spanish legacy is still felt throughout the region.

STANDARDS: 3.1   1

EL ESPAÑOL—¿POR QUÉ?

There are many reasons for learning to speak Spanish. Which of these reasons is most important to you?

Parque El Retiro en Madrid, España

Each language has its own personality. To really get to know someone, you have to speak that person's language. Someday you may travel to a Spanish-speaking country. Whatever your reason for going, you'll get a lot more out of your stay if you can speak the language.

You're living in one of the major Spanish-speaking countries right now—the United States! Learning Spanish can open up a whole new world of information, entertainment, and adventure. Spanish-language movies, books, videos, magazines, TV shows, and music are all around you.

Playa en Chile

One of the best reasons for studying Spanish is for satisfaction. Studying another language is a challenge to your mind. And you get a great feeling of accomplishment the first time you have a conversation in Spanish!

Festival en la Calle Ocho en Miami

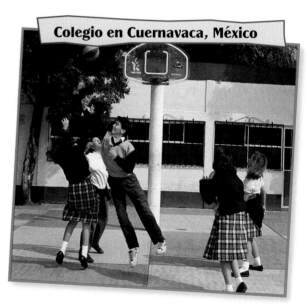
Colegio en Cuernavaca, México

¿SABÍAS...?

Spanish language and culture are important parts of our national history. As you begin your study of Spanish, you should be aware that . . .

▼ the Spanish were among the first European explorers in what is today the United States.

▼ the Spaniards founded St. Augustine (**San Agustín**), Florida, the first European settlement in the United States, in 1565.

▼ parts of the U.S. once belonged to Mexico.

▼ Spanish is the second most frequently spoken language in the U.S.

NUEVA ESPAÑA

Río MISSISSIPI

GOLFO DE MÉXICO

● San Agustín
FLORIDA

Spanish Territory in North America in 1785

0 200 400 Kilómetros
0 200 400 Millas

1 Herencia hispana
Answers will vary. Possible answers below:

Working in small groups, discuss the following topics. Share your findings with the class.

1. Many cities in the U.S. have Spanish names. Name four cities that you know of with Spanish names. (Hint: Many begin with San, Los, and Las.)
2. Many foods common in the U.S. come from Spanish-speaking countries. List two foods from a Spanish-speaking country that you've eaten or have heard of.
3. Using the maps on pages xvii–xxiii, name two Spanish-speaking countries that you've heard something about. Choose one country and list at least two things you know about it.
4. Can you name three famous Spanish-speaking people? They can be a movie star, a singer, an athlete . . .

1. Los Angeles, San Diego, San Antonio, Albuquerque, Santa Fe, Las Vegas, San Francisco 2. taco, enchilada, burrito, salsa, chocolate, tortilla, fajita
3. Answers will vary. 4. Antonio Banderas, Gloria Estefan, Sergi Bruguera, Jennifer López

¡ADELANTE!

tres 3

BACKGROUND
St. Augustine, Florida, was founded in 1565 by Pedro Menéndez de Avilés, a Spaniard. It is considered the first permanent European settlement in what is today the United States. St. Augustine is on the northeastern coast of Florida just south of Jacksonville.

HISTORY LINK
In 1848 the Mexican Congress signed **el Tratado de Guadalupe Hidalgo,** ending the Mexican-American War. With this treaty Mexico ceded to the United States more than one-third of Mexico's total territory—the present-day states of Texas, California, Arizona, New Mexico, Nevada, Utah, and part of Colorado.

SUGGESTION
1 You may wish to make this a homework assignment.

LANGUAGE NOTE
The word **chocolate** came into Spanish from Nahuatl, an indigenous language spoken in central and western Mexico. **Xocolatl** (*sho-ko-la-tul*), meaning *bitter water,* is the Nahuatl word for a drink made from the cacao plant. The Aztec nobility drank it without sugar. Today, there are over one million native Nahuatl speakers in Mexico.

CRITICAL THINKING

Point out that Spanish speakers in the United States and much of Latin America come from diverse backgrounds. Spanish speakers' ancestors came from all parts of the world, including Africa, the Americas, Asia, Europe, and the Middle East. Ask students how they think such diverse people got to Latin America and why.

HISTORY LINKS

• **Simón Bolívar** was born before Venezuela became an independent nation in 1821. Explain to students that even though we say he was born in Venezuela, the modern nation did not exist at that time.

• **La reina Isabel** *(Queen Isabella of Castile)* was also responsible for commissioning the first Spanish grammar. In 1492, at her request, **Antonio de Nebrija** wrote a guide to Castilian, which became the first published Romance language grammar.

SUGGESTION

Ask students to describe briefly other famous Spanish speakers or people of Hispanic heritage. Have classmates guess who they are describing. (Gloria Estefan, César Chávez, Edward James Olmos, Rosie Perez, Emilio Estevez, Martin Sheen (b. Ramon Estevez), Tish Hinojosa, Antonia Novello)

¿LOS CONOCES? PA p. 1 Act. 1

Spanish speakers from all over the world have made valuable contributions in science, sports, politics, and the arts.

Miguel de Cervantes y Saavedra (1547–1616) was the author of *Don Quixote*, one of the great works of Spanish literature. He wrote very realistic stories about life in Spain at the end of the 16th century.

Ivan "Pudge" Rodriguez (b. 1971), from Manatí, Puerto Rico, is a catcher for the Texas Rangers. He is an 8 time member of American League All-Star Team.

Simón Bolívar (1783–1830), born in Caracas, Venezuela, led a brilliant struggle against Spanish colonialism that helped win independence for most of South America. Today he is honored as **el Libertador**, The Liberator.

La Reina Isabel (Isabel I of Spain; 1451–1504) helped unite what is today modern Spain by marrying Fernando, King of Aragon. We know her best for paying for Columbus's voyage to the New World.

Frida Kahlo (1907–1954), a Mexican artist, is most famous for the paintings she made of herself. Like her husband, the famous painter and muralist Diego Rivera, Frida Kahlo painted the history and political life of her country.

Rigoberta Menchú (b. 1959), a Guatemalan Quiché woman, won the 1992 Nobel Prize for speaking out against the inhumane treatment of the indigenous people of Central America.

Desiderio (Desi) Arnaz (1917–1986), a native of Cuba, is best known as Ricky Ricardo on the 1950s TV show *I Love Lucy*. The 3-camera system he created for *I Love Lucy* set the standard for television filming and is still used today.

Arantxa Sánchez Vicario (b. 1971) is one of Spain's hottest tennis stars. She has won both the French and U.S. Opens. With over eight tournament titles, she is well on her way to being one of the world's leading tennis players.

¡ADELANTE!

HISTORY LINK

A memorable figure in Mexican history is Benito Pablo Juárez (1806–1872). Mexicans regard him as one of their greatest presidents, much as Americans regard Abraham Lincoln. During his presidency (1861–1872) he was responsible for leading the campaign that ended French occupation in Mexico. Today Mexicans celebrate **el Cinco de mayo** to commemorate this.

SCIENCE LINK

A noted figure in science is Spanish engineer Juan de la Cierva (1895–1936). His invention of the hinged flapping rotor blade and autogyro set the stage for the development of the modern-day helicopter.

MOTIVATING ACTIVITY
Ask students if they can think of any Spanish names that are not on the list. Have a volunteer write them on the board or on an overhead transparency.

SUGGESTIONS
• Play **¿Cómo te llamas?** on Audio CD 1 Track 1. Have students listen without responding. Then replay the tape and have student repeat the names for practice.

• You may want to assign Spanish names for student to use in class. They can select a Spanish equivalent or assume a completely new Spanish name.

• Emphasize that Spanish and English do not sound the same. Encourage students to listen carefully to the tape and to your pronunciation of their names. Students should try to mimic correct pronunciation as closely as possible. For longer names, you may wish to have the students do "backward buildup." (Wilfredo: -do, **-fredo**, Wil**fredo**).

• Emphasize the importance of practice. Language is a skill learned gradually, like playing a sport or an instrument.

SUGGESTION
2 Have students find and list ten different Spanish last names from the phone book.

¿CÓMO TE LLAMAS? p. 1 Act. 2

Here are some common names from Spanish-speaking countries. Choose a name for yourself from the list if you wish. Script is the list of names on these two pages.

CD 1 Tr. 1

Me llamo Teresa.

Adela
Alicia (Licha)
Ana, Anita
Ángela, Angélica
Beatriz
Carmen
Catalina (Cata)
Claudia
Cristina (Tina)
Daniela
Dolores (Lola)
Elena (Nena)
Graciela (Chela)
Inés

Isabel (Isa)
Juana
Luisa
Margarita
María
Marisol (Mari)
Marta
Mercedes (Merche)
Natalia
Paloma
Pilar
Rosario (Charo)
Sara
Susana
Teresa
Verónica (Vero)

Me llamo Ema.

2 Mis amigos
Find and write Spanish names from pages six and seven that match the names of at least six of your family members, friends, or classmates. Check to see that you've written the accents in the correct places.
Answers will vary, see names on these pages.

Alberto

Alejandro (Alejo)

Andrés

Antonio (Toño)

Carlos

Cristóbal

Me llamo Pablo.

Diego

Eduardo (Lalo)

Francisco (Paco)

Gregorio

Guillermo

Ignacio (Nacho)

Jaime

Jesús (Chuy)

Jorge

José (Pepe)

Juan

Julio

Lorenzo

Luis

Manuel

Mario

Miguel

Me llamo César.

Pablo

Pedro

Rafael (Rafa)

Ricardo

Roberto (Beto)

Santiago

Tomás

3 **Nombres en español** Script on p. T69

CD 1 Tr. 2

Listen to a series of names in Spanish and repeat them aloud after the speaker. Try to guess the English equivalent of each one. Does your name have an equivalent in Spanish?

4 **Me llamo...**

Form a name chain in your row. The first person turns to a classmate and asks his or her name. That person answers with a chosen name in Spanish, and then asks the next person's name. Keep going to the end of the row.

MODELO   —¿Cómo te llamas?
          —Me llamo Carlos.
          ¿Cómo te llamas?

Los acentos

You may have noticed the accent mark (´) and the tilde (~) on letters in the name chart. They're used to help you pronounce the words correctly. You'll learn more about these and other special marks, including the upside-down question mark and exclamation point, in Chapter 1.

GAME

4 Have students line up in alphabetical order according to their chosen Spanish name. They are only allowed to say their Spanish name and are not allowed to speak in English.

CHALLENGE

After reviewing these two pages of Spanish names, have students go around a circle saying Spanish names in alphabetical order. For example, if the first student says Alberto, then the next would say Beatriz, the third Carmen, and so on.

CULTURE NOTE

It is very popular in the Dominican Republic to give children Russian names. (Vladimir, Katirina, Ivan, Tavia) It is also popular to give children name of countries and cities. (América, Venecia, Roma, Australia)

LANGUAGE NOTE

An **apodo** is an affectionate nickname, such as **el gallo**, or **la rubia**, which is frequently given to fellow students in school.

MOTIVATING ACTIVITY

To build confidence, help students identify the Spanish cognates such as **ciclismo**, **ensalada**, **examen**, or **violín**.

SUGGESTION

- Before students try to produce the sounds themselves, have them point to the corresponding letter and picture as they listen to the **Alfabeto** on Audio CD 1 Track 3.
- A recitation of the alphabet in Spanish is on the Preliminary Chapter segment of the video.

AUDITORY LEARNERS

Students may like to chant rhymes or make up rap tunes to learn the correct sounds. **(A-E-I-O-U, Yo me llamo María. ¿Cómo te llamas tú?)** As their vocabulary increases, encourage students who respond well to this approach to revise their rhymes to include new words.

NATIVE SPEAKERS

Have native speakers begin a notebook in which they write down words that are commonly misspelled. Have them focus on the following letters or combinations of letters, one page for each: *b, ce, ci, ge, gi, h, j, ll, s, v, z.* Point out that the pronunciation of a word will help them spell it, but words with these letters must be memorized.

EL ALFABETO

Script on p. T69
CD 1 Tr. 3

PA p. 2
Act. 3

The Spanish alphabet isn't quite the same as the English one. What differences do you notice? Listen to the names of the letters and repeat after the speaker.

Although **ch** and **ll** have been officially dropped from the Spanish alphabet, dictionaries and glossaries published before 1994 will continue to show them as separate entries.

A
águila

B
bandera

C
ciclismo

CH
chaleco

D
dinero

E
ensalada

F
fruta

G
geografía

H
helicóptero

I
iguana

J
jabón

K
karate

L
lámpara

LL
llanta

5 Los cognados

Cognates are words in Spanish and English that look similar. Although they're pronounced differently, they often have the same meaning—but not always! For example, **asistir** means *attend,* not *assist.* There are seven cognates in this ad. Can you find them?

correspondencia, inteligente, sincera, sociable, música, teléfono, televisión

☛ **Busco amigo por correspondencia**

Me llamo Catalina. Soy inteligente, sincera y muy sociable. Me gusta leer, escuchar música, hablar por teléfono y mirar televisión.

M máscara	**N** naranja	**Ñ** castañuelas	**O** oso
P piñata	**Q** quetzal	**R** toro	**RR** burro
S salvavidas	**T** teléfono	**U** uvas	**V** violín
W Walter	**X** examen	**Y** yate	**Z** zapatos

6 **Por teléfono** Script on p. T69

Imagine that you work as a receptionist answering the phone. Listen as six Spanish speakers spell their names for you. Write CD 1 Tr. 4 each name as you hear it spelled.

7 **¿Cómo se escribe...?**

Spell each of the following items to your partner, in Spanish. Your partner will write each word as you spell it. Switch roles when you're done. Answers will vary.

1. your first name
2. your last name
3. the name of your school

¡ADELANTE!

nueve **9**

SUGGESTIONS
- Dictate the spelling of words and have students find them in the illustrations.
- Dictate a list of items for students to remember on a trip to the grocery store. (**jabón, fruta, naranja, uvas, dinero**)

CHALLENGE
6 Spell students' last names out loud in Spanish and ask them to raise their hands when they recognize their own names.

SUGGESTION
7 Teach students **con mayúscula**. Point out that names are capitalized in Spanish just as they are in English. Teach **con acento** or **lleva acento** as well. (**eme con mayúscula, a, ere, i con acento, a: María**)

LANGUAGE NOTES
- Although the **Real Academia** deleted the letters *ch* and *ll* from the alphabet, many dictionaries still have separate entries for these letters. The vocabulary lists in this book follow the new rules, with *ch* and *ll* in sequence: "*ce...ch...ci*" and "*li...ll...lo.*"
- Although in the Americas *rr* is commonly recognized as a separate letter, the **Real Academia** does not officially recognize it.

STANDARDS: 1.2, 1.3, 4.1, 5.1   **9**

FRASES ÚTILES

PA p. 2 Act. 4

Para escuchar   Script on p. T69

Miren la pizarra.

Here are some phrases you'll probably hear regularly in Spanish class. Learn to recognize them and answer appropriately.

CD 1 Tr. 5

Abran el libro (en la página 20), por favor.	Open your books (to page 20), please.
Levántense, por favor.	Please stand up.
Siéntense, por favor.	Please sit down.
Levanten la mano.	Raise your hands.
Bajen la mano.	Put your hands down.
Escuchen con atención.	Listen closely.
Repitan.	Repeat.
Saquen una hoja de papel.	Take out a sheet of paper.
Silencio, por favor.	Silence, please.
Miren la pizarra.	Look at the chalkboard.

8 Simón dice   Script on p. T69

CD 1 Tr. 6

Listen to some commands and do what the person says, such as raising your hand or opening your book. Respond only if the speaker says **Simón dice**.

9 ¿Qué dice?

Get together with a partner and find the phrase from the list that Mrs. Mercado, the new Spanish teacher, would use in the following situations.   Answers in side column

1. She wants the students to sit down.
2. She wants everyone to be quiet.
3. She wants everyone to open their books.
4. She wants everyone to take out a sheet of paper.
5. She wants everyone to listen carefully.
6. She wants everyone to stand up.

Para decir · Script on p. T69

Tengo una pregunta.

Here are some phrases that you'll need to use often. Learn as many as you can and use them when they're appropriate.

CD 1 Tr. 7

Buenos días.	*Good morning.*
Buenas tardes.	*Good afternoon.*
¿Cómo se dice… en español?	*How do you say . . . in Spanish?*
¿Cómo se escribe…?	*How do you spell . . .?*
Más despacio, por favor.	*Slower, please.*
¿Puedo ir por mi libro?	*Can I go get my book?*
No entiendo.	*I don't understand.*
No sé.	*I don't know.*
¿Puede repetir, por favor?	*Can you repeat, please?*
Perdón.	*Excuse me.*
Tengo una pregunta.	*I have a question.*

10 ¿Qué haría?

What would Mr. García, the Spanish teacher, do if one of his students said each of the following? Match each item with an appropriate answer.

1. Más despacio, por favor. c
2. Tengo una pregunta. e
3. No entiendo. b
4. ¿Puede repetir, por favor? d
5. ¿Cómo se dice *Good morning* en español? a

a. He would say **Buenos días**.
b. He would explain the lesson another way.
c. He would speak slower.
d. He would repeat what he just said.
e. He would ask what the question is.

11 Situaciones

What would you say in the following situations? Choose your responses from the list above.   Answers in side column

1. You see your teacher at the store one afternoon.
2. You don't understand the directions.
3. Your teacher is talking too fast.
4. You don't know the answer.
5. You'd like to ask a question.
6. You need to hear something again.

¡ADELANTE!

once **11**

ADDITIONAL VOCABULARY

Para escuchar If you use an overhead transparency instead of a chalkboard, you may wish to teach the phrase **Miren la transparencia**. Another command you may find helpful is **¡Libros al suelo!**

Para decir Additional phrases you may wish to teach your students are **¿Qué quiere decir…?**; **No oigo**; **¿Puedo ir al baño?**; **¿Puedo ir a la oficina?**

Answers to Activity 11

1. Buenas tardes.
2. No entiendo.
3. Más despacio, por favor. / ¿Puede repetir, por favor?
4. No sé.
5. Tengo una pregunta.
6. ¿Puede repetir, por favor?

LOS COLORES

PA p. 3
Act. 7

p. 3
Act. 7

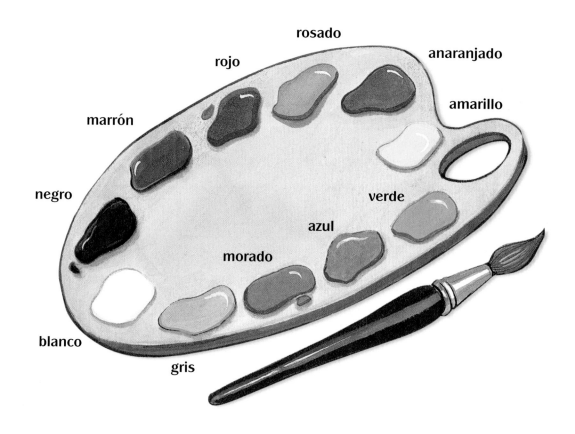

rosado

rojo

anaranjado

marrón

amarillo

negro

verde

azul

morado

blanco

gris

SUGGESTIONS

• Let students be creative in the colors they say but ask them to explain their choices. For example, leaves may be red, orange, or yellow in the fall and strawberries have a green stem and black spots.

• For personalization, point to various clothing items worn by students as you say the corresponding color.

• Ask students to name the colors of various classroom items. To evaluate listening comprehension, have students respond **cierto** or **falso** to your statements about colors in the room. For example, **El libro *Adelante* es amarillo. (cierto)**

• Some of your students may be colorblind (unable to distinguish between two or more of the colors red, green, and blue). With a colorblind student, you should stress color associations (fruits, plants, holidays) rather than color distinctions.

ADDITIONAL VOCABULARY

café; pardo   *brown*
(café) claro   *light (brown)*
(azul) oscuro   *dark (blue)*
oro   *gold*
plata   *silver*

12 Colores típicos

What colors come to mind when you think of the following things? Say them in Spanish.   Answers will vary. Possible answers:

1. a zebra blanco, negro
2. the sky azul, blanco, gris
3. coffee marrón
4. a banana amarillo, verde, negro
5. grape juice morado
6. a tire negro

7. a traffic light rojo, amarillo, verde
8. grass verde
9. a strawberry rojo
10. a pumpkin anaranjado
11. a cloudy day gris, blanco
12. snow blanco

13 ¿Qué cosas son de este color?

 Get together with a partner. For each of the following colors, name three things that are that color.   Answers will vary. Possible answers:

1. azul blueberries, the sky, bluebirds
2. rojo cherries, fire engines, cardinals
3. morado grapes, violets, eggplants

4. negro coal, newsprint, the night sky
5. verde celery, spinach, grass
6. amarillo the sun, squash, lemons

EL CALENDARIO p. 3 Act. 8

Los días de la semana

enero
semana 1

1	lunes	5	viernes
2	martes	6	sábado
3	miércoles	7	domingo
4	jueves		

14 ¿Qué día es?

If **el lunes** is *Monday*, what days do you think the following are?

1. el jueves Thursday   2. el viernes Friday   3. el miércoles Wednesday

Which days in Spanish are the following?

4. Sunday el domingo   5. Tuesday el martes   6. Saturday el sábado

Los meses del año p. 4 Act. 9

Which month is *March*?[1]

la primavera
- marzo
- abril
- mayo

el invierno
- diciembre
- enero
- febrero

el verano
- junio
- julio
- agosto

el otoño
- septiembre
- octubre
- noviembre

15 ¿En qué mes estamos?

 Talk to your partner about what months of the year and what season it might be when these things happen.   Answers will vary. Possible answers:

1. It snows outside.
2. People celebrate Thanksgiving.
3. You and your friends go swimming.
4. You don't have school.
5. Leaves fall off the trees.
6. It rains a lot outside.

---

[1]*March* is **marzo**.

1. diciembre, enero, febrero, el invierno
2. noviembre, el otoño
3. junio, julio, agosto, el verano
4. junio, julio, agosto, el verano
5. septiembre, octubre, noviembre, el otoño
6. marzo, abril, mayo, la primavera

¡ADELANTE!

trece **13**

SUGGESTION
Write the following phrases on a bulletin board:
  Ayer fue
  Hoy es
  Mañana será
Write the days of the week on seven different index cards, one day per card. Make it a daily assignment for students to update the bulletin board, a different student each day.

TEACHER NOTE
Point out to your students that **el** is used with days of the week.

ADDITIONAL PRACTICE
Call out a month in Spanish and have students raise their hands if they were born in that month.

KINESTHETIC LEARNERS
Teach the phrase **¿En qué mes naciste?** Have students ask each other this question and line themselves up in order by month.

 GAMES
See pages T72–T73 for games to practice this material.

COOPERATIVE LEARNING

17 Have students write other numbers on scraps of paper. Collect the scraps and have students divide into groups of four or five. Shuffle and give each student four or five numbers. Students take turns dictating the number they receive, and the members of the group write the number as it is read. After verifying answers, the next student dictates, and so on.

GAMES

El número secreto Write the numerals 1 to 30 on pieces of paper or self-adhesive notes and attach them to students backs. Teach students **¿del...al?** so they may ask the range of their number. For example, one student asks another **¿del 1 al 10?** and the other responds **sí** or **no.** With that new information, the guesser asks another question, **¿del 5 al 10?,** for example. Have students keep playing for five minutes or until everyone has guessed his or her own number.

Adivina qué número Have one student think of a number between 1 and 30. Have students try to guess the number. When they guess, the person with the secret number gives them hints by saying **más** or **menos.** The person who guesses the number correctly gets to choose the next number.

See pages T72–T73 for games to practice this material.

LOS NÚMEROS

PA p. 4 Act. 10

| cero | uno | dos | tres | cuatro | cinco |

| seis | siete | ocho | nueve | diez |

16 Números de todos los días

What numbers come to mind when you look at each of the following items? Make up your own for the last item.

1. a pair of tennis shoes dos
2. your fingers cinco, diez
3. a tricycle tres
4. a pack of soft drink cans seis
5. an octopus ocho
6. a rectangle cuatro
7. a week siete
8. ¿? Answers will vary.

17 Números de teléfono Script on p. T69

 Listen as four Spanish speakers tell you their telephone numbers. Based on what you hear, CD 1 Tr. 8 match each speaker's name with the right number.

1. Nicolás   3. Miguel
2. Juana   4. Cristina

Miguel
745-08-12

Juana
391-23-46

Cristina
510-57-24

Nicolás
473-00-16

Del once al treinta

11 once	*16* dieciséis	*21* veintiuno	*26* veintiséis
12 doce	*17* diecisiete	*22* veintidós	*27* veintisiete
13 trece	*18* dieciocho	*23* veintitrés	*28* veintiocho
14 catorce	*19* diecinueve	*24* veinticuatro	*29* veintinueve
15 quince	*20* veinte	*25* veinticinco	*30* treinta

18 Datos importantes

Use numbers in Spanish to give the following information.

Answers will vary.

1. your age
2. your telephone number and area code
3. your zip code
4. the number of students in your row

19 Placas y permisos en México

Your partner will read a number or name a color from these license stickers and plates. If you hear a number, name a color from the license plate that has that number, and vice versa. Switch roles after four or five tries. Answers will vary.

MODELO —¿QZB 7829?
—Verde.
—¡Sí!

a

997 FEV
DF   03   MEX

c

996 FEP
DF   03   MEX

b

QZB 7829
MEX MEX

d

KZY 8762
D F MEX

BACKGROUND

19 Items **a.** and **c.** are registration stickers that change yearly. Item **b.** is a license plate from the State of Mexico, and item **d.** is from Distrito Federal. Cars keep the same plates for ten years. Registration stickers are placed on the inside of the windshield. Cars from Mexico City and surrounding areas have to show that they have passed the six-month smog inspection. Cars must also have a sticker (not shown in text, but on the Level 1 *Videodisc Program*) for pollution control. It is called **la calcomanía** or **el engomado** and says **Hoy No Circula**. This sticker designates the day of the week when the car may not be driven.

¡Ven conmigo a España!

LOCATION OPENER CHAPTERS 1, 2

PRINT

Video Guide Level 1A
• Activity Masters and Suggestions, pp. 3–4

MEDIA

Video Program Level 1A
Videocassette 1

Interactive CD-ROM Tutor
Disc 1

go.hrw.com
WV3 ESPANA

¡Ven conmigo! Level 1
DVD Tutor, Disc 1

You may wish to point out the following images as students view the España Location Opener. These images will be seen on both the Video Program and the DVD Program. If you are using the DVD Program they may be freeze-framed for presentation and discussion purposes.

The **acueducto de Segovia** is an example of Roman engineering in Spain. Built in the second century BC, this structure is made up of interlocking granite blocks that are held in place without mortar. It carried water to the city until modern times.

The **Castillo de Alcázar**, in Segovia, was constructed as a fortress in the 12th century. When it was restored after a 19th-century fire, some of the most decorative elements of the castle were added, making it look more like a fairy-tale castle than a fortress.

El Templo de la Sagrada Familia in Barcelona was begun as a neo-Gothic construction in 1882 and was taken over by Antonio Gaudí y Cornet in 1891. Gaudí's plan for the cathedral included towers that resembled trees and vines instead of traditional pillars. Gaudí passed away at an early age in 1926, but the cathedral is still under construction to this day.

Every year in March, Valencia celebrates **las Fallas**, a tradition dating back to the Middle Ages when carpenters burned wood shavings in bonfires to honor Saint Joseph, patron saint of woodworkers. The tradition evolved into current celebrations in which huge satirical structures of wood, papier mâché, and cardboard are constructed and eventually burned.

Many cities in Spanish-speaking countries have a central square called the **plaza mayor**. Children, teens and older people, gather in the **plaza** to walk and talk. In Madrid, **la Plaza Mayor** is a popular meeting place for people of all ages.

PROJECT

EL ARTE ÁRABE

Many buildings in southern Spain show Arabic influence in their designs and ornamentation. The elaborate geometric figures of the Alhambra are a good example. Explain to students that the designs don't include people or animals as the Islamic religion forbids the portrayal of human or animal figures. Have students draw one of the geometric patterns portrayed on the walls of the Alhambra.

Materials students may need

- ◆ Drawing paper
- ◆ Drawing compass (to make circles)
- ◆ Pencils, pens, and colored markers
- ◆ Rulers

Sequence

1. Present students with pictures of the **Alhambra** from an encyclopedia or reference book. Show students several examples of the geometric patterns.
2. Point out that the patterns are repeated geometric shapes. Many patterns are based upon a circle, using the center point as the anchor for a particular shape.
3. Have each student choose one figure they would like to draw and make a pattern for the shape that is repeated.

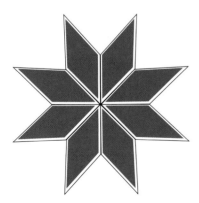

Challenge

The following is an example of a more complex pattern of geometric shapes from the Alhambra. For a challenge, have students make the three patterns for the design, trace the outline of the geometrical shapes on paper, and color them in. Hint: Have students trace the shape that looks like a three-legged starfish first, and then trace the star and hexagon shapes.

Grading the project

Suggested point distribution (total = 100 points):

Overall appearance **25**
Neatness **25**
Creativity **25**
Artistic design **25**

¡Ven conmigo a España!

LOCATION OPENER CHAPTERS 1, 2 (cont.)

Using the Map

- Have students find the capital of Spain. (Madrid)
- Have students identify the other country occupying the Iberian Peninsula. (Portugal) Explain that the Portuguese language is related to Spanish and is similar in many ways.
- Have students identify Spain's neighbors to the north, west, and south. (France, Andorra, Portugal, Morocco)
- Have students find the areas on the map where other languages of Spain are spoken.
- Have students locate Gibraltar. Ask them if they have heard of the Rock of Gibraltar, a large limestone mass that occupies most of Gibraltar's 2.3 square miles. You may want to point out that Gibraltar has been a British possession since 1713.
- Point out the short distance between Spain and Morocco. A distance of only 8 miles separates the Spanish town of Algeciras from the coast of North Africa. (about one hour by ferry)
- Point out Ceuta, part of Spain that is in Africa.

Critical Thinking

Ask students what language the majority of the people in the U.S. speak. Then tell them we speak English because England colonized the U.S. Have them compare and contrast what would have happened had the French colonized. Have students think about that for a moment. Then ask students if they know what language is spoken in most of Latin American countries. If they can tell you Spanish, have them think about why. Tell them that it's because Spain colonized most of Latin America.

History Link

The North Africans who conquered Spain in the early 700s were Muslims (**musulmanes**), followers of Islam. These Arabic-speaking people brought with them very sophisticated science, mathematics, architecture, culture, and medicine.

Slower Pace

Have students study the photograph of the Segovia castle on pages 16–17. Ask them to describe what they see. Lead a discussion about the differences between what is portrayed in the photo and the land, buildings, and culture in the city where they live.

NATIVE SPEAKER

Ask native speakers if they know about some customs or regional idioms from Spain. Some examples are **Vale** for *OK,* **patata** for **papa**. What are some other examples that students know?

You may wish to have students do the above map activities using the Atlas Interactivo Mundial at **go.hrw.com**.

go.hrw.com — MAPQUEST.COM

Language Notes

- In 1492, the Catholic kings reconquered the remaining Moorish territories on the Iberian Peninsula and expelled the Jewish people. Many fled to the Balkans and Israel. Today, those people (Sephardic Jews) still speak a Castilian-like language called Ladino. It contains many elements of 15th-century Castilian that are no longer present in today's Spanish. For example, **hijo** is *fijo,* **hablar** is *fablar,* and **ahora** is *agora.* Like Yiddish, Ladino is written using the Hebrew alphabet.

- Many words in the Spanish language that begin with **al-** are Arabic in origin:

alcalde (m.)	*mayor, judge*	**almohada**	*pillow*
almacén (m.)	*store*	**alquilar**	*to rent*
alfombra	*rug*	**albóndiga**	*meatball*

- Just as U.S. English differs from British English, so too does Latin American Spanish differ from Peninsular Spanish. Furthermore, the varieties of Spanish spoken in countries within Latin America differ from each other in both vocabulary and pronunciation.

Culture Note

Madrid, the capital of Spain, has many attractions to keep a tourist busy. One can sit and enjoy a **tortilla española** in a café, row boats on the lake in the **Parque del Retiro,** visit the fashionable shops downtown, or spend a quiet afternoon in the world-renowned **Museo del Prado.**

Multicultural Link

Have students name some annual celebrations from your area. (Thanksgiving, New Year's, etc.) Ask students if they are familiar with annual celebrations in other countries. This is an opportunity for students of other backgrounds to share their heritage with the class. Ask students if they have ever heard of the Running of the Bulls. It is a celebration known as **El Día de San Fermín** in Pamplona where it is held every July. Bulls are set loose in the streets, where only the most daring try to outrun them without getting hurt.

¡Ven conmigo a España!

VIDEO INTEGRATION

Adelante LEVEL 1A
Video Program
Videocassette 1, 4:50–7:24

¡Ven conmigo! LEVEL 1
DVD Tutor, Disc 1

MOTIVATING ACTIVITY

Before students open their books, have them brainstorm about what they think Spain is like. Then have them compare their guesses to what they see in the photographs on pages 16–19.

BACKGROUND

The word **alcázar** means *fortified palace* or *fortress* in Arabic. The **Castillo de Alcázar** in Segovia was constructed as a fortress in the 13th century. In 1474, **la Princesa Isabel** left the **Alcázar** to be crowned the queen of Castile. In the 16th century, the tower was used as a state prison. The **Castillo de Alcázar** is one of 1,400 castles and palaces in Spain.

Segovia has one of the best-preserved Roman aqueducts. The aqueduct was used to bring water to the city from the **Río Frío**. It is almost 100 feet tall at its highest point. The Romans built this aqueduct around 50 A.D.

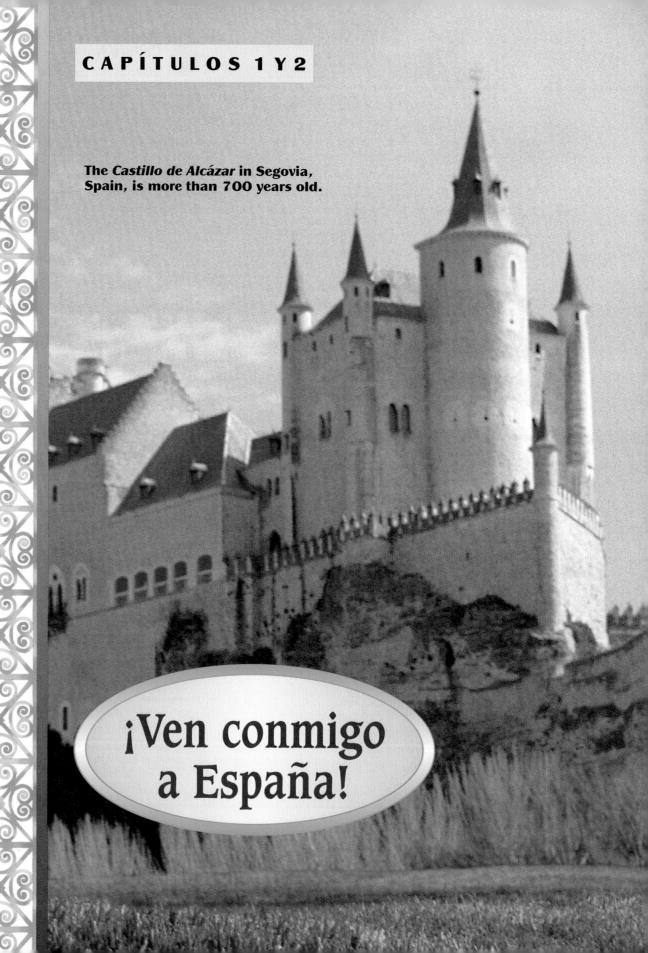

The *Castillo de Alcázar* in Segovia, Spain, is more than 700 years old.

¡Ven conmigo a España!

España

Population: 40,000,000

Area: 504,788 kms² (194,898 sq. mi.). Spain is larger than California, but smaller than Texas.

Capital: Madrid; population: about 3 million

Government: constitutional monarchy (King Juan Carlos I since 1975), with an elected parliament

Industries: food products, automobiles, steel, ships, textiles

Monetary unit: euro

Main languages: Spanish, Catalan, Basque, Galician

Map labels

Océano Atlántico del Norte
FRANCIA
Pirineos
Cordillera Cantábrica
Bilbao
León
ANDORRA
ESPAÑA
Madrid
Barcelona
PORTUGAL
Valencia
Islas Baleares
Sevilla
Mar Mediterráneo
Gibraltar (Br.)
Ceuta (Esp.)
Melilla (Esp.)
ARGELIA
MARRUECOS
Islas Canarias
N
0 100 200 Kilómetros
0 50 100 Millas

---

internet

MARCAR: go.hrw.com
PALABRA CLAVE:
WV3 SPAIN

go.hrw.com — **HRW ATLAS INTERACTIVO MUNDIAL**

MAPQUEST.COM

Have students go to the interactive atlas at **go.hrw.com** to find out more about the geography of Spain.

USING THE ALMANAC

- **Government:** The king serves as Spain's head of state. Although he does not have a direct role in running the government, he is an advisor.

- **Main Languages:** Although Castilian Spanish (**el castellano**) is the official language, there are also three other major languages. Catalan (**el catalán**) is spoken in the region around Barcelona; Basque (**el vasco**), also called Euskera, is spoken in the region around Bilbao, and Galician (**el gallego**) is spoken in the northwest region of Spain bordering Portugal.

CNNenEspañol.com

Have students check the CNN en español Web site for news on Spain. The CNN en español site is also a good source of timely, high interest readings for Spanish students.

diecisiete 17

USING THE PHOTO ESSAY

1 In mountainous northern Spain people enjoy many outdoor sports such as white water rafting, hiking, climbing, and camping.

2 The Costa Brava is a beautiful coastal zone north of Barcelona with steep cliffs, small coves, and finely grained sand. People from all over the world come to enjoy its beaches.

3 The Pyrenees Mountains (**los Pirineos**) stretch over 270 miles with a maximum width of about 100 miles. They form the boundary between France and Spain. Only Switzerland surpasses Spain as Europe's most mountainous country. The **Pico de Aneto** in Aragon is the tallest peak in the Pyrenees, at 11,169 feet. This peak is as tall as 11 Empire State buildings.

MOTIVATING ACTIVITY

Can students think of any regions in the United States that have large mountains? (the Colorado Rockies, the Adirondacks, the Appalachians)

ESPAÑA

CD-ROM
DISC 1

What comes to mind when you think of Spain? Spain is known for its beautiful architecture and rich cultural history dating back tens of thousands of years. The different regions of Spain have distinct landscapes and cultures. Many of these regions still retain their own languages.

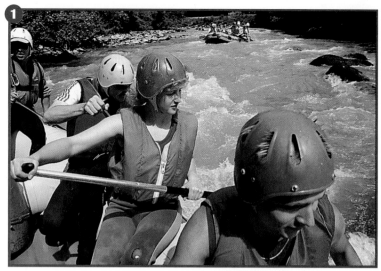

▲ **Aventuras en los ríos**
The swift waters and rugged terrain in northern Spain are ideal for white water rafting adventures.

◄ **Las playas de la Costa Brava**
The beaches of the Costa Brava in northeastern Spain are very popular.

Esquiar en los Pirineos ►
The Pyrenees Mountains form a natural border separating Spain from the rest of Europe. Abundant snowfall on the higher peaks makes them an excellent location for winter sports.

18 *dieciocho*

Chapters 1 and 2 will intro-duce you to some students who live in Madrid, the capital of Spain. Located in the center of the country, Madrid is a large, modern city of about three million people. Both visitors and **madrileños** (the residents of Madrid) love to explore the city's cultural treasures, parks, and cafés.

▲ Los parques de Barcelona
Barcelona, like many cities in Spain, has beautiful parks where families and friends go to relax.

El baile flamenco ▶
This young woman is wearing a traditional costume of Andalucía. Costumes like these are often worn to dance flamenco, a music and dance tradition that originated with the gypsies in southern Spain.

4 One of the most famous parks in Barcelona is Güell Park, which was designed by Antonio Gaudí, a Catalonian architect (1852–1926). It has curved benches, decorative staircases, and a breathtaking view of the city.

5 **Flamenco**, a lively tradition in **Andalucía,** is a dance of complex rhythms that involves acoustic guitar, hand-clapping, clicking castanets, and heel-stomping. The art of flamenco is a prime example of the blend of cultures that occurred in Spain. Experts continue to debate about the exact contri-butions of Andalusian popular songs, gypsy rhythms, Jewish laments, and Arabic style to the development of flamenco. While it is true that much of Andalusian food, culture, and architecture is the result of 800 years of Moorish influence, it is only part of the story for the flamenco song, dance, and guitar tradition.

MOTIVATING ACTIVITY
Play *Pin the Flag on Spain*. Mount an enlarged copy of the world map on pages xviii–xix or project Map Transparency 2 (**Europa y las Américas**) on the wall. Have students tape a small flag of Spain in the appropriate place on the map. For an advanced challenge, students can pin a flag on other Spanish-speaking countries.

CAPÍTULO 1

¡Mucho gusto!
CHAPTER OVERVIEW

De antemano pp. 22–25	*¡Me llamo Francisco!*			
	FUNCTIONS	**GRAMMAR**	**VOCABULARY**	**RE-ENTRY**
Primer paso pp. 26–33	• Saying hello and goodbye, p. 27 • Introducing people and responding to an introduction, p. 29 • Asking how someone is and saying how you are, p. 31	• **Gramática**: Punctuation marks, p. 30 • **Gramática**: Subject pronouns **tú** and **yo**, p. 32		• Accents (from **Capítulo preliminar**)
Segundo paso pp. 34–39	• Asking and saying how old someone is, p. 35 • Asking where someone is from and saying where you're from, p. 38	• **Nota gramatical**: **Soy, eres**, and **es**, p. 38 • **Nota gramatical**: Asking questions, p. 39	• Numbers 0–30, p. 36	• Numbers 0–30 (from **Capítulo preliminar**)
Tercer paso pp. 42–49	• Talking about what you like and don't like, p. 43	• **Gramática**: Nouns and definite articles, p. 46	• Sports, p. 44 • Classes at school, p. 44 • Musical genres, p. 45 • Foods, p. 45	

Letra y sonido	p. 49	The vowels	**Dictado**: Audio CD 1 Tracks 22–26	
Enlaces	p. 50	**Las ciencias sociales y la geografía**		
Vamos a leer	pp. 52–53	**Categorías**	**Reading Strategy**: Using cognates	
Review	pp. 54–57	**Repaso**, pp. 54–55	**A ver si puedo...**, p. 56	**Vocabulario**, p. 57

Culture
• **Nota cultural**: First and last names in Spanish, p. 26
• **Nota cultural**: First names and Catholicism, p. 27
• **Nota cultural**: Saint's Days, p. 30
• **Nota cultural**: Greetings, p. 33
• **Nota cultural**: Handwriting in Spanish-speaking countries, p. 34
• **Panorama cultural**: ¿De dónde eres?, pp. 40–41
• **Nota cultural**: Snack foods in Spain, p. 42

PRINT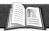

Lesson Planning

One-Stop Planner
Lesson Planner with Substitute Teacher
Lesson Plans, pp. 5–8

Listening and Speaking

Listening Activities
- Student Response Forms for Listening Activities, pp. 46–48
- Additional Listening Activities 1-1 to 1-6, pp. 2–4
- Additional Listening Activities (song), p. 5
- Scripts and Answers, pp. 26–28

Video Guide
- Teaching Suggestions, pp. 6–7
- Activity Masters, pp. 8–10
- Scripts and Answers, pp. 49–50, 63

Activities for Communication
- Communicative Activities, pp. 1–6
- Realia and Teaching Suggestions, pp. 38–42
- Situation Cards, pp. 70–71

¡Ven conmigo! Level 1
TPR Storytelling Book, pp. 1–4

Reading and Writing

Reading Strategies and Skills, Chapter 1
¡Lee conmigo! 1, Chapter 1
Practice and Activity Book, pp. 5–14

Grammar

Grammar and Vocabulary Workbook, pp. 1–8

¡Ven conmigo! Level 1
Grammar Tutor for Students of Spanish
Chapter 1

Assessment

Testing Program
- Paso Quizzes and Chapter Test, pp. 1–12
- Score Sheet, Scripts and Answers, pp. 13–18

Grammar and Vocabulary Quizzes
- Quizzes 1-1A, 1-2A, 1-3A
- Alternative Quizzes 1-1A, 1-2A, 1-3A

Alternative Assessment Guide
- Portfolio Assessment, p. 12
- Performance Assessment, p. 19
- CD-ROM Assessment, p. 26

¡Ven conmigo! Level 1
Standardized Assessment Tutor
- Reading, pp. 1–3
- Writing, p. 4
- Math, pp. 25–26

Native Speakers

¡Ven conmigo! Level 1
Cuaderno para hispanohablantes, pp. 1–5

MEDIA

Online Activities
- Juegos interactivos
- Actividades internet

Video Program
- Videocassette 1
- Videocassette 3 *(captioned version)*

¡Ven conmigo! Level 1
DVD Tutor, Disc 1

Audio Compact Discs
- Textbook Listening Activities, CD 1, Tracks 9–27
- Additional Listening Activities, CD 1, Tracks 33–38
- Assessment Items, CD 1, Tracks 28–32

Interactive CD-ROM Tutor, Disc 1

Teaching Transparencies
- Situations 1-1 to 1-3
- Vocabulary 1-A to 1-C
- Grammar and Vocabulary Workbook

One-Stop Planner CD-ROM

Use the **One-Stop Planner CD-ROM with Test Generator** to aid in lesson planning and pacing.

For each chapter, the **One-Stop Planner** includes:
- Editable lesson plans with direct links to teaching resources
- Printable worksheets from resource books
- Direct launches to the HRW Internet activities
- Video and audio segments
- Test Generator
- Clip Art for vocabulary items

¡Mucho gusto!
TECHNOLOGY

DVD/VIDEO

Videocassette 1, Videocassette 3 (captioned version)
DVD Tutor, Disc 1 See Video Guide, pages 5–10.

De antemano • ¡Me llamo Francisco!
Paco is hoping that Ramón, the mail carrier, is going to bring a letter from his new pen pal. Ramón pretends not to have a letter for Paco because the letter is addressed to "Francisco," Paco's full name. While Paco is reading the letter and daydreaming about his pen pal, his friend Felipe stops by for a visit.

¿De dónde eres?
Students from various parts of the Spanish-speaking world tell us where they are from.

A continuación
Paco and Felipe go to meet Mercedes, Paco's pen pal. She arrives at the pizzeria with her friend Juanita. Paco and Mercedes know each other from school as Paco and Merche. After some awkward moments, they realize that they are one another's pen pal, but under their full names, Francisco and Mercedes.

Videoclips
• **Colombia:** promotional piece directed by Edgar González

INTERACTIVE CD-ROM TUTOR

Activity	Activity Type	Pupil's Edition Page
En contexto	*Interactive conversation*	
1. Así se dice	¿Que falta?	pp. 27, 29, 31
2. Así se dice	Patas arriba	pp. 27, 29, 31
3. Vocabulario	¡Super memoria!	p. 36
4. Gramática	¡A escoger!	pp. 38–39
5. Vocabulario	Imagen y sonido ¡Exploremos! ¡Identifiquemos!	pp. 36, 38
6. Vocabulario	¿Cuál es?	pp. 44–45
Panorama cultural	¿De dónde eres? ¡A escoger!	pp. 40–41
¡A hablar!	*Guided recording*	pp. 54–55
¡A escribir!	*Guided writing*	pp. 54–55

Teacher Management System
Launch the program, type "admin" in the password area and press RETURN. Log on to **www.hrw.com/CDROMTUTOR** for a detailed explanation of the Teacher Management System.

DVD-ROM TUTOR ¡Ven conmigo! Level 1

The *DVD Tutor* contains all material from the Level 1 *Video Program*. Spanish captions are available for use at your discretion for all sections of the video. The *DVD Tutor* also provides a variety of video-based activities that assess students' understanding of the **De antemano, A continuación,** and **Panorama cultural.**

This part of the *DVD Tutor* may be used on any DVD video player connected to a television or video monitor.

In addition to the video material and the video-based comprehension activities, the *DVD Tutor* also contains the entire Level 1 *Interactive CD-ROM Tutor* in DVD-ROM format. Each DVD disc contains the activities from all 12 chapters of the *Interactive CD-ROM Tutor.*

This part of the *DVD Tutor* may be used on a Macintosh® or Windows® computer with a DVD-ROM drive.

One-Stop Planner CD-ROM

To preview all resources available for this chapter, use the **One-Stop Planner CD-ROM,** Disc 1.

MARCAR: go.hrw.com
PALABRA CLAVE:
WV3 SPAIN-1

INTERNET CONNECTION

*Have students explore the **go.hrw.com** Web site for many online resources covering all chapters. All Chapter 1 resources are available under the keyword **WV3 SPAIN-1.** Interactive games help students practice the material and provide them with immediate feedback. You will also find a printable worksheet that provides Internet activities that lead to a comprehensive online research project.*

JUEGOS INTERACTIVO

You can use the interactive games in this chapter

- to practice grammar, vocabulary, and chapter functions
- as homework
- as an assessment option
- as a self-test
- to prepare for the Chapter Test

ACTIVIDADES INTERNET

Students look for information about famous Spanish-speakers online and record a little about each person, using the vocabulary and phrases from the chapter.

- In preparation for the **Hoja de actividades,** have students review the dramatic episode on Videocassette 1 or redo the activities in the **Panorama cultural** on page 31.

- After completing the activity sheet, have students work with a partner and share the information they gathered in activity B on that sheet. Then ask each pair of students to share what they learned with the class.

Proyecto

Have students list five things they enjoy doing and then exchange their list with another student. With their new lists, have the students search online for five Spanish-language Web sites that describe, show, or advertise those activities. Have each student record those URLs and return the list of sites to the list's creator.

CAPÍTULO 1

¡Mucho gusto!

TEXTBOOK LISTENING ACTIVITIES SCRIPTS

For Student Response Forms, see Listening Activities pp. 46–49

PRIMER PASO   pp. 26–33

5 Saludos y despedidas   p. 27

1. — Hasta luego, Miguel Ángel. Tengo que irme.
   — ¡Chao, Alicia!
2. — Hola, Santiago.
   — ¿Qué tal, Miguel Ángel?
3. — Buenos días, don Alonso.
   — Hola, Miguel Ángel.
4. — Adiós, Mariana.
   — Sí, hasta mañana, Miguel Ángel.
5. — Buenas tardes, doña Luisa. ¿Cómo está?
   — Buenas tardes. Estoy bien, gracias.
6. — Bueno, tengo clase.
   — ¡Hasta luego, David!

Answers to Activity 5

1. Alicia: leaving	4. Mariana: leaving
2. Santiago: arriving	5. Doña Luisa: arriving
3. Don Alonso: arriving	6. David: leaving

8 ¿Cómo respondes?   p. 29

1. Mucho gusto.
2. Me llamo Abel. ¿Y tú? ¿Cómo te llamas?
3. Éste es mi amigo. Se llama Felipe.
4. Ésta es Evita, la estudiante del programa internacional.
5. Encantada.
6. Soy la señora Rivas.

Answers to Activity 8

1. Igualmente.	4. ¡Mucho gusto!/ Encantado(a).
2. Me llamo...	5. Igualmente.
3. ¡Mucho gusto!/Encantado(a).	6. Encantado(a)./¡Mucho gusto!

12 ¿Cómo estás?   p. 31

1. SARA   ¿Cómo estás, Daniel?
   DANIEL   Ay, muy mal.
2. SARA   ¿Qué tal, Marta?
   MARTA   Más o menos, Sara. ¿Y tú?
3. SARA   Buenos días, Elena. ¿Cómo estás?
   ELENA   Estoy muy bien, gracias, Sara.
4. SARA   Hola, José Luis. ¿Qué tal?
   JOSÉ LUIS   Pues, muy bien, Sara. ¿Y tú?
5. SARA   Buenas tardes, Carlos. ¿Cómo estás?
   CARLOS   ¡Excelente!
6. SARA   ¿Qué tal, Juan?
   JUAN   Pues, estoy muy mal, amiga, muy mal.

Answers to Activity 12

bien	regular	mal
Elena	Felipe (modelo)	Daniel
José Luis	Marta	Juan
Carlos		

SEGUNDO PASO   pp. 34–39

20 Edades   p. 37

DANIEL   Ésta es Marisa y tiene catorce años. Éste es José.

ADRIANA   ¿Cuántos años tiene?

DANIEL   Tiene seis años.

ADRIANA   ¿Y éste? ¿Cómo se llama?

DANIEL   Se llama David. Tiene once años.

ADRIANA   ¿Y ésta?

DANIEL   Se llama Anita. Tiene veinticinco años.

ADRIANA   ¿Y éste?

DANIEL   ¡Éste es Daniel! ¡Sí, soy yo! En esta foto tengo un año.

Answers to Activity 20

a. Marisa	c. Anita	e. José
b. Daniel	d. David	

23 ¿De dónde es?   p. 38

1. — Es Gabriela, ¿no?
   — Sí, es Gabriela. Es de Buenos Aires, Argentina.
2. — ¿Y ésta es Maricarmen?
   — Sí, es Maricarmen y es de Santiago de Chile.
3. — ¿De dónde es David?
   — David es de Madrid, España.
4. — ¿Cómo te llamas?
   — Me llamo Antonio y soy de Quito, Ecuador.
5. — ¿Y tú? Eres Laura, ¿verdad?
   — Sí, Laura Alicia, encantada. Yo soy de San José, Costa Rica.
6. — ¿De dónde es Pedro?
   — Pedro es de Bogotá, Colombia.

Answers to Activity 23

1. Gabriela: **b** Es de Buenos Aires, Argentina.
2. Maricarmen: **d** Es de Santiago de Chile.
3. David: **a** Es de Madrid, España.
4. Antonio: **c** Es de Quito, Ecuador.
5. Laura: **f** Es de San José, Costa Rica.
6. Pedro: **e** Es de Bogotá, Colombia.

TERCER PASO   pp. 42–49

28 Planes   p. 43

CARLOS ¿Te gusta el voleibol?

ELENA Bueno, no. No me gusta mucho.

CARLOS ¿Te gusta la pizza?

ELENA No, no me gusta.

CARLOS Oye, ¿te gusta la música pop?

ELENA Pues, no me gusta.

CARLOS Bueno, entonces, ¿qué te gusta?

ELENA A ver... ¿te gusta la comida mexicana?

CARLOS Sí, me gusta.

ELENA ¡Estupendo! A mí también me gusta. ¿Te gusta el restaurante El Mercado?

CARLOS Mmm..., no, no me gusta mucho.

ELENA Ah, bueno...

Answers to Activity 28

1. voleibol—Elena doesn't like it.
2. pizza—Elena doesn't like it.
3. la música pop—Elena doesn't like it.
4. la comida mexicana—Carlos and Elena both like it.
5. el restaurante El Mercado—Carlos doesn't like it.

29 Una fiesta   p. 45

AMIGO ¿Te gustan los deportes?

DIANA Sí, me gusta el béisbol. Y me gusta mucho el tenis. No me gusta mucho la natación.

AMIGO Bueno, y ¿qué comida te gusta?

DIANA Mmm, no me gusta la fruta. Me gusta la comida italiana. Y la ensalada. ¡Me gusta mucho la ensalada!

AMIGO Y a ti te gusta bastante la música, ¿verdad?

DIANA Sí, me gusta la música pero no me gusta el jazz. Me gusta más la música rock.

Answers to Activity 29

Answers will vary. Possible answers:

el béisbol, la comida italiana, la ensalada, la música rock

LETRA Y SONIDO   p. 49

For the scripts for Parts A and C, see page 49. The dialogue for Part B is below.

B. Dictado

— Buenos días, Marta. ¿Qué tal?
— Muy bien, Ana. ¿Cómo estás?
— Bien. Bueno, tengo que irme.
— Hasta luego.
— Chao.

REPASO   pp. 54–55

1 p. 54

MODELO Me llamo Mariana Castillo. Soy de España. Tengo quince años y me gusta mucho la música rock. No me gusta el tenis.

— Hola. Me llamo <u>Liliana Rivera</u>. Soy de <u>Santiago de Chile</u> y tengo <u>dieciséis años</u>. Me gusta mucho <u>el tenis</u> pero no me gusta hacer <u>la tarea</u>.

— Hola, ¿qué tal? Soy <u>Pablo García</u>. Soy de <u>Monterrey, México</u>, y tengo <u>quince años</u>. Me gusta mucho <u>el inglés</u>. No me gusta <u>la música clásica</u>, pero <u>la música rock</u>, sí.

¡Mucho gusto!

PROJECTS

COLLAGE

In this activity students will create picture collages of some of their favorite things to use as visual support when they introduce themselves and say how old they are in Spanish. Suggest to students that they consider saving the collage in their portfolios.

Materials students may need

- ◆ Poster board
- ◆ Glue
- ◆ Old magazines
- ◆ Photos
- ◆ Removable tape or paper clips
- ◆ Scissors

Sequence

1. Ask students what they are interested in when they meet a new friend. What do they want to find out or know about someone new?

2. Working individually, students make a list in English of what things they like and don't like. For Spanish vocabulary, students can refer to the Additional Vocabulary on pp. 275–280.

3. Students write sentences in Spanish about their likes and dislikes.

4. Students find pictures in magazines or make their own drawings to illustrate their likes and dislikes.

5. Students may mount their illustrations above or around the text on a large sheet of paper. Paper clips or small pieces of removable tape are helpful to hold the illustrations in place until they decide on the final layout.

6. Have students peer-edit their Spanish captions and make corrections before final mounting.

7. Student arrange their illustrations with the appropriate descriptions and rehearse the collage presentation.

Grading the project

Suggested point distribution (total = 100 points):

Completion of all steps **15**
Self or peer-edit **30**
Visual presentation **15**
Grammar **25**
Pronunciation **15**

NOTE

You may suggest that students save the collages in their Portfolio (see pp. T52–T53). If the projects are for the Portfolio, tell students beforehand to save their English notes, the first draft of the Spanish text, and the final draft of the Spanish text.

FAMILY LINK

Students may show their projects to a family member or a friend who is not taking Spanish. Ask students if they are able to make themselves understood by showing the pictures and Spanish text.

TEACHER NOTE

Keep in mind when giving assignments that entail the disclosure of personal information that some students and their families may consider family matters private. In some cases, you may want to give students the option of discussing a make-believe family.

PASSPORT

In this activity students will create a passport for themselves or for an imaginary person. Passports are recognized worldwide as a form of identification. Have students discuss when and where they might use a passport and why they think passports are important. Have them do research to find out how they would go about getting a passport (where they would go, what forms they might need, and how long they would need to wait).

Materials students may need

- ◆ A recent photo of themselves
- ◆ A pocket size notebook
- ◆ Pens or markers
- ◆ Stickers or ink pad and stamps
- ◆ Old magazines
- ◆ Construction paper
- ◆ Tape
- ◆ Glue
- ◆ Scissors

Sequence

To create their passports, students may use a cutout from a magazine if they are making a passport for an imaginary person. Students may also wish to draw their own portraits. Explain that passport photos must be a headshot. Students should then choose a country of origin.

1 Have students design a cover for their passport. It should display the name of the country and an official seal or emblem. If a student chooses an actual country, you may wish to have him or her do library research to find out what its official seal looks like.

2 Remind students that their passport should contain blank pages at the back for visas.

3 Have students prepare a sketch of the body of their passport before beginning. They should use expressions from this chapter in place of words like **nombre** (**me llamo...**), **edad** (**tengo...años**), and **nacionalidad** (**soy de...**).

4 Students first make a rough draft for peer review in which they sketch the images they plan to use and the way they plan to use them. Students exchange rough drafts for peer review and then turn in revised drafts for teacher review and suggestions.

5 Students complete the final draft leaving several blank pages at the end for visas. The idea of the passport can continue. Students can design their own stickers and stamps as they progress through different locations of *¡Ven conmigo!*

FAMILY LINK

If a family member or guardian has a passport, students may wish to compare their own passport to that one. They may also wish to invite them to bring their passport in to show the class. Or they could ask other teachers or school personnel if they have a passport.

Grading the project

Suggested point distribution (total = 100 points):

Creativity **15**
Appearance. **25**
Originality **25**
Peer-editing. **15**
Accurate use of chapter expressions **20**

✂ LAS FICHAS

A good beginning project for any foreign language class is to create flash cards. They may be used at home, in groups, or in class for games and review.

Materials students may need

- ◆ An index card box or sealable plastic pencil bag
- ◆ Index cards
- ◆ Pens or markers
- ◆ Old magazines

1 One set of cards could include pictures of things students like in order to practice "**me gusta**".

2 Another set could have questions on one side of the card and an appropriate answer on the other. For Chapter 1, include greetings, goodbyes, introductions, or any of the functional expressions from the chapter.

3 Vocabulary from each **paso** should be included on the cards. Point out that using a picture on one side and the Spanish vocabulary word on the other will stimulate their visual recall, helping them to remember more.

Grading the project

Flash cards may be placed in students' portfolios.

Suggested point distribution: (total = 100 points):

Originality and design **25**
Spelling **25**
Variety of vocabulary and expressions **25**
Grammar **25**

CAPÍTULO 1

¡Mucho gusto!

GAMES

¿DÓNDE ESTÁ?

*The objective of this game is to familiarize students with Spanish-speaking countries and their major cities. This may be played after the **Panorama cultural** on pages 82–83.*

Materials you may need

◆ Wall map of the world or a globe
◆ Slips of paper
◆ Container for folded slips of paper

Procedure

On each slip of paper, write the name of a major city or country in which Spanish is spoken. Divide the class into two teams, Team A and Team B. Choose one student to be the scorekeeper. A member of Team A draws a name from the container and says to a member of Team B, **¿Dónde está _____?** A member of Team B must point to the country or city on the map within ten seconds. If he or she is unsuccessful, the turn goes to Team A. If successful, Team A receives the point. If neither is successful, then the teacher or another student supplies the correct information and neither team scores. Team B then draws a new slip of paper and the game continues. The team with the most points wins.

¿QUÉ TE GUSTA?

This word scramble can be played to quickly review vocabulary presented in Chapter 1.

Procedure

Students unscramble seven words from the chapter vocabulary list to find the answer to the question **¿Qué te gusta?** Students place one letter in each blank to form the words. Students then arrange the circled letters to unscramble the answer to the question **¿Qué te gusta?**

Materials you may need

◆ Chapter vocabulary list
◆ Pencils or pens
◆ Copy of word scramble

ME GUSTA LA

Ⓟ I Z Z Ⓐ   ZAZPI
F R U T Ⓐ   ARFTU
E N S A Ⓛ A D A   NSAEALAD
T E L E V I Ⓢ I Ó N   STIVNIÓLEE
C L A S Ⓔ   ESLAC
M A Ⓝ A N A   ANAMÑA
C Ⓞ M I D A   DCIMOA
SOLUCIÓN: ME GUSTA EL E S P A Ñ O L.

PONGA

This game, which is played exactly like Bingo®, gives students the opportunity to practice numbers in Spanish while enjoying a familiar game. Use it to practice the numbers on page 36.

Materials students may need

◆ Index cards or cardboard
◆ Permanent ink pen
◆ Paper scraps

Procedure

Students prepare their own PONGA card by drawing a card similar to a Bingo® card on a sheet of paper. Cards should have five horizontal spaces and five vertical spaces. Students write a number between 0 and 30 in each space on the card. Read a number between 0 and 30 in Spanish and record it. Students cover or cross off numbers as they are called. When a player has marked off an entire row of numbers, he or she says "PONGA," then reads the numbers back to the teacher in Spanish. If the numbers are correct, that student is the winner. You may want to laminate the cards and reuse them with future classes. Students can use paper scraps to cover the numbers (if they have been written on before lamination) or write with a water-based marker.

P	O	N	G	A
12	9	30	27	0
20	15	4	2	7
1	23	18	25	18
17	13	5	16	3

DERECHA / IZQUIERDA

This is a game to practice the alphabet, as well as to introduce the vocabulary for left and right. It may be played in small or large groups.

Procedure

A group leader stands in the middle of the circle. He or she points to a person and says **izquierda** and begins counting. That person must say the name of the person to his or her left and spell it before the leader counts off the full circle. If the leader points to a person and says **derecha,** that person must say the name of the person to his or her right and spell it. If the person fails to say the letters correctly, he or she takes the role of leader and comes to the center of the circle. The former leader takes the empty chair.

NÚMEROS EN LÍNEA

Preparation

Have students prepare index cards with numbers written out as words in Spanish.

Materials students may need
◆ Index cards   ◆ Markers

Procedure

Randomly pass out cards to students. Instruct students to line up in numerical order in complete silence, then read off their numbers.

Repeat the lineup with even numbers (**pares**) on one side of the room and odd numbers (**nones, impares**) on the other. Or, ask them to line up in reverse order (**del 30 al 1**), or by every other number (**por dos**). Again, ask students to read off their number after they've lined up.

LA PAPA CALIENTE

Make a **"papa caliente"** using a battery operated alarm clock in a small box. Be sure to make the box top removable and choose an alarm or timer that ticks loudly.

Materials you may need
◆ A small box   ◆ A battery-operated alarm clock

Procedure

When students enter the classroom, pass the **"papa"** to one of the students with the instructions, "I have just handed you a timer set to go off at any moment. If you're holding it when it does you're out of the game." The only way you can get rid of it is to correctly introduce yourself to someone else, say where you're from, and find out that person's name and where he or she is from. Then, you may give that person the **"papa."** Continue the game until the timer goes off, then reset as often as needed until all of the students have taken part in the activity.

ANSWERS TO CHAPTER 1 ACTIVITIES

Answers not listed here appear on corresponding pupil pages. Listening activity answers appear with the Scripts for this chapter on pages 19E–19F.

SEGUNDO PASO   pp. 34–39

21 Answers will vary. Possible answers:
1. Tiene cinco años.
2. Tiene dieciocho años.
3. Tiene trece años.
4. Tiene doce años.
5. Tiene diecinueve años.
6. Tiene dieciséis años.
7. Tiene diez años.

24
1. María Luisa es de Honduras.
2. Daniel es de Perú.
3. Patricia es de El Salvador.
4. Fabiola es de Ecuador.
5. Tú eres de Paraguay.
6. Yo soy de...

TERCER PASO   pp. 42–49

30 Answers will vary. Possible answers:
1. deportes - Me gusta la natación. No me gusta el baloncesto.
2. comida - Me gusta la comida mexicana. No me gusta la pizza.
3. música - Me gusta el jazz. No me gusta la música pop.
4. clases - Me gusta la clase de español. No me gusta la tarea.

32 Answers will vary. Possible answers:
1. Me llamo...
2. Estoy bien, gracias.
3. Tengo... años.
4. No, no me gusta el béisbol.

VAMOS A LEER   pp. 52–53

A Answers will vary. Possible answers:
Videos
Natura
Arte
Música
Humor

B
1. Trivia
2. Tecnología
3. Humor
4. Tu Estilo Personal
5. Arte
6. Música
7. Pasatiempos
8. Ecología
9. Videos
10. Natura

Cognados falsos
real—*royal* not *real*
grupo—*group*
ropa—*clothes* not *rope*
disgusto—*displeasure* not *disgust*
sopa—*soup* not *soap*
The words **real, disgusto, ropa,** and **sopa** are false cognates.

A VER SI PUEDO...   p. 56

1 Answers will vary. Possible answers:
1. Buenos días, señor/a.
2. Bueno, tengo clase.
3. Hasta mañana.

2 Answers will vary. Possible answers:
1. Me llamo...
2. Mucho gusto; Encantado/a.
3. Igualmente.

3 Answers will vary. Possible answers:
1. ¿Qué tal?; ¿Cómo estás?
2. Bien; Regular.

4 Answers will vary. Possible answers:
1. ¿Cuántos años tienes?
2. Tengo ... años.
3. Juan tiene ... años.

5 Answers will vary. Possible answers:
1. Soy de Minnesota.
2. ¿De dónde eres?
3. Juan es de Puerto Rico.

6 Answers will vary. Possible answers:
1. ¿Te gusta el voleibol? Sí, me gusta...; No me gusta...
2. ¿Te gusta el béisbol?
3. ¿Te gusta la comida italiana?
4. ¿Te gusta la música pop?
5. ¿Te gusta el baloncesto?

🏠 HOMEWORK SUGGESTIONS

Chapter Section	Presentation	Homework Options
Primer paso	**Así se dice,** p. 27	*Pupil's Edition,* p. 28, Activity 6 *Grammar and Vocabulary,* p. 1, Activity 1
	Así se dice, p. 29	*Pupil's Edition,* p. 29, Activity 9 *Practice and Activity Book,* p. 6, Activity 4 *Grammar and Vocabulary,* p. 1, Activity 2
	Así se dice, p. 31	*Pupil's Edition,* p. 32, Activity 13 *Practice and Activity Book,* p. 7, Activities 5–6 *Grammar and Vocabulary,* p. 3, Activities 6–7 *CD-ROM,* Disc 1, Chapter 1, Activity 2
	Gramática, p. 30	*Grammar and Vocabulary,* p. 2, Activities 3–5
	Gramática, p. 32	*Practice and Activity Book,* p. 8, Activities 7–8 *Grammar and Vocabulary,* p. 4, Activities 8–10
Segundo paso	**Así se dice,** p. 35	*Practice and Activity Book,* p. 9, Activity 10
	Vocabulario, p. 36	*Practice and Activity Book,* p. 9, Activity 9 *Grammar and Vocabulary,* p. 5, Activities 11–13 *CD-ROM,* Disc 1, Chapter 1, Activity 3
	Así se dice, p. 38	*Practice and Activity Book,* p. 10, Activity 13
	Nota gramatical, p. 38	*Grammar and Vocabulary,* p. 6, Activity 14
	Nota gramatical, p. 39	*Pupil's Edition,* p. 39, Activities 25–26 *Practice and Activity Book,* p. 10, Activity 12 *Grammar and Vocabulary,* p. 6, Activity 15 *CD-ROM,* Disc 1, Chapter 1, Activity 4
Tercer paso	**Así se dice,** p.43	*Practice and Activity Book,* p. 11, Activity 14
	Vocabulario, pp. 44–45	*Grammar and Vocabulary,* p. 7, Activities 16–17 *CD-ROM,* Disc 1, Chapter 1, Activity 6
	Gramática, p.46	*Practice and Activity Book,* pp. 11–12, Activities 15–17 *Grammar and Vocabulary,* p. 8, Activities 18–20

¡Mucho gusto!

MOTIVATING ACTIVITY

Ask students the following: What do you say to someone you've just met? What would you write in a letter introducing yourself to a pen pal? How would your greetings differ if you were meeting someone face to face as opposed to introducing yourself by mail?

PHOTO FLASH!

① Pilar and Eva are from the province of Ciudad Real, in the region of Castilla-La Mancha. The girls have just finished dancing a **jota**, a traditional Castilian dance. The girls danced in a city park in Madrid to a chorus of traditional songs sung by other park visitors. Such impromptu performances are not unusual in Spain, where many people learn the traditional songs and dances of their region as children and dance them at parties and festivals throughout their lives.

CRITICAL THINKING

Ask students to observe from the background where each photo might have been taken. (restaurant, park, city street) What clues tell where the photos were taken?

CAPÍTULO

¡Mucho gusto!

FRANCISCO

RAMON

MERCED

① **Me llamo Pilar. Soy de Ciudad Real. Ésta es mi amiga Eva.**

In this chapter you will learn to

PRIMER PASO

- say hello and goodbye
- introduce people and respond to an introduction
- ask how someone is and say how you are

SEGUNDO PASO

- ask and say how old someone is
- ask where someone is from and say where you're from

TERCER PASO

- talk about what you like and don't like

internet

go.hrw.com

MARCAR: go.hrw.com
PALABRA CLAVE:
WV3 SPAIN-1

② **Hola, soy yo. Soy Ana. ¿Qué tal?**

③ **¿Te gusta el voleibol?**

TEACHER NOTE
Some activities suggested in the *Annotated Teacher's Edition* ask students to contact various people and organizations in the community. It is advisable to request parental permission for these activities. In some cases, you may also want to obtain permission from the parties the student will be asked to contact.

FOCUSING ON OUTCOMES
- Have students read the list of objectives for this chapter, then match the first three learner outcomes to a photo. (Photo 1: introductions; photo 2: saying hello and asking how someone is; photo 3: talking about likes and dislikes.)
- Have students identify as many English expressions as possible to say hello and goodbye. When would they use each expression? What gesture, if any, do they use with these greetings? (a handshake, a kiss, a hug)

PHOTO FLASH!
② Ask students to guess what the girl in this photo is saying and who she's speaking to. Ask students why someone might need to make telephone calls from a telephone booth. Point out that although almost every household in the U.S. has a telephone, telephone service in Spain and Latin America is much more expensive and fewer people have telephones.

VIDEO INTEGRATION

Adelante LEVEL 1A

Video Program

Videocassette 1, 7:25–11:28 OR
Videocassette 3, 00:22–4:24
(captioned version)

¡Ven conmigo! LEVEL 1
DVD Tutor, Disc 1

TEACHER NOTE

The **fotonovela** is an abridged version of the video episode.

VIDEO SYNOPSIS

Paco is waiting for Ramón, the mail carrier, to bring a letter from his new pen pal. Paco sees Ramón coming and runs through his parents' fruit and vegetable store. Paco bumps into his mother, apologizes, and goes to get the letter. The mailman pretends not to have a letter for Paco because the letter is addressed to "Francisco," Paco's full name. Back in his room, Paco reads the letter and daydreams about his pen pal. Then Paco's friend Felipe stops by for a visit.

MOTIVATING ACTIVITY

Ask students if they have ever anxiously awaited a call or letter. How did they feel?

SUGGESTION

Refer to page T58 for names and addresses of pen pal organizations. Have students begin corresponding with a pen pal throughout the year.

STANDARDS: 1.1, 1.2, 3.2, 5.1

DE ANTEMANO

Reminder: Read the highest bubble first.

¡Me llamo Francisco!

CD 1 Trs. 9–10

Look at the characters in the **fotonovela**, or photo story. Where are they? What are their occupations? What do you think they're talking about? What do you suppose will happen in the story?

PA p. 5 Acts. 1–2

Paco

Felipe

Ramón

1

¡Ay, Paco!

¡Lo siento, mamá!

2

Hola, buenos días, Paco. ¿Cómo estás?

Muy bien, gracias. ¿Hay una carta para mí?

DE ANTEMANO

veintitrés **23**

PRESENTATION

Have students scan the speech bubbles and find up to eight words whose meaning they think they can guess. Point out that **pizza** and **voleibol** are cognates (words that are similar in two languages). Tell students that looking and listening for cognates will help them understand. Then discuss each of the following:

1. What do you think the following words or phrases mean? **¡Buenos días! ¿Cómo estás! ¡Hola!**

2. What do you think Paco is expecting from Ramón? Can you guess what word means *letter*?

3. What kinds of things do you think Mercedes is telling Paco in her letter?

4. Play the video or audio recording a second time, then break the class into pairs for students to practice reading the dialogues and role-playing the parts of the different characters. As you circulate, check pronunciation.

CHALLENGE

❺ Using the letter as a model, have students write a similar letter about themselves or about an alter ego.

LANGUAGE NOTE

Characters in this video episode speak with a Spanish accent. Point out that through the *Video Program* they will hear many accents from around the Spanish-speaking world.

NATIVE SPEAKERS

Explain to native speakers from Latin America that Spaniards have an additional sound in the language, similar to the *th* in the English word *think*. Model how Spaniards would distinguish between these word pairs: **casa** *(ka sa)*, **caza** *(ka tha)*; **siento** *(syen to)*, **ciento** *(thyen to)*, **coser** *(ko ser)*, **cocer** *(ko ther)*

A continuación

You may choose to continue with *¡Me llamo Francisco! (a continuación)* at this time or wait until later in the chapter. At this point, Paco and Felipe go to meet Mercedes. Francisco and Mercedes know each other from school as Paco and Merche, and they realize that they are pen pals under their full names. You may wish to have pairs of students predict what they think will happen in the second part of the video.

1 ¿Comprendes?

How well do you understand what is happening in the **fotonovela**? Check by answering these questions in English. Don't be afraid to guess.

1. Who are the people in the **fotonovela**? Make a list of them. How are they related to Paco?
2. Why does Paco run out of the store?
3. What do you know about the family business?
4. What do you think will happen next?

These activities check for global comprehension only. Students should not yet be expected to produce language modeled in **De antemano**.

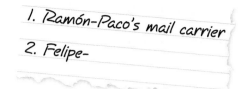

1. Ramón–Paco's mail carrier
2. Felipe–

1. Ramón, Paco's mail carrier; Felipe, Paco's friend; Mamá, Paco's mother; Paco, main character
2. To see if the mail carrier has a letter for him.
3. They operate a fruit and vegetable store.
4. Paco will tell Felipe about his new pen pal Mercedes.

2 Cortesías

Match the English phrase to the Spanish phrase the characters use in the **fotonovela.**

1. Hello. f
2. Good morning! c
3. I like volleyball a lot. b
4. My name is . . . a
5. Thank you. e
6. Goodbye. d

a. Me llamo...
b. Me gusta mucho el voleibol.
c. ¡Buenos días!
d. Adiós.
e. Gracias.
f. Hola.

3 ¡Soy yo!

Find the sentences in the **fotonovela** and fill in the blanks.

PACO   ¿Hay una ___1___ para mí?

RAMÓN   No, ésta no es. Esta carta es para ___2___.

PACO   ¡Sí, soy yo! Yo ___3___ Francisco pero me llaman Paco.

RAMÓN   ___4___, don Francisco Xavier López Medina.

1. carta
2. el señor Francisco Xavier López Medina
3. soy
4. Adiós

SUGGESTIONS

1 Have students work with a partner. Allow approximately five minutes for pairs to prepare answers to the questions. Review with the entire class.

2 You might ask students to write the Spanish expressions in Activity 2. In the early stages of language acquisition, copying is a valid writing activity. Assure students that it is normal for the skills of speaking and writing (productive skills) to develop more slowly than the skills of listening and reading (receptive skills). Allow time for students to develop their receptive skills before asking them to speak and write sentences of their own creation. Not all students will develop their productive skills at the same pace.

COOPERATIVE LEARNING

Once students have seen the video twice and have had the chance to practice the dialogue, divide them into groups of three or four. Have each team appoint a scribe. Allow about eight to ten minutes for them to complete exercises 2 and 3; the scribe will record the group's answers. At the end of the allotted time, have groups exchange their answers and correct them as a class. Everyone in the group will earn the same grade. Repeat this type of activity after watching subsequent videos. Stress teamwork.

VIDEO INTEGRATION

Adelante LEVEL 1A

Video Program
Videocassette 1, 8:43–8:59 OR
Videocassette 3, 1:40–1:56
(captioned version)

¡Ven conmigo! LEVEL 1
DVD Tutor, Disc 1

Bell work

Have students refer to the **fotonovela** on pages 22–24 and write all of the expressions they can find to greet someone and to say goodbye.

SUGGESTIONS

• After reading the **Nota cultural**, ask volunteers to say what their last name would be if they used this naming convention. To create a comfortable and nonthreatening atmosphere, it is best to ask only volunteers to provide such personal examples.

• As an additional challenge, ask students where their last name would be listed in the phone book using both parents' last names. (It would be listed by the first letter of their father's last name: Smith Anderson, Smith Brown, Smith Cole, Smith Davis, etc.)

PRIMER PASO

Storytelling Book
pp. 1, 4

WV3 SPAIN-1

Saying hello and goodbye; introducing people and responding to an introduction; asking how someone is and saying how you are

4 ¿Qué pasa?

What greeting does the mail carrier use in this photo? How does Paco answer? Put the following phrases in the correct order.

3 Muy bien, gracias.

2 ¿Cómo estás?

1 Hola. Buenos días.

Nota cultural

Spaniards and Latin Americans often use both their first and middle names. They also generally use two last names: first the father's (in Paco's case, López) and then the mother's maiden name (for Paco, it's Medina). In the phone book, Paco's name would be listed under "**L**" as **López Medina, Francisco.** What would your full name be in a Spanish-speaking country?

ASÍ SE DICE   Saying hello and goodbye

To greet someone, say:

¡Hola! *Hello!*

Buenos días, señor.
Good morning, sir.

Buenas tardes, señorita.
Good afternoon, miss.

Buenas noches, señora.
Good evening/Good night, ma'am.

To say goodbye to someone, say:

Adiós.	*Goodbye.*
Bueno, tengo clase.	*Well, I have class.*
Chao.	*'Bye.*
Hasta luego.	*See you later.*
Hasta mañana.	*See you tomorrow.*
Tengo que irme.	*I have to go.*

PA
p. 6
Act. 3

GV
p. 1
Act. 1

1-1

5 Saludos y despedidas   *Script and answers on p. 19E*

Miguel Ángel talks with various people throughout his day. Listen and decide if each person he speaks with is leaving or arriving.

CD 1 Tr. 11

MODELO   —¡Hola, Miguel Ángel!
—Buenos días, señora López. *(arriving)*

1. Alicia
2. Santiago
3. don Alonso
4. Mariana
5. doña Luisa
6. David

Recuerdo del bautizo de
María Magdalena Montoya Ramírez
13 de mayo de 1998
Padrinos: José Antonio Muñoz Ruiz y
Ana María Cervantes Banderas

🌎 Nota cultural

Many people in Spain and Latin America are Roman Catholic. This influences the names that families give their children. Common first names are José and Juan Pablo for males, María José and Magdalena for females. Many girls' names commemorate the Virgin Mary: Ana María and María del Socorro. Some common Jewish names include Miriam and Ester for girls and Isaac and Jacobo for boys. Islamic names include Ómar and Ismael for boys and Jasmín and Zoraida for girls. Do you know the origin of your first name?

☀ MOTIVATE

Ask pairs of volunteers to demonstrate in front of the class how they greet people. Have them do this as if they were greeting close friends of the same or opposite sex, parents, grandparents, the school principal, a small child, or a new student in school.

☀ TEACH

PRESENTATION
ASÍ SE DICE

(TPR) Model the expressions using appropriate gestures and expressions. Then call out the new functional phrases. Students show comprehension by acting out the phrases. (You say, **¡Hasta luego!** and students pretend to leave, wave, etc.)

SUGGESTION

5 Discuss the value of being a good listener. Play the recording, then verify answers with students. Play the recording again and have them repeat the Spanish. Encourage them to imitate the pronunciations they hear as closely as possible.

28

STANDARDS: 1.1, 1.2, 1.3, 5.1

PAIR WORK

6 Ask students to work in pairs. Have them come up with as many **saludos** and **despedidas** as they can, referring to what they've learned so far.

NATIVE SPEAKERS

Ask native speakers if they know of any other **saludos** and **despedidas**. Have them share them with the class. Point out that **¡Hola!** as a greeting is spelled with an *h,* and that the word for *wave* is spelled **ola,** without the *h.* Ask them to add **hola** to their list of words that begin with silent *h.*

Answers to Activity 6

a. —Buenos días, señorita;
—Buenos días.
b. —¡Hola!;
—¡Hola!;
—Bueno, tengo clase.
c. —Buenas tardes, señor;
—Buenas tardes.
d. —Adiós;
—Hasta mañana.
e. —Adiós;
—Chao;
—Hasta luego;
—Hasta mañana;
—Tengo que irme.
f. —Buenas noches;
—Buenas noches;
—Hasta mañana.

6 ¡Buenos días!

How would you say hello or goodbye to the following people? How would they respond to your greetings? Choose your phrases from **Así se dice** on page 27.   Answers will vary. Possible answers in side column

a

b

c

d

e

f

7 Entre clases

 Work with a partner. Imagine you just ran into each other in the hall between classes. Greet each other briefly. Tell your partner you have to go and then say goodbye. Switch roles and have the conversation again. This time use different expressions.

MODELO

TÚ	¡Hola!
TU AMIGO/A	¡Buenos días!
TÚ	Bueno, tengo clase.
TU AMIGO/A	¡Hasta luego!

Answers will vary. Possible answers:
—¡Hola!
—¡Hola!
—Tengo clase. ¡Adiós!
—Hasta luego.

ASÍ SE DICE

Introducing people and responding to an introduction

To introduce yourself, say:

Me llamo... *My name is . . .*

Soy... *I am . . .*

¿Y tú? ¿Cómo te llamas?
And you? What's your name?

To introduce others, say:

Éste es mi amigo...
This is my (male) friend . . .

Ésta es mi amiga...
This is my (female) friend . . .

Se llama... *His/Her name is . . .*

To respond to an introduction, say:

¡Mucho gusto! *Nice to meet you!*

Encantado/a.[1]
Delighted to meet you.

To respond to **Mucho gusto** or **Encantado/a,** say:

Igualmente. *Same here.*

8 ¿Cómo respondes? Script and answers on p. 19E

CD 1 Tr. 12

Look over the **Así se dice** section above. Then listen as some people at a party introduce themselves to you. Use the phrases in the box to answer what each person says. You will use some phrases more than once.

> **Igualmente.**   **Me llamo...**
>
> **¡Mucho gusto!**   **Encantado/a.**

9 Te presento a...

A friend wants to introduce you to a new student. Work with two other classmates to act out the conversation with words and phrases you've learned. Then change roles and try it again.

CHRIS   Hola.

LUPE   ___1___ Hola.

CHRIS   Ésta es mi amiga Patricia.

LUPE   ___2___, Patricia. Mucho gusto

PATRICIA   Igualmente. ¿Y tú? ¿Cómo te llamas?

LUPE   Me ___3___ Lupe. llamo

CHRIS   Bueno, ___4___ clase. Tengo que irme. tengo

LUPE   Hasta ___5___. luego

PATRICIA   ___6___.   Answers will vary. Possible answer: Adiós.

---

[1] If you're male, use **Encantado.** If you're female, use **Encantada.**

PRESENTATION
ASÍ SE DICE
Walk around the room greeting various students, using the suggested phrases. Encourage students to respond using the appropriate expression. Ask several students **¿Cómo te llamas?** As they respond, shake each student's hand and reply **¡Mucho gusto!** or **Encantado/a.** Then introduce them to the class by saying **Éste/a es** or **Se llama.** Ask for student volunteers to model the phrases.

SUGGESTION
9 For additional practice, students can go back to **Así se dice** and copy words and phrases or make picture flash cards. As a follow-up, or to correct the activity, have groups of three read the completed dialogue to the class.

30

PRESENTATION

GRAMÁTICA

Point out to students that the inverted question and exclamation marks used in Spanish signal the tone of a sentence before you start to read it. Explain that Spanish accent marks are part of the spelling of the words, and that accent marks sometimes change the meaning of a word. (**qué** = *what* **que** = *that*). Ask students how many of these new punctuation marks they can find in the **Así se dice** boxes on pages 27 and 29.

SUGGESTION

10 This pair-work activity is best done orally. Allow approximately three minutes for students to complete this activity.

CHALLENGE

10 Have students create their own dialogues and perform them for the class. They should change the setting (school, outside, home, or at the mall). After a pair has presented their dialogue, ask the class to paraphrase what they said.

p. 2
Acts. 3–5

GRAMÁTICA   Punctuation marks

1. Questions and exclamations in Spanish begin and end with punctuation. Spanish uses upside-down punctuation marks to begin a question (¿) and an exclamation (¡). Questions and exclamations end with question marks (?) and exclamations (!).

   ¿Cómo te llamas?   **¡Mucho gusto!**

2. An accent mark is sometimes needed over a vowel (á, é, í, ó, ú). This shows which syllable is stressed.

3. The mark on the **ñ** (as in **mañana**) is called the **tilde**. It indicates the sound *ny* as in *canyon.*

10 Mini-situaciones

What would you say in the following situations? First find the words and phrases you need in **Así se dice**. Then, with a partner, act out each mini-situation. Be sure to use gestures to make your dialogue more authentic.   Answers will vary. Possible answers:

1. A friend introduces you to a new student. ¡Mucho gusto!; Hola; Me llamo...
2. You want to ask a classmate what his or her name is. ¿Cómo te llamas?
3. You've just been introduced to your new Spanish teacher. Mucho gusto.
4. Your new counselor has just said **"Mucho gusto."** Igualmente.
5. You want to introduce your friend Ana to your partner. Ésta es mi amiga Ana.
6. You want to say "His name is Daniel." Se llama Daniel.

Nota cultural

Roman Catholics in Latin America and Spain celebrate the feast day of the Christian saint they are named after. Spanish speakers have a celebration on their birthday, and often a second celebration on their Saint's Day. For example, a girl named Susana might celebrate her **Día de Santo** on August 11 in honor of St. Susan. How many of the saints' names in this calendar do you recognize?

agosto

DOM	LUN	MAR	MIER	JUE
1	2	3	4	5
Sta. Esperanza	N.S. de los ángeles	Sta. Lydia	Sto. Domingo de G.	San Esperanza
8	9	10	11	12
San Emiliano	San Román	Sta. Paula	Sta. Susana	Sta. Clara
15	16	17	18	19
La asunción	San Esteban	San Jacinto	Sta. Beatriz	San Sixto III

ASÍ SE DICE — Asking how someone is and saying how you are

PA pp. 7–8 Acts. 5–8

GV pp. 3–4 Acts. 6–7

1-1

To find out how a friend is, ask:

¿Cómo estás? *How are you?*

¿Y tú? *And you?*

¿Qué tal? *How's it going?*

Your friend might say:

Estoy (bastante) bien, gracias. *I'm (pretty) well, thanks.*

Yo también. *Me too.*

Estupendo/a. *Great.*

Excelente. *Great.*

Regular. *Okay.*

Más o menos. *So-so.*

(Muy) mal. *(Very) bad.*

¡Horrible! *Horrible!*

PRESENTATION

ASÍ SE DICE
Model these expressions, and have students repeat after you, imitating your gestures. (**regular**—thumb up; **horrible**—thumb down; **más o menos**—hand rocking side to side with palm down; **estupendo** and **excelente**— emphatic gestures)

SUGGESTION
11 Draw faces on the chalkboard or on flashcards to practice the new vocabulary. Have students call out an appropriate response to a smiling face, a sad face, etc.

VISUAL LEARNERS
• Use gestures or sketch visual cues on index cards to represent each functional phrase.

• If students are developing their own flash cards, they should make some representing the phrases in **Así se dice.** They can use the cards to verify comprehension and also for pair and small-group practice.

---

11 ¿Qué tal?

Look at the faces on the right and decide how the characters might answer the greeting ¿Cómo estás? ¿Qué tal? Match the letter of each face to a phrase below. You may use some of the faces more than once.

1. Estoy bien, gracias. b
2. Estoy horrible. d
3. Estoy mal. a

4. Regular, ¿y tú? c
5. Estupendo. b
6. Más o menos. c

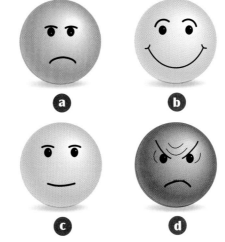

---

12 ¿Cómo estás? Script and answers on p. 19E

CD 1 Tr. 13

As each friend tells Sara how he or she is, write the person's name under the appropriate heading. The names are listed in the box below.

MODELO   —Buenas tardes, Felipe.
                    ¿Qué tal?
                —Regular, gracias. ¿Y tú?

bien   regular   mal
Felipe

Juan   Carlos   Sara
José Luis   Elena
Marta   Daniel

---

13 **¿Cómo contestas?**

Work with your partner to practice saying and answering the following phrases. Answers will vary. Possible answers:

1. ¡Hola! ¿Qué tal? Bien, gracias.
2. Ésta es mi amiga Charín. Mucho gusto, Charín.
3. ¿Cómo estás? Regular.
4. Soy Eduardo Robledo. ¿Y tú? Me llamo...
5. ¡Hasta luego! Adiós.

G V
p. 4
Acts.
8–10

GRAMÁTICA — Subject pronouns **tú** and **yo**

1. Use the pronoun **yo** to refer to yourself. In Spanish, **yo** *(I)* is not capitalized except at the beginning of a sentence. Use **tú** *(you)* when you're talking to another student, to a friend, or to someone who is about your own age. Notice that **tú** has an accent.

2. In Chapter 4 you'll learn a different pronoun to use when speaking to someone older than you or to a stranger. You'll also discover that subject pronouns like these aren't used as often in Spanish as in English.

¿Tú te llamas Maribel?

Sí, yo me llamo Maribel.

14 **¿Tú o yo?**

Which pronoun (**tú** or **yo**) is understood but not stated in each sentence?

MODELO   ¿Cómo estás? (tú)

1. ¿Cómo te llamas? tú
2. Me llamo Mercedes Margarita. yo
3. Soy Francisco. yo
4. ¿Cómo estás, Francisco? tú
5. Estoy bien, gracias. yo
6. ¿Estás bien, Merche? tú

15 ¿Quién es?

Imagine it's the first day of school in Madrid and several people are introducing themselves. Fill in the blanks with the pronouns **tú** or **yo** to complete the students' conversation.

—___1___ te llamas Enrique, ¿no? Tú

—Sí, ___2___ me llamo Enrique. yo

—Yo me llamo Raquel. ¿Y ___3___? tú
¿Cómo te llamas?

—Me llamo Sandra. ¿Cómo estás?

—Estoy bien. ¿Y ___4___? tú

—Bien, gracias. Bueno, tengo clase. ¡Adiós!

16 Charla

Mercedes is talking to a new classmate. Using words or phrases you've learned, write their conversation. Answers will vary. Possible answers:

MERCEDES	*greets her friend* ¡Hola, Elena! ¿Qué tal?
ELENA	*responds and introduces her friend Pedro* Muy bien, Mercedes. Éste es mi amigo Pedro.
MERCEDES	*says it's nice to meet Pedro* Mucho gusto, Pedro.
PEDRO	*responds and asks Mercedes how she is* Igualmente. ¿Cómo estás?
MERCEDES	*responds and says she has class* Muy bien, gracias, pero tengo clase.
ELENA	*says she also has to go* Sí, yo tengo que irme.
ALL	*say goodbye* ¡Adiós! ¡Hasta luego!

Nota cultural

In Spanish, there are many informal ways to greet friends and ask how they're doing. You might hear **¿Qué pasa?** *(What's happening?)* and **¿Qué hay?** or **¿Qué tal?** *(What's up?)*. Other greetings include **¿Qué onda?** and **¿Qué hubo?** or **¿Qué húbole?**, as well as **¡Epa, 'mano!** What do you say when you greet your friends?

VIDEO INTEGRATION

Adelante LEVEL 1A
Video Program
Videocassette 1, 9:30–10:15 OR
Videocassette 3, 2:27–3:12
(captioned version)

¡Ven conmigo! LEVEL 1
DVD Tutor, Disc 1

SUGGESTION
Show the video without sound.
Ask students if they remember
what's happening in the story
at this point.

Bell work
Have students use
Mercedes' letter as a model.
They should rewrite it and
personalize it.

17 Have a discussion with
students asking what they
would write to a pen pal.
What would they tell about
themselves? What would they
want to ask their pen pal?

SEGUNDO PASO Storytelling Book pp. 2, 4

WV3 SPAIN-1

Asking and saying how old someone is; asking where someone is from and saying where you're from

Madrid 3 de septiembre

¡Hola Francisco!
Me llamo Mercedes Margarita
Alvarez García y soy de Madrid.
Tengo 15 años. Me gusta la
pizza y me gusta mucho el
voleibol. ¿Cuántos años tienes?
¿Qué te gusta a ti?

Mercedes

Sr. Francisco Xavier López Medina
C/Echegaray 21. 1º.D
28014 Madrid.

Nota cultural

Handwriting in Spanish-
speaking countries is
slightly different from handwriting in the U.S. Note the
m, s, p, and **z** in Mercedes'
letter. Also, look at the number one (written with a tail)
in the letter and on the envelope. What other differences
can you find? Share your
findings with the class.

17 ¿Qué escribe ella?

Find and copy the phrases Mercedes uses . . .

1. to tell Francisco how old she is Tengo 15 años.
2. to tell him where she's from Soy de Madrid.
3. to ask him how old he is ¿Cuántos años tienes?

ASÍ SE DICE — Asking and saying how old someone is

p. 9
Act. 10

1-2

To ask how old someone is, say:

¿Cuántos años tienes?
How old are you?

¿Cuántos años tiene?
How old is (he/she)?

To answer, say:

Tengo... años.
I'm . . . years old.

Tiene... años.
(He/She) is . . . years old.

18 Conversación

Using the dialogue bubbles, rewrite the dialogue on your paper, putting the sentences in the correct order. Answers in side column.

5 — Tengo trece años. ¿Y tú?

4 — Igualmente. ¿Cuántos años tienes?

1 — ¡Hola! Me llamo Lupe. ¿Cómo te llamas?

7 — ¡Chao!

3 — Mucho gusto.

2 — Me llamo Raúl.

6 — Tengo doce años. Bueno, tengo clase. ¡Adiós!

☀ MOTIVATE

Discuss coming of age in our society and some of the rites of passage connected with it. Some examples are a bar or bat mitzvah, confirmation, a first summer job, first time to babysit, first time to buy one's own clothes, a **quinceañera** celebration, and getting a driver's license.

☀ TEACH

PRESENTATION
ASÍ SE DICE

Ask each of several students how old he or she is. Model the correct response. Continue practicing until students feel comfortable with the phrases. Then ask a volunteer to tell you a classmate's age. The volunteer should say "*(Student's name)* **tiene...años.**"

Answers to Activity 18

1. ¡Hola! Me llamo Lupe. ¿Cómo te llamas?
2. Me llamo Raúl.
3. Mucho gusto.
4. Igualmente. ¿Cuántos años tienes?
5. Tengo trece años. ¿Y tú?
6. Tengo doce años. Bueno, tengo clase. ¡Adiós!
7. ¡Chao!

PRESENTATION

VOCABULARIO

Have all students stand. Give a foam ball or some other light object to a student and ask him or her to begin the count with **uno**. The student then tosses the ball to another student and sits down. The student who caught the ball calls out the next number in the sequence, throws the ball to a classmate, and sits down. Continue the game until all students are seated. As you repeat the game, vary the rules by setting time limits of 45–60 seconds or by having students count by twos or threes.

♜ GAME
¿Cuántos años tienes?
Write numbers out as numerals or as words on flashcards. Give one to each student and have students pretend that the number represents their age. Students then put themselves in order according to age by asking **¿Cuántos años tienes?**

CHALLENGE
19 Teach students the phrase **Pienso en un número entre uno y treinta** and the words **más**, and **menos**. Then play a guess-the-number game with the class, or have the students play the game with a partner.

VOCABULARIO

p. 9
Act. 9

Los números del 0 al 30

p. 5
Acts.
11–13

1-A

cero   uno   dos   tres

cuatro   cinco   seis   siete

ocho   nueve   diez

11 once	**12** doce	**13** trece	**14** catorce
15 quince	**16** dieciséis	**17** diecisiete	**18** dieciocho
19 diecinueve	**20** veinte	**21** veintiuno	**22** veintidós
23 veintitrés	**24** veinticuatro	**25** veinticinco	**26** veintiséis
27 veintisiete	**28** veintiocho	**29** veintinueve	**30** treinta

19 Número secreto

 You and a partner should each write five secret numbers between 0 and 30. Then take turns trying to guess each other's numbers in Spanish, one number at a time. If a guess is wrong, your partner will say **más** to mean higher, or **menos** to mean lower. Keep trying until you guess right. Answers will vary.

20 Edades Script and answers on p. 19E

Daniel is showing Adriana pictures in the family album. Listen as he tells how old each relative is. Then match the correct picture to the age he gives.

CD 1 Tr. 14

Marisa   José   David
Anita   Daniel

a

b

c

d

e

21 ¿Cuántos años tienen?

 Daniel has some other cousins whose ages he's not sure about. Read the information given. Then write a sentence telling how old each cousin probably is. Answers on p. 19K

MODELO   Chela just learned how to walk.
Tiene un año.

1. Miguel just started kindergarten.
2. Teresa graduated from high school last spring.
3. Lalo just started eighth grade.
4. Rosario just started seventh grade.
5. Diego started college last year.
6. Raquel just got her driver's license.
7. Gabriela is in fifth grade.

22 Presentaciones

 Introduce yourself to the two classmates sitting closest to you. Greet them and ask each one's name and age. Then introduce your two new friends to the class. Answers will vary.

CHALLENGE
Have students call out in Spanish the number of students in the classroom, the number of windows in the room, the number of desks, the number of certain objects in the rooms, and so on.

SLOWER PACE
22 Before having the students break into groups, briefly review expressions for introductions, how people are, and ages on pages 29, 31, and 35.

SUGGESTION
22 Have students create imaginary names and origins for themselves. You also may point to Spanish-speaking countries on a map and have students answer that they are from that country by saying **Soy de...**

ADDITIONAL PRACTICE
22 As homework, have students interview at least three people (school staff, faculty members, or other students). Have them ask the three people their names and their country of origin. The students will draw a picture of the people they interview and write captions underneath. For example, **Ésta es la señora Corrales. Es de California** or **Éste es Nico. Es de El Salvador.**

PA
p. 10
Acts.
11–13

CD-ROM
DISC 1
1-2

ASÍ SE DICE

Asking where someone is from and saying where you're from

To find out where someone is from, ask:

¿De dónde eres?
Where are you from?

¿De dónde es...?
Where is . . . from?

To answer, say:

Soy de los Estados Unidos.
I'm from the United States.

Es de...
(She/He) is from . . .

23 ¿De dónde es?
Script and answers on p. 19F

CD 1 Tr. 15

You'll overhear students talking at a party. Match the name of the person with the sentence that tells where he or she is from.

1. Gabriela
2. Maricarmen
3. David
4. Antonio
5. Laura
6. Pedro

a. Es de Madrid, España.
b. Es de Buenos Aires, Argentina.
c. Es de Quito, Ecuador.
d. Es de Santiago de Chile.
e. Es de Bogotá, Colombia.
f. Es de San José, Costa Rica.

España

Ecuador

Argentina

Colombia

Costa Rica

Chile

CD-ROM DISC 1

NOTA GRAMATICAL

The words **soy, eres,** and **es** are all forms of the verb **ser**, which is one way to say *to be* in Spanish. When talking about where someone is from, use these forms.

GV
p. 6
Act. 14

24 Nuevos amigos

You're writing a letter to your pen pal in Madrid about some new students in your school. Write a sentence that tells your pen pal what country each student is from.

MODELO Juana – España
Juana es de España.

1. María Luisa – Honduras
2. Daniel – Perú
3. Patricia – El Salvador
4. Fabiola – Ecuador
5. Tú – Paraguay
6. Yo – ¿? Answers on p. 19K

NOTA GRAMATICAL

p. 6
Act. 15

So far, you've asked questions using several different words.

¿Cómo estás?

¿Cómo te llamas?

¿Cuántos años tienes?

¿De dónde eres?

To ask questions like these, put the question word at the beginning of the sentence. These question words have accents.

¿Cuántos años tienes?

25 El comienzo de una amistad

It's the first day of school for Ana, a new student at a school in Madrid. Complete the following sentences with the correct word.

ANA   Buenos días. ¿___1___ (Cómo/Cuántos) estás? Cómo

FEDERICO   Bien, ¿y tú?

ANA   Regular. Oye, soy Ana. Y tú, ¿___2___ (de dónde/cómo) te llamas? cómo

FEDERICO   Me llamo Federico. Tú no eres de aquí, ¿verdad? ¿___3___ (Cuántos/De dónde) eres? De dónde

ANA   Soy de Andalucía. ¿___4___ (Cuántos/Cómo) años tienes? Cuántos

FEDERICO   Tengo trece años. ¿Y tú?

ANA   Yo tengo trece años también.

26 Una encuesta

A   Imagine that you're listening to Javier as he's being interviewed over the phone for a survey. Below are the answers Javier gave. Match the correct question to the answer he gave.

1. Bien, gracias. c
2. De Madrid. d
3. Catorce. a
4. Javier Francisco González. b

B   Next, take a survey in your class. Ask three students these same questions. Are there any similarities? differences?

a. ¿Cuántos años tienes?

b. ¿Cómo te llamas?

c. ¿Cómo estás?

d. ¿De dónde eres?

PRESENTATION

NOTA GRAMATICAL

Model pronunciation and the various usages of the question words. Toss a soft foam ball to students while asking a question. Whoever catches it answers your question. He or she then tosses it to another student while asking a different question. Students do this exercise while standing and should sit after speaking.

☀ CLOSE

Have students suggest several situations where they might need to use the functional phrases from **Así se dice** on pages 35 and 38. (age, origin, introductions)

☀ ASSESS

▸ Testing Program, pp. 3–4
Quiz 1-2
Audio CD 2, Tr. 29

▸ Grammar and Vocabulary Quizzes
Quiz 1-2A or
Alternative Quiz 1-2A

▸ Alternative Assessment Guide, p. 19

PERFORMANCE ASSESSMENT

In small groups, have students create a situation in which they introduce themselves and another student to the class. Students tell their name, age, and where they are from.

VIDEO INTEGRATION

Adelante LEVEL 1A
Video Program
Videocassette 1, 16:45–18:42

¡Ven conmigo! LEVEL 1
DVD Tutor, Disc 1

TEACHER NOTES

• Each **Panorama cultural** section consists of authentic video interviews shot on location in different parts of the Spanish-speaking world. The *Video Program* and *DVD Program* include numerous interviews in addition to those featured in the Pupils Edition. See *Level 1A Video Guide* for activity masters and teaching suggestions.

• Remind students that cultural material may be included in the Quizzes and Chapter Test.

• The language of the people interviewed represents informal, unrehearsed speech. Occasionally, text has been edited for clarity.

Panorama cultural

CD 1
Trs. 16–19

¿De dónde eres?

Panorama cultural will introduce you to real Spanish speakers from around the globe, including Europe, Latin America, and the United States. In this chapter, we asked some people to tell us who they are and where they're from.

Mariano and his friend Renata are from Mexico City, the largest Spanish-speaking city in the world.

Marcelo is from the country of El Salvador. Can you name two countries that border on El Salvador?

● **Mariano y Renata**
Ciudad de México, México CD 1 Tr. 17

Me llamo Mariano Mañón Talamantes. Tengo trece años. Soy de aquí, de México. Ella se llama Renata.

Hola. ¿Qué tal?

● **Marcelo**
San Salvador, El Salvador
CD 1 Tr. 18

Mi nombre es Marcelo Antonio Comedo Valencia, y yo vengo de El Salvador en Centroamérica.

40 STANDARDS: 1.2, 3.1, 3.2

Valeria and Alejandra are sisters. They're from the island of Puerto Rico, in the Caribbean Sea.

● Valeria y Alejandra

San Antonio, Texas

CD 1 Tr. 19

Yo soy de Puerto Rico. Ahora yo vivo en San Antonio. Yo tengo catorce años. Ésta es mi hermana Alejandra.

1 What country is Mariano referring to when he says, **"Soy de aquí"**? México

2 What phrase does Renata use to ask the interviewer how she is? ¿Qué tal?

3 How many last names does Marcelo use? What are they? Which one represents his mother's last name? two; Comedo Valencia; Valencia

4 What region of Latin America is Marcelo from?
a. South America
b. Central America

5 What expression does Valeria use to introduce Alejandra? Ésta es mi hermana Alejandra.

6 How old is Valeria? 14 years old

Para pensar y hablar... Answers will vary.

A. What three things do you most want to know about people when you meet them for the first time? What questions would you ask Mariano, Renata, Marcelo, Valeria, and Alejandra?

B. Work with a partner to find the places the interviewees are from. Use the maps on pages xvii–xxiii. Each of you should write three ideas you have about what these places are like. Compare your ideas, and be ready to share them with the class.

C. Where would you turn to find more information on the geography, history, and culture of these countries?

MOTIVATING ACTIVITY
Ask several students where they are from. Encourage a discussion of whether or not it is preferable to live in one place or to move frequently. Ask for volunteers to tell how many different places they have lived. Some students may prefer not to discuss this topic. Since it may be a private subject, do not penalize students for not participating.

PRESENTATION
Before showing the video, have students read through the speech bubbles and identify the words and phrases that they have learned in the first two **pasos.** After showing the video, have the students use the phrases they have learned to answer these questions as you ask them:

1. **¿Cómo se llama el chico de El Salvador?** (Marcelo)

2. **¿De dónde es Valeria?** (Puerto Rico) **¿Cuántos años tiene?** (14)

3. **¿Cómo se llama el chico de México?** (Mariano)

4. **¿Cómo se llama la chica de México?** (Renata)

41

TERCER PASO
(TPR) Storytelling Book pp. 3, 4

WV3 SPAIN-1

Talking about what you like and don't like

Bell work
Have students answer the following questions in writing: **¿Cómo te llamas? ¿De dónde eres? ¿Cuántos años tienes?**

SUGGESTION
Write the letter on the board or on a transparency leaving out the following words: **15, pizza, voleibol,** and **Mercedes.** Have students rewrite the letter filling in the missing words with their own information.

Tengo 15 años. Me gusta la pizza y me gusta mucho el voleibol. ¿Cuántos años tienes? ¿Qué te gusta a ti?

Mercedes

27 ¿Qué te gusta?
Complete the questions asking Mercedes what she likes. Use the words from the box.
1. ¿Te gusta el ___voleibol___?
2. Me ___gusta___ mucho el voleibol.
3. ¿Te gusta la ___pizza___?
4. Sí, ___me___ gusta mucho la pizza.

me	voleibol
gusta	pizza

Nota cultural

Spain has many pizzerias and fast food restaurants. These foods are popular but not traditional. One type of traditional fast food in Spain is **tapas**. **Tapas** can include marinated olives, meatballs, mussels, snails, anchovies, cheese, a serving of Spanish **tortilla** (omelet with potatoes), and many other foods. Snacks are particularly important in Spain as dinner is served late, often after 9 P.M. Have you tasted any of the foods that are traditionally served as **tapas**?

ASÍ SE DICE   Talking about what you like and don't like

p. 11 Act. 14

1-3

To find out what a friend likes, ask:

¿Qué te gusta?
What do you like?

Your friend might answer:

Me gusta la comida mexicana.
I like Mexican food.

Me gusta mucho el tenis.
I like tennis a lot.

No me gusta la natación.
I don't like swimming.

¿Te gusta el fútbol?
Do you like soccer?

Sí, pero me gusta más el béisbol.
Yes, but I like baseball more.

28 Planes   Script and answers on p. 19F

CD 1 Tr. 20

Elena and her cousin Carlos are making plans for her visit to the city next weekend. As you listen to them talk, take notes about which items Elena likes and doesn't like by writing the number of the photo under the categories **Me gusta** or **No me gusta**. Is there anything she and Carlos both like?

1. el voleibol

2. la pizza

3. la música pop

4. la comida mexicana

5. el restaurante El Mercado

TERCER PASO

cuarenta y tres **43**

☀ MOTIVATE

Write *Food, Sports,* and *School* as column heads across the top of a transparency. Ask students to name some things in English that they like and dislike in each category. Write their responses under the category heads. Have students fill in the Spanish equivalents after the presentation of the **Vocabulario** on pages 44–45.

☀ TEACH

PRESENTATION
ASÍ SE DICE

Model pronunciation and sentence construction with **gustar.** Then, using the transparency from MOTIVATE, point to a word and mime whether or not you like the item using **(No) me gusta...** and the Spanish equivalent of the activity.

SUGGESTION

28 Have students take on the identity of either Carlos or Elena and write a paragraph about themselves based on what they heard.

STANDARDS: 4.1

PRESENTATION

VOCABULARIO

Model pronunciation by teaching a word's last syllable first and then building "backwards." (**-ción, -tación, natación**) Then, with one hand, hold up a visual of an item on the list. Use a puppet to ask silly comprehension questions. For example, while you are holding up a picture of a salad, the puppet asks **¿Qué es esto? ¿Una pizza?** You respond **No, no es una pizza, es una ensalada.**

SUGGESTIONS

• Use Vocabulary Transparency 1-B for further practice with this vocabulary.

• Students can use *CD-ROM* Chapter 1, Activity 6 to practice this vocabulary further. The Teacher Management System provides an effective way to track students' work and progress.

VOCABULARIO

p. 12
Acts. 16–17

1-B

Los deportes

el fútbol • el béisbol • el voleibol • la natación • el baloncesto • el tenis • el fútbol norteamericano

Las clases

el español • la tarea • la clase de inglés • ¿Qué tal? • Shakespeare

La música

el jazz

la música clásica

MOZART

la música de...

la música pop/rock

La comida

la cafetería

la pizza
la fruta
la ensalada
la comida mexicana
la comida china
el chocolate

la comida italiana   *Italian food*

29 **Una fiesta**   Script and answers on p. 19F

CD 1 Tr. 21

You're in charge of planning a party for Diana. Listen as a friend asks Diana what she likes and doesn't like. Take notes. Then, based on your list, name one sport, one food, and one kind of music you would include in a party to please her.

TERCER PASO

cuarenta y cinco   **45**

1-C

VISUAL LEARNERS

Have students make review cards for new vocabulary. They can draw or paste pictures of sports, food, or school-related items on the face of each card and write the Spanish word on the back of the card.

SUGGESTION

You might want to play **¿Qué te gusta?** from page 19l at this time.

46

PRESENTATION GRAMÁTICA

Model a few of the vocabulary words from this chapter and ask students to supply the correct definite article. Then have students identify the nouns and accompanying definite articles in the **fotonovela** on pages 22–24.

SUGGESTION

Have students keep a log of vocabulary. They can record the words in their notebooks, in their word boxes, or on a computer disk. At some point, you may want to have students do a bulletin board project with regional variants.

CHALLENGE

30 Have students poll three to five people about their likes and dislikes. They should use sports, food, and school vocabulary. Have students report their findings to the class in an oral or written presentation in Spanish. You might have them organize their collective results into a graph or chart.

TEACHER NOTE

The **Vocabulario extra** sections contain supplemental vocabulary. Words that appear in these sections will not be included on Chapter Tests.

p. 11
Act. 15

p. 8
Acts. 18–20

GRAMÁTICA   Nouns and definite articles

All the vocabulary words on pages 44–45 are nouns—words used to name people, places, and things. As you can see, all the nouns in the list have **el** or **la** *(the)* before them. Most nouns ending in **–o** (and nouns referring to males) are called *masculine*. Most nouns ending in **–a** (and nouns referring to females) are called *feminine*. When learning new nouns, always learn the definite article that goes with the noun at the same time.

MASCULINE NOUNS: **el amigo, el tenis**
FEMININE NOUNS: **la amiga, la natación**

30 Gustos personales

Get together with two classmates. For each category listed, write a sentence stating one thing in the category that you like and another that you don't like. Be sure to use the correct definite article (**el** or **la**) in your sentence. Compare answers with the others in your group. Are there any similarities? differences?

MODELO   deportes   Answers on p. 19K
1. **Me gusta el tenis.**
2. **No me gusta el fútbol.**

a. deportes   **b.** comida   **c.** música   **d.** clases

VOCABULARIO EXTRA

el arte   *art*
las arvejas   *peas*
la carne asada   *roast beef*
el ciclismo   *cycling*
la coliflor   *cauliflower*
el espagueti   *spaghetti*
la biología   *biology*
la lucha libre   *wrestling*
la historia   *history*
el taller   *shop*

31 La nueva estudiante

Felipe is interviewing the new student from Managua, Nicaragua, for the Spanish newspaper. Take the role of the new student and write his or her part. *Answers will vary. Possible answers:*

FELIPE   ¡Hola! Me llamo Felipe. ¿Cómo te llamas?

ESTUDIANTE   1. ¡Mucho gusto! Me llamo...

FELIPE   ¿Cómo estás?

ESTUDIANTE   2. Estoy bien, gracias.

FELIPE   ¿Y cuántos años tienes?

ESTUDIANTE   3. Tengo doce años.

FELIPE   El fútbol es muy popular en Nicaragua. ¿Te gusta el fútbol?

ESTUDIANTE   4. No, no me gusta el fútbol.

FELIPE   Personalmente, me gusta más el béisbol. ¿Te gusta el béisbol también?

ESTUDIANTE   5. Sí, me gusta el béisbol también.

FELIPE   Bueno, gracias y hasta luego.

ESTUDIANTE   6. Adiós. .

32 ¡Mucho gusto!

Work with a partner and take turns playing the roles of two new friends, Pilar and Miguel. Use the photos as a cue to answer each other's questions about your name, age, where you're from, and what kinds of things you like. Then switch roles.
Answers on p. 19K

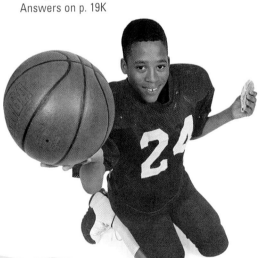

Miguel, 14 años
Los Gatos, California

Pilar, 12 años
Lima, Perú

ADDITIONAL PRACTICE

32 Have students use cutouts from magazines or drawings to create a collage of the things they like and don't like. They can use their collages instead of the photos in the textbook to interview one another.

TERCER PASO

cuarenta y siete   47

SUGGESTION

33 Tell your students that they may pretend they have a different name and are from a Spanish-speaking country for these interviews. The list of names in the Preliminary Chapter gives them examples of new names. The maps at the front of the book can give the students ideas for their new countries of origin.

PORTFOLIO

33 **Oral** Suggest this activity as a potential oral portfolio item. For Portfolio suggestions, see *Alternative Assessment Guide*, page 12.

PHOTO FLASH!

The person pictured is Arantxa (pronounced *a-rán-cha*) Sánchez Vicario. She is an outstanding professional tennis player from Spain who has won silver medals at the Olympic Games.

SUGGESTION

34 You may wish to provide a list of famous men and women from which to choose. Students could also use the library or media center to research names. As an alternative, students choose a hero or heroine or a role model and explain their choice.

EN MI CUADERNO

35 For an additional journal entry suggestion for Chapter 1, see *Practice and Activity Book*, p. 75.

33 ¡Entrevista!

Interview a classmate. Find out your partner's name, age, and where he or she is from. Also find out at least three things your partner likes and doesn't like. Be prepared to act out your interview for the class.   Answers will vary.

¿Cómo te llamas?

¿Cuántos años tienes?

¿De dónde eres?   ¿Qué te gusta?

¿Qué no te gusta?

34 ¿Qué les gusta a las estrellas?

Make a list of three famous people and write what you think they probably would like and not like. Then share your list with your partner. Are your lists similar? Are there any differences?

MODELO   1. A _____ le gusta el tenis.
           A _____ no le gusta el baloncesto.
           Answers will vary.

Arantxa Sánchez Vicario

35 En mi cuaderno

Write a letter to a pen pal. Introduce yourself and give your age and where you're from. List three or four things that you like and don't like. Then ask your pen pal at least three questions. Keep a copy of this letter in your journal.   Answers will vary.

Querido amigo / Querida amiga,

Me llamo . . .   Tengo. . .
Me gusta . . .   pero no . . .

También me . . .   pero. . . más

Con abrazos,

LETRA Y SONIDO

Script on p. 19F

A. The Spanish vowels (**a, e, i, o, u**) are pronounced clearly and distinctly. Learn to pronounce them by mimicking the recording or your teacher.

CD 1
Trs. 22–26

1. a: as in *father,* but with the tongue closer to the front of the mouth

| Ana | cámara | amiga | tarea | llama |

2. e: as in *they,* but without the *y* sound

| este | eres | noche | excelente | café |

3. i: as in *machine,* but much shorter

| íntimo | isla | legítimo | Misisipi | día |

4. o: as in *low,* but without the *w* sound

| hola | moto | años | dónde | color |

5. u: as in *rule*

| fruta | uno | fútbol | único | música |

B. Dictado
Ana has just met several new friends in Madrid and is practicing the new phrases she has heard. Write what you hear.

C. Trabalenguas
¡A, e, i, o, u! Arbolito del Perú, ¿cómo te llamas tú?

SUGERENCIA

The dictionary in the back of this book can be a helpful tool as you learn Spanish. For example, some of the words in **Letra y sonido** might be new to you. A dual-language dictionary will usually have the Spanish to English section first, followed by the English to Spanish section. Try looking up the word **isla** in the back of the book. Begin with the Spanish-English Vocabulary section that starts on page 277. Look in the alphabetized **i** section (ignore the article **la** when checking alphabetical order) and write down what **isla** means. Now look up the word **carpeta**. Does it mean what you might think it does?

AUDITORY LEARNERS
Tongue twisters and songs can help students focus on pronunciation. The tongue twister that practices vowel pronunciation can be a helpful mnemonic device for students.

☀ CLOSE
Conduct a short question-and-answer session in which students say what they like and don't like. They should use as much of the vocabulary from this **paso** as possible.

☀ ASSESS
▸ Testing Program, pp. 5–6
Quiz 1-3
Audio CD 3, Track 30
▸ Grammar and Vocabulary Quizzes
Quiz 1-3A or
Alternative Quiz 1-3A
▸ Alternative Assessment Guide, p.19

PERFORMANCE ASSESSMENT
In pairs, have students role-play a situation where one is a famous sports figure and the other is a reporter. The reporter asks questions about the star's likes and dislikes (sports and food vocabulary) and the star answers the questions.

The **Enlaces** pages are an interdisciplinary feature. It links the study of Spanish and Spanish-speaking culture with other subjects that students might be studying. These subjects include social studies, mathematics, science, literature, and history.

PRESENTATION

Ask students the following questions: What is a census? Why does the government conduct a census every ten years? What useful information do they find out in a census? How would they use that information?

ADDITIONAL PRACTICE

2 As a class wrap-up activity, make a chart for the entire class based on the information gathered from the small groups. List all the countries mentioned by the students. Then make a chart of the different backgrounds of students in the class.

CIENCIAS SOCIALES

1 ¿De dónde son?

Did you know that over 30 million people of Spanish-speaking origin live in the United States? What countries do they come from? Use the information in the pie chart to complete these sentences.

Spanish-speaking Countries of Origin

México	**58.5%**
Puerto Rico	**9.6%**
Cuba	**3.5%**
República Dominicana	**2.2%**
El Salvador	**1.9%**
Colombia	**1.3%**
Guatemala	**1.1%**
Ecuador	**.7%**
Perú	**.7%**
Honduras	**.6%**
Nicaragua	**.5%**
Argentina	**.3%**
Panamá	**.3%**
Chile	**.3%**
España	**.3%**
Venezuela	**.3%**
All other Hispanics*	**17.3%**

*Hispanic respondents who did not give a detailed answer in the 2000 census. Due to rounding, sum does not equal 100%

1. Most Spanish speakers in the United States are from ———. Mexico

2. The three largest Spanish-speaking groups in the United States come from ———, ———, and ———. Mexico, Puerto Rico, Cuba

3. The largest group of Central American Spanish speakers comes from ———. El Salvador

4. The largest group of South American Spanish speakers comes from ———. Colombia

2 ¿De dónde somos?

Work in groups of five. Find out what countries each student and his or her parents, grandparents, or great-grandparents came from. First decide who takes the following roles: Answers will vary.

- Interviewer: asks the question about countries
- Note taker: writes down everyone's answers
- Mathematician: adds up the number of people from each country
- Artist: draws the countries (see the world map in the front of the book, pp. xviii–xix)
- Presenter: tells the class about the list of countries and the maps

GEOGRAFÍA

3 Mira el mapa

Read the clues below aloud to your partner. Identify where each Spanish-speaking student lives. Use the maps in the beginning of the book on pages xvii through xxii to figure out what country each student is describing.

Norte

Oeste   *Este*

Sur

I'm from South America. My country doesn't have a border next to an ocean. Peru and Chile are to the west and to the east is Brazil. To the south is Argentina.
Bolivia

Me llamo Carolina. Vivo en América del Sur. ¿De dónde soy?

I'm from a country in Central America. To the north is Mexico and to the east, Belize. To the south are El Salvador and the Pacific Ocean. Guatemala

Me llamo Alberto. Vivo en Centroamérica. ¿De dónde soy?

I'm from the Spanish-speaking half of an island between Cuba and Puerto Rico. It's in the Caribbean Sea. Haiti is the other half of the island. La República Dominicana

Me llamo Graciela. Vivo en el Caribe. ¿De dónde soy?

Me llamo Paloma. Vivo en Europa. ¿De dónde soy?

I'm from Europe. They speak Portuguese in the country to the west. To the east is the Mediterranean Sea. España

ENLACES

cincuenta y uno **51**

PRESENTATION
Ask students if they know anyone from a Spanish-speaking country. You may begin the discussion by talking about someone you know. If students do not know anyone personally, they may make up a fictitious person from Spain or Latin America. Point out the country on a classroom map or have students find it on the maps on pages xvii–xxiii of their textbooks.

VISUAL LEARNERS
3 Have students trace a map of a Spanish-speaking country or region. For example, have student trace the map of South America from their textbook to learn where the Spanish-speaking countries are located on that continent.

ADDITIONAL PRACTICE
3 Have students write new clues for imaginary teens named Lola, Manolo, Adriana or Federico. Students may decide which country this imaginary person is from. One partner reads the clues as the other tries to guess what country the imaginary person is from using as few clues as possible. Then the partners switch roles.

TEACHER NOTE
Explain that **vivo** means *I live.*

STANDARDS: 1.2, 3.1, 5.1   **51**

READING STRATEGY

Using cognates to determine meaning. Tell students that the tips they learn in this section can be applied to any reading.

☀ PREREADING

A In each **Vamos a leer** section, the activities under **¡A comenzar!** focus on prereading skills and offer an opportunity to practice the targeted reading strategy.

MOTIVATING ACTIVITY

Have students glance through English-language magazines, looking only at the headlines. What kind of information is in a headline? What could they tell a friend about the message just from looking at the headline?

TEACHER NOTE

Be aware of your students' skill level in English. Students may need help acquiring good reading skills in a second language if they lack those same skills in their native language. Additionally, if you have students who have difficulty listening or spelling in Spanish, they may have similar difficulties in English. Talk to other teachers and to the students themselves to assess native-language abilities or challenges and develop strategies for remediation.

VAMOS A LEER

Estrategia

Cognates

Spanish shares many words with English. Words with similar meanings and spellings in both languages are called *cognates* *. Recognizing cognates can help you understand more Spanish words.

¡A comenzar!

A These headlines are from different Spanish-language magazines. Find five Spanish/English cognates. Compare your list with a classmate's and discuss the English meaning of each headline. Look up any words you're not sure of in the dictionary beginning on page 277. Answers on p. 19K

Al grano Answers on p. 19K

B The following are descriptions of articles from these magazines. In which magazine would you look to find the following information?

1. interesting facts about famous personalities
2. the latest in compact disc players
3. jokes and riddles
4. mural paintings in East Los Angeles
5. the new album by a Spanish rap group
6. suggestions about what to do on your next free Saturday
7. how to organize your school to do a neighborhood cleanup
8. reviews of movies to watch at home
9. building a birdhouse

Cognados falsos

C Some words look the same but don't mean the same thing in both languages. For example, **vaso** means *drinking glass,* not *vase.* List a similar English word for each Spanish word below. Then look up the Spanish words in the Spanish-English dictionary beginning on page 281 to see what they actually mean. How many are false cognates? Answers on p. 19K

real	**disgusto**
grupo	**sopa**
ropa	**teatro**

---

* So-called false cognates can be misleading. For example, **librería** means *bookstore,* not *library.*

VIDEOS

natura

Música

arte

TRIVIA

pasatiempos

humor

TECNOLOGÍA

ecología

 READING

COOPERATIVE LEARNING

B Put students in groups of four. Ask them to choose a discussion leader, a scribe, a proofreader, and an announcer (or assign these roles). Give students three to five minutes to complete Activity C. Monitor the groups' work as you walk around. Help students as necessary. At the end of the activity, call on the announcer to read the group's results. Remind students that they will receive a common group grade. This will keep each person on task and engaged in the total process.

POSTREADING

COGNATES

C After doing Activities A and B, have students brainstorm to find as many English-Spanish cognates as they can in three minutes. Review their lists as a class. Clarify the meaning of any **cognados falsos** *(false cognates)*.

NATIVE SPEAKERS

Ask native speakers to bring in Spanish-language magazines or newspaper clippings. Preview the reading materials for age-appropriate content. Then have students look for cognates.

TEACHER NOTE

For additional reading, see *Practice and Activity Book*, page 13.

STANDARDS: 1.2, 3.2, 4.1   53

The **Repaso** reviews and integrates all four skills and culture in preparation for the Chapter Test.

SUGGESTION

Before beginning the **Repaso**, have students turn to page 21 and review the chapter objectives. Ask them if they feel they have learned what was intended. Proceed through the **Repaso** activities. Encourage both group and individual work.

ADDITIONAL PRACTICE

1 Have students create a third card and fill it out for themselves. Then have students fill out a card for a partner, to practice asking in the **tú** form and reporting in the **él** or **ella** form.

TEACHER NOTE

The **¡A hablar!**, **¡A escribir!**, and **En contexto** sections from the CD-ROM provide students with an excellent opportunity to integrate and practice chapter material.

REPASO

internet

go.hrw.com

MARCAR: go.hrw.com
PALABRA CLAVE:
WV3 SPAIN-1

CD-ROM DISC 1

1 Imagine that you work for a pen pal service. Your job is to complete a set of cards with information left by the clients on the answering machine. One card has been done for you as an example. Create two other cards and fill them in as you listen to the messages. *Script and answers on p. 19F*

CD 1
Tr. 27

> NOMBRE: Mariana Castillo
> ORIGEN: Es de España.
> EDAD: Tiene 15 años.
> LE GUSTA: la música rock
> NO LE GUSTA: el tenis

2 Read the following letter from a client looking for a pen pal (**amigo por correspondencia**). Then decide which of the three candidates in Activity 1 would be a good pen pal for him. Base your decision on what they like and don't like. *Pablo García would be a good match because they both like rock music and neither one likes classical music.*

> Hola. Busco un amigo por correspondencia. Me llamo José Luis Bazán. Tengo trece años y soy de Guatemala. Me gusta mucho el fútbol y el béisbol. También me gusta la música rock, pero no me gusta la música clásica.

3 Make a chart of what you like and don't like for each of the categories in the word box. Present your information on a poster. Share with the class. Look at the **Vocabulario** on pages 44–45 for help. *Answers will vary.*

> comida   música
> deportes   clases

4 What is Andrés López Medina's father's last name? What is his mother's last name? Can you explain the system of last names to someone who has not studied Spanish? Write your answer out and present it to the class.

Father's last name: López; Mother's last name: Medina

```
                                                    LOPEZ - 89
        LOPEZ MATEOS, N. - Galileo, 21 ...................................  248 9093
        »  MATEOS, J. - Alonso Cano, 33 .................................  730 1883
        »  MATUTE, R. - Giralda, 204 ......................................  775 8964
        »  MAYORAL, A. - Palencia, 101 ...................................  263 3276
        »  MAYORAL, C. - Luis Buñuel, 12 ................................  437 1806
        »  MEDIAVILLA, P. - Embajadores, 78 ...........................  711 8419

        LOPEZ MEDINA, A. - Av. S. Eloy, 301 ..........................  472 4932
        »  MEDINA, F. - Amor Hermoso, 69 .............................  326 3771
        »  MEDINA, R. - Echegaray, 21 ....................................  775 8964
        »  MEDINA, T. - Av. Valle, 35 .......................................  464 7691
        »  MEDRANO, A. - Cerro Blanco, 14 ...........................  558 2220

        LOPEZ MEGIA, J. - Bolivia, 35 ...................................  471 4936
        »  MEIRA, L. - Libertad, 45 .........................................  792 2039
```

5 The editor of your Spanish class newspaper has asked you to come up with a standard questionnaire for interviewing new students. Create an interview form that asks for their name, age, where they're from, and what they like and don't like. Then try your questionnaire out on a classmate.   Answers will vary.

¿Cómo te llamas?	¿Cómo estás?	¿Cuántos años tienes?	¿De dónde eres?
1.			
2.			

6 **S I T U A C I Ó N**

You've been asked to introduce the new student from Ecuador to your class. Role play the scene with a partner, using the information given. Be sure to ask for his or her name and age, where he or she is from, and several things that he or she likes and doesn't like. Then introduce your new friend to the class.

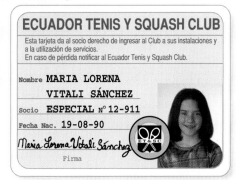

ECUADOR TENIS Y SQUASH CLUB

Esta tarjeta da al socio derecho de ingresar al Club a sus instalaciones y a la utilización de servicios.
En caso de pérdida notificar al Ecuador Tenis y Squash Club.

Nombre **MARIA LORENA VITALI SÁNCHEZ**
Socio **ESPECIAL N° 12-911**
Fecha Nac. **19-08-90**

Maria Lorena Vitali Sánchez
Firma

PORTFOLIO
5 **Written** Activity 5 may be used as a Portfolio entry. For Portfolio suggestions, see *Alternative Assessment Guide*, p. 12.

A VER SI PUEDO...

Answers on p. 19K

WV3 SPAIN-1

Can you say hello and goodbye?
p. 27

Can you introduce people and respond to an introduction?
p. 29

Can you ask how someone is and say how you are?
p. 31

Can you ask and say how old someone is?
p. 35

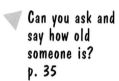

Can you ask where someone is from and say where you're from? p. 38

Can you talk about what you like and don't like? p. 43

1 How would you greet or say goodbye to these people?

1. the principal before class
2. a classmate as the bell rings
3. a friend at the end of the school day

2 What would you say in the following situations?

1. The new Spanish teacher asks your name.
2. You've just been introduced to Juan, the new student from Spain.
3. Juan has just said, "Mucho gusto."

3 Juan has just joined your class and you want to get to know him. How would you . . .?

1. ask him how he's doing
2. tell him how you're doing

4 How would you . . .?

1. ask Juan how old he is
2. tell him how old you are
3. tell your friend how old Juan is

Juan Fernández Jiménez

5 Can you . . .?

1. tell Juan where you're from
2. ask him where he's from
3. tell your friend where Juan is from

6 You'd like to ask Juan to do something with you on Saturday, but you don't know what he likes. Ask him if he likes these things, and tell him which ones you like.

1. volleyball
2. baseball
3. Italian food
4. pop music
5. basketball

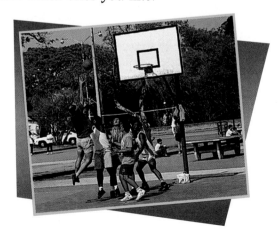

VOCABULARIO

PRIMER PASO

Saying hello and goodbye

Adiós. *Goodbye.*
Buenas noches. *Good night.*
Buenas tardes. *Good afternoon.*
Bueno, tengo clase. *Well, I have class (now).*
Buenos días. *Good morning.*
Chao. *'Bye.*
Hasta luego. *See you later.*
Hasta mañana. *See you tomorrow.*
¡Hola! *Hello!*
señor *sir, Mr.*
señora *ma'am, Mrs.*
señorita *miss*
Tengo que irme. *I have to go.*

Introducing people and responding to an introduction

¿Cómo te llamas? *What's your name?*
Encantado/a. *Delighted to meet you.*
Ésta es mi amiga. *This is my friend. (to introduce a female)*
Éste es mi amigo. *This is my friend. (to introduce a male)*
Igualmente. *Same here.*
Me llamo... *My name is . . .*
Mucho gusto. *Nice to meet you.*
Se llama... *His/Her name is . . .*
Soy... *I am . . .*
¿Y tú? *And you? (familiar)*

Asking how someone is and saying how you are

¿Cómo estás? *How are you? (to ask a friend)*
Estoy (bastante) bien, gracias. *I'm (pretty) well, thanks.*
Estupendo/a. *Great./Marvelous.*
Excelente. *Great./Excellent.*
Gracias. *Thanks.*
Horrible. *Horrible.*
Más o menos. *So-so.*

(Muy) mal. *(Very) bad.*
¿Qué tal? *How's it going?*
Regular. *Okay.*
tú *you (informal)*
¿Y tú? *And you?*
yo *I*
Yo también. *Me too.*

SEGUNDO PASO

Asking and saying how old someone is

¿Cuántos años tiene? *How old is (he/she)?*
¿Cuántos años tienes? *How old are you?*
el número *number*
Tengo ... años. *I'm . . . years old.*
Tiene ... años. *He/She is . . . years old.*

Asking where someone is from and saying where you're from

¿De dónde eres? *Where are you from?*
¿De dónde es? *Where is he/she from?*
Es de... *He/She is from . . .*
ser *to be*
Soy de... *I'm from . . .*

Numbers 0–30

See p. 36

TERCER PASO

Talking about what you like and don't like

el baloncesto *basketball*
el béisbol *baseball*
la cafetería *cafeteria*
el chocolate *chocolate*
la clase de inglés *English class*
la comida mexicana/italiana/china *Mexican/Italian/Chinese food*
el *the*
la ensalada *salad*
el español *Spanish*
la fruta *fruit*
el fútbol *soccer*
el fútbol norteamericano *football*
el jazz *jazz*
la *the*
más *more*
Me gusta... *I like . . .*
Me gusta más... *I prefer . . .*
mucho *a lot*
la música clásica/pop/rock *classical/pop/rock music*
la música de... *music by . . .*
la natación *swimming*
no *no*
No me gusta... *I don't like . . .*
pero *but*
la pizza *pizza*
¿Qué te gusta? *What do you like?*
sí *yes*
la tarea *homework*
¿Te gusta...? *Do you like . . .?*
el tenis *tennis*
el voleibol *volleyball*

CHAPTER 1 ASSESSMENT

▶ **Testing Program**
Chapter Test, pp. 7–12
Audio Compact Discs, CD 1, Trs. 32–33
Speaking Test, p. 112

▶ **Alternative Assessment Guide**
Performance Assessment, p. 19
Portfolio Assessment, p. 12
CD-ROM Assessment, p. 26

▶ **Interactive CD-ROM Tutor, Disc 1**
¡A hablar!
¡A escribir!

▶ **Standardized Assessment Tutor**
Chapter 1

▶ **One-Stop Planner, Disc 1**
Test Generator
Chapter 1

¡Organízate!

CHAPTER OVERVIEW

De antemano pp. 60–63	¡Mañana es el primer día de clases!			

	FUNCTIONS	GRAMMAR	VOCABULARY	RE-ENTRY
Primer paso pp. 64–71	• Talking about what you want or need, p. 66	• **Así se dice: Quiero, Quieres**, p. 66 • **Gramática:** Noun plurals, p. 67; Plural indefinite articles, p. 68 • **Notas gramaticales:** Indefinite articles, p. 66; Subject pronouns, **él** and **ella**, p. 70	• School supplies, p. 65	• Subject pronouns: **tú** and **yo** (from **Capítulo 1**) • Definite articles: **el** and **la** (from **Capítulo 1**)
Segundo paso pp. 74–81	• Saying what's in your room, p. 76	• **Así se dice:** Using **hay**, p. 76 • **Gramática:** Agreement of **mucho** and **¿cuánto?**, p. 78	• The contents of your room, p. 75	• Talking about likes and dislikes (from **Capítulo 1**) • Numbers 0–30 (from **Capítulo preliminar**)
Tercer paso pp. 84–89	• Talking about what you need and want to do, p. 85	• **Así se dice: Necesitar, querer** + infinitive, p. 85 • **Nota gramatical:** Identifying infinitives, p. 86	• Things you do, p. 86 • Numbers 31–199, p. 88	• Numbers 0–30 (from **Capítulo preliminar**) • Using cognates (from **Capítulo 1**)

Letra y sonido	**p. 89**	The letter **d**	**Dictado:** Audio CD 2 Tracks 11–15	
Enlaces	**pp. 90–91**	**La historia y las matemáticas**		
Vamos a leer	**pp. 92–93**	**Portadas**	**Reading Strategy:** Reading titles	
Review	**pp. 94–97**	**Repaso**, pp. 94–95	**A ver si puedo...**, p. 96	**Vocabulario**, p. 97

Culture	• **Nota cultural:** Extended family, p. 63 • **Nota cultural:** School uniforms, p. 65 • **Encuentro cultural: Los saludos**, pp. 72–73 • **Nota cultural:** Apartments in Spain/Sharing TV set, p. 75	• **Nota cultural:** Exclamations, p. 79 • **Panorama cultural: ¿Qué necesitas para el colegio?**, pp. 82–83 • **Realia:** Spanish currency, p. 88

Lesson Planning

One-Stop Planner
Lesson Planner with Substitute Teacher
Lesson Plans, pp. 9–13

Listening and Speaking

Listening Activities
- Student Response Forms for Listening Activities, pp. 49–51
- Additional Listening Activities 2-1 to 2-6, pp. 6–8
- Additional Listening Activities (song), p. 9
- Scripts and Answers, pp. 29–31

Video Guide
- Teaching Suggestions, pp. 11–13
- Activity Masters, pp. 14–17
- Scripts and Answers, pp. 51–53, 63–64

Activities for Communication
- Communicative Activities, pp. 7–12
- Realia and Teaching Suggestions, pp. 43–47
- Situation Cards, pp. 72–73

¡Ven conmigo! Level 1
TPR Storytelling Book, pp. 5–8

Reading and Writing

Reading Strategies and Skills, Chapter 2
¡Lee conmigo! 1, Chapter 2
Practice and Activity Book, pp. 15–26

Grammar

Grammar and Vocabulary Workbook, pp. 9–17

¡Ven conmigo! Level 1
Grammar Tutor for Students of Spanish
Chapter 2

Assessment

Testing Program
- Paso Quizzes and Chapter Test, pp. 19–30
- Score Sheet, Scripts and Answers, pp. 31–36

Grammar and Vocabulary Quizzes
- Quizzes 2-1A, 2-2A, 2-3A
- Alternative Quizzes 2-1A, 2-2A, 2-3A

Alternative Assessment Guide
- Portfolio Assessment, p. 13
- Performance Assessment, p. 20
- CD-ROM Assessment, p. 27

¡Ven conmigo! Level 1
Standardized Assessment Tutor
- Reading, pp. 5–7
- Writing, p. 8
- Math, pp. 25–26

Native Speakers

¡Ven conmigo! Level 1
Cuaderno para hispanohablantes, pp. 6–10

MEDIA

Online Activities
- Juegos interactivos
- Actividades internet

Video Program
- Videocassette 1
- Videocassette 3 *(captioned version)*

¡Ven conmigo! Level 1
DVD Tutor, Disc 1

Audio Compact Discs
- Textbook Listening Activities, CD 2, Tracks 1–16
- Additional Listening Activities, CD 2, Tracks 22–28
- Assessment Items, CD 2, Tracks 17–21

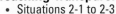
Interactive CD-ROM Tutor, Disc 2
Teaching Transparencies
- Situations 2-1 to 2-3
- Vocabulary 2-A to 2-C
- Grammar and Vocabulary Workbook

One-Stop Planner CD-ROM

Use the **One-Stop Planner CD-ROM with Test Generator** to aid in lesson planning and pacing.

For each chapter, the **One-Stop Planner** includes:
- Editable lesson plans with direct links to teaching resources
- Printable worksheets from resource books
- Direct launches to the HRW Internet activities
- Video and audio segments
- Test Generator
- Clip Art for vocabulary items

CAPÍTULO 2
¡Organízate!
TECHNOLOGY

DVD/VIDEO

**Videocassette 1, Videocassette 3 (captioned version)
DVD Tutor, Disc 1 See Video Guide, pages 11–16.**

De antemano • ¡Mañana es el primer día de clases!
Paco explains to his grandmother that he needs to buy school supplies. His grandmother gives him money to buy what he needs but tells him he has to clean his room first. Paco tries to clean his room quickly by throwing everything in his desk drawer and under his bed. When he finishes, he realizes he has lost the money his grandmother gave him.

A continuación
Paco begins to tear apart his room looking for the lost money. His grandmother comes in and is shocked at the mess. While helping him look for the money, his grandmother realizes that Paco already has most of the school supplies he thought he needed. After finding the money, Paco and his friend Felipe go shopping for the things he still needs for school.

 ¿Qué necesitas para el colegio?
Students from various Spanish-speaking countries tell us about what they need to buy for school.

 Los saludos en el mundo hispano

 Videoclips
• **Analfabetismo:** public service message about illiteracy

INTERACTIVE CD-ROM TUTOR

Activity	Activity Type	Pupil's Edition Page
En contexto	*Interactive conversation*	
1. Vocabulario	Imagen y sonido ¡Exploremos! ¡Identifiquemos!	p. 65
2. Gramática	¿Que falta?	pp. 66–68
3. Vocabulario	¿Cuál es?	p. 75
4. Gramática	¡A escoger!	p. 78
5. Así se dice	¡Super memoria!	p. 85
6. Vocabulario	Patas arriba	p. 88
Panorama cultural	¿De dónde eres? ¡A escoger!	pp. 82–83
¡A hablar!	*Guided recording*	pp. 94–95
¡A escribir!	*Guided writing*	pp. 94–95

Teacher Management System
Launch the program, type "admin" in the password area and press RETURN. Log on to **www.hrw.com/CDROMTUTOR** for a detailed explanation of the Teacher Management System.

DVD-ROM TUTOR ¡Ven conmigo! Level 1

 The *DVD Tutor* contains all material from the Level 1 *Video Program*. Spanish captions are available for use at your discretion for all sections of the video. The *DVD Tutor* also provides a variety of video-based activities that assess students' understanding of the **De antemano, A continuación**, and **Panorama cultural.**

This part of the *DVD Tutor* may be used on any DVD video player connected to a television or video monitor.

 In addition to the video material and the video-based comprehension activities, the *DVD Tutor* also contains the entire Level 1 *Interactive CD-ROM Tutor* in DVD-ROM format. Each DVD disc contains the activities from all 12 chapters of the *Interactive CD-ROM Tutor.*

This part of the *DVD Tutor* may be used on a Macintosh® or Windows® computer with a DVD-ROM drive.

One-Stop Planner CD-ROM

To preview all resources available for this chapter, use the **One-Stop Planner CD-ROM**, Disc 1.

MARCAR: go.hrw.com
PALABRA CLAVE: WV3 SPAIN-2

INTERNET CONNECTION

*Have students explore the **go.hrw.com** Web site for many online resources covering all chapters. All Chapter 2 resources are available under the keyword **WV3 SPAIN-2**. Interactive games help students practice the material and provide them with immediate feedback. You will also find a printable worksheet that provides Internet activities that lead to a comprehensive online research project.*

JUEGOS INTERACTIVO

You can use the interactive activities in this chapter

- to practice grammar, vocabulary, and chapter functions
- as homework
- as an assessment option
- as a self-test
- to prepare for the Chapter Test

ACTIVIDADES INTERNET

Students search online bookstores for books written about subjects they like. They then create a dialogue about going to the store for school supplies.

- To prepare students for the **Hoja de actividades,** have them complete the Cuaderno de actividades activities from the **Primer** and **Tercer pasos.**

- Once students complete the activity sheet, have them make an inventory of the school supplies they are carrying today. Then, ask them to estimate how many more of each item they are likely to need before the school year is out.

Proyecto

Have students search online stores for items they would like in an ideal bedroom. On a search engine, they can enter the chapter vocabulary or the word **hogar** *(home).* You might have them start at a large site like www.elcorteingles.es (a large department store in Spain). Have them save images of lamps, beds, radios, and so on to their hard drive, and then attach the images to a brief description of each item.

For Student Response Forms, see Listening Activities pp. 49–51

PRIMER PASO   pp. 64–71

5 Arturo y Sumiko   p. 65

ARTURO   Para las clases, necesito unas gomas de borrar, cuadernos y libros, claro. Tú, ¿qué necesitas?

SUMIKO   Necesito lápices y cuadernos, y una regla nueva.

Answers to Activity 5

una mochila
unos cuadernos—A, S
unos lápices—S
un libro—A
un diccionario
un bolígrafo
una calculadora
una carpeta
una regla—S
papel
unas gomas de borrar—A

6 ¿Qué necesita Blanca?   p. 66

Necesito papel, una calculadora, lápices y una carpeta. Ya tengo una mochila, varios cuadernos, los libros y los bolígrafos.

Answers to Activity 6

Blanca necesita papel, una calculadora, lápices y una carpeta.

SEGUNDO PASO   pp. 74–81

19 ¿Qué hay?   p. 76

En mi cuarto hay dos camas. También tengo un escritorio y un armario. Tengo tres revistas y dos carteles. También hay una radio y dos sillas.

Answers to Activity 19

dos camas
tres revistas
dos carteles
dos sillas

32 Victoria y Tomás necesitan...   p. 86

Primero les digo lo que necesito hacer yo. Necesito organizar mi cuarto, poner la ropa en el armario y encontrar mi mochila. Necesito hacer muchas cosas. Mi hermano Tomás también necesita hacer muchas cosas. Él necesita ir al centro comercial para comprar una mochila nueva, pero primero necesita hacer la tarea.

Answers to Activity 32

1. B
2. T
3. T
4. V
5. V
6. V
7. T

For the scripts for Parts A and C, see page 89. The script for Part B is below.

B. Dictado

Quiero ir de compras. Necesito varias cosas: diez lápices, una calculadora, dos cuadernos y un diccionario. No necesito bolígrafos; ya tengo cinco. Y carpetas, ya tengo cuatro. ¿Qué más? Ah sí, ¡necesito el dinero!

1 p. 94

Para las clases necesitas muchas cosas. Necesitas una mochila, cuatro cuadernos, cinco carpetas, diez bolígrafos, seis lápices y un diccionario.

Answers to Repaso Activity 1

a. cuatro cuadernos
b. un diccionario
c. diez bolígrafos
d. cinco carpetas
e. seis lápices
f. una mochila

¡Organízate!
PROJECTS

DESEOS Y NECESIDADES

*This activity allows for written production while calling for higher-order thinking skills as students determine their wants and needs. Students are to set up a budget for **deseos y necesidades** as if they, or some imaginary person, were going to boarding school. If they wish, native speakers can share insights with you and the class.*

Introduction

Initiate a short discussion in English concerning the role the media (television, radio, movies, etc.) play in determining who we should be and how we should look. Encourage them to discuss how they determine what they really need.

Materials students may need

◆ Exchange rate information
◆ Budget example
◆ Pencils or pens
◆ Graph paper

Sequence

1 Students use the currency exchange rate to determine how many **euros** they can buy for 20 dollars and how many they can buy for 100 dollars.

2 Students list their wants and needs and find out their respective prices in dollars, then convert the prices of those items to **euros.**

3 Students list all the items they need to buy in their 20-dollar scenario and all the items they want to buy in their 100-dollar scenario.

4 You may decide to have students work on this project individually, entirely outside of class, or in groups that prepare a single budget to present to the class.

5 Assign a date for the rough draft, which may be peer reviewed in pairs for corrections, then specify a final date to present budgets for partners to evaluate orally.

6 The final written copy and the partner evaluation are turned in to the teacher.

Grading the project

Suggested point distribution (total = 100 points):

Vocabulary use **40**
Creativity and appearance **20**
Correct exchange rate **10**
Oral presentation **30**

EL REGRESO A CLASES

*In this activity, students will use all four skills to create full-page magazine ads in Spanish. The theme of students' ads may be "Back to School" (**El regreso a clases**). Have students discuss how advertising affects what they decide to buy. Ask them what types of advertising they prefer and have them identify ways in which advertisers target certain consumer groups at certain times of the year.*

Introduction

Tell students they will be able to use the vocabulary they have learned for school supplies and classroom items to create their ads. Ask them to make the ads appealing but accurate for the back-to-school theme. Help students brainstorm the key information an ad should contain: product name, benefits to the consumer, price, and when to buy it.

Materials students may need

◆ Large sheets of paper
◆ Old magazines
◆ Exchange rate information
◆ Internet access
◆ Tape
◆ Scissors
◆ Markers
◆ Glue

Sequence

1 Have students work individually or in groups. To create their ads, they need pictures of vocabulary items listed on page 97. Students cut pictures out of magazines or draw the items and list a price in **pesetas** at the current exchange rate. Have students research the exchange rate in a recent national newspaper or on the Internet.

2 Describe the project and assign a date for the rough draft. Assign a date for them to complete the ad and a date for oral presentations. Distribute a project assignment sheet and post a copy in the classroom, or write the assignment on the board.

3 If they will be working in groups, give students time in class to brainstorm and organize their ideas. Monitor their progress frequently.

4 Have students complete their first drafts for peer review and suggestions before turning them in.

5 Students complete the final drafts, present their ads to the class, and submit their written ads to the teacher.

FAMILY LINK

If students have worked individually on the project, they may also wish to present their ads to their families. Have them ask family members if they would buy the product based on the information in the ad. Why or why not?

Grading the project

Suggested point distribution (total = 100 points):

Chapter vocabulary use in ad	40
Creativity and appearance	20
Correct exchange rate	10
Oral presentation	30

NOTES

- You may wish to devote bulletin board space to finished products.
- Students may want to put their ads in their individual portfolios.
- Oral presentations may be recorded on audio- or videotape.

EL DINERO

*The following activity introduces students to the different monetary units used in Spanish-speaking countries. You may wish to have students refer to the **Enlaces** section on page 90 to introduce some currencies used in other countries.*

Materials students may need

- ◆ Encyclopedias
- ◆ Internet information (see page 15A)
- ◆ Paper or poster board
- ◆ Actual currency (optional)

Sequence

1 Point out the opportunity to learn new Spanish words, as well as interesting historical and cultural information about different countries through this research project.

2 Have students conduct library or Internet research on a particular currency.

3 Each student produces a poster with a visual replica of the country's money large enough for the class to see and a report on that currency.

4 Students look for the following information:
- the color of the bill
- who is pictured on the bill
- why the person pictured is important
- the names of any monuments on the bill
- the current exchange rate

5 Remind students that all labels must be in Spanish.

Grading the project

Suggested point distribution (total = 100 points):

Historical information	40
Creativity and appearance	20
Located currency reproduction	10
Oral presentation	30

NOTES

Some bulletin board space may be devoted to the finished products. You may decide to put their ads in students individual portfolios. Oral presentations may be videotaped.

CAPÍTULO 2

¡Organízate!

GAMES

LA TORRE DE BLOQUES

This game is good for learners with high visual/spatial intelligence. It promotes memory and Spanish-speaking skills.

Materials students may need
◆ Building blocks

Procedure

1. The object of the game is to make the highest stack of blocks without the tower falling over.

2. Students should sit in a circle on the floor or around a table with a bucket of blocks. Each block must go on top of the previous block.

   Before each student adds a block he or she must tell the group what all the students before him or her said in the same order without making a mistake and add a statement of his or her own. For example:

   RAFAEL   Necesito un bolígrafo. *(Adds a block)*

   VICENTE   Rafael necesita un bolígrafo y yo necesito papel. *(Adds a block)*

   CARMELA   Rafael necesita un bolígrafo, Vicente necesita papel y yo necesito un lápiz. *(Adds a block)*

3. Have students continue until they use all the blocks or the tower falls.

EL CUARTO IMAGINARIO

This game may be played in pairs with students sitting back to back, or as a game show with groups of students in front of the classroom and the rest of the class as the audience. It is designed to review indefinite articles and vocabulary from this chapter. It also introduces students to new vocabulary in a meaningful setting.

Materials students may need
◆ Paper
◆ Pens or pencils
◆ Chapter vocabulary lists
◆ Large spinner (for game show)
◆ Index cards with dollar amounts

Procedure 1
Pair work:

1. Have two students each prepare a list of items that might be found in their imaginary rooms. They may include any of the vocabulary items from the Preliminary Chapter through Chapter 2, as well as cognates the teacher may suggest, or an item they locate the meaning for in the dictionary. (They must explain to their partners.)

2. Sitting back to back with a partner, one student must guess if an item is found in his partner's imaginary room. For example **¿Tienes un armario?**

3. His or her partner responds with a **sí** or **no**. For every correct answer, the person guessing receives 10 points.

4. Then, the roles are reversed and the other student will ask about the items in his or her partner's imaginary room.

Procedure 2
Game show:

1. A large spinner with dollar amounts written in Spanish is handy for a variety of game shows, or you may have the game show host draw index cards with dollar amounts.

2. Divide students into groups and choose a moderator for the game show **El cuarto imaginario.**

3. Each team chooses a name and must prepare a list of items as indicated above. Each team member will contribute at least one item to the list.

4. The moderator then introduces the show and chooses two groups at a time to compete.

5. Team members sit back to back, and the moderator announces the value of each answer, **Por diez dólares, ¿qué hay en el cuarto imaginario?**

6 Each team member guesses one at a time the items selected by the other team, who will answer with **sí** or **no**.

7 This game promotes creative thinking because the correct answer is up to the individuals who make the list of items in the imaginary room.

8 Encourage students to be as original as possible. Mention a few cognates and personalized vocabulary items in the chapters to get them started, such as:

un cartel de (favorite actor, actress, musician, or band)

un reloj

una fotografía de (favorite actor, actress, musician, or band)

una alfombra (color)

una guía telefónica

SOBRE LA MESA

This game allows students to work in teams and to practice vocabulary from Chapter 2.

Materials you may need

◆ As many items from **Vocabulario** on page 65 as possible

Procedure

1 Place the items on a table or desk and cover them with a cloth. Divide students into teams.

2 Have all students gather around the table as you remove the cloth. Give students two minutes to study the items on the table. At the end of two minutes, replace the cloth and have them regroup into their teams. They are to make a list in Spanish of as many of the items as they can remember.

3 You many wish to provide students with a second look if they need to add to their lists. The teams with the most correct list wins.

Challenge

Remove one or two of the items and hide them. Students must then say which items are missing. This can also be played as a team activity.

LA BÚSQUEDA

*This game is a scavenger hunt to reinforce the vocabulary of Chapter 2, and to re-enter colors from the **Capítulo preliminar**. It will work best in classrooms where the students have access to common supplies.*

Materials students may need

◆ Six or more different types of common school supplies

Procedure

1 Divide the class into small groups. Each group should make up a list of classroom supplies for another group. Tell them that lists should be as realistic as possible, but may include colors and numbers as modifiers as well. The items on the list are restricted to vocabulary from the chapter that is available in the classroom. (**una calculadora, dos lápices amarillos, una mochila roja, dos carpetas...**)

2 Have groups exchange lists and allow time for a scavenger hunt for the items on their list. At the end of the time limit (five minutes, for example), have groups show their supplies while reading off the list. The group that has found the most items on its list is the winner.

ANSWERS TO CHAPTER 2 ACTIVITIES

Listening activity answers appear on Scripts pages 57E–57F. Answers to all other activities appear on corresponding pupil pages.

PRIMER PASO   pp. 64–71

8
1. Quiero una calculadora.
   Pero Paco, ya tienes tres calculadoras.
2. Necesito unos lápices.
   Ya tienes once lápices.
3. Quiero unos cuadernos.
   Ya tienes nueve cuadernos.
4. Necesito una mochila.
   Ya tienes dos mochilas.
5. Necesito unos bolígrafos.
   Ya tienes quince bolígrafos.
6. Necesito una carpeta.
   Ya tienes cinco carpetas.
7. Necesito unas gomas de borrar.
   Ya tienes veinte gomas de borrar.
8. Necesito una regla.
   Pero ya tienes cuatro reglas.

15 Answers will vary. Possible answers:
1. Necesito un diccionario, un bolígrafo y unos papeles.
2. Necesito una carpeta y un cuaderno.
3. Necesito papel, unos marcadores, pintura y un pincel.
4. Necesito una calculadora.
5. Necesito una mochila.
6. Necesito un diccionario.
7. Necesito un bolígrafo.
8. Necesito papel, un lápiz, una goma de borrar y un marcador.

SEGUNDO PASO   pp. 74–81

20 Answers will vary. Possible answers:

hay	no hay
una mesa	un armario
una silla	un televisor
una puerta	una cama
un reloj	una radio
una ventana	una lámpara

21 Answers will vary. Possible answers:
1. En el cuarto de Débora hay tres revistas.
2. Débora tiene cuatro lápices.
3. En el cuarto de Débora hay una silla.
4. Débora tiene una cama.
5. Débora tiene un reloj.

TERCER PASO   pp. 84–89

34 Answers will vary. Possible answers:
1. Necesita comprar un reloj.
2. Necesita organizar el cuarto.
3. Necesita comprar un diccionario de español.
4. Necesita ir a la librería.
5. Necesita conocer a nuevos amigos.
6. Necesita comprar ropa.
7. Necesita comprar una lámpara.
8. Necesita comprar zapatillas de tenis.

35 Answers will vary. Possible answers:
1. ¿Quieres comprar un reloj?
2. ¿Quieres organizar el cuarto?
3. ¿Quieres comprar un diccionario de español?
4. ¿Quieres ir a la librería?
5. ¿Quieres conocer a nuevos amigos?
6. ¿Quieres comprar ropa?
7. ¿Quieres comprar una lámpara?
8. ¿Quieres comprar zapatillas de tenis?

A VER SI PUEDO...   p. 96

1
1. Juanita, ¿necesitas unos bolígrafos y papel?
   Sí, necesito unos bolígrafos y papel.
2. Paco, ¿necesitas una calculadora?
   No, no necesito una calculadora.
3. Felipe, ¿necesitas unos cuadernos?
   Sí, necesito unos cuadernos.

2
1. ¿Cuánto papel necesitas?
2. ¿Cuántos libros necesitas?
3. ¿Cuántas reglas necesitas?
4. ¿Cuántos cuadernos necesitas?
5. ¿Cuántas carpetas necesitas?
6. ¿Cuántos lápices necesitas?

3
¿Tienes un armario en tu cuarto?
¿Tienes una cama en tu cuarto?
¿Tienes un estéreo en tu cuarto?
¿Tienes un televisor en tu cuarto?

4
1. Necesita organizar su cuarto. Quiero organizar mi cuarto.
2. Necesita poner las zapatillas en el armario. Quiero poner las zapatillas en el armario.
3. Necesita comprar unos cuadernos. Quiero comprar unos cuadernos.
4. Necesita conocer a muchos nuevos amigos. Quiero conocer a muchos nuevos amigos.
5. Necesita comprar zapatillas de tenis. Quiero comprar unas zapatillas de tenis.

HOMEWORK SUGGESTIONS

Chapter Section	Presentation	Homework Options
Primer paso	**Vocabulario,** p. 65	*Grammar and Vocabulary,* p. 9, Activities 1–2
	Así se dice, p. 66	*Practice and Activity Book,* p. 17, Activity 5
	Gramática, p. 67	*Grammar and Vocabulary,* p. 11, Activities 5–6 *Practice and Activity Book,* p. 18, Activity 7 *CD-ROM,* Disc 1, Chapter 2, Activity 2
	Gramática, p. 68	*Pupil's Edition,* pp. 68–69, Activities 10, 12 *Grammar and Vocabulary,* p. 12, Activities 7–8 *Practice and Activity Book,* p. 18, Activity 8
	Nota gramatical, p. 70	*Grammar and Vocabulary,* p. 13, Activities 9–10
Segundo paso	**Vocabulario,** p. 75	*Pupil's Edition,* p. 75, Activity 18 *Grammar and Vocabulary,* p. 14, Activities 11–12 *Practice and Activity Book,* p. 19, Activity 9 *CD-ROM,* Disc 1, Chapter 2, Activity 3
	Así se dice, p. 76	*Pupil's Edition,* p. 76, Activity 20 *Practice and Activity Book,* p. 19, Activities 9–10
	Gramática, p. 78	*Pupil's Edition,* p. 78, Activity 23 *Grammar and Vocabulary,* p. 15, Activity 13 *Practice and Activity Book,* pp. 20–21, Activities 11–13 *CD-ROM,* Disc 1, Chapter 2, Activity 4
Tercer paso	**Así se dice,** p. 85	*Pupil's Edition,* p. 85, Activity 30 *Practice and Activity Book,* p. 22, Activities 14–15 *CD-ROM,* Disc 1, Chapter 2, Activity 5
	Vocabulario, p. 86	*Pupil's Edition,* pp. 86–87, Activities 33–34 *Practice and Activity Book,* pp. 22–24, Activities 16–18 *Grammar and Vocabulary,* p. 16, Activity 14
	Nota gramatical, p. 86	*Grammar and Vocabulary,* p. 16, Activity 15
	Vocabulario, p. 88	*Pupil's Edition,* pp. 88–89, Activities 37–38 *Practice and Activity Book,* p. 24, Activity 19 *Grammar and Vocabulary,* p. 17, Activities 16–17

¡Organízate!

MOTIVATING ACTIVITIES

• Ask students what they do to get ready to go back to school and what they usually need to buy. What do they keep from year to year and what do they have to buy each year?

• Have students list in English the items in the photo that they need for school. In pairs, have them compare their lists. Students should refer to the lists at the end of the chapter to see what they've learned.

PHOTO FLASH!

(1) Ask students if they know any words in English ending in **-ería**. Try to get them to come up with pizzeria. Tell them that **papel** means paper and ask them to try to figure out what a **papelería** is. What other products would they expect to find in a **papelería**?

RE-ENTRY

Ask students how the girl in the photo would tell her friend that she likes her new notebook. How would she ask if he likes it?

AUDITORY LEARNERS

Ask students to point to the items in the photo as you read aloud: **fotos, mapas, diccionarios,** and **globos.** Point out that some of these are cognates.

CAPÍTULO

2

¡Organízate!

(1) **Necesito dos libros. ¿Qué necesitas tú?**

58 *cincuenta y ocho*

In this chapter you will learn to

PRIMER PASO

- talk about what you want and need

SEGUNDO PASO

- say what's in your room

TERCER PASO

- talk about what you need and want to do

internet

go.hrw.com

MARCAR: go.hrw.com
PALABRA CLAVE:
WV3 SPAIN-2

② ¡Hombre! Necesitas organizar tus cosas.

③ ¿Qué hay en tu cuarto?

59

FOCUSING ON OUTCOMES

Explain to students that in this chapter they will be learning to communicate to others what they need and want. Have them read the learner outcomes and match them to the photos. (Photo 1: talking about what you need. Photo 2: talking about what you need to do. Photo 3: saying what's in your room.) Ask students to think of several items they want at the beginning of a new school year and several more they really need.

PHOTO FLASH!

② This photo is taken from the video episode for Chapter 2. **Abuela** tells Paco that his room is a mess and that he needs to put his things away before he goes shopping.

ADDITIONAL VOCABULARY

almohada *pillow*
manta, frazada *blanket*
sobrecama *bedspread*
cortinas *curtains*
cuadro *picture, portrait*
animal (m.) de peluche/un peluche *stuffed animal*
alfombra *carpet*
cómoda *dresser*
espejo *mirror*

VIDEO INTEGRATION

Adelante LEVEL 1A
Video Program
Videocassette 1, 23:31–28:29 OR
Videocassette 3, 9:55–14:41
(captioned version)

¡Ven conmigo! LEVEL 1
DVD Tutor, Disc 1

TEACHER NOTE
The **fotonovela** is an abridged version of the video episode.

VIDEO SYNOPSIS
Paco explains to his grandmother that he needs to buy school supplies. His grandmother tells him to straighten his room first and gives him money to buy what he needs. While straightening his room, Paco discovers that he doesn't really need everything he thought he did. His grandmother tells him to buy only what he needs. But then Paco can't find the money.

MOTIVATING ACTIVITY
Have students predict what is going to happen in the **fotonovela.**

CULTURE NOTE
In Spanish-speaking countries fewer teenagers have part-time jobs or receive allowances. Therefore, they need to ask their parents for spending money.

DE ANTEMANO

 ¡Mañana es el primer día de clases!

CD 2 Trs. 1–2   Look at the pictures in the **fotonovela.** Who are the characters? Where are they? Is there a problem? What are the clues that tell you this?

p. 15
Acts. 1–2

Paco

Abuela

60 *sesenta*

4 Paco, mira. ¡Tu cuarto es un desastre! Primero... organiza tu cuarto.

Aquí tienes el dinero, pero para las cosas que necesitas.

5 Y ves, ya tienes lápices.

6 Gracias, abuelita. Pero... ¿organizar mi cuarto?

7 Abuela ¡ya estoy lista!

Bueno, no necesito lápices... ni necesito bolígrafos. Y ya tengo una calculadora. Pero no tengo mucho papel... y necesito más cuadernos.

8 Necesito también unas zapatillas de tenis. Y necesito una mochila.

61

PRESENTATION
Play the video or audio recording for students as they follow along in their books. Then read the **fotonovela** frame by frame, modeling the language while students repeat after you. Encourage students to guess meaning from context and visual clues. Students need not master structures and vocabulary at this point as they will be presented and practiced in the **pasos**.

KINESTHETIC LEARNERS
Pick up or point to the following items in the classroom: **mochila, cuaderno, lápiz, libro, papel, bolígrafo, calculadora, diccionario, zapatillas de tenis.** Then ask students to show you each article by picking it up or pointing it out. (**Muéstrame una calculadora.**) To review names and personalize the activity, ask **¿Quién tiene una calculadora?** Then have students ask other students the question.

TEACHER NOTE
Throughout *¡Ven conmigo!*, students learn vocabulary variants (such as **zapatillas de tenis**) that are appropriate to the chapter's geographical setting. If you prefer another local term, be aware that the *Testing Program* calls for forms presented in the *Pupil's Edition*.

CAPÍTULO 2

LANGUAGE NOTES

- The word **goma** means both *eraser* and *rubber*. Use **borrador** for a chalkboard eraser.

- In some countries such as Puerto Rico, **bulto** is used for *backpack* and in Spain **lapicero** means *pen*. In South America, **carpeta** is also used to mean *notebook*.

CRITICAL THINKING

Ask students to think of different possible endings for the **fotonovela** episode.

A continuación

You may choose to continue with *¡Mañana es el primer día de clases! (a continuación)* at this time or wait until later in the chapter. After Paco's grandmother helps find the money, Paco and Felipe shop for school supplies and a gift for Paco's grandmother. You may wish to discuss with students where they buy school supplies and differences between stores in Spain and the U.S.

Cuaderno para hispanohablantes, pp. 6–10

1 ¿Comprendes?

Check your understanding of the **fotonovela**. Choose the best answer to each question.

1. Where does the story take place?
   a. Paco's school
   (b) Paco's house
2. What does Paco's grandmother tell him to do?
   (a) clean his room
   b. do his homework
3. At the end of the scene, which items does Paco find out that he does <u>not</u> need?
   a. an eraser and a ruler
   (b) pencils and pens
4. How does the scene end?
   a. Paco makes a phone call.
   (b) Paco can't find his money.

2 ¿Cierto o falso?

Based on the **fotonovela**, respond to each statement with **cierto** (true) or **falso** (false).

1. Mañana es el primer día de clases. cierto
2. Paco no necesita más cuadernos. falso
3. Paco no necesita más lápices. cierto
4. La abuela organiza el cuarto de Paco. falso
5. Paco necesita unas zapatillas de tenis. cierto

3 ¿Listos?

Complete the following paragraph about Paco with the correct words from the box.

Ay, ¡mañana es el primer día de ___1___! Bueno, no ___2___ lápices ni necesito bolígrafos, y ya tengo una ___3___. Pero no tengo mucho ___4___ y necesito más cuadernos. Y también necesito unas ___5___ de tenis. Ahora, ¿dónde está el dinero?

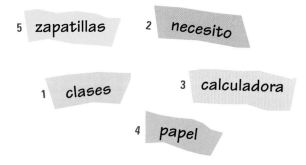

5 **zapatillas**   2 **necesito**

1 **clases**   3 **calculadora**

4 **papel**

These activities check for global comprehension only. Students should not yet be expected to produce language modeled in **De antemano**.

Nota cultural

It's common for extended families to live together in Spain and Latin America. Like Paco, many young people grow up in homes with parents, grandparents, and even an aunt or uncle. What are the advantages and disadvantages of living with many relatives? How does this compare with your family or your friends' families?

COOPERATIVE LEARNING

1 *through* **3** Have students work through these exercises together in groups of two to four. Their answers should be identical. This means they need to agree upon their answers. Let them know that you will randomly choose only one sheet from each group. Every member will receive the grade from the sheet.

CHALLENGE

2 If a statement is false, students should change it to make it true.

SUGGESTIONS

1 Ask for volunteers to ask and answer questions. Have the class indicate whether answers are correct with thumbs up or thumbs down.

2 Write the words and phrases that make up these sentences on magnetic or felt board strips. Then ask students to manipulate the sentences to change negative sentences into positive ones and vice-versa.

ADDITIONAL PRACTICE

Have partners make a shopping list for Paco. The list should include only the items he decides he needs after he has straightened his room. Ask students how much money Paco will have to spend on his school supplies. Ask pairs to compare their lists.

64

PRIMER PASO

(TPR) Storytelling Book pp. 5, 8

go.hrw.com

WV3 SPAIN-2

Talking about what you want and need

SUGGESTION

As students watch the video, ask them to identify an expression other than **necesito** that implies something Paco needs. (**No tengo mucho papel.**)

Bell work
Have students make two columns in their notebooks with the heads **Paco tiene** and **Paco no tiene**. Based on the **fotonovela**, students complete these columns with the different school supplies Paco has and does not have.

NATIVE SPEAKERS

For some native speakers **carpeta** might mean *desk*, for others it might mean *carpet*. Point out that **el pupitre** is also used for *desk* and that **la alfombra** is standard for *carpet*.

☀ MOTIVATE

Ask students which items in the word box for Activity 4 are things they need for school. Ask if there is anything they still need.

Bueno, no necesito lápices... ni necesito bolígrafos. Y ya tengo una calculadora. Pero no tengo mucho papel... y necesito más cuadernos.

Necesito también unas zapatillas de tenis. Y necesito una mochila.

4 La lista de Paco

Look at the word box. List the five school supplies that Paco mentions in the photo above. calculadora, lápices, papel, cuadernos, bolígrafos

libros   calculadora   bolígrafos   regla

papel   cuadernos   lápices

CD-ROM DISC 1

p. 16
Act. 3

p. 9
Acts. 1–2

2-A

CAPÍTULO 2

VOCABULARIO

Cosas para el colegio en la librería...

una mochila

una calculadora

un cuaderno

La Historia

un lápiz

un libro

Diccionario

un diccionario

un bolígrafo

una regla

una goma de borrar

una carpeta

papel

5 Arturo y Sumiko

CD 2 Tr. 3

Follow the instructions to find out about Arturo and Sumiko's shopping trip. Script and answers on p. 57E

a. Make sure you have a separate piece of paper with a list of the eleven school supplies shown above.

b. Then, listen as Arturo and Sumiko talk about the supplies they need for school.

c. Write an **A** by every item Arturo needs and an **S** by every item Sumiko needs.

d. Finally, circle the item that both Arturo and Sumiko need.

Nota cultural

To prepare for school, many students in Spanish-speaking countries buy pens and notebooks just as you do. However, many of these students also need to buy school uniforms. You'll notice photos of students wearing school uniforms as you work with this book. Do you or any of your friends wear a uniform to school? What are some good things and bad things about school uniforms?

TEACH

PRESENTATION

VOCABULARIO

Fill a backpack with objects from the **Vocabulario** and walk into class. Sit at an empty desk and model the pronunciation of each item by saying **Tengo...** as you take them out. Once you are done, practice asking students **¿Tienes...?** Have them respond with **Sí, tengo...** or **No, no tengo...** Ask them to hold up the supplies in order to verify that their answers are correct.

SUGGESTION

Have students follow up by doing *CD-ROM,* Activity 1, an **Imagen y sonido** activity.

CRITICAL THINKING

After students have read the **Nota cultural,** ask them why students might wear a uniform. Explain that students in many countries wear uniforms and that uniforms help provide a form of equality among all students. This is especially important in countries with big disparities between the rich and the poor.

PA pp. 16–17 Acts. 4–5

2-1

ASÍ SE DICE   Talking about what you want and need

To find out what someone wants, ask:

   ¿Qué quieres?

   ¿Paco quiere una mochila?

To answer, say:

   Quiero una mochila.

   Sí, él **quiere** una mochila.

To find out what someone needs, ask:

   ¿Qué necesitas?

   ¿Necesitas papel?

   ¿Qué necesita Merche?

To answer, say:

   Necesito un cuaderno.

   No, **ya tengo** papel.
   No, I already have paper.

   ¡Ella necesita muchas cosas!
   She needs a lot of things!

6 ¿Qué necesita Blanca?   Script and answers on p. 57E

Blanca needs to buy school supplies before school starts. Listen as she talks about her list. Then write her shopping list as she would write it. Ignore the things she already has and write only the things she needs. Start your answer with **Blanca necesita...**

CD 2 Tr. 4

GV p.10 Acts. 3–4

NOTA GRAMATICAL

Un and **una** mean *a* or *an.* Use **un** with masculine nouns.
   un cuaderno
Use **una** with feminine nouns.
   una mochila
Many masculine nouns end with -**o** and many feminine nouns end with -**a.** Do you remember two ways to say *the* in Spanish?[1]

el cuaderno

la mochila

[1]**El** and **la** mean *the.*

7 Cosas para el colegio

Elena is telling her father what she has and what she needs for school. Complete each sentence with **un** or **una.**

Tengo ___1___ libro de matemáticas pero necesito ___2___ cuaderno. Tengo ___3___ bolígrafo, ___4___ goma de borrar y ___5___ carpeta. Necesito ___6___ diccionario, ___7___ calculadora, una regla y ___8___ lápiz. Y quiero ___9___ mochila nueva *(new),* por favor.

1. un
2. un
3. un
4. una
5. una
6. un
7. una
8. un
9. una

GRAMÁTICA · Making nouns plural

1. So far, you've been talking about single things. To make a noun plural, add **-s** if it ends in a vowel: **diccionario → diccionarios.** If the noun ends in a consonant, add **-es: papel → papeles.**

2. If a noun ends in **-z**, change **-z** to **-c** and add **-es: lápiz → lápices.**

3. How would you make these nouns plural?[1]

   a. cruz   b. luz   c. vez

PA
p. 18
Act. 7

GV
p.11
Acts. 5–6

8 ¡Necesito muchas cosas!

With a partner, play the roles of Paco and a friend. Each time Paco says he wants an item, his friend reminds him he already has several. Use the numbers in parentheses. Answers on p. 57K

MODELO libro de béisbol (6)
—Quiero un libro de béisbol.
—Pero Paco, ¡ya tienes seis libros de béisbol!

1. calculadora (3) 3. cuaderno (9) 5. bolígrafo (15) 7. goma de borrar (20)
2. lápiz (11)   4. mochila (2)   6. carpeta (5)   8. regla (4)

9 Una lista

Work in pairs. Look at the drawings below. Make a list of at least five items you have and five items you need. Compare your lists with a partner. What items do you have in common? Which supplies do you both need? Answers will vary.

MODELO ¿Necesitas una goma de borrar?
Sí, necesito una goma de borrar.

La lista de Marta
1. una goma de borrar

---

[1] The plurals are **cruces, luces,** and **veces.**

PRIMER PASO

sesenta y siete **67**

CAPÍTULO 2

PRESENTATION GRAMÁTICA

Ask students to make plural each of the vocabulary items on page 65. Practice by holding up one or more of the items on the list and asking students to say **un** or **una.**

MULTICULTURAL LINK

Have students interview exchange students or others who have studied in Spanish-speaking countries. Ask if students in those countries follow the same kind of schedule as students in your school. Do they stay in the same room all day? How does this affect what they bring to school? Do students wear uniforms? If there are no exchange students in your school, your students might ask these questions of pen pals. See page T58 for pen pal information.

SLOWER PACE

8 Before students join their partner, have them write the words for the numerals describing how many items Paco has. Allow them to use the written responses as they role-play Paco and his friend.

STANDARDS: 1.1, 1.3, 4.2   **67**

GRAMÁTICA

Indefinite articles (un, una, unos, unas)

1. You've already learned that **un** and **una** mean *a* or *an*. **Unos** and **unas** mean *some* or *a few*. This chart shows how the four forms of the indefinite article are used.

	SINGULAR	PLURAL
MASCULINE	un bolígrafo	unos bolígrafos
FEMININE	una mochila	unas mochilas

PA
p. 18
Act. 8

GV
p. 12
Acts. 7–8

2. Use **unos** with a masculine plural noun. When referring to a group that includes both males and females, the masculine plural is used (**unos estudiantes**).

3. In a negative sentence, **un, una, unos,** and **unas** are often dropped.
   ¿Necesitas unos bolígrafos?   No, no necesito bolígrafos.

PRESENTATION
GRAMÁTICA

TPR Model the usage of indefinite articles by walking around the room and picking up various items and then saying what you have. **(Tengo un bolígrafo. Tengo unos lápices.)** Then tell students **Saquen un lápiz.** Follow it with **Saquen unos lápices.** Repeat the activity with other vocabulary items.

KINESTHETIC LEARNERS
10 After completing this activity, have students team up with a partner. Students should check their answers and then role-play the conversation. Students then use props to act out the conversation without looking in their books.

10   Hablando con Felipe

It's the first day of school. Complete Paco and Felipe's phone conversation. Use the correct indefinite article (**un, una, unos,** or **unas**) with each missing word.

un diccionario

PACO   Felipe, ¿necesitas _____?

unos cuadernos

FELIPE   Sí. También necesito _____.

una calculadora   unas reglas

PACO   Yo necesito _____ y _____ para la clase

unas gomas de borrar

de matemáticas. Ah, y ¿quieres _____?

unos lápices

FELIPE   Sí, y necesito _____ también.

VISUAL LEARNERS
Have students label their school supplies by copying the words for them onto adhesive labels or onto strips of paper, then affixing them to the corresponding item. The class can also do this for other objects in the room.

ADDITIONAL PRACTICE
Divide students into groups of four. Explain that they will be setting up their own **tienda.** They need to come up with a name and a sign for their **tienda.** There should be two people working and two people shopping. After each pair has three exchanges, they should switch roles. Students will buy and sell different class supplies using the vocabulary they already know.

11   ¿Qué necesitas?

What school supplies do you need for your classes? With a partner, take turns asking each other what you need for the following classes. Name at least two items.   Answers will vary. Possible answers below:

MODELO   la clase de arte
—¿Qué necesitas para la clase de arte?
—Necesito unos lápices y una goma de borrar.

1. la clase de español un bolígrafo y un cuaderno
2. la clase de matemáticas una regla y una calculadora
3. la clase de inglés un cuaderno y un diccionario
4. la clase de historia una carpeta y un cuaderno
5. la clase de ciencias una lupa y un microscopio
6. la clase de computación una computadora y un cuaderno

VOCABULARIO EXTRA

la **computadora**   *computer*
la **enciclopedia**   *encyclopedia*
la **lupa**   *magnifying glass*
el **microscopio**   *microscope*

12   ¿Dónde está la mochila?

Paco lost his new backpack with all his school supplies in it. Help him out by making a list of at least five things he needs to replace. Remember that he'll need more of some items than others, so tell him exactly how many you think he needs.

MODELO   Necesitas diez lápices.

Answers will vary. Possible answers: Necesitas tres cuadernos, cinco bolígrafos, una calculadora, una mochila y una regla.

PRESENTATION

NOTA GRAMATICAL

Point to yourself and say **Yo tengo unos bolígrafos.** Then ask someone, **¿Necesitas un bolígrafo?** After the student answers, point to him or her and ask the class **¿Él (Ella) necesita un bolígrafo?** Repeat until students understand the usage and meaning of **él** and **ella**.

CLOSE

Fill a shopping basket with multiple classroom objects presented in this **paso**. One by one, have students come up to the basket. Tell each person what he or she is to select. Use either **Necesitas** or **Quieres** with the name of an item or items in the basket. If you say **Miguel, necesitas cuadernos,** Miguel is to pick notebooks from the basket and say a sentence using the **yo** form of **necesitar** and **cuadernos. (Necesito unos cuadernos.)**

Él necesita una mochila.

Ella necesita una calculadora.

GV p.13 Acts. 9–10

NOTA GRAMATICAL

In Chapter 1 you learned to use the subject pronoun **yo** when talking about yourself and **tú** when talking to another student or someone your own age. When you want to talk about someone else, use **él** to mean *he* and **ella** to mean *she*.

13 ¿Él o ella?

Complete each of the sentences with **él** or **ella,** as appropriate.

MODELO   ¿Felipe? ¿Qué tiene ======? **(él)**

1. ¿Paco? ====== ya tiene papel. Él
2. ¿Merche? ====== quiere una mochila. Ella
3. ¿Leticia? No, ====== no necesita un cuaderno. ella
4. ¿Juan Antonio? ¿Qué quiere ======? él
5. ¿Noemí? Sí, ====== necesita bolígrafos. ella
6. ¿Ignacio? ====== no necesita lápices. Él
7. ¿Verónica? ====== ya tiene unas gomas de borrar. Ella

14 Memoria

 Work in groups of three. Each person takes turns saying one school supply he or she needs. Next, everyone says what the person on the right needs, using **tú**. Then all say what the other person in the group needs, using **él** or **ella.** Answers will vary.

MODELO   Yo necesito una carpeta.
Tú necesitas unos papeles. (*to* the person on your right)
Ella necesita un lápiz. (*about* the person on your left)

15 ¿Qué necesitas para...?

 Get together with a partner. Take turns saying what items you need to do the activities listed below. Use the items in the **Vocabulario** on page 65 and the words in the **Vocabulario extra** box.   Answers on p. 57K

MODELO   to do math homework
Necesito un libro, un papel, una calculadora, una goma de borrar y una regla.

1. to write a report
2. to carry loose papers
3. to make a poster for art class
4. to add up some numbers
5. to carry your books
6. to look up unknown words
7. to write in your journal
8. to make a birthday card for your friend

VOCABULARIO
EXTRA

el lápiz de color   *colored pencil*
el marcador   *marker*
el pincel   *paintbrush*
la pintura   *paint*

16 Comparaciones

Look at the school supplies that Anabela and Juan have in the photos. Take turns describing to your partner what Juan and Anabela have or need. You may also say something about an item they both have or an item they both need. Each of you should say at least three things about the photos.   Answers will vary. Possible answers below:

MODELO   1. **Anabela tiene una carpeta. Juan necesita una carpeta.**
         2. **Juan necesita unos lápices de color y Anabela necesita unos lápices de color también.**

1. Juan tiene una regla. Anabela necesita una regla.
2. Juan tiene un libro. Anabela necesita una calculadora.
3. Anabela tiene un diccionario. Juan necesita un diccionario.

PRIMER PASO

setenta y uno **71**

♜ GAME
Dibujos To review material from this **paso**, divide the class into two teams. Be sure to keep a record of each item for scoring. Ask the first player from team one to go to the board. Show the student a vocabulary word. The student draws a picture of the word and his or her team says the word in Spanish, including the correct definite article (**el** or **la**). The team has one minute to draw and guess the word before the opposing team may try. The successful team gets the point. Repeat with the other team, but this time ask for indefinite articles. Alternate teams and definite and indefinite articles.

☀ ASSESS

▸ Testing Program, pp. 19–20
  Quiz 2-1
  Audio CD 2, Tr. 17

▸ Grammar and Vocabulary
  Quizzes
  Quiz 2-1A or
  Alternative Quiz 2-1A

▸ Alternative Assessment
  Guide, p. 20

PERFORMANCE ASSESSMENT
List on the board ten school supplies that students typically bring to school, and have students copy it. Put these ten supplies in a backpack. Then take out an item, and at the same time call out a number (**uno** for the first item, **diez** for the last). Ask students to write the number you call next to the name of the item on the list they copied.

STANDARDS: 1.1, 1.2, 5.1   **71**

VIDEO INTEGRATION

Adelante LEVEL 1A

Video Program
Videocassette 1, 35:50–38:11

TEACHER NOTE
Even-numbered chapters have an **Encuentro cultural,** in which a young Spanish speaker introduces students to a variety of customs and cultural themes from around the Spanish-speaking world. The textbook pages are coordinated with a video presentation.

PRESENTATION
Have your students think about the ways people greet one another in our culture. Point out that they greet friends in quite a different way than they greet teachers, parents, or adults they don't know. How do they greet people their own age that they're meeting for the first time? What do they think are some of the factors that determine how two people will greet one another? (age, gender, circumstances, familiarity, etc.)

ENCUENTRO CULTURAL

Los saludos en el mundo hispano

In Spain there are many ways to greet people. You can shake hands with someone you're meeting for the first time, or give a friend or a member of your family a hug or kiss on the cheek.

1 ¿Qué dijo?
Ana explains several ways that people greet one another. Read what she says and see if you can guess what kind of greeting she's describing in the following sentences.

¡Hola! Yo me llamo Ana y soy de Sevilla. En España es muy común darle dos besos cuando ves a un amigo o una amiga que ya conoces. Cuando los hombres se ven, se dan un abrazo fuerte, u otra señal de cariño. Entre familia nos saludamos con mucho cariño.

"En España es muy común **darle dos besos**".

"Cuando los hombres se ven, se dan **un abrazo fuerte**".

"Entre familia nos saludamos **con mucho cariño**".

1. Ana says that in Spain **"se dan dos besos"**. What do you think that means? two kisses

2. Ana says men sometimes give each other **un abrazo fuerte** when they greet each other. What do you think **un abrazo fuerte** means?
   a. a big hug
   b. a firm handshake

3. How does Ana say family members greet one another? with a lot of affection

2 ¡Piénsalo!

1. Look at the photos on these two pages. Is there one that shows ways in which you also greet someone? Do any of the photos show something you don't do when you meet someone?

2. Using what you know about how people greet one another in Spain, what is Ana's relation to each of the people she's greeting below? How do you know?

1. Answers will vary. Possible answers:
Do: hugging, shaking hands, or kissing cheek
Don't: kiss friends on the cheek

2. The woman and young man are close friends or relatives. The older man is an acquaintance or someone Ana has just met.

3 ¿Y tú?

1. Describe how the following people would greet each other. Mention gestures as well as phrases they might use. Would the greetings be different depending on whether the people were in Spain or Latin America? How? Answers will vary. Possible answers:
   a. two old friends seeing each other unexpectedly two kisses (one kiss in Latin America) or a big hug
   b. a student meeting a teacher for the first time shake hands
   c. a young person greeting his or her grandparent kisses and hugs

2. On the first day of school this year, how did you greet friends whom you hadn't seen all summer? How did you greet teachers you knew? Answers will vary.

3. Imagine two situations in which you might need to know how Spanish speakers greet each other. Answers will vary. Possible answers: meeting a foreign exchange student from a Spanish-speaking country; studying abroad in a Spanish-speaking country

ENCUENTRO CULTURAL

setenta y tres **73**

CRITICAL THINKING

2 Have students imagine that they're writing an etiquette guide for exchange students from Spain or Latin America who will be attending their school. Have them write a short section on the do's and don'ts of greetings in their community, including information such as how to greet friends, family, teachers, and new people.

CHALLENGE

3 For an added challenge, have students mention phrases that people might use to greet each other in these three situations.

Using what they now know about greetings, have your students discuss how Spanish-speaking teens might behave under the same circumstances.

MULTICULTURAL LINK

Have students research ways to greet people in other cultures, particularly non-Western cultures. The richest source of information for them will probably be people from other countries and in other language communities.

SUGGESTION

Show the video sequence of Paco greeting Merche or show other footage of Spanish-speaking people greeting one another to illustrate culturally appropriate displays of affection.

VIDEO INTEGRATION

Adelante LEVEL 1A
Video Program
Videocassette 1, 29:02–29:50 OR
Videocassette 3, 15:14–16:02
(captioned version)

¡Ven conmigo! LEVEL 1
DVD Tutor, Disc 1

Bell work
Ask students to list the school supplies they have either in their backpacks, their desks, or their lockers. (**En mi mochila tengo...**)

SUGGESTION
17 This scene from the video shows Paco and his grandmother in his room. Have students watch the scene or look closely at the photo to determine what Paco has and doesn't have.

☀ MOTIVATE

• Ask students to envision their ideal room; have several students describe the way they see it. How do they envision their own rooms when they get to high school?

• Ask students to jot down five things they consider essential for any student's room. Tally the number of times each item is listed, and put the most frequently listed items first when introducing this lesson.

SEGUNDO PASO

TPR

Storytelling Book
pp. 6, 8

WV3 SPAIN-2

Saying what's in your room

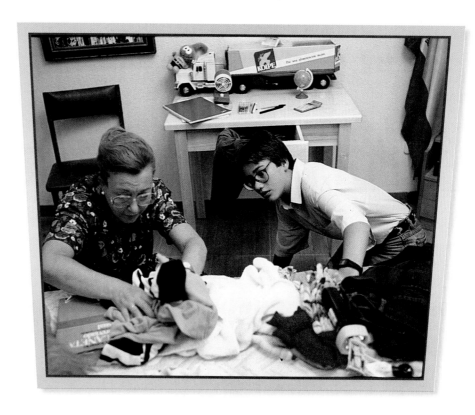

17 ¿Qué hay en el cuarto de Paco?

Look at the photo. Find three items from the choices below that are in the photo above. Then write a sentence saying what Paco has in his room. Begin your sentence with **Paco tiene...**

una calculadora

una mochila

el dinero

un libro

un lápiz

unos bolígrafos

un cuaderno

Answers will vary. Possible answer: Paco tiene una calculadora, unos bolígrafos y un cuaderno.

VOCABULARIO

El cuarto de Débora

CD-ROM DISC 1

p. 19
Act. 9

GV
p.14
Acts.
11–12

2-B

- el reloj
- la ventana
- la lámpara
- el cartel
- el escritorio
- la puerta
- la silla
- el armario
- la ropa
- la radio
- la cama
- la revista
- el televisor
- la mesa
- la zapatilla de tenis

18 En mi cuarto tengo...

List five items from Débora's room that you have in your room. How many of each item do you have?

MODELO Tengo una cama, un armario, una radio, dos ventanas y tres carteles.

Answers will vary.

Nota cultural

In Spain, most people live in **pisos** *(apartments)* in cities or towns. Bedrooms are often smaller, and sisters or brothers will sometimes have to share a room. Generally, the family shares a single TV and a single phone. It's not common for younger family members to have a TV or phone of their own. What's positive and negative about sharing a TV or phone with the family?

PA
p. 26
Acts.
21–22

p. 19
Act. 10

2-2

PRESENTATION

ASÍ SE DICE

Draw a picture of a room on a transparency and describe it. (**En el cuarto hay una cama, una silla...**) Then ask students personalized questions about their rooms. (**Pepe, ¿tienes una ventana en tu cuarto?**) Put students at ease by assuring them that their answers can refer to an imaginary or an ideal room.

VISUAL LEARNERS

19 Label vocabulary items found in your classroom to help students remember the words.

LANGUAGE NOTE

Las zapatillas de tenis is the common term for *tennis shoes* in Spain. In other countries the words **los zapatos de tenis** and **los tenis** are common.

MUSIC LINK

To the tune of a favorite song, students can write their own lyrics describing their **cuarto ideal**. (Here's an example using the tune of **La bamba: En mi cuarto hay mesas, tengo yo una cama, una ventana, una lámpara grande.**)

ASÍ SE DICE   Saying what's in your room

To find out what there is in someone's room, ask:

To answer, say:

¿Qué hay en tu cuarto?

Tengo una mesa y dos sillas **en mi cuarto.** *I have a table and two chairs in my room.*

¿Qué hay en el cuarto de Paco? *What is there in Paco's room?*

Hay libros y cuadernos **en su cuarto.** *There are books and notebooks in his room.*

¿Tienes un televisor? *Do you have a TV set?*

No, **no tengo** televisor.

¿Qué tiene Merche **en su cuarto?** *What does Merche have in her room?*

Merche **tiene** unos carteles y una radio **en su cuarto.**

---

19 ¿Qué hay?   Script and answers on p. 57E

CD 2 Tr. 5

First read the list of items below. Then, listen as Julio describes what's in his room. Julio has more than one of some items. Use the list to help you write the four items he says he has several of. For each of the four items you have listed, write how many he has.

1. una cama
2. una mesa
3. un reloj
4. una silla
5. una revista
6. una lámpara
7. un escritorio
8. una radio
9. un armario
10. un cartel

tres revistas

20 En la sala de clase

Which of the things in Débora's room on page 75 are also found in your classroom?

hay	no hay
una ventana	un armario

Answers on p. 57K

21 Describir el cuarto

 Look at the drawing on page 75. With your partner, take turns telling him or her how many of each item Débora has in her room. Find four items that she has in her room. Start with **En el cuarto de Débora hay...** or **Débora tiene...** Your partner should also find four different items to tell you about.

Answers on p. 57K

VOCABULARIO

EXTRA

el estéreo   *stereo*
el teléfono   *telephone*
la videocasetera   *VCR*

ADDITIONAL PRACTICE
21 Display Teaching Transparency 2-2 to give students more practice saying what's in a room.

SLOWER PACE
22 Pair students with different abilities beforehand. Have one student write what the other one dictates.

VISUAL LEARNERS
Have students draw a floor plan of their **cuarto ideal**, including images of the things that are in it. Their plans should be large, labeled, and in color. As a challenge, have them present their plan to the class and describe what's in the room.

22 Un cuarto perfecto

Look at the photo of this bedroom. Imagine that it's your room and write a sentence describing it. Begin your description with **En mi cuarto hay...**   Answers will vary. Possible answers below:

En mi cuarto hay una cama, una radio, muchos
carteles, una ventana y un reloj.

GRAMÁTICA

Agreement of mucho and cuánto with nouns

1. Many nouns and adjectives have the following endings:

	SINGULAR	PLURAL
MASCULINE	-o	-os
FEMININE	-a	-as

pp. 20–21
Acts. 11–13

p. 15
Acts. 13

Making the endings of adjectives and nouns match is called *agreement in gender* (masculine/feminine) and *number* (singular/plural).

2. **¿Cuánto?** and **¿Cuánta?** mean *how much?* **¿Cuántos?** and **¿Cuántas?** mean *how many?* Like other adjectives, **¿cuánto?** matches the noun it describes.

   ¿Cuántas carpetas necesitas?
   ¿Cuántos bolígrafos?
   ¿Cuánto papel?
   ¿Cuánta tarea tienes?

3. The forms of **mucho** mean *a lot, much,* or *many*. Like **cuánto, mucho** changes to match the noun it modifies.

   No necesito muchas carpetas, pero necesito muchos bolígrafos.
   Tengo mucha tarea.

23 ¿Cuántas cosas tengo?

Patricia has just moved to a new town, and her classmate David wants to know more about her. Complete their conversation using forms of **cuánto** and **mucho**.

DAVID   ¿Te gusta el colegio? ¿___1___ clases tienes? Cuántas ¿Hay mucha tarea?

PATRICIA   Me gusta el colegio. Tengo siete clases y sí, ¡hay ___2___ tarea! mucha

DAVID   ¿Te gusta tu cuarto? ¿Hay ___3___ ventanas? muchas

PATRICIA   No hay ___4___ ventanas. Sólo *(only)* hay una. muchas

DAVID   ¿___5___ carteles hay? ¿Y cuántos libros tienes? Cuántos

PATRICIA   Tengo muchos carteles y ___6___ libros. Pero David... muchos no tengo ___7___ amigos. muchos

DAVID   Ay, Patricia... ¡yo soy tu amigo!

24 David y Patricia

Now try acting out the roles of Patricia and David. Use the dialogue from the previous activity as a script.

25 Comparación de cuartos

Work with a partner. Imagine that one of you is staying in the **Hotel Dineral** and the other is staying in the **Hotel Pocovale**. Pretend that you're talking to each other on the telephone, comparing your rooms. Tell your partner four things that are in your room, then list four things that are not there. *Answers in side column*

MODELO   —En mi cuarto hay dos camas.
　　　　　—No tengo televisor.

Hotel Dineral

Hotel Pocovale

Nota cultural

In Spanish-speaking countries, it's common for people to use many expressions in addition to hand gestures. There are a variety of ways that people say they like something a lot, such as **¡Genial!**, **¡Increíble!** or **¡Qué padre!** If they think something is all right, they might say **Está bien.** If people think something is terrible they might use expressions such as **¡Qué horrible!**, **¡Qué pesado!** or **¡Pésimo!** What expressions do you and your friends use to show that you like something a lot or think something is terrible?

¡Esta música es genial!

CAPÍTULO 2

LANGUAGE NOTE
25 Point out that when saying, "There isn't a . . . ," the indefinite article is often omitted: **No hay televisor.**

CULTURE NOTE
Additional phrases for expressing that something is impressive include **¡Qué chévere!** (Venezuela), **¡Fenomenal! ¡Bárbaro!** (Spain), **¡Bacán!** (Peru and Ecuador).

Answers to Activity 25
Answers will vary. Possible answers:

Hotel Pocovale
1. En mi cuarto hay un teléfono, pero no hay una radio.
2. En mi cuarto hay una ventana grande.
3. Tengo dos lámparas.
4. Tengo una silla pero no tengo una mesa.

Hotel Dineral
1. En mi cuarto tengo una mesa y cuatro sillas.
2. En mi cuarto no hay una radio, pero tengo un televisor.
3. En mi cuarto hay una cama grande, pero no tengo videocasetera.

STANDARDS: 1.1, 2.1, 4.1   **79**

26 La sala de clase ideal

Work with two classmates to find out what items would be in the ideal classroom. List at least six items. Be prepared to tell the class what kind of classroom your group would have.

MODELO   En la sala ideal de mi grupo (*my group*) hay...

Answers in side column

una pecera

una planta

un videojuego

VOCABULARIO
EXTRA

un disco compacto   *C D*
un estante   *bookshelf*
una pecera   *fish bowl*
una planta   *plant*
un tocador de discos compactos   *C D player*
un videojuego   *videogame*

un disco compacto

un tocador de discos compactos

¿Te acuerdas?

Look on pages 65 and 75 for more ideas of what to put in your ideal classroom. See also additional vocabulary on pages 275–280.

un estante

Robertín

Rosa

Magdalena

27 ¿Quién es?

With a partner, make a list with three columns. At the top of the columns, write the names **Rosa, Robertín,** and **Magdalena.** Then decide which person in the photos is best described by each statement and write the number of the sentence in that column. Choose the answer you think is best.   Answers will vary. Possible answers:

1. Tengo catorce años.
2. Tengo un diccionario inglés-español.
3. Tengo cinco años.
4. Necesito una mochila.
5. Tengo ocho años.
6. Tengo una calculadora.
7. En mi cuarto, hay una muñeca *(a doll)*.
8. Quiero un teléfono en mi cuarto.
9. Tengo lápices de color.

Rosa	Robertín	Magdalena
3, 7, 9	4, 5	1, 2, 6, 8

28 El cuarto de mis sueños

Choose a photo or drawing of your ideal room from a magazine, or draw a room yourself. Then write a description of it, including how many of various things you have.

MODELO En mi cuarto ideal hay dos carteles...   Answers will vary.
Possible answer:
En mi cuarto ideal hay un televisor,
un estéreo y treinta discos compactos...

Try making Spanish labels for things you use every day at school and at home (your school supplies, things in your room, etc.). This way, every time you look at an item you'll be reminded of how to say it in Spanish. And don't forget to include **el** and **la** to remind you of which words are masculine and which ones are feminine.

SEGUNDO PASO

ochenta y uno **81**

CAPÍTULO 2

AUDITORY LEARNERS
27 Convert this into a listening activity by having students cover up the sentences in the book while you read them aloud.

☀ CLOSE

To review the material introduced in this **paso**, use Teaching Transparencies 2-B and 2-2. Have students identify new vocabulary as you point to it, asking **¿Qué es esto?, ¿Qué hay en el cuarto?, ¿Tiene un televisor?**, and so on.

☀ ASSESS

▸ Testing Program, pp. 21–22
Quiz 2-2
Audio CD 2, Tr. 18

▸ Grammar and Vocabulary Quizzes
Quiz 2-2A or
Alternative Quiz 2-2A

▸ Alternative Assessment Guide, p. 20

PERFORMANCE ASSESSMENT
Divide students into groups of three. Assign or let students choose these roles: librarian, scribe, proofreader. The librarian looks up words as needed, the scribe writes the description, and the proofreader checks for accuracy. Give each group a picture of a bedroom cut from a magazine. After discussing the things in the picture, each groups writes a description of the room based on their discussion. All members of a group receive the same grade.

STANDARDS: 1.1, 1.2, 1.3, 5.1   **81**

VIDEO INTEGRATION

Adelante LEVEL 1A
Video Program
Videocassette 1, 38:12–41:13

¡Ven conmigo! LEVEL 1
DVD Tutor, Disc 1

TEACHER NOTES

- See *Video Guide* for suggestions on different ways to use this versatile resource in the classroom and for activities related to the **Panorama cultural**.

- Remind students that cultural material may be included in the Quizzes and Chapter Test.

- The language of the people interviewed represents informal, unrehearsed speech. Occasionally, text has been edited for clarity.

MOTIVATING ACTIVITY

Using the new vocabulary from Chapter 2, have students list the supplies necessary for school. Write their suggestions on the board or on a transparency.

Panorama cultural

CD 2
Trs. 6–9

¿Qué necesitas para el colegio?

In this chapter, we asked some people what they need to buy before the school year starts.

What does Héctor say he needs for school? What does he already have?

● Héctor
Ciudad de México, México
CD 2 Tr. 8

[Necesito] un uniforme. Lo que tengo es un diccionario, ...un cuaderno, un marcador color verde, un lápiz y una pluma.

Bárbara likes to shop at the mall for school supplies. Is this similar to how you get ready to go back to school? What does she need to buy?

● Bárbara
Sevilla, España
CD 2 Tr. 7

Necesito comprar una mochila, unos colores, ...dos bolígrafos, un sacapuntas y unas tijeras.

Do you buy any of the same supplies that Jorge does?

Jorge

San Antonio, Texas CD 2 Tr. 9

Normalmente tengo que comprar una mochila, cuadernos, también bolígrafos, lápices y una carpeta... mi libro de francés... y también mi calculadora gráfica.

1 What does Héctor wear to school? a uniform

2 How many things does Héctor have to write with? What are they? three: a marker, a pencil, and a pen

3 How does Bárbara carry her school supplies? a backpack

4 Bárbara mentions having to buy **colores** and **tijeras** *(scissors)*. What class does she probably have? art

5 What language class does Jorge have? French

6 What tells you that Jorge takes math? calculator

Para pensar y hablar... Answers will vary.
A. What supplies do you need to buy for school? Are they the same as those mentioned by Bárbara, Héctor, and Jorge? Explain.
B. Héctor mentions having to buy a uniform. Design your ideal school uniform. What would it look like?

Cuaderno para hispanohablantes, p. 10

PRESENTATION
Have students watch the video without looking at the written interview. Have them recall the supplies that they heard named. Check the items off the list from the Motivating Activity. Then have students read the interviews while listening to the videotape a second time and check the answers that were given.

CULTURE NOTE
Schools in Latin American countries often don't provide as many materials as schools in the United States do. For example, you might point out that many schools in Spain and Latin America require uniforms and that often the students must purchase them. It's common for students to have to purchase their books because schools don't always provide them.

CHALLENGE
Play the interviews and have students listen for words they don't recognize. See if it's clear to them what **marcador, tijeras,** and **sacapuntas** are.

STANDARDS: 1.2, 2.1, 3.2, 4.2 **83**

VIDEO INTEGRATION

Adelante LEVEL 1A
Video Program
Videocassette 1, 24:35–25:36 OR
Videocassette 3, 10:59–12:00
(captioned version)

¡Ven conmigo! LEVEL 1
DVD Program, Disc 1

Bell work
Display Teaching Transparency 2-2. Give students five minutes to describe the room, listing as many items as they can.

☀ MOTIVATE

Ask students to list in English the things they need to do *(make the bed, do the dishes,* etc.), and a list of things they want to do *(watch a movie, go out for lunch,* etc.)

TERCER PASO Storytelling Book pp. 7, 8

WV3 SPAIN-2

Talking about what you need and want to do

¿Qué necesita comprar Paco?

29 **Las compras de Paco**

Look at the choices below. Find the four items that Paco can most likely buy at a bookstore. unos libros, unos cuadernos, papel, una mochila

una pizza   un chocolate   papel

unos libros   unas zapatillas de tenis

una mochila   unos cuadernos

ASÍ SE DICE   Talking about what you need and want to do

Acts.
14–15

To find out what someone needs to do, ask:

¿Qué necesitas hacer?

To answer, say:

Necesito organizar mi cuarto.
I need to organize my room.

¿Y qué **necesita** hacer Paco?

Necesita ir a la librería.
He needs to go to the bookstore.

2-3

To find out what someone wants to do, ask:

¿Qué quieres hacer?

No sé, pero no quiero hacer la tarea.
I don't know, but I don't want to do homework.

¿Y qué **quiere hacer** Merche?

Quiere ir a la pizzería.

30 ¿Necesitas o quieres? 🏠

Find Miguel's answer to each of his grandmother's questions.

Preguntas

1. ¿Necesitas cuadernos? c
2. ¿Qué cosas necesitas hacer? b
3. ¿Qué quieres comprar? a
4. ¿Necesitas dinero? d

Respuestas

a. Quiero comprar unas zapatillas de tenis.
b. Necesito organizar mi cuarto.
c. No, no necesito cuadernos.
d. Sí, ¡necesito mucho!

31 Tú y tu abuela

With a partner, act out the roles of a student and his or her grandmother. Use the dialogue from the previous activity. Then switch roles and this time try to use different phrases.

TERCER PASO

ochenta y cinco   **85**

CAPÍTULO 2

☀ TEACH

PRESENTATION

ASÍ SE DICE

Model the expressions in **Así se dice** for correct pronunciation and intonation. Have students repeat after you. Then give them one minute to role-play the first exchange with a partner. After the minute, ask them to report what they found out about their partner using the third person forms as shown in **Así se dice**.

SUGGESTION

31 Check students' answers to Activity 30 before students role-play.

CHALLENGE

To model the concept of first, second, and third person, count off students in groups of three. Have them model the expressions in **Así se dice** according to the following model:

JUAN	María, ¿qué necesita Pablo?
MARÍA	No sé. Pablo, ¿qué necesitas?
PABLO	Necesito un cuaderno.
MARÍA	Juan, Pablo necesita un cuaderno.

STANDARDS: 1.1, 1.2, 5.1   **85**

PRESENTATION

VOCABULARIO

Model the pronunciation of the phrases and have students repeat after you. Then ask the class **¿Necesitas poner la ropa en el armario?** Have the class answer all together first, then call on some individual students. Next practice **¿Quieres ir al centro comercial esta tarde?** and **¿Quieres comprar muchas cosas? ¿Necesitas** muchas cosas o solamente *quieres* muchas cosas? Then have students practice using the new phrases in pairs.

AUDITORY LEARNERS

32 After writing the answers, have students check answers orally in pairs, asking each other what the various people need. (**¿Qué necesita hacer Victoria? Necesita comprar una mochila.**) Ask them how well prepared they think both **Victoria** and **Tomás** are.

Answers to Activity 33

Answers will vary. Possible answers:
1. Necesito organizar mi cuarto.
2. Quiero ir a clase.
3. Necesito comprar un diccionario de español.
4. Quiero encontrar el dinero.
5. Necesito hacer la tarea para mañana.

---

pp. 22–24
Acts. 16–18

GV
p. 16
Act. 14

2-C

VOCABULARIO

Necesito...

poner la ropa en el armario   **encontrar** el dinero primero

Quiero...

ir al centro comercial   **conocer** a muchos nuevos amigos   **comprar** muchas cosas

NOTA GRAMATICAL

Comprar, poner, conocer, and **ir** are infinitives. The infinitive is the form of the verb found in a dictionary. There are three kinds of infinitive endings in Spanish: **-ar, -er,** and **-ir.**

GV
p. 16
Act. 15

---

32 Victoria y Tomás necesitan... Script and answers on p. 57F

CD 2 Tr. 10 First, read the list of things to do. Listen as Victoria lists seven things she and Tomás need to do before Monday. For each item, write **V** if it's something Victoria needs to do, or write **T** if it's something Tomás needs to do. Write **B** if it's something they both need to do.

1. hacer muchas cosas
2. ir al centro comercial
3. comprar una mochila
4. organizar el cuarto
5. encontrar la mochila
6. poner la ropa en el armario
7. hacer la tarea

33 Mis planes

Write five sentences telling what you plan to do this week. Use verbs from the first column with phrases from the second. Start each sentence with **Necesito...** or **Quiero...** Compare your sentences with a partner's.
Answers in side column

poner
hacer
comprar
organizar
ir
encontrar

mi cuarto
a clase
la tarea para mañana
el dinero
un diccionario de español
mi libro en la mochila

34 Problemas

The following people need your help. Write what each person needs to do, wants to buy, or where each one needs to go. Use as many new expressions as you can.   Answers on p. 57K

MODELO   Mingo's clothes are scattered all over his room.
   Necesita poner la ropa en el armario.

1. Juanita never knows what time it is.
2. Isabel can't find tomorrow's homework in her cluttered room.
3. Rafael is trying to build his vocabulary for Spanish class.
4. Diego is out of pens, pencils, and paper.
5. Inés is new in town and feeling lonely.
6. María doesn't have enough clothes.
7. Jorge's room is too dark.
8. Adelaida is not prepared for physical education.

35 ¿Qué necesitas hacer?

Work in pairs. Tell your partner what each person in Activity 34 needs to do. Then find out if your partner wants or needs to do the same things. Answer your partner's questions. Switch roles after number four.   Answers on p. 57K

MODELO   —Diego necesita ir a la librería. ¿Y tú? ¿Quieres ir a la librería?
   —Sí, quiero ir a la librería. Necesito cuadernos.

36 El anuncio

Work with your group to design an ad for school supplies. Have a member of your group draw a picture of the product. Then label your product and write the price. Share your ad with the class.

reglas $3.50

SUGGESTION

35 Have students imagine that they're getting ready to go back to school. Ask them **¿Necesitas comprar muchas cosas?** If they answer **sí,** then ask **¿Qué necesitas comprar?** If they answer **no,** ask them **¿Qué tienes ya?** Next have them imagine that they're packing their backpacks the night before school starts. Ask **¿Qué necesitas poner en la mochila?**

ADDITIONAL PRACTICE

The packing activity from **Suggestion** (above) can be used in groups of two to four, with one student asking questions and the others answering. The role of questioner alternates.

KINESTHETIC LEARNERS

Prepare a set of cards with vocabulary and expressions from **Así se dice** as well as some with punctuation marks written on them. Have students line up in order to form sentences according to cues you call out. (Example: You say, **"No tengo papel."** Students line up to form the sentence **Necesitas comprar papel.**)

PA p. 22 Act. 19

VOCABULARIO

¿Cuánto es en dólares?

GV p. 17 Acts. 16–17

31	treinta y uno	**40**	cuarenta	**101**	ciento uno
32	treinta y dos	**50**	cincuenta	**102**	ciento dos
33	treinta y tres	**60**	sesenta	**103**	ciento tres
34	treinta y cuatro	**70**	setenta		...
35	treinta y cinco	**80**	ochenta		...
36	treinta y seis	**90**	noventa		...
...		**100**	cien	**199**	ciento noventa y nueve

Uno at the end of a number changes to **un** before a masculine noun and **una** before a feminine noun: **veintiún dólares** *(dollars)*, **veintiuna pesetas**.

---

37 **¿Cuánto tienes?**

Indicate how much money you have, using the Spanish words for the numbers.

MODELO (38 euros)

—Tengo treinta y ocho euros.

Answers in side column

① **②** **③**

88 *ochenta y ocho*

CAPÍTULO 2 ¡Organízate!

38 ¿Cuántos años tiene?

Write a sentence giving the ages of the following people, following the **Modelo**. If you don't know, you'll have to ask! If you can't ask, just guess.   Answers will vary.

MODELO   your uncle
Él tiene treinta y dos años.

1. your parent or guardian
2. your principal
3. the person sitting next to you
4. a TV star
5. the President
6. a grandparent or elderly person
7. the person in your family nearest your age
8. your favorite singer or musician

39 En mi cuaderno

Do you need to get more organized? In your journal, write a paragraph about what you need to do this week. Include at least four things you need to do and where you need to go.

LETRA Y SONIDO

Script on p. 57F

CD 2
Trs. 11–15

A. The letter **d** in Spanish represents two possible pronunciations.

1. At the very beginning of a phrase, or after an *l* or *n*, it sounds like the *d* in the English word *did* except with the tip of the tongue closer to the back of the teeth.

dinero   diez   diccionario   dar   andar   dónde   el día   falda

2. Anywhere else in the word or phrase (especially between vowels) its pronunciation is softened and is similar to the *th* in the English word *they*.

qué día   cerdo   modo   cada   verdad   estudiar   calculadora

B. Dictado
Adriana is making a shopping list. Complete her list based on what she says.

Tengo...   Necesito...

C. Trabalenguas
Pronounce this tongue twister after your teacher or after the recording.

**Cada dado da dos dedos,
dice el hado, y cada lado
de dos dados, o dos dedos,
da un dos en cada uno de los lados.**

NATIVE SPEAKERS
Have native speakers write the tongue twister in the **Letra y sonido** as you dictate it. After they have finished, ask them to look at the text to correct their work.

☀ CLOSE

Set up a **papelería** in the classroom with a variety of classroom objects "for sale" at various prices. Ask students to take the role of salesclerk and shopper and to practice buying items in the store.

☀ ASSESS

▶ Testing Program, pp. 23–24
  Quiz 2-3
  Audio CD 2, Tr. 19

▶ Grammar and Vocabulary Quizzes
  Quiz 2-3A or
  Alternative Quiz 2-3A

▶ Alternative Assessment Guide, p. 20

PERFORMANCE ASSESSMENT
Write **organizar el cuarto** on a sheet of paper. Students are to describe the steps that need to be accomplished to complete the task. This can be done orally, or in writing.

PRESENTATION

Begin by asking students questions about the United States dollar. What color is it? (green) Are all bills the same color? (yes) Whose pictures are on the various bills? Have they seen the new designs for some of the bills? What do they think of them?

HISTORY LINKS

- **La Reina Isabel** (*Queen Isabella*) of Spain sent the explorer **Cristóbal Colón** (*Christopher Columbus*) west in search of India. Most Europeans didn't know about the American continents until he reached them by sailing west in 1492. Today, the currencies in both Costa Rica and El Salvador are named **colón** in his honor.

- **Sor Juana Inés de la Cruz** (**Juana de Asbaje y Ramírez**) was a very intelligent woman who lived in colonial Mexico. At that time, women were not allowed to attend universities. Juana's mother opposed her desperate plan to go to the university disguised as a man. Because of her passion for learning, Sor Juana abandoned her life in the courts of the Viceroy of Mexico to pursue studies in math, geometry, science, philosophy, and literature as a nun.

LA HISTORIA

1 Las figuras históricas

Many Latin American countries have pictures of important historical figures on their coins and paper bills, just as we have a picture of Abraham Lincoln on the five-dollar U.S. bill. Match the following people in Latin American history to the currencies that were named for them or that carry their pictures.

1. **Lempira,** the chief of the Lenca people, who fought heroically against the Spanish conquerors. c
2. **Sor Juana Inés de la Cruz (Juana de Asbaje),** a nun who was a devoted scholar and poet in seventeenth-century Mexico. b
3. **Francisco Hernández de Córdoba,** a Spanish explorer who founded the colonial cities of Granada and León. a

a. **córdoba:** Nicaragua

b. **peso:** México

c. **lempira:** Honduras

2 ¡Te toca a ti!

Pretend your state is actually a country. Work with a partner to create money for your "country." Include drawings of famous people and symbols that are important in your state. Draw examples of both sides of a coin or the paper money. Present the money you designed to the class. Can your classmates identify your symbols and colors and explain what they mean?

3 De compras *(Shopping)*

In most Spanish-speaking countries you can shop in neighborhood shops that specialize in one type of food or item. Large stores are common in big cities. Smaller shops and open markets are still popular, however, and they're within walking distance from most homes. Imagine you have 1500 **bolívares venezolanos (Bs.)** to spend on fruit at the local fruit stand **(la frutería)**. Answers will vary.

(Bs. 1500)

1. Decide which kinds of fruit to buy.
2. Calculate how much change you will get back.
3. Where would you go to buy fruit in your hometown?

Bs. 400

Bs. 230

el mango

la papaya

Bs. 500

Bs. 370

La frutería

la sandía

la piña

HISTORY LINK
Simón Bolívar was a leader who helped many regions of South America win their independence from Spain. The **bolívar** is the national currency in Venezuela and the **boliviano** is the monetary unit of Bolivia.

MATH LINK
Have students look up exchange rates for the Mexican **peso** on the Internet or in a national newspaper. Show them a school supply advertisement from a local newspaper and have them figure out what the school supplies would cost in **pesos**.

CRITICAL THINKING
Remind students that a store that sells paper (**papel**) is called a **papelería**, and that a store that sells books (**libros**) is called a **librería**. Have students guess what a store is called that sells shoes (**zapatos**), flowers (**flores**), and watches (**relojes**). (**zapatería, florería, relojería**)

⊕ CULTURE NOTE
In many Spanish-speaking countries people grow fruit trees in their backyards. They grow fruits like **mango, guanábana, limón,** and **tamarindo.**

STANDARDS: 2.2, 3.1   **91**

READING STRATEGY
Using pictures, titles, and subtitles before reading.

☀ PREREADING

MOTIVATING ACTIVITY
Ask students to brainstorm the names of any books and movies from other countries that they might be familiar with.

☀ READING

TEACHING SUGGESTION
C Ask students to choose three of the items. What kinds of people would like these as gifts? (**50 cosas que los niños pueden hacer para salvar la tierra:** people who are interested in nature, animals, oceans, recycling)

CRITICAL THINKING
Ask students what they think they could learn from each of the items. Other than what the titles say, what information might be included?

Answers to C
1. Los dinosaurios; su descubrimiento
2. Enciclopedia ilustrada de los animales
3. Mundo marino
4. Las nuevas aventuras de Mofli

VAMOS A LEER

Estrategia
Scanning
Look at pictures, titles, and subtitles before you begin to read. Also look for other words that "stand out" (bold or large print). By looking at these first, you can often tell what a passage is about without reading every word.

Portadas
A trip to the bookstore to buy school supplies is also a good opportunity to browse through some other interesting and fun items.

¿Te acuerdas?

Remember the strategy you learned in Chapter 1. **Use cognates to figure out meaning.**

¡A comenzar!
A Look at the photos and titles on the next page. Are these items . . .?
1. advertisements no
2. movie reviews no
3. books and video tapes yes
4. posters no

B By looking at just the photos and drawings on the covers, can you tell which item is about . . .?
1. the environment
2. kids on an island
3. life in the ocean

1. 50 cosas que los niños pueden hacer para salvar la Tierra
2. La isla del terror
3. Mundo marino

Al grano
Now take a little more time and look at the words in bold print.

C Which item would you buy as a gift for each of these people? Remember to rely only on photos and drawings, titles, and subtitles!

For someone who . . .
1. is interested in dinosaurs
2. likes animals
3. wants to be a marine biologist
4. likes to watch cartoons on TV
Answers in side column

D Now read the information accompanying each picture and answer the questions.
1. Look at the *Enciclopedia ilustrada de los animales.* Is the book illustrated? Is it in color? Write the cognates that told you this.
2. Look at *50 cosas que los niños pueden hacer para salvar la Tierra.* What's this book about? How do you know?
3. Look at *Mundo Marino.* This item isn't a book. What cognate tells you what it is?

1. Yes, the book is illustrated and is in color. The cognates are *ilustrada* and *color*.
2. The book is about 50 things that children can do to save the Earth. The number 50, the picture of the planet Earth, and the English phrase, *The earth works group* provide the clues.
3. Video.

Educar para el futuro. ▶
50 COSAS QUE LOS NIÑOS PUEDEN HACER PARA SALVAR LA TIERRA
The earth works group.
Ed Emecé.

▲ **LOS DINOSAURIOS. SU DESCUBRIMIENTO.**
Transportados en la máquina del tiempo.
METROVIDEO.

◀ Mamíferos, aves, reptiles, anfibios y peces son los protagonistas de esta enciclopedia compuesta por tres tomos y magníficamente ilustrada.
ENCICLOPEDIA ILUSTRADA DE LOS ANIMALES
Ed. Everest

BILLIKEN PRESENTA: MUNDO MARINO
Video documental filmado en el oceanario de San Clemente del Tuyú.
ATLÁNTIDA ◀

▲ **LA ISLA DEL TERROR**
Autor: Tony Koltz
Ilustró: Ron Wing

LAS NUEVAS AVENTURAS DE MOFLI
GATIVIDEO
Dibujos animados.
Doblada al español.
Duración: 90 minutos.

Cuaderno para hispanohablantes, pp. 6–8

☀ POSTREADING

SUGGESTION
Ask students to think about their favorite book. What is the title? What do they like about the book? Can they tell from the title what the book is about?

NATIVE SPEAKERS
Ask native speakers to bring in a favorite Spanish language book or video. You may want to preview the materials that students bring in for age-appropriate content. See if non-native speakers can determine what it is about by reading the title. Then ask native speakers to describe its contents and why they like it.

The **Repaso** reviews and integrates all four skills and culture in preparation for the Chapter Test.

ADDITIONAL PRACTICE

1 After they complete the first activity, have students pair up. Students should list five items they need including how many of each without discussing it with the partner. After completing their lists, one partner reads his or her list aloud. The other partner should listen and write down the items mentioned. Then, the student who read aloud should check the answers. After checking the answers students should switch roles.

📁 PORTFOLIO

2 **Written** Suggest that students write a paragraph about a member of their own family or a fictional family using vocabulary and functions learned in this chapter. A complete paragraph should include the following: what the person likes, what he or she needs or wants to buy, and places he or she needs or wants to go. For Portfolio suggestions, see the *Alternative Assessment Guide*, page 13.

REPASO

MARCAR: go.hrw.com
PALABRA CLAVE:
WV3 SPAIN-2

Script and answers on p. 57F

1 Imagine that it's the first day of school and your Spanish teacher is telling you what supplies you will use for the year. Based on what he tells you, how many of each item do you need? Write the numbers as words.

CD 2
Tr. 16

   a. cuaderno   **d.** carpeta

   b. diccionario   **e.** lápiz

   c. bolígrafo   **f.** mochila

2 With a partner, look at the photos and match each statement below to the person who made it. Make up a description for the remaining photo.

   1. Tengo veintiocho años. Me gusta la música clásica y tengo muchos discos compactos. ¿Quién soy? d

   2. Me gusta ir al centro comercial. Necesito zapatillas de tenis. Tengo quince años. ¿Quién soy? c

   3. Me gusta ir al centro comercial. Necesito un libro, pero primero necesito encontrar mi dinero. Tengo cuarenta años. ¿Quién soy? b

a

b

c

d

3 It's time to go shopping for school supplies! Write a conversation that you might have with a parent. Say two things you want and two things you need. Imagine what the parent would say to answer. Write at least four lines for each character. Be sure to use **quiero** and **necesito**. Answers will vary.

4 Your homeroom class has raised $150 for improvements to the local community center. You and your partner should each write a list of items you want to buy. Tell your partner how you would spend the money. Start your sentence with **Quiero comprar…** Work together to produce one list that includes items from both lists. Answers will vary.

una silla	$10.00	un cartel	$3.00	una radio	$40.00
una mesa	$20.00	un voleibol	$15.00	un reloj	$20.00
una lámpara	$15.00	un televisor	$100.00		

5 What would Enrique, a 13-year-old living in Spain, do to greet his uncle? What would Alicia, an 11-year-old living in Paraguay, do to greet a friend?
Enrique will give his uncle a hug. Alicia would kiss her friend once on the cheek.

6 **S I T U A C I Ó N**

Get together with two or three classmates. Imagine that you're students from different Spanish-speaking countries, with new names and ages. Introduce yourself to the group in Spanish. Ask your partners questions about where they're from, what things they have in their room, what they like and don't like, and what they want to do this weekend.

Cuaderno para hispanohablantes, p. 9

PAIR WORK
3 After they create their individual written dialogues, have students pair up. One partner takes the role of the student and the other of the parent. The partners choose which dialogue to perform first. After performing the first partner's dialogue, they switch roles and perform the other one.

VISUAL LEARNERS
4 Have students list the items before beginning this activity. If possible, label items in the classroom with prices.

CHALLENGE
In pairs, each student thinks of two things he or she needs and a reason why it might be difficult to get. Students describe the problem and what they need using chapter vocabulary. (**No tengo dinero. Necesito un cuaderno.**) The partner should then offer a solution, also using the phrases and vocabulary from the chapter. (**Necesitas ir al banco. Necesitas comprar un cuaderno.**) After one partner has presented two problems and the other has presented two solutions, have students switch roles.

A VER SI PUEDO...

WV3 SPAIN-2

▼ **Can you talk about what you want and need?** p. 66

1 How would you ask these students if they need the items listed? How would the students answer? Answers on p. 57K

MODELO Adriana / some pencils (no)
Adriana, ¿necesitas unos lápices?
No, no necesito lápices.

1. Juanita / some pens and paper (sí)
2. Paco / a calculator (no)
3. Felipe / some notebooks (sí)

2 Tomorrow is the first day of class. Ask a friend how much or how many he or she needs of each item. How would your friend answer? Answers on p. 57K

1. paper
2. books
3. rulers
4. notebooks
5. folders
6. pencils

▼ **Can you say what's in your room?** p. 76

3 1. Describe your ideal room and include the items pictured below. Answers on p. 57K
2. You want to ask a friend if he or she has these items in his or her room. Write the question you would use.

▼ **Can you talk about what you need and want to do?** p. 85

4 Paco isn't very well prepared for the first day of class. How would you say he needs to do the following things? How would you say you want to do the same things? Answers on p. 57K

1. to straighten up his room
2. to put his tennis shoes in the closet
3. to buy some notebooks
4. to meet some new friends
5. ¿?

VOCABULARIO

PRIMER PASO

Talking about what you want and need

el bolígrafo *ballpoint pen*
Bueno... *Well . . .*
la calculadora *calculator*
la carpeta *folder*
el colegio *high school*
el cuaderno *notebook*
el diccionario *dictionary*
él *he*
ella *she*
la goma de borrar *eraser*
el lápiz *pencil*
la librería *bookstore*
el libro *book*
la mochila *book bag, back-pack*
necesita *he/she needs*
necesitar *to need*
necesitas *you need*
necesito *I need*
el papel *paper*
querer (ie) *to want*
quiere *he/she wants*
quieres *you want*
quiero *I want*
la regla *ruler*
un *a, an* (masc. sing.)
una *a, an* (fem. sing.)
unas *some, a few* (fem. pl.)
unos *some, a few* (masc. pl.)
ya *already*

SEGUNDO PASO

Saying what's in your room

el armario *closet*
la cama *bed*
el cartel *poster*
¿cuánto/a? *how much?*
¿cuántos/as? *how many?*
el cuarto *room*
el escritorio *desk*
hay *there is, there are*
la lámpara *lamp*
la mesa *table*
mi *my*
mucho/a *a lot (of); a lot*
muchos/as *many, a lot of*
la puerta *door*
¿Qué hay en... *What's in . . .?*
la radio *radio*
el reloj *clock; watch*
la revista *magazine*
la ropa *clothing*
la silla *chair*
su *his; her*
el televisor *TV set*
tener (ie) *to have*
tengo *I have*
tiene *he/she has*
tienes *you have* (familiar)
tu *your* (familiar)
la ventana *window*
las zapatillas
  de tenis *tennis shoes* (Spain)

TERCER PASO

Talking about what you need and want to do

el centro
  comercial *shopping mall*
comprar *to buy*
conocer *to get to know* (someone)
la cosa *thing*
el dinero *money*
el dólar *dollar*
encontrar (ue) *to find*
hacer *to do, to make*
ir *to go*
No sé. *I don't know.*
nuevos amigos *new friends*
organizar *to organize*
la pizzería *pizzeria*
poner *to put*
primero *first*

Numbers 31–199
See p. 88

ADDITIONAL PRACTICE

(TPR) Call out school items and have students hold them up as you say them. Start out by holding up a book and say, "**¡Libro!**" Move on to holding up other objects.

CHAPTER 2 ASSESSMENT

▶ **Testing Program**
Chapter Test, pp. 25–32
Audio Compact Discs, CD 2, Trs. 20–21
Speaking Test, p. 112

▶ **Alternative Assessment Guide**
Performance Assessment, p. 20
Portfolio Assessment, p. 13
CD-ROM Assessment, p. 27

▶ **Interactive CD-ROM Tutor, Disc 1**
¡A hablar!
¡A escribir!

▶ **Standardized Assessment Tutor**
Chapter 2

▶ **One-Stop Planner, Disc 1**
Test Generator
Chapter 2

STANDARDS: 1.2, 5.1   97

¡Ven conmigo a México!

LOCATION OPENER CHAPTERS 3, 4

PRINT

MEDIA

Video Guide Level 1A
- Activity Masters and Suggestions, pp. 18–19

Video Program Level 1A
Videocassette 1

Interactive CD-ROM Tutor
Disc 1

go.hrw.com
WV3 MEXICO

¡Ven conmigo! Level 1
DVD Tutor, Disc 1

You may wish to point out the following images as students view the México Location Opener. These images will be seen on both the Video Program and the DVD Program. If you are using the DVD Program they may be freeze-framed for presentation and discussion purposes.

Teotihuacán, which means *the place where people become gods* in Nahuatl, was already an ancient ruin when the Spaniards arrived. According to myth, the gods met here to create the sun and the moon. A huge pyre was built, and the brave god Nanahuatzin threw himself without fear into the fire and became the sun. The god Tecciztecatl, who had boasted of his bravery, hesitated before casting himself into the flames. He became the pale moon.

The two great pyramids—the Pyramid of the Sun (**la pirámide del sol**) and the Pyramid of the Moon (**la pirámide de la luna**)—are the most prominent structures in Teotihuacán. The Pyramid of the Sun stands 215 feet tall. The smaller Pyramid of the Moon is 147 feet tall.

Taxco is a colonial silver-mining town about 70 miles southwest of Mexico City and is the oldest mining town in North America. The entire town was declared a national monument by the Mexican government—making it illegal to construct buildings that are not in the same style as existing ones.

The Central Library of the **Universidad Nacional Autónoma de México** (UNAM) has a stone mosaic designed by Juan O'Gorman in 1950 to symbolize the history of Mexican culture. In the mosaic, O'Gorman used such materials as stone, colored cement, tile, and blown glass.

Mexico has about 6,320 miles (10,170 kms) of coastline. By comparison, the continental United States has only 4,993 miles (8,035 kms). Many Mexican coastal cities such as **Acapulco, Cancún,** and **Puerto Vallarta,** have become important tourist destinations because of their comfortable climates and attractive beaches.

97A LOCATION OPENER CHAPTERS 3, 4

PROJECTS

MAPA DE PRODUCTOS E INDUSTRIAS

This activity introduces students to industries and agricultural products of Mexico that are mentioned in the Almanac Box. Students will produce a map that illustrates the products and their location within Mexico.

Introduction

Mexico is a land rich in natural resources and agricultural products. Talk with students about the importance of natural resources and the development of new industries. Ask students if they know of any major crops that come from Mexico. Ask students if anyone has visited Mexico and has seen the landscape and agriculture. Explain that students will be looking for information about products that come from Mexico and that they will be making a map to illustrate their findings.

Materials students may need

- ◆ Poster board
- ◆ Overhead transparencies
- ◆ Markers—fine and wide tip
- ◆ Transparency pens
- ◆ Rulers, pencils

Sequence

1 Divide students into groups of four. Within each group, assign the roles of Librarian, Cartographer, Researcher, and Reporter.

2 Groups draw a map outline of Mexico. They produce a list of agricultural products and locate on the map where they are grown. Students list natural resources of Mexico that have contributed to the growth of industry and illustrate them on the map.

3 The group Librarian is in charge of getting materials for the group; The Cartographer is in charge of drawing the outline map; the Researcher is in charge of researching and illustrating products mentioned in the Almanac on page 99; and the Reporter explains the findings to the class.

4 Groups may produce overhead transparencies to teach the class. Other groups may produce large posters that can be displayed in the classroom and later used as a teaching tool and a reference to the economy of Mexico.

Grading the project

Suggested point distribution (total = 100 points):

Map	30
Content	30
Oral presentation	30
Group effort	10

¡Ven conmigo a México!
LOCATION OPENER CHAPTERS 3, 4 (cont.)

Using the Map

Refer students to the map of Mexico on page xxii to answer the following questions.

1 Have students point out countries that border Mexico. (the United States, Guatemala, Belize)

2 Have students point out **el D.F.** (**Teotihuacán** is about 30 miles from **el D.F.**)

3 Have students locate **Monterrey,** an important industrial center.

4 Have students locate **Guadalajara,** an important agricultural and industrial center.

5 Have students locate **Acapulco, Cozumel, Mazatlán,** and **Puerto Vallarta.** Ask if they have visited these popular places.

HISTORY LINK

According to legend, the god Huitzilopochtli told the Aztecs to establish their capital, **Tenochtitlán,** where they saw an eagle perched on a cactus with a serpent in its mouth. They saw this on an island in the middle of Lake Texcoco, a large salt lake surrounded by volcanic peaks. Some parts of Tenochtitlán, now Mexico City, were built on artificial garden-islands known as **chinampas,** which also provided much of the city's food supply. The Spanish conquerors were astounded at how developed Tenochtitlán was and took over the city for their own capital. Ask students to say where there is a famous salt lake in the United States. (Utah)

Culture Notes

El día de las madres (el 10 de mayo), in Mexico is a day the entire extended family comes together to celebrate. Family members serenade the mother from beneath her window in the early hours of the morning. They sing **Madrecita querida** and other songs honoring mothers. The mother also receives flowers and presents from her children and grandchildren. The family eats a late afternoon meal called a **merienda,** including dishes like **mole de pollo** or **mole de puerco con arroz y frijoles.**

Guadalajara is the lively capital of Jalisco. It's famous for preserving its traditional Mexican culture of **mariachis,** folk dances, and Orozco murals. José Clemente Orozco, a famous Mexican muralist, was born in Guadalajara, and he painted several huge murals on buildings in his home town.

Geography Link

Tell students that many buildings in Mexico City are very slowly sinking because the Spanish built Mexico City over the Aztec city, **Tenochtitlán,** which had been constructed on artificial islands on Lake Texcoco. The Spanish drained the lake, and Mexico City expanded out onto the flat plains, which had formerly been a muddy lake bed. As the city's population grew, and as more water was taken from wells, the ground underneath some parts of the city became compressed. As a result, many buildings have begun to sink. The soft soils of the former lake bed are especially unstable during earthquakes. This is why destruction from earthquakes can be so dramatic in Mexico City.

You may wish to have students do the above map activities using the Atlas Interactivo Mundial at **go.hrw.com.**

go.hrw.com — MAPQUEST.COM

Multicultural Link

Explain to students the difference between the Egyptian pyramids and those in the Americas. In the Americas, pyramids have steps, flat tops, and were used as temples. In Egypt, they have smooth sides, pointed tops, and were used as tombs and monuments.

ART LINK

Ask students if they know what a mural is. (a large picture painted on a wall or a ceiling) Can they describe a mosaic? (pictures or designs made by inlaying small bits of colored stone, glass, tile, etc., in mortar) Who are some famous Mexican muralists? (Diego Rivera, José Clemente Orozco, David Siqueiros)

Multicultural Link

The Olmecs are noted for their contribution to the development of the calendar. Ask students what other ancient cultures developed calendars. (Egyptian, Babylonian, Roman, Arabs, Aztecs, Chinese) Ask them why they think calendars are important. Why do we need calendars?

Critical Thinking

Ask students to think about why most of Latin America is Spanish-speaking. Help them draw a parallel between North and South America. (The British colonized the north; the Spanish, the south.)

Multicultural Link

Ask students if they know about traditional dances from any other country such as Scotland, India, Ghana, or folk dances from the United States.

Critical Thinking

Ask students to compare Chapultepec Park to a park they know. Do both parks have many trees? Are they near water? Do people like to go there to relax? If students don't know of a park, have them go to the library or media center to get information.

SCIENCE LINK

Have students get some information on earthquakes to find out what causes them. Have them find out where in the Americas earthquakes occur. (California, Alaska, Chile, Nicaragua, Costa Rica, etc.) If you live in an area subject to earthquakes, have students review how to prepare for one and what to do if one strikes. Tell students that some words for earthquake in Spanish are **el terremoto, el temblor,** and **el sismo**.

¡Ven conmigo a México!

VIDEO INTEGRATION

Adelante LEVEL 1A
Video Program
Videocassette 1, 42:07–44:38

¡Ven conmigo! LEVEL 1
DVD Tutor, Disc 1

MOTIVATING ACTIVITY

Use Map Transparency 5, **México**, to introduce students to the major regions and cities. Ask if any students have ever been to Mexico. What are the people like? What do they do for entertainment? Do students know anything about the indigenous or native people of Mexico? Have them compare their guesses to what they see in the photographs on pages 98–101.

BACKGROUND INFORMATION

The **jarabe tapatío** is a well-known folk dance of Jalisco, Mexico. It has been called the "Mexican Hat Dance" in English because of the special role of the large **sombreros** that the men wear. In the middle of the dance the men place their **sombreros** on the floor and dance around them with their partners. This is one of many traditional regional dances that are performed by the **Ballet Folklórico.**

98   STANDARDS: 1.1, 1.2, 3.1, 3.2, 5.1

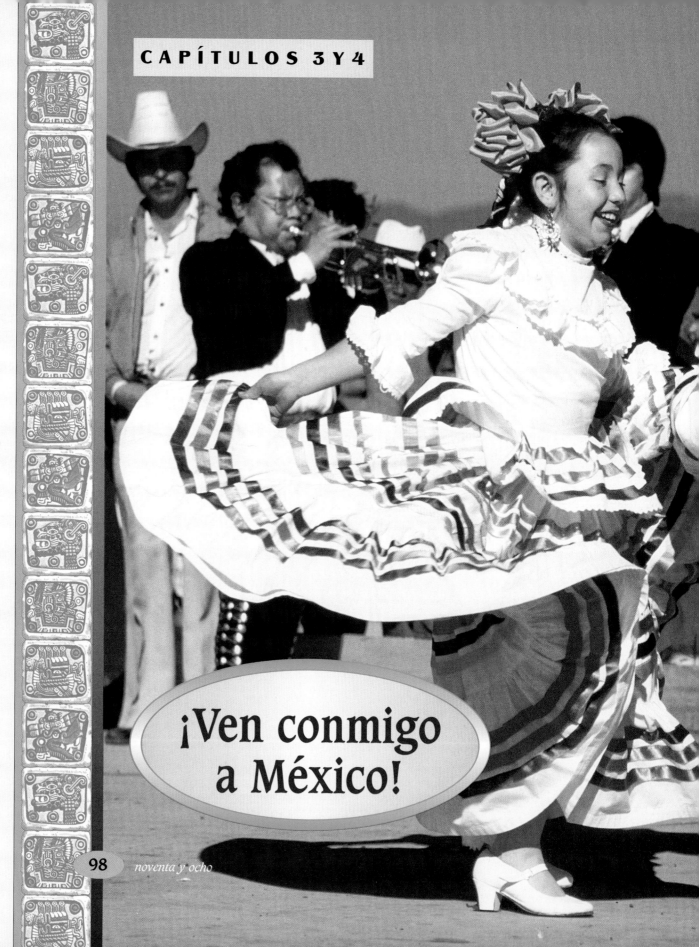

CAPÍTULOS 3 Y 4

¡Ven conmigo a México!

98   *noventa y ocho*

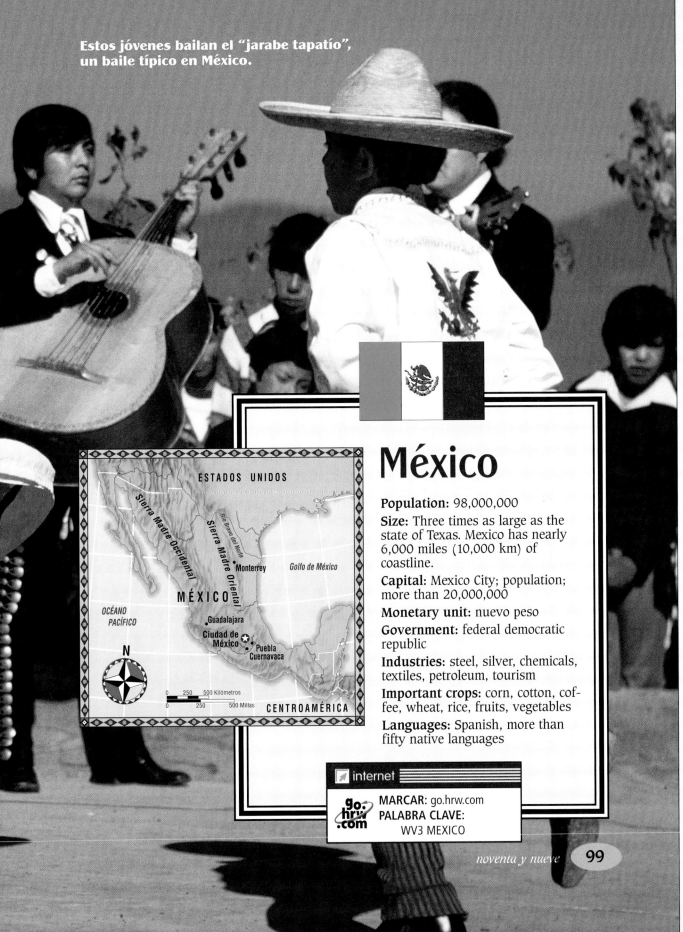

Estos jóvenes bailan el "jarabe tapatío", un baile típico en México.

México

Population: 98,000,000

Size: Three times as large as the state of Texas. Mexico has nearly 6,000 miles (10,000 km) of coastline.

Capital: Mexico City; population; more than 20,000,000

Monetary unit: nuevo peso

Government: federal democratic republic

Industries: steel, silver, chemicals, textiles, petroleum, tourism

Important crops: corn, cotton, coffee, wheat, rice, fruits, vegetables

Languages: Spanish, more than fifty native languages

ESTADOS UNIDOS

Sierra Madre Occidental

Sierra Madre Oriental

Río Bravo del Norte

• Monterrey

Golfo de México

MÉXICO

OCÉANO PACÍFICO

• Guadalajara

Ciudad de México ★ • Puebla
Cuernavaca

N

0   250   500 Kilómetros
0   250   500 Millas

CENTROAMÉRICA

internet

go.hrw.com
MARCAR: go.hrw.com
PALABRA CLAVE:
WV3 MEXICO

 HRW ATLAS INTERACTIVO MUNDIAL

MAPQUEST.COM

Have students go to the interactive atlas at **go.hrw.com** to find out more about the geography of Mexico.

 USING THE ALMANAC

- **La bandera:** The emblem in the center of the flag commemorates the legend of the founding of **Tenochtitlán,** the Aztec capital and the site of present-day Mexico City.

- **Industrias: acero** *steel;* **plata** *silver;* **productos químicos** *chemicals;* **electrodomésticos** *electrical household appliances;* **caucho** *rubber*

- **Cosechas principales: algodón** *cotton;* **café** *coffee;* **trigo** *wheat;* **arroz** *rice;* **caña de azúcar** *sugarcane*

- **Idiomas:** Spanish is the official language of Mexico. The main indigenous languages are **maya, mixteco, náhuatl, otomí, purépecha,** and **zapoteca.**

CNNenEspañol.com

Have students check the CNN en español Web site for news on Spain. The CNN en español site is also a good source of timely, high interest readings for Spanish students.

USING THE PHOTO ESSAY

1 In Oaxaca you can find indigenous black pottery and Spanish-style green-glazed pottery. Also for sale in the **mercados** are weavings, textiles, filigree jewelry, ceramics, sculptures, baskets, and colorful native dresses called **huipiles**. **Oaxaca** is a Zapotec word. The *x* is pronounced like the *x* in **México**.

2 Masks are used for more than just wall decoration in Mexico. They have been used in religious ceremonies since long before the Spanish arrived. Currently, masks are used in many celebrations throughout the year, such as **Carnaval**, **Semana Santa**, and **Corpus Christi**, as well as in local festivals. People use them to act out the stories of the celebrations. Masks are usually made of papier mâché or wood. **Guerrero**, **Oaxaca**, and **Michoacán** are the states where most masks are made.

3 **El Parque de Chapultepec** is a favorite spot for Mexicans, especially on Sunday afternoons. It covers 40 square miles. Chapultepec has an amusement park, three lakes, and eight museums, including the famous **Castillo de Chapultepec**, where the president lived until 1940. In Nahuatl, the language of the Aztecs, **chapultepec** means *grasshopper hill.*

MEXICO

Mexico is a nation rich in natural resources, culture, and history. The diverse population includes indigenous, or native, people and those whose ancestors came from Europe, Africa, the Middle East, and Asia.

▲ **Los mercados de Oaxaca**
The markets of Oaxaca are excellent places to find colorful pottery, weavings, jewelry, ceramics, and baskets.

◄ **Máscaras especiales para las fiestas**
There are many festivals in Mexico. During some festivals, people wear hand-painted masks. What festivals and special community events are there where you live?

El Parque de ► Chapultepec
In Mexico, parks are favorite spots to see friends, get exercise, have a picnic, or read a book. The largest and best known is Chapultepec Park in Mexico City.

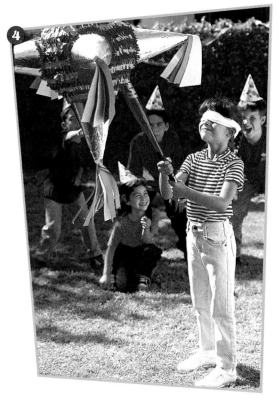

In Chapters 3 and 4 you will meet several students who live in Cuernavaca, the capital of the Mexican state of Morelos. People from all over the world come to Cuernavaca to study Spanish. Young people from Mexico City come to Morelos for fun-filled weekends of water sports, shopping, and visiting historical sites like the *Palacio de Cortés*.

▲ Las piñatas

Piñatas are very popular at children's parties. Piñatas are made of papier mâché and filled with candy.

▲ La charrería

These women are dressed in the typical *amazona* costume worn at Mexican *charrería*, or rodeo, festivals. The biggest rodeo rings in Mexico are in Mexico City and Guadalajara.

ciento uno 101

4 Piñatas are used in a traditional Mexican party game, especially around Christmastime. **Piñatas** are containers in the shape of animals or other figures and are filled with confetti, fruit, nuts, coins, candy, and toys. Blindfolded children take turns hitting the **piñata** with a stick until it breaks open. Then the children rush to catch the **piñata** contents as they fall. Traditionally **piñatas** were made of clay, but now they're usually made of papier mâché.

ART LINK
Have the class get together and make a **piñata** for a classroom celebration.

5 Charreadas are rodeo-like competitions popular in western Mexico. The male horsemen, called **charros,** wear suits made of doeskin or velvet with a short jacket known as a **bolero,** and riding pants with gold or silver buttons down the sides. The **charras** wear a feminine version of the **charro** suit, and the **amazonas** wear long, colorful dresses.

CAPÍTULO

3

Nuevas clases, nuevos amigos
CHAPTER OVERVIEW

De antemano pp. 104–107	*¡Bienvenida al colegio!*

	FUNCTIONS	GRAMMAR	VOCABULARY	RE-ENTRY
Primer paso pp. 108–115	• Talking about classes and sequencing events, p. 110 • Telling time, p. 112	• **Nota gramatical:** Plural definite articles **los** and **las,** p. 109 • **Gramática:** Telling time, p. 113	• School subjects, p. 109	• Present tense of **tener** • Numbers 0–99 • School supplies • Forming questions
Segundo paso pp. 118–123	• Telling at what time something happens, p. 119 • Talking about being late or in a hurry, p. 122	• **Nota gramatical:** The preposition **de,** p. 121	• Time expressions, p. 119	• Present tense of **tener** • Noun-adjective agreement • Forms of **necesitar** and **querer**
Tercer paso pp. 124–133	• Describing people and things, p. 125 • Talking about things you like and explaining why, p. 129	• **Nota gramatical:** The verb **ser,** p. 126 • **Gramática:** Adjective agreement, p. 127 • **Nota gramatical:** Tag questions, p. 131	• Words that describe people and things, p. 125 • Free-time activities and things you like, p. 130	• Talking about likes and dislikes • Question formation with **¿cómo?**

Letra y sonido p. 133	The letters *g*, *h*, and *j*	**Dictado:** Audio CD 3 Tracks 12–16
Enlaces pp. 134–135	Time zones and the 24-hour clock	
Vamos a leer pp. 136–137	**Calificaciones y horarios**	**Reading Strategy:** Using background knowledge
Review pp. 138–141	**Repaso,** pp. 138–139	**A ver si puedo...,** p. 140 **Vocabulario,** p. 141

Culture
- **Nota cultural:** Class schedules, p. 108
- **Nota cultural:** Grades, p. 110
- **Nota cultural:** The **siesta**, p. 115
- **Panorama cultural:** ¿Cómo es un día escolar típico?, pp. 116–117

- **Nota cultural:** Regional vocabulary for objects, p. 121
- **Nota cultural:** Titles of respect, p. 124

Lesson Planning
One-Stop Planner
Lesson Planner with Substitute Teacher
Lesson Plans, pp. 14–18

Listening and Speaking
Listening Activities
- Student Response Forms for Listening Activities, pp. 52–54
- Additional Listening Activities 3-1 to 3-6, pp. 10–12
- Additional Listening Activities (song), p. 13
- Scripts and Answers, pp. 32–34

Video Guide
- Teaching Suggestions, pp. 21–22
- Activity Masters, pp. 23–25
- Scripts and Answers, pp. 53–55, 64

Activities for Communication
- Communicative Activities, pp. 13–18
- Realia and Teaching Suggestions, pp. 48–52
- Situation Cards, pp. 74–75

¡Ven conmigo! Level 1
TPR Storytelling Book, pp. 9–12

Reading and Writing
Reading Strategies and Skills, Chapter 3
¡Lee conmigo! 1, Chapter 3
Practice and Activity Book, pp. 27–38

Grammar
Grammar and Vocabulary Workbook, pp. 18–26

¡Ven conmigo! Level 1
Grammar Tutor for Students of Spanish
Chapter 3

Assessment
Testing Program
- Paso Quizzes and Chapter Test, pp. 37–48
- Score Sheet, Scripts and Answers, pp. 49–54, 121–124
- Midterm Exam, pp. 115–120

Grammar and Vocabulary Quizzes
- Quizzes 3-1A, 3-2A, 3-3A
- Alternative Quizzes 3-1A, 3-2A, 3-3A

Alternative Assessment Guide
- Portfolio Assessment, p. 14
- Performance Assessment, p. 21
- CD-ROM Assessment, p. 28

¡Ven conmigo! Level 1
Standardized Assessment Tutor
- Reading, pp. 9–11
- Writing, p. 12
- Math, pp. 25–26

Native Speakers
¡Ven conmigo! Level 1
Cuaderno para hispanohablantes, pp. 11–15

 Online Activities
- Juegos interactivos
- Actividades internet

 Video Program
- Videocassette 1
- Videocassette 3 *(captioned version)*

 ¡Ven conmigo! Level 1
DVD Tutor, Disc 1

Audio Compact Discs
- Textbook Listening Activities, CD 3, Tracks 1–17
- Additional Listening Activities, CD 3, Tracks 25–30
- Assessment Items, CD 3, Tracks 18–24

 Interactive CD-ROM Tutor, Disc 2
Teaching Transparencies
- Situations 3-1 to 3-3
- Vocabulary 3-A to 3-C
- Grammar and Vocabulary Workbook

 One-Stop Planner CD-ROM

Use the **One-Stop Planner CD-ROM with Test Generator** to aid in lesson planning and pacing.

For each chapter, the **One-Stop Planner** includes:
- Editable lesson plans with direct links to teaching resources
- Printable worksheets from resource books
- Direct launches to the HRW Internet activities
- Video and audio segments
- Test Generator
- Clip Art for vocabulary items

Nuevas clases, nuevos amigos
TECHNOLOGY

DVD/VIDEO

Videocassette 1, Videocassette 3 (captioned version)
DVD Tutor, Disc 1 See Video Guide, pages 19–21.

De antemano • ¡Bienvenida al colegio!

Claudia is starting the year at a new school. She meets the school principal, who introduces her to the students in her first class. While waiting for her teacher to arrive, Claudia talks with her new classmates, Fernando and María Inés. María Inés stands at the front of the class and jokingly begins to imitate the teacher, not realizing that he is standing in the doorway of the classroom.

¿Cómo es un día escolar típico?

Students from Costa Rica, Argentina, Venezuela and other Spanish-speaking countries tell us about their school day.

A continuación

María Inés receives an extra assignment from her teacher. After school, Fernando and María Inés introduce Claudia to some of their friends, including Luis. Claudia, Luis, and María Inés decide to go to the park to buy popsicles.

Videoclips

• **I.C.E.:** advertisement for lower telephone rates during the holidays

INTERACTIVE CD-ROM TUTOR

Activity	Activity Type	Pupil's Edition Page
En contexto	*Interactive conversation*	
1. Así se dice	patas arriba	pp. 110, 112
2. Gramática	¡Super memoria!	p. 113
3. Vocabulario	¡A escoger!	p. 109
4. Así se dice	¿Qué falta?	pp. 119, 120
5. Así se dice	¿Cuál es?	pp. 125, 129
6. Vocabulario	Imagen y sonido ¡Exploremos! ¡Identifiquemos!	p. 125
Panorama cultural	¿Cómo es un día escolar típico?	pp. 116–117
¡A hablar!	*Guided recording*	pp. 138–139
¡A escribir!	*Guided writing*	pp. 138–139

Teacher Management System

Launch the program, type "admin" in the password area and press RETURN. Log on to **www.hrw.com/CDROMTUTOR** for a detailed explanation of the Teacher Management System.

DVD-ROM TUTOR ¡Ven conmigo! Level 1

The *DVD Tutor* contains all material from the Level 1 *Video Program*. Spanish captions are available for use at your discretion for all sections of the video. The *DVD Tutor* also provides a variety of video-based activities that assess students' understanding of the **De antemano, A continuación,** and **Panorama cultural.**

This part of the *DVD Tutor* may be used on any DVD video player connected to a television or video monitor.

In addition to the video material and the video-based comprehension activities, the *DVD Tutor* also contains the entire Level 1 *Interactive CD-ROM Tutor* in DVD-ROM format. Each DVD disc contains the activities from all 12 chapters of the *Interactive CD-ROM Tutor.*

This part of the *DVD Tutor* may be used on a Macintosh® or Windows® computer with a DVD-ROM drive.

To preview all resources available for this chapter, use the **One-Stop Planner CD-ROM,** Disc 1.

internet

MARCAR: go.hrw.com
PALABRA CLAVE:
WV3 MEXICO-3

INTERNET CONNECTION

*Have students explore the **go.hrw.com** Web site for many online resources covering all chapters. All Chapter 3 resources are available under the keyword **WV3 MEXICO-3.** Interactive games help students practice the material and provide them with immediate feedback. You will also find a printable worksheet that provides Internet activities that lead to a comprehensive online research project.*

JUEGOS INTERACTIVO

You can use the interactive activities in this chapter

- to practice grammar, vocabulary, and chapter functions
- as homework
- as an assessment option
- as a self-test
- to prepare for the Chapter Test

ACTIVIDADES INTERNET

Students find out what kinds of classes schools in other countries offer and create a schedule of classes they would take if they were exchange students.

- As preparation for the **Hoja de actividades,** have students review the **Primer paso** or watch the **Panorama cultural** on Videocassette 1 or CD-ROM, Disc 1.
- After completing the activity sheet, ask students to create a schedule for an exchange student coming to their school for a year. Have them include classes and activities offered at their school that they think a foreign student would like.

Proyecto
Have students post the schedule they create for the **Hoja de actividades** on a personal Web site. Ask them to create a link from each class to the page on the Web where they learned about that class. If this is not possible, have students include with each class a list of two things covered in that course. (From the site of a school in Spain, they might find an art class that covers Goya and Velázquez.)

TEXTBOOK LISTENING ACTIVITIES SCRIPTS

For Student Response Forms, see Listening Activities pages 52–54.

PRIMER PASO   pp. 108–115

5 ¡Tenemos la misma clase!   p. 109

— Hola, Lupita. ¿Qué tal?
— Hola, Álvaro. ¿Cómo estás?
— Bien, ¿y tú?
— Bueno, más o menos. Es el primer día de clase y ya tengo mucha tarea.
— ¿Qué clases tienes?
— Tengo ciencias, francés, arte, matemáticas, computación, educación física e historia con el profesor Maldonado. ¿Qué clases tienes tú?
— Yo tengo historia con la profesora Vásquez, álgebra, biología, computación y geografía.
— ¿A qué hora tienes clase de computación?
— A la una menos cinco.
— ¡Qué bien! Estamos en la misma clase, entonces.
— ¡Ay, no, llegamos tarde!
— ¡Vamos!

Answer to Activity 5

They have their computer science (**computación**) class together.

10 El reloj   p. 112

1. — Oye, Bernardo, ¿qué hora es?
   — Son las dos y media.
2. — Bernardo, dime, ¿qué hora es?
   — Son las tres y cuarto.
3. — No tengo reloj, Bernardo. ¿Qué hora es?
   — Son las seis.
4. — ¿Qué hora es, por favor?
   — Es la una y cuarto.
5. — Ahora, ¿qué hora es?
   — Son las diez. Vete a jugar.
6. — Bueno, Geraldo. ¡Despiértate!
   — ¿Qué hora es?
   — Son las ocho.

7. — Ya es tarde.
   — Pero, Bernardo, ¿qué hora es?
   — Son las ocho y media.
8. — Bernardo, ¿qué hora es?
   — Son las cuatro. ¡Vamos al parque!

Answers to Activity 10

   1. h   **2.** f   **3.** g   **4.** a   **5.** c   **6.** e   **7.** b   **8.** d

15 ¿Qué clase tengo ahora?   p. 114

1. Ya son las nueve y cuarto. Tengo la clase de arte.
2. Ahora tengo ciencias sociales. Son las ocho y venticinco.
3. Son las once y cuarenta. Por fin tengo almuerzo.
4. ¡Ya es la una! Tengo clase de matemáticas.
5. Ya son las dos menos cinco. Tengo educación física.
6. Son las tres menos cuarto. Tengo la clase de francés.
7. ¿Son las diez y cinco? ¡Tengo geografía!

Answers to Activity 15

   1. d, arte
   2. g, ciencias sociales
   3. b, almuerzo
   4. f, matemáticas
   5. c, educación física
   6. e, francés
   7. a, geografía

SEGUNDO PASO   pp. 118–123

19 Horarios   p. 119

1. Necesito ir a clase. ¿Qué hora es?
2. ¿A qué hora es el descanso?
3. Necesito organizar mi cuarto. ¿Ya son las tres?
4. ¿A qué hora es el almuerzo?
5. ¿A qué hora necesitas ir a la clase de inglés?
6. Quiero ir al centro comercial. ¿Qué hora es?

Answers to Activity 19

   1. b   **2.** b   **3.** a   **4.** b   **5.** a   **6.** b

39 Patricia y Gregorio   p. 130

— Hola, Patricia, soy Gregorio. ¿Cómo estás?

— Muy bien. ¿Y tú?

— Bien. Oye, ¿qué haces esta tarde? Hay una fiesta a las ocho.

— ¡Ay, no, una fiesta no, por favor! No me gustan las fiestas. Pero me gustan los partidos de fútbol.

— Este, pues... No me gustan los partidos de fútbol. No son interesantes. Pero, a ver... me gustan los videojuegos. ¿A ti te gustan?

— Los videojuegos no me gustan. Bueno, Gregorio, ¿te gustan los partidos de tenis?

— Es que no me gustan los deportes. Pero me gustan los conciertos.

— ¡Ay, sí! Me encantan los conciertos. ¿Qué música te gusta? ¿Te gusta la música rock?

— Sí, me gusta la música rock. ¡Vamos a un concierto!

Answers to Activity 39

1. cierto   **2.** falso   **3.** falso   **4.** cierto

For the scripts for Parts **A** and **C**, see page 133. The script for Part **B** is below.

B. Dictado

Necesito una goma de borrar y una regla en matemáticas. En geografía, necesito un bolígrafo y un cuaderno.

1 p. 138

1. MIGUEL   Mañana tengo la clase de geografía a las diez y cuarto.

2. EDGARDO   Y yo tengo la clase de arte a las once en punto. Me gusta la clase de arte porque el profesor es muy cómico.

3. MIGUEL   Yo tengo almuerzo a las doce menos diez. ¿A qué hora es tu descanso?

4. EDGARDO   El descanso es a la una y cuarto.
    MIGUEL   ¿Y a qué hora es el examen de ciencias?

5. EDGARDO   El examen de ciencias es a las dos y veinte.

Answers to Repaso Activity 1

1. c   **2.** d   **3.** b   **4.** a   **5.** e

Nuevas clases, nuevos amigos
PROJECTS

 ## MI DICCIONARIO

Making a Spanish picture dictionary is an easy and entertaining way to review and increase vocabulary. Encourage students to seek out words for those things they're most interested in learning. Invite them to be creative by drawing their own pictures or using magazine cutouts. They can look at the alphabet presentation on pages 8–9 for a sample. For any words that your students are unable to find in their own dictionaries, encourage them to consult other resources, such as dictionaries in the library, or suggest that they ask native speakers.

Materials students may need

◆ Spiral notebook or notebook paper   ◆ Scissors
◆ Old magazines   ◆ Glue
◆ English-Spanish dictionary   ◆ Markers

Sequence

1 This project may be done individually or in groups.

2 If students work in groups, each group could be assigned to research a particular category for a class dictionary. If students work individually, specify a minimum number of categories and words.

3 Suggest a table of contents similar to the Additional Vocabulary on pages 275–277. Include categories such as:

Nombres comunes (suggest they find names other than those in this book)
Frases útiles
Me gusta/Me gustan
No me gusta/No me gustan
Mi casa

Mi cuarto
La clase de español
España
México
Para describir a la gente
Para describir las cosas

4 Review basic dictionary skills by looking at different types of dictionary entries in an English-Spanish dictionary.

5 Go over all abbreviations to make sure students can identify nouns, verbs, and adjectives. Alert students to the basic problems associated with finding words in the dictionary. Discourage literal translations, and always have them cross-reference any new words they find.

6 Once students have chosen categories and entries and have found illustrations for them, they should design the pages. Allow for individual creativity.

Grading the project

Suggested point distribution (total = 100 points):

Dictionary format **15**
Neatness **20**
Accuracy of definitions **15**
Spelling **15**
Originality **20**
Number of words included **15**

UN FOLLETO PARA ESTUDIANTES

In this activity students will create a brochure of their school or town. This project may be done in class or as an outside assignment. Tell students to imagine that they are creating the brochures for a foreign exchange program. Exchange students in Spanish-speaking countries will use the information in the brochures to decide where in the United States they would like to live and attend school.

Materials students may need

◆ Old magazines   ◆ Scissors
◆ Old newspapers   ◆ Glue or tape
◆ Construction paper   ◆ Colored markers
◆ A camera

Sequence

1. Students obtain pictures to illustrate the brochure. They may draw them, take photos, or cut pictures from magazines and newspapers. Each group decides which pictures to use.

2. Students prepare a short written description in Spanish of each picture used. Each student is responsible for writing at least one description. Review the **Vocabulario** on page 141.

3. Groups design a preliminary two-page layout in which they indicate where pictures and descriptions will go.

4. Each group member proofreads the group's layout for accuracy. Option: Groups might critique each other's work at this point.

5. Groups glue or tape pictures on construction paper and write descriptions by the pictures. Groups also design a cover and a title for their brochures.

6. Each student reads the descriptions she or he has written to the class.

Grading the project

Suggested point distribution (total = 100 points):

Brochure content **40**
Correct vocabulary and grammar **20**
Originality **20**
Oral presentation **20**

TEACHER NOTE

If your class has a pen pal program, students might send the brochure to their pen pals' school and ask for one in return.

✂️ MI HORARIO ESCOLAR

This project enables students to review the school-related vocabulary and compare their school schedules with those of students from Mexico. They will prepare a poster that illustrates a weekly schedule for a student in the United States and a poster that illustrates a weekly schedule for a Mexican student.

Introduction

Discuss the differences between academic schedules for students in Mexico and for your own students. In the United States, do students attend the same classes each day? In Mexico, do students attend the same classes each day? How many subjects does a typical student take in the U.S.? How may subjects does a typical Mexican student take? Discuss the advantages or disadvantages of each system.

Materials students may need

◆ Colored poster board   ◆ Meter sticks
◆ Markers

Sequence

1. Divide students into pairs. One will be the Artist, the other will be the Writer. Each pair of students should think of an ideal schedule to put into draft form. The Writer will write a draft of the schedule that they have created. Students should refer to the **Vocabulario** on page 141. Each draft should include:
   - the days of the week
   - times from the beginning to the end of the school day (to represent class periods or blocks)
   - at least six to eight class subjects

2. The Artist will prepare the chart and transfer the information from the draft to a poster (preferred) or to an overhead transparency.

3. Each pair will present its schedule to the class, pointing out the differences and similarities between class schedules in the United States and Mexico.

Grading the project

Suggested point distribution (total = 100 points):

Overall appearance, neatness **30**
Information and content **20**
Accuracy of information, spelling, gender correctness **30**
Group participation and cooperation **20**

Nuevas clases, nuevos amigos
GAMES

DE SÍLABAS A PALABRAS

This game provides an opportunity to practice pronunciation. It can also be used to review vocabulary from this or any chapter.

Materials you may need

◆ An ample supply of unruled index cards

◆ Pens or markers

Preparation

Review the definition of a syllable as a short unit of speech. Every syllable contains at least one vowel sound, and at least one or more consonant sounds. Break up the vocabulary words from the chapter into syllables and have the students write each syllable on an index card using large letters. For example, make three cards for **mar - ca - dor**, two cards for **com - prar**, etc.

Procedure

1 Shuffle the cards and pass them out among students.

2 Either the teacher or a selected student says **de sílabas a palabras.**

3 Give the students a specific amount of time (one minute) to find other people with whom they can form a word.

4 Tell students to call out **¡Palabra!** when they have formed a word.

5 The group must say their word in unison as you point to them.

6 Students who are not in a word group may clap, tap with a pen or pencil, or use their fingers to count syllables as they repeat the words.

7 Collect all the index cards, shuffle them, and redistribute them to play again.

¿QUÉ HORA ES?

The following game practices telling time. It's easy to set up and can be used by pairs of students or by small groups to practice telling time.

Materials you may need

◆ Paper plates
◆ Brads (metal clasps available at most office supply stores)
◆ Markers
◆ Index cards

Preparation

Have students write various times on the index cards in Spanish. They should use a variety of times including full hours, half hours, quarter hours, before and after the hour, as well as special expressions such as:

La hora de la clase de español
La hora de ir a la escuela
¡Ahora!

Procedure

1 Place index cards face down.

2 Have one student draw an index card with a specific time.

3 First the student must read the time aloud and set the clock to the correct time.

4 If the clock is set correctly the student wins one point.

PALABRAS REVUELTAS

This game is especially good for tactile learners. The objective is for students to be able to construct at least five Spanish words from scrambled letters.

Materials you may need

10 small squares of paper for each student

Procedure

1 Divide the class into two teams.

2 Each person on the team looks up a Spanish word from the **Vocabulario** on page 141 and writes the letters that make up that word on squares of paper, one letter per square.

3 Then they scramble their letters.

4 Ask for members from each team to exchange their letters.

5 Students try to immediately arrange the letters in the correct order.

6 The student who unscrambles his or her word before his or her opponent wins a point for his or her team.

CADENA

This game, which helps students review vocabulary, is good for auditory learners.

Procedure

1 Have all students stand up.

2 Begin by saying **Este semestre tengo geografía.**

3 The first student then says **Este semestre tengo geografía y física.**

4 The second student repeats what has already been said, adding a new school subject to the sentence.

5 When someone says the "chain" incorrectly, he or she sits down.

6 This sequence continues until no one can add any more school subjects to the sentence. Then begin a new sentence, such as **Me gusta el arte.**

7 The winners are the last three students to be left standing.

¿ES LA HORA?

This game is especially good for auditory learners. The objective is for students to be able to distinguish between a las and son las.

Preparation

Prepare twenty to thirty flashcards with questions in Spanish about time. For example, **¿A qué hora es la clase de español?** or **Compro el almuerzo. ¿Qué hora es?**

Procedure

1 Divide the class into two teams. Allow them to pick a name for their team.

2 Hand the representative from first team a card with a question. They ask the representative from the second team the question, and he or she must answer correctly using **a las...** or **son las...**

3 Then have a representative from Team 2 ask a question. Have the team representatives change every question so that everyone can participate.

ANSWERS TO CHAPTER 3 ACTIVITIES

Answers to listening activities appear on pages 101E–101F. Answers to all other activities appear on corresponding pupil pages.

PRIMER PASO   pp. 108–115

9 Answers will vary. Possible answers:
(1A) Hola, ¿qué tal?
(2A) Estoy bien. ¿Cómo estás?
(1B) Bien, gracias. ¿Qué clases tienes este semestre?
(2B) Tengo el francés, la biología y la geografía. ¿Qué clases tienes hoy?
(1C) Primero tengo la clase de español. Luego tengo la computación.
(2C) Me gusta la clase de biología.
(1D) Bueno, tengo que irme. Hasta luego.
(2D) Adiós.

SEGUNDO PASO   pp. 118–123

21 1. —¿A qué hora es la clase de matemáticas?
—Es a las once menos veinticinco de la mañana.
2. —¿A qué hora es la clase de computación?
—Es a las dos y diez de la tarde.
3. —¿A qué hora es la clase de educación física?
—Es a las doce menos diez de la mañana.
4. —¿A qué hora es la clase de francés?
—Es a las cuatro menos veinte de la tarde.
5. —¿A qué hora es la clase de arte?
—Es a la una y media de la tarde.
6. —¿A qué hora es la clase de geografía?
—Es a las ocho y veinticinco de la mañana.

22 Answers will vary. Possible answers:
STUDENT 1   Hola, ¿cómo estás?
STUDENT 2   Muy bien. ¿Y tú?

STUDENT 1   Bien, gracias. ¿De dónde eres?
STUDENT 2   Soy de Cuernavaca. ¿Qué clases tienes este semestre y a qué hora son?
STUDENT 1   Tengo geografía y francés. La clase de geografía es a las nueve y la clase de francés es a las diez.

27 Answers will vary. Possible answers:
—Hola, Marcos, ¿cómo estás?
—Muy bien. ¿Y tú?
—Más o menos. ¿Cómo es tu clase de francés?
—Es buena, pero tengo que irme.
—Y ¿cómo es el profesor?
—Es simpático, pero tengo mucha prisa. Estoy atrasado.
—Bueno, hasta luego.

TERCER PASO   pp. 124–133

36 Answers will vary. Possible answers:
1. —¿Cómo es tu libro de ciencias sociales?
—Es grande pero interesante.
2. —Oye, ¿cómo es la comida en la cafetería?
—Mira, es buena.
3. —Oye, ¿cómo es la clase de inglés?
—Mira, es aburrida, pero me gusta.
4. —Oye, ¿cómo es la tarea de español?
—Bueno, hay mucha, pero es fácil.
5. —¿Cómo son tus amigos?
—Son muy simpáticos.
6. —Oye, ¿cómo es la música de...?
—Es buena.

ENLACES   pp. 134–135

1 1. Son las cuatro de la tarde.
2. Son las cinco de la mañana.
3. Son las tres y media de la tarde.
4. Son las ocho y cuarto de la noche.

VAMOS A LEER   pp. 136–137

B 1. report cards
2. report cards
3. report cards and schedules
4. schedules
5. report cards and schedules
6. neither
7. report cards
8. neither
9. report cards and schedules

C 1. her conduct
2. Óscar: 8.8; Juana: 9
3. Óscar
4. Óscar

D 1. Gloria: 9; Óscar: 8; Juana: 7
2. Answers will vary.
3. A las siete y media.

REPASO   pp. 138–139

2 1. La clase de español de Gabriela es a las doce y media. La clase de español de Martín es a las trece y media.
2. Gabriela tiene primero la clase de ciencias sociales. Martín tiene primero la clase de francés.
3. Después del almuerzo Gabriela tiene la clase de español. Después del almuerzo Martín tiene la clase de ciencias sociales.

A VER SI PUEDO...   p. 140

5 Answers will vary. Possible answers:
Yolanda es inteligente y morena.
Gabriela es alta y rubia.
Simón es joven y cómico.
Bruto es grande y simpático.

HOMEWORK SUGGESTIONS

Chapter Section	Presentation	Homework Options
Primer paso	**Vocabulario**, p. 109	*Grammar and Vocabulary*, p. 18, Activities 1–2 *CD-ROM*, Disc 1, Chapter 3, Activity 3
	Nota gramatical, p. 109	*Grammar and Vocabulary*, p. 19, Activities 3–5
	Así se dice, p. 110	*Pupil's Edition*, pp. 110–111, Activities 6–8 *Practice and Activity Book*, pp. 28–29, Activities 4, 6
	Así se dice, p. 112	*Practice and Activity Book*, p. 30, Activity 7 *CD-ROM*, Disc 1, Chapter 3, Activity 1
	Gramática, p. 113	*Pupil's Edition*, pp. 113–115, Activities 12–14, 17 *Grammar and Vocabulary*, p. 20, Activities 6–7 *CD-ROM*, Disc 1, Chapter 3, Activity 2
Segundo paso	**Así se dice**, p. 119	*Pupil's Edition*, p. 120, Activity 20
	Vocabulario, p. 119	*Practice and Activity Book*, pp. 31–32, Activities 9–10 *Grammar and Vocabulary*, p. 21, Activities 8–9
	Nota gramatical, p. 121	*Grammar and Vocabulary*, p. 22, Activities 10–11
	Así se dice, p. 122	*CD-ROM*, Disc 1, Chapter 3, Activity 4 *Pupil's Edition*, pp. 122–123, Activities 24–26 *Practice and Activity Book*, pp. 32–33, Activities 11–12
Tercer paso	**Así se dice**, p. 125	*Pupil's Edition*, p. 125, Activity 29 *Practice and Activity Book*, p. 35, Activity 15
	Vocabulario, p. 125	*Pupil's Edition*, pp. 127–128, Activities 33–34, 37 *Practice and Activity Book*, pp. 35–36, Activities 16–17, 19 *CD-ROM*, Disc 1, Chapter 3, Activity 6
	Nota gramatical, p. 126	*Grammar and Vocabulary*, p. 23, Activities 12–13
	Gramática, p. 127	*Grammar and Vocabulary*, p. 25, Activity 17
	Así se dice, p.129	*Pupil's Edition*, p. 129, Activity 38 *Practice and Activity Book*, pp. 36, Activity 18 *CD-ROM*, Disc 1, Chapter 3, Activity 5
	Vocabulario, p. 130	*Grammar and Vocabulary*, p. 26, Activities 18–19

Nuevas clases, nuevos amigos

MOTIVATING ACTIVITIES

- Ask students to list in English what they might say to each other on the first day of a new school year. What might they ask new and old friends?

- Have students briefly discuss the classes they have this year and which they anticipate to be the best, hardest, most useful, most enjoyable, or most interesting.

- Ask students how they think they would feel about starting the year in a new school. Would they be excited about making new friends, or would they miss their old school?

FOCUSING ON OUTCOMES

Have students look at the chapter outcomes and match them with the three photos. (Photo 1 represents describing people and things; photo 2 represents telling at what time something happens, telling time, and talking about class schedules; and photo 3 represents talking about class schedules.) Point out to students that many of the people they meet are at school, and much of their time is spent there, so it is important to be able to talk about these things.

CAPÍTULO

3 Nuevas clases, nuevos amigos

① **Mis compañeros de clase son simpáticos.**

In this chapter you will learn to

PRIMER PASO

- talk about classes
- sequence events
- tell time

SEGUNDO PASO

- tell at what time something happens
- talk about being late or in a hurry

TERCER PASO

- describe people and things
- talk about things you like and explain why

internet

MARCAR: go.hrw.com
PALABRA CLAVE:
WV3 MEXICO-3

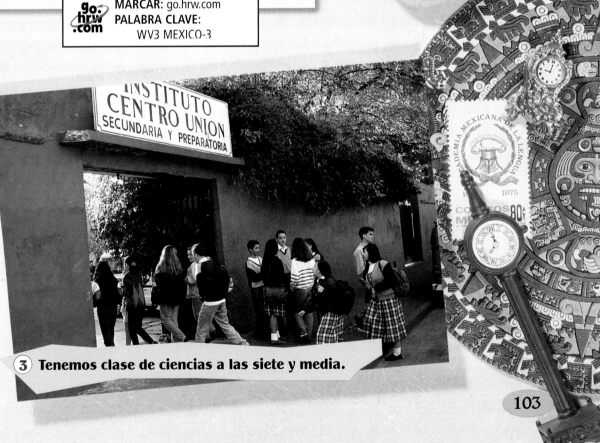

2 ¿A qué hora es la clase?

3 Tenemos clase de ciencias a las siete y media.

103

NATIVE SPEAKERS
If any of your students have lived in or visited Mexico, ask them if they would be willing to share some of their experiences. Ask them how Mexico is similar to the United States. What foods are similar? Which stores do the two countries have in common? Which sports are the same? What are Mexican schools like compared with those in the United States? Are there more or fewer classes each day? Is the schedule the same or a bit different? How many students are there in a class?

VIDEO INTEGRATION

Adelante LEVEL 1A
Video Program
Videocassette 1, 44:39–50:08 OR
Videocassette 3, 21:48–27:08
(captioned version)

¡Ven conmigo! LEVEL 1
DVD Tutor, Disc 1

TEACHER NOTE
The **fotonovela** is an abridged version of the video episode.

VIDEO SYNOPSIS
Claudia is starting the year at a new school. She meets the school principal, who introduces her to the students in her first class. While they wait for their teacher to arrive, Claudia talks with her new acquaintances. The students are friendly, and one is particularly mischievous.

MOTIVATING ACTIVITY
Divide students into small groups. Have students use the photos to predict what is going to happen in the **fotonovela.** Ask them to make their predictions by answering questions based on *who? how old? what? where?* and *why?* This may be done in English or in Spanish, depending on students' proficiency, but remember that your main purpose is to engage the students' interest and focus their attention on the **fotonovela.**

DE ANTEMANO

¡Bienvenida al colegio!

CD 3 Trs. 1–2

Look at the photos that accompany the story. Where and when do you think these scenes are taking place? What clues tell you this? What do you think will happen in the story?

p. 27
Acts. 1–2

María Inés, Fernando y Claudia

Director Altamirano

Profesor Romanca

1

DIRECTOR Bueno, ya son las ocho menos cinco. Aquí tienes el horario. Ahorita tienes clase de ciencias sociales... y a las ocho y cincuenta tienes clase de francés. El descanso es a las nueve y cuarenta...

DIRECTOR Muchachos, buenos días. Ella es una compañera nueva. Se llama Claudia Obregón Sánchez. Es de la Ciudad de México.

MARÍA INÉS Me llamo María Inés.

FERNANDO Y yo soy Fernando. Encantado. Y ¡bienvenida a Cuernavaca!

MARÍA INÉS Eres de la Ciudad de México, ¡ay, qué padre! Hay muchas cosas interesantes allá, ¿no?

CLAUDIA Sí, la capital es muy divertida. Mira, me gusta ir al parque... visitar los museos... y también me gusta mucho jugar al basquetbol.

FERNANDO Miren, ya son las ocho. ¿Dónde está el profesor? Está atrasado.

PRESENTATION

Have students follow along as you read the captions or play the audio recording. Next, have students repeat the dialogue after you. In their same groups from the Motivating Activity, encourage students to guess the meaning of the captions. Ask groups to revise their original predictions. Play the video and then have students describe what is happening in each frame of the **fotonovela.**

LANGUAGE NOTE

Explain some colloquial words in the **fotonovela** that might be unfamiliar to students.
¡Qué padre! *Cool!*
¡Mira! *Look!* or *Hey!*
¡Híjole! *Gosh!*

SUGGESTIONS

• Point out that **bienvenida** in the title refers to Claudia, and that **bienvenido** changes in gender and number depending on who is being addressed.

• After students read the **fotonovela,** ask them if they have ever been in a similar situation (a new student in another country or simply in a new school). If so, how did they handle it? What were some of the differences they found?

ADDITIONAL PRACTICE

Have students scan the text in the **fotonovela** for ten cognates. On this page, they should be able to recognize **clase, horrible, favorita, exámenes, profesor/a, estudiar.**

CRITICAL THINKING

Have students try to guess what will happen to María Inés. What is her teacher, Profesor Romanca, likely to say to her? How might she respond to what he says?

A continuación

You may choose to continue with *¡Bienvenida al oologio! (a continuación)* at this time or wait until later in the chapter. At this point, María Inés receives an extra assignment from the teacher. After school María Inés meets more of Claudia's friends. You may wish to discuss with students differences between schools in Mexico and the U.S.

CLAUDIA	Fernando, ¿cómo es esta clase?
FERNANDO	Ay, es horrible. El profesor es muy aburrido... ¡y no le gustan los exámenes fáciles!
MARÍA INÉS	No te preocupes, Claudia, no es verdad. Esta clase es mi favorita. Es muy interesante, y el profesor, pues, es... así.

⑤

⑥

MARÍA INÉS	Señor Rodríguez, una pregunta. ¿Le gustan las ciencias sociales?
FERNANDO	Sí, "profesora"... me gustan.
MARÍA INÉS	¿Y le gusta estudiar?
FERNANDO	Sí, me gusta estudiar.
MARÍA INÉS	Entonces, ¿por qué no le gusta estudiar las ciencias sociales?

⑦

⑧

⑨

¡Ay, no!

106 *ciento seis*

1 ¿Comprendes?

Check your understanding of the **fotonovela** by answering these questions.

These activities check for global comprehension only. Students should not yet be expected to produce language modeled in **De antemano**.

1. What time is it when the story begins? How do you know?
   a. 7:55   because director Altamirano states the time and the
   b. 8:00   clock shows 7:55
2. What do you think the principal is discussing with Claudia?
   a. the bus schedule
   b. her class schedule
3. What kind of photographs is Claudia showing Fernando and María Inés?
   a. pictures of Mexico City
   b. pictures of Cuernavaca
4. What do María Inés and Fernando think of this class?
   a. Fernando really likes it and María Inés thinks it's awful.
   b. Fernando thinks it's horrible and María Inés thinks it's interesting.
5. The **fotonovela** ends with . . .
   a. María Inés walking into the wrong classroom.
   b. the teacher walking in while María Inés is imitating him.

2 ¿Quién es?

Match the name of the person with the sentence that describes him or her.

1. María Inés d
2. Claudia a
3. Fernando b
4. el señor Romanca c

a. Ella es de la Ciudad de México.
b. A él no le gusta la clase de ciencias sociales.
c. Es el profesor de ciencias sociales.
d. A ella le gusta la clase de ciencias sociales.

3 ¡Opiniones!

Using the **fotonovela** as a guide, complete this conversation between two students with the words from the box.

—Tengo la clase de ___1___ a las ocho. No me ___2___ la clase. ¡Es ___3___ y los exámenes son difíciles!
—¿Ah, sí? Pues, es mi clase ___4___. ¡Es muy ___5___!

interesante   gusta

horrible

favorita

ciencias sociales

1. ciencias sociales
2. gusta
3. horrible
4. favorita
5. interesante

SUGGESTION

1 Have students review questions with a partner. Then ask for volunteers to answer the questions. Ask the class to use thumbs up if the answer is correct and thumbs down if the answer is incorrect.

ADDITIONAL PRACTICE

2 Put words and phrases that make up the following sentences on sentence strips or a felt board, and have students move the words to make the false sentences true and correct false ones.

Fernando es de la Ciudad de México.

La compañera nueva se llama María Inés.

La clase es de matemáticas.

María Inés es la profesora de la clase.

Señor Romanca es el profesor de la clase.

VIDEO INTEGRATION

Adelante LEVEL 1A
Video Program
Videocassette 1, 45:23–46:24 OR
Videocassette 3, 22:32–23:33
(captioned version)

¡Ven conmigo! LEVEL 1
DVD Tutor, Disc 1

Bell work

Write the following questions on the board and have students write their answers.

¿Qué necesitas para el colegio?

¿Cuántos cuadernos necesitas?

¿Cuántas carpetas necesitas?

¿Tienes una calculadora?

¿Tienes muchos bolígrafos?

CULTURE NOTE

Point out that a **siesta** isn't necessarily a nap. It can be just some time to relax. Also, in larger cities, it may be some extra time to commute to and from home for the midday meal. Nine-to-five schedules without a **siesta** are increasingly common.

PRIMER PASO ⓉⓅⓇ

Storytelling Book
pp. 9, 12

WV3 MEXICO-3

*Talking about classes and sequencing events;
telling time*

DIRECTOR Bueno, ya son las ocho menos cinco. Aquí tienes el horario. Ahorita tienes clase de ciencias sociales... y a las ocho y cincuenta tienes clase de francés. El descanso es a las nueve y cuarenta...

4 El horario de Claudia

Help Claudia complete part of her class schedule.

Claudia Obregón Sánchez

7:55 – la clase de <u>ciencias sociales</u>

8:50 – la clase de <u>francés</u>

9:40 – <u>descanso</u>

🌐 Nota cultural

Some students in Spanish-speaking countries go home for lunch and a **siesta** (*nap* or *rest*) in the middle of the school day. They then go back to school in the afternoon. These students may not get out of school for the day until 4:30 or 5:00. Other students attend school only in the morning, while a second group of students attends school only in the afternoon. What do you think the ideal school schedule is? Why?

VOCABULARIO

¿Qué materias estudias?   *What subjects are you studying?*

CD-ROM DISC 1

PA
p. 28
Act. 3

GV
p. 18
Acts. 1–2

3-A

el francés

la geografía

las matemáticas

el almuerzo

la educación física

el arte

las ciencias

el descanso

la computación

las ciencias sociales

NOTA GRAMATICAL

With nouns referring to more than one thing, like **libros** or **clases,** use **los** or **las. Los** is for masculine nouns. **Las** is for feminine nouns. Both words mean *the.*

Tengo **los** libros.

¿Tienes **las** gomas de borrar?

Also use **los** when referring to a group of people that includes both males and females.

Los profesores son de México.

PA
p. 29
Act. 5

GV
p. 19
Acts. 3–5

5 ¡Tenemos la misma clase!

CD 3 Tr. 3

Script and answers on p. 101E

Listen to Álvaro and Lupita discuss their new class schedules. What class do they have together?

Álvaro	Lupita

PRIMER PASO

ciento nueve **109**

☀ MOTIVATE

Ask students what their favorite and least favorite subjects are. As they mention different subjects, respond with **Entonces te gusta... / no te gusta...**

☀ TEACH

PRESENTATION

VOCABULARIO

Have students scan the vocabulary for recognition. Then ask ¿**Quién tiene clase de arte?** Ask for a show of hands. Repeat for the other subjects. Continue by asking individuals if they like certain subjects.

TEACHER NOTE

Teach students some extra vocabulary for classes, such as: **el coro** *choir,* **la banda** *band,* **la orquesta** *orchestra,* and **el taller** *shop.*

PRESENTATION

NOTA GRAMATICAL

Remind students that nouns in Spanish are either masculine or feminine. Review **el** and **la** and introduce **los** and **las.** Ask students to call out the appropriate article for objects you hold up. (**carpeta, cuadernos, bolígrafo,** etc.) Vary the number and gender of objects you hold up.

pp. 28–29
Acts. 4, 6

ASÍ SE DICE   Talking about classes and sequencing events

To find out what classes a friend has, ask: Your friend might answer:

¿Qué clases tienes este semestre?
What classes do you have this semester?

Bueno, **tengo** matemáticas, inglés, español y ciencias sociales.

¿Qué clases tienes hoy?
What classes do you have today?

Primero tengo geografía, **después** computación y **luego** francés.
First I have geography, afterwards computer science, and then French.

¿Y cuándo tienes un día libre?
And when do you have a day off?

¡Mañana, por fin, tengo un día libre!
Tomorrow, at last, I have a day off!

---

6 ¿Qué clase tiene primero? H

Alma is talking about her class schedule with a friend. Read the conversation. Then list the items in the box in the order she'll need them, based on her schedule. Label the first item she'll need number one, and the last item she'll need number five.   Answers in side column

—Primero tengo la clase de matemáticas.

—¿Y después tienes la clase de geografía?

—Sí, y después del almuerzo, tengo educación física. Luego tengo la clase de ciencias.

—Y por último tienes la clase de arte, ¿verdad?

zapatillas de tenis
lápices de color
un mapa de México
libro de biología
una calculadora

p. 38
Act. 21

Nota cultural

How would you feel if you got a score of 18 on a test? In Peru, this would actually be a high grade, equivalent to a 90. Peruvian schools use a scale of 1 to 20, with 11 the lowest passing score. Mexican schools use a scale of 1 to 10, with 6 as passing. What would your grades be if you went to school in Peru? In Mexico?

AÑO	ASIGNATURAS	1o Lapso Calif.	1o Lapso Inas.	2o Lapso Calif.	2o Lapso Inas.	3o Lapso Calif.	3o Lapso Inas.	Calificación Definitiva
9no	Castellano	12		11		11		11
	Biología	14		12		10		12
	Inglés	18		16		16		17
	Geografía de Venezuela	13		12		13		13
	Cátedra Bolivariana	14		10		11		12
	Química	16		10		12		13
	Física	11		15		15		14
	Matemáticas	10		10		13		11
	Educación Física	05		14		11		10
	Psicopedagogía	15		16		17		16
	Computación	11		12		13		12
	Servicio	10		13		12		12

Using a hand puppet, ask: **Lulú, ¿qué clases tienes este semestre?** Have the puppet "answer" you: **Bueno, tengo computación, ciencias sociales, inglés,** and so on. Continue to model the sentences in this manner, then have the class repeat them after you.

SUGGESTION

Have students role-play the dialogue from **Así se dice**. Limit the time to one or two minutes.

ADDITIONAL PRACTICE

Practice the adverbs **primero, después, luego,** and **por fin** in a conversation with students. (**Carlos, ¿qué clase tienes primero? ¿Y qué tienes después? ¿Luego qué clase tienes?**) Then have students practice with a partner for three to four minutes.

SUGGESTION

6 Have students work in pairs to see if they have the same classes that are mentioned in the activity. If not, have them compare classes they have in common.

Answers to Activity 6

1. una calculadora
2. un mapa de México
3. zapatillas de tenis
4. libro de biología
5. lápices de color

---

7 Primero tiene...

Complete this description of Eduardo's weekly morning schedule using the words below. Two answers are interchangeable. *Answers in side column*

luego   primero   después

hoy   mañana

Eduardo Bello González			
	LUNES	**MARTES**	**MIÉRCOLES**
8:00	Matemáticas	Matemáticas	Matemáticas
9:00	Ciencias Sociales	Ciencias Sociales	Ciencias Sociales
10:00	descanso	descanso	descanso
10:30	Computación	Educación Física	Computación
11:30	Ciencias	Ciencias	Ciencias
12:30	almuerzo	almuerzo	almuerzo
1:00	Francés	Arte	Francés
2:00	Español	Español	Español

____1____ Eduardo tiene siete clases.
____2____ tiene la clase de matemáticas con la profesora Lares. ____3____ tiene las ciencias sociales y un descanso. ____4____ tiene la computación, las ciencias y el almuerzo. ____5____ tiene educación física a las 10:30 y arte a la 1:00.

8 El día de Julia

First, rewrite Julia's schedule, putting everything in order. Then write three things that *you* do showing the order in which you do them. Use the words from Activity 7 to write your sentences, and put them in order with **primero, luego,** and **después**. *Personalized answers will vary.*

a. Luego tengo descanso. 3
b. Después del descanso tengo arte. 4
c. Primero tengo ciencias. 1
d. ¡Por fin no tengo más clases! 5
e. Después de ciencias tengo 2 español.

9 Pues, tengo...

Get together with a partner. Create a conversation in which you greet one another and find out what classes you each have and in what order you have them. Use words like **primero, luego,** and **después**. Follow the guide below. *Answers will vary. Possible answers on p. 101K*

Tú

Greet your friend. --------→

Respond that you're doing well. Ask what class he or she has this semester.

Tell your partner what class you have first and then what you have afterwards.

Say goodbye.

Tu compañero/a

Respond to your partner's greeting and ask how he or she is doing.

Answer your partner's question. Ask your partner what classes he or she has today.

Tell your partner which class you like.

Say goodbye.

📖 EN MI CUADERNO
7 Have students write a description of their class schedule in their journals. Ask them to use the adverbs **primero, después, luego,** and **por fin** for sequencing the classes. For an additional journal entry suggestion for Chapter 3, see *Practice and Activity Book,* p. 77.

MATH LINK
7 Take a poll to find out how many students have other classes in common. Ask the class for a show of hands as you ask questions like **¿Quién tiene geografía?** Write the results on the board. Have students use the results to create a bar graph labeled in Spanish.

🌎 CULTURE NOTE
Students in Spain often receive comments instead of number or letter grades: **sobresaliente, bien, suficiente, suspendido,** or **deficiente**.

SLOWER PACE
9 You might want to write days of the week on the board and have students structure their conversation around them. (**¿Qué clases tienes hoy?** or **¿Qué clases tienes mañana?**)

Answers to Activity 7
1. Hoy
2. Primero
3. Luego *or* Después
4. Luego *or* Después
5. Mañana

p. 30
Act. 7

ASÍ SE DICE   Telling time

To find out what time it is, ask:

¿Qué hora es?

To answer, say:

Son las ocho.
It's eight o'clock.

Son las once y media.
It's 11:30.

Es la una y cuarto.
It's 1:15. (It's a quarter after one.)

¡Ay! ¿**Ya son** las tres?
Yikes! Is it already three o'clock?

Sí, es tarde. ¡Vamos!
Yes, it's late. Let's go!

10 El reloj

CD 3 Tr. 4

Bernardo is babysitting today. You'll hear his brother at different times throughout the day asking him what time it is. Match each time mentioned with the correct clock below. Scripts and answers on p. 101E

GRAMÁTICA Telling time

p. 30
Act. 8

1. To tell the hour (except for times around 1:00), use **Son las...** plus the hour.

   Son las ocho. *It's 8:00.*

2. For times after the hour, follow this pattern:

   Son las siete y **cuarto.** *It's a quarter after seven.*
   Son las ocho y **veinticinco.** *It's 8:25.*
   Son las once y **media.** *It's 11:30.*

p. 20
Acts. 6–7

3. For times before the hour, say:

   Es la una **menos veinte.**
   It's twenty minutes to one.
   Son las doce **menos cuarto.**
   It's a quarter to twelve.
   Son las ocho **menos diez.**
   It's ten minutes to eight.

4. For times including 1:00, use **Es la una...**

   Es la una y veinte. *It's 1:20.*

PRESENTATION
GRAMÁTICA
Before beginning this section, prepare large flashcards. On each card write a time, such as 3:00. As you hold up each card, have students tell you whether to use **son las** or **es la**. Say the time with them: **Son las tres.** Next, show the cards one at a time and have the class tell you the time in unison in Spanish. Students can do *CD-ROM,* Activity 2 as a follow up.

11 ¿Qué hora es?

With a partner, take turns asking and telling each other what time it is on each watch.

1. Son las tres y media.
2. Son las doce menos veinte.
3. Son las cinco.
4. Son las diez y cuarto.
5. Son las seis y cinco.
6. Son las diez menos cinco.

SUGGESTION
11 Tell students there are different ways to tell time. For example, instead of saying **Son las ocho menos diez,** they may say **Son las siete y cincuenta** for 7:50. You may point out that director Altamirano in **De antemano** uses **a las ocho y cincuenta** rather than **a las nueve menos diez** when he tells Claudia about the class schedule.

12 La hora

Read the sentences and match each one with the correct time.

1. Son las diez menos cinco. c
2. Son las ocho y cuarto. e
3. Son las nueve menos diez. a
4. Son las siete menos seis. d
5. Es la una menos cuarto. b

a. 8:50
b. 12:45
c. 9:55
d. 6:54
e. 8:15

ADDITIONAL PRACTICE
13 Have students work with a partner to practice telling time in Spanish. One partner draws the hands of a clock or the numbers for a digital clock and asks **¿Qué hora es?** The other partner answers **Es la...** or **Son las...** After one partner has practiced telling time in Spanish about five times, the partners switch roles.

KINESTHETIC LEARNERS
14 Have one or two volunteers pantomime several of the actions mentioned in this activity while the rest of the class guesses the associated time.

ADDITIONAL PRACTICE
15 Write all daily class period times on the board in digital numbers. (8:15, 10:10, 11:30, and so on) In pairs, have students ask questions about each other's schedules. For example:
—**Son las once y media. ¿Qué clase tienes?**
—**Tengo la clase de matemáticas.**

13 Relojes

Draw a clock that corresponds to each of the times given below.
Then copy the time in words below your drawing.

1. Son las once menos cuarto. (10:45)
2. Son las cuatro. (4:00)
3. Son las tres y media. (3:30)
4. Son las diez menos veinte. (9:40)
5. Es la una y media. (1:30)
6. Son las dos menos diez. (1:50)

14 ¿Qué hora es cuando...?

Generally, what time is it when . . .? Answers will vary. Possible answers below

Son las siete de la tarde.

Son las once de la noche.

Son las siete de la mañana.

Es la una de la tarde.

Son las siete y media de la mañana.

Son las doce de la tarde.

15 ¿Qué clase tengo ahora? Scripts and answers on p. 101E

Imagine that you're talking with your new friend Alberto about a typical school day. Listen as he tells you about his schedule. Write the class that he has for each of the times listed.

CD 3 Tr. 5

MODELO —Son las doce y diez. Tengo la clase de computación.
(h, computación)

a. 10:05   c. 1:55   e. 2:45   g. 8:25
b. 11:40   d. 9:15   f. 1:00   h. 12:10

Nota cultural

In Spanish-speaking countries, especially those with warmer climates, you might find that people's schedules are a little different from yours. A **siesta** after lunch makes it possible for people to eat dinner later and stay up later, too. The **siesta** is a time when stores and businesses close for around two hours at noon. They then stay open a little later in the evening. The dinner hour is also later, usually between 8:00 and 10:00. In many areas, however, this is changing. Many businesses are now open from 9:00 to 5:00. Do you think a **siesta** is a good idea? Why or why not?

16 Son las...

Take turns reading each item to your partner and asking and answering what time it is. More than one time may be appropriate for some items. Create your own item for number 6.

MODELO   Tienes clase de matemáticas. → Son las nueve menos diez.

1. Es la hora del almuerzo.
2. Necesitas hacer la tarea.
3. Necesitas ir al colegio.
4. Hay un descanso.
5. Tienes la clase de español.
6. ¿?

Answers will vary.
Possible answers:
1. Son las doce de la tarde.
2. Son las cuatro de la tarde.
3. Son las ocho de la mañana.
4. Son las dos y media de la tarde.
5. Son las diez de la mañana.

17 Las clases

Adela and Martín are talking before school in the morning. Show the order of their conversation by writing the letters of each item in the correct order.

3 **a.** —Primero tengo la clase de matemáticas. Luego tengo la clase de ciencias a las nueve y media. Y tú, ¿cuántas clases tienes hoy?

2 **b.** —Estoy bien, Adela. ¿Qué clase tienes primero?

4 **c.** —Yo tengo seis clases hoy. Mañana tengo siete porque tengo educación física. Oye, Adela, ¿qué hora es?

6 **d.** —¡Ay! Es tarde. Tengo clase. ¡Vamos!

1 **e.** —Hola, Martín. ¿Cómo estás?

5 **f.** —Son las ocho menos cuarto.

CAPÍTULO 3

☀ CLOSE

17 Ask students comprehension questions, such as, **¿Qué clase tiene primero Adela?; ¿Cuántas clases tiene Martín hoy?;** or **¿Cuántas clases tiene Martín mañana?** Then, ask several students the same questions about their own schedules, **¿Qué clase tienes primero?; ¿Cuántas clases tienes hoy?;** or **¿Cuántas clases tienes mañana?** Next, assign pairs in which students write and perform a dialogue based on this conversation between Adela and Martín.

☀ ASSESS

▸ Testing Program, pp. 37–38
   Quiz 3-1
   Audio CD 3, Track 18

▸ Grammar and Vocabulary Quizzes
   Quiz 3-1A or
   Alternative Quiz 3-1A

▸ Alternative Assessment Guide, p. 21

PERFORMANCE ASSESSMENT

In pairs, have students describe their schedules to each other as they would to a new friend. They should tell which classes they have at what time and indicate the order of their classes using **primero, después, luego,** and **por fin.** Have students present their dialogues to the class or record them on audiocassette or videocassette.

PRIMER PASO ... ciento quince 115

PRIMER PASO

ciento quince **115**

STANDARDS: 1.1, 1.3, 4.2   **115**

VIDEO INTEGRATION

Adelante LEVEL 1A
Video Program
Videocassette 1, 55:27–58:22

¡Ven conmigo! LEVEL 1
DVD Tutor, Disc 1

TEACHER NOTES
- See the *Video Guide* for activities related to **Panorama cultural.**
- Remind students that cultural information may be included in the Quizzes and the Chapter Test.
- The language of the people interviewed represents informal, unrehearsed speech. Occasionally, text has been edited for clarity.

MOTIVATING ACTIVITY
Ask students what a typical school day is like for them. What times do their classes start? What electives can they take? What subjects do they like? What do they do after class?

PRESENTATION
Have students look at the interviews to find five words about schedules, five words about classes and one about an elective.

Panorama cultural

CD 3
Trs. 6–9

¿Cómo es un día escolar típico?

In this chapter, we asked some students at what time they usually go to school, what they do after class, and which classes they like.

N

Rodrigo's school day starts at 5:45 A.M., and he has several classes. What is a typical day at your school like?

In Spain, students almost always go home for lunch. They sometimes have an hour and a half.

● **Rodrigo**
San Miguel,
Costa Rica
CD 3 Tr. 7

[Tengo] español, estudios, ciencias, matemáticas, agricultura y religión. [Mi clase favorita es] ciencias.

● **Elizabeth**
Sevilla, España
CD 3 Tr. 8

Voy desde las nueve de la mañana hasta las dos del mediodía y luego voy a mi casa a comer.

As soon as she gets to school, Renata greets her teachers. Do you say hello to your teachers when you begin the school day?

Renata CD 3 Tr. 9
*Ciudad de México,
México*

Bueno, pues, entrar a las ocho en punto a la escuela, saludar a las maestras, empezar a trabajar en matemáticas, después en español, después en ciencias naturales y geografía.

1 How many classes does Rodrigo have? 6

2 What classes does Rodrigo take that you don't? Answers will vary.

3 Elizabeth starts school much later than Rodrigo. What time does she start? She starts at 9:00 A.M.

4 At 2:00 P.M., Elizabeth goes ===== for lunch.
a. home
b. to the cafeteria

5 What time does Renata start school?
a. around 8:00 A.M.
b. at 8:00 on the dot

6 What classes do you have in common with Renata? Answers will vary.

Para pensar y hablar... Answers will vary.

A. Which student has classes or a school routine most like yours? Explain.

B. In a group of three or four, talk about a normal day at school. What do you like about the class schedule at your school? What would you change about it if you could?

Cuaderno para hispanohablantes, p. 14

VIDEO INTEGRATION

Adelante LEVEL 1A
Video Program
Videocassette 1, 47:25–48:50 OR
Videocassette 3, 24:34–25:59
(captioned version)

¡Ven conmigo! LEVEL 1
DVD Tutor, Disc 1

Bell work
Write the following questions on the board or on a transparency and have students write their answers:
¿Qué materias tienes este semestre?
¿Qué clases tienes hoy?
¿Qué clase tienes ahora?
¿Qué hora es?

SUGGESTION
Ask students what happens if they are late to a class. What are some of the reasons they might be late? What are some reasons a teacher might be late?

☀ MOTIVATE
Ask students when they need to know at what time something starts. (to watch a TV program or to get to a movie or concert on time) Are they ever late? When do they feel the need to hurry to get somewhere? In this **paso** they will learn to talk about these things in Spanish. Have them list three things for which they need to know the starting time.

SEGUNDO PASO ⓉⓅⓇ

Storytelling Book
pp. 10, 12

go.
hrw
.com
WV3 MEXICO-3

Telling at what time something happens;
talking about being late or in a hurry

CLAUDIA Sí, la capital es muy divertida. Mira, me gusta ir al parque... visitar los museos... y también me gusta mucho jugar al basquetbol.

FERNANDO Miren, ya son las ocho. ¿Dónde está el profesor? Está atrasado.

18 ¿Dónde está el profesor?
Answer the questions according to what Fernando says.

1. ¿Qué hora es?
   a. 7:55
   b. 8:00
2. ¿Está en la clase el profesor?
   a. Sí, ya está en la clase.
   b. No, no está en la clase.
3. ¿Quién está atrasado?
   a. el profesor
   b. Fernando

Una plaza en la Ciudad de México

ASÍ SE DICE

Telling at what time something happens

PA
p. 31
Act. 9

To find out at what time something happens, ask:

¿A qué hora es la clase?
At what time is the class?

¿A qué hora es el almuerzo?

To answer say:

(Es) a las tres de la tarde.
(It's) at three in the afternoon.

¡Es ahora! Son las doce en punto.
It's now! It's twelve o'clock on the dot.

PA
pp. 31–32
Act. 10

GV
p.21
Acts. 8–9

VOCABULARIO

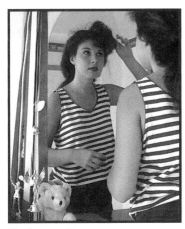

de la mañana
in the morning (A.M.)

de la tarde
in the afternoon (P.M.)

de la noche
in the evening (P.M.)

19 Horarios Script and answers on p. 101E

Two new students are discussing their daily schedules. Listen to each question. Then choose the best answer for each question.

CD 3 Tr. 10

1. a. Es la una de la mañana.
   b. Son las ocho de la mañana.

2. a. A las siete de la mañana.
   b. A las doce y media de la tarde.

3. a. Sí, son las tres de la tarde.
   b. Sí, son las tres de la mañana.

4. a. A las seis de la tarde.
   b. A las doce menos cuarto.

5. a. A la una y cuarto de la tarde.
   b. A las dos de la mañana.

6. a. Son las tres de la mañana.
   b. Son las cinco de la tarde.

SEGUNDO PASO

ciento diecinueve **119**

TEACH

PRESENTATION
ASÍ SE DICE
Create a list in Spanish of upcoming school-related activities. Make a calendar and enter the activities and the times they start. Ask students to practice asking a partner what time an event takes place.
—¿A qué hora es el partido de fútbol?
—A las siete.

VOCABULARIO

Using the new vocabulary items, ask students when they have different classes:
—Julia, ¿a qué hora tienes la clase de arte?
—Tengo arte a las dos y media de la tarde.

ADDITIONAL PRACTICE
To practice the vocabulary, ask students questions and have them clarify whether the activity takes place in the morning, afternoon, or evening. **¿Practicas el fútbol a las cinco? ¿A las cinco de la mañana o de la tarde? (A las cinco de la tarde.)**

CULTURE NOTE
Throughout a great deal of the Spanish-speaking world, the idea of the afternoon is a little different. The afternoon for many Spanish speakers can be as late as 7:00 P.M.

GROUP WORK

20 This activity requires file cards and several TV schedule listings. Put students in groups of five. Have each group write the name and time (in numerals) of five of their favorite TV programs, one on each card. Give each group a TV schedule so that they may verify the program times. Then have them exchange their file cards with another group. On the back of each card, the group receiving it will write out the time of the program in Spanish. After completing the times in Spanish, they give the cards back to the group that created them for peer review.

ADDITIONAL PRACTICE

To practice the difference between **¿Qué hora es?** and **¿A qué hora...?** bring in a watch and a schedule listing (a bus schedule, for example) and place them on your desk. Have volunteers come forward one at a time. Ask them either **¿A qué hora es...?** or **¿Qué hora es?** The volunteer shows his or her understanding by consulting either the watch (which you reset for each student) or the schedule to answer your question.

20 La tele

Complete the conversation between Sandra and Juan Carlos with the words from the word box. One word will be used more than once. Use the TV schedule to help you.

1. gusta
2. qué
3. siete
4. después
5. a las
6. a qué hora
7. de la noche
8. gusta

SANDRA	A mí me ___1___ *Beetlejuice*.
JUAN CARLOS	¿A ___2___ hora es?
SANDRA	A las ___3___. Y ___4___ de *Beetlejuice* es *Batman*.
JUAN CARLOS	Es ___5___ siete y media, ¿no? Y ¿___6___ es *Intriga Tropical*?
SANDRA	A las ocho ___7___. ¿Te gusta *Intriga Tropical*?
JUAN CARLOS	Sí, me ___8___ mucho.

Word box:
de la noche   gusta   a qué hora
qué   después   a las   siete

TV schedule (Jueves, DIC.30 NOCHE):

7:00 **5** BEETLEJUICE. Dibujos animados.
NOCHE **7** ALF. Comedia.
9 ESPECIAL MUSICAL. Variedades. "Timbiriche".
11 HOY EN LA CULTURA Entrevista especial a Octavio Paz. Premio Nobel de Literatura y Orgullo de México. Conducción: Sari Bermúdez.
7:30 **2** ¡LLÉVATELO! Concursos para toda la familia, con Paco Stanley y Gabriela Ruffo.
5 BATMAN. Dibujos animados.
7 SALVADO POR LA CAMPANA. Aventuras.
11 EL HOMBRE Y LA INDUSTRIA. Reportajes. Juventud.
13 SEÑORA. Telenovela.
22 POR AQUI PUEDEN PASAR. Animación infantil. Cuentos alrededor del mundo: Rumpelstkin.
7:50 **22** ENCUADRE. Cartelera cinematográfica. Con Leonardo García Tsao y Nelson Carro.
8:00 **4** LOS INTOCABLES. Aventuras policíacas.
5 INTRIGA TROPICAL. Aventuras de un ex-agente antinarcóticos y su socia detective. Rob Stewart "Nick Slaughter", Carolyn Dunn "Sylvie Girard", Pedro Armendáriz "Lt. Carrillo".
7 LOS SIMPSONS Dibujos animados.
9 LOLITA AYALA, FERNANDO SCHWARTZ. Muchas Noticias.

21 ¿A qué hora es la clase?

With a partner, take turns asking each other when these classes meet. Use the times given for each course.

MODELO ¿A qué hora es la clase de ciencias?
A las nueve menos cuarto de la mañana.

Answers on p. 101K

1. 10:35 de la mañana

2. 2:10 de la tarde

3. 11:50 de la mañana

4. 3:40 de la tarde

5. 1:30 de la tarde

6. 8:25 de la mañana

22 Entrevista

Get together with a classmate. Imagine that you've just met. Exchange greetings and then find out the following information about each other. After you've interviewed each other, write down each other's schedules. Answers on p. 101K

a. how each of you is feeling today
b. where each of you is from
c. what classes you each have today and at what time they meet

p. 33
Act. 13

p. 22
Acts. 10–11

NOTA GRAMATICAL

In Spanish, to show that something belongs to someone, use **de**.

> **los zapatos de David**
> *David's shoes*

> **las clases de Eva**
> *Eva's classes*

De combines with **el** to form the contraction **del**.

> el perro **del** profesor
> *the teacher's dog*

> la directora **del** colegio
> *the school's director*

Nota cultural

In Spain, sneakers are referred to as **zapatillas de tenis**. In Latin America, they're called **zapatos de tenis**. In fact, the word **zapatillas** means slippers in Latin America. Spanish sometimes has more than one word for an object, depending on the country. English is like this, too. For example, in England an elevator is called a lift. Can you think of other examples in English where there is more than one word for something?

23 Una encuesta

With your partner, take turns completing the sentences below. Be ready to report your and your partner's choices to the class. Answers will vary.

MODELO   LUIS   Mi actor favorito es Andy García.
         TÚ   El actor favorito de Luis es Andy García.

1. Mi actor favorito es...
2. Mi actriz *(actress)* favorita es...
3. Mi libro favorito es...
4. Mi deporte favorito es...
5. Mi color favorito es...
6. Mi programa de televisión favorito es...

SEGUNDO PASO

ciento veintiuno **121**

PRESENTATION

NOTA GRAMATICAL
First, have the students read the grammar explanation. Then walk around the class and pick up various objects. Ask for volunteers to answer questions such as **¿De quién es este libro?** Elicit answers such as **Es el libro de Beth** or **Es de Beth.**

SUGGESTION
22 Have students work in pairs, or suggest that students alternate asking questions around their circle of three. Each student will then have an opportunity to both ask and answer questions. Students may need an example of an interview dialogue:
—**¿Cómo estás?** —**Estoy bien.**
—**¿De dónde eres?** —**Soy de aquí.**
—**A las ocho ¿qué clase tienes?** —**Tengo la clase de arte a las ocho.**

FAMILY LINK
Ask students to get together with someone at home and write out that person's daily schedule. Does the person do the same things at the same time every day, or does his or her schedule vary? Have students report their findings to the class, describing in Spanish a typical day in a family member's life. Remind them that they can substitute an imaginary family member if they wish.

STANDARDS: 1.3, 2.2, 4.1, 5.1   **121**

pp. 32–33
Acts. 11–12

CD-ROM DISC 1

ASÍ SE DICE Talking about being late or in a hurry

To tell someone you are late, say:

Estoy atrasada. *(if you're female)*

Estoy atrasado. *(if you're male)*

To tell someone you are in a hurry, say:

Tengo prisa.

To say that someone else is late, say:

La profesora de biología **está atrasada.**

El director del colegio **está atrasado.**

To tell a friend to hurry up, say:

¡Date prisa!

24 ¡Date prisa! H

Everyone's running late today! Match the correct photo to each caption below.

a

b

c

d

1. ¡Ay! Son las nueve y cuarto. Estoy atrasado. c
2. Buenas tardes, señor Altamirano. Tengo prisa porque la clase de ciencias sociales es a la una. b
3. ¿Estás atrasado, Julio? ¿A qué hora tienes clase? a
4. ¡Date prisa, Claudia! También quiero ir al centro comercial. d

25 ¡Es tarde!

Leopoldo left his watch at home and is having a hard day.
Complete the conversation below.

son
hora
clase
prisa
atrasado

LEOPOLDO   La __1__ de español es a   clase
las dos. ¿Qué __2__ es?   hora

CARLA   Ya __3__ las dos y cinco.   Son

LEOPOLDO   ¡Ay! Estoy __4__.   atrasado

CARLA   ¡Date __5__!   prisa

26 Los planes

Luisa and Juan are talking on the telephone. Write Juan's part of
the conversation. You might also want to draw a picture of Juan
on a piece of paper and write his answers to her questions beside
your picture as in the drawing of Luisa.

Answers will vary.
Possible answers:
—Sí, me gusta la comida
   mexicana.
—Es a las siete de la noche.
—Sí, a las siete en punto.
—Bueno, hasta luego.

Luisa

27 Lo siento, no tengo tiempo.

Imagine that you and your partner have just run into each other
at a shopping mall. Write a conversation in which one of you
keeps on talking about his or her schedule while the other tries to
end the conversation. Practice the conversation with your partner.   Answers on p. 101K

Primero tengo clase de
matemáticas a las...

Luego tengo literatura a las...

Lo siento, pero estoy
atrasado/a.

¡Tengo prisa! Tengo un
examen ahora.

VISUAL LEARNERS
26 Write sentences on
paper strips that reflect both
sides of the conversation. Test
student comprehension by mix-
ing up the sentences and having them put the sentences in
the correct order.

☀ CLOSE

Ask your students: **¿A qué hora
es la clase de español?, ¿A
qué hora es el almuerzo?,** or
**Tienes la clase de español a
las ocho. Son las ocho y
media. ¿Estás atrasado/a?** Use
Teaching Transparency 3-2 and
Teaching Transparency 3-A to
further review the material
from this **paso.**

☀ ASSESS

▸ Testing Program, pp. 39–40
  Quiz 3-2
  Audio CD 3, Tr. 19

▸ Grammar and Vocabulary
  Quizzes
  Quiz 3-2A or
  Alternative Quiz 3-2A

▸ Alternative Assessment
  Guide, p. 21

**PERFORMANCE
ASSESSMENT**
Make up an age-appropriate
TV schedule and pass out a
copy to each student. Have
students work in pairs to prepare a dialogue in which one
asks the times of various programs, which the other student
provides. Students are to present their dialogues to the
class or record them on an
audio- or videocassette.

Describing people and things; talking about things you like and explaining why

> **CLAUDIA** Fernando, ¿cómo es esta clase?
>
> **FERNANDO** Ay, es horrible. El profesor es muy aburrido... ¡y no le gustan los exámenes fáciles!
>
> **MARÍA INÉS** No te preocupes, Claudia, no es verdad. Esta clase es mi favorita. Es muy interesante, y el profesor, pues, es... así.

28 ¿Clase favorita?

Based on the scene above, choose the correct answer.

1. ¿A quién le gusta la clase?
   a. a Claudia
   b. a Fernando
   c. a María Inés

2. ¿A quién no le gusta la clase?
   a. a María Inés
   b. a Claudia
   c. a Fernando

3. A María Inés le gusta la clase porque es...
   a. horrible
   b. muy interesante
   c. muy aburrida

4. Fernando dice (*says*) que el profesor es...
   a. muy interesante
   b. muy travieso
   c. muy aburrido

Nota cultural

Titles of respect are often used in Spanish-speaking countries. Teachers are frequently addressed as **profesor/a** or **maestro/a**. Some other titles are **licenciado**, used usually for someone with a bachelor's degree, **ingeniero** (*engineer*), or **arquitecto** (*architect*). The title **doctor** is used for medical doctors, and also for others who have received an advanced degree from a university. What other titles can you think of?

VIDEO INTEGRATION

Adelante LEVEL 1A
Video Program
Videocassette 1, 48:51–49:28 OR
Videocassette 3, 26:00–26:37
(*captioned version*)

¡Ven conmigo! LEVEL 1
DVD Tutor, Disc 1

Bell work
Write these questions on the board or on a transparency and have students write their answers.
¿Qué hora es?
¿A qué hora tienes el almuerzo?
¿Te gusta el español?
¿Qué clase tienes después del español?
¿Te gusta?

MOTIVATING ACTIVITY
Ask students what their favorite subjects are and why they like them. Which subject do they like best? As an introduction you could have students raise their hands to answer how many like art, math, English, physical education, Spanish, etc.

SUGGESTION
Names of additional professions can be found in the Additional Vocabulary on pages 275–277.

ASÍ SE DICE Describing people and things

PA
p. 35
Act. 15

To find out what people and things are like, ask:

¿Cómo es tu compañero/a nuevo/a?
What's your new friend like?

¿Cómo es la clase?

¿Cómo son los profesores?
What are the teachers like?

To tell what someone or something is like, say:

Él es alto.
He's tall.
Ella es alta.
She's tall.
Es excelente. **No es aburrida.**
It's excellent. It's not boring.

No te preocupes. Ellos no son muy estrictos.
Don't worry. They aren't very strict.

VOCABULARIO

GV
p. 24
Acts.
14–16

3-B

antipático/a	*disagreeable*
bueno/a	*good*
cómico/a	*funny*
difícil	*difficult*
divertido/a	*fun, amusing*
fácil	*easy*
guapo/a	*good-looking*
inteligente	*intelligent*
interesante	*interesting*
malo/a	*bad*
nuevo/a	*new*
simpático/a	*nice*

29 ¿Cómo es?

Write four questions asking what the characters in the drawing are like. Then answer each of your questions. Answers will vary. Possible answers:

MODELO —¿Cómo es Oso? —Él es muy feo.

1. ¿Cómo es el señor Medina?
   Es muy guapo.
2. ¿Cómo es la abuela?
   Es muy simpática.
3. ¿Cómo es Panchito?
   Es bajo.
4. ¿Cómo es Lupita Reyes?
   Es bonita.

TERCER PASO

ciento veinticinco **125**

☀ MOTIVATE

Ask students to pretend that they have to provide a description of an imaginary friend. What words or phrases in English would they use to say what the person looks like? to indicate that the person is male or female?

☀ TEACH

PRESENTATION
ASÍ SE DICE
VOCABULARIO

Present the functional phrases and vocabulary by describing to the class several people in Teaching Transparency 3-3 or in magazine photos. Then play Twenty Questions using three pictures taped to the board. Say that you're thinking of one of the people, and have students ask yes-or-no questions until they can guess the name of the person you're thinking about. You might have students play the game in small groups.

TPR Post magazine pictures of people in the front of the room. Describe one, **Él es moreno y alto,** for example, and have a student come forward and point to the correct picture.

P A p. 36 Act. 19

G V p. 23 Acts.12–13

NOTA GRAMATICAL

You're familiar with the singular forms of **ser** *(to be)*. Here are all the forms of the verb.

(yo) **soy**	(nosotros) (nosotras) **somos**
(tú) **eres**	(vosotros) (vosotras) **sois**
(usted) (él) **es** (ella)	(ustedes) (ellos) **son** (ellas)

30 ¿Quién es?

Efraín is describing people to his mother. What does he say about each person? Complete each sentence by matching the person with the description.

a **1.** Rosalinda
d **2.** Nosotros
c **3.** Yo
b **4.** Mis amigos
e **5.** Tú

a. es inteligente y divertida.
b. son divertidos.
c. soy interesante.
d. somos cómicos.
e. eres bonita y simpática.

31 ¿Cómo son?

Match each drawing with an appropriate description.

1. Es nuevo pero es aburrido. c
2. Son bajos y muy cómicos. d
3. Son pequeños pero son muy malos. a
4. Es alto y feo. b

32 Ella es bonita

With a partner, take turns describing three of the characters on page 125. Have your partner guess who you're describing.

MODELO —Es bonita, morena y joven.   Answers will vary.
—Es Lupita Reyes.

GRAMÁTICA   Adjective agreement

pp. 35–36
Acts.
16–17

p. 25
Act. 17

Have you noticed that adjectives such as **divertido** change to match the nouns they modify?

	MASCULINE	FEMININE
SINGULAR	un libro **divertido**	una clase **divertida**
PLURAL	unos libros **divertidos**	unas clases **divertidas**

1. To describe one person or thing, use **es** + a singular adjective.
   El libro **es divertido.**   La clase **es divertida.**

2. To describe more than one person or thing, use **son** + a plural adjective.
   Los libros **son buenos.**   Las clases **son buenas.**

3. If you're describing a group of males and females, use a masculine plural adjective.
   María y Daniel **son simpáticos.**

4. Adjectives ending in -**e** or a consonant such as **l, r,** or **n** have only two forms: singular and plural. To make these adjectives plural, add -**s** if the word ends with a vowel, as **interesante** does.
   El libro es **interesante.** → Los libros son **interesantes.**
   For words ending with a consonant, like **difícil,** add -**es.**
   La clase es **difícil.** → Las clases son **difíciles.**

33 La carta de Claudia

Claudia is writing to her cousin Marisa, telling her about her new school and her friends there. Complete her letter by choosing the appropriate adjectives from the word box. Use each adjective only once.

bonita   simpáticos
inteligentes   interesantes
divertidas   difíciles
guapo   cómica

Querida Marisa,
¡Hola! ¿Cómo estás? Bueno, aquí estoy en el Instituto Centro Unión. Me gusta mucho. Las clases son __1__ y __2__ pero no son __3__. Los profesores son muy __4__. Los estudiantes en este colegio son __5__. Mi amiga María Inés es __6__ y __7__. Fernando es el amigo de María Inés. Él es muy __8__. Bueno, ahora tengo clase. ¡Ya estoy atrasada!

                    ¡Hasta luego!
                    Claudia

1. interesantes
2. divertidas
3. difíciles
4. inteligentes
5. simpáticos
6. bonita
7. cómica
8. guapo

PRESENTATION
GRAMÁTICA
Use pictures of people from magazines or stick figures on the board to practice gender and number. For example, draw or show two female figures and write the adjective **bonito.** Ask **¿Cómo son?** and have students respond **Son bonitas.**

SUGGESTION
Have students cut out pictures of famous people from magazines. Place them in a bag and have one student go to the front of the room. Select a picture from the bag and tape it on the student's back. Other students take turns making up a descriptive sentence hinting at who the famous person is. After each sentence, the student who is "it" must guess the name of the celebrity.

ADDITIONAL PRACTICE
33 Using Claudia's letter as a model, have students write a brief description of school, their friends, classes, and teachers.

LANGUAGE NOTE
You might point out to students that **rubio/a** and **moreno/a** may also be used to describe someone's complexion.

Answers to Activity 34

1. Mis clases no son difíciles. Son fáciles.
2. La clase de español no es aburrida. Es interesante.
3. Mi cuarto no es pequeño y feo. Es grande y bonito.
4. Los profesores no son antipáticos. Son simpáticos.
5. Alberto no es aburrido. Es interesante.
6. Mis amigos no son malos. Son buenos.

34 ¡Al contrario!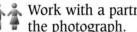

You wrote in your diary when you were in a really bad mood, and now you feel different. Change each statement to say the opposite of what you wrote.   Answers in side column

MODELO   Fernando es antipático. → No, no es antipático. Es simpático.

1. Mis clases son difíciles.
2. La clase de español es aburrida.
3. Mi cuarto es pequeño y feo.
4. Los profesores son antipáticos.
5. Alberto es aburrido.
6. Mis amigos son malos.

35 Descripciones

 Work with a partner and write at least three sentences describing the photograph.   Answers will vary. Possible answers:

1. Pepe es muy malo.
2. Marisol es muy bonita.
3. Dolores es rubia.

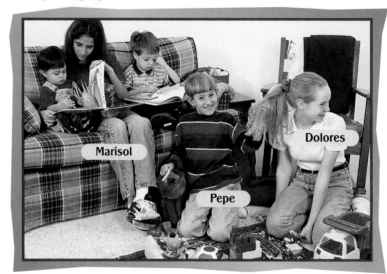

Marisol · Dolores · Pepe

36 Mis amigos son...

 Work with a partner. Take turns asking and answering questions about the following people and things. Be prepared to share your opinions with the class.   Answers on p. 101K

MODELO   —Oye, ¿cómo es tu cuarto?
            —Mira, es pequeño pero bonito.

1. el libro de...
2. la comida en la cafetería
3. la clase de...
4. la tarea de...
5. tus amigos
6. la música de...

37 ¡Escribamos!

Write a short paragraph of six or seven sentences describing your classes, teachers, and friends at school this year. How many classes do you have? At what time are they? Can you describe your teachers and friends?   Answers will vary.

ASÍ SE DICE Talking about things you like and explaining why

p. 36
Act. 18

To find out if a friend likes more than one thing, ask:

¿**Te gustan** las clases?

¿**Cuál es** tu clase favorita?
Which is your favorite class?

¿**A Claudia le gustan** las ciencias?
Does Claudia like science?

¿**Por qué?**
Why?

Your friend might answer:

Sí, **me gustan.** Son fáciles.

Mi clase **favorita** es inglés.

Sí. **Le gustan** mucho y también **le gusta** la geografía.

Porque son muy interesantes.
Because it's very interesting.

38 ¿Te gustan?

Match each question with the appropriate answer.

1. ¿Cuál es tu deporte favorito? c
2. ¿Por qué? g
3. ¿Cuál es tu comida favorita? a
4. ¿A Sandra le gustan las clases? f
5. ¿Por qué le gusta a Claudia la capital? h
6. ¿Por qué te gusta ir al centro comercial? e
7. ¿Tc gusta la música rock? b
8. ¿A ti te gustan los zapatos de tenis? d

a. Me gusta mucho la pizza.
b. Sí, me gusta mucho. No es aburrida.
c. Es la natación.
d. No, no me gustan porque son feos.
e. Porque me gusta comprar ropa.
f. Sí, le gustan porque son interesantes.
g. Porque es divertida.
h. Le gusta porque los parques y museos son divertidos.

De Nuevo a Clases

N$259

N$199

N$219

A precios sin competencia

la línea de zapatos "Deportes"

MOTIVATING ACTIVITY
Ask students to list three things they like and three things they don't like. Have them think about why. (fun, not fun, interesting, boring, and so on)

PRESENTATION
ASÍ SE DICE
Review the singular forms of **gustar:**
Me gusta el arte.
¿**Te gusta el arte?**
Then introduce **le gusta(n)** and tell students it means *he, she, you (formal) like(s).* For example:
A Rebeca le gusta el arte.
Ask students individual questions to elicit these forms.
—¿**Te gusta el arte, Rebeca?**
—**Sí, me gusta el arte.**
—**Juan, ¿a Rebeca le gusta el arte?**
—**Sí, le gusta el arte.**
Then do plural forms.

SUGGESTION
38 Have students work in pairs to answer the questions in ¿**Te gustan?** verbally. Also, have them each write two or three questions of their own to ask each other. Spot-check student work by circulating around the classroom and by asking for volunteers to report their partners' likes and dislikes.

VOCABULARIO

GV p. 26 Acts. 18–19

3-C

el baile

el concierto

los deportes

el examen (pl. **los exámenes**)

la fiesta

la novela

el partido de...

el videojuego

39 Patricia y Gregorio
Script and answers on p. 101F

CD 3 Tr. 11

Patricia and Gregorio have just met at school. First, read the true and false statements about their conversation. Then, listen to Patricia and Gregorio as they try to decide what to do. Based on their conversation, respond to these statements with **cierto** or **falso.**

1. A Patricia no le gustan las fiestas.
2. A Gregorio le gustan los partidos de fútbol porque son interesantes.
3. A Patricia no le gustan los conciertos.
4. A Gregorio le gusta la música rock.

NOTA GRAMATICAL

p. 34
Act. 14

One way of asking a question is by adding **¿no?** or **¿verdad?** to the end of a sentence. These are called *tag questions.*

> La clase es difícil, **¿no?**
> *The class is difficult, isn't it?*

> Te gustan las fiestas, **¿verdad?**
> *You like parties, don't you?/ right?*

¡Una Fiesta de Cumpleaños!

40 ¿Por qué te gusta? Answers will vary.

Take turns asking each other whether or not you like the things in the list below. When your partner answers, ask "why?" and listen to the reason. Use the adjectives from the word box in your explanation.

MODELO —Te gustan los bailes, ¿no?
—Sí, me gustan mucho.
—¿Por qué?
—Porque son divertidos.

1. la música pop
2. los exámenes
3. el basquetbol
4. las fiestas
5. los deportes
6. los videojuegos
7. el tenis

antipático/a   bueno/a
cómico/a   difícil
divertido/a   fácil   malo/a
interesante   simpático/a
nuevo/a

41 La fiesta de cumpleaños Answers will vary.

 You're helping your friend plan a birthday party. Ask your partner at least four questions to try to find out what activities he or she might like at the party. Use tag questions like **¿no?** and **¿verdad?** in two of your questions. Then reverse roles.

MODELO —Te gusta la música popular, ¿verdad?
—Sí, me gusta la música popular en inglés y en español.

TERCER PASO

ciento treinta y uno **131**

PRESENTATION

NOTA GRAMATICAL

Model the use of tag questions verbally and on the board. For example, **Paul Rodríguez es cómico, ¿verdad?** or **Homer Simpson es muy delgado, ¿no?** You may wish to play the section of the video where María Inés models the use of **¿no?** or point out her question in **De antemano** on page 105.

SLOWER PACE

40 If students are having trouble remembering vocabulary, put pictures of famous people on the board and number each one. Ask students to write a list of adjectives for each picture. It may be helpful for them to associate an image with adjectives. Then, have them check their adjective endings to be sure the form is correct.

PORTFOLIO

43 Written Point out to students that this activity would be an appropriate entry for their written portfolio. For Portfolio suggestions, see *Alternative Assessment Guide,* p. 14.

SUGGESTION

43 Ask students to write to the Mexican Embassy or the Mexican Government Tourism Office (see page T58) to obtain information on Mexico. They might ask for information on specific cities such as Cuernavaca. Students may also supplement their knowledge with travel books on Mexico from bookstores or public libraries.

42 Soy...

Form a group of five. On a sheet of paper, write a detailed description of yourself. In your description, include your age, what kind of person you are, what you look like, and things you like and don't like. Don't include your name, and try to disguise your handwriting. Fold your paper in half. Shuffle all the papers. Each group member picks one paper, reads it aloud and tries to guess who it is. If you get your own paper, pick again.   Answers will vary.

43 De visita

A Imagine that you're a student at the **Instituto Centro Unión** in Cuernavaca, Mexico. Prepare a list of at least six questions that you can use to interview students from the U.S. who are visiting your class. Write at least one question about each of the following.

how old he or she is
—¿Cuántos años tienes?

what classes he or she has this semester
—¿Qué clases tienes este semestre?

what his or her friends are like
—¿Cómo son tus amigos?

what he or she likes
—¿Qué te gusta?

what his or her teachers are like
—¿Cómo son tus profesores?

what he or she doesn't like
—¿Qué no te gusta?

B Now work with a partner and decide who will play the student from Cuernavaca and who will be a student from the U.S. Interview your partner using the questions you've prepared. Then switch roles.

44 En mi cuaderno

In your journal, write seven or eight sentences about what you need and want to do at different times tomorrow. Include such items as going to class, doing homework, and going shopping. Use **necesito** and **quiero**. Answers will vary.

MODELO   Mañana necesito hacer la tarea de inglés a las cuatro y media. También quiero...

LETRA Y SONIDO

Script on p. 101F

CD 3
Trs. 12–16

A. 1. **h:** The letter **h** in Spanish is always silent.

| hora | ahora | héroe | Hugo | hijo | hospital |

2. **j:** The letter **j** in Spanish represents a sound that has no matching sound in English. It's pronounced like the *h* in the English word *house*, but much stronger.

| jugar | jefe | ají | joven | pasaje | caja | juego |

3. **g:** The letter **g** before the vowels **e** and **i** has the same sound as the letter *j* in the examples above.

| gente | general | geografía | gimnasio | corregir | agitar |

4. Before the vowels **a, o,** and **u** the letter **g** is pronounced like the *g* in the English word *go.*

| ángulo | tengo | gusto | mango |

Between vowels this sound is much softer.

| haga | agua | agotar | mucho gusto |

5. The **g** is pronounced "hard," like the *g* in *get,* when it's part of **gue** or **gui.**

| guerra | llegué | guitarra | guía |

B. Dictado
Jimena describes for us what she needs in two of her classes. Write what Jimena is saying.

C. Trabalenguas
La gente de San José generalmente juega a las barajas con ganas de ganar.

EN MI CUADERNO
44 For an additional Chapter 3 journal entry suggestion, see *Practice and Activity Book,* page 77.

ADDITIONAL PRACTICE
44 Have student brainstorm first, to think of vocabulary for what they need and want to do.

☀ CLOSE

Hold up photos of famous people clipped from magazines. Ask students to describe the people. For example, while holding a photo of a famous athlete, ask: **¿Quién es? ¿Cómo es él/ella? ¿Es alto/a? ¿Es guapo/a? ¿moreno/a? ¿simpático/a? ¿Qué le gusta a él/ella? ¿Le gustan los deportes?** Repeat with various photos to review a variety of adjectives.

☀ ASSESS

▸ Testing Program, pp. 41–42
  Quiz 3-3
  Audio CD 3, Tr. 20

▸ Grammar and Vocabulary Quizzes
  Quiz 3-3A or
  Alternative Quiz 3-3A

▸ Alternative Assessment Guide, p. 21

PERFORMANCE ASSESSMENT
Bring in ads from a magazine for students to critique. What do they like about the ad? (**Me gustan los colores. Son bonitos.**) What would they change? (**No me gusta el hombre. No es cómico.**)

MOTIVATING ACTIVITY

Ask for volunteers to say whether they know people in other parts of the United States. Do they have relatives or friends in other states? Have they ever lived in a different state?

PRESENTATION

Using a map of the United States, explain to students what a time zone is. If they don't already know, have them determine which time zone they live in. Then ask them if they know people who live in other time zones. Do they have to account for a time change if they want to call someone in another time zone? Ask them to consider why someone living in San Francisco should probably not call someone in Washington, D.C. too late in the evening.

CULTURE NOTE

Making long distance phone calls can be a very different experience in another country. Fewer people have long distance service because it is extremely expensive. Many countries have long distance calling centers where people wait in line to access special telephone booths. An operator makes the call and directs the customer to a booth.

LAS MATEMÁTICAS/LA GEOGRAFÍA

1 ¿Qúe hora es?

Look at the time zone map and note how many hours difference there is between different areas of the world. Next look at the times and places in the questions below. For each item, say what time it is in the Latin American country given. Answers on p. 101K

MODELO Son las cuatro de la tarde en Miami. ¿Qué hora es en Caracas?

The time zone map shows it's one hour later in Caracas than in Miami.

$$\begin{array}{r} 4:00 \text{ P.M.} \\ + 1:00 \text{ hora} \\ \hline 5:00 \text{ P.M.} \end{array}$$

Son las cinco de la tarde en Caracas.

En los Estados Unidos

1. Es la una de la tarde en San Francisco.
2. Son las tres de la mañana en Denver.
3. Son las dos y media de la tarde en Chicago.
4. En Nueva York son las nueve y cuarto de la noche.

En la América Latina

¿Qué hora es en Bogotá?

¿Qué hora es en La Habana?

¿Qué hora es en la Ciudad de Panamá?

¿Qué hora es en la Ciudad de México?

2 La llamada

You're on a trip in Latin America and planning to call your friend back home. If you call from Caracas at 5:00 P.M. on Saturday, what time is it in your home town? Choose another Latin American city to visit and another time to call your friend. What time would it be then in your home town? Answers will vary.

BOGOTÁ

Son las 4:00 de la tarde aquí en Bogotá.

CHICAGO

Son las 3:00 de la tarde en Chicago.

LAS MATEMÁTICAS

How the 24-hour system works:

3:00   8:30   12:00   19:30   23:00

Many countries around the world use schedules based on a 24-hour clock. This allows travelers to look quickly at schedules and know the difference between 9:00 A.M. and 9:00 P.M. For example, using a 24-hour clock for a train schedule, a morning train would leave at 9:00 and a night train would leave at 21:00.

3 Convertir a 24 horas

How would you write the following times using the 24-hour system? For P.M. hours, add 12:00 to the hour. For A.M. hours, write the same hour but without using the abbreviation "A.M."

MODELO   2:35 A.M.   **2:35**

1. 7:20 A.M.   **3.** 9:25 P.M.   **5.** 11:00 A.M.

2. 3:15 P.M.   **4.** 4:30 P.M.   **6.** 8:15 P.M.

```
  1:05 P.M.
+ 12:00
  13:05
```

1. 7:20
2. 15:15
3. 21:25
4. 16:30
5. 11:00
6. 20:15

4 Convertir de 24 horas

Rewrite these times using A.M. and P.M. For times before 12:00, add A.M. to the end. For times after 12:59, subtract 12:00 from the hour and add P.M. at the end of the result.

MODELO   2:35   **2:35 A.M.**

1. 23:40   **3.** 1:15   **5.** 20:39

2. 17:55   **4.** 15:25   **6.** 5:42

```
  13:05
- 12:00
  1:05 P.M.
```

1. 11:40 P.M.
2. 5:55 P.M.
3. 1:15 A.M.
4. 3:25 P.M.
5. 8:39 P.M.
6. 5:42 A.M.

5 Horario de aviones

Answer the following questions using the 12-hour system (A.M. and P.M.).

1. What time does flight AO 444 to Madrid leave?   1:10 P.M.

2. If you got to the airport at 2:00 P.M., would you have enough time to catch the flight to Barcelona? Why or why not?   no; it departs at 2:05 P.M.

3. If you got out of school at 3:00 P.M., which flight to Melilla would you be able to catch?

the second flight, which leaves at 4:15 P.M.

VUELO FLIGHT	SALIDAS DESTINO TO	HORA TIME
IB 346	MADRID	1250
AO 444	MADRID	1310
IB 834	BARCELONA	1405
AO 452	P.MALLORCA	1445
AAN106	P.MALLORCA	1450
IB 387	MELILLA	1500
IB 397	MELILLA	1615

PRESENTATION

Ask students how many hours there are in a day. Ask them what the next hour after 12:00 noon is. What would happen if we didn't start over again with one? What would the next number be? What would be the advantages of using 13:00 instead of 1:00? Explain that when using a 24-hour clock, 0:00 is midnight. Then put 1:00 on the board and ask students if it is 1:00 A.M. or 1:00 P.M. Once it becomes clear that 1:00 is 1:00 A.M., ask students how they think 1:00 P.M. would be represented.

TEACHER NOTE

You may want to mention that in the U.S. the 24-hour clock is also referred to as *military time*.

VAMOS A LEER

p. 37
Act. 20

Estrategia
Using background knowledge

As soon as you know the topic of a reading, spend a couple of minutes just thinking about the topic. What do you already know about it? The reading should then be easier to understand, and you'll be better able to guess unknown words and make sense of difficult passages.

¡A comenzar!

A You'll probably be familiar with the topics of these items. Skim them briefly and then complete the following statement.

These items are

a. TV schedules and sports scores
b. report cards and TV schedules
c. sports scores and class schedules
d. class schedules and report cards

B Draw three columns on your paper. Title one <u>schedules</u>, the next <u>report cards</u>, and the third <u>neither</u>. Read the items below and decide if they would be found in report cards, in schedules, or in neither. Write the number of each item below in the correct column. Some items may belong under both <u>schedules</u> and <u>report cards</u>.

1. letter grades   Answers on p. 101K
2. parents' names
3. class names

4. days of the week   Answers on p. 101K
5. student's name
6. textbook names
7. numerical grades
8. best friend's name
9. class times

Now look at the report cards and schedule above and find the mentioned items.

Al grano

C Look at the last columns of each report card.   Answers on p. 101K

1. The numerical grades are the achievement grades for the class. There are also letter grades. What do the letter grades on Juana's report card represent?
2. What is the highest grade each student got in science?
3. Who did better in physical education?
4. Who did better in Spanish?

D Contesta las siguientes preguntas.
1. ¿Cuántas clases tiene Gloria? ¿Óscar? ¿Juana?
2. ¿Te gustan las clases de Gloria? ¿Por qué?
3. ¿A qué hora empiezan *(begin)* las clases de Gloria?
   Answers on p. 101K

READING STRATEGY
Using background knowledge

MOTIVATING ACTIVITY
Discuss with students the basic reasons for having schedules and report cards. What information do they contain? What would schools be like without them?

☀ PREREADING

USING PRIOR KNOWLEDGE
- You may wish to review the 24-hour clock, which is explained in the previous **Enlaces** on page 135.
- Ask students what information is listed on their report cards. (student name, classes, grades) What is the grading system that is most commonly used in the United States? What do the letters A, B, C, D, and F mean?

NATIVE SPEAKERS
If you have students who have studied in other countries, ask them to talk about the grading system in the countries where they lived. Was it a system of numbers or letters? What were the numbers or letters used and what did they mean?

MULTICULTURAL LINK
Discuss with students ways to get schedules and report cards from other countries. Students can write to an education agency in Mexico (see page T58).

ÓSCAR GONZÁLEZ LÓPEZ (MÉXICO)

MATRÍCULA B0847842	SEPT.	OCT.	NOV.	ENE.	FEB.	MAR.
ESPAÑOL	7.7	9.8	9.5	9.5	9.2	8.4
MATEMÁTICAS	8.8	8.2	9.0	6.4	7.1	8.0
LENG.A.A/ESPAÑOLA	8.5	6.5	7.5	9.0	10.0	10.0
C. NATURALES	7.2	7.4	7.6	8.1	8.8	7.7
C. SOCIALES	9.0	7.7	9.6	10.0	9.7	9.4
EDUC. FÍSICA	10.0	7.5	10.0	9.5	9.6	9.5
EDUC. ARTÍSTICA	10.0	10.0	10.0	10.0	9.5	9.5
EDUC. TECNOLÓGICA	10.0	10.0	10.0	10.0	10.0	10.0

ALUMNA: JUANA ACOSTA RUIZ (ESPAÑA)

Segundo De B.U.P.	PRIMERA EVALUACIÓN			TERCERA EVALUACIÓN		
	Faltas de asistencia	conoci-mientos	Actitud	Faltas de asistencia	conoci-mientos	Actitud
Español		7	C		8	C
Francés		8	B	1	6	B
Geografía Humana		8	C		7	C
Matemáticas		5	C		5	C
Ciencias		9	B		6	C
Religión		7	C		7	B
Educ. Física y Deportes					6	C

El horario de Gloria (México)

Hora	lunes	martes	miércoles	jueves	viernes
7:30–8:20	música	civismo	geografía	biología	historia
8:30–9:20	español	inglés	inglés	matemáticas	matemáticas
9:30–10:20	matemáticas	español	historia	educación física	civismo
10:30–11:20	historia	música	matemáticas	geografía	educación física
11:30–12:20	inglés	descanso	descanso	descanso	español
12:30–13:20	biología	matemáticas	español	español	biología
13:30–14:20					

Cuaderno para hispanohablantes, pp.11–13

VAMOS A LEER

☀ READING

Have students work in groups of three. Ask them to scan the reading to find as many cognates as they can. Set a time limit of three minutes.

SLOWER PACE

Before they work with all the schedules, have students work with just one until they understand its parts and the vocabulary it uses.

☀ POSTREADING

Have students review the start and finish times of the class schedules from this reading in groups of three. Have students talk about the advantages and disadvantages of the times the classes start and end. As a group, have them decide which schedule they would prefer. Then, have them present their choice to the class and explain why they like it best. Students may vote on which schedule is most appealing.

CRITICAL THINKING

Have students design their own grading system. Would they use numbers, letters, or another system? How would they decide which work was excellent and which needed improvement?

TEACHER NOTE

For additional readings, see *Practice and Activity Book*, p. 37.

The **Repaso** reviews and integrates all four skills and culture in preparation for the Chapter Test.

PRELISTENING

1 As a prelistening warm-up, have students brainstorm questions about classes and schedules. Write the schedule-related vocabulary that they generate on the board. Ask volunteers to say a few sentences about their schedules.

• Have students make a checklist of the kinds of questions they might hear. As they hear the questions in the conversation, have them check them off.

• Ask students to role-play this dialogue to practice chapter vocabulary and functions. Limit the time to one or two minutes.

ADDITIONAL PRACTICE

Divide the class into pairs. Tell them that they will create a conversation for a classroom competition. One of each pair plays a student who has recently arrived from Mexico to study at your school. The new student is unfamiliar with U.S. school schedules, classes, and what should be done at what time. The partner answers the new student's questions. Partners present their conversations to the class. At the end of the competition, the class votes on which pair has the most spontaneous, interesting, or humorous conversation.

  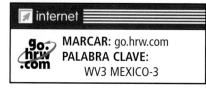

internet

MARCAR: go.hrw.com
PALABRA CLAVE:
WV3 MEXICO-3

CD 3
Tr. 17

1 Listen as Miguel and Edgardo are talking on the phone about their plans for tomorrow.   Script and answers on p. 101F

A. First, match each of the sentences you hear with one of the drawings below.

ⓐ

ⓑ

ⓒ

ⓓ

ⓔ

B. Now listen to their conversation again. This time, write one of the times from the list next to each item number on a sheet of paper.

3 11:50   5 2:20   4 1:15

2 11:00   1 10:15

Hora	Martín	Gabriela
7:50 - 8:40	Francés	Ciencias sociales
8:40 - 9:30	Geografía	Computación
9:30 - 9:40	DESCANSO	DESCANSO
9:40 - 10:30	Arte	Inglés
10:30 - 11:20	Computación	Geografía
11:20 - 11:40	Inglés	Arte
11:40 - 12:30	ALMUERZO	ALMUERZO
12:30 - 13:20	Ciencias sociales	Español
13:20 - 13:30	DESCANSO	DESCANSO
13:30 - 14:20	Español	Educación física

2 These are the classes that Martín and Gabriela have on Monday. Answer the following questions in Spanish.

1. ¿A qué hora es la clase de español de Gabriela? ¿Y la clase de español de Martín?

2. ¿Qué clase tiene Gabriela primero? ¿Y Martín?

3. ¿Qué clase tiene Gabriela después del almuerzo? ¿Y Martín?   Answers on page 101K

3 Answer the following questions according to what you've read in this chapter.

1. Would you be pleased if you got a 16 on your report card in Peru? *maybe*
2. And if you got a 9 on your report card in Mexico? *yes*

4 # Vamos a escribir

You and your friend want to join a pen pal club. You've offered to send in the required information for both of you. Write a paragraph with five sentences that tells what you like and don't like. Then do the same for your friend. Before writing, try organizing your ideas with a cluster diagram.

Estrategia

Cluster diagrams are a useful way to get organized. Draw a circle and label it **a mí me gusta.** Then draw 2 or 3 other circles around it, each connected to the circle labeled **a mí me gusta.** Label each with an activity you like. Repeat the process with **a mí no me gusta.** Now organize your ideas about your friend's likes and dislikes with circles that say **a (mi amigo/a) le gusta** and **a (mi amigo/a) no le gusta.** Answers will vary.

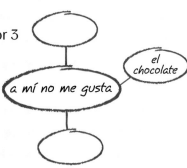

5 # SITUACIÓN

Working with a partner, create a scene in which two friends who have known each other since elementary school meet while shopping in your town. One of the friends has been living in Cuernavaca for the past year. Find out what's new with each other by

1. asking each other about classes (¿**Qué clases tienes este semestre?**) and schedules (¿**A qué hora es tu clase de...?**)
2. asking each other what class he or she likes (¿**Cuál es tu clase favorita?**) and why (¿**Por qué?**)

End the conversation by having one friend say he or she is late and in a hurry. Answers will vary.

Cuaderno para hispanohablantes, p. 14

📁 **PORTFOLIO**

4 Written Mention to your students that this essay would be an appropriate entry for their Portfolios.

5 Oral You may suggest that students include the **Situación** interview in their Portfolio. For Portfolio information, see *Alternative Assessment Guide,* p. 14.

ADDITIONAL PRACTICE
Prepare color-coded cards. (verb = red, noun = blue, adjective = green) Prepare various forms of each part of speech. For example, **bonito, bonita, bonitos, lápiz, lápices,** etc. Arrange the cards to form complete sentences. Then replace a card and have students replace any other necessary cards. For example, create the sentence **Me gusta la fiesta.** Then replace the word **fiesta** with **fiestas**. Students must then replace **la** with **las** and **gusta** with **gustan**.

A VER SI PUEDO...

WV3 MEXICO-3

Answers to Activity 1

Hoy tengo primero la clase de...
Luego tengo la clase de...
Después del almuerzo tengo la clase de... Mañana...

Answers to Activity 2

a. Son las diez.
b. Son las seis.
c. Son las ocho y media.
d. Son las tres y quarto.

Answers to Activity 3

Answers will vary. Possible answers:

1. —Sofía, ¿qué clases tienes y a qué hora?
   —Tengo educación física a las ocho y trece de la mañana y arte a las dos y diez de la tarde.
2. —Tengo la clase de francés a las doce menos veinte y la clase de geografía a las dos y veinticinco.
3. —Tengo la clase de ciencias a las nueve y siete y la clase de matemáticas a las tres y cuarto.
4. —Tengo la clase de español a las once menos veintidós y la computación a la una menos seis.

Answers to Activity 4

1. Tengo prisa.
2. Estoy atrasado/a.
3. Está atrasado/a.
4. ¡Date prisa!

Can you talk about classes and sequencing events? p. 110

Can you tell time? p. 112

Can you tell at what time something happens? p. 119

Can you talk about being late or in a hurry? p. 122

Can you describe people and things? p. 125

Can you talk about things you like and explain why? p. 129

1 How would you tell a classmate what order you have your classes in today? And tomorrow? Answers in side column

2 Write the time shown on each clock. Answers in side column

a   b   c   d

3 How would you ask each of these students what classes they have and at what time they meet? How would each student answer? Answers in side column

1. Sofía
   physical education (8:13)
   art (2:10)
2. César
   French (11:40)
   geography (2:25)
3. Simón
   science (9:07)
   mathematics (3:15)
4. Adela
   Spanish (10:38)
   computer science (12:54)

4 How would you . . .? Answers in side column

1. say you're in a hurry
2. say that you're late
3. say that a friend is late
4. tell a friend to hurry up

5 Look at the photos. Write a sentence describing each person or animal. Answers on p. 101K

Yolanda   Gabriela   Simón   Bruto

6
1. How would you say why you like or don't like your math class? (No) me gusta la clase de matemáticas porque es...
2. How would you ask a friend why he or she likes or doesn't like science? ¿Por qué (no) te gustan las ciencias?
3. How would you tell another person why your friend likes or doesn't like math? A mi amigo (no) le gusta la clase de matemáticas porque es...

VOCABULARIO

PRIMER PASO

Talking about classes and sequencing events

el almuerzo *lunch*
el arte *art*
las ciencias *science*
las ciencias sociales *social studies*
la computación *computer science*
¿Cuándo? *When?*
el descanso *recess, break*
después *after*
un día libre *a day off*
la educación física *physical education*
el francés *French*
la geografía *geography*
hoy *today*
las, los *the (pl.)*
luego *then*
mañana *tomorrow*
las matemáticas *mathematics*
la materia *subject*
por fin *at last*
primero *first*
¿Qué clases tienes? *What classes do you have?*
el semestre *semester*

Telling time

Es la una. *It's one o'clock.*
menos cuarto *quarter to (the hour)*
¿Qué hora es? *What time is it?*
Son las... *It's . . . o'clock*
tarde *late*
¡Vamos! *Let's go!*
y cuarto *quarter past (the hour)*
y media *half past (the hour)*

SEGUNDO PASO

Telling at what time something happens

ahora *now*
¿A qué hora es...? *At what time is . . . ?*
de *of, from*
del *of the, from the*
de la mañana *in the morning (A.M.)*
de la noche *in the evening (P.M.)*
de la tarde *in the afternoon (P.M.)*
en punto *on the dot*

Talking about being late or in a hurry

¡Date prisa! *Hurry up!*
Está atrasado/a. *He/She is late.*
Estoy atrasado/a. *I'm late.*
Tengo prisa. *I'm in a hurry.*

TERCER PASO

Describing people and things

aburrido/a *boring*
alto/a *tall*
antipático/a *disagreeable*
bajo/a *short (to describe people)*
bonito/a *pretty*
bueno/a *good*
cómico/a *funny*
¿Cómo es...? *What's . . . like?*
¿Cómo son...? *What are . . . like?*
el (la) compañero/a *friend, pal*
difícil *difficult*
divertido/a *fun, amusing*
Él/Ella es... *He/She is . . .*
ellas, ellos *they*
Ellos/Ellas son *They are . . .*
estricto/a *strict*
fácil *easy*
feo/a *ugly*
grande *big*
guapo/a *good-looking*
inteligente *intelligent*
interesante *interesting*
malo/a *bad*
moreno/a *dark-haired, dark-skinned*
No es aburrido/a. *It's not boring.*
No te preocupes. *Don't worry.*
nuevo/a *new*
pequeño/a *small*
el (la) profesor, -a *teacher*
rubio/a *blond*
simpático/a *nice*
somos *we are*

Talking about things you like and explaining why

el baile *dance*
el concierto *concert*
¿Cuál? *Which?*
¿Cuál es tu clase favorita? *Which is your favorite class?*
los deportes *sports*
el examen *exam (pl. los exámenes)*
favorito/a *favorite*
la fiesta *party*
le gusta(n) *he/she likes*
me gustan *I like*
¿no? *isn't it?/right?*
la novela *novel*
el partido de... *game of . . . (sport)*
¿Por qué? *Why?*
porque *because*
te gustan *you like*
¿verdad? *don't you?/right?*
el videojuego *videogame*

♜ GAME

¿A qué hora es...? Post a mock class schedule. Divide the class into two teams. A member of Team A asks a member of Team B what time a class begins. Teams get one point for each correct response.

CHAPTER 3 ASSESSMENT

▶ **Testing Program**
Chapter Test, pp. 42–48
Audio Compact Discs, CD 3, Trs. 21–22
Speaking Test, p. 113

▶ **Alternative Assessment Guide**
Performance Assessment, p. 21
Portfolio Assessment, p. 14
CD-ROM Assessment, p. 28

▶ **Interactive CD-ROM Tutor, Disc 1**
¡A hablar!
¡A escribir!

▶ **Standardized Assessment Tutor**
Chapter 3

▶ **One-Stop Planner, Disc 1**
⚡ Test Generator
✍ Chapter 3

▶ **Midterm Exam**
Testing Program, pp. 115–120
Audio CD 3, Trs. 23–24

¿Qué haces esta tarde?
CHAPTER OVERVIEW

De antemano pp. 144–147	¿Dónde está María Inés?			
	FUNCTIONS	**GRAMMAR**	**VOCABULARY**	**RE-ENTRY**
Primer paso pp. 148–157	• Talking about what you and others like to do, p. 149 • Talking about what you and others do during free time, p. 152	• **Gramática:** Present tense of regular **-ar** verbs, p. 150 • **Nota gramatical: con, conmigo, contigo,** p. 155 • **Nota gramatical:** Relative pronoun **que,** p. 157	• Things you like to do, p. 154	• Present tense of **tener** • Present tense of **gustar**
Segundo paso pp. 160–167	• Telling where people and things are, p. 161	• **Nota gramatical:** The verb **estar,** p. 162 • **Gramática:** Subject pronouns, p. 166	• Places in town and their location, p. 163	• Subject pronouns **yo, tú, él, ella** • Describing with **ser**
Tercer paso pp. 170–175	• Talking about where you and others go during free time, p. 171	• **Nota gramatical:** The verb **ir,** p. 172 • **Nota gramatical:** Days of the week, p. 174	• The days of the week, p. 174	• Telling time • Days of the week

Letra y sonido	**p. 175**	The letters **b** and **v**	**Dictado:** Audio CD 4 Tracks 13–17	
Enlaces	**pp. 176–177**	**La música y los deportes**		
Vamos a leer	**pp. 178–179**	**Línea directa**	**Reading Strategy:** Scanning for information	
Review	**pp. 180–183**	**Repaso,** pp. 180–181	**A ver si puedo...,** p. 182	**Vocabulario,** p. 183

Culture
- **Nota cultural:** Hispanic athletes, p. 154
- **Nota cultural:** Referring to or greeting friends, p. 156
- **Encuentro cultural:** Un recorrido por la Plaza de las Armas, pp. 158–159
- **Nota cultural: tú** and **usted,** p. 166
- **Panorama cultural: ¿Te gusta pasear con tus amigos?,** pp. 168–169
- **Nota cultural:** Mail service, p. 170

Lesson Planning

One-Stop Planner
Lesson Planner with Substitute Teacher
Lesson Plans, pp. 19–23

Listening and Speaking

Listening Activities
- Student Response Forms for Listening Activities, pp. 55–57
- Additional Listening Activities 4-1 to 4-6, pp. 14–16
- Additional Listening Activities (song), p. 17
- Scripts and Answers, pp. 35–37

Video Guide
- Teaching Suggestions, pp. 27–28
- Activity Masters, pp. 29–32
- Scripts and Answers, pp. 55–58, 65

Activities for Communication
- Communicative Activities, pp. 19–24
- Realia and Teaching Suggestions, pp. 53–57
- Situation Cards, pp. 76–77

¡Ven conmigo! Level 1
TPR Storytelling Book, pp. 13–16

Reading and Writing

Reading Strategies and Skills, Chapter 4
¡Lee conmigo! 1, Chapter 4
Practice and Activity Book, pp. 39–50

Grammar

Grammar and Vocabulary Workbook, pp. 27–36

¡Ven conmigo! Level 1
Grammar Tutor for Students of Spanish
Chapter 4

Assessment

Testing Program
- Paso Quizzes and Chapter Test, pp. 55–66
- Score Sheet, Scripts and Answers, pp. 67–72

Grammar and Vocabulary Quizzes
- Quizzes 4-1A, 4-2A, 4-3A
- Alternative Quizzes 4-1A, 4-2A, 4-3A

Alternative Assessment Guide
- Portfolio Assessment, p. 15
- Performance Assessment, p. 22
- CD-ROM Assessment, p. 29

¡Ven conmigo! Level 1
Standardized Assessment Tutor
- Reading, pp. 13–15
- Writing, p. 16
- Math, pp. 25–26

Native Speakers

¡Ven conmigo! Level 1
Cuaderno para hispanohablantes, pp. 16–20

Online Activities
- Juegos interactivos
- Actividades internet

Video Program
- Videocassette 2
- Videocassette 3 *(captioned version)*

¡Ven conmigo! Level 1
DVD Tutor, Disc 2

Audio Compact Discs
- Textbook Listening Activities, CD 4, Tracks 1–18
- Additional Listening Activities, CD 4, Tracks 24–29
- Assessment Items, CD 4, Tracks 19–23

Interactive CD-ROM Tutor, Disc 1

Teaching Transparencies
- Situations 4-1 to 4-3
- Vocabulary 4-A to 4-C
- Grammar and Vocabulary Workbook

 One-Stop Planner CD-ROM

Use the **One-Stop Planner CD-ROM with Test Generator** to aid in lesson planning and pacing.

For each chapter, the **One-Stop Planner** includes:
- Editable lesson plans with direct links to teaching resources
- Printable worksheets from resource books
- Direct launches to the HRW Internet activities
- Video and audio segments
- Test Generator
- Clip Art for vocabulary items

¿Qué haces esta tarde?
TECHNOLOGY

DVD/VIDEO

Videocassette 2, Videocassette 3 (captioned version)
DVD Tutor, Disc 1 See Video Guide, pages 25–27.

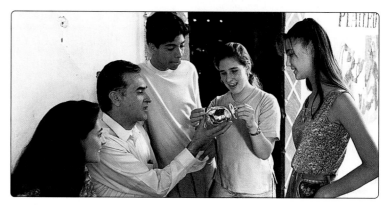

De antemano • ¿Dónde está María Inés?
Claudia and Luis plan to go to Taxco with Claudia's sister Rosa. Knowing that María Inés enjoys Taxco, Claudia and Luis decide to invite her to go with them. They look for María Inés at all the places she usually goes on Saturdays. Unfortunately they miss her by just a few minutes at each place.

¿Te gusta pasear con tus amigos?
People from various Spanish-speaking countries tell their opinions about the *paseo*.

A continuación
After failing to find María Inés, Claudia and Luis return to Claudia's house, where María Inés meets up with them. They go sightseeing in Taxco and visit Claudia's uncle, a local silversmith. He makes a special gift for Claudia to take back for her mother's birthday.

Un recorrido por la Plaza de las Armas

Videoclips
• **Banco Popular:** advertisement by a bank promoting respect for people with disabilities

INTERACTIVE CD-ROM TUTOR

Activity	Activity Type	Pupil's Edition Page
En contexto	*Interactive conversation*	
1. Vocabulario	¿Cuál es?	p. 149
2. Gramática	¿Qué falta?	p. 150
3. Así se dice	Patas arriba	p. 161
4. Gramática	¿Qué falta?	p. 162
5. Gramática	¡A escoger!	p. 172
6. Vocabulario	¡Super memoria!	p. 174
Panorama cultural	¿Te gusta pasear con tus amigos? ¡A escoger!	pp. 168–169
¡A hablar!	*Guided recording*	pp. 180–181
¡A escribir!	*Guided writing*	pp. 180–181

Teacher Management System
Launch the program, type "admin" in the password area and press RETURN. Log on to **www.hrw.com/CDROMTUTOR** for a detailed explanation of the Teacher Management System.

DVD-ROM TUTOR ¡Ven conmigo! Level 1

The *DVD Tutor* contains all material from the Level 1 *Video Program*. Spanish captions are available for use at your discretion for all sections of the video. The *DVD Tutor* also provides a variety of video-based activities that assess students' understanding of the **De antemano, A continuación,** and **Panorama cultural.**

This part of the *DVD Tutor* may be used on any DVD video player connected to a television or video monitor.

In addition to the video material and the video-based comprehension activities, the *DVD Tutor* also contains the entire Level 1 *Interactive CD-ROM Tutor* in DVD-ROM format. Each DVD disc contains the activities from all 12 chapters of the *Interactive CD-ROM Tutor.*

This part of the *DVD Tutor* may be used on a Macintosh® or Windows® computer with a DVD-ROM drive.

One-Stop Planner CD-ROM

To preview all resources available for this chapter, use the **One-Stop Planner CD-ROM,** Disc 1.

internet

MARCAR: go.hrw.com
PALABRA CLAVE:
WV3 MEXICO-4

INTERNET CONNECTION

*Have students explore the **go.hrw.com** Web site for many online resources covering all chapters. All Chapter 4 resources are available under the keyword **WV3 MEXICO-4**. Interactive games help students practice the material and provide them with immediate feedback. You will also find a printable worksheet that provides Internet activities that lead to a comprehensive online research project.*

JUEGOS INTERACTIVO

You can use the interactive activities in this chapter

- to practice grammar, vocabulary, and chapter functions
- as homework
- as an assessment option
- as a self-test
- to prepare for the Chapter Test

ACTIVIDADES INTERNET

Students write about the activities they would do on a weekend if they were an exchange student in Mexico.

- In preparation for the **Hoja de actividades,** have students review the chapter vocabulary on page 135. You might have them complete the vocabulary activities in the **Cuaderno de gramática.**

- After they have completed the activity sheet, have students create a similar schedule of activities appropriate for a grandparent or older person visiting Mexico City.

Proyecto

Have students work with a partner to find a tourism Web site for a Mexican city. Ask them to find activities that the city promotes. Then ask the pairs to create a brief brochure that highlights city activities they think appeal to people their age. You might have them create an online brochure: have them post descriptions and images on a personal Web site.

¿Qué haces esta tarde?

TEXTBOOK LISTENING ACTIVITIES SCRIPTS

For Student Response Forms, see Listening Activities, pp. 55–57.

PRIMER PASO   pp. 148–157

6 Actividades   p. 150

1. Hola. Me llamo Tomás. Me gusta comprar muchas cosas. Por eso me gusta ir de compras.
2. ¿Qué tal? Me llamo Arturo. No me gustan las fiestas porque son muy aburridas.
3. Yo soy Bárbara. A mí me gusta hablar por teléfono... ¡día y noche!
4. Hola. Soy Patricia. No me gusta estudiar mucho, pero me gusta mirar la televisión.

Answers to Activity 6

1. A Tomás le gusta comprar cosas.
2. A Arturo no le gusta bailar en las fiestas.
3. A Bárbara le gusta hablar por teléfono.
4. A Patricia le gusta mirar la televisión.

10 El tiempo libre   p. 152

1. Hola, soy Carmen. Escucho música y miro la televisión en mi cuarto.
2. Me llamo Javier. Hablo por teléfono con Sofía, Manuel, Rebeca y Raúl...
3. Soy Armando. Ana y yo estudiamos en la biblioteca día y noche.
4. Me llamo Susana. Después de clases, practico el béisbol y el tenis.
5. Soy Pablo. En el tiempo libre, bailo y canto con mis amigos. Toco la guitarra también.

Answers to Activity 10

1. d   2. b   3. a   4. e   5. c

SEGUNDO PASO   pp. 160–167

23 ¿Dónde está?   p. 161

1. ¿El correo? Está en la Plaza de la Constitución.
2. Necesito encontrar mi mochila. No está en mi cuarto.
3. Hola. ¿Qué tal? Estoy atrasado. Todavía estoy en el trabajo.
4. ¡Mira, José! ¡Allí está la plaza!

Answers to Activity 23

1. d   2. c   3. b   4. a

27 ¿Quiénes son y dónde están?   p. 164

MODELO   Paco es bajo y moreno. Le gusta jugar con su perro.

1. Marisa y Ana Luisa son guapas y morenas. Tienen catorce años.
2. El señor Contreras es bajo y le gusta comprar ropa.
3. Eva es muy inteligente y le gusta estudiar matemáticas.
4. Isabel tiene seis años y le gustan los videos cómicos.
5. Mario y José son antipáticos. Siempre necesitan hablar con el director del colegio.
6. Anabel nada muy bien. Tiene treinta y cinco años y es muy bonita.
7. Guillermo es alto y rubio. Juega mucho al basquetbol con sus amigos.

Answers to Activity 27

1. f   2. g   3. e   4. c   5. h   6. b   7. d

TERCER PASO pp. 170–175

37 **¿Cuál es la pregunta? p. 171**

1. Julio va al centro comercial.
2. Voy a estudiar en la biblioteca.
3. La biblioteca está al lado del correo.
4. Primero voy a nadar en la piscina y después voy a la casa de Jorge.
5. Mi hermana Sandra va al restaurante italiano.
6. Esteban está en la tienda con su hermana.

Answers to Activity 37

1. b   **2.** a   **3.** c   **4.** a   **5.** b   **6.** c

38 **¿Adónde vamos? p. 172**

1. — Y Pedro, ¿adónde va él?
   — Él va a la casa de Graciela.
2. — David y Luisa, entonces. ¿Adónde van ellos?
   — Ellos van al gimnasio.
3. — Y tú, Alicia, ¿adónde vas?
   — Voy a la piscina. Trabajo allí hoy.
4. — Y Carlos, ¿va al cine?
   — Sí, Carlos va al cine.
5. — Hola, Carlos.
   — Hola, Filiberto. ¿Adónde vas?
   — Voy al cine. ¡Contigo!

Answers to Activity 38

1. a la casa de Graciela

2. al gimnasio

3. al gimnasio

4. a la piscina

5. al cine

6. al cine

LETRA Y SONIDO p. 175

For the scripts for Parts A and C, see page 175. The script for Part B is below.

B. Dictado

veinte, bolígrafo, librería, basura, el tiempo libre, jueves

REPASO pp. 180–181

1 **p. 180**

MODELO   Hola, soy Carlos. El sábado vamos al parque para jugar al tenis. Vamos a las 10:00. ¿Quieres ir también?

1. Buenos días. Soy Carmen. Enrique y yo vamos a estudiar en la biblioteca hoy a las tres y media. ¿Quieres ir con nosotros?
2. Hola. Soy Gaby. ¿Cómo estás? Voy a la piscina mañana a las cuatro y media. ¿Quieres ir conmigo?
3. Buenos días. Soy Victoria. ¿Cómo estás? Sara y yo vamos al cine el domingo a las tres. A ti te gustan las películas, ¿no? Pues, ¡vamos!

Answers to Repaso Activity 1

1. c   **2.** a   **3.** b

¿Qué haces esta tarde?
PROJECTS

UN MAPA DE MI CIUDAD

This activity, excellent for visual/spatial intelligence learners, provides students with the opportunity to use chapter vocabulary to show imaginary Spanish speakers visiting important places in town. Students will create a map and use it to present an oral guided tour.

Introduction

Talk to students about the importance of being able to use Spanish to explain where things are and to ask where things are when they travel. Ask students if they have ever been on a guided tour. What did the tour guide say? Which buildings, parks, and important places should be part of a guided tour of your town?

Materials students may need

- Poster board
- Blank overhead transparencies
- Markers
- Rulers
- Pens and pencils
- Toy vehicle (optional)

Sequence

1. Divide students into groups of four. Within each group assign the roles of Script-writer, Proofreader, Tour guide, and someone to point out the route on the map.

2. Groups will cooperatively draw a map of your town or the area around the school on poster board or an overhead transparency. The map will be used in the tour presentation and should include as many of the locations as possible from the **Vocabulario** on page 183.

3. Next, the Script-writer works with the other students to create a script in Spanish for the guided tour. The script should include what to say as they arrive at a location and a short description of each site (what it is near or next to; what it looks like; what they like to do there).

4. The Proofreader edits the script.

5. In front of the class, the Tour Guide narrates the trip. The person demonstrating the route on the map points to or

moves a toy vehicle to each location as the tour guide mentions it.

Grading the project

Suggested point distribution (total = 100 points):

Map appearance	**30**
Appropriate chapter vocabulary and detail	**30**
Spelling and grammar accuracy	**10**
Guided Tour	**30**

MI TIEMPO LIBRE

This project reinforces leisure activity vocabulary that students learn in this chapter. Students create posters that are visual representations of specific vocabulary.

Introduction

Discuss what leisure activities students take part in during the weekends, after school, and during vacations. Do they like to spend time with their friends, their families, or by themselves? What do they like to do in their free time? Play sports? Read? Watch TV? See friends? Students will make a collage of at least seven of their favorite activities by illustrating the activity and labeling the poster in Spanish. This project will consist of two parts: creating the poster and presenting it orally to the class.

Materials students may need

- Colored poster board
- Markers or colored pencils
- Pencils
- Rulers
- Scissors
- Cutouts from magazines
- Glue sticks

Sequence

1. Each student will draft a list of at least seven activities that he or she likes to do. The list should include activities

they do after school, during the weekend, and during vacations.

2 Students will look for pictures that illustrate the activities on their list or draw the activities on the poster themselves.

3 Students may arrange the illustrations or pictures in collage format or in order of preference. They should label illustrations and pictures in Spanish and title it **MI TIEMPO LIBRE**.

4 Students will share their leisure activities with the class by making oral presentations.

Grading the project

Suggested point distribution (total = 100 points):

Neatness **20**
Creativity and artistic design. **20**
Information and content **15**
Spelling and grammar accuracy. **15**
Oral presentation **30**

NUESTRA CIUDAD IDEAL

This activity taps into students' interpersonal and visual/spatial intelligence. It requires the planning, design, and hands-on construction of different locations within a city. Students work together to arrange the city buildings, park, and other places as a cooperative effort among all members of the class.

Introduction

Students decide what buildings or public spaces will make up their ideal city. Then they cooperatively construct models of buildings, and arrange the buildings and spaces according to their plan.

Materials students may need

- ◆ Shoe boxes or other larger cardboard boxes
- ◆ Construction paper
- ◆ Glue
- ◆ Colored markers
- ◆ Markers—fine tip and wide tip
- ◆ Magazines for decoration pictures
- ◆ Poster board

Sequence

1 Do the students like the city or town where they live? What do they like about it and what would they change? Brainstorm with them to get their ideas about what an ideal city would be. Would it have movie theaters? parks? libraries? shopping malls? schools?

2 Students choose a structure to build with a partner. (For example: a bank, a restaurant, a post office) They may construct building models using shoe boxes or larger cardboard boxes. Students label each building in Spanish. They may decorate the building with markers and magazine pictures.

3 Both partners will present their model to the class orally in Spanish.

4 Next, lead students through a city planning brainstorm. Have them think about the town in which they live. What is near the fire station? Where is the gas station? Where are the office buildings? Ask them more questions about their ideal city. Would their school be next to their house? the mall? a video arcade? a grocery store?

5 Using the ideas from the city planning brainstorm, the class will then decide how to organize the building models to design **Nuestra ciudad ideal.** As the class decides where to place the buildings, have one or two students draw the city plan on the board.

6 The ideal city can be placed on a table or in a corner of the room and can be on permanent display in the class.

Grading the project

Suggested point distribution (total = 100 points):

Model appearance, neatness **25**
Creativity, artistic design **25**
Information and content **20**
Oral presentation **20**
Partner cooperation **10**

FAMILY LINK

Suggest that students practice their presentation with a family member or friend who may be able to suggest some things to say about why that object is important.

4

¿Qué haces esta tarde?

GAMES

¿DÓNDE ESTÁ?

*This game reviews classroom vocabulary and practices the verb **estar**. It's especially good for students with spatial intelligence.*

Procedure

One student hides a pen, a book, or a notebook in the front of the room while the other students close their eyes. The rest of the class must ask the student questions in order to find the object. (**¿Está debajo de la mesa? ¿Está cerca del escritorio?**) The student who guesses correctly is the next person to hide an object.

CEREBRO

This game, played like Concentration®, helps students learn and review vocabulary by using the skills of concentration and recall.

Preparation

Have each student make three pairs of cards:

1 On one card students write a question from any **Así se dice** and on its mate they write an appropriate response.

2 On one card students write a verb (conjugated or infinitive) from the chapter, and on its mate they draw a stick figure that depicts the action.

3 On one card students write a verb from the second shaded word box from Activity 15 on page 155. On its mate they write an appropriate phrase from the third box. (Make sure that there is only one phrase from the third box that matches.)

Procedure

Divide the class into pairs or small groups. Have students place a combined set of their cards in a pattern on the desk, face down. Players take turns turning over two cards each. If the cards match, the player takes them. Play continues until all the cards have been matched. The player with the most matches wins. For a challenge, have students make additional sets of cards.

FAMILY LINK

 Have students teach a relative or friend Spanish phrases using the **Cerebro** cards. Students are assigned to take home their own set of six **Cerebro** cards and teach someone the three Spanish phrases on them by playing the game. Have students report orally how their **estudiante** is doing.

BINGO®

This quick game of word Bingo® is an enjoyable way to reinforce familiar vocabulary from the chapter. It can be played in the last ten minutes of any class, when students have finished their work. It can be played with verbs or nouns in Spanish or from English to Spanish.

Preparation

1 Make a set of Bingo® cards to be used by students at any time, for any lesson. Using a piece of 8 1/2 × 11 paper, divide the sheet into quarters. Within each quarter, draw a tic-tac-toe grid. (two horizontal lines, two vertical lines)

2 Cut the quarters to be used as mini-sheets to play bingo.

3 Designate vocabulary to be used by students to play the game: -**ar** verbs, **ir, estar,** or locations in the city. Give the page references to students to access vocabulary. For this chapter, **Vocabulario** is on page 183.

4 The students write one Spanish word in each box.

5 Call out a word in Spanish. Students mark off the word they hear. The student who completes his card first wins and calls out "¡Bingo®!"

Alternatives

You can also write the words in Spanish, call the words in English, or write the words in English and call out the words in Spanish.

EL JUEGO DE CONJUGACIÓN

This game makes students think about the correlation between the personal pronoun and the personal ending of the conjugated verb. Students have fun while getting used to changing the ending of each verb, and it is excellent for body/kinesthetic and interpersonal intelligences.

Materials students may need

◆ Red, blue, green, and yellow index cards   ◆ Markers

Preparation

Make index cards with the following:

• 9 personal pronouns (**yo, tú, usted, él, ella, nosotros, ustedes, ellos, ellas**), each on a red (**rojo**) card.

• 5 personal endings (**o, as, a, amos, an**) on blue (**azul**) cards.

• 15 verb stems (**descans, dibuj, escuch, lav, mir, nad, sac, habl, pint, practic, prepar, trabaj, regres, bail, toc**) on green (**verde**) cards.

• 20 conjugated English verb forms *(I work, we draw, they speak, etc.)* on yellow (**amarillo**) cards.

Sequence

1 Divide the class into groups: **el grupo rojo**, pronouns; **el grupo azul**, personal endings, **el grupo verde**, stems.

2 Pass one card to each student. Cards remain in their group category.

3 Read the English from a yellow card. For example, *He works.* Students from **el grupo rojo** must find the pronoun **él**; students from **el grupo verde** must find the verb stem **trabaj**; and students in **el grupo azul** must find the ending -**a**, to cooperatively make the correct conjugation for the English translation.

CATEGORÍAS

The following game is patterned after the game Scattergories®. It is good for reinforcing vocabulary.

Materials students may need

◆ A timer   ◆ Pencils and paper for scoring
◆ Index cards

Preparation

1 Make a list of categories on transparencies to teach the game to the class. Number lists so students use a different list for each round. Make index cards with the letters of the alphabet on them.

2 Use categories of vocabulary already learned:

• **materias/clases**   • **palabras descriptivas**
• **deportes y pasatiempos**   • **colores**
• **en la ciudad**   • **números**
• **instrumentos musicales**   • **nombres**

3 Students prepare a sheet of paper with three numbered columns, one for each of the three rounds of play, numbered from one to the number of categories on the list. All students use the same list of categories.

Sequence

1 The object of the game is to quickly fill out a category list with items beginning with the same letter. Students score points if no other player matches their answers.

2 Display the transparency list of the categories. One student chooses a letter card from the stack of index cards. The student calls out the letter to be used in this round. A student sets the timer for one minute and the round begins.

3 For each category, students quickly fill in the answer sheet with appropriate people, places, or things that begin with the key letter. When the timer rings, students must immediately stop writing.

4 To score a round, students in turn read their answers aloud to the group. The students circle acceptable answers that **do not** match anyone else's. They continue until all categories have been scored. Then, score one point for each of the circled answers and record the score at the top of the first column of the answer sheet.

5 After three rounds, students total the scores on their answer sheets. The player with the highest score wins. This game may also be played with one small group competing against another in which each group produces a single list.

ANSWERS TO CHAPTER 4 ACTIVITIES

Listening activity answers appear on Scripts pages 141E–141F. Answers to all other activities appear on corresponding pupil pages.

PRIMER PASO pp. 148–157

5
1. Sí, a Claudia le gusta cantar en el coro.
2. Sí, a Luis le gusta jugar al basquetbol.
3. Sí, a María Inés le gusta practicar el baile folklórico.
4. A mí me gusta...

12 Answers will vary. Possible answers:
1. En su tiempo libre, Marcus, Lee y Jeffrey nadan en la piscina.
2. Mi amiga Patricia escucha música popular.
3. Roberto pinta en el parque después de clases.
4. Después de clases, Lian habla por teléfono.
5. Franklin y Raquel lavan el carro del papá de Franklin.
6. Answers will vary.

SEGUNDO PASO pp. 160–167

24
1. —¡Hola, Lupe! ¿Cómo estás?
   —Estoy bien. ¿Dónde estás?
   —Oye, estoy en el centro. Esta tarde quiero montar en bicicleta.
   —¡Qué bueno! Yo quiero ir también.
2. —Hola, Señora Montes. ¿Está Mariana en casa?
   —No, Alicia, no está.
   —¿Dónde está?
   —Está con Paco. Están en la biblioteca.
   —Gracias. ¡Hasta luego!

27
   b. Ella está en la piscina.
   c. Ella está en casa.
   d. Ellos están en el gimnasio.
   e. Ella está en la biblioteca.
   f. Ellas están en el restaurante.
   g. Él está en la tienda.
   h. Ellos están en la escuela.

33
1. nosotros *or* nosotras
2. ellos *or* ellas
3. ella
4. yo
5. él
6. tú
7. usted
8. ustedes *or* vosotros/as
9. usted

ENLACES pp. 176–177

4
1. Gervasio Deferr
2. Columbia
3. 18 points
4. Sailing–Men's Mistral
5. 0.25 (1/4) kilometers per minute

A VER SI PUEDO... p. 182

3
1. Caminamos en el parque.
2. Montamos en bicicleta.
3. Pasamos el rato con amigos.
4. Estudiamos en la biblioteca.
5. Escuchamos música.
6. Miramos la televisión.

4
1. Ella está en la biblioteca.
2. Ella está en el centro comercial.
3. Ellos están en el parque.
4. Ella está en el parque.
5. Estamos en la piscina.

5
1. El supermercado está al lado del parque.
2. La librería está lejos del colegio.
3. El gimnasio está cerca de la biblioteca.

6 Answers will vary. Possible answers:
1. Ella va a la librería.
2. Lupe va al gimnasio.
3. Ellos van al correo.

¿Qué haces esta tarde?

 HOMEWORK SUGGESTIONS

CAPÍTULO
4

Chapter Section	Presentation	Homework Options
Primer paso	**Así se dice,** p. 149	*Pupil's Edition*, p. 149, Activity 5
	Vocabulario, p. 149	*Practice and Activity Book,* pp. 38–40, Activity 4 *Grammar and Vocabulary*, p. 27, Activities 1–2 *CD-ROM*, Disc 1, Chapter 4, Activity 1
	Gramática, p. 150	*Pupil's Edition*, p. 151, Activities 8–9 *Grammar and Vocabulary*, pp. 28–29, Activities 3–6 *CD-ROM*, Disc 1, Chapter 4, Activity 2
	Así se dice, p. 152	*Pupil's Edition*, pp. 152–153, Activities 11–12 *Practice and Activity Book*, p. 42, Activity 5
	Vocabulario, p. 154	*Pupil's Edition*, p. 154, Activity 14 *Grammar and Vocabulary*, p. 29, Activity 7
	Nota gramatical, p. 157	*Grammar and Vocabulary*, p. 30, Activity 9
Segundo paso	**Así se dice,** p. 161	*CD-ROM*, Disc 1, Chapter 4, Activity 3
	Nota gramatical, p. 162	*Practice and Activity Book*, p. 43, Activity 8 *Grammar and Vocabulary*, p. 31, Activities 10–11
	Vocabulario, p. 163	*Grammar and Vocabulary*, p. 32, Activities 12–13
	Gramática, p. 166	*Pupil's Edition*, p. 167, Activity 34 *Grammar and Vocabulary*, p. 33, Activities 14–16 *CD-ROM*, Disc 1, Chapter 4, Activity 4
Tercer paso	**Así se dice,** p.171	*Pupil's Edition*, p. 172, Activity 39
	Nota gramatical, p. 172	*Practice and Activity Book*, p. 46, Activities 11–12 *Grammar and Vocabulary*, p. 34, Activities 17–18 *CD-ROM*, Disc 1, Chapter 4, Activity 5
	Vocabulario, p.174	*Grammar and Vocabulary*, p. 35, Activities 19–20 *CD-ROM*, Disc 1, Chapter 4, Activity 6
	Nota gramatical, p. 174	*Practice and Activity Book,* pp. 47–48, Activities 13–16 *Grammar and Vocabulary*, p. 36, Activities 21–23

¿Qué haces esta tarde?

MOTIVATING ACTIVITY

Ask students what they do on weekends. Have them discuss some of their favorite and least favorite free-time activities. Do they like to watch TV? take out the trash? listen to music?

PHOTO FLASH!

(1) Soccer is a very popular sport for both young people and adults in Latin America. Young people often play on organized teams, but they also participate in informal neighborhood soccer games. At school, girls and boys usually take separate physical education classes in Latin America and Spain.

TEACHER NOTE

Refer students to the **Deportes y pasatiempos** section of the Additional Vocabulary, pp. 275–277.

 MULTICULTURAL LINK

Discuss with students the tradition in Spain and Latin America of spending Sundays with the family. Hispanic teens in the United States often spend Sundays with their families as well. Ask students how they generally spend Sundays. (Do they sleep late? go to the park? visit grandparents?)

CAPÍTULO

4
¿Qué haces esta tarde?

(1) **En el tiempo libre, ellas practican deportes.**

142 *ciento cuarenta y dos*

In this chapter you will learn to

PRIMER PASO

- talk about what you and others like to do
- talk about what you and others do during free time

SEGUNDO PASO

- tell where people and things are

TERCER PASO

- talk about where you and others go during free time

internet

go.hrw.com

MARCAR: go.hrw.com
PALABRA CLAVE:
WV3 MEXICO-4

② ¿El correo? Está en la Plaza de la Constitución.

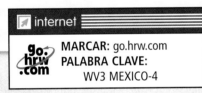

③ ¿Adónde vamos?

FOCUSING ON OUTCOMES
Have students look at the photos and match them with the learner outcomes. Photo 1 represents talking about what you and others like to do during free time; photo 2 represents telling where something is, and photo 3 represents talking about where you and others go during free time.

PHOTO FLASH!
③ The photo of the teenagers packing the van is taken from the *Video Program*. They go to Taxco to visit relatives and to sightsee.

CULTURE NOTE
Point out that families in Spanish-speaking countries often do not own more than one car. It is common for parents to take the bus, train, or subway to work. In many cases, the public transportation system may be more convenient than a car. Teenagers walk, take the bus, or ride a moped to get where they need to go.

CRITICAL THINKING
Would walking or taking the bus (as teenagers do in Spanish-speaking countries) create more or less air pollution than driving to school or work? (driving cars would cause more air pollution than taking a bus, riding a moped, or walking)

143

VIDEO INTEGRATION

Adelante LEVEL 1A
Video Program
Videocassette 2, 1:16–7:58 OR
Videocassette 3, 32:42–39:12
(captioned version)

¡Ven conmigo! LEVEL 1
DVD Tutor, Disc 1

TEACHER NOTE
The **fotonovela** is an abridged version of the video episode.

VIDEO SYNOPSIS
Claudia and her friends decide to spend Saturday in Taxco. Knowing that María Inés enjoys Taxco, they try to find her by going to all the places she usually goes on Saturdays.

MOTIVATING ACTIVITY
Ask students what they generally do with new friends. Ask them to talk about where they might take friends who are new in town. What would they do? Who would they introduce them to?

BACKGROUND
Located in the hills of the southern Sierra Madre, Taxco has been declared a Mexican national monument. Much of its charm comes from its cobblestone streets, blossoming bougainvillea, stucco houses, and red tile roofs. The Taxco mines were a main source of silver for the Spaniards in the early 1600s.

DE ANTEMANO

 ¿Dónde está María Inés?

You met Claudia and her new friends in Chapter 3. Look at the **fotonovela.** What do you think happens in this story? Where do you think Claudia and her new friends are going? Read the story and find out!

CD 4 Trs. 1–2

p. 39
Acts. 1–2

María Inés

Luis

Rosa y Claudia

1
Papi, él es mi amigo Luis. Después de clases, yo canto en el coro con Luis.

Sí, los miércoles y los viernes, ¿verdad?

No, papi, los martes y los jueves.

Ah... Entonces, Luis... ¿vas a Taxco con Claudia y Rosa?

Sí, señor... voy con ellas.

2
Hola, Luis. Claudia habla mucho de ti. Tú juegas al basquetbol muy bien, ¿no?

Pues... no sé.

Bueno, Luis, vamos a Taxco porque mi tío Ernesto tiene un regalo especial para mamá.

PRESENTATION

Have students read the **fotonovela** in pairs and list ten words they know or recognize: either cognates or material from previous chapters. Based on the photos and the words they know, have them guess what's happening.

BACKGROUND

- Taxco is a beautiful city in the state of Guerrero. The church of Santa Prisca was ordered built in 1751 by José (Joseph) de la Borda, a Frenchman made wealthy by developing the local silver mines.

- Folk dancing is a tradition carried on by many contemporary Mexicans. Numerous regional dances are performed by men, women, and children in traditional costumes at festivals throughout the year. The **Ballet Folklórico de México** performs regional Mexican dances in the Palacio de Bellas Artes in Mexico City and in theaters throughout the world.

PHOTO FLASH!

❺ In Chapter 2 students learned the phrase **necesito ir al centro comercial.** Here María Inés says, **"Necesito ir al correo."** Ask students to look at what María Inés is holding and then have them guess what the **correo** is. (post office)

145

CAPÍTULO 4

KINESTHETIC LEARNERS

After students watch the video, have them break into groups to practice introducing a friend to their parent(s). Have one or two assume the role of the parent(s) and the other student introduces a friend. Groups should use the vocabulary from Chapter 1 and follow the example of Claudia introducing Luis from **De antemano.**

LANGUAGE NOTE

The word **papi** is used often in Spanish and is similar in meaning to the English word *daddy.*

A continuación

You may choose to continue with *¿Dónde está María Inés? (a continuación)* at this time or wait until later in the chapter. At this point in the story, Claudia and Luis return home, where María Inés meets up with them. The three friends go to Taxco for the afternoon with Rosa, where they visit relatives and go sightseeing. You may wish to discuss with students the types of places they might visit or activities they might pursue in their free time.

Cuaderno para hispanohablantes, pp. 16–20

146 ciento cuarenta y seis

1 ¿Comprendes?

Do you understand who the characters in the **fotonovela** are and what they're doing? See if you can answer these questions. Don't be afraid to guess!

1. Where in Cuernavaca does the story begin? Claudia's house
2. Where do Luis, Claudia, and Rosa plan to go? Taxco
3. Who are Luis and Claudia looking for? María Inés
4. Where do they look? At the dance school, post office, and library.

2 ¿Cierto o falso?

Based on the **fotonovela,** respond to these statements with **cierto** or **falso.**

1. Claudia canta en el coro con Luis. cierto
2. Luis juega al basquetbol. cierto
3. A María Inés no le gusta Taxco. falso
4. María Inés no está en el correo. cierto
5. Claudia y Luis van al centro comercial. falso

3 ¿Dónde está ella?

In the **fotonovela,** Luis and Claudia go to many places around Cuernavaca looking for María Inés. Put the following events in the order they occur. c, d, b, a

a. Claudia y Luis van a la biblioteca.
b. Claudia y Luis van al correo.
c. Luis va a la casa de Claudia.
d. Ellos van a la clase de baile.

These activities check for global comprehension only. Students should not yet be expected to produce language modeled in **De antemano.**

NATIVE SPEAKERS
Have students list in their spelling notebook five words from the **fotonovela** with the letter *b* and five with the letter *v*. Have them pronounce the phrases **Buena idea** and **Tengo una muy buena idea** and concentrate on the pronunciation of *b*. Have them do the same with **¡Vamos!** and **¿Adónde vamos?,** concentrating on the *v*. Point out that any change in pronunciation does not affect spelling. Note that some Spanish-English bilinguals pronounce the *v* in Spanish as in English.

CHALLENGE
2 Have students correct any false statements.

AUDITORY LEARNERS
3 Have students close their books and listen as you read the sentences aloud. Read all of the sentences once, then read them again slowly, asking students to number the lettered sentences in order.

VIDEO INTEGRATION

Adelante LEVEL 1A
Video Program
Videocassette 2, 2:22–2:49 OR
Videocassette 3, 33:48–34:15
(captioned version)

¡Ven conmigo! LEVEL 1
DVD Tutor, Disc 1

Bell work

Write the following sentences on the board or a transparency and have students write one-sentence answers.

1. ¿Te gustan los bailes?
2. ¿Te gustan los deportes?
3. ¿Te gustan los exámenes?
4. ¿Te gusta el arte?

ADDITIONAL PRACTICE

4 Give students the following sentences with the verb underlined and ask them to change the underlined verb to the **yo** form.

Lavamos el carro.
Estudias español.
Compran muchas cosas.
Practicamos voleibol.
Escuchas música.

PRIMER PASO

Storytelling Book
pp. 13, 16

Talking about what you and others like to do; talking about what you and others do during free time

4 ¿Qué dice ella?

You already know how to talk about yourself using **yo.** Now use what you know to help you with the activity below.

A 1. Find and copy on a sheet of paper the sentence in which Claudia uses **yo.** Después de clases, yo canto en el coro con Luis.
   2. In the sentence you copied, circle the word that comes right after **yo.** canto
   3. What is the last letter in this word? -o

B Now look at the sentences in the word box. Based on the word that you circled in Part A, write the sentences that Claudia would use to talk about herself. How did you know which ones to choose? Estudio inglés. Necesito el dinero. The verbs both end in **o.**

> ¿Practicas el béisbol?　　　Estudio inglés.
>
> 　　Necesito el dinero.　　Compras muchos libros.

ASÍ SE DICE

Talking about what you and others like to do

p. 40
Act. 3

To find out what a friend likes to do, ask:

¿A ti qué te gusta hacer?

Your friend might answer:

A mí me gusta pintar.
I like to paint.

4-1

¿A Manuel le gusta estudiar?
Does Manuel like to study?

No, **no le gusta** estudiar.
No, he doesn't like to study.

Pero le gusta **hablar por teléfono.**
But he likes to talk on the phone.

¿A quién le gusta bailar y cantar?
Who likes to dance and sing?

A mí me gusta bailar y cantar.
I like to dance and sing.

Por eso me gustan las fiestas.
That's why I like parties.

5 ¿Te gusta...?

Based on the **fotonovela**, what can you assume the characters like or don't like? Answer the last question for yourself. Answers on p. 141K

1. ¿A Claudia le gusta cantar en el coro?
2. ¿A Luis le gusta jugar al basquetbol?
3. ¿A María Inés le gusta practicar el baile folklórico?
4. ¿Qué te gusta hacer?

pp. 40–41
Act. 4

p. 27
Acts. 1–2

4-A

VOCABULARIO

cuidar a tu hermano/a

descansar en el parque

dibujar

escuchar música

lavar el carro

lavar la ropa

mirar la televisión

nadar en la piscina

sacar la basura

☀ MOTIVATE

Ask students to think about why they like or don't like the things mentioned in *Bell work* from page 148. Is it because they like or don't like *to do* certain things? What do they like to do? When do they do them? Who do they do them with?

☀ TEACH

PRESENTATION
ASÍ SE DICE

Refer students to what they wrote in *Jump Start!* from page 148 and ask them to find phrases in **Así se dice** to explain why. **Me gusta el arte porque me gusta pintar.** Then have them find out what a partner likes and why. They should report those findings to the class. Display Teaching Transparency 4-1. Point to a person and have students say whether the person likes what he or she is doing. **¿Le gusta hacerlo?**

VOCABULARIO

Display Teaching Transparency 4-A. Point to a scene and have students identify the action depicted using the infinitive. Have students work in pairs to find out which activities their partner likes to do.

6 Actividades Script and answers on p. 141E

CD 4 Tr. 3

Based on what you hear, combine phrases to write a true statement about each person.

1. A Tomás
2. A Arturo
3. A Bárbara
4. A Patricia

| no le gusta | le gusta |

hablar por teléfono
bailar en las fiestas
comprar cosas
mirar la televisión

7 ¿A quién le gusta...?

Get together with a partner and take turns asking and answering the following questions. Fill in the blanks with words from the **Vocabulario** on page 149. Answers will vary.

Questions

1. ¿Qué te gusta hacer?

2. ¿A tu amigo/a le gusta _____?

3. ¿A quién le gusta _____?

Answers

a. A mí me gusta _____.
   También me gusta _____.
   Pero no me gusta mucho _____.
b. No, no le gusta _____.
   Pero le gusta _____.
   También le gusta _____.
c. A *(friend's name)* le gusta _____.
   También le gusta _____,
   pero no le gusta _____.

GRAMÁTICA Present tense of regular -ar verbs

1. In Spanish and English, verbs change depending on the *subject* (the person doing the action). This is called *conjugating* the verb.
2. In Spanish, there are three main groups of verbs; their infinitives (the unchanged form of a verb) end in -ar, -er, or -ir. The first group of verbs in Spanish you'll learn to conjugate is the -ar verbs: habl**ar** *(to speak)*, trabaj**ar** *(to work)*, estudi**ar** *(to study)*.
3. To conjugate **hablar** or any other regular -ar verb, take the part of the verb called the *stem* (**habl**-) and add these endings:

GV
pp. 28–29
Acts. 3–6

(yo)	habl**o**	(nosotros) (nosotras)	habl**amos**
(tú)	habl**as**	(vosotros) (vosotras)	habl**áis**
(usted) (él) (ella)	habl**a**	(ustedes) (ellos) (ellas)	habl**an**

8 ¿Qué hacen?

Look at the drawings to see what different people are doing. Then match the letter for each drawing to the sentence that describes it.

1. Ellos cantan muy bien. i
2. El señor Cheng pinta muy bien. c
3. Le gusta bailar. d
4. ¡Tú hablas por teléfono mucho! g
5. La señora Bayamón escucha música. f
6. Tú estudias mucho, ¿no? a
7. Yo cuido a mi hermana todos los días. e
8. Tú y tu amigo sacan la basura. b
9. Cristina y yo nadamos en la piscina. h

9 Los sábados

Conjugate each of the following verbs in parentheses to say what you and others do on Saturdays.

1. Tú (cuidar) a tu hermano. cuidas
2. Él (escuchar) música rock. escucha
3. Ella (lavar) el carro. lava
4. Eva y yo (mirar) la televisión. miramos
5. María y Claudia (dibujar) mucho. dibujan
6. Nosotros (nadar) en la piscina. nadamos
7. Ustedes (sacar) la basura. sacan
8. Yo (descansar) en el parque. descanso

NATIVE SPEAKERS
Point out that **hacer** and **hablar** and all their forms begin with an *h*. Also point out that the forms of **hacer** are spelled with *c* and sometimes with *z* (**hizo**), but never with *s*. Have them add these to their spelling notebook.

KINESTHETIC/ VISUAL LEARNERS
8 Act out an activity and have students say what you're doing, using the **usted** form. Then have a volunteer stand up and act out an activity. Students say what the volunteer is doing using the **él** or **ella** form. Have pairs act out activities to practice plural forms.

AUDITORY LEARNERS
9 Read the completed sentences aloud to students and have them indicate who the subjects are.

p. 42
Act. 5

ASÍ SE DICE
Talking about what you and others do during free time

To ask what a friend does after school, say:

Your friend might answer:

¿Qué haces después de clases?

¡Descanso!
I rest!

¿Tocas el piano?
Do you play the piano?

No, pero **toco la guitarra.**
No, but I play the guitar.

¿Baila María Inés antes de regresar a casa?
Does María Inés dance before returning home?

Sí, ella baila con su grupo de baile.

¿Practican deportes Luis y Carmen **en su tiempo libre?**
Do Luis and Carmen practice sports during their free time?

No, ellos no **practican** deportes.

PRESENTATION
ASÍ SE DICE

Role-play the first exchange with a volunteer. Then have students role-play the exchange with a partner. Next have them role-play the exchange again but this time replacing **descanso** with the **yo** form of a verb of their choice. Have them report what their partner does to another classmate or to the class.

ADDITIONAL PRACTICE
10 Have students write sentences about what each student probably does after school.

SLOWER PACE
11 Write the correct answers to these items on the board and have students match them to the correct sentences.

10 El tiempo libre Script and answers on p. 141E

CD 4 Tr. 4 Listen as the following people tell you what they do during their free time. Match each person with the correct activity.

1. Carmen
2. Javier
3. Armando y Ana
4. Susana
5. Pablo

a. estudiar en la biblioteca
b. hablar con amigos
c. bailar con sus amigos
d. escuchar música
e. practicar deportes

11 Después de clases

Read what each of the following people likes. Then write a sentence telling what he or she probably does after school.

MODELO   A Reynaldo le gustan los quehaceres *(chores)*.
Reynaldo saca la basura.   Answers will vary. Possible answers:

1. A Ema le gustan los días bonitos en el parque. Ema descansa en el parque.
2. A Luisa le gusta la clase de arte. A Ramón le gusta el arte también. Luisa y Ramón dibujan.
3. A Tyrone le gusta mucho la música rock. A Marcela le gusta la música también. Tyrone y Marcela escuchan música.
4. A Pablo le gustan muchos programas de televisión. Pablo mira la televisión.
5. A Joaquín le gusta mucho la natación. Joaquín nada en la piscina.

152 *ciento cincuenta y dos*   CAPÍTULO 4   ¿Qué haces esta tarde?

152 STANDARDS: 1.2, 3.1, 5.1

12 Hacemos un poco de todo

Your pen pal in Cuernavaca wants to know what everyone does in their free time. Write sentences based on the photos. Write one extra sentence saying what you like to do in your free time. Answers on p. 141K

1. Marcus, Lee y Jeffrey

2. Patricia

3. Roberto

4. Lian

5. Franklin y Raquel

13 ¡Te toca a ti!

With a partner, take turns asking and answering questions using the words below. Be sure to ask each other at least four questions. Also, use words that describe when or how things are done. Answers will vary.

MODELO —¿Dibujas bien?
—Sí, dibujo muy bien.

hablar español
bien
practicar deportes
nadar
tocar el piano
cantar
todos los días
mal
con tu amigo/a
dibujar
bailar
en mi tiempo libre
pintar
regular

p. 42
Acts. 6–7

p. 29
Act. 7

4-B

PRESENTATION

VOCABULARIO

After they look at the pictures, ask students to raise their hands to answer the following questions about their own activities: **¿A quién le gusta montar en bicicleta? ¿A quién no le gusta preparar la cena? ¿A quién le gusta caminar con el perro? ¿Quiénes de ustedes no toman el refresco _____? ¿Ustedes pasan el rato con amigos?**

KINESTHETIC LEARNERS

Have students play charades to familiarize themselves with the new vocabulary.

SUGGESTION

14 Have students write about four activities they usually do with their friends using the vocabulary on page 149 and on this page.

VOCABULARIO

pasar el rato con amigos

caminar con el perro

montar en bicicleta

trabajar en un restaurante

tomar un refresco

tomar un helado

preparar la cena

14 ¿Dónde?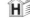

Read the sentences below. Then match them with the places where the activities might take place. You may use each place more than once.

a. en una fiesta
b. en el parque
c. en casa

1. Camino con el perro con mi amiga. b
2. Preparas la cena con tus padres. c
3. Montamos en bicicleta los sábados. b
4. Paso el rato con amigos los viernes. a, b, c
5. Miramos la televisión con mamá y papá. c
6. Bailamos a la música rock. a, c

Nota cultural

Soccer, bike riding, tennis, and baseball are especially popular in Spanish-speaking countries. In the United States, athletes like tennis star Mary Joe Fernández and baseball great Fernando Valenzuela have thrilled sports fans with their skills and spirit. Can you name any other outstanding Spanish-speaking athletes?

154 *ciento cincuenta y cuatro*   CAPÍTULO 4   ¿Qué haces esta tarde?

154 STANDARDS: 1.2, 5.1

15 Combina las frases

Combine words and phrases from each of the boxes to write five original sentences. Remember to conjugate the verbs! Answers will vary.

yo tú ella él nosotros ellos ustedes ellas	trabajar montar caminar con el perro tomar pasar el rato preparar practicar escuchar tocar	la cena el piano un refresco música deportes un helado en bicicleta	con amigos en una fiesta en el parque en un restaurante en la piscina

16 ¿Qué hacen tus amigos?

Look at the photos on page 154. Write a complete sentence for each photo about what everyone is doing. Use words like **él, ella, ellos,** etc.

MODELO   Ellos pasan el rato con amigos.   Answers will vary.

NOTA GRAMATICAL

p. 30
Act. 8

To talk about doing things with someone else, **con** is used with a pronoun like **él** or **ella.** The expressions *with me* and *with you* have special forms.

¿Quién estudia **contigo?**
Who studies with you?

Mi amigo Miguel estudia **conmigo.**
My friend Miguel studies with me.

17 ¡Conmigo!

Ask a partner to say who (**Quién**) does the following activities with him or her. Then switch roles and answer the questions. Notice that **Quién** always takes the **él/ella** form of the verb.

MODELO   practicar deportes   Answers will vary.
          —¿Quién practica los deportes contigo?
          —Juan practica los deportes conmigo.

1. montar en bicicleta
2. dibujar
3. estudiar
4. mirar la televisión
5. escuchar música
6. caminar con el perro
7. tomar un helado
8. practicar el basquetbol
9. tocar la guitarra

KINESTHETIC LEARNERS

15 Write subject pronouns, conjugated verb forms, direct objects, and prepositional phrases on index cards and pass them out among students. Students then have to get together with other students to make a complete sentence. Once they have formed their group, a representative will read the sentence aloud. You will need to use some verbs and subjects more than once when preparing cards.

PRESENTATION

NOTA GRAMATICAL
Teach students that **solo/a** means alone. Then ask them yes-or-no questions such as **¿Estudias? ¿Nadas? ¿Escuchas música? ¿Montas en bicicleta?** If they say yes, ask them if they do these things alone. (**¿solo/a?**) If they say that they don't do them alone, ask them **¿Con quién?**

LANGUAGE NOTE

Teach students this riddle: What's a funny way to say in Spanish "a dog with a gorilla on the beach"? (**un can con King Kong en Cancún**) The word **can** is an alternate word for **perro.**

RE-ENTRY

18 Have students use days of the week (from **Capítulo preliminar**) in their answers.

CULTURE NOTE
Explain to students that in Mexico and other Spanish-speaking countries, people often take a long lunch at midday. That means that schoolchildren often have at least an hour off for lunch. This gives families time to have their main meal together. In areas with hot weather, this break may include a **siesta**. This custom of the **siesta** allows people to stay out of the sun during the hottest part of the day.

ADDITIONAL PRACTICE
19 Have students role-play the conversation as if they were conducting a television interview. If possible, have them record the interview on audio- or videotape. Suggest that students include the recording in their porfolios.

18 ¿Con quién?

Write a short note to Claudia describing three of your friends. Mention three activities they do with you or others. End your note by asking Claudia who studies with her. Look at the example below for help.   Answers will vary.

> Hola Claudia,
>   Mi amigo David es muy inteligente. Estudia conmigo en la biblioteca. También vamos al c

Nota cultural

In Spain and Latin America, there are many different ways of referring to or greeting friends. Friends often call each other 'mano/a (short for **hermano/a**) or **compañero/a**. In Peru, friends sometimes say **¡Hola, pata!** Some Mexican expressions for friends include **chamaco/a, chavo/a,** or **cuate.** Throughout Latin America, men often call each other **compadre.**

19 ¿Qué haces después de clases?

Work in pairs. Find out what your partner does in his or her free time with friends. Ask two questions using the expressions **después de clases** and **en el tiempo libre.** Report your partner's answer for each question in writing. Switch roles and answer your partner's questions.   Answers will vary.

MODELO   —¿Qué haces con tus amigos después de clases?
             —Después de clases tomo un refresco con mi amiga Carolina.
             (You write:) Toma un refresco con su amiga Carolina.

156   *ciento cincuenta y seis*   CAPÍTULO 4   ¿Qué haces esta tarde?

156   STANDARDS: 2.1, 3.2, 5.1

NOTA GRAMATICAL

GV
p. 30
Act. 9

Que is a very common word in Spanish. It can refer to either people or things and can mean *that, which,* or *who*.

Tengo una amiga **que** canta bien.

La música **que** me gusta escuchar es rock en español.

20 ¿Quién es?

Match the description of the person in the first column to his or her name from the second column.

1. Es una persona que canta bien. b
2. Es una persona que trabaja en la televisión. d
3. Son personas que practican deportes en Denver, Colorado. e
4. Soy una persona que estudia español. c
5. Es una persona que trabaja en tu colegio. a

a. el/la profesor/a de matemáticas

b. Gloria Estefan

c. yo

d. Daisy Fuentes

e. los "Broncos"

21 Preferencias

With a partner, create questions from the phrases below. Then take turns asking and answering these questions. Be sure to use **que** in your answer. Answers will vary.

MODELO clase / te gusta más
—¿Cuál es la clase que te gusta más?
—La clase que me gusta más es el español.

1. música / te gusta escuchar
2. programa de televisión / te gusta mirar
3. cosa / necesitas comprar
4. deporte / te gusta practicar

El deporte que me gusta practicar es el béisbol.

PRIMER PASO

ciento cincuenta y siete **157**

PRESENTATION

NOTA GRAMATICAL

Write the following sentences on the board:
Tengo <u>un amigo</u>.
<u>Mi amigo</u> canta muy bien.

Point out that if they mean the same person when they say **amigo**, they can put the two sentences together with **que**: **Tengo <u>un amigo</u> que canta muy bien.**

Have them put the following pairs of sentences together:
1. **Tengo una clase; la clase me gusta.**
2. **Tengo un amigo; mi amigo es simpático.**
3. **Quiero el libro; el libro es interesante.**

☀ CLOSE

Use Teaching Transparency 4-1 or 4-A to review activities and verb forms with the class.

☀ ASSESS

▶ Testing Program, pp. 55–56
Quiz 4-1
Audio CD 4, Tr. 19

▶ Grammar and Vocabulary Quizzes
Quiz 4-1A or
Alternative Quiz 4-1A

▶ Alternative Assessment Guide, p. 22

PERFORMANCE ASSESSMENT
Have students describe their preferences for free-time activities and those of the ideal "roommate" at summer camp orally or in writing.

STANDARDS: 1.1, 4.1, 5.1   **157**

MOTIVATING ACTIVITY
Ask students where they go to get together with friends. Where would they go to mail a letter? Where would they go to buy clothes?

PRESENTATION
The project **Un mapa de mi ciudad** on page 141G would be a good introduction to the topic of this **Encuentro cultural**. The project **Nuestra ciudad ideal** on page 141H would be a good culminating activity to use after presenting this **Encuentro cultural**.

ENCUENTRO CULTURAL

Un recorrido por la Plaza de las Armas

Ofelia es de Cuernavaca, México. A ella le gusta ir a la Plaza de las Armas con sus amigas para pasear y ver a la gente. ¿Adónde te gusta ir con tu familia o con tus amigos?

1 ¿Qué dijo?
Ofelia describes the **plaza** in different ways. Read what she says and see if it sounds like a place in your neighborhood.

Ésta es la Plaza de las Armas. Es bonita, ¿verdad? Las oficinas del gobierno están en ese edificio. Mi tío trabaja allí. Al lado del Palacio del Gobierno está el correo. Cerca del correo hay una zapatería.

Mi colegio no está muy lejos de aquí. Mucha gente viene a la plaza para pasear, leer, hacer compras, tocar música, jugar y pasar el rato entre amigos.

"Las **oficinas del gobierno** están en ese edificio."

"**Cerca del correo** hay una **zapatería.**"

"**Mucha gente viene a la plaza** para **pasear, leer, hacer compras, tocar música, jugar y pasar el rato entre amigos.**"

1. Ofelia's uncle probably works:
   a. in an office
   b. in a classroom
   c. on a farm

2. In Cuernavaca, there is a shoe store near the post office. Can you walk from the post office to a shoe store where you live?
   Answers will vary.

3. Name three things people like to do when they come to the Plaza de las Armas.
   Answers will vary. Possible answers: read, go shopping, spend time with friends

158 *ciento cincuenta y ocho* CAPÍTULO 4 ¿Qué haces esta tarde?

158 STANDARDS: 1.2, 3.2, 5.1

2 ¡Piénsalo!

Use Ofelia's Web page to answer the following questions.   Answers in side column

1. Ofelia says the name of her city comes from an ancient Mexican language, not Spanish. Can you name five U.S. cities or states whose names do not come from English?

2. According to Ofelia's Web page, where in Cuernavaca would you go if you wanted to see fine art?

3. If you could send Ofelia an e-mail message, what two things would you ask about her city?

¡Bienvenidos a la página web de Ofelia!

¡Hola! Me llamo Ofelia y vivo en Cuernavaca. ¡Me encanta mi ciudad!

Cuernavaca viene de la palabra náhuatl Cuauhnáhuac, que quiere decir "cerca de la arboleda". Náhuatl es el idioma de los aztecas. Cuernavaca es una ciudad muy bonita.

El **Palacio Cortés** fue construido en el siglo dieciséis. Hoy en día se llama el Museo Cuauhnáhuac. Tiene pinturas de Diego Rivera y Frida Kahlo.

En el **zócalo**, puedes comprar de todo: libros, carteles, discos compactos, plantas. Mi favorito es un raspado de fresa.

Regresar

Avanzar

Página inicial

3 ¿Y tú?

What would you say to Ofelia to describe what you do in your free time?

Answers will vary.

1. En mi tiempo libre, a mí me gusta _____.

2. Un lugar de mi ciudad adonde va la gente a pasear, comer y hacer compras es _____.

3. Un lugar de mi barrio que me gusta es _____. Me gusta porque _____.

CHALLENGE

2 Have students work in groups to research the history of the city or town they live in. Assign each group one of the following questions:
1. What is the origin of the town's name? What language does it come from?
2. When was the town founded?
3. How many people lived in the town 50 years ago?
4. How many people live here now?

NATIVE SPEAKERS

Have native speakers scan this reading for one word with that begins with *h,* one that begins with *j,* and two words that begin with *v.* They should add those words to their spelling notebooks. (**hacer, jugar, vamos, viene**)

Answers to Activity 2

1. Answers will vary. Possible answers: San Diego, Massachusetts, Baton Rouge, Colorado, Minnesota
2. to the Museo Cuauhnáhuac
3. Answers will vary.

Telling where people and things are

22 ¿Qué pasa?

Use the photo above to answer the following questions.

1. Who is Claudia looking for?
2. What words does she use to ask if María Inés is there?
3. What words does Claudia use to ask where the post office is?
4. Where is the post office?

1. María Inés.
2. ¿Está aquí María Inés Hernández?
3. ¿Dónde está?
4. En la Plaza de la Constitución.

ASÍ SE DICE Telling where people and things are

PA
p.43
Act. 8

CD-ROM
DISC 1

To find out where someone or something is, ask:

¿Dónde estás?
Where are you?

¿No está en la escuela de baile?
Isn't she at dance school?

Your friend might answer:

Estoy en el centro. Necesito encontrar a María Inés.
I'm downtown. I need to find María Inés.

No, no está aquí.
No, she's not here.

Está en el trabajo. *She's at work.*

23 ¿Dónde está? Script and answers on p. 141E

Listen to these people talk about where things are. Match each statement you hear with the correct drawing.

CD 4 Tr. 5

a

b

c

d

24 El teléfono Answers on p. 141K

Put each of the following telephone conversations in order.

1

—Estoy bien.
¿Dónde estás?

—¡Qué bueno!
Yo quiero ir también.

—¡Hola, Lupe! ¿Cómo estás?

—Oye, estoy en el centro.
Esta tarde, quiero montar
en bicicleta.

2

—No, Alicia, no está.

—Está con Paco. Están en
la biblioteca.

—Gracias. ¡Hasta luego!

—Hola, señora Montes.
¿Está Mariana en casa?

—¿Dónde está?

☀ MOTIVATE

Ask students when it is necessary to know where something or someone is. (when you're meeting someone or giving directions) What expressions are needed to ask and to say where something is?

☀ TEACH

PRESENTATION
ASÍ SE DICE

Write each of the following places on two different slips of paper: **la clase de arte, la clase de español, la clase de computación, la clase de inglés, la clase de matemáticas, la clase de ciencias sociales, el cuarto, el centro, el trabajo, Madrid, Cuernavaca, el centro comercial, la cafetería, la pizzería, casa.** You may need more if you have more than 30 students. Shuffle the slips of paper and pass them out to students. The word on the paper represents where they are right now. Without showing each other their papers, have them find the other person who is in the same place by asking **¿Dónde estás? Estoy en...** Follow up by asking them where they and their partners and classmates are.

PRESENTATION

NOTA GRAMATICAL

Replay the activity from **PRESENTATION** on page 161. Practice all forms of **estar** by asking students where you, they, and their partners and classmates are.

ENGLISH LINK
One of the few instances in which students can clearly see the conjugation process at work in English is with the verb *to be*. Point out that in English, when asking where people and things are, the verb *to be* changes depending on the person just as it does in Spanish.

SUGGESTION
Use the Taxco hotel advertisement to give students more practice reading in Spanish. Before students begin reading, ask them what they would expect to find in an ad for a hotel. What aspects of the hotel would the ad promote? Then have them read looking for words describing the hotel's features.

Answers to Activity 25

1. estás
2. está
3. está
4. está
5. están
6. están

NOTA GRAMATICAL
The verb **estar** *(to be)* is used to talk about where people and things are. Here are the present tense forms of the verb.

p.43
Act. 8

(yo)	est**oy**	(nosotros)(nosotras)	est**amos**
(tú)	est**ás**	(vosotros)(vosotras)	est**áis**
(usted)(él)(ella)	est**á**	(ustedes)(ellos)(ellas)	est**án**

GV
p. 31
Acts. 10–11

25 Vamos a Taxco
This is the first time Luis has been to Taxco, so María Inés is describing the city to him as she shows him around. Use **estar** to complete her sentences.

Luis, es la primera vez que tú ___1___ en Taxco, ¿no? Bueno, allá ___2___ el parque, y allá ___3___ la biblioteca. El museo ___4___ en la Plaza Borda. Hay muchos buenos hoteles en esta ciudad. Muchos ___5___ en la calle Hidalgo. Dos tiendas muy buenas ___6___ en la Plazuela de San Juan.

Answers in side column

26 ¿Quiénes o qué?
 Work with a partner. Take turns asking each other who is in each of the following places. Answer by naming three people or things that are in each of the following places right now. Answers will vary.

MODELO ¿Quiénes están en la clase de matemáticas?
—Jimena y Esteban están en la clase de matemáticas.
¿Qué está en la clase de matemáticas?
—La calculadora está en la clase de matemáticas.
—La profesora está en la clase de matemáticas.

1. en la clase de español
2. en tu cuarto
3. en tu casa
4. en México

Hotel Agua Escondida

UNICO EN EL ZOCALO DE TAXCO

- Restaurant "LA HACIENDA" Comida nacional e internacional con sabor casero. Menús especiales
- Estacionamiento cubierto
- Alberca
- Salones para convenciones y banquetes
- Tres amplias terrazas panorámicas

GUILLERMO SPRATLING No. 4

al lado de *next to;*
   to one side of, beside
allá *there*
aquí *here*

cerca de *near*
debajo de *under; beneath*
encima de *on top of*
lejos de *far from*

PRESENTATION

VOCABULARIO

Use local places to present the new vocabulary. (**El cine "Expo" está en la calle Guadalupe. Clase, ¿dónde están otros cines?**) Students respond with the names of other theaters. Check comprehension by having students correct false statements. (**—El cine "Expo" está en la avenida Lincoln. —No, profesora, está en la calle Guadalupe.**) Have students practice with a partner: one gives a new vocabulary word and the other responds with the proper name of a local place.

VISUAL/AUDITORY LEARNERS

Have students look at the city scene in the **Vocabulario**. Make statements about the town and ask students to tell you if they are **cierto** or **falso**. Have students correct false statements. For example,

1. **El supermercado está cerca del parque. (cierto)**
2. **El cine está lejos del supermercado. (falso)**
3. **La piscina está encima del gimnasio. (cierto)**
4. **La tienda está lejos del gimnasio. (falso)**

AUDITORY/VISUAL LEARNERS

27 Read the following sentences and have students match each statement with the correct picture.

1. Carlos y Marcos no están en la clase. Están en la oficina del director. (h)
2. Mario y Fernando están en el gimnasio. (d)
3. Mariana está en el gimnasio también. Está en la piscina. (b)
4. Federico y su perro Bandido están en el parque. (a)
5. María y Claudia están en el restaurante. (f)
6. El señor Pérez está en la tienda de ropa. (g)
7. Elena está en la biblioteca. (e)

ADDITIONAL PRACTICE

28 Have students bring in drawings or photos of their room or an imaginary one. Have them identify the things in it and where they are in relation to each other.

27 ¿Quiénes son y dónde están? Script and answers on p. 141E

 A Listen as Luis Miguel describes his friends and family to you. Match each drawing with the description you hear.

CD 4 Tr. 6

MODELO Paco es bajo y moreno. Le gusta jugar con su perro. **(a)**

B Now look at the drawings again. Write a sentence saying where each person is. Answers on p. 141K

MODELO **a.** Él está en el parque.

28 En mi cuarto

Look at the drawing. Then match the items with their locations below.

1. El lápiz e
2. El reloj a
3. Los zapatos b
4. El cuaderno f
5. El papel c
6. Los bolígrafos d

a. está lejos de la cama.
b. están debajo de la mesa.
c. está cerca de los zapatos.
d. están encima del cuaderno.
e. está al lado del libro.
f. está debajo del bolígrafo.

164 *ciento sesenta y cuatro*   CAPÍTULO 4   ¿Qué haces esta tarde?

164 STANDARDS: 1.2

29 Necesito un...

You and your friends are visiting a new town. Help your friends decide where to go to do a variety of activities. Write a complete sentence that tells where each friend should go. Come up with your own suggestion of what you want to do and where you need to go for the last item. Answers will vary. Possible answers in side column

MODELO Blanca y Ángel quieren estudiar.
Necesitan ir a la biblioteca.

1. Yo quiero comprar ropa.
2. Melissa y Ana quieren caminar con el perro.
3. Deon necesita comprar estampillas *(stamps)*.
4. Paula y David quieren nadar.
5. Josh quiere comprar una pizza.
6. Tú quieres ¿?

30 ¿Dónde está?

Now help your friends find their way around the new town by giving them directions. First look at the map on page 163. Match the location in the first column with the directions in the second column.

MODELO la biblioteca
Está al lado del correo.

1. el parque d
2. la tienda e
3. el cine f
4. el correo a
5. el restaurante b
6. la piscina c

a. Está cerca del cine, al lado de la biblioteca y lejos del gimnasio.
b. Está al lado de la biblioteca, cerca de la tienda y lejos del parque.
c. Está encima del gimnasio.
d. Está cerca del supermercado, el cine y el gimnasio.
e. Está al lado del gimnasio y debajo de la piscina.
f. Está al lado del supermercado y cerca del parque.

31 ¿Dónde están tus cosas?

Get together with two other classmates. Using the words shown here and other words you know, take turns describing where four things are in your own room. While one person describes, the other two draw what they hear on a sheet of paper. Then compare the drawings and make corrections: **No, el reloj no está allí. Está encima de la mesa.** Answers will vary.

el escritorio
el reloj
la cama
el cuaderno
la mochila
la radio

ciento sesenta y cinco **165**

(TPR) Have students take out the following items: **un lápiz, un bolígrafo, papel, un libro, un diccionario, una goma de borrar.** Teach the command **¡Pongan!** and practice the prepositions from the **Vocabulario** on page 163 by having students follow your instructions. **Pongan el lápiz al lado del bolígrafo. Pongan el papel lejos del lápiz,** etc. Have them follow up by using the question **¿Dónde está?** and these vocabulary words.

VISUAL LEARNERS
29 Display Teaching Transparency 4-C. Instead of having students speak or write a response, have volunteers point to the place where each person needs to go.

GAME
31 Have students play **¿Dónde está?** from page 141I to practice the prepositions from **Vocabulario** page 163.

Answers to Activity 29

1. Necesita ir a la tienda.
2. Necesitan ir al parque.
3. Necesita ir al correo.
4. Necesitan ir a la piscina.
5. Necesitan ir al restaurante.
6. Answers will vary.

PA
p. 45
Act. 10

GV
p. 33
Acts. 14–16

GRAMÁTICA   Subject pronouns

In Spanish, you don't need to use subject pronouns as often as you do in English. That's because the verb ending usually shows the subject of the verb. But the pronoun may be used to clarify or emphasize the subject.

yo	compr**o**	nosotros nosotras	compr**amos**
tú	compr**as**	vosotros vosotras	compr**áis**
usted		ustedes	
él	compr**a**	ellos	compr**an**
ella		ellas	

1. In general, **tú** is used to speak to people with whom you're on a first-name basis. Use **usted** with adults and people in authority.

2. In Spain, **vosotros/as** is the plural of **tú**, while **ustedes** is the plural of **usted.** In Latin America, **ustedes** is the plural of both **tú** and **usted.**

   SPAIN   Vosotros sois de San José, ¿verdad?
   LATIN AMERICA   Ustedes son de San José, ¿verdad?

3. The masculine forms (**nosotros** and **vosotros**) are used to refer to groups of males or groups including both males and females. The feminine forms **nosotras** and **vosotras** refer to groups that include only females.

   —José y María, ¿de dónde sois vosotros?
   —Nosotros somos de Madrid.

32 ¿Quién es?

What subject pronoun would you use to replace the names below?

MODELO   Pedro→él

1. Natalia y Hugo ellos
2. tú y Felicia ustedes
3. el señor Ling él
4. Robert y yo nosotros
5. la señora Ryan ella
6. Julia y Tamara ellas

Nota cultural

The use of **tú** and **usted** varies from country to country. Children in some areas are likely to address a parent as **usted**, while children in other areas use **tú**. If you're in a Spanish-speaking area, listen to others and try to use **tú** and **usted** as they do. When in doubt, use **usted** and wait for the other person to invite you to be less formal. How would you address your principal in Spanish?

33 Yo, tú, ella... Answers on p. 141K

Which pronoun would you use if you were talking *about* . . .?

1. you and your friends
2. your next-door neighbors
3. a teacher who is a woman
4. yourself
5. your grandfather

Which pronoun would you use if you were talking *to* . . .?

6. your little brother
7. your doctor
8. your three cousins
9. your principal

34 ¡Zapatos nuevos!

Complete the conversation by filling in the subject pronouns that are missing.

—___1___ necesito comprar unos zapatos en una tienda en el centro comercial. Yo

—¿Ah, sí? ___2___ quiero zapatos nuevos también. Yo

—¿___3___ quieres ir a la tienda esta tarde? Mi familia tiene Tú
que comprar muchas cosas. ___4___ vamos a las tres. Nosotros/Nosotras

—¡Sí! ___5___ quiero ir. ¿Quiere ir Marta también? Yo

—No, ___6___ está en el gimnasio. Bueno, hasta luego. ella

—¡Adiós!

35 Buenos días

During the course of the day, Octavio greets several people and asks how they are. Write both Octavio's greetings and the people's responses. Include the subject pronouns in your sentences.

Answers will vary.

❶   ❷   ❸   ❹

☀ CLOSE

COOPERATIVE LEARNING

Divide the class into groups of three. Each group will choose two verb phrases using verbs they have learned. Each of the three students is responsible for two pronouns and two verb forms so that all six forms are covered by the group. Cards should have one verb phrase and the two pronouns on the front (for example, **hablar español—yo/usted**), and two completed sentences on the back. (**Yo hablo español./ Usted habla español.**) Every group will end up with two complete sets of cards.

☀ ASSESS

▶ Testing Program, pp. 57–58
Quiz 4-2
Audio CD 4, Tr. 20

▶ Grammar and Vocabulary Quizzes
Quiz 4-2A or
Alternative Quiz 4-2A

▶ Alternative Assessment Guide, p. 22

PERFORMANCE ASSESSMENT

In groups, students develop a conversation in which they tell a new student where to find various people and rooms in the school and some of their favorite places around town.

STANDARDS: 1.1, 1.2, 1.3, 5.1   **167**

VIDEO INTEGRATION

Adelante LEVEL 1A
Video Program
Videocassette 2, 18:46–21:29

¡Ven conmigo! LEVEL 1
DVD Tutor, Disc 1

TEACHER NOTES

• Remind students that cultural information may be included in the Quizzes and the Chapter Test.

• The language of the people interviewed represents informal, unrehearsed speech. Occasionally, text has been edited for clarity.

MOTIVATING ACTIVITIES

• Ask students to discuss what they and their friends do together. Where do they go to see and be seen by others?

• Using the new vocabulary from Chapter 4, have students make a list of places in a town. Write their suggestions on the board or on a transparency.

Panorama cultural

CD 4
Trs. 7–10

¿Te gusta pasear con tus amigos?

The **paseo** is a tradition in Spanish-speaking countries; people stroll around the **plaza** or along the streets of a town in the evening to socialize, and to see and be seen by others. In this chapter, we asked some teens about the **paseo**.

After school, Alejandra and her friends get together. Where does she say they like to go?

Sevilla, where Álvaro lives, has many parks and outdoor cafés. They're perfect for hanging out with friends.

● **Alejandra**
San Antonio, Texas
CD 4 Tr. 8

Sí, me encanta pasear. A mí me gusta ir al cine, al parque. Nos juntamos y hablamos mucho de lo que pasó en la escuela.

● **Álvaro**
Sevilla, España
CD 4 Tr. 9

Sí, me encanta pasear. Voy al parque de María Luisa porque es muy divertido. Todo el mundo va a pasear.

Fernando likes to do active things, such as rent a rowboat in Chapultepec Park.

Fernando CD 4 Tr. 10
Ciudad de México,
México

Sí. Mi papá, mi hermano y mi mamá y yo vamos a remar *(row)* a Chapultepec; [hacemos] cosas muy divertidas.

1 What are two places where Alejandra goes? movies, park

2 When Alejandra goes walking with her friends, what do they talk about? what happened in school

3 Why does Álvaro go walking in the park? because it's fun

4 What's the name of the park where Álvaro goes? María Luisa

5 What activity does Fernando mention? rowing

6 How can you tell that Fernando likes to go out with his family? he says they do "cosas divertidas"

Para pensar y hablar... Answers will vary.

A. What activities do you do together with your family? Do you ever go somewhere to watch people and talk with friends?

B. Name one place where all the interviewees go to socialize. Who do they go there with? Do you think it's a good idea for people from a neighborhood to get together and socialize on a regular basis? Why or why not?

Cuaderno para hispanohablantes, p. 20

PRESENTATION
Remind students of the reading strategies they have learned: recognizing cognates, scanning titles, and using previous knowledge. Have them go through the interviewees' answers to find five cognates. They may not know what **juntamos** means, but encourage them to identify the **nosotros** form. Have them use context and background knowledge to guess the meaning of the word **juntamos**. Compare **me encanta** (which both Alejandra and Álvaro use) and **me gusta** to show students their shared verb structure. Then show students the video so they may hear the language in context.

CULTURE NOTE
Although the **paseo** is no longer a tradition in very large Latin American cities, urban families may still take strolls in their **barrio**. Urban neighborhoods in Latin American countries often have the feel of small towns, with family-owned shops and small cafés and restaurants. This is also true in urban Spanish-speaking neighborhoods of the United States, such as those in New York.

170
STANDARDS: 2.1

VIDEO INTEGRATION

Adelante LEVEL 1A
Video Program
Videocassette 2, 5:07–5:45 OR
Videocassette 3, 36:33–37:11
(captioned version)

¡Ven conmigo! LEVEL 1
DVD Tutor, Disc 1

Bell work
On the board write two columns of phrases. Students will match the phrases correctly to form sentences. (Column one: **El libro está, Claudia y Luis están, Nosotros estamos, Los lápices no están;** Column two: **en el gimnasio, encima del escritorio, en la escuela, debajo de la mesa**)

PREVIEWING
36 Have students read these questions as a previewing activity.

TERCER PASO

Storytelling Book
pp. 15, 16

WV3 MEXICO-4

Talking about where you and others go during free time

36 Juan y María Inés

Match each question with the correct answer.

1. ¿Adónde va Juan? c
2. ¿Adónde necesita ir María Inés? a
3. ¿Quiere ir María Inés con Juan? b

a. Necesita ir al correo.
b. No quiere ir con Juan.
c. Va al centro.

Nota cultural

In most Spanish-speaking cities, people don't receive mail delivery at their homes. In most cases, people have a mail box at a central post office where they go to pick up their mail. The address on these letters identifies an **apartado** or **casilla** (post office box) with a number, instead of a street address. Because it's not convenient to travel to the central post office every day, there are many couriers who deliver mail and packages. These couriers often travel on mopeds, and make deliveries to offices and homes. How does your family get its mail?

ASÍ SE DICE

Talking about where you and others go during free time

To ask where someone goes, say:

¿Adónde vas?
Where do you go?

Your friend might answer:

Voy a la biblioteca **para estudiar.**
I go to the library in order to study.

¿Adónde va María Inés?
Where does María Inés go?

María Inés va a la piscina. Luego va al cine **para ver una película.**
María Inés goes to the pool. Later, she goes to the theater to see a movie.

37 **¿Cuál es la pregunta?** Script and answers on p. 141F

CD 4 Tr. 11

Listen to the following people as they answer questions about where they and others go during free time. Then choose the question that each one answered. You may use each question more than once.

a. ¿Adónde vas?

b. ¿Adónde va?

c. ¿Dónde está?

¿Oye, adónde vas?

Voy a la clase de música y después voy al parque.

TERCER PASO

ciento setenta y uno **171**

NOTA GRAMATICAL

Ir *(to go)* is an irregular verb; the conjugation follows its own pattern. To ask where someone is going, use the question word **¿adónde?** *(where to?)*.

PA
p. 46
Acts. 11–12

GV
p. 34
Acts. 17–18

(yo)	**voy**	(nosotros) (nosotras)	**vamos**
(tú)	**vas**	(vosotros) (vosotras)	**vais**
(usted) (él) (ella)	**va**	(ustedes) (ellos) (ellas)	**van**

38 ¿Adónde vamos?

CD 4 Tr. 12

Listen as Filiberto asks his friends where they're going this afternoon after school. On a sheet of paper, write where each person is going. Use the phrases from the word box. Script and answers on p. 141F

el gimnasio — la piscina — la casa de Graciela — el cine

1. Pedro
2. David
3. Luisa
4. Alicia
5. Carlos
6. Filiberto

39 En Taxco

Answers in side column

Claudia and her friends are visiting Taxco and everyone is going to a different place. Fill in the blanks with the correct form of the verb **ir.**

ROSA   Claudia ___1___ a la casa de su tío y yo ___2___ con ella. Luis, ¿adónde ___3___ tú?

LUIS   Yo ___4___ al parque. Oye, María Inés, ¿adónde ___5___ tú?

MARÍA INÉS   Yo ___6___ al centro.

LUIS   ¿A qué hora ___7___ ustedes a la casa del tío?

CLAUDIA   ¡Nosotras ___8___ a la casa de mi tío a las nueve!

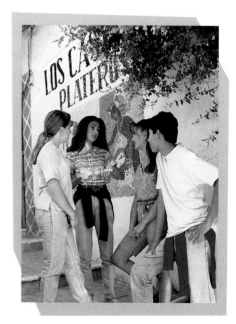

172   *ciento setenta y dos*   CAPÍTULO 4   ¿Qué haces esta tarde?

172   STANDARDS: 1.2, 4.1, 5.1

40 Los planes de todos

You need to keep track of what everyone is doing today. Write five sentences using the information below. Combine words from each column. Be sure your sentences make sense! *Answers will vary.*

Felipe y yo	va	al centro	para jugar al voleibol
Inocencia	van	al supermercado	para pasar el rato con amigos
Mis amigos	voy	al parque	para comprar fruta
Tú	vas	a la tienda	para comprar ropa
Yo	vamos	a la casa	para tomar un refresco

41 Cosas que hacer

You're trying to think of something to do this weekend. Look at the entertainment guide and say where you or your friends have decided to go. Base your answers on the newspaper clipping below.

MODELO   Te gusta nadar.
Answers will vary. Possible answers:
Voy a las piscinas
Municipales Aluche.

1. Te gusta jugar al tenis. Voy al Club de Tenis Las Lomas.
2. A tu amigo/a le gusta nadar. Mi amigo/a va a las piscinas Municipales Aluche.
3. Quieres hacer ejercicios aeróbicos *(aerobics)*.   Voy al Gimnasio García.
4. Quieres ver una película. Voy a Cines Lumiere.

CINE

CINES LUMIERE.
Pasaje Martín de los Heros o Princesa, 5. Tel. 542 11 72. Acceso directo desde el parking. Precio por sesión, 500 ptas. y otra película sin determinar. Confirmar cambios de horarios y película en taquilla.

GIMNASIOS

GIMNASIO GARCÍA.
Andrés Bello, 21-23. Teléfono. 312 86 01. Karate (club campeón de España), clases de aeróbicos, gimnasia, jazz, voleibol, basquet-bol y baile. Máquinas Polaris.

PISCINAS

MUNICIPALES ALUCHE
(Latina). A. General Fanjul, 14 (metro Aluche, autobuses 17, 34 y 39). Tel. 706 28 68.

TENIS

CLUB DE TENIS LAS LOMAS.
Avenida de Las Lomas. Tel. 633 04 63. Escuela de tenis. Todos los niveles. Todos los días de la semana.

42 Destinos

Write six sentences naming places where you, your friends, and your parents (**mis padres**) go in your free time.   *Answers will vary.*

MODELO   Voy al parque para montar en bicicleta.

AUDITORY LEARNERS

40 Create random sentences using the elements in these boxes, some that make sense and some that don't. Read them aloud and have students indicate whether they are **lógico** (thumbs up) or **ilógico** (thumbs down).

 RE-ENTRY

41 Have students recycle question formation as well as previously-learned vocabulary in an oral variation. (**¿Vas a la piscina? Sí, voy a la piscina. ¿A qué hora vas? Voy a las cuatro.**)

PRESENTATION

VOCABULARIO

Teach the phrases **Ayer fue**
_____, **Hoy es** _____,
and **Mañana será** _____.
Display Teaching Transparency 4-3 (or 4C). Ask the question **¿Qué día es hoy?**
Point to a day and model the answer. Then ask **¿Qué día fue ayer?** Have a volunteer give the answer. Then ask **¿Qué día será mañana?**

NOTA GRAMATICAL

Have all students stand up. Call out a day of the week and toss a foam ball to a student. That student calls out the next day in the sequence, tosses the ball to another student, and sits down. Continue until all students are seated. If a student is unsure of the next day, he or she says **paso**, tosses the ball to a classmate, remains standing, and waits for another turn.

VISUAL LEARNERS

Ask students to develop a Spanish calendar for the current month, putting the days of the week and the dates in their proper places. Remind them that the days of the week are not capitalized. Have them fill in one week of the calendar with a sentence for each day, telling what they or someone they know usually does on that day.

VOCABULARIO

p. 35
Acts.
19–20

4-C

Los días de la semana

Monday					el fin de semana	
lunes	martes	miércoles	jueves	viernes	sábado	domingo
1	2	3	4	5	6
7	8	9	10	11	12	13

OCTUBRE

43 Los días

A With a partner, take turns saying the days of the week in Spanish. For each day, your partner will say the name of that day in English.   Answers will vary.

B Next, say a day of the week in Spanish, and your partner will name the following day in Spanish.   Answers will vary.

pp. 47–48
Acts. 13–16

p. 36
Acts. 21–23

4-3

NOTA GRAMATICAL

1. Always use **el** before a day of the week except when stating what day it is. **Hoy es martes.**
2. To say *on Monday, on Tuesday,* etc., use **el lunes, el martes**.
3. To say *on Mondays, on Tuesdays, the weekends,* etc., use **los lunes, los martes, los fines de semana**.
4. To make **sábado** and **domingo** plural, add -**s**: **los sábados, los domingos**.
5. Days of the week are not capitalized in Spanish.

Los sábados por la mañana ellos trabajan en el jardín *(garden)*.

44 ¡Una encuesta!

Take a survey of three classmates to find out where they go on the weekend. Write the name of each person and at least two places where he or she goes. Be prepared to present the class with the results of your survey.   Answers will vary.

MODELO —Kevin, ¿adónde vas los fines de semana?
—Voy al parque y al cine.
Kevin va al parque y al cine.

45 Si son las ocho, ¿dónde estás?

Compare schedules with a partner. Ask each other where you are at the following times during the week. Answers will vary.

MODELO   ¿Dónde estás los lunes a las ocho de la mañana?
—Estoy en la clase de inglés.

1. los viernes a las cuatro de la tarde
2. los sábados a las diez y media de la mañana
3. los martes a la una de la tarde
4. los jueves a las once de la mañana
5. los lunes por la mañana
6. los miércoles por la noche

46 En mi cuaderno

Write a short description of a typical week in your life. Start by making a calendar for the week and include at least one activity for each day. Then write a paragraph describing your week. Answers will vary.

miércoles	jueves	viernes
ir a la casa de María, hacer la tarea		jugar al fútbol

LETRA Y SONIDO

Script on p. 141F

A. The letters **b** and **v** in Spanish represent the same sound. That single sound has two possible variations.

CD 4
Trs. 13–17

1. At the beginning of a phrase, or after an **m** or an **n,** these letters sound like the *b* in the English word *bean.*

   biblioteca   basquetbol   bailar   invierno   viernes

2. Between vowels and after other consonants, their pronunciation is softened, with the lower lip slightly forward and not resting against the upper teeth.

   lobo   lo bueno   uva   Cuba

3. Note that the **b** and **v** in the following pairs of words and phrases have exactly the same pronunciation.

   tubo/tuvo   los huevos/los suebos   a ver/haber   botar/votar

B. Dictado
Pablo hasn't learned to spell words that use **b** and **v** yet. As he says the words he's not sure of, write what you hear.

C. Trabalenguas
El lobo sabe bailar bien el vals bajo el árbol.

 CULTURE NOTE
In many Spanish-speaking countries, calendars often begin with **el lunes** *(Monday),* not **el domingo** *(Sunday).*

 PORTFOLIO
45 **Oral** You may wish to suggest this activity to your students as an appropriate oral Portfolio entry. For Portfolio suggestions, see *Alternative Assessment Guide,* p. 15.

☼ CLOSE

Use Teaching Transparency 4-3 to review material in this **paso.**

☼ ASSESS

▸Testing Program, pp. 59–60
  Quizzes
  Quiz 4-3
  Audio CD 4, Tr. 21

▸ Grammar and Vocabulary Quizzes
  Quiz 4-3 or
  Alternative Quiz 4-3A

▸ Alternative Assessment Guide, p. 22

PERFORMANCE ASSESSMENT
In pairs, have students role-play the following situation: You are going to spend the weekend with a friend in a neighboring town. Call a relative and let him or her know your plans. Your relative asks where you and your friend are going and what times you expect to be at each location. Plan at least four activities for the weekend.

STANDARDS: 1.1, 1.2 **175**

Enlaces

LA MÚSICA

1 Los instrumentos

People in Spanish-speaking countries play many different musical instruments. Some of these instruments are described below. Look at the photographs as you read the descriptions.

el charango

la flauta

1. La **flauta** azteca es un instrumento muy bonito. Es parecida al *(it looks like)* clarinete.

2. El **charango** es popular en los Andes. Es parecido a la guitarra.

3. El **güiro** es un instrumento percusivo *(percussion instrument).* ¡Pero es muy diferente al tambor *(drum)*!

4. En muchos países el **arco** se usa *(is used)* para tocar el violín. En Centroamérica el **arco** es un instrumento musical.

el güiro

el arco

2 ¿De qué se hace?

People have always made musical instruments from materials that are readily available. For example, people have made pottery flutes from clay and percussion instruments from gourds. If you had to make your own musical instrument from materials you have around your classroom, what materials would you use? What instrument would you make? Share your answers with a partner. Answers will vary.

Estos músicos en la región de Asturias, España, tocan las gaitas *(bagpipes).*

176   *ciento setenta y seis*   CAPÍTULO 4   ¿Qué haces esta tarde?

176   STANDARDS: 2.2, 3.1

LAS MATEMÁTICAS/LAS CIENCIAS SOCIALES

3 Los deportes

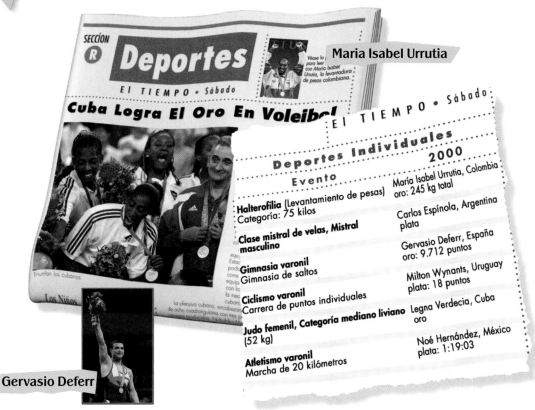

SECCIÓN R
Deportes
EL TIEMPO • Sábado

Véase la para leer con María Isabel Urrutia, la levantadora de pesas colombiana.

Maria Isabel Urrutia

Cuba Logra El Oro En Voleibol

Triunfan los cubanos
Los Niños
la ofensiva cubana, encabezada de ocho cuadrangulares con tres p

Gervasio Deferr

EL TIEMPO • Sábado

Deportes Individuales 2000

Evento	
Halterofilia (Levantamiento de pesas) **Categoría:** 75 kilos	María Isabel Urrutia, Colombia oro: 245 kg total
Clase mistral de velas, Mistral masculino	Carlos Espínola, Argentina plata
Gimnasia varonil Gimnasia de saltos	Gervasio Deferr, España oro: 9.712 puntos
Ciclismo varonil Carrera de puntos individuales	Milton Wynants, Uruguay plata: 18 puntos
Judo femenil, Categoría mediano liviano (52 kg)	Legna Verdecia, Cuba oro
Atletismo varonil Marcha de 20 kilómetros	Noé Hernández, México plata: 1:19:03

el atletismo track and field
la carrera the race
la categoría mediano liviano
  half lightweight
femenil women's
la halterofilia weightlifting

el oro gold
la plata silver
los puntos points
varonil men's
las velas sailing

4 Héroes olímpicos históricos   Answers on p. 141K

1. What male athlete won a gold medal in the 2000 Olympics?

2. Where is champion weightlifter María Isabel Urrutia from?

3. How many points did the Uruguayan cyclist earn to win the silver?

4. What did an Argentinian athlete win a silver medal for?

5. How fast—in kilometers per minute—did Noé Hernández walk in the Track and Field event? (Hint: Convert the time into minutes. Divide the number of kilometers by the total number of minutes to find his speed in kilometers per minute.)

CAPÍTULO 4

MOTIVATING ACTIVITY
Ask students who watched or heard about the 2000 Olympic Games held in Australia: What countries do you remember and why? What sports or activities did you watch or hear about? Which did you like best? What is the purpose of the Olympic games?

PRESENTATION
In pairs, have students use the new vocabulary from this page to ask each other about their likes and dislikes. For example, **¿Te gusta el judo?** or **¿Te gusta el ciclismo?** Tell students to be ready to report on their partner's likes and dislikes, for example, **A María le gusta el ciclismo.**

HISTORY LINK
Cuba, Chile, Spain, Mexico, Colombia, Argentina, Uruguay and Costa Rica all won Olympic medals at the 2000 Olympics in Sydney. The Cuban volleyball team won a gold medal. Other countries won medals in a variety of sports such as soccer, judo, track and field, wrestling, taekwondo, basketball, canoe/kayak, fencing, weightlifting, sailing, field hockey, cycling, gymnastics, and swimming.

STANDARDS: 1.1, 1.2, 3.1, 5.1   **177**

VAMOS A LEER........................

Estrategia

Scanning for specific information means looking for one thing at a time, without worrying about the other information in the reading. For example, you scan when looking up the spelling of a word in a dictionary or looking through the TV listing to see what time a certain show comes on.

¡A comenzar!
The ads on these pages are for pen pals. They come from *Tú*, a magazine for Spanish-speaking teens. Before doing any scanning, gather some general information.

¿Te acuerdas?

Use your background knowledge before you read in depth.

A If you were writing an ad for a pen pal, what would you tell about yourself? The items below are examples of what you might want to write about. Answers will vary.

- your name
- your best friend's name
- your address
- the name of your school
- your age
- what you look like
- what your parents do
- your hobbies

B Now look briefly at the ads. Of the eight possibilities listed above, which four are included in the ads? name, address, age, hobbies

Al grano
Now that you have a general overview of the pen pal ads, you can scan for more details.

C Imagine that you're setting up a letter exchange for your Spanish class. Your classmates have listed the kinds of things they're looking for in a pen pal. Which pen pal would be best for each classmate?

1. someone from Venezuela Wilmer
2. someone who's 11 years old Juan
3. a boy from Panama Esteban
4. a 13-year-old girl Susana
5. someone from the United States Gerardo
6. someone who lives in the city of Buenos Aires Julia
7. a 13-year-old boy Wilmer

D Now it's time to choose a pen pal for yourself. You're hoping to develop a long-term friendship with someone who shares your own interests and hobbies. Who will you choose if you . . .?

1. like to dance Gerardo or Susana
2. like to play sports Esteban or Julia
3. like to listen to music
   Wilmer, Juan, Gerardo, or Julia
Who won't you choose if you . . .?
4. don't like to study Wilmer
5. don't like video games Esteban
6. don't like to swim Julia

LÍNEA DIRECTA

Nombre: Wilmer Ramírez
Edad: 13 años
Dirección: Urb. Las Batallas, Calle
La Puerta #2, San Félix,
Edo. Bolívar, VENEZUELA.
Pasatiempos: Leer tiras cómicas,
escuchar música y estudiar.

Nombre: Susana Tam
Edad: 13 años
Dirección: 4ta. Ave., N #41-07,
La Flora, Cali, COLOMBIA.
Pasatiempos: Ir al cine, a fiestas,
a bailar y hablar por teléfono.
Pueden escribirme en inglés.

Nombre: Juan Dos Santos
Edad: 11 años
Dirección: 55 mts sur, Bomba
Gasotica, Pérez Zeledón,
COSTA RICA.
Pasatiempos: Escuchar música
rock, hablar con los turistas.

Nombre: Gerardo Vargas
Edad: 14 años
Dirección: P.O. Box 2002,
Borrego Springs, California 92004,
ESTADOS UNIDOS.
Pasatiempos: Leer, bailar y
escuchar música rock en español.
Mantener correspondencia con
chicas de otros países.

Nombre: Esteban Hernández
Edad: 15 años
Dirección: Apartado 8-3009,
El Dorado, PANAMÁ
Pasatiempos: Ir al cine, practicar
deportes, jugar a los videojuegos.

Nombre: Julia Ileana Oliveras
Edad: 15 años
Dirección: Yapeyú 9550
(1210) Cap. Fed. Buenos Aires,
ARGENTINA
Pasatiempos: Escuchar la radio,
leer, nadar y jugar al tenis. Pueden
escribirme también en inglés y en
alemán.

Cuaderno para hispanohablantes, pp. 16–18

VAMOS A LEER

ciento setenta y nueve **179**

CRITICAL THINKING
Ask students why they see so
many cognates in Spanish.
(English uses many words of
French origin and both Spanish
and French come from Latin.
Also, modern Spanish adopts
many Anglicisms because of
the universality of English in
the fashion, travel, and business worlds.) Encourage students with this fact: Spanish
may be easier to learn than
they think!

NATIVE SPEAKERS
Have native speakers find five
words that contain *b* and five
that contain *v* to include in
their spelling notebook.

TEACHER NOTE
For additional readings, see
Practice and Activity Book,
p. 49, and *Native Speaker
Activity Book*, pp. 16–19.

☀ POSTREADING

SUGGESTION
D Have students copy their
pen pal ads without putting
their names or street addresses
on them and turn them in.
Randomly number the anony-
mous ads. Tape the ads around
the room. Have students walk
around and find the ad of
someone they'd like to get to
know. They should copy the
number of the ad they like and
that of their own ad and sit
down. Then call out the numbers of the ads and ask whose
they are. Students may be surprised at the people they've
picked.

The **Repaso** reviews and integrates all four skills and culture in preparation for the Chapter Test.

SUGGESTION

2 Have students write questions about the contents of the letter. With a partner, have them write five questions that Isabel's mother could have asked her about the letter. Each pair then role-plays the conversation between the mother and Isabel. They may wish to include the expression **Silvia dice** _____ or simply **Dice** _____.

internet

MARCAR: go.hrw.com
PALABRA CLAVE:
WV3 MEXICO-4

1 Listen to these messages left on Pedro's answering machine. Match the person in Column A with the activity he or she mentions in Column B.   Script and answers on p. 141F

CD 4
Tr. 18

MODELO   Carlos—ir al parque
1. Carmen
2. Gaby
3. Victoria

a. ir a la piscina
b. ir al cine
c. ir a la biblioteca

2 Complete Silvia's letter to her friend Isabel using the verbs in the word box. Use each verb only once.

6 practican   1 estoy   3 vamos   7 camino
2 gusta   5 trabajan   4 voy

Querida Isabel,
   Aquí __1__ yo en St. Louis. Me __2__ mucho mi colegio. Mis amigos son muy simpáticos. Nosotros __3__ al partido de fútbol los viernes, y yo __4__ al centro comercial los sábados. Mis hermanos Teresa y Andrés __5__ en el cine porque necesitan dinero, pero __6__ deportes todas las tardes a las cuatro. Después de clases yo __7__ con el perro.
   Bueno, voy a estudiar. Tengo un examen mañana.. ¡Hasta luego!

                    Un abrazo,
                                Silvia

3 Based on what you have learned in this chapter, choose two reasons why the **paseo** is popular in Latin America.
   a. People have an opportunity to get together with friends.
   b. Everyone thinks the food is great.
   c. The weather is better in Latin America.
   d. Families can spend time together.

4 Vamos a escribir

Write a paragraph explaining where different places in your school are located. Use words like **al lado de**, **cerca de**, and **lejos de.** Answers will vary.

Estrategia

Using drawings can help you write. Try drawing a map of your school and its surroundings to help you organize your thoughts. Then choose the best words to describe where things are on your map.

la cafetería

el auditorio

la oficina del director

la sala de clase

la biblioteca

el gimnasio

la sala de clase

la sala de clase

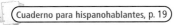
Cuaderno para hispanohablantes, p. 19

5 S I T U A C I Ó N

Work with a classmate to create this conversation in Spanish. One of you will be **Student A** and the other will be **Student B.** Answers will vary.

Student A: Ask your friend if he or she studies in the library on weekends.

Student B: Answer that you study in the library on Saturdays. Ask your friend if he or she goes to the park on weekends.

Student A: Answer that you go to the park on Sundays. Tell your friend two different activities you do there. Ask your friend if he or she goes to the park on weekends.

Student B: Answer that you go to the park on Sundays, too. Tell your friend two different activities you do there.

📁 PORTFOLIO

4 Written Your students may want to consider this activity as a potential Portfolio item. For Portfolio suggestions, see *Alternative Assessment Guide,* pp. 9 and 15.

CHALLENGE

5 Have students do the dialogue in the **Situación** using their own information, and not the cues provided.

A VER SI PUEDO...

WV3 MEXICO-4

ADDITIONAL PRACTICE

1 To review **gustar,** have students role-play a disagreement about where they should go on a day off.

GAME

Clave Divide the class into two teams. On a dry-erase board, chalkboard, or flipchart paper, write various Spanish phrases, verbs, and nouns. Give a verbal clue describing one of the items listed. (**los días sábado y domingo**) A representative from each team points to the words described. (**el fin de semana**) The first to correctly identify it circles the item with that team's colored marker. The team with the most words circled at the end wins.

Answers to Activity 1

1. Le gusta nadar.
2. Le gusta comprar.
3. Le gusta bailar.
4. Te gusta caminar.
5. Me gusta estudiar.

Answers to Activity 2

1. Toco la guitarra.
2. Preparo la cena.
3. Lavo el carro.
4. Miro la televisión.

 Can you talk about what you and others like to do?
p. 149

 Can you talk about what you and others do during free time?
p. 152

 Can you tell where people and things are?
p. 161

 Can you talk about where you and others go during free time?
p. 171

1 How would you tell what these people like to do at the place given? Answers will vary. Possible answers in side column

MODELO   el señor López—la oficina
           Le gusta trabajar.

1. Cecilia—la piscina
2. Gustavo—el centro comercial
3. Berta—la fiesta
4. tú—el parque
5. Yo—la biblioteca

2 How would you tell someone that you . . .? Answers in side column

1. play the guitar
2. make dinner
3. wash the car
4. watch television

3 How would you say that you and someone else. . .? Answers will vary. Possible answers on p. 141K

1. walk in the park
2. ride bicycles
3. spend time with friends
4. study in the library
5. listen to music
6. watch television

4 Can you tell where the following people are? Answers will vary. Possible answers on p. 141K

1. Rosa estudia.
2. Claudia compra un regalo.
3. Geraldo y Fernando caminan con el perro.
4. Sofía monta en bicicleta.
5. Tú y tus amigos nadan.

5 How would you tell a visitor who needs directions that . . .? Answers on p. 141K

1. the supermarket is next to the park
2. the bookstore is far from the school
3. the gym is near the library

6 Write a sentence telling where each person is going. Answers on p. 141K

MODELO   Mr. Súarez is really thirsty.
           Va al restaurante para tomar un refresco.

1. Mariana wants to buy some books and magazines.
2. Lupe wants to lift weights.
3. Carlos and Adriana need to buy stamps.

VOCABULARIO

PRIMER PASO

Talking about what you and others like to do

A mí me gusta + inf.
  I (emphatic) like to . . .
¿A quién le gusta...? *Who likes to . . .?*
¿A ti qué te gusta hacer?
  What do you (emphatic) like to do?

bailar *to dance*
cantar *to sing*
cuidar a tu hermano/a *to take care of your brother/sister*
descansar en el parque *to rest in the park*
dibujar *to draw*
escuchar música *to listen to music*
estudiar *to study*
hablar por teléfono *to talk on the phone*
lavar el carro *to wash the car*
lavar la ropa *to wash the clothes*
me gusta(n) *I like*
mirar la televisión *to watch TV*
nadar *to swim*
pintar *to paint*
la piscina *swimming pool*
por eso *that's why, for that reason*
¿Quién? *Who?*
sacar la basura *to take out the trash*

Talking about what you and others do during free time

antes de *before*
caminar con el perro *to walk the dog*

la cena *dinner*
con *with*
conmigo *with me*
contigo *with you*
descansar *to rest*
después de *after*
la guitarra *guitar*
el helado *ice cream*
montar en bicicleta *to ride a bike*
pasar el rato con amigos *to spend time with friends*
el piano *piano*
practicar *to practice*
preparar *to prepare*
que *that, which, who*
¿Qué haces después de clases?
  What do you do after school?
el refresco *soft drink*
regresar *to return, go back, come back*
el restaurante *restaurant*
(en) el tiempo libre *(during) free time*
tocar *to play an instrument*
tomar *to drink, to take*
trabajar *to work*

SEGUNDO PASO

Telling where people and things are

al lado de *next to, to one side of, beside*
allá *there*
aquí *here*
la biblioteca *library*
la casa *house, home*
el centro *downtown*
cerca de *near*
el cine *movie theater*
el correo *post office*

debajo de *under, beneath*
¿Dónde? *Where?*
encima de *on top of*
estar *to be*

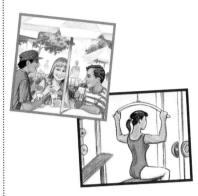

el gimnasio *gym*
lejos de *far from*
nosotros/nosotras *we*
el parque *park*
el paseo *walk, stroll*
el supermercado *supermarket*
la tienda *store*
el trabajo *work, job*
usted *you (formal)*
ustedes *you (plural, formal)*
vosotros/vosotras *you (plural, informal)*

TERCER PASO

Talking about where you and others go during free time

¿Adónde? *Where (to)?*
¿Adónde vas? *Where are you going?*
al *to the*
el día *day*
el domingo *Sunday*
el fin de semana *weekend*
el jueves *Thursday*
el lunes *Monday*
el martes *Tuesday*
el miércoles *Wednesday*
para + infinitive *(in order) to*
la película *movie*
el sábado *Saturday*
la semana *week*
ver *to see*
el viernes *Friday*

GAME
Play **Mímica** to review verbs and prepositions. Write action verbs and prepositional phrases on cards. (**nadar, debajo de la mesa**) Divide the class into teams and give one card to each student. Taking turns, students act out their word or words while the other team guesses in Spanish. You may consider limiting the time that each team has to guess.

CHAPTER 4 ASSESSMENT

▸ **Testing Program**
Chapter Test, pp. 61–68
 Audio Compact Discs, CD 4, Trs. 22–23
Speaking Test, p. 113

▸ **Alternative Assessment Guide**
Performance Assessment, p. 22
Portfolio Assessment, p. 15
CD-ROM Assessment, p. 29

▸ **Interactive CD-ROM Tutor, Disc 1**
 ¡A hablar!
¡A escribir!

▸ **Standardized Assessment Tutor**
Chapter 4

▸ **One-Stop Planner, Disc 1**
   Test Generator
   Chapter 4

¡Ven conmigo a la Florida!
LOCATION OPENER CHAPTERS 5, 6

PRINT	MEDIA
Video Guide Level 1A • Activity Masters and Suggestions, pp. 33–34	**Video Program Level 1A** Videocassette 2 **Interactive CD-ROM Tutor** Disc 2 **go.hrw.com** WV3 FLORIDA **¡Ven conmigo! Level 1** **DVD Tutor,** Disc 1

You may wish to point out the following images as students view the Florida Location Opener. These images will be seen on both the Video Program and the DVD Program. If you are using the DVD Program they may be freeze-framed for presentation and discussion purposes.

Little Havana, or **la Pequeña Habana,** stretches along several blocks of **Calle Ocho** through downtown Miami. In mid-March, **Calle Ocho** fills with people celebrating Cuban culture and heritage. This festival features music, dancing, food, and special activities for children. The *Guinness Book of World Records* states that in the 1988 **Calle Ocho** Festival, 119,986 people formed the longest conga dance line ever.

The quickest way to get around Miami is on the Metrorail, a train that glides on a 21-mile track connecting downtown Miami with several suburbs. The **Metromover,** a monorail, makes two loops in downtown Miami, and has 4.4 miles of track with 12 stations at major business and shopping centers.

Art Deco was a decorative and architectural style of the period between 1925 and 1940, characterized by bold colors and the use of industrial materials. Miami's Art Deco architects developed a unique style called **Tropical Deco** which included the use of tropical colors and etched-glass panels featuring mermaids, sea horses, flamingos, pelicans, and palm trees.

The **Everglades** extend from Lake Okeechobee to Florida Bay and include land covered by shallow water and saw grass in the northern part, and saltwater marshes and mangrove swamps in the southern region. Alligators, deer, fish, panthers, pelicans, and snakes inhabit the Everglades. The Seminole Indians have reservations in the Everglades. Many residents of the Everglades offer airboat tours of the area.

Alligators were once common along the Gulf of Mexico and the Atlantic coast from Florida to North Carolina. So many were hunted for their hides that they nearly became extinct. In 1967, the U.S. Fish and Wildlife Service classified them as an endangered species. By 1977, the population had increased so much that they were reclassified from endangered to threatened; however, alligator hunting is still tightly restricted.

PROJECTS

UNA VISITA A LA FLORIDA

This activity will familiarize students with the geography of the southern United States, primarily Florida. It will emphasize Spanish speakers' linguistic, social, and cultural contributions to this state.

Introduction

Ask students if they are familiar with Spanish-speaking influence in this part of the South. Show students a detailed map of Florida and ask them to pick out names of cities that look or sound Spanish in origin. Ask them why they think so many people in the Miami area speak Spanish as their native language. Ask them if they know of sports, foods, music, art, or leisure activities that are of Hispanic origin. Have students imagine that they are planning a family vacation to Florida. Popular tourist destinations include Orlando, Miami, and Saint Augustine. Have students learn about these and other places by writing to the Chamber of Commerce of a given city or by checking on the Internet. From the information gathered, students will prepare a bulletin board to be used as a reference for Chapters 5 and 6.

Materials students may need

- Brochures on Florida
- Large sheets of construction paper
- Large- and medium-point felt-tipped markers
- Strips of posterboard
- Thumbtacks
- Pictures of Florida
- Map of Florida

Sequence

1. Divide students into groups. Within each group, assign the roles of Researcher, Cartographer, and Reporter.
2. Groups gather information about a specific city in Florida. The Researcher writes to the Chamber of Commerce for information. The group members decide which information to illustrate or cut out to put on the class bulletin board. The Researcher can also use the Internet or library resources for material.
3. Topics that student groups should consider include Hispanic influence on this city, activities, food, climate, attractions, weather, map of the city, sports, and airport connections with other cities in the U.S.
4. The Cartographer from each group begins preparing the bulletin board for the class. The Cartographer draws a large map of Florida and identifies the researched cities on the map.
5. The Cartographer in the group makes labels in Spanish to emphasize the categories of interest for each city. He or she puts the labels on the bulletin board, along with the visuals.
6. Before the Cartographers have prepared the bulletin board of the map of Florida, be sure to emphasize the proximity to Cuba. Have them include the island of Cuba as a part of the map.
7. The Reporter for each group presents the findings of his or her group to the class. Reporters can imagine that they are doing an on-the-spot live interview for a TV network station to promote their city.

Grading the project

Suggested point distribution (total = 100 points):

Research information	**30**
Map	**30**
Oral presentation	**30**
Group effort	**10**

CHAPTERS 5, 6   LOCATION OPENER   **183B**

LOCATION 3

¡Ven conmigo a la Florida!

LOCATION OPENER CHAPTERS 5, 6 (cont.)

⬥ Using the Map

You may want to have students refer to the maps on pages xxi and xxiii.

- Ask students to identify the two states that border Florida. (Alabama and Georgia)
- Have students measure the distance between Miami and **La Habana** (approximately 200 miles). What significance might this short distance have? (The culture in Miami has a lot of Cuban influence.)
- Tourism is crucial to Florida's economy. Ask students to locate some of the tourist spots on the map and to discuss their attractions.

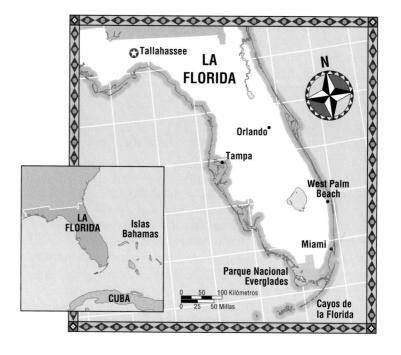

History/Geography Links

- Explain to students that Havana is the capital of Cuba.
- Florida and the states bordering Mexico bear the unmistakable stamp of Spanish influence. Ask students which areas in the United States reveal a strong French heritage. (Louisiana, Northern New England)
- Ask students if they can think of a Caribbean island that was colonized by both the French and the Spanish. (Hispaniola—divided between Haiti, a former French colony, and the Dominican Republic, a former Spanish colony) Have them locate it on the map on page xxi.

You may wish to have students do the above map activities using the Atlas Interactivo Mundial at **go.hrw.com**.

go.hrw.com ⸺ MAPQUEST.COM

Culture Notes

• Southern Florida has a diverse population with an overall Hispanic flavor. Many of the state's Hispanic residents are of Cuban heritage and came to the United States to escape the communist policies of Fidel Castro after 1959. Cubans and Cuban Americans have often overcome difficult circumstances to excel in politics, business, sports, art, and entertainment. (mayor of Miami Xavier Suárez; baseball player Tony Oliva; actor Andy Garcia; salsa musician Celia Cruz, and pop singer Gloria Estefan)

• Thanks to its Cuban influence, southern Florida is virtually bilingual. Spanish is heard everywhere: in schools and shops, on the streets, and over the airwaves. Spanish-language radio, television, and newspapers are popular and profitable. Florida's bilingualism is doubtless a strong attraction for Spanish-speaking tourists and businesspeople from around the world.

• The beaches of Miami are famous for their size and beauty. On weekends, it is common to see families and groups of people at the beach having cookouts, listening to music, and, of course, swimming in the ocean.

Art Link

Explain that Art Deco was a popular architectural style between 1925 and 1940 that used geometric designs, bold colors, chrome, plastic, and other industrial materials. It was used mostly in architecture, furniture, jewelry, pottery, and textiles. Ask students if they can name any famous buildings that have Art Deco style. (the Empire State Building and Radio City Music Hall in New York City) Ask students to research and report on Hispanic influence on architecture in the southwestern United States.

¡Ven conmigo
a la Florida!

**VIDEO
INTEGRATION**

Adelante LEVEL 1A
Video Program
Videocassette 2, 22:40–24:42

¡Ven conmigo! LEVEL 1
DVD Tutor, Disc 1

MOTIVATING ACTIVITY

Ask your students what images, words, or ideas make them think of Florida. What do they know about Florida's culture and people? Point out that Spanish is spoken widely in southern Florida, and that in these chapters they will learn how prevalent Latino culture is in this region of the United States.

BACKGROUND

This photo features the Art Deco District of Miami Beach. Art Deco fans lobbied to have the area recognized as a national treasure, and in 1979 it was placed on the *National Register of Historic Places,* becoming the youngest historic district in the nation.

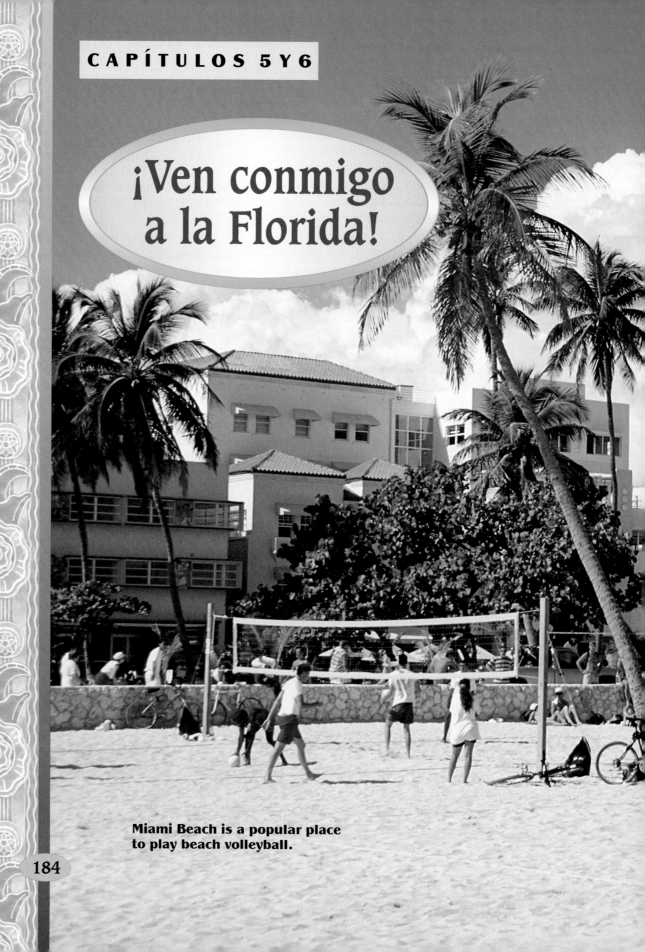

CAPÍTULOS 5 Y 6

¡Ven conmigo
a la Florida!

**Miami Beach is a popular place
to play beach volleyball.**

184

La Florida

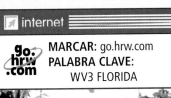

Population: More than 16,000,000 inhabitants. More than 15% are of Hispanic origin.

Area: 58,664 sq. mi.

Capital: Tallahassee

Major city: Miami, with a metropolitan area population of more than 3,711,000

Climate: subtropical

Industries: tourism, citrus fruit products, commercial fishing, electronics, and sugarcane products

History: Populated by Native Americans before the arrival of the Spanish explorer Ponce de León in 1513. A Spanish colony was established in 1565 at St. Augustine. The Seminole arrived in the 18th century. Spain ceded the territory to the United States in 1819.

internet

MARCAR: go.hrw.com
PALABRA CLAVE:
WV3 FLORIDA

HRW ATLAS INTERACTIVO MUNDIAL

MAPQUEST.COM

Have students go to the interactive atlas at **go.hrw.com** to find out more about the geography of Florida.

 USING THE ALMANAC

- **La bandera:** The Florida state flag features crossed diagonal red bars on a white field. Its centerpiece is the state seal with a Native American woman strewing flowers, a sabal palm (the state tree), a steamboat, and the rising sun.

- **Los seminole:** The Seminole fled from the British in Georgia and Alabama and settled in south Florida in the 18th century. In 1829, the U.S. government ordered them deported to the Oklahoma Indian Territory. Most Seminole were ultimately killed, forcibly resettled, or driven deep into the Everglades. A few descendants still live there today.

- **La colonia española:** In 1565, the Spanish founded St. Augustine, the first permanent European settlement in what would become the United States.

CNNenEspañol.com

Have students check the CNN en español Web site for news on Florida.

USING THE PHOTO ESSAY

② The internationally known beach at Varadero, Cuba, has beautiful white-sand beaches and clear blue waters. During the 1800s, many sailors would land their boats on its shore, which is where the name **Varadero** *(shipyard)* comes from. Cuba was a travel destination for many North American tourists earlier this century. People enjoyed going to the beaches, listening to live music, and relaxing.

ADDITIONAL VOCABULARY

You may want to present the following words:
bucear *to scuba dive*
la sombrilla *parasol*
jugar al ajedrez *to play chess*
jugar al dominó *to play dominoes*
el arrecife de coral *coral reef*
el pantano *wetland*
la garza *heron*

BACKGROUND

The Florida East Coast Railroad was extended to Miami and completed in 1896. The railway boosted tourism and business in the region and enabled Miami to reach a population of 250,000 over the next fifty years. Miami is now an international financial center linking Latin America to the United States. It is also a major crossroads of international travel.

☀ LA FLORIDA

CD-ROM DISC 2

Florida has many attractions, such as the Kennedy Space Center, the wetlands of the Everglades, and hundreds of miles of beaches. The local culture has been deeply colored by the many Spanish-speaking immigrants and visitors that have come since the 1500s. In addition, Florida has a rich variety of other ethnic heritages, including Native American and African American.

▲ **Un cafecito**
This *cafetería* in Little Havana caters to Cuban Americans. People order Cuban coffee or sandwiches at a walk-up window and drink and eat standing up.

▲ **Un mural**
This mural in Miami commemorates the famous Varadero beach in Havana, Cuba.

186 *ciento ochenta y seis*

Chapters 5 and 6 will introduce you to Patricia, José Luis, and Raquel, some students who live in Miami. Spanish speakers make up the majority of this city's population, with those of Cuban heritage forming the largest group. You'll have a chance to find out about everyday life in this energetic and well-known North American city.

▲ El buceo

Florida has 1,350 miles of coastline and some of the most beautiful beaches in the U.S. It's the perfect place for scuba diving, water skiing, and other water sports.

▼ Los caimanes

Alligators are common in the Florida Everglades, a national park about 25 miles west of Miami. It is home to many species of other animals including manatees, deer, storks, and bald eagles.

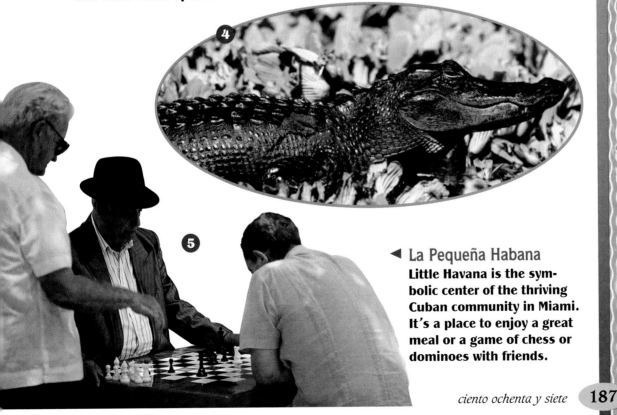

◀ La Pequeña Habana

Little Havana is the symbolic center of the thriving Cuban community in Miami. It's a place to enjoy a great meal or a game of chess or dominoes with friends.

ciento ochenta y siete 187

LOCATION OPENER
CAPÍTULOS 5 Y 6

LANGUAGE NOTE
The English word *alligator* comes from the Spanish **el lagarto** *(lizard)*.

❸ Tell students that Florida is the site of the first undersea park in the continental U.S., the John Pennekamp Coral Reef State Park near Key Largo. Ask them why Florida is naturally more attractive to beach goers and divers than other coastal states. (Florida is warm year-round and has more ocean coastline than any other state except Alaska. Its beaches are exceptionally clean and beautiful.)

❹ At the turn of the century Miami began to boom, and the Everglades were in danger of being destroyed. In 1916, the Florida Federation of Women's Clubs purchased the first 4,000 acres of what would become Everglades National Park and set them aside for preservation. In recent years, the commitment to save the Everglades has included expansion of the park and restoration of a more natural water flow to the wetlands.

❺ **El parque Máximo Gómez,** better known as Domino Park, is located on **la Calle Ocho,** in the heart of Miami's Little Havana. The park is popular with members of the Cuban-American community who come to play dominoes and chess.

El ritmo de la vida
CHAPTER OVERVIEW

De antemano pp. 190–193	*¿Cómo es el ritmo de tu vida?*			
	FUNCTIONS	**GRAMMAR**	**VOCABULARY**	**RE-ENTRY**
Primer paso pp. 194–199	• Discussing how often you do things, p. 195	• **Gramática:** Negation, p. 196 • **Nota gramatical:** The question words **¿quién?** and **¿quiénes?**, p. 198		• Present tense of regular **-ar** verbs • Negation with **no** • **¿quién?**
Segundo paso pp. 202–211	• Talking about what you and your friends like to do together, p. 203 • Talking about what you do during a typical week, p. 209	• **Nota gramatical:** The pronoun **les**, p. 206 • **Gramática: -er** and **-ir** verbs, p. 207	• Weekend activities, p. 204 • Frequency terms, p. 208	• **gustar** • Subject pronouns
Tercer paso pp. 212–219	• Giving today's date, p. 213 • Talking about the weather, p. 216	• **Nota gramatical:** The formula for giving today's date, p. 213	• The seasons and the months, p. 214 • Weather expressions, p. 216	• Days of the week

Letra y sonido	p. 219	Accent marks		**Dictado:** Audio CD 5 Tracks 11–15
Enlaces	pp. 220–221	**Las ciencias sociales y las ciencias**		
Vamos a leer	pp. 222–223	**Deportes en el agua**	**Reading Strategy:** Using context to guess meaning	
Review	pp. 224–227	**Repaso,** pp. 224–225	**A ver si puedo...,** p. 226	**Vocabulario,** p. 227

Culture
- **Nota cultural:** Leisure-time activities, p. 194
- **Panorama cultural: ¿Cómo es una semana típica?,** pp. 200–201
- **Nota cultural:** Meeting places, p. 208
- **Nota cultural:** Weather reports, p. 212
- **Nota cultural:** The seasons of the year in South America, p. 215

PRINT

Lesson Planning
One-Stop Planner
Lesson Planner with Substitute Teacher
Lesson Plans, pp. 24–28

Listening and Speaking
Listening Activities
- Student Response Forms for Listening Activities, pp. 58–60
- Additional Listening Activities 5-1 to 5-6, pp. 18–20
- Additional Listening Activities (song), p. xx
- Scripts and Answers, pp. 38–40, 21

Video Guide
- Teaching Suggestions, pp. 36–37
- Activity Masters, pp. 38–40
- Scripts and Answers, pp. 58–60, 65–66

Activities for Communication
- Communicative Activities, pp. 25–30
- Realia and Teaching Suggestions, pp. 58–62
- Situation Cards, pp. 78–79

¡Ven conmigo! Level 1
TPR Storytelling Book, pp. 17–20

Reading and Writing
Reading Strategies and Skills, Chapter 5
¡Lee conmigo! 1, Chapter 5
Practice and Activity Book, pp. 51–62

Grammar
Grammar and Vocabulary Workbook, pp. 37–44

¡Ven conmigo! Level 1
Grammar Tutor for Students of Spanish
Chapter 5

Assessment
Testing Program
- Paso Quizzes and Chapter Test, pp. 73–84
- Score Sheet, Scripts and Answers, pp. 85–90

Grammar and Vocabulary Quizzes
- Quizzes 5-1A, 5-2A, 5-3A
- Alternative Quizzes 5-1A, 5-2A, 5-3A

Alternative Assessment Guide
- Portfolio Assessment, p. 16
- Performance Assessment, p. 23
- CD-ROM Assessment, p. 30

¡Ven conmigo! Level 1
Standardized Assessment Tutor
- Reading, pp. 17–19
- Writing, p. 20
- Math, pp. 25–26

Native Speakers
¡Ven conmigo! Level 1
Cuaderno para hispanohablantes, pp. 21–25

MEDIA

Online Activities
- Juegos interactivos
- Actividades internet

Video Program
- Videocassette 2
- Videocassette 3 *(captioned version)*

¡Ven conmigo! Level 1
DVD Tutor, Disc 2

Audio Compact Discs
- Textbook Listening Activities, CD 5, Tracks 1–16
- Additional Listening Activities, CD 5, Tracks 22–27
- Assessment Items, CD 5, Tracks 17–21

Interactive CD-ROM Tutor, Disc 2

Teaching Transparencies
- Situations 5-1 to 5-3
- Vocabulary 5-A to 5-C
- Grammar and Vocabulary Workbook

One-Stop Planner CD-ROM

Use the **One-Stop Planner CD-ROM with Test Generator** to aid in lesson planning and pacing.

For each chapter, the **One-Stop Planner** includes:
- Editable lesson plans with direct links to teaching resources
- Printable worksheets from resource books
- Direct launches to the HRW Internet activities
- Video and audio segments
- Test Generator
- Clip Art for vocabulary items

CAPÍTULO 5

El ritmo de la vida
TECHNOLOGY

DVD/VIDEO

Videocassette 2, Videocassette 3 (captioned version)
DVD Tutor, Disc 1 See Video Guide, pages 33–38.

De antemano • ¿Cómo es el ritmo de tu vida?

Students in Miami prepare a news broadcast program for their high school. José Luis gives the national weather forecast, and Raquel interviews students about what they do during their free time. After Raquel's last interview, there is a problem with the camera in the studio and the broadcast is interrupted.

¿Cómo es una semana típica?

Teenagers from Ecuador, Venezuela, Argentina and other Spanish-speaking countries tell us what a typical week is like for them.

A continuación

The students resolve the camera problem and finish their news broadcast. The next day they show Armando, the new student from Panama, around the gardens of Vizcaya.

Videoclips

• **Pronóstico del tiempo:** weather report from Costa Rica

INTERACTIVE CD-ROM TUTOR

Activity	Activity Type	Pupil's Edition Page
En contexto	Interactive conversation	
1. Así se dice	Imagen y sonido ¡Exploremos! ¡Identifiquemos!	p. 195
2. Gramática	¡A escoger!	p. 196
3. Vocabulario	¡Super memoria!	p. 204
4. Gramática	¿Qué falta?	p. 207
5. Vocabulario	¡Super memoria!	pp. 214, 216
6. Vocabulario	¡A escoger!	p. 214
Panorama cultural	¿Cómo es una semana típico? ¡A escoger!	pp. 200–201
¡A hablar!	Guided recording	pp. 224–225
¡A escribir!	Guided writing	pp. 224–225

Teacher Management System

Launch the program, type "admin" in the password area and press RETURN. Log on to **www.hrw.com/CDROMTUTOR** for a detailed explanation of the Teacher Management System.

DVD-ROM TUTOR ¡Ven conmigo! Level 1

The *DVD Tutor* contains all material from the Level 1 *Video Program*. Spanish captions are available for use at your discretion for all sections of the video. The *DVD Tutor* also provides a variety of video-based activities that assess students' understanding of the **De antemano, A continuación,** and **Panorama cultural.**

This part of the *DVD Tutor* may be used on any DVD video player connected to a television or video monitor.

In addition to the video material and the video-based comprehension activities, the *DVD Tutor* also contains the entire Level 1 *Interactive CD-ROM Tutor* in DVD-ROM format. Each DVD disc contains the activities from all 12 chapters of the *Interactive CD-ROM Tutor.*

This part of the *DVD Tutor* may be used on a Macintosh® or Windows® computer with a DVD-ROM drive.

One-Stop Planner CD-ROM

To preview all resources available for this chapter, use the **One-Stop Planner CD-ROM,** Disc 2.

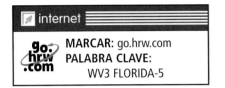

⟍↑⟋ internet

go.hrw.com
MARCAR: go.hrw.com
PALABRA CLAVE:
WV3 FLORIDA-5

INTERNET CONNECTION

*Have students explore the **go.hrw.com** Web site for many online resources covering all chapters. All Chapter 5 resources are available under the keyword **WV3 FLORIDA-5**. Interactive games help students practice the material and provide them with immediate feedback. You will also find a printable worksheet that provides Internet activities that lead to a comprehensive online research project.*

JUEGOS INTERACTIVO

You can use the interactive activities in this chapter

- to practice grammar, vocabulary, and chapter functions
- as homework
- as an assessment option
- as a self-test
- to prepare for the Chapter Test

ACTIVIDADES INTERNET

Students find out what the weather is like today in Miami. Based on their findings, they write activities they would like to do there.

- To prepare for the **Hoja de actividades,** have students watch the dramatic episode on Videocassette 2.
- After completing the activity sheet, ask students to choose a Spanish-speaking city with a very different climate than Miami's and do the same activity. Encourage students to learn more about that city than just the weather: what can they do there? what are typical leisure activities? what do people do at other times of year?

Proyecto

Students work in pairs: one student is a travel agent, and the other is a client. The agent asks the client what activities he or she enjoys. Based on that information, the pair searches online together for a Spanish-speaking city that offers those activities this time of year. They plan a three-day vacation for the client. You might have them post the itinerary on a personal Web site.

CAPÍTULO 5

El ritmo de la vida

TEXTBOOK LISTENING ACTIVITIES SCRIPTS

For Student Response Forms, see Listening Activities pp. 58–60.

PRIMER PASO   pp. 194–199

5 El cine   p. 195

CARLOS Hola, Teresa. Hola, Maité, ¿qué tal?

TERESA Bien, Carlos, ¿y tú?

CARLOS Estoy muy bien. Oye, hoy por la tarde voy a ir al cine.

TERESA ¿Otra vez? ¿Con qué frecuencia vas al cine?

CARLOS Yo voy todos los viernes. ¿Y tú, Maité?

MAITÉ No me gustan mucho las películas pero sí me gusta ir al centro comercial. Muchas veces voy al centro comercial los sábados. ¿Quieres ir conmigo este sábado por la tarde, Teresa?

TERESA No gracias, Maité. Tengo clase de música. Practico el piano todos los sábados y miércoles.

Answers to Activity 5

1. c
2. b
3. a

SEGUNDO PASO   pp. 202–211

15 Mejores amigos   p. 203

GLORIA Oye, Carlos, ¿qué deportes les gustan a ti y a Eddie?

CARLOS Bueno, a mí me gusta esquiar.

EDDIE A mí me gusta mucho acampar.

GLORIA Hmmm, entonces, a Carlos le gusta esquiar y a Eddie le gusta acampar. ¿Qué les gusta hacer juntos? ¿Les gusta bucear juntos?

CARLOS Pues sí, nos gusta bucear juntos. Especialmente los fines de semana.

GLORIA ¿Y les gusta pescar juntos?

CARLOS ¿Pescar? No, no pescamos nunca.

Answers to Activity 15

1. b
2. d
3. a
4. c

24 Un día típico   p. 209

Típicamente Miguel bebe jugo y hace un poco de tarea por la mañana, antes de ir al colegio. Él va al colegio en bicicleta. ¡Nunca toma el autobús! Por la tarde, típicamente come ensalada y frutas cuando hace la tarea de matemáticas.

Answers to Activity 24

a. cierto
b. falso
c. falso

31 **¿Qué fecha es hoy?**   p. 213

1. Hoy es el veinticinco de diciembre.
2. Hoy es el veintiséis de abril.
3. Hoy es el treinta y uno de octubre.
4. Hoy es el veintiséis de noviembre.
5. Hoy es el catorce de febrero.
6. Hoy es el cuatro de julio.

Answers to Activity 31

1. b	**3.** a	**5.** e
2. d	**4.** f	**6.** c

LETRA Y SONIDO   p. 219

For the scripts for parts A, B, and D see page 219. The script for part C is below.

C. Dictado

Voy al almacén hoy porque necesito una cámara nueva. Pero, ¿dónde está mi suéter? ¿Y el cinturón para mi falda? Ah, aquí están. ¿Tú quieres ir conmigo?

1 **p. 224**

1. Hoy en Nueva York, hace mal tiempo. No hace mucho frío, pero está lloviendo muchísimo.
2. En Chicago hace mucho viento otra vez. No va a llover hoy, y la temperatura va a llegar a los setenta grados.
3. En Miami va a ser un día maravilloso. Hace buen tiempo. Hace sol y la temperatura es de ochenta grados, un buen día para la playa.
4. Hace frío en las montañas de Colorado. La temperatura es de treinta y dos grados. Un día perfecto para esquiar.

Answers to Repaso Activity 1

1. c
2. d
3. a
4. b

CAPÍTULO 5

El ritmo de la vida
PROJECTS

CALENDARIO DEL DÍA

*One way to constantly reinforce vocabulary about the days of the week, the months, the weather, and the seasons is a **Calendario del día**. This can be a poster large enough to be read from the opposite end of the room. This daily reinforcement keeps the days and months fresh in students' working vocabulary and reinforces necessary structures.*

Introduction

Initiate a discussion on the importance of dates and calendars. Ask students to think of three or four reasons why calendars are important. Can they think of a reason other than keeping appointments? (to be able to plan for harsh-weather seasons) Explain that in this project they will create a poster that will keep them aware of the current date and weather in Spanish. You might have students do research on weather seasons in Spanish-speaking countries to find out what seasons Spanish speakers need to plan for.

Materials students may need

◆ Large matte boards that can be free-standing on a chalkboard

◆ Colored poster board cut into strips or number cards

◆ 3 × 5 or 4 × 6 index cards—preferably colored

◆ Colored markers—large tip

◆ Manila envelopes cut in half to make pockets

Sequence

1 Have students write the following questions on the matte board. Where a blank is indicated, have them leave room for a pocket (made from the manila envelope) that will hold an index card with an appropriate answer. (Velcro® can be used on the cards instead of the envelopes)
¿Qué día es hoy?   Hoy es _____.
¿Cuál es la fecha?   Es el _____ de _____.
¿Qué tiempo hace hoy?   Hoy hace _____.

2 Have them make answer cards for each of the following categories and write them so that the text is visible with the cards resting in a manila envelope pocket.
Numbers: 1–31
Days of the week: **lunes, martes, miércoles, jueves, viernes**
Months of the year: **enero, febrero, marzo, abril, mayo, junio, septiembre, octubre, noviembre, diciembre**
Weather conditions: **hace frío, hace calor, hace mal tiempo, hace buen tiempo, llueve, nieva, hace viento, hace sol, está nublado**

3 Each day, a different student can ask his or her classmates questions and change the cards as necessary to keep the display current.

ESTOY ACTIVO/A TODO EL AÑO

*This mini-poster will give students the opportunity to discuss the activities they and their friends like to do during leisure time throughout the year. The mini-poster will be a visual representation of the vocabulary they have learned in this chapter using **me, te, le, nos, les gusta** + infinitive.*

Introduction

This activity should be done in pairs. Each student selects eight activities he or she likes to do during the year. They cut out pictures from magazines or illustrate the activities themselves. Each illustration is labeled in Spanish using **me, te, le, nos, les gusta** + infinitive linked to the season of the year: **En la primavera me gusta pasear en el campo.** Each student presents his or her mini-poster to a partner or the pairs can present the posters orally to the whole class.

Materials students may need

- Colored posterboard
- Magazines
- Colored pencils, large-tip markers for title
- Glue sticks
- Fine-point felt-tipped markers

Sequence

1. The pairs will write eight sentences in Spanish describing their favorite leisure activities. The sentences should include the season in which they do the activity: **Me gusta practicar el fútbol en el otoño.** Use the vocabulary from page 227 as well as previously learned vocabulary.

2. Students should make a diagram of the four seasons of the year, label the seasons, and include their favorite activities in each one. One way to do this is to divide the poster board into four quadrants, each representing a season.

3. Have students either find magazine pictures of those activities or draw them on the poster board. Preview their magazine clippings for appropriate content.

4. Use the posters or mini-posters to create a bulletin board in the classroom or a presentation for a school display case.

5. As students look at each other's posters, they may want to make a graph that outlines likes and dislikes.

Grading the project

Suggested point distribution (total = 100 points):

List of vocabulary	30
Poster	30
Oral presentation	40

✂ ¿QUÉ TIEMPO HACE?

This simulated TV broadcast has students practice basic structures to express different weather conditions locally, nationally, or around the world.

Introduction

Have students imagine what it would be like to be a well-known weatherperson on TV. Explain that they will put together the weather segment of a news broadcast. Have them choose from the following topics:

1) A U.S. weather report on five cities from coast to coast

2) A global weather report on five major cities around the Spanish-speaking world, including three continents

Students work in pairs or small groups to present their weather report to the class.

Materials students may need

- Markers
- Posterboard
- Atlas or map
- A world almanac or other source of seasonal weather information
- Double-sided removable adhesive tape

Sequence

1. Groups should decide which weather report they would like to give and use a map that represents that forecast area. They may use an atlas, or prepare a map on an overhead transparency. If students choose a national or world setting, have them choose five cities to report about, each in a different area of the globe.

2. Make a list of the current temperatures and weather conditions in those cities. Check a national newspaper or the Internet for the latest information.

3. Have anchors greet one another. One asks the other: **¿Qué tiempo hace en Madrid?**

4. The other responds **Hace mal tiempo en Madrid. La temperatura está a 10 grados y hace mucho viento.**

5. Anchors should say goodnight to each other and sign off.

6. If your school has video equipment available, ask an audiovisual technician to videotape the presentations. Show the weather reports to the class.

Grading the project

Suggested point distribution (total = 100 points):

Map	30
Accuracy of weather reports	40
Pronunciation	15
Dramatic presentation, originality	15

CAPÍTULO 5

El ritmo de la vida
GAMES

PREGUNTAS

*This game can be used to practice and reinforce the vocabulary presented in the **Así se dice** sections of this chapter. You may also choose to include phrases from the **Así se dice** sections of preceding chapters.*

Procedure

1 Divide the students into two teams. Each team is to develop a list of the answers to the questions presented in **Así se dice**. Then play begins with one student from each team facing off.

2 The Team 1 player reads the first answer from his or her list. If the Team 2 player asks a question that would be appropriate for the answer, Team 2 receives a point. Then players switch roles. If the Team 1 player is successful, Team 1 receives a point. The lists are then passed to the second player on each team and play continues.

LA FECHA EN DIEZ PREGUNTAS

This game gives students the opportunity to practice asking questions and to use their critical thinking skills to determine the proper questions.

Procedure

Write several dates (day and month) on a piece of paper. Students take turns asking **sí-no** questions to determine the date. Students who can determine the date with ten questions or fewer are the winners.

Suggestion

Explain that the best way to win is to ask focused questions. Questions should include the word **antes** or **después.** For example, **¿Es antes de junio? ¿Es después de marzo? ¿Es antes del 15?**

Challenge

You may wish to challenge students to determine the date with only five questions.

¡DIBÚJALO!

This game provides a thorough review of nouns, verbs, and adjectives from Chapters 1–5. It also creates team spirit within the class.

Materials students may need

◆ Index cards   ◆ Colored markers

Preparation

1 Divide the class into five equal groups of students. Each group of students selects 20–25 vocabulary items from one chapter in the textbook.

2 Give each group index cards and colored markers. Groups write one vocabulary word from the assigned chapter on each card. Students look for verb infinitives, (**hablar, estudiar, jugar**) nouns, (**lápiz, mesa, casa**) or adjectives (**nuevo, malo, feo**).

3 Combine all cards from each group and shuffle.

Procedure

1 Divide the class into two teams. You will need one scorekeeper and one timekeeper.

2 Give the first team a card with the Spanish word written on it. (**jugar al fútbol**).

3 That team member goes to the board and must illustrate the word within 15 seconds.

4 The next three people in line from that person's team are allowed one guess each. If one of the three people guesses correctly, the team scores a point. If they cannot guess, the question goes to the next person on the other team. The other team is allowed only one guess.

5 If the student shown the card does not know what the Spanish word means, the team defaults its turn, and the opportunity to play the word goes to the other team.

6 **Dibújalo** can be played by the whole class, or a small group for vocabulary review. It can also serve for testing purposes or for enrichment.

ANDA A PESCAR

This is a pair activity that reviews vocabulary from various chapters. It is a way to reinforce learned vocabulary visually and orally, using a familiar game. Playing the game reinforces verbal commands as well.

Materials students may need

◆ Index cards (40 per student pair)
◆ Colored pencils or fine-tipped markers
◆ General interest magazines

Preparation

1 Students choose a partner. Each pair makes 20 cards from the Chapter 5 **Vocabulario.**

2 Students prepare two cards for each vocabulary word selected on the list. On both cards they write the verb, noun, or adjective in Spanish and illustrate the word with a drawing or magazine clipping. Students may draw their own pictures or cut out photos from magazines. Labeling the picture reinforces the vocabulary especially for visual learners.

3 You may decide to have students use this game to practice conjugating the new verbs they have learned this chapter, or have them use **¿Te gusta?** and the noun or verb vocabulary.

Procedure

1 One partner shuffles the deck of cards and deals out seven cards each. He or she puts the remaining cards in the center of the table.

2 The object of the game is for each player to match similar cards and try to be the first to get rid of all his or her cards. For example, if Player A has the card with the noun **papas fritas,** he or she would ask Player B, **¿Comes papas fritas?** If Player B also has the card **papas fritas,** he or she gives it to Player A. Player A puts this pair on the table. Then Player A gets to ask another question: **¿Escribes cartas?**

3 If Player B does not have the card **cartas,** he or she responds **No, ¡anda a pescar!** and Player A picks up a card from the stockpile.

4 Then Player B, who has the noun **jugo,** asks Player A **¿Bebes jugo?**

5 The game continues with each student accumulating as many points as possible from matching cards.

6 The first player to successfully match all cards and discard his or her final card wins.

CAPÍTULO
5

El ritmo de la vida

ANSWERS TO CHAPTER 5 ACTIVITIES

Listening activity answers appear on Scripts pages 187E–187F. Answers to all other activities appear on corresponding pupil pages.

PRIMER PASO   pp. 194–199

12 1. ¿Quién habla por teléfono? Zoraida habla por teléfono.
2. ¿Quiénes preparan la cena? La señora Vivanco y Anita preparan la cena.
3. ¿Quiénes caminan por el parque? La señora Chávez y Luis caminan por el parque.
4. ¿Quiénes compran ropa? Sarah y tú compran ropa.
5. ¿Quién practica al fútbol? Jaime practica al fútbol.
6. ¿Quién toca el piano? Alejandra toca el piano.
7. ¿Quiénes montan en bicicleta? Patty y yo montamos en bicicleta.

SEGUNDO PASO   pp. 202–211

17 1. leer / escribir / recibir
2. comer / recibir
3. leer / recibir
4. beber
5. asistir a
6. comer

20 1. ¿A ellas les gusta practicar deportes?
2. ¿A ellos les gusta escuchar música clasica?
3. ¿A ellos les gusta bailar?
4. ¿A ellos les gusta comer la comida china?
5. ¿A ella le gusta beber el jugo de frutas?
6. ¿A ustedes les gusta escuchar la música pop?

23 Answers will vary. Possible answers:
1. Ustedes corren juntos por el parque los sábados.
2. Tú y tu familia comen juntos todos los días.
3. Nosotros leemos juntos las tiras cómicas del periódico de vez en cuando.
4. La señora Pérez escribe tarjetas postales cada tres días durante las vacaciones.
5. Ellas asisten a una clase de ejercicios aeróbicos todos los martes por la tarde.
6. Elisa lee novelas a menudo.

TERCER PASO   pp. 212–219

38 1. true
2. false. Elsa swims in a pool every day.
3. true
4. false. Elsa runs in the morning when it's cooler.

VAMOS A LEER   pp. 222–223

C 1. **rápidamente**   *rapidly*
2. **divertido**   *fun*
3. **cubierta**   *covered*
4. **diversión**   *fun*
5. **lecciones**   *lessons*
6. **barcos**   *boats*

REPASO   pp. 224–225

2 Answers will vary. Possible answers:

En Asunción hace fresco y hace sol. Vamos a caminar en el parque.

En Bogotá está lloviendo a cántaros. Voy a leer una novela en casa.

En Buenos Aires hace mucho viento. Vamos a volar una cometa.

En La Paz hace mucho frío. Voy a mirar la televisión.

4 1. el veinticuatro de junio
2. el treinta de marzo
3. el doce de septiembre
4. el primero de febrero
5. el dieciocho de noviembre
6. el ocho de agosto

A VER SI PUEDO...   p. 226

3 Answers will vary. Possible answers:

Típicamente preparamos el desayuno los sábados. Los domingos, voy a la casa de mi amiga. Después leo una novela. Durante la semana, voy al colegio. Por la tarde, hago la tarea y miro la televisión.

5 1. Está lloviendo y hace frío.
2. Hace frío y hace mucho viento.
3. Está nevando. / Nieva mucho hoy.
4. Hace calor y mucho sol.
5. Está nublado.
6. Hace fresco.

El ritmo de la vida

CAPÍTULO
5

🏠 HOMEWORK SUGGESTIONS

Chapter Section	Presentation	Homework Options
Primer paso	**Así se dice,** p. 195	*Pupil's Edition*, p. 195, Activity 6 *Practice and Activity Book,* p. 52, Activity 2; p. 54, Activity 7 *CD-ROM,* Disc 2, Chapter 5, Activity 1
	Gramática, p. 196	*Pupil's Edition*, pp. 196–197, Activities 7–8, 10 *Grammar and Vocabulary,* pp. 37–38, Activities 1–3 *CD-ROM,* Disc 2, Chapter 5, Activity 2
	Nota gramatical, p. 198	*Pupil's Edition*, p. 198, Activity 11 *Grammar and Vocabulary,* p. 38, Activity 4
Segundo paso	**Así se dice,** p. 203	*Practice and Activity Book,* pp. 55–56, Activities 8–10 *Grammar and Vocabulary,* p. 39, Activity 5
	Vocabulario, p. 204	*Pupil's Edition*, p. 205, Activity 18 *Grammar and Vocabulary,* p. 39, Activity 6 *CD-ROM,* Disc 2, Chapter 5, Activity 3
	Nota gramatical, p. 206	*Pupil's Edition*, p. 206, Activity 20 *Grammar and Vocabulary,* p. 40, Activity 7
	Gramática, p. 207	*Grammar and Vocabulary,* pp. 40–41, Activities 8–10 *Practice and Activity Book,* p. 56, Activity 11 *CD-ROM,* Disc 2, Chapter 5, Activity 4
	Así se dice, p. 209	*Pupil's Edition*, p. 211, Activity 29 *Practice and Activity Book,* p. 57, Activity 12
Tercer paso	**Así se dice/Nota gramatical,** p. 213	*Pupil's Edition*, p. 213, Activity 32 *Grammar and Vocabulary,* pp. 42–43, Activities 12–14
	Vocabulario, p.214	*Pupil's Edition*, p. 214, Activity 33 *Grammar and Vocabulary,* p. 42, Activity 11 *Practice and Activity Book,* pp. 58–59, Activities 13–15 *CD-ROM,* Disc 2, Chapter 5, Activity 6
	Así se dice/ Vocabulario, p. 216	*Pupil's Edition*, pp. 217–218, Activities 37–38 *Grammar and Vocabulary,* p. 44, Activities 15–16 *Practice and Activity Book,* pp. 59–60, Activities 16–18 *CD-ROM,* Disc 2, Chapter 5, Activity 5

El ritmo de la vida

MOTIVATING ACTIVITY
Have students list what they typically do with friends and family during an average week. Ask them to share what they have to do, what they choose to do, and how often they do it.

BACKGROUND
The southern part of Florida depends on rain for fresh water. It receives a drenching 40 to 65 inches a year, largely from May to October. You may wish to ask students how this compares with the amount typically received in the area where you live. (They could get this information from a weather forecaster.)

PHOTO FLASH!
① This is a photo of Armando and Raquel, two video characters from Chapters 5 and 6.

SCIENCE LINK
Have students research the damaging effects of draining fresh water from the Everglades. (Draining fresh water allows saline sea water to flow into the Everglades and destroy the plant and animal life there.)

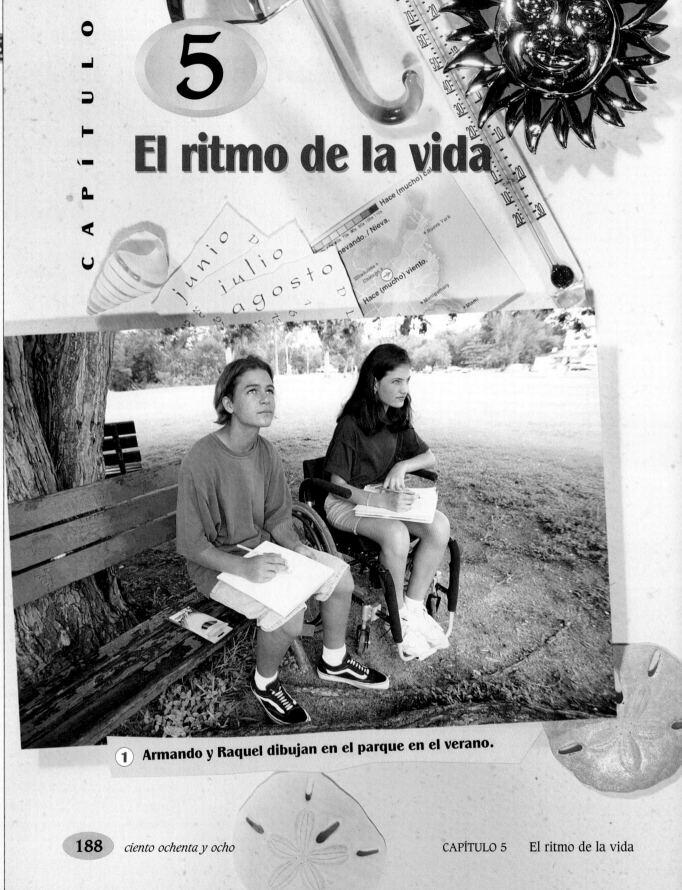

CAPÍTULO

5
El ritmo de la vida

① **Armando y Raquel dibujan en el parque en el verano.**

In this chapter you will learn to

PRIMER PASO

- discuss how often you do things

SEGUNDO PASO

- talk about what you and your friends like to do together
- talk about what you do during a typical week

TERCER PASO

- give today's date
- talk about the weather

internet

MARCAR: go.hrw.com
PALABRA CLAVE:
WV3 FLORIDA-5

② Todos los días hacemos ejercicio en el club deportivo.

③ ¡Está lloviendo a cántaros!

ciento ochenta y nueve **189**

FOCUSING ON OUTCOMES

- Have students look at the chapter outcomes and match them with the three photos. (Photo 1: talking about what you and your friends do together; Photo 2: discussing how often you do things; Photo 3: talking about the weather)

- Ask students to talk about their plans for this week and how often they plan to do certain events.

- Bring in the weather map and the forecast from a local newspaper to provide students with some first-hand information about what the weather will be in their area. Students can identify the expressions they will need to know in order to discuss the forecast in Spanish.

- Tell students that they will learn how to talk about these subjects in Spanish in this chapter.

SUGGESTION

③ You may want to teach your students **el impermeable** to discuss this photo.

LANGUAGE NOTE

A **cántaro** is a large, narrow-mouthed pitcher. Therefore the expression **está lloviendo a cántaros** is the equivalent of the English expression "it's raining cats and dogs," or "it's pouring."

VIDEO INTEGRATION

Adelante LEVEL 1A
Video Program
Videocassette 2, 24:43–28:50 OR
Videocassette 3, 47:04–51:00
(captioned version)

¡Ven conmigo! LEVEL 1
DVD Tutor, Disc 1

TEACHER NOTE
The **fotonovela** is an abridged version of the video episode.

VIDEO SYNOPSIS
In this episode, students in Miami prepare a news-broadcast program for their high school. They present a national weather forecast, interviews with students and a teacher about their free-time activities, and an interview with a new student. At the end of the episode, a problem with the camera interrupts the broadcast.

MOTIVATING ACTIVITY
Have students imagine that a reporter has stopped them on the street to interview them about their free-time activities. Have students make a list: What questions might the reporter ask? How might they answer?

DE ANTEMANO

¿Cómo es el ritmo de tu vida?

CD 5 Trs. 1–2

Look at the pictures in the **fotonovela.** Can you tell what Patricia, José Luis, and Raquel are doing? Where are they? Does something go wrong? How can you tell?

p. 51
Act. 1

Patricia   **José Luis**

Raquel

1 ¡Bienvenidos! Hoy es el seis de noviembre y ¡ésta es la nueva edición de "Noticias Colegio Seminole"! Soy Patricia Carter...

Y yo soy José Luis Jiménez. Como siempre, tenemos un programa muy interesante para ustedes esta semana.

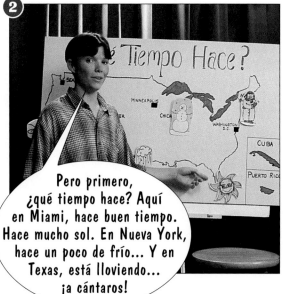

2 Pero primero, ¿qué tiempo hace? Aquí en Miami, hace buen tiempo. Hace mucho sol. En Nueva York, hace un poco de frío... Y en Texas, está lloviendo... ¡a cántaros!

3 Gracias, José Luis. Ahora, vamos al reportaje especial de Raquel. Esta semana, ella habla con la gente del colegio sobre el ritmo de sus actividades en una semana típica.

RAQUEL ¡Hola! Raquel Villanueva a sus órdenes. Todos estamos aquí, en el colegio, durante las horas de clase. ¿Pero qué hacemos cuando no estamos aquí? Ramón... ¿qué haces por la tarde?

RAMÓN Bueno... los martes y los jueves, trabajo en el restaurante de mis padres. Y cuando no trabajo, hago la tarea o paso el rato con mis amigos.

RAQUEL ¿Qué tal, Anita y Josué? Dime, Anita... ¿qué haces típicamente los domingos?

ANITA Eh... todos los domingos, descanso y leo el periódico. Y Josué y yo siempre corremos juntos por la tarde.

RAQUEL Ah, ¿sí? ¿Y corren mucho?

JOSUÉ Sí, mucho. Nos gusta correr. ¡Pero en el verano no, porque hace demasiado calor!

RAQUEL Buenos días, profesor Williams. ¿Qué hace usted por la noche cuando está en casa?

PROFESOR WILLIAMS Bueno, Raquel...primero la señora Williams y yo preparamos la cena. Después, a veces escucho música o escribo cartas.

PRESENTATION

Have students break into pairs before they read the **fotonovela** to discuss in detail the visual clues in the photos that help them predict what's going on. Then play the audio recording or read aloud the different characters' parts, having students repeat each character's lines after you as they read along in the book. Then have the students practice with each other, taking turns reading the parts of different characters in the story. Finally, play the video. Have students see if the predictions they made based on the visual cues in the photos were accurate.

LANGUAGE NOTES

• Ramón's pronunciation of **mis amigos** is an example of aspiration, pronouncing the final **-s** of a syllable as an **-h** or not pronouncing it at all. It is very common in many Spanish dialects.

• The expression **a sus órdenes** is a traditional way of saying *at your service*.

• Professor Williams speaks Spanish with an American-English accent.

DE ANTEMANO

ciento noventa y uno **191**

CRITICAL THINKING

On a current weather map from a newspaper or from The Weather Channel Homepage (http://www.weather.com/twc/homepage.twc), ask students to locate a report on Miami. Is the weather in Miami today the same as it is in the **fotonovela**? You might have students also compare the weather in the additional locations mentioned in the **fotonovela** with the current weather in those places.

A continuación

You may choose to continue with *¿Cómo es el ritmo de tu vida? (a continuación)* at this time or wait until later in the chapter. At this point, the students resolve the camera problems and clean up the spilled papers. Later they take Armando to the Vizcaya Gardens. You may wish to discuss with students attractions in their hometown that they would show to a visitor from another country.

7

RAQUEL	¡Tenemos un nuevo estudiante en el Colegio Seminole! ¿Quién es? Es Armando Tamayo, y es de Panamá. Armando, ¿qué haces en tu tiempo libre?
ARMANDO	En mi tiempo libre, yo pinto y dibujo.
RAQUEL	¿En serio? A mí también me gusta mucho pintar y dibujar. Qué casualidad, ¿no?

RAQUEL
Bueno, amigos... aquí termina mi reportaje. Quiero recibir tarjetas postales de ustedes. ¿Les gusta el programa? ¡Escríbanme! ¡Y hasta la próxima!

8

9

Noticias Colegio Sem...

¿Hay un problema con la cámara?

Gracias, Raquel, y ahora... ¿qué pasa?

10

1 ¿Comprendes?

Answer the questions below. If you're not sure about what's happening in the **fotonovela**, make an educated guess!

These activities check for global comprehension only. Students should not yet be expected to produce language modeled in **De antemano.**

1. What are the teenagers in the story doing? Filming a TV show.
2. What kind of report does José Luis give? A weather report.
3. What does Raquel do in her special report? She interviews people about free-time activities.
4. How do you think the crew will deal with the accident at the end of the broadcast? Answers will vary.

2 ¿Cuál es la verdad?

For each pair of sentences below, choose the letter of the sentence that is true.

1. **a.** Patricia y José Luis están en Nueva York.
   (b) Patricia y José Luis están en Miami.
2. **(a)** Hace un poco de frío en Nueva York.
   b. Está lloviendo en Nueva York.
3. **a.** En su tiempo libre, Armando juega al voleibol.
   (b) Armando pinta y dibuja en su tiempo libre.
4. **(a)** Josué y Anita corren por la tarde.
   b. Josué y Anita trabajan en un restaurante.

3 ¿Cómo se dice?

Use the **fotonovela** to help you match a sentence in English with its corresponding sentence in Spanish.

1. to say the weather is nice c
2. to ask a friend what he or she usually does on Sundays d
3. to tell someone you write letters a
4. to tell someone you listen to music e
5. to say you spend time with your friends b

   a. Escribo cartas.
   b. Paso el rato con mis amigos.
   c. Hace buen tiempo.
   d. ¿Qué haces típicamente los domingos?
   e. Escucho música.

RE-ENTRY
Ask volunteers to introduce the characters in the **fotonovela** using skills they have learned in Chapters 1 through 4. Have them give each character's name, age, country of origin, and after-school activities.

CHALLENGE
3 Ask students to cover the right column and answer the questions.

COOPERATIVE LEARNING
3 In groups of three to four, students write statements similar to the ones in this activity. After proofreading them and writing the correct answers, students pass the questions to another group. Every group edits another group's questions and checks their answers.

VIDEO INTEGRATION

Adelante LEVEL 1A
Video Program
Videocassette 2, 27:37–27:58 OR
Videocassette 3, 49:58–50:19
(captioned version)

¡Ven conmigo! LEVEL 1
DVD Tutor, Disc 1

Bell work
To review material from Chapter 4, ask students to write five things they do in their free time. Next to each activity have them write how often they do it. (**Juego al baloncesto con mis amigos. Always.**)

CULTURE NOTE
In small towns in many Latin American countries, communities pool their resources to build homes for one another. They also work together to improve the community by planting trees and flowers in central **plazas**. Lead a discussion about what the class could do together to benefit the school or the community.

LANGUAGE NOTE
In Mexico, kites are called **los papalotes**.

PRIMER PASO Storytelling Book pp. 17, 20

WV3 FLORIDA-5

Discussing how often you do things

RAQUEL	Buenos días, profesor Williams. ¿Qué hace usted por la noche cuando está en casa?
PROFESOR WILLIAMS	Bueno, Raquel... primero la señora Williams y yo preparamos la cena. Después, a veces escucho música o escribo cartas.

4 El profesor Williams
Write what Mr. Williams says he does when he gets home in the evenings.
preparamos la cena, escucho música, escribo cartas

Nota cultural

In Spanish-speaking countries, young people and adults enjoy doing a variety of activities in their free time. Dominoes is a popular game throughout Latin America; it's common to see the game being played on the side of the street or in a **plaza** in small towns. **Plazas** are a great place to roller skate, or for a village to hold a dance. As in the United States, many activities depend on the weather. In windy weather, children often go out to fly kites (**volar cometas**). During hot weather, they swim. Is there a place in your neighborhood where people go to have fun? What activities are popular?

ASÍ SE DICE — Discussing how often you do things

p. 52
Act. 2,
p. 54
Act. 7

To find out how often a friend does things, ask:

¿Con qué frecuencia desayunas?
How often do you eat breakfast?

¿Siempre organizas tu cuarto?
Do you always organize your room?

¿Y qué haces **durante la semana?**
And what do you do during the week?

¿Todavía tocas la guitarra?
Do you still play the guitar?

Your friend might respond:

Desayuno todos los días.
I eat breakfast every day.

Nunca organizo mi cuarto.
I never organize my room.

A veces cuido a mi hermano.
Sometimes I take care of my brother.

Muchas veces ayudo en casa.
Often I help at home.

Sí, pero **sólo cuando** no tengo tarea.
Yes, but only when I don't have homework.

5 El cine · Script and answers on p. 187E

Listen as Teresa, Maité, and Carlos talk about what they do in their free time. Match each person with how often he or she participates in the activity. · CD 5 Tr. 3

1. Teresa practica el piano
2. Maité va al centro comercial
3. Carlos va al cine

a. todos los viernes.
b. muchas veces los sábados.
c. todos los sábados y miércoles.

6 ¿Qué haces tú durante la semana?

Write four sentences. Choose phrases from each word box to say what you do, and when, how often, and where you do each activity.

Answers will vary.

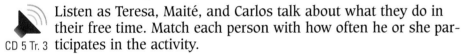

A veces	desayuno	en el centro comercial
Todos los días	estudio matemáticas	en casa
Los sábados (domingos,...)	practico la natación (el fútbol,...)	en el colegio
Muchas veces	preparo la cena	en el parque
Todos los...	voy al cine	en la piscina
Nunca	compro...	en ¿ ?

☀ MOTIVATE

Ask students how often they and their friends and family do different things such as have a cookout, or go to the beach or lake. Remind them that their answers may be fictional.

☀ TEACH

PRESENTATION
ASÍ SE DICE

Write the days of the week in Spanish on the board or on a transparency. Beneath each one list a few activities you do each day of the week. Write the new adverbs of frequency next to your weekly schedule. Describe to the class how often you do these different activities. Use only **-ar** verbs. Then have the students write sentences describing how often you do them. (**Usted siempre monta en bicicleta los sábados.**) Model the expressions by asking several questions and have students answer them. Then, have students ask and answer the questions in **Así se dice** with a partner.

SUGGESTION
5 Have students read these phrases as advance organizers.

PRESENTATION
GRAMÁTICA

Say **Nunca bailo en el escritorio.** Emphatically shake your head as you make this statement and other negative ones. Then call on students to make statements and others to negate them.

SUGGESTIONS

Tira cómica First, ask your students to scan the comic for cognates and familiar words. What do they think is happening?

7 Have students write six statements of their own using **siempre, nunca, nada,** and **nadie.** Each writes three true statements and three false statements about what they like to do. Then, in pairs, one reads his or her statements and the other guesses whether they are **cierto** or **falso.** After guessing all six, the partners switch roles.

RE-ENTRY

Write these words on the board or on a transparency: **Siempre, Muchas veces, A veces, Nunca.** Ask students to use Chapter 4 vocabulary to write as many activities as they can under each heading. Then discuss what students always, often, sometimes, and never like to do.

GRAMÁTICA   Negation

In Chapter 2 you learned to make sentences negative by putting **no** before the verb. To say *never* or *not ever,* put **nunca** before the verb.

> **Nunca** tomo el autobús.   *I never take the bus.*

pp. 52–53
Acts. 3–5

In Spanish, you'll often use **no** and **nunca** or **no** and **nada** together in the same sentence. In that case, be sure to put **no** in front of the verb, and **nunca** or **nada** after the verb.

> **No** tomo el autobús **nunca.**   *I never take the bus.*
> Los sábados **no** hago **nada.**   *On Saturdays I don't do anything.*

pp. 37–38
Acts. 1–3

Another negative word is **nadie** *(no one)*. It's always used with the **él** or **ella** form of the verb.

> **No** toca la guitarra **nadie.**
> **Nadie** toca la guitarra. } *Nobody plays the guitar.*

7 ¿Cierto o falso?

Read the following sentences and respond **cierto** if the sentence is true or **falso** if it's false. Change the false sentences to make them true.   Answers will vary.

MODELO   Nadie habla inglés. (falso)
Nosotros hablamos inglés todos los días.

1. Nadie estudia español.
2. Nunca escuchamos música en las fiestas.
3. Siempre preparamos la cena en la clase de matemáticas.
4. Los profesores no bailan nunca.
5. Siempre hago mi tarea.
6. Nadie en esta clase tiene ropa amarilla.

> Nunca practico la guitarra.

> ¡No es cierto! Practicas todas las tardes, ¿verdad?

8 Mi semana

What do you do during a typical week? Write six sentences using activities from the word box. Be sure to explain how often you do each activity. Answers will vary.

MODELO —Practico el basquetbol todos los días.

tocar un instrumento

ir al colegio

escuchar música rock

desayunar

practicar un deporte

pintar   ir al centro comercial

cuidar a tu hermano/a

9 Una encuesta

 Interview three classmates to find out how often they do the activities listed below. Your classmates will answer by using phrases from both columns. Answers will vary.

MODELO —¿Con qué frecuencia miras la televisión?
—Miro la televisión sólo cuando tengo tiempo.

Actividad	Frecuencia
practicar la natación	a veces
practicar el fútbol	sólo cuando tengo tiempo
ir al centro comercial	los lunes, los martes,...
patinar	los fines de semana
escuchar música	todos los días
hablar por teléfono	nunca

10 ¿Quién?

Look at the photographs. Then, for each activity below, write a sentence about who is doing it, or say if no one is doing the activity. Answers in side column

1. desayunar
2. estudiar
3. practicar el piano
4. hablar
5. escuchar
6. hablar por teléfono
7. practicar el béisbol
8. mirar la televisión
9. montar en bicicleta

Miguel

Graciela y Ana

el señor Guzmán y Adolfo

ADDITIONAL PRACTICE

8 Ask students to imagine a list left by a parent or guardian asking the student to do three things immediately. Ask students to create such a note, using the activities from the word box. They can begin the list with **Necesitas...**

MATH LINK

9 After groups have completed their surveys, ask them to compile the results. Then ask each group to graph the results. Display the graphs labeled in Spanish for the entire class.

VISUAL LEARNERS

9 If you have access to a video camera, have students videotape one another interviewing classmates, or do the videotaping yourself. A good time to do this would be during a class **fiesta** or during group work.

Answers to Activity 10

1. Nadie desayuna./No desayuna nadie.
2. Graciela y Ana estudian.
3. Nadie practica el piano./No practica el piano nadie.
4. El señor Guzmán habla con Adolfo.
5. Adolfo escucha al señor Guzmán.
6. Nadie habla por teléfono./No habla por teléfono nadie.
7. Miguel practica el béisbol.
8. Nadie mira la televisión./No mira la televisión nadie.
9. Nadie monta en bicicleta. /No monta en bicicleta nadie.

PRESENTATION

NOTA GRAMATICAL

Write five questions on the board. (**¿Quiénes estudian el arte? ¿Quién es cómico/a? ¿Quiénes son altos? ¿Quién es bajo/a? ¿Quiénes son divertidos?**) Elicit oral answers from several students. Next have them write answers to the questions on a sheet of paper. They then compare their answers to a classmate's. Point out that students should use **¿Quién?** if they expect the answer to be one person and **¿Quiénes?** if they expect it to be more than one.

SLOWER PACE

11 Point out the clues in the text that show how many people the speaker is talking about. In item 1, students may choose **¿Quién?** based on **chico.** In item 2, students may choose **¿Quiénes?** based on **las chicas.**

COOPERATIVE LEARNING

Have students draw or cut out pictures of people doing different activities and name the people in each picture. They should present their work to their small group and ask them **¿Quién/es?** and an activity. (**¿Quién practica la guitarra?**) Their classmates respond with the appropriate phrase.

¿Quiénes miran la televisión?
Roberto y Laura.

PA
p. 54
Act. 6

GV
p. 38
Act 4

NOTA GRAMATICAL

You've already learned the question word **¿quién?** *(who?).* **¿Quién?** is used to ask about one person. When asking about more than one person, use **¿quiénes?** Compare the two sentences below.

> **¿Quién** es el chico rubio?
> *Who is the blond boy?*

> **¿Quiénes** son las chicas altas?
> *Who are the tall girls?*

11 **¿Quiénes son?**

Complete Sandra and Melisa's conversation during lunch in the cafeteria. Fill in the blanks with **quién** or **quiénes.**

SANDRA ¿___1___ es el chico con la ropa negra? Quién

MELISA Se llama Daniel. Es un estudiante nuevo.

SANDRA ¿Y ___2___ son las chicas que están cerca de la puerta? quiénes

MELISA Se llaman Sonia y Eva. Están en mi clase de ciencias. Oye, ¿ ___3___ van al cine hoy? quiénes

SANDRA María y yo. ¿Quieres ir?

MELISA Sí, claro. ¿Qué película van a ver?

SANDRA La nueva película de aventuras.

MELISA ¿ ___4___ es la estrella *(star)*? Quién

SANDRA Lupita Cárdenas. ¡Es excelente!

SUGERENCIA

At first, it's often hard to write in a foreign language. Remember that learning to write is like learning other skills in Spanish. Take it slowly, and go in small steps. Begin by writing short messages. For example, you can write brief reminders to yourself about what you need to do, or try writing out your weekly schedule in Spanish. Start now by making a list of three or four activities you usually do during a particular day—for example, on Mondays.

hoy
estudiar para el examen de ciencias
hablar por teléfono con Susana
practicar la guitarra
escuchar el disco compacto de José Miquel
montar en bicicleta con Raúl
sacar la basura

12 ¿Quién hace eso?

With a partner, take turns asking and answering questions about the people and activities shown in the drawings. Answers on p. 187K

MODELO ¿Quiénes nadan en la piscina?
Julia y Silvia nadan en la piscina.

1. hablar / teléfono
2. preparar / la cena
3. caminar / por el parque
4. comprar / ropa

5. practicar / el fútbol
6. tocar / el piano
7. montar / bicicleta

Alejandra

Jaime

la señora Vivanco y Anita

Zoraida

tú y Sarah

Patty y yo

la señora Chávez
y Luis

13 ¿Tienes buena memoria?

Work in groups of four. On three slips of paper write the categories **siempre, a veces,** and **nunca.** Under each category write two activities. Next, shuffle the papers. Each person draws three slips and asks who does one of the activities that are written. Everyone tries to guess who wrote the activities on each slip.

MODELO ¿Quién toca el piano siempre?

☀ CLOSE

On a small piece of paper, write activities and expressions of frequency. Make enough to give one to each student. List some activities only once and others on several pieces of paper with different adverbs of frequency. If you use **mirar la televisión,** ask **¿Quién no mira la televisión nunca?** Students with this activity and **nunca** raise their hands. Then have a student ask another question. (**¿Quién siempre escucha música?**)

☀ ASSESS

▸ Testing Program, pp. 73–74
Quiz 5-1
Audio CD 5, Tr. 17

▸ Grammar and Vocabulary Quizzes
Quiz 5-1 or
Alternative Quiz 5-1A

▸ Alternative Assessment Guide, p. 23

PERFORMANCE ASSESSMENT

Ask students to write a letter in Spanish to a friend who is spending the year in Mexico. Ask them to include information about what three of their friends are doing this year including the day of the week or how often the friend does the activity. The letter might begin with **Querido/a** _____ and end with **Un saludo de** _____.

VIDEO INTEGRATION

Adelante LEVEL 1A
Video Program
Videocassette 2, 33:24–35:40

¡Ven conmigo! LEVEL 1
DVD Tutor, Disc 1

TEACHER NOTES

- See *Video Guide* for activities related to the **Panorama cultural.**
- Remind students that cultural information may be included in the Quizzes and Chapter Test.
- The language of the people interviewed represents informal, unrehearsed speech. Occasionally, text has been edited for clarity.

MOTIVATING ACTIVITY

Ask students what they imagine the daily routines of teenagers in Spain and Latin America to be like. Do they think they are the same or different from their own? Why?

LANGUAGE NOTE

Point out that it's possible to use infinitives to list activities as Juan Fernando does.

Panorama cultural

CD 5
Trs. 4–7

¿Cómo es una semana típica?

In this chapter, we asked some students what they usually do during the week and on weekends.

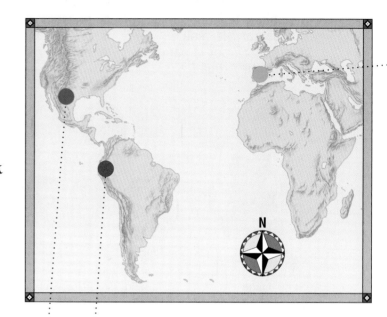

Verónica trabaja todos los fines de semana en casa. ¿Qué haces tú para ayudar en casa?

● **Verónica**
*San Antonio,
Texas*
CD 5 Tr. 5

[Yo] hago mi tarea, estudio, como con mi familia, duermo... Cada sábado, tengo que organizar mi cuarto, entonces limpio la cocina.

Juan Fernando hace algunas actividades durante la semana y otras durante el fin de semana. ¿Qué haces tú los fines de semana?

● **Juan Fernando**
Quito, Ecuador
CD 5 Tr. 6

De lunes a viernes... ir al colegio, hacer las tareas y descansar un poco. Los sábados y domingos practico deportes.

Después de sus clases en el colegio, Bárbara toma una clase más. ¿Qué haces tú por la tarde?

● **Bárbara**

Sevilla, España
CD 5 Tr. 7

Pues, regreso a casa, almuerzo, después descanso un tiempo, estudio un par de horas, y seguidamente voy a danza clásica.

1 ¿Con quién come Verónica? Come con su familia.

2 ¿Cómo ayuda Verónica en casa los sábados? Limpia su cuarto y limpia la cocina.

3 ¿Qué hace Juan Fernando los fines de semana? Practica los deportes.

4 ¿Qué hace Juan Fernando después del colegio? Descansa y hace las tareas.

5 ¿Adónde va Bárbara a comer durante la semana? Va a comer en casa.

6 ¿Qué hace Bárbara después del almuerzo? Estudia y va a la clase de danza.

Para pensar y hablar... Answers will vary.
A. Look at all three interviews again. See if you can find three things they **all** do that you also do during the week or on the weekend. What are they?
B. Two of the interviewees mention relaxing during the week. Is your weekly schedule busy? Do you have time to relax? Why or why not?

Cuaderno para hispanohablantes, p. 24

PRESENTATION
Have students read the six introductory questions on the page to focus their viewing. After they watch the video, assign quotes for the students to read in unison using the video as a model. Then play the video again and have students answer the questions in **Para pensar y hablar...**

NATIVE SPEAKERS
Have native speakers listen for the different pronunciations of the speakers. Are some easier to understand than others?

CRITICAL THINKING
Have students use the context of Bárbara's response to deduce the meaning of **un par de horas** and **seguidamente.** (a couple of hours; immediately)

VIDEO INTEGRATION

Adelante LEVEL 1A
Video Program
Videocassette 2, 27:12–27:36 OR
Videocassette 3, 49:33–49:57
(captioned version)

¡Ven conmigo! LEVEL 1
DVD Tutor, Disc 1

Bell work
Before class, write several phrases from Chapter 4 on the board or on a transparency. Put blanks in for some of the letters. Have students complete them.
(m_ _ta_ _n _i_ _cl_t_
= montar en bicicleta)

MOTIVATING ACTIVITY
Write the following questions on the board: **¿Quiénes hacen ejercicio? ¿Quiénes van a la biblioteca? ¿Quiénes van al centro comercial los sábados?** Students need to copy them down then write their answers.

CHALLENGE
Write some well-known Spanish sayings without the English equivalents on the board before class. **Lo bueno, si breve, dos veces bueno.** *Keep it short and sweet.* **Querer es poder.** *Where there's a will, there's a way.* **Más ven cuatro ojos que dos.** *Two heads are better than one.* Ask if students can figure out what some of the words mean and if they can think of the English equivalents.

SEGUNDO PASO

 Storytelling Book pp. 18, 20

go.
hrw
.com
WV3 FLORIDA-5

Talking about what you and your friends like to do together; talking about what you do during a typical week

RAQUEL   ¿Qué tal, Anita y Josué? Dime, Anita... ¿qué haces típicamente los domingos?

ANITA   Eh... todos los domingos, descanso y leo el periódico. Y Josué y yo siempre corremos juntos por la tarde.

RAQUEL   Ah, ¿sí? ¿Y corren mucho?

JOSUÉ   Sí, mucho. Nos gusta correr. ¡Pero en el verano no, porque hace demasiado calor!

14   ¿Qué hacen?
Complete each sentence with one of the words below, according to what Anita, Raquel, and Josué say. Two words will not be used.

1. Los domingos Anita ————. descansa
2. Anita y Josué siempre ———— por la tarde. corren
3. Anita dice *(says):* "Josué y yo siempre corremos ———— por la tarde". juntos
4. ¿Qué haces ———— los domingos? típicamente

típicamente   juntos   verano
corren   descansa   calor

ASÍ SE DICE

Talking about what you and your friends like to do together

pp. 55–56
Acts. 8–10

p. 39
Act. 5

5-2

So far, you've been using **gustar** with the pronouns **me, te,** and **le** to talk about what just one person likes and dislikes.

To find out what a group of your friends likes to do, ask:

Your friends might answer:

¿Qué **les gusta** hacer, chicos?
What do you guys like to do?

Nos gusta hacer ejercicio o correr por la playa.
We like to exercise or run on the beach.

¿Les gusta acampar y pescar?
Do you like to camp and fish?

Sí, **especialmente** durante **las vacaciones.**
Yes, especially on vacation.

Y a los señores Bello, ¿**les gusta esquiar?**
And Mr. and Mrs. Bello, do they like to ski?

No sé, pero les gusta **bucear juntos.**
I don't know, but they like to scuba dive together.

15 Mejores amigos   Script and answers on p. 187E

Gloria is interviewing Carlos and Eddie on the radio about sports. Listen to their interview. Then match the people that like each sport with the photo of that sport.

CD 5 Tr. 8

1. Carlos   **2.** Eddie   **3.** Carlos y Eddie   **4.** Nadie

a   b   c   d

※ MOTIVATE

Tell students to imagine they have just met a group of teenagers from Chile who speak no English. Have students jot down in English what types of questions they might want to ask the visitors. What would they want to be able to say to them in Spanish?

※ TEACH

PRESENTATION
ASÍ SE DICE
Ask individual volunteers **¿Qué te gusta hacer?** Then begin asking groups of students or the entire class **¿Qué les gusta hacer?** Elicit responses from them by acting out swimming, dancing, etc. Point to everyone and yourself and say **Nos gusta (nadar, bailar, etc.).**

SUGGESTION
Have students do a find-your-twin activity. Pass out two sets of cards with the verbs from **Así se dice.** Students must go around the room asking and responding to the question **¿Qué te gusta hacer?** until they find the student with the identical verb. Then ask each pair **¿Qué les gusta hacer?**

204

PRESENTATION

VOCABULARIO

Model the new vocabulary by bringing in props, using Transparency 5-2 or 5-A, or by acting them out. Point at yourself while you read the comics and say **Me gusta leer las tiras cómicas en el periódico.** Then point to several people as you act out reading the comics and say **Les gusta leer las tiras cómicas.** Then point to everyone including yourself and say **Nos gusta leer las tiras cómicas.**

ADDITIONAL PRACTICE

Vocabulario Ask students to work with a partner. Ask them to report to the class the activities that they both like to do and the activities that neither likes to do. (**Nos gusta asistir a una clase de ejercicios aeróbicos.**) If one student likes to do the activity and the other does not, ask them to report that as well. (**A mí me gusta comer papas fritas pero a Jackie no le gusta.**)

Answers to Activity 16

1. nos
2. pescar
3. nunca
4. juntos
5. siempre

16 Elena y su abuelo

Elena is telling Manuel about her vacation with her grandparents. Look at this drawing and fill in the blanks to complete the conversation. Use the words in the word box.

ELENA   Cuando estoy con mis abuelos, ___1___ gusta acampar.

MANUEL   ¿Dónde acampas?

ELENA   Cerca del río *(river)*. A mi abuelo y a mí nos gusta ___2___. Pero mi abuela ___3___ pesca.

MANUEL   Pues, ¿tú y tu abuelo pescan ___4___?

ELENA   Sí, mis vacaciones con ellos ___5___ son buenas.

Answers in side column

nos   juntos   pescar

siempre   nunca

p. 39
Act. 6

5-A

VOCABULARIO

asistir a una clase de ejercicios aeróbicos

beber agua o jugo

comer un sándwich o una hamburguesa con papas fritas

leer las tiras cómicas en el periódico

escribir tarjetas postales

recibir cartas

17 Pienso en...

Write a verb that corresponds to each item. Some phrases may have more than one possible answer. Be prepared to explain your choices. Answers on p. 187K

MODELO la tarea de inglés—escribir

1. una carta a...
2. una pizza
3. una revista
4. un jugo de frutas
5. un concierto de música rock
6. una ensalada

18 ¿Qué les gusta hacer?

Tell what you and your friends like to do at each of these times and places. For each answer, choose at least one item from the **Vocabulario** on page 204. Answers will vary.

MODELO después de correr
Después de correr, nos gusta descansar y beber jugo.

1. en el tiempo libre
2. el sábado por la tarde
3. después de la clase de ejercicios aeróbicos
4. después de escribir cartas
5. en el gimnasio después de las clases

19 Preferencias

Work in pairs. Using the cues, ask a series of questions to find out which activities your partner likes to do and how often (**con qué frecuencia**). Switch roles after three questions. Be prepared to tell the class what you learned. For activities you both like to do, use **nos gusta**. Answers will vary.

MODELO correr: playa / parque
—¿Te gusta correr por la playa o por el parque?
—Bueno, me gusta correr por el parque pero no me gusta correr por la playa.
—¿Y con qué frecuencia? ¿Todos los días?
—No, sólo a veces.

1. escribir: cartas / tarjetas postales
2. recibir: notas de amigos / cartas de tu abuela
3. comer: ensalada / un sándwich
4. leer: revistas / periódico
5. asistir: a clases / a un concierto de...
6. beber: jugo / agua

¿Te gusta correr por la playa?

ADDITIONAL PRACTICE

Have volunteers call out infinitives from **Vocabulario** on page 204. The class responds with the corresponding noun. For example, the volunteer says **leer**, and the class says **el periódico**.

ADDITIONAL PRACTICE

18 Have students work in pairs to find three things that they both like to do. Then have the pairs interview each other by asking each other what they like to do. Have the pairs practice these plural forms for about three minutes.

SUGGESTIONS

19 Divide the class into teams. Use a big clock or draw one on the board. Ask a student what he or she likes to do at the indicated time. The student pantomimes the action, as students from the same team guess what activity is being acted out. The team earns a point if they guess correctly. For example: **Le gusta hablar por teléfono a las nueve.**

19 Encourage students to add personalized information to their answers. For example, **Me gusta leer revistas de deportes.**

CHALLENGE

Ask students to create a **tira cómica** that incorporates vocabulary from this chapter.

GV
p. 40
Act. 7

NOTA GRAMATICAL

Look at the examples in the **Así se dice** box on page 203. Notice that the same pronoun, **les,** can be used to mean both *to them* and *to you* (plural). The phrases **a ustedes** and **a ellos** or **a ellas** are sometimes added for clarification or emphasis.

Look at the literal translations of these questions.

> **¿A ustedes les gusta nadar?**
> *Is swimming pleasing to you?*
>
> **¿A ellos les gusta preparar la cena juntos?**
> *Is preparing dinner together pleasing to them?*

What would the nonliteral English translations be?[1]

¿A ustedes les gusta el videojuego nuevo?

A los amigos de Maritza les gusta pasar el rato juntos.

20 Necesitas preguntarle a...

You're in charge of planning a party at your local recreation center. Your neighbor señora Sánchez knows everybody better than you. Write how you would ask her if the following people would like some of the refreshments and activities you had in mind. Answers on page 187K

MODELO   A Cristina y a Rodrigo — videojuegos
                ¿A ellos les gusta practicar los videojuegos?

1. A Norma y a Susana — deportes
2. A los señores Silva *(Mr. and Mrs. Silva)* — música clásica
3. A Beto y a Carlos — bailar en las fiestas
4. A Adriana y a Paco — la comida china
5. A la señora Bello — el jugo de frutas
6. A ustedes — la música pop

---

[1] *Do you like to swim? Do they like to fix dinner together?*

GRAMÁTICA -er and -ir verbs

p. 56
Act. 11

pp. 40–41
Acts.
8–10

1. In Chapter 4 you learned how to conjugate -ar verbs, such as **hablar**. Now look at the conjugation of **comer** to see how -**er** verbs work.

(yo)	com**o**	(nosotros) (nosotras)	com**emos**
(tú)	com**es**	(vosotros) (vosotras)	com**éis**
(usted) (él) (ella)	com**e**	(ustedes) (ellos) (ellas)	com**en**

2. Escribir is a regular -**ir** verb.

escrib**o**	escrib**imos**
escrib**es**	escrib**ís**
escrib**e**	escrib**en**

3. You already know the verb **ver**. It is regular except in the (**yo**) form.

v**eo**	v**emos**
v**es**	v**eis**
v**e**	v**en**

21 De vacaciones en Miami

Match the following people with what they do when they go to Miami.

1. Carolina d
2. Yo a
3. Esteban y yo b
4. Mamá y papá c

a. como mucha comida cubana *(Cuban)*.
b. corremos por la playa.
c. escriben tarjetas postales a mis abuelos.
d. lee libros románticos.

22 ¿Qué hacen?

Tell your partner what the following people do during their free time. Use the correct form of the verbs in the word box.   Answers will vary.

1. Tu mejor amigo/a y tú
2. Tus padres
3. Una estrella de cine *(choose a movie star's name)*
4. Tu profesor/a
5. Tú

comer   leer

asistir a   correr

recibir   escribir

PRESENTATION
GRAMÁTICA

To practice these verb forms begin by asking a student **¿Qué comes?** The student answers **Como un sándwich.** Then ask another student **¿Qué come él?** and that student responds **Come un sándwich.** To practice plural forms, ask two students **Juan y Gloria, ¿qué comen ustedes?** Juan and Gloria answer together **Comemos un sándwich.** Ask **¿Qué comen ellos?** Students answer **Comen un sándwich.** Repeat the pattern with **escribir,** then have students ask and answer each other to use all of the forms.

CRITICAL THINKING
Ask students which two endings are not identical for both types of verbs.

VISUAL/KINESTHETIC LEARNERS
22 Conjugate six verbs for each pronoun and write the verbs and pronouns on notecards. Distribute the notecards to the students and then read a sentence in English. Students with the cards **tú** and **lees** move to the front of the room as the class checks their answer. Practice this several times with all the cards.

208

NATIVE SPEAKERS

Have students write the present tense of the verb **ver** in their spelling notebook. You may teach them this rhyme: **V de vaca, B de burro, viajar con biajaca y no escribas con apuro.** (**biajaca** is a Cuban freshwater fish)

CULTURE NOTE

The tendency to relocate or move is not as common in Latin America as it is in the United States. Therefore families may stay in the same city for several generations. Teens are often friends with the children of their parents' friends, which often provides a family-like relationship.

CHALLENGE

To model the concept of first, second, and third person, count off students in groups of three. Have them work through this dialogue according to the following model:

JUAN   María, ¿qué come Pablo?
MARÍA   No sé. Pablo, ¿qué comes?
PABLO   Como una naranja.
MARÍA   Juan, Pablo come una naranja.

---

23 ¡Todos juntos!

 For each photo, write a sentence describing what the people are doing and how often they do this activity. Use the phrases in the **Vocabulario extra** box below.   Answers on p. 187K

1. ustedes

2. tú y tu familia

3. nosotros

4. la señora Pérez

5. ellas

6. Elisa

VOCABULARIO EXTRA

de vez en cuando   *once in a while*

todo el tiempo   *all the time*

a menudo   *often*

pocas veces   *not very often*

cada (dos, tres…) dias   *every (two, three . . .) days*

tres veces por semana   *three times a week*

Nota cultural

Spending time with a group of friends is an important part of life for young teens in the Spanish-speaking world. It's more common to meet friends in public than at one's house. People often get together in parks and cafés. The streets of many Spanish-speaking towns are usually lively, and often crowded, both day and night. Where do you spend time with your friends?

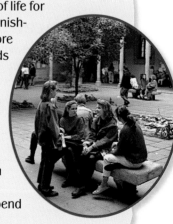

ASÍ SE DICE Talking about what you do during a typical week

p. 57
Act. 12

5-1

To find out what your friends typically do during the week, ask:

¿Qué haces **típicamente** durante el día?

¿Qué hace Josué **por la mañana**?
What does Josué do in the morning?

¿Hacen ustedes ejercicio juntos?

¿Y qué hacen Raquel y Anita **por la noche?**
And what do Raquel and Anita do at night?

Some responses might be:

Asisto a clases, trabajo y paso el rato con amigos.

Corre **dos millas** por la playa.
He runs two miles on the beach.

Sí, pero sólo **por la tarde.**
Yes, but only in the afternoon.

A veces van a un restaurante.

24 Un día típico   Script and answers on p. 187E

Listen as Miguel's mother describes a typical day in his life. Look at each drawing and answer **cierto** if it shows what she says. If the drawing doesn't represent what she says, answer **falso**.

CD 5 Tr. 9

(a)

(b)

(c)

25 Por la mañana...

Raquel is a newscaster for her school's radio show. While preparing for a broadcast about what she does on a typical day, Raquel got her script notes all mixed up. Help put what she says in the correct order. Write the letters in order on your paper. d, b, c, a

a. A veces comemos en un restaurante por la noche.
b. Típicamente, asisto a mis clases por la mañana.
c. Leo cartas de mis amigas por la tarde.
d. Antes de ir al colegio, bebo mucho jugo con mi desayuno.

PRESENTATION
ASÍ SE DICE

Tell the class a story about yourself, highlighting the vocabulary in **Así se dice** and using Transparency 5-1. You may want to write the story on the board ahead of time for visual learners. Use props such as a Spanish book, a map, and tennis shoes to give students a visual link to the topics. **Típicamente, trabajo aquí en el colegio desde las siete hasta las cuatro. Por la mañana enseño español, y por la tarde enseño...** Continue your story with expressions such as **por la tarde, por la noche,** and **típicamente**. Then ask the students to respond to comprehension questions:
—**Clase, ¿qué hago típicamente por la mañana?**
—**Usted enseña español.**
—**¿Y qué hago por la tarde?**
Extend the pattern to several students, asking questions based on **Así se dice**.

PRELISTENING

24 To focus students' listening, ask them to describe what Miguel is doing in each drawing before playing the audio recording.

26 ¿Quién lo hace?

Work in small groups. Try to identify at least one person in your partners' circle of friends who does each of the activities listed. Then find out how often each person does the activity. Take notes, and try to find activities that your friends have in common. If nobody does the activity, use **nadie** in your answer.

MODELO   —Juana, ¿quién lee revistas?   Answers will vary.
—Nadie, pero Juan lee el periódico todos los días porque le gustan los deportes.

leer: revistas, las tiras cómicas, el periódico, novelas

escribir: poemas, cartas, tarjetas postales

comer: ensaladas, fruta, hamburguesas

correr: en el parque, después de clases, cinco millas

VOCABULARIO EXTRA

los poemas   *poems*
los cuentos de aventuras
   adventure stories
la ciencia ficción   *science fiction*
el misterio   *mystery*

27 La tarjeta

Pretend that you're writing a postcard to a close friend who is on vacation. Write at least three sentences about activities that you're doing.

28 ¿Cómo pasas tú los días?

Interview a partner to find out how he or she spends a typical weekday. Ask about morning, afternoon, and evening activities. Switch roles and answer your partner's questions about a typical weekend morning, afternoon, or evening. Be prepared to tell the class two of your partner's activities.

MODELO —¿Qué haces los lunes por la mañana?
—Los lunes asisto al colegio y hablo con mis amigos.
—Mirla asiste al colegio los lunes y habla con sus amigos.

correr por el parque   estudiar   mirar la televisión

asistir al colegio / a una clase de ejercicios aeróbicos   escribir tarjetas

comer en un restaurante   leer libros / las tiras cómicas

Hablo con mis amigos todos los sábados.

29 Los sábados

With whom do you usually spend Saturdays? Write a paragraph about things you typically do on Saturday. Be sure to tell what time of day it is when you do each activity, and who does each activity with you. Use the expressions in the word box to help you write.

siempre	luego
especialmente	después
típicamente	vamos a
primero	nos gusta
nunca	
por fin	
a veces	

SEGUNDO PASO

doscientos once **211**

SUGGESTION

28 To practice negation, vary Activity 28 so that students explain what they don't do on weekdays and weekends. (**En el colegio no miro la tele-visión, no escucho música... Los fines de semana nunca tengo clases...**)

☀ CLOSE

Ask students to form groups. Give each group a list of several activities. Have students divide the activities into three categories—**por la mañana, por la tarde,** and **por la noche**—according to the time of day that they do each. Ask a spokesperson for each group to report when the activities are done.

☀ ASSESS

▶ Testing Program, pp. 75–76
Quiz 5-2
Audio CD 5, Tr. 18

▶ Grammar and Vocabulary Quizzes
Quiz 5-2A or
Alternative Quiz 5-2A

▶ Alternative Assessment Guide, p. 23

PERFORMANCE ASSESSMENT

Ask each student to make a daily planner for the coming weekend. Ask them to list the day of the week and use **por la mañana, por la tarde,** or **por la noche** with any activity they plan for that day.

VIDEO INTEGRATION

Adelante LEVEL 1A
Video Program
Videocassette 2, 25:40–26:29 OR
Videocassette 3, 48:01–48:50
(captioned version)

¡Ven conmigo! LEVEL 1
DVD Tutor, Disc 1

Bell work
On the board or a transparency, write several simple addition and subtraction problems using numbers in written form from **uno** to **treinta y uno**. Have students solve the problems and write the answers in Spanish.

VISUAL LEARNERS
30 Have students cover José Luis's speech bubble and answer the questions by looking at the weather map.

☀ MOTIVATE

Ask students to list five dates that are important to them and to explain why.

TERCER PASO

 Storytelling Book pp. 19, 20

WV3 FLORIDA-5

Giving today's date; talking about the weather

> Pero primero, ¿qué tiempo hace? Aquí en Miami, hace buen tiempo. Hace mucho sol. En Nueva York, hace un poco de frío... Y en Texas, está lloviendo... ¡a cántaros!

30 ¿Qué tiempo hace?

Fill in the blanks to complete what José Luis says about the weather.

1. En Texas, está ===== a cántaros.
2. En Miami, hace mucho =====.
3. En Nueva York, hace un poco de =====.

1. lloviendo
2. sol
3. frío

Nota cultural

In many parts of the tropics, weather reports are uncommon. There is little variety in weather from day to day. Because there is little change in temperature over the course of the year, people don't rely on a forecast to figure out what to wear. However, during hurricane season in the Caribbean, people pay close attention to warnings. Do you listen to weather forecasts regularly? Do you adjust what you plan to wear or do based on the forecast?

ASÍ SE DICE — Giving today's date

To find out today's date, ask:

> ¿Cuál es la fecha?
> ¿Qué fecha es hoy?

To give today's date, say:

> **Hoy es el primero de diciembre.**
> *Today is the first of December.*

> **Es el quince de enero.**
> *It's the fifteenth of January.*

To tell on what date something happens, say:

> **El cuatro de este mes hay** un examen.
> *On the fourth of this month there's a test.*

p. 58
Act. 14

NOTA GRAMATICAL

The formula for giving today's date is **el** + *number* + **de** + *month:* **el quince de junio.** The first day of the month is called **el primero.** Note that in Spanish no preposition is needed in expressions like *on the fifth.*

> **La fiesta es el cinco.**
> *The party is on the fifth.*

GV

pp. 42–43
Acts. 12–14

31 ¿Qué fecha es hoy?   Script and answers on p. 187F

Listen and match the date you hear with the correct drawing.

CD 5 Tr. 10

 a

 b

 c

 d

 e

 f

32 Las fechas

Complete each sentence with the correct date.   Answers will vary.

1. La Navidad *(Christmas)* es...
2. Mi cumpleaños es...
3. El Día de los Enamorados *(Valentine's Day)* es...
4. El cumpleaños de mi mamá es...
5. El primer día del año *(year)* es...
6. El Día de la Independencia *(Independence Day)* es...
7. El cumpleaños de mi mejor *(best)* amigo/a es...

✵ TEACH

PRESENTATION

ASÍ SE DICE
Write the date on the board and say **Hoy es el... de...** Then ask the class to answer in unison, **¿Cuál es la fecha?** and **¿Qué fecha es hoy?** Ask volunteers to share dates that are important to them. Write the dates and why they are important on the board.

NOTA GRAMATICAL
Call out dates of holidays in Spanish and have students say what holiday it is. For example, **El diecisiete de marzo.** (St. Patrick's Day) Next, call out holidays and have students give the dates.

RE-ENTRY
Have students write the days of the week leaving two lines between each day. Then have them write what their friends or family members like to do on those days.

SLOWER PACE
31 Before playing the audio recording, have students look at the pictures and come up with possible statements.

PA
pp. 58–59
Acts. 13, 15

GV
p. 42
Act. 11

5-B

PRESENTATION

VOCABULARIO

Use Transparency 5-B or pictures from magazines to represent the four seasons as you ask what season it is. Have students read the **Nota cultural** on page 215. Then write four sentences on the board or a transparency. (**Los meses de verano son...**, and so on for each season) Ask students to complete each statement for the Northern then for the Southern Hemisphere.

ADDITIONAL PRACTICE

Have students write their birthdate in Spanish on one side of a card and their name on the other. Collect the cards and have a volunteer shuffle and pass them out. Call on students to ask the first question using the date on their paper: **¿Quién cumple años el... de...?** The student recognizing his or her birthday answers **Yo cumple años el... de...** If no one answers, the student asks individual students until he or she finds the right person.

VOCABULARIO

la primavera
• marzo
• abril
• mayo

el verano
• junio
• julio
• agosto

el otoño
• septiembre
• octubre
• noviembre

el invierno
• diciembre
• enero
• febrero

◆ El otoño es una estación.
◆ Hay cuatro estaciones en un año.

◆ Octubre es un mes.
◆ Hay doce meses en un año.

33 Actividades

What do you usually do during various seasons of the year? Write a sentence for each season by combining words and phrases from each column. Answers will vary.

MODELO En el verano voy a la playa.

	hacer ejercicio	en el colegio
En el invierno	comer	en el gimnasio
En la primavera	nadar	en el parque
En el verano	montar en bicicleta	en la cafetería
En el otoño	bucear	en la playa
	estudiar	en la biblioteca
	beber agua	en el centro comercial
	leer	

34 ¿Cuál es la fecha?

Make a list of five dates, including at least one from each season. Then read them to your partner one at a time. Your partner will tell you what season each is in, and at least one activity he or she associates with that time of year.

MODELO —Es el treinta de abril.
—Es la primavera y juego al béisbol.

Es el 3 de enero. La familia Sánchez juega en la playa en Puerto Rico.

Es el 27 de julio. Mi amigo Daniel esquía en las montañas de Chile.

Nota cultural

The seasons in the southern part of South America are opposite to the seasons north of the equator. In the south, summer begins in December and winter begins in June. The tropical region of South America, which is on or near the equator, has only two seasons: rainy and dry. In the equatorial lowlands the temperature stays warm all year round. However, in the mountains near the equator (such as the Andes), it is generally cool and often gets quite cold. The temperature is determined by altitude rather than by latitude. Look at the dates on the photos. What is the weather like on those dates where you live?

35 Las estaciones

Pretend that you live in the following places. Write what season it is. You may want to look at the maps on pages xviii–xx.

MODELO   Es el 12 de noviembre. Estoy en Sacramento, California. **Es el otoño.**

1. Es el 7 de julio. Estoy en Buenos Aires, Argentina. Es el invierno.
2. Es el 8 de agosto. Estoy en Chicago, Illinois. Es el verano.
3. Es el 23 de diciembre. Estoy en Asunción, Paraguay. Es el verano.
4. Es el 2 de mayo. Estoy in Portland, Oregón. Es la primavera.
5. Es el 22 de septiembre. Estoy en Montevideo, Uruguay. Es la primavera.
6. Es el 30 de octubre en Albuquerque, Nuevo México. Es el otoño.

ADDITIONAL PRACTICE
34 Have students look at the maps at the beginning of the book and then write similar sentences. Their partner writes what season it is.

SUGGESTION
35 Tell students that in Argentina and Chile fall begins March 20 or 21; winter begins June 21 or 22; spring begins September 22 or 23; summer begins December 22 or 23.

CRITICAL THINKING
Explain latitude and longitude to students. (latitude lines run side to side and longitude run up and down) Ask if altitude or latitude has more effect on the weather in Latin America. (altitude, especially in the Andes and other high mountains)

GEOGRAPHY LINK
35 Using the dates from this activity, have students write a short report about the weather in Cuzco, Peru; in Guadalajara, Mexico; or in San Juan, Puerto Rico.

SCIENCE LINK
Ask students to explain why the seasons occur at opposite times of the year in the Southern and Northern Hemispheres. (Due to tilt of the earth's axis, sunlight is more direct in the Southern Hemisphere in December and more direct in the Northern Hemisphere in June.)

5-3

ASÍ SE DICE   Talking about the weather

To find out what the weather is like, ask:

To answer, say:

¿Qué tiempo hace?

Hace buen tiempo.
Hace muy mal tiempo hoy.

pp. 59–60
Acts.
16–18

p. 44
Acts.
15–16

5-C

VOCABULARIO

Hace frío.

Hace sol.

Hace fresco.

Está nevando. / Nieva.

Está lloviendo. / Llueve.

Hace viento.

Hace calor.

Está nublado.

36 ¿Qué tiempo hace?

Get together with a partner. Take turns asking and answering what the weather is usually like where you live during the following months and seasons. Answers will vary.

MODELO   —¿Qué tiempo hace en diciembre?
            —Hace mucho frío y nieva.

1. julio
2. la primavera
3. octubre
4. marzo
5. el verano
6. febrero
7. agosto
8. el otoño

37 El pronóstico del tiempo

Look at the weather map and match the weather to the corresponding city. Each city can match with more than one kind of weather.

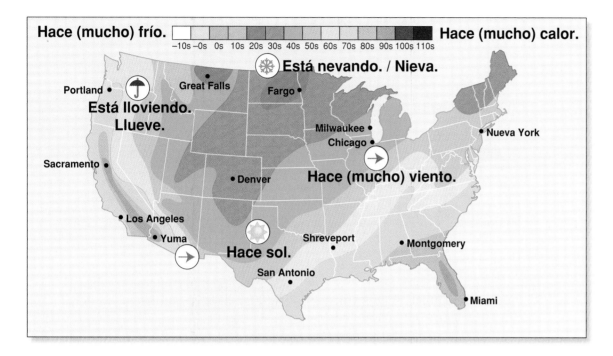

Hace (mucho) frío.　−10s −0s 0s 10s 20s 30s 40s 50s 60s 70s 80s 90s 100s 110s　Hace (mucho) calor.

Está nevando. / Nieva.

Está lloviendo.
Llueve.

Hace (mucho) viento.

Hace sol.

1. En Miami... a, c, d, h
2. En Nueva York... i
3. En Fargo... g
4. En Sacramento... a, c, d, h
5. En Shreveport... a, c
6. En Chicago... e

a. hace sol y hace buen tiempo.
b. está lloviendo.
c. hace buen tiempo.
d. hace calor y hace sol.
e. hace viento.
f. hace mucho frío.
g. hace frío y está nevando.
h. hace calor.
i. hace fresco.

VOCABULARIO EXTRA

¡Hace un frío tremendo!
It's incredibly cold!

¡Hace un calor espantoso!
It's terribly hot!

Está lloviendo a cántaros.
It's raining cats and dogs.

Hace un tiempo precioso.
It's a beautiful day.

SLOWER PACE
37 Have students follow along in their books as you talk about the weather map. Ask them to point to the city as you talk about it. (**En Portland está lloviendo...**)

ADDITIONAL PRACTICE
37 Ask each student to bring in a weather map from a recent copy of a local newspaper. In pairs, students ask each other simple yes or no questions about current weather conditions. Then ask students about the weather in various parts of the country. The symbols on the map can also be used to help practice weather expressions.

KINESTHETIC LEARNERS
Divide students into groups of three or four. Give each group a piece of paper with a month or a season on it. They are to develop a pantomime based on their month or season, and the class is to guess which one it is. Each student in the group should play a part in the pantomime.

38 Cuando hace calor...

Elsa lives in Santiago de Chile. Read a part of the letter she wrote to her pen pal in Albany, New York. Then say if the sentences about the letter are true or false. Correct the false statements.

Answers on p. 187K

> Hola Ricardo,
>
> Hace mucho calor este verano. Voy con mi amiga Sonia a la piscina todos los días. A veces los fines de semana voy con mi familia a la playa. Nos gusta acampar. Cuando acampamos en la playa corro por la mañana antes de desayunar. A esa hora no hace mucho calor.
>
> Y tú, ¿cómo estás? Vemos en la televisión que hace muy mal tiempo donde tú vives. ¿Está nevando mucho? ¿Te gusta esquiar?

1. It's summer in Santiago.
2. Ricardo probably will go swimming in a lake after school today.
3. Elsa likes to camp on the beach.
4. Elsa likes to run when it's hot.

39 ¿Qué haces cuando...?

Find out what your partner does in the following kinds of weather. Be prepared to report your findings to the class.   Answers will vary.

MODELO —¿Qué haces cuando hace calor?
—Cuando hace calor descanso en el parque y bebo muchos refrescos.

40 En mi cuaderno

Write two paragraphs describing your favorite season and explain why you like it. First, tell what the months are in that season and describe the weather. In the second paragraph, write about the activities that you and your friends like to do, and any special places where you go at that time. Answers will vary.

En el verano, a Mireli y a sus hermanos les gusta jugar a las cartas en la playa.

LETRA Y SONIDO

Script on p. 187F

CD 5
Trs. 11–15

A. One purpose of accent marks is to show which syllable to stress.

1. Words ending in a vowel, **n,** or **s** are stressed on the next to the last syllable.

examen	**hablan**	**discos**	**toma**	**quiero**

2. Words ending in any consonant besides **n** or **s** are stressed on the last syllable.

animal	**feliz**	**Madrid**	**hablar**

3. Exceptions to rules 1 and 2 get an accent mark over the syllable to be stressed.

semáforo	**lápices**	**rápido**	**lámpara**	**música**	**Víctor**	**suéter**

4. All question words have an accent mark.

¿qué?	**¿cuándo?**	**¿quién?**	**¿cómo?**	**¿cuánto?**	**¿dónde?**

B. Some words have an accent mark to tell them apart from a similar word.

mi *my* **mí** *me* **tu** *your* **tú** *you* **si** *if* **sí** *yes*

C. Dictado

Listen and read the phone conversation, and rewrite the words that need accent marks.

Voy al almacen hoy porque necesito una camara nueva. Pero, ¿donde esta mi sueter? ¿Y el cinturon para mi falda? Ah, aqui estan. ¿Tu quieres ir conmigo?

D. Trabalenguas

Tin marín dedós pingüé, cúcara, mácara, títere fue

EN MI CUADERNO

40 For an additional journal entry suggestion, see *Practice and Activity Book,* page 79.

PORTFOLIO

40 **Written** This is an appropriate portfolio entry. For portfolio suggestions, see *Alternative Assessment Guide,* p. 16.

☀ CLOSE

Read statements and ask students to illustrate each. **Es el invierno, hace frío y nieva mucho. Hace sol y mi amigo y yo nadamos.**

☀ ASSESS

▸ Testing Program, pp. 77–78
  Quiz 5-3
  Audio CD 5, Tr. 19

▸ Grammar and Vocabulary Quizzes
  Quiz 5-3A or
  Alternative Quiz 5-3A

▸ Alternative Assessment Guide, p. 23

PERFORMANCE ASSESSMENT

Ask pairs of students to role-play the following: One is a cousin from Argentina visiting the United States. The Argentinean asks about the weather and what they usually do in order to know what to bring. The cousin from the U.S. asks when the cousin plans to come in order to describe the weather.

PRESENTATION
Ask students where they think the word Sunday comes from. (sun's day) Saturday, Sunday, and Monday are from Roman days of the week (Latin). They come from Saturn's day, sun's day, and moon's day, respectively. Most of the English days of the week are named after gods from Germanic mythology. Tuesday from Tiu's day, Wednesday from Woden's day, Thursday from Thor's day, Friday from Frigg's day. Have students compare these origins to the origins of the Spanish days of the week.

CULTURE NOTE
Dates are abbreviated using a combination of Arabic and Roman numerals in some Spanish-speaking countries. For example, March 16, 2005 would be written 16-III-05. Most other Spanish-speaking countries put the day first also, but use Arabic numbers for the month. For example, 16-03-05.

TEACHER NOTE
Many seventh-grade social studies classes talk about the Americas. Check to see if you can coordinate with the social studies teacher on the Americas unit.

LAS CIENCIAS SOCIALES

Los calendarios   Most of the days of the week in Spanish come from Latin. Look at the chart to see the roots of the Spanish words. Then answer the questions that follow.

lunes	martes	miércoles	jueves	viernes	sábado	domingo
Latin: *lunae*	Latin: *Martis*	Latin: *Mercurii*	Latin: *Jovis*	Latin: *Veneris*	Hebrew: *shabbat*	Latin: *dominus*
moon	Mars: Roman god of war	Mercury: Roman messenger of the gods	Jupiter: Roman king of the gods	Venus: Roman goddess of love	sabbath	Lord's day

1 Los planetas

¿Qué planeta corresponde a cada día de la semana?

1. viernes b   **3.** jueves a   **a.** Júpiter   **c.** Mercurio

2. miércoles c   **4.** martes d   **b.** Venus   **d.** Marte

2 El calendario azteca

The Aztec Sun Calendar, the **xihuital** (shee-wee-TAL) or "count of the years," is similar to ours. Both are 365 days long, the number of days it takes the earth to orbit the sun. The **xihuital,** however, has 18 months of 20 days each, with extra "unlucky days" at the end of the year.

1. Can you find the ring on the Sun Calendar that represents the twenty days?

2. Since 18 months of 20 days each do not add up to 365 days, what is the number of "unlucky days" at the end of the year?

    1. The ring is the next circle out from the center face.
    2. 5 days

LAS CIENCIAS

El huracán Hurricanes are violent tropical thunderstorms with extremely heavy rains and high wind speeds of up to 186 mph. Hurricanes usually occur in the Atlantic Ocean, the Gulf of Mexico, and the Caribbean Sea between June 1 and November 30. During the worst hurricanes, streets become rivers, whole cities lose their electricity, and people must sometimes leave their homes and go to higher ground. The word *hurricane* comes from *hurakán,* the storm god of the Caribbean Taino Indians.

Floods from Hurricane Gert in Tampico, Mexico

3 ¿Dónde están los huracanes?

Use the information in the table to track Hurricane Dolly on graph paper. Draw a line connecting the points of the hurricane's path. Put a dot on the map where the latitudes and longitudes listed cross on your graph. Find out which country it hit. See the example of Hurricane Hortense drawn on the chart. Dolly struck Mexico.

Day	Latitude	Longitude
1	19° N	88° W
2	19.5° N	90° W
3	21° N	95° W
4	22° N	99° W

Hurricane Dolly

ENLACES

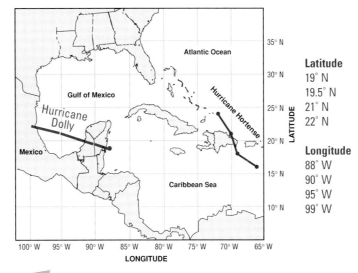

Latitude
19° N
19.5° N
21° N
22° N

Longitude
88° W
90° W
95° W
99° W

4 ¿Cómo se llama?

Each tropical storm of the season is given a name. The names are chosen ahead of time, and they alternate between female and male names in alphabetical order. For example, the first storm would be Alex, the next Brenda, and so on. Write Spanish names for the first ten tropical storms of the season. Would a hurricane named Rosa be early or late in the hurricane season? Answers will vary.
Rosa would be late in the season.

doscientos veintiuno 221

CAPÍTULO 5

LANGUAGE NOTE
Hurricanes are known by different terms in different parts of the world. In the Pacific Ocean this kind of tropical storm is called a *typhoon.* Around the Indian Ocean, they are called *cyclones.* Australians call them *willy-willies.* Have students look at the world maps on pages xviii–xix with partners to locate those regions of the world.

HURACÁN EN UNA BOTELLA
Materials you may need
• Two empty 2–3 liter plastic soft drink bottles with their lids
• Glue
• Hammer and nail
• Water

Sequence
1. Glue the lids of two 2–3 liter plastic soft drink bottles together top to top. Make a hole through the center of the lids with a hammer and nail.
2. Fill one bottle three-quarters full with water and screw the connected lids on tightly. Screw the empty bottle to the bottle full of water.
3. Turn the connected bottles upside down. Swirl the bottles in a circle. Then place the connected bottles, empty one down, on a steady, flat surface and watch the vortex form as the water goes into the other bottle.

STANDARDS: 3.1   221

VAMOS A LEER

MOTIVATING ACTIVITY
Ask students to list the types of water activities they enjoy, and which they would like to try some day.

☀ PREREADING

A Ask students to look at the pictures to guess what the reading will be about. Ask them what their favorite water sport is and if it is pictured here. Also, ask them which words are cognates.

TEACHER NOTE
For additional readings, see *Practice and Activity Book,* p. 61.

CHALLENGE
Ask students to write an original paragraph describing their favorite sport. Have them write which sport it is, how often they practice it, and during what season.

NATIVE SPEAKERS
Have native speakers scan the reading for two words with an accent on the letter *a*, two with an accent on the letter *i*, and two with an accent on the letter *o*. Have them find the only word in the reading with an accent on the letter *e*. (**océano**) They will learn more about accent marks in Level 1B **En camino.**

PA
p. 61
Act. 19

Estrategia
Using context
As you know, it's easy to understand pictures, cognates, and words you've already studied. You can understand many other words, too, based on how they're used in the sentence or paragraph. When you come to an unknown word, try to guess its meaning based on context (the other words around it).

¡A comenzar!

A Before you do any in-depth reading, first remember to get the general idea and to recall your background knowledge of the topic. It should be easy to tell what these readings are about based on the pictures.

¿Te acuerdas?

Look at pictures and titles first.
What is the reading on page 223 about?
a. a sporting goods store
b. racing
c. water sports
d. the environment

Al grano

B Imagine that your family will be vacationing in Miami this summer. Each of you wants to try out a different sport. Read the passages and decide which sport would be best for each member of your family.

1. your father, who loves high speeds   el motoesquí
2. your mother, who likes the most popular of all water sports   la natación
3. your sister, who likes small, one- or two-person boats   el kayak
4. your brother, who wants to take lessons to learn something new   el windsurf

C Your parents are trying to read the descriptions of these sports, but they don't know Spanish as well as you do. They underlined the words they didn't know so that you could help them. Use your knowledge of context to help them guess the meanings of these words.   Answers on p. 187K

D Tus padres dicen *(say)* que tienes el día libre para participar en tu deporte acuático favorito. ¿Cuál de estos cuatro deportes prefieres? ¿Por qué?   Answers will vary.

DEPORTES EN EL AGUA

EL MOTOESQUÍ corre muy rápidamente. Es fácil usar esta máquina. Se puede usar en el océano, el río o el lago. Es muy divertido usarlo en las olas.

LA NATACIÓN es un deporte favorito durante el verano. Es posible nadar en el océano, en un lago o en la piscina. Se puede nadar en una piscina cubierta durante el invierno, el otoño y la primavera. Algunas personas usan la natación como diversión y otros la usan como ejercicio.

Si no tienes experiencia con el **WINDSURF** es muy importante tomar lecciones de un instructor. Tu primera experiencia debe ser en el verano porque el viento es ideal. En la primavera hace demasiado viento para las personas que no tienen experiencia en el deporte.

En la primavera y en el verano, hay muchos **KAYAKS** en el agua. Son barcos pequeños para una o dos personas. Generalmente se operan en los ríos, pero también hay kayaks de océano.

Cuaderno para hispanohablantes, pp. 21–23

VAMOS A LEER

doscientos veintitrés **223**

✷ READING

MAIN IDEA
C Tell students to focus on the main idea of each sentence as they read through the first time. The second time through, have them look up words in the Spanish-English glossary in their book and write a list of words they don't know. Then have them write one sentence to summarize each paragraph.

✷ POSTREADING

ADDITIONAL PRACTICE
D As a follow-up activity, put students in groups of two or three, give them a picture of a different sport from those listed here, and have them write a brief description.

AUDITORY LEARNERS
Write the names of the sports illustrated in the photos on a transparency or on the board. Have students close their books. Then read a portion of the description of each photo from the text and ask students to identify the sport you are describing.

The **Repaso** reviews and integrates all four skills and culture in preparation for the Chapter Test.

2 Ask students to read or listen to the local weather forecast and to prepare their own brief **pronóstico del tiempo** for your city or town for the following day. It could be done as an audio or video recording or as a newspaper article. (You may wish to bring in a newspaper in case some students do not have access to a forecast.)

ADDITIONAL PRACTICE

2 After students have done Activity 2, ask them whether one could normally expect to do a given activity on a given date, in a given city or country. (**—¿Nadan en Buenos Aires en julio? —No, porque hace frío.**)

internet

go.hrw.com

MARCAR: go.hrw.com
PALABRA CLAVE:
WV3 FLORIDA-5

1 For each weather report you hear, determine which of the photos is being described.
Script and answers on p. 187F

CD 5
Tr. 16

2 Look at the weather map. Then, complete a sentence by matching each city with a phrase. Use the information on the map, and the phrases in the boxes.
Answers on p. 187K

En Asunción
En Bogotá
En Buenos Aires
En La Paz

está lloviendo a cántaros
hace mucho frío
hace mucho viento
hace fresco y hace sol

Voy a mirar la televisión.
Vamos a volar una cometa *(fly a kite)*.
Vamos a caminar en el parque.
Voy a leer una novela en casa.

Caracas   35°C/95°F
Bogotá   20°C/68°F
Quito   23°C/74°F
Lima   19°C/66°F
La Paz   2°C/35°F
Asunción   17°C/63°F
Santiago   12°C/53°F
Buenos Aires   16°C/61°F
Montevideo   10°C/50°F

3 Vamos a escribir

Write a paragraph about what you would typically do on a Monday in January and another paragraph about what you would do on a Saturday in May. Write what season it is, what the weather is usually like, and what activities you are likely to do. Start by making an outline.

Estrategia

Outlining is a way for you to organize what you want to write about before you write it. Put your ideas in related groups. In this case it could be the month, the weather, and the activities you do.

> I. Un lunes en enero
>   A. El tiempo
>   B. Mis actividades
>
> II. Un sábado en mayo

4 Write the following dates as they would be written in Spanish. Write the numbers as words. Answers on p. 187K

1. June 24
2. March 30
3. September 12
4. February 1
5. November 18
6. August 8

5 Where do young people in Spanish-speaking countries more commonly spend time together?

a. at a friend's house   **(b.)** in the **plaza**   c. at the mall

6 SITUACIÓN

Imagine that you're the host of your own late night talk show. With a partner, choose a famous person and role-play the interview. Be sure to ask what your guest does during certain times of the year, what he or she likes to do on vacation, where he or she likes to go, and why.

MODELO   —Típicamente, ¿qué haces durante el invierno?
             —Me gusta esquiar con mis amigos.
             —Y a ti y tu familia, ¿les gusta ir de vacaciones juntos?
             —Siempre...

> Cuaderno para hispanohablantes, pp. 23–24

ADDITIONAL PRACTICE

3 After students have completed this activity on their own, have them work in pairs to create a dialogue. In the conversation, they will talk about five activities they typically do each week. At the end, they decide to get together the evening or weekend day when they are free.

PORTFOLIO

3 Written You may wish to suggest this activity as an appropriate entry for your students' Portfolio. For Portfolio suggestions, see *Alternative Assessment Guide,* pages 9 and 16.

SUGGESTION

6 You might like to videotape the interview, in which one student assumes the role of a late night talk show host and the other pretends to be a famous person. Then partners can switch roles.

PORTFOLIO

6 Oral You might suggest that students include the **Situación** interview in their portfolio. For portfolio information, see *Alternative Assessment Guide,* pages 9 and 16.

A VER SI PUEDO...

WV3 FLORIDA-5

Answers to Question 1

1. Nunca nado.
2. Siempre desayuno.
3. A veces hablo con Luisa los fines de semana.
4. A veces voy al cine los viernes.

Answers to Question 2

Answers will vary. Possible answers:

1. ¿A ustedes les gusta correr juntas en el parque?
2. ¿A ustedes les gusta bucear juntos?
3. ¿Te gusta leer novelas?
4. ¿Les gusta esquiar juntas?
5. ¿Te gusta hacer ejercicio en el gimnasio?
6. ¿Te gusta escribir cartas?

Answers to Question 4

1. el cinco de marzo
2. el catorce de septiembre
3. el veintisiete de enero

▼ **Can you discuss how often you do things?** p. 195

1 How would José Luis say that . . .? Answers in side column

1. he never swims
2. he always eats breakfast
3. he sometimes talks to Luisa on weekends
4. he sometimes goes to the movies on Fridays

▼ **Can you talk about what you and your friends like to do together?** p. 203

2 How would you ask these people if they like to do the activities mentioned? How would they answer you?

1. Cristina and Marta / run in the park   Answers in side column
2. Geraldo and Esteban / scuba dive
3. Pablo / read novels
4. Linda and Laura / ski
5. Daniel / exercise in the gym
6. Isabel / write letters

▼ **Can you talk about what you do during a typical week?** p. 209

3 How would you tell a classmate about five activities you typically do each week?
Answers on p. 187K

▼ **Can you give today's date?** p. 213

4 How would you tell a classmate the date of the following things?   Answers in side column

1. the Spanish test—March 5
2. the football game—September 14
3. the birthday party—January 27

▼ **Can you talk about the weather?** p. 216

5 How would you describe the weather if it were . . .?

1. rainy and cold
2. cold and windy
3. snowy
4. hot and sunny   Answers on p. 187K
5. a cloudy day
6. cool

6 What would be a typical weather description in your hometown during the following times of year?   Answers will vary.

1. el otoño
2. el invierno
3. la primavera
4. el verano

VOCABULARIO

PRIMER PASO

Discussing how often you do things

a veces *sometimes*
ayudar en casa *to help at home*
la chica *girl*
el chico *boy*
¿con qué frecuencia? *how often?*
desayunar *to eat breakfast*
durante *during*
muchas veces *often*
nada *nothing*
nadie *nobody*
nunca *never*
¿Quiénes? *Who? (plural)*
la semana *week*
siempre *always*
sólo cuando *only when*
todavía *still, yet*
todos los días *every day*
tomar el autobús *to take the bus*

SEGUNDO PASO

Talking about what you and your friends like to do together

a ellos/as *to them*
a ustedes *to you (plural)*
acampar *to camp*
el agua (f.) *water*
asistir a *to attend*
beber *to drink*
bucear *to scuba dive*
la carta *letter*
una clase de ejercicios aeróbicos *aerobics class*
comer *to eat*
correr *to run*
escribir *to write*

especialmente *especially*
esquiar *to ski*
hacer ejercicio *to exercise*
la hamburguesa *hamburger*
el jugo *juice*
juntos/as *together*
leer *to read*
Les gusta + infinitive *They/you (pl.) like to . . .*
Nos gusta + infinitive *We like to . . .*
las papas fritas *french fries*
el periódico *newspaper*
pescar *to fish*
por la playa *along the beach*
recibir *to receive*
el sándwich *sandwich*
las tarjetas postales *postcards*
las tiras cómicas *comics*
las vacaciones *vacation*

Talking about what you do during a typical week

la milla *mile*
por la mañana *in the morning*
por la noche *at night (in the evening)*
por la tarde *in the afternoon*
típicamente *typically*

TERCER PASO

Giving today's date

abril *April*
agosto *August*
el año *year*
¿Cuál es la fecha? *What is today's date?*
diciembre *December*
El... de este mes hay... *On the (date) of this month, there is / are . . .*
enero *January*

Es el... de... *It's the (date) of (month).*
las estaciones *seasons*
febrero *February*
Hoy es el... de... *Today is the (date) of (month).*
el invierno *winter*
julio *July*
junio *June*
marzo *March*
mayo *May*
el mes *month*

noviembre *November*
octubre *October*
el otoño *fall*
la primavera *spring*
el primero *the first (of the month)*
¿Qué fecha es hoy? *What's today's date?*
septiembre *September*
el verano *summer*

Talking about the weather

Está lloviendo. *It's raining.*
Está nevando. *It's snowing.*
Está nublado. *It's cloudy.*
Hace buen tiempo. *The weather is nice.*
Hace calor. *It's hot.*
Hace fresco. *It's cool.*
Hace (mucho) frío. *It's (very) cold.*
Hace mal tiempo. *The weather is bad.*
Hace sol. *It's sunny.*
Hace (mucho) viento. *It's (very) windy.*
Llueve. *It's raining.*
Nieva. *It's snowing.*
¿Qué tiempo hace? *What's the weather like?*

VOCABULARIO *doscientos veintisiete* **227**

SUGGESTION

See Games pages 187I–187J for games to review this chapter's material.

CHAPTER 5 ASSESSMENT

▶ **Testing Program**
Chapter Test, pp. 79–84
 Audio Compact Discs, CD 5, Trs. 20–21
Speaking Test, p. 114

▶ **Alternative Assessment Guide**
Performance Assessment, p. 23
Portfolio Assessment, p. 16
CD-ROM Assessment, p. 30

▶ **Interactive CD-ROM Tutor, Disc 2**
¡A hablar!
¡A escribir!

▶ **Standardized Assessment Tutor**
Chapter 5

▶ **One-Stop Planner, Disc 2**
 Test Generator
Chapter 5

227

Entre familia
CHAPTER OVERVIEW

De antemano pp. 230–233	*¿Cómo es tu familia?*			

	FUNCTIONS	**GRAMMAR**	**VOCABULARY**	**RE-ENTRY**
Primer paso pp. 234–241	• Describing a family, p. 236	• **Gramática:** Possessive adjectives, p. 237	• Members of the family, p. 235 • Pets and the words to describe them, p. 241	• **hay** • Possessive adjectives • Demonstrative adjectives • Use of **de**
Segundo paso pp. 244–251	• Describing people, p. 245 • Discussing things a family does together, p. 248	• **Gramática:** The verbs **hacer** and **salir**, p. 249 • **Nota gramatical:** The personal **a**, p. 250	• Words that describe people, pp. 245, 248	• Colors • Descriptions of people • Pastimes/hobbies • **¿Con qué frecuencia?** • Adjective agreement
Tercer paso pp. 254–259	• Discussing problems and giving advice, p. 255	• **Así se dice:** Present tense of **decir: dice,** p. 255 • **Nota gramatical:** The verb **deber,** p. 255 • **Nota gramatical:** The verb **poner,** p. 257	• Household chores, p. 256	• Forming questions with **¿cómo?** and **¿cuántos?**

Letra y sonido	p. 259	The Spanish *r*	**Dictado:** Audio CD 6 Tracks 9–13
Enlaces	pp. 252–253	**La familia**	
Vamos a leer	pp. 262–263	**Diversiones en la Pequeña Habana**	**Reading Strategy:** Using context and cognates
Review	pp. 264–267	**Repaso,** pp. 264–265	**A ver si puedo...,** p. 266 **Vocabulario,** p. 267

Culture	• **Nota cultural:** El compadrazgo, p. 239 • **Encuentro cultural:** La importancia de la familia hispana, pp. 242–243	• **Nota cultural:** Diminutive names, p. 247 • **Panorama cultural:** ¿Cuántas personas hay en tu familia?, pp. 260–261

PRINT

Lesson Planning
One-Stop Planner
Lesson Planner with Substitute Teacher
Lesson Plans, pp. 29–33

Listening and Speaking
Listening Activities
- Student Response Forms for Listening Activities, pp. 61–63
- Additional Listening Activities 6-1 to 6-6, pp. 22–24
- Additional Listening Activities (song), p. 25
- Scripts and Answers, pp. 41–43

Video Guide
- Teaching Suggestions, pp. 42–43
- Activity Masters, pp. 44–47
- Scripts and Answers, pp. 60–62, 66

Activities for Communication
- Communicative Activities, pp. 31–36
- Realia and Teaching Suggestions, pp. 63–67
- Situation Cards, pp. 80–81

¡Ven conmigo! Level 1
TPR Storytelling Book, pp. 21–24

Reading and Writing
Reading Strategies and Skills, Chapter 6
¡Lee conmigo! 1, Chapter 6
Practice and Activity Book, pp. 63–74

Grammar
Grammar and Vocabulary Workbook, pp. 45–52

¡Ven conmigo! Level 1
Grammar Tutor for Students of Spanish
Chapter 6

Assessment
Testing Program
- Paso Quizzes and Chapter Test, pp. 91–102
- Score Sheet, Scripts and Answers, pp. 103–108, 125–138
- Final Exam, pp. 125–132

Grammar and Vocabulary Quizzes
- Quizzes 6-1A, 6-2A, 6-3A
- Alternative Quizzes 6-1A, 6-2A, 6-3A

Alternative Assessment Guide
- Portfolio Assessment, p. 17
- Performance Assessment, p. 24
- CD-ROM Assessment, p. 31

¡Ven conmigo! Level 1
Standardized Assessment Tutor
- Reading, pp. 21–23
- Writing, p. 24
- Math, pp. 25–26

Native Speakers
¡Ven conmigo! Level 1
Cuaderno para hispanohablantes, pp. 26–30

MEDIA

Online Activities
- Juegos interactivos
- Actividades internet

Video Program
- Videocassette 2
- Videocassette 3 *(captioned version)*

¡Ven conmigo! Level 1
DVD Tutor, Disc 2

Audio Compact Discs
- Textbook Listening Activities, CD 6, Tracks 1–18
- Additional Listening Activities, CD 6, Tracks 27–33
- Assessment Items, CD 6, Tracks 19–26

Interactive CD-ROM Tutor, Disc 2

Teaching Transparencies
- Situations 6-1 to 6-3
- Vocabulary 6-A to 6-C
- Grammar and Vocabulary Workbook

One-Stop Planner CD-ROM

Use the **One-Stop Planner CD-ROM with Test Generator** to aid in lesson planning and pacing.

For each chapter, the **One-Stop Planner** includes:
- Editable lesson plans with direct links to teaching resources
- Printable worksheets from resource books
- Direct launches to the HRW Internet activities
- Video and audio segments
- Test Generator
- Clip Art for vocabulary items

DVD/VIDEO

Videocassette 2, Videocassette 3 (captioned version)
DVD Tutor, Disc 1 See Video Guide, pages 39–44.

De antemano • ¿Cómo es tu familia?
Armando goes to Raquel's house, and she shows him photos of her family. She describes what her family is like and what they like to do together. While she is showing Armando the photos, they are interrupted by a loud crash.

¿Cuántas personas hay en tu familia?
Teenagers from various Spanish-speaking countries describe their families and what they do to help around the house.

A continuación
Raquel discovers that her dog, Pepe, has come into the house and knocked something over in the other room. She scolds him and sends him outside. Later, she cannot find him and is afraid that he has run away. After Raquel and her friends scour the neighborhood, they finally find Pepe hiding under a table in Raquel's living room.

La importancia de la familia hispana

Videoclips
• **Estar en familia:** public service message supporting spending time with family

INTERACTIVE CD-ROM TUTOR

Activity	Activity Type	Pupil's Edition Page
En contexto	*Interactive conversation*	
1. Vocabulario	¡Super memoria!	p. 235
2. Gramática	¡A escoger!	p. 237
3. Gramática	¿Qué falta?	p. 249
4. Así se dice	Imagen y sonido ¡Exploremos! ¡Identifiquemos!	p. 245
5. Vocabulario	¡Super memoria!	p. 256
6. Gramática	¿Qué falta?	pp. 255, 257
Panorama cultural	¿Cuántas personas hay en tu familia? ¡A escoger!	pp. 260–261
¡A hablar!	*Guided recording*	pp. 264–265
¡A escribir!	*Guided writing*	pp. 264–265

Teacher Management System
Launch the program, type "admin" in the password area and press RETURN. Log on to **www.hrw.com/CDROMTUTOR** for a detailed explanation of the Teacher Management System.

DVD-ROM TUTOR ¡Ven conmigo! Level 1

The *DVD Tutor* contains all material from the Level 1 *Video Program*. Spanish captions are available for use at your discretion for all sections of the video. The *DVD Tutor* also provides a variety of video-based activities that assess students' understanding of the **De antemano, A continuación,** and **Panorama cultural.**

This part of the *DVD Tutor* may be used on any DVD video player connected to a television or video monitor.

In addition to the video material and the video-based comprehension activities, the *DVD Tutor* also contains the entire Level 1 *Interactive CD-ROM Tutor* in DVD-ROM format. Each DVD disc contains the activities from all 12 chapters of the *Interactive CD-ROM Tutor.*

This part of the *DVD Tutor* may be used on a Macintosh® or Windows® computer with a DVD-ROM drive.

One-Stop Planner CD-ROM

To preview all resources available for this chapter, use the **One-Stop Planner CD-ROM,** Disc 2.

internet

MARCAR: go.hrw.com
PALABRA CLAVE:
WV3 FLORIDA-6

INTERNET CONNECTION

*Have students explore the **go.hrw.com** Web site for many online resources covering all chapters. All Chapter 6 resources are available under the keyword **WV3 FLORIDA-6.** Interactive games help students practice the material and provide them with immediate feedback. You will also find a printable worksheet that provides Internet activities that lead to a comprehensive online research project.*

JUEGOS INTERACTIVO

You can use the interactive activities in this chapter

- to practice grammar, vocabulary, and chapter functions
- as homework
- as an assessment option
- as a self-test
- to prepare for the Chapter Test

ACTIVIDADES INTERNET

Students will create the script for a television show that is about two families coming together.

- Have students prepare for the **Hoja de actividades** by reviewing the vocabulary from the **Primer paso.** You might also have them complete the Listening Activities for that **Paso.**
- When students have finished the activity sheet, have them describe their show's cast and plot (the family activities they chose in activity A).

Proyecto

Have students search Spanish-language Web sites such as television networks or online magazines for images and descriptions of actors. They should choose possible cast members for their show about families from the **Hoja de actividades.** For each person they cast, have students describe his or her physical appearance and say which role each would play.

CAPÍTULO 6

Entre familia 🔊

TEXTBOOK LISTENING ACTIVITIES SCRIPTS

For Student Response Forms, see Listening Activities pp. 62–64

PRIMER PASO   pp. 234–241

5 ¿Quién es quién?   p. 235

1. Es una familia bastante grande. Hay nueve personas en total.
2. La familia es muy simpática. Tiene un perro muy travieso.
3. Hay dos personas en la familia. Tienen dos gatos y un perro también.
4. Hay cuatro en la familia. El padrastro es muy simpático.
5. Los chicos son muy buenos. El gato también.

Answers to Activity 5

1. b
2. d
3. ninguna foto
4. c
5. a

SEGUNDO PASO   pp. 244–251

17 ¿Ciencia o ficción?   p. 245

1. Alma tiene veintidós años y tiene el pelo blanco.
2. Guillermo es pelirrojo. Tiene los ojos negros.
3. Olivia tiene el pelo rubio y tiene ojos azules.
4. Adolfo tiene ochenta y cinco años. Tiene el pelo negro.
5. Liliana tiene los ojos blancos y el pelo verde.
6. Anselmo tiene pelo rubio y ojos de color café.

Answers to Activity 17

1. improbable
2. improbable
3. probable
4. improbable
5. improbable
6. probable

19 ¿Cómo son tus amigos?   p. 246

1. Es pelirrojo, tiene ojos azules y es muy alto.
2. Es muy simpática y guapa. Tiene pelo negro y ojos de color café.
3. Ella es baja, tiene pelo rubio y ojos verdes. Él es alto y tiene ojos verdes también.
4. Es una persona muy especial. Es muy cariñosa conmigo. Tiene cincuenta años, pero se ve joven.
5. Son muy cómicos cuando están juntos. Uno de ellos es delgado y el otro es un poco gordo. Son muy traviesos.

Answers to Activity 19

1. David
2. Rebeca
3. Conchita y Gabriel
4. Maki
5. Simón y Quique

25 Con la familia   p. 249

1. Durante el verano mi familia y yo hacemos un viaje. Casi siempre visitamos a nuestros primos. Ellos viven en Colorado.
2. Salgo con frecuencia con mis amigos. A veces vamos a la playa.
3. Soy muy atlética. Hago ejercicio por la mañana con mis amigos. A veces los sábados corro con ellos en el parque.
4. Mi familia y yo salimos a comer juntos todos los viernes. Nos gusta hablar sobre nuestras actividades, las clases y el trabajo.

Answers to Activity 25

1. b
2. d
3. c
4. a

33 Los problemas de Mónica   p. 255

Mi tía es divorciada y vive con nosotros. Ella dice que mi mamá trabaja demasiado. Mi mamá sale de la casa a las siete de la mañana y regresa a las nueve de la noche. Debe descansar más, ¿verdad? Mi hermana es muy inteligente. Estudia ciencias y siempre está en la biblioteca con sus libros. Debe salir con amigos a veces. ¿Y yo? Pues, soy bastante perezosa. Toco la guitarra pero toco muy mal. Claro, debo practicar más.

Answers to Activity 33

1. c
2. a
3. b
4. not pictured

35 El sábado   p. 257

MAMÁ   Buenos días, mis hijos queridos.

BERNARDO   Buenos días, mamá. Queremos ir a patinar en línea esta mañana.

MAMÁ   Hoy es sábado y primero necesitan hacer los quehaceres de la casa.

LUISA   Después de desayunar, voy a hacer mi cama.

MAMÁ   ¡Excelente! Esta semana, le toca a Daniel limpiar la cocina. Bernardo debe pasar la aspiradora en la sala y Luisa debe cortar el césped.

BERNARDO   Voy a cuidar al gato. Se ve que quiere su desayuno también.

Answers to Activity 35

1. no
2. sí
3. sí
4. no
5. sí
6. sí

For the scripts for Parts A and C, see page 259. The script for Part B is below.

B. Dictado

Rafael Ramírez es rubio y tiene ojos verdes. Él corre muy rápido en sus zapatos rojos de rayas.

1 p. 264

Roberto, ésta es mi familia. Ésta es mi madre. Lee muchas novelas y lee el periódico todos los días. Y éste es mi padre. Es artista y trabaja en un museo. Debe trabajar menos. Ésta es mi hermana. Ella es muy lista pero debe estudiar más. Éste es mi tío Miguel. A él le gusta tocar la guitarra día y noche. Éste es nuestro perro. Es un poco gordo porque come demasiado. Y finalmente éste soy yo. Yo soy muy responsable y siempre limpio mi cuarto.

Answers to Repaso Activity 1

1. el perro
2. el padre
3. la madre
4. Marcos
5. el tío Miguel
6. la hermana

Entre familia

PROJECTS

 EL ÁLBUM DE MI FAMILIA

This project invites students to illustrate their families in book or collage form.

Introduction

Ask your students how they define family. Who are the people in a family? Uncles? Neighbors? Grandmothers? Guardians? Friends?

Materials students may need

- White 8 1/2 x 11 paper
- Colored markers
- Glue sticks
- Photos of family members
- Magazines

Sequence

1. Have students use the vocabulary from Chapter 6 to list nuclear or extended family. Students may consider pets as part of their families as well. Allow students to make up an imaginary family for this activity.

2. Have students draw portraits, use magazine pictures, or bring in photographs of the members of their families for the album.

3. Have students label the pictures or photos and write a brief descriptive sentence in Spanish about each family member using vocabulary from this chapter and Chapter 3. For example, **Mi madre es creativa y simpática.** Students should use two adjectives for each person.

4. The cover of the album should have a title, a dedication, and a by-line.

5. When students have completed the project, assign them to groups of four. Have students show their albums to each other and give an oral presentation in Spanish.

Grading the project

Suggested point distribution (total = 100 points):

Neatness **20**
Creativity **20**
Correct grammar **20**
Imaginative descriptions **20**
Oral presentation **20**

 EL ÁRBOL GENEALÓGICO

With this hands-on project, students make a mobile that reinforces vocabulary about the family from this chapter. Students prepare a visual representation of their family members and share the information about them orally with classmates.

Introduction

Students make mobiles that illustrate the main characteristics of their family members, including pets. Lead a brainstorming session about what family means to the students. What members make up a family for them? How would they describe their family members to a new friend? Do they include pets as part of their definition of a family?

Materials students may need

- Clothes hangers
- Colored paper
- Glue sticks
- Scissors
- Markers
- String or yarn
- Single-hole punch

Sequence

1 Have each student make a list in Spanish of five family members to describe. They write a descriptive sentence about each person. For example: **Mi padre es bajo y atlético.**

2 Have students cut out five shapes from the colored paper large enough to glue the pictures, photos, or drawings to. They then punch a hole in the top. Afterwards, they select photos of their family members, use cutouts from magazines, or draw them and glue them to the paper. They can write the person's name and a short description over or under the picture.

3 Have students punch holes at the top of their colored-paper shapes and use yarn or string to tie them to a coat hanger. They can use different lengths of string for variety.

4 When the mobile is complete, students present it to the class by describing their family members.

5 Mobiles can be displayed from the ceiling in the classroom to reinforce this chapter's vocabulary.

Grading the project

Suggested point distribution (total = 100 points):

Overall appearance, neatness 20
Creativity 20
Information and content 20
Spelling, gender agreement 20
Oral presentation 20

LOS JUEGOS DE MESA

In this challenging activity students use listening, speaking, reading, and writing to create their own board game. This will be a group project involving cooperative learning, delegating tasks, and creative organization of ideas.

Introduction

Ask students to think of all the board games they have played. Ask which are their favorites and why. Bring in various games in Spanish to show the class if you have them, or ask your students to bring some.

Materials students may need

◆ Poster board or cardboard
◆ Toy cars, play figures, or other game pieces
◆ Markers
◆ Index cards
◆ Old magazines

Sequence

1 Have students work in groups of four. Each group selects a game to imitate or creates a new one.

2 Give students time to brainstorm. Suggest that they check the rules of board games they are familiar with.

3 Students may use the format of a game you have already played in class, but they must design a gameboard to go with it. Encourage them to be creative, but mention the possibility of using a favorite classic board game as a model. Some examples are Monopoly®, Go to the Head of the Class®, Clue®, and Payday®.

4 Set a date for a game proposal to be peer-reviewed by another group. This proposal should include basic rules and how they propose to create the game.

5 Have a game day when groups play their game, then exchange with other groups.

Grading the project

Suggested point distribution (total = 100 points):

Vocabulary use 20
Appearance. 20
Creativity 20
Grammar usage 20
Rules easy to understand 20

CAPÍTULO 6

Entre familia

GAMES

¡DIBÚJALO!

In this game students review chapter vocabulary by drawing pictures of the vocabulary words and naming them in Spanish. It is a very effective review method for visual learners.

Materials you may need
◆ Markers ◆ Index cards

Preparation
Make index cards for family vocabulary and adjectives. For example: **madre, hijo, cómico, guapo**.

Procedure
1 Divide the class into two teams. Remind students that drawing a family tree can be useful to show family relationships.
2 Have a student from Team A come forward to pick a vocabulary card and begin drawing for his or her team to guess. Members of Team A call out the possible word in Spanish. If they guess it within the two-minute time limit, they win a point.
3 Repeat steps one and two for Team B. Be sure each team member has a chance to draw. The team with the higher score wins.
4 For a challenge, give students a noun and an adjective to draw simultaneously. For example: **madre** and **alta**.

¿ERES MI HERMANO?

This game reinforces new vocabulary related to the family and descriptive adjectives. It can be played any time after the Primer paso.

Preparation
1 Draw a large family tree on the board or use the family tree in Teaching Transparency 6-A.
2 Include additional words such as **divorciado/a** *divorced* and **adoptado/a** *adopted*.

Procedure
1 Divide the class into two teams. One player from each team chooses a person on the tree that he or she will be. The Team A player announces aloud the person he or she is going to be. The Team B player tells only you.
2 The Team A player asks the Team B player five questions to find out his or her identity, but never uses any names on the tree. (**¿Eres viejo o joven? ¿Tienes hijos? ¿Cuántos hermanos tienes? ¿Eres mi madre?**)
3 If the Team A player guesses the Team B player's identity, Team A gets one point. If not, Team B gets one point. The next round, the teams reverse roles.

CHALLENGE
After the **Segundo paso,** write descriptions of some of the people on the tree you made for **¿Eres mi hermano?** Have a student from each group come to the front. Describe a person on the tree using a string of relationships, never mentioning the name of the person. Start out with simple sentences and gradually make your sentences more complicated. **Este hombre es bajo...** One of the two students will respond **Es el abuelo de Jaime.** The player who identifies the person first gets one point and both players return to their seats. Then call up two more players and describe another person.

UNA PALABRA MÁS

The object of this game is for students to build logically on words to make complete sentences. The sentences can be odd or funny, but they should be grammatically correct.

Procedure
1 Divide the class into two or more teams. Write one word on the board to begin a sentence, for example, **Mi.** Have a student from another team write a word to continue the sentence, for example, **hermano.** The next team's player should write another word, for example, **tiene.**
2 Play continues until the sentence is long. Students may add words either before or after previous ones. For example, a later student could write **inteligente** between **hermano** and **tiene.** Each time a student adds a word correctly, his or her team gets a point.

¡NO HAY SUJETO!

*The object of this game is for students to identify the grammatical subject of a sentence from context. It may be used at any time to review the vocabulary of the **paso** you are working on.*

Preparation

1 Cut out a small slip of paper for each student.

2 Write a Spanish sentence on each slip, leaving out the subject in each and using the vocabulary of the **paso** you are working on. For the **Primer paso,** you might write sentences such as **Mi _____ es el hijo de mis abuelos.** Place all the slips in a hat.

Procedure

1 Divide the class into two teams. Have a player from Team A draw a slip, read it aloud, and supply the missing subject. For this example, the Team A player could say **Mi padre es el hijo de mis abuelos.**

2 Follow the same procedure with Team B. Have teams alternate turns until each student has had a chance to make a complete sentence. Teams score one point for each sentence they make with a correct subject. The winner is the team with the highest score.

EL RITMO

Use this game to review a variety of vocabulary and vocabulary categories.

Preparation

1 Write categories on the board, for example, **la familia, las descripciones, los quehaceres.**

2 Demonstrate the following four-beat rhythm. On beat 1, slap your hands on your thighs. On beat 2, clap your hands. On beat 3, snap with the fingers of your left hand. On beat 4, snap with the fingers of your right hand.

3 Have students copy the four-beat rhythm.

Procedure

1 One person begins by calling out a category, such as **la familia,** on beats three and four.

2 The next student adds an appropriate vocabulary item such as **el hijo** on the subsequent count of three and four. The next student adds **el tío,** and so on.

 If the rhythm breaks down, stop and start again with a new category.

LA GEOGRAFÍA

This game may be used to review basic geography, forming questions (Chapter 1), telling where things are (Chapter 4), and pronunciation. It also calls upon higher-order thinking skills.

Preparation

Tell students to pretend they are in training to become experts in world geography to assist a team of Spanish-speaking scientists on a trip around the world.

Procedure

1 Write questions like the following on the board: **¿Qué país está al sur de España? ¿Cuántos océanos hay en el mundo? ¿Dónde está la Argentina? ¿Cuántos países hay en Sudamérica?**

2 Divide students into groups and choose a leader for each. The leader begins the game by asking a question that can be answered by looking at the map. (one from the board or one of his or her own design)

3 The other students in the group try to answer the question. Allow students to look at the maps on pages xvii–xxiii if they need to, but insist they try to answer without looking at the book first. The first student to answer correctly becomes the leader.

ANSWERS TO CHAPTER 6 ACTIVITIES

Listening Activity answers appear on Scripts pages 227E–227F. Answers to all other activities appear on corresponding pupil pages.

DE ANTEMANO   pp. 230–233

3
1. ¿Cómo es tu familia?
2. Éstos son mis padres.
3. ¿Y cuántos viven aquí?
4. Nosotros hacemos cosas juntos los domingos.
5. Alguna vez debes probar la barbacoa que prepara mi mamá.

PRIMER PASO   pp. 234–241

8
1. nuestra
2. su
3. tus
4. su
5. mi
6. nuestra
7. nuestros

9 Answers will vary. Possible answers:
1. Sí, es nuestro primo.
2. Sí, es nuestra abuela *or* Sí, es su madre.
3. No, no son mis tíos.
4. Sí, son sus hijas.
5. Sí, es nuestro tío *or* Sí, es su esposo.
6. Sí, nuestros amigos son mucho más altos que mis hermanos.

ENCUENTRO CULTURAL   pp. 242–243

2
1. Answers will vary. Possible answer: 3
2. Answers will vary. Possible answers: grandfather, granddaughter, mother, son, aunt, niece
3. preparing the cornhusks, fill the cornhusks, rolling up and folding the tamales

SEGUNDO PASO   pp. 244–251

24
1. hacen
2. salimos
3. cenamos
4. comida
5. algo
6. hacemos
7. viaje

ENLACES   pp. 252–253

1
1. Cabrera: 3; Miró: 3
2. Cabrera: father, mother and daughter; Miró: father, mother, and child
3. Answers will vary.

3
1. Se llaman Xavier y Leticia.
2. Los abuelos paternos se llaman Gustavo Lomas Mendoza y Estela Muñoz de Lomas.
3. Se llama Ana Díaz de Lomas.

4
1. Antonio Lomas Muñoz
2. Pablo Lomas Díaz

TERCER PASO   pp. 254–259

37 Answers will vary. Possible answers:
a. Pablo no debe poner la mesa en la cama. Debe poner la mesa en la cocina.
b. Diana y Lola no deben trabajar en la sala. Deben trabajar en el jardín.
c. Federico no debe pasar la aspiradora en el jardín. Debe pasar la aspiradora en la sala.
d. Miguelito no debe poner la basura en el armario. Debe sacar la basura.
e. Frida no debe cuidar la planta. Debe cuidar al perro.

38 Answers will vary. Possible answers:
1. Mi hermana y yo debemos cuidar al gato y al perro.
2. Mis abuelos deben trabajar en el jardín.
3. Mi primo debe cuidar a mis hermanos.
4. Mi hermano debe preparar la cena.
5. Debo cortar el césped.
6. Debemos planchar la ropa.

A VER SI PUEDO...   p. 266

4 Answers will vary. Possible answers:
1. Casi siempre cenamos juntos.
2. A veces los sábados visitamos a mi tía Elena.
3. Todos los domingos en el verano salimos juntos a pescar.

5 Answers will vary. Possible answers:
1. Debe limpiar su cuarto.
2. Debe trabajar menos.
3. Deben preparar la cena.

Chapter Section	Presentation	Homework Options
Primer paso	**Vocabulario,** p. 235	*Grammar and Vocabulary,* p. 45, Activities 1–2 *Practice and Activity Book,* p. 63, Activities 3–4 *CD-ROM,* Disc 2, Chapter 6, Activity 1
	Así se dice, p. 236	*Pupil's Edition,* p. 236, Activity 6 *Practice and Activity Book,* p. 65, Activity 5
	Gramática, p. 237	*Pupil's Edition,* p. 237, Activity 8 *Grammar and Vocabulary,* p. 46, Activities 3–4 *CD-ROM,* Disc 2, Chapter 6, Activity 2
Segundo paso	**Así se dice,** p. 245	*Practice and Activity Book,* p. 67, Activity 9 *CD-ROM,* Disc 2, Chapter 6, Activity 4
	Vocabulario, p. 245	*Pupil's Edition,* pp. 247–248, Activities 21, 23 *Grammar and Vocabulary,* p. 47, Activities 5–6 *Practice and Activity Book,* p. 67, Activity 10
	Así se dice, p. 248	*Pupil's Edition,* p. 248, Activity 24 *Practice and Activity Book,* p. 69, Activity 13
	Gramática, p. 249	*Grammar and Vocabulary,* p. 48, Activity 8 *CD-ROM,* Disc 2, Chapter 6, Activity 3
	Nota gramatical, p. 250	*Pupil's Edition,* p. 250, Activity 28
Tercer paso	**Así se dice,** p. 255	*Pupil's Edition,* p. 255, Activity 32 *Practice and Activity Book,* pp. 70–71, Activities 14–15
	Nota gramatical, p. 255	*Grammar and Vocabulary,* p. 50, Activities 11–12
	Vocabulario, p. 256	*Grammar and Vocabulary,* p. 51, Activities 13–15 *Practice and Activity Book,* pp. 71–72, Activities 16–17 *CD-ROM,* Disc 2, Chapter 6, Activity 5
	Nota gramatical, p. 257	*Pupil's Edition,* p. 257, Activity 36 *Grammar and Vocabulary,* p. 52, Activities 16–17 *CD-ROM,* Disc 2, Chapter 6, Activity 6

Entre familia

MOTIVATING ACTIVITY
Ask students to discuss what they do with their families. (weddings, birthdays, baseball games, etc.) Do members of their families advise each other? Who gives whom advice? Do they mostly solve problems alone, or do they seek help from friends and family?

LANGUAGE NOTE
1 **Jesús** is often used as a first name in Spanish. Some common nicknames for **Jesús** in Spanish-speaking countries are **Chucho** and **Chuy.**

RE-ENTRY
1 Use this photo to review numbers, **tener,** and **llamarse,** asking several students to tell the class how many cousins they have and what their names are. (**Tengo tres primos. Se llaman Susan, Bill y Joe.**)

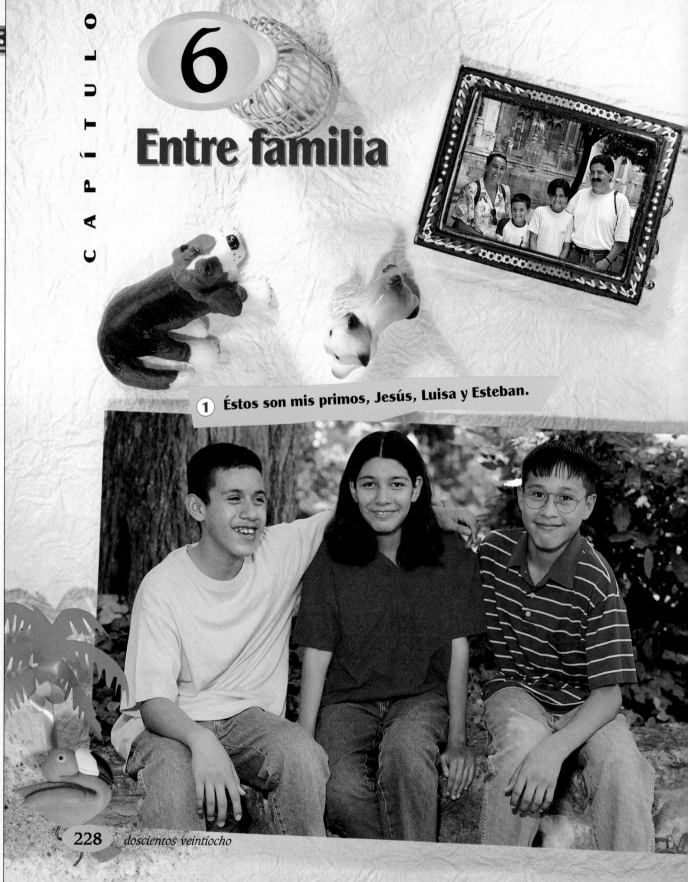

CAPÍTULO

6

Entre familia

1 Éstos son mis primos, Jesús, Luisa y Esteban.

228 *doscientos veintiocho*

In this chapter you will learn to

PRIMER PASO

- describe a family

SEGUNDO PASO

- describe people
- discuss things a family does together

TERCER PASO

- discuss problems and give advice

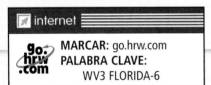

internet

MARCAR: go.hrw.com
PALABRA CLAVE:
WV3 FLORIDA-6

② **Tiene pelo negro y ojos de color café.**

③ **Si tienes problemas, debes hablar conmigo.**

229

FOCUSING ON OUTCOMES

Refer students to the photos and have them match the outcomes with photos. (Photo 1: describing your family; Photo 2: describing people; Photo 3: discussing problems and giving advice) Then have students look at these photos and describe the people. Ask volunteers to describe their family members.

CRITICAL THINKING

② Ask students if they can guess what color **ojos de color café** are. They can indicate some students in the class who have brown eyes using the correct form of the verb **tener.** (**María tiene ojos de color café.**)

CULTURE NOTE

In Spanish-speaking countries, **la familia** often includes aunts, uncles, cousins, grandparents, and godparents. The extended family in the United States often includes members who are not biological relatives: stepparents, stepsiblings, stepgrandchildren, for example. In the United States, three or more generations do not live in the same house as often as they do in Spanish-speaking countries.

CAPÍTULO 6

VIDEO INTEGRATION

Adelante LEVEL 1A
Video Program
Videocassette 2, 36:54–41:06 OR
Videocassette 3, 55:49–59:49
(captioned version)

¡Ven conmigo! LEVEL 1
DVD Tutor, Disc 1

TEACHER NOTE
The **fotonovela** is an abridged version of the video episode.

VIDEO SYNOPSIS
Armando is visiting Raquel's house and she is describing her family to him. As they look at a photo album, he asks her questions about her family members and she tells him about them and their interests. At the end of the scene, she is describing her dog when they are interrupted by a loud crash.

MOTIVATING ACTIVITY
Ask students if they keep a photo album of their friends and families. Ask them to bring in their photo albums and write captions for photos in Spanish. See **El álbum de mi familia** on page 227G.

DE ANTEMANO

 ¿Cómo es tu familia?

CD 6 Trs. 1–2

 Look at the photos below. What is going on? Who is Raquel talking about with Armando? Does something surprising happen at the end? What could have happened?

PA
p. 63
Acts. 1–2

Raquel

Armando

Pepe

1

A ver, Raquel, ¿cómo es tu familia?

Bueno, es bastante grande... tengo tres hermanos, una hermana... y muchísimos primos...

¿Y cuántos viven aquí?

Somos ocho en casa: mis padres, todos mis hermanos menos uno, una abuela y una tía.

2

¿Y cómo son tus padres? ¿Son simpáticos?

Sí, son muy simpáticos. ¿Por qué no miramos mi álbum de fotos? Así puedes conocer a toda la familia.

230 *doscientos treinta*

Éstos son mis padres.
Ellos son de Cuba. Les gusta
mucho trabajar en el jardín.
Mi mamá es muy buena cocinera.
Alguna vez debes probar
la barbacoa que ella prepara.
¡Es fenomenal!

Éstos son mis
hermanos mayores.
Y ella es
mi hermana menor.

Nosotros hacemos muchas cosas juntos,
especialmente los domingos. Primero,
vamos a la iglesia. Después, comemos
juntos y salimos a alguna parte. En
esta foto, salimos al parque.

PREVIEWING

Ask students some previewing
questions based on the photos
and captions on these pages:
**¿Cómo se llaman los chicos?
¿Cuántas personas hay en la
familia de Raquel? ¿De dónde
son los papás de Raquel? ¿Qué
deporte practican los hermanos
de Raquel?**

PRESENTATION

Have students look at the
fotonovela. What do they
think is going on in the
story? What visual cues
help them make intelligent
guesses? Next, play the
video. Have students work
with a partner to see if
they agree about what is
happening. Discuss the plot
with the whole class, then
have them repeat the lines
after you or the audio
recording. If time permits,
ask volunteers to read the
lines aloud.

ADDITIONAL PRACTICE

After you have presented the
fotonovela, have students
review the learner outcomes
listed on page 229. Ask them
to identify the phrases in the
fotonovela that describe family
and other people. Discussing
problems and giving advice are
functions modeled in the con-
tinuation of the **fotonovela** in
the *Video Program.*

STANDARDS: 1.2, 3.2   231

VISUAL LEARNERS

After students have seen the video and answered the questions, have them close their books and draw a picture of Raquel's family, and identify the members. Then have them open their books and see how many they were able to remember.

NATIVE SPEAKERS

Check with native speakers to see if they would like to give a presentation on their families using drawings, photos, or props.

A continuación

You may choose to continue with *¿Cómo es tu familia? (a continuación)* at this time or wait until later in the chapter. At this point, Raquel discovers that her dog, Pepe, has made a mess. Later Raquel cannot find Pepe. She and her friends search the neighborhood for the dog. You may wish to have pairs of students predict where they think Raquel will find Pepe.

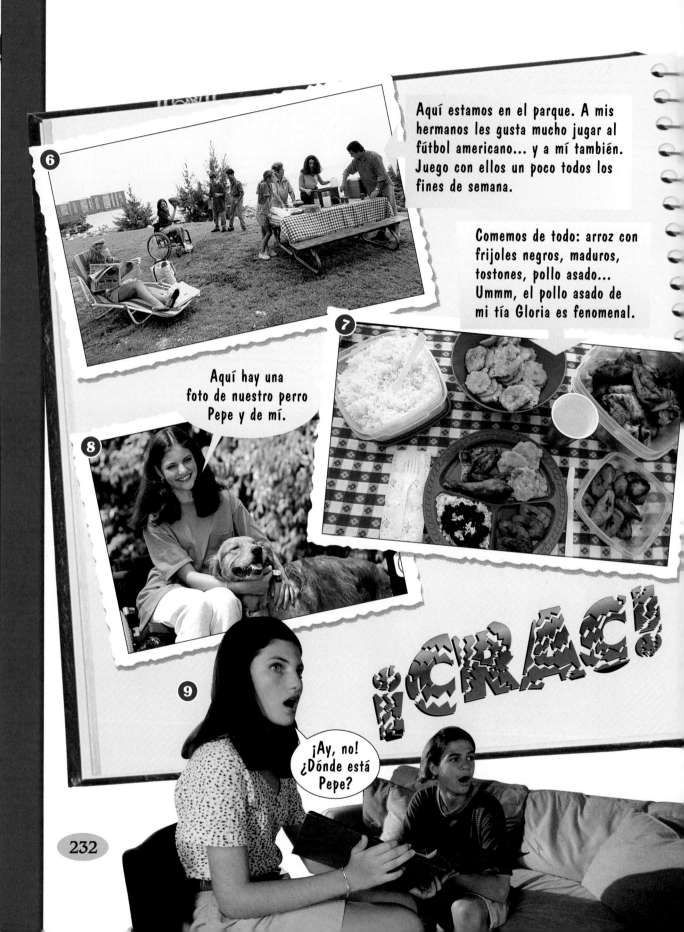

6 Aquí estamos en el parque. A mis hermanos les gusta mucho jugar al fútbol americano... y a mí también. Juego con ellos un poco todos los fines de semana.

Comemos de todo: arroz con frijoles negros, maduros, tostones, pollo asado... Ummm, el pollo asado de mi tía Gloria es fenomenal.

7

Aquí hay una foto de nuestro perro Pepe y de mí.

8

9

¡Ay, no! ¿Dónde está Pepe?

¡CRAC!

1 ¡Contesta las preguntas!

These questions will help you check your understanding of the **fotonovela.** Don't be afraid to guess.   Answers in side column

1. Where are Raquel and Armando?
2. What are Raquel and Armando talking about?
3. What do Raquel and her family do together on Sundays?
4. Who is Pepe?

2 ¿Cierto o falso?   Answers in side column

Con base en la fotonovela, contesta **cierto** o **falso.** Explica tus respuestas.

MODELO   A Raquel no le gustan los deportes.
         Falso. Le gusta el fútbol americano.

1. Armando y Raquel son hermanos.
2. El hermano mayor toca el piano.
3. Pepe es el primo de Raquel.
4. A los hermanos de Raquel les gusta mucho el fútbol americano.
5. Los padres de Raquel son de Cuba.
6. Hay cuatro personas en la familia de Raquel.

These activities check for global comprehension only. Students should not yet be expected to produce language modeled in **De antemano.**

3 ¿Cómo se dice?

Look through the **fotonovela** and find the words and phrases you think the characters are using . . .   Answers on p. 227K

1. to ask what someone's family is like
2. to point out his or her parents in a photo
3. to ask a friend how many people live in his or her house
4. to say that she and a family member do things together on Sundays
5. to tell a friend that he or she should try your mom's barbecue

SUGGESTION
2 Have students identify the scene that proves or disproves each statement.

LANGUAGE NOTE
Ask students to compare the Spanish word **esposo/a** with the English word *spouse.* (Spanish cognates often have an **e** before initial **sp** or **st.**) You may also hear **mujer** for **esposa,** a term that is used affectionately in Spanish.

ADDITIONAL PRACTICE
Have students clip pictures from magazines and create imaginary families. Ask them to describe each family member by using the expressions Raquel used.

Answers to Activity 1

1. Están en la casa de Raquel.
2. Hablan de la familia de Raquel.
3. Van a la iglesia, van a comer, y salen para alguna parte.
4. Pepe es el perro de Raquel.

Answers to Activity 2

1. falso; son amigos
2. falso; toca la guitarra
3. falso; es el perro
4. cierto
5. cierto
6. falso; son ocho

PRIMER PASO (TPR)

Storytelling Book
pp. 21, 24

WV3 FLORIDA-6

Describing a family

A ver, Raquel, ¿cómo es tu familia?

Bueno, es bastante grande... tengo tres hermanos, una hermana... y muchísimos primos...

¿Y cuántos viven aquí?

Somos ocho en casa: mis padres, todos mis hermanos menos uno, una abuela y una tía.

4 ¿Cómo es la familia de Raquel?

Complete this paragraph about Raquel's family with the words below.

La familia de Raquel es bastante ___1___. Son ___2___ en su casa. Ella tiene tres hermanos y una ___3___. Su abuela y una ___4___ viven con ellos. Un ___5___ ya no vive en casa.

3 **hermana** 2 **ocho** 4 **tía**

5 **hermano** 1 **grande**

VIDEO INTEGRATION

Adelante LEVEL 1A

Video Program
Videocassette 2, 38:20–38:46 OR
Videocassette 3, 57:13–57:39
(captioned version)

¡Ven conmigo! LEVEL 1
DVD Tutor, Disc 1

Bell work
On the board or on a transparency, write the expressions **Nos gusta... juntos** and **No nos gusta... juntos.** Have students write five sentences listing what their families like or don't like to do together.

AUDITORY LEARNERS
4 Have students write their answers on a separate sheet of paper as they listen to the audio portion of this scene.

LANGUAGE NOTES
• The word **bastante** means *enough* but very often implies *quite* or *plenty.* When Raquel says her family is **bastante grande,** she means *quite* or *very big.*

• Point out that **ser** is often used to indicate the number of people in a group:
—¿**Cuántos son?** *How many of you are there?*
—**Somos ocho.** *There are eight of us.*

CD-ROM DISC 2

p. 64
Acts. 3–4

p. 45
Acts. 1–2

6-A

Ésta es la **familia** de Miguel: su **madre**, su **media hermana** (*half sister*) y su **gato**.

La familia Pérez es grande. Aquí están el **padre** y su **esposa** (*wife*), los dos **hijos** y una **hija** (*daughter*), la **abuela** (*grandmother*) y el **tío** (*uncle*) de los chicos. La **tía** (*aunt*) Catalina y el **abuelo** no están en la foto.

En mi casa hay cuatro personas: mi **medio hermano**, mi madre y yo, y el **esposo** (*husband*) de mamá, Rolando. Es mi **padrastro** (*stepfather*).

Soy María. Aquí están mis **padres** (mi **padre** y mi **madre**) y mi **perro** Chuleta.

los abuelos	*grandparents*	los hermanos	*brothers and sisters*
la hermanastra	*stepsister*	los hijos	*children*
el hermanastro	*stepbrother*	la madrastra	*stepmother*

5   ¿Quién es quién?   Script and answers on p. 227E

CD 6 Tr. 3   Imagine that you're on the phone with the photographer who took the family portraits above. First, study the photos to see how many people are in each family and what they're like. Then, as the photographer describes members of each family, find the photo that matches. If no photo matches, answer **ninguna foto**.

⁜ MOTIVATE

Have students talk about their family, the people they live with, or the family members from a popular movie or TV show. List in English as many words as possible that show family relationships. *(mother, father, cousin, aunt, uncle)* Have them put this list in a notebook. As they learn new vocabulary, they write it next to its English meaning.

⁜ TEACH

PRESENTATION

VOCABULARIO

Draw your family tree on a transparency. Beneath the tree, write the vocabulary you will use. Before you show the class your over-head, describe it in detail in Spanish. Then do the same using the overhead. Students write down meanings of vocabulary as they are described. You can also use Teaching Transparency 6-A or 6-1 to introduce basic family vocabulary.

NATIVE SPEAKERS

Point out that the word **pa-rientes** is a false cognate meaning relatives. Ask whether students remember the Spanish word for parents. (**padres** or **papás**)

STANDARDS: 1.2, 4.2, 5.1   **235**

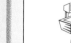
pp. 65–66
Acts. 5, 8

6-1

ASÍ SE DICE   Describing a family

To find out about a friend's family, ask:

¿Cuántas personas hay en tu familia?

Your friend might answer:

Hay cinco personas **en mi familia.** Mi abuela **vive** con nosotros también.
My grandmother lives with us too.

Somos cinco.

También **tenemos** un perro.
We also have a dog.

¿Cómo es tu familia?

Nuestra familia es muy grande.
Tenemos muchos **primos.**
We have lots of cousins.

Somos muy **unidos.**
We're very close-knit.

6 ¿Cómo es tu familia?

Look at the sentences below. Find which family tree each sentence best describes. For each description, write the name of the family.

MODELO Mi hermano se llama Andrés. (Andrade)

1. Somos ocho en casa. Andrade
2. Somos seis personas en mi familia: mis padres, mi tía, mis dos hermanos y yo. Canales
3. Somos tres hermanas, dos hermanos, mis padres y mi abuelo. Andrade
4. Mi hermana menor tiene tres años y es rubia. Andrade
5. La hermana de mi papá vive con nosotros. Canales

la familia Andrade

papá   abuelo   mamá

la familia Canales

tía Rosa   papá   mamá

Alberto   Rosario   Zenaida

Leticia   Andrés   Rosa

Felipe   Esperanza

7 Retrato de familia

Work in pairs. Pretend that you're a member of the Andrade or Canales family in Activity 6. Tell about yourself and the other members of your family. Your partner will pretend to be a member of the other family. Then switch roles.

MODELO   Me llamo Leticia y tengo dos hermanos...

GRAMÁTICA   Possessive adjectives

You've been using **mi(s)**, **tu(s)**, and **su(s)**, which are *possessive adjectives.*
Here are some others:

nuestro(s)	*our*
nuestra(s)	
vuestro(s)	*your (when "you" is plural)*
vuestra(s)	
su(s)	*your (when "you" is plural)*
su(s)	*their*

1. Note that **nuestro** and **vuestro** have a feminine form:

   Nuestra familia es pequeña.

2. Like **mi**, **tu**, and **su**, these forms add an -s when they modify a plural noun: **sus primos, nuestros gatos.**

Y aquí está Verónica con sus abuelos.

pp. 65–66
Acts. 6–7

pp. 46
Acts. 3–4

8 En nuestra familia...

Liang and Tranh are looking at pictures of Liang's family. Complete their conversation using the correct possessive adjective.

TRANH   ¿Quiénes están contigo en esta foto?

LIANG   Aquí está (1. <u>nuestra</u>/nuestro) abuela conmigo y con mis primos.

TRANH   ¿Y quién es este señor?

LIANG   ¿Con mi tía? Es (2. <u>su</u>/sus) esposo. Es el padrastro de mis primos.

TRANH   Es bastante grande la familia de (3. tu/<u>tus</u>) primos, ¿verdad?

LIANG   Sí, (4. <u>su</u>/sus) familia es grande. Hay siete personas. En (5. <u>mi</u>/mis) familia somos cuatro.

TRANH   En (6. <u>nuestra</u>/nuestras) casa somos cuatro también. Pero si contamos *(count)* (7. nuestro/<u>nuestros</u>) perros, ¡somos siete!

doscientos treinta y siete   237

**PRESENTATION
GRAMÁTICA**

Walk up to a student's desk and hold up his or her book. Ask **¿De quién es este libro?** Elicit **Es su libro**. Look at that person and ask **¿Es tu libro?** Continue this with various school items and incorporate the other possessive adjectives. After practicing several times, write **nuestro, nuestros, nuestra,** and **nuestras** on the board. Demonstrate their meaning by eliciting sentences in which students talk about people and objects belonging to the whole class or school. (**nuestra cafetería, nuestro gimnasio**)

VISUAL LEARNERS

For additional practice with family relations and possessive adjectives, display Teaching Transparency 6-1. Assume the role of one of the family members named on the transparency. As you point to other people on the transparency, have students indicate the person's relationship to you. For example, if you take the role of Mario, point to Rosa and ask students **¿Quién es?** Encourage students to use the appropriate possessive adjective in their answer. (**Es Rosa; es su hermana.**)

STANDARDS: 1.1, 1.3, 4.1   237

238

SLOWER PACE

9 Have students refer to the pictures on page 235 and develop questions based on the people shown. You might have them work in pairs and alternate asking and answering questions about the pictures.

CHALLENGE

10 Prepare a series of pairs of cards according to the following pattern.

Card 1: **Tú eres baja y rubia. Tu tío es alto y guapo.**

Card 2: **Tú eres alto y guapo. Tu sobrina es baja y rubia.**

Shuffle and pass out one card to each student. Have them use the information to find their missing relative.

CULTURE NOTE

It's not at all unusual for aunts and uncles to be addressed **tío** or **tía**. For example, a nephew or niece might greet an aunt or uncle with **Hola, tía** or **Hola, tío.**

Answers to Activity 10

Answers will vary. Possible answers:
1. alto
2. baja
3. rubia
4. inteligente
5. guapa
6. cómico

---

9 Una reunión familiar

Your partner doesn't know your family well. Answer his or her questions using the correct possessive adjectives. Use the hints in parentheses to help you answer. Then switch roles.

MODELO —¿Quién es ella? ¿Es su tía? (sí)
—Sí, es nuestra tía. Se llama Melinda. Answers on p. 227K

1. ¿El chico alto es el primo de ustedes? (sí)
2. ¿Es ella la madre de Melinda? (sí)
3. ¿Los señores son tus tíos? (no)
4. ¿Quiénes son ellas? ¿Son las hijas de tía Melinda? (sí)
5. Es el esposo de tía Melinda, ¿no? (sí)
6. Y nuestros amigos, ¿son más altos que tus hermanos? (sí)

Ésta es nuestra tía Melinda.

10 La familia de Cristina

Cristina is describing her family to you. Use the word box to help you complete the sentences. Remember to use the correct form of the adjective! Answers in side column

Mi tío Martín es muy ___1___. Aquí está mi prima Mayra. Es ___2___ y ___3___. A mi abuelita le gusta leer. Es ___4___ y ___5___ y tiene canas. Mi hermano Jacobo es ___6___, ¿verdad?

> guapo/a
> bonito/a
> alto/a
> bajo/a
> simpático/a
> cómico/a
> inteligente
> rubio/a

STANDARDS: 1.2, 4.2, 5.1

11 ¿Quién en tu familia es...?

Work in pairs. Pretend that your partner is a member of the family pictured on page 238. Ask your partner three questions using **¿Quién en tu familia es...?** and adjectives like those in the box on page 238. Then switch roles.

MODELO ¿Quién en tu familia es cómico?
Mi hermano Jacobo es cómico.

12 Una entrevista

A Work in a group. Create a questionnaire with four or five questions about someone's family. Include questions about what people look like, what they're like, what their house is like, and if they have a dog or a cat. Take turns interviewing each other.

B Then make a list of what is similar about all the families. Be prepared to share your list with the rest of the class. Keep your questionnaire for use in Activity 14.

1. ¿Cuántos son en tu familia?

2. ¿Tienes un perro o un gato?

3. ¿Quién es la persona más alta de tu familia?

Nota cultural

When a man and a woman serve as **padrino** (godfather) and **madrina** (godmother) at a baby's baptism, it's understood that they'll have a special lifelong relationship with their godchild. The godparents give their **ahijados** (godchildren) love, advice, and even help with education and careers. **El compadrazgo** is the relationship between the child's parents and godparents. The father and the godfather call each other **compadre** and the mother and the godmother call each other **comadre. Compadres** and **comadres** often consider each other family. Is there someone that you think of as a relative but who isn't related to you?

CULTURE NOTE
Many Spanish-speaking families ask close friends to be the godparents of their children; however, they also frequently choose family members. The godfather (**el padrino**) is often an uncle or an older cousin whereas the godmother (**la madrina**) may be an aunt or an older cousin. Not only is there a special relationship between the child and their godparents but also between the parents and godparents.

PHOTO FLASH!
This is a photo of a baptism on Olvera Street in Los Angeles, California. Olvera Street is the oldest street in Los Angeles and the site of the oldest house. It is near the **Pueblo de los Ángeles,** where the city began in 1781. In 1930, it was restored as a Mexican-style marketplace for pedestrians only.

13 Cuestionario sobre la familia

 Based on what you see in the questionnaire below, work with your partner to describe the family.   Answers in side column

1. Ésta es una familia...
2. En la familia hay...
3. Viven *(They live)* en...
4. Probablemente tienen...
5. Les gusta...
6. Sus hermanos tienen...

Información Personal

1 Datos personales

a. Nombre completo:

Apellido   Young

Nombre(s)   Kelly

b. Edad: 14   años

c. Domicilio:

una casa ☐

un apartamento ☒

2 Vivo

a. con unos parientes ☐
b. con una familia extensa ☐
c. en una familia nuclear ☒

3 Datos familiares

a. ¿Tienes hermanos?   sí
   ¿Cuántos?   2
b. ¿Cuántos años tiene cada uno?

Mi hermano mayor Mike tiene 16 años

Mi hermana menor Lynn tiene 12 años

4 Actividades

a. pescar
b. visitar a los parientes
c. ir al cine   todos los viernes
d. limpiar la casa
e. acampar   a veces durante el verano
f. ir de vacaciones

14 ¿Cómo es tu familia?

A Work with a partner. Each of you should think of a fictional family (from a book, movie, or TV show). Choose which member of the family you'll be.

B Interview each other using the questionnaire you wrote in Activity 12. Fill in the blanks as you go. After your partner interviews you, compare answers to see what your families have in common. Be prepared to share your findings with the rest of the class.

15 Mi mascota

Could your pet be the next Pet of the Week? Write a description of your real or imaginary pet to be featured in **La mascota de la semana.** You should write at least four sentences. Be sure to mention your pet's name, color, age, and at least one interesting thing your pet does.

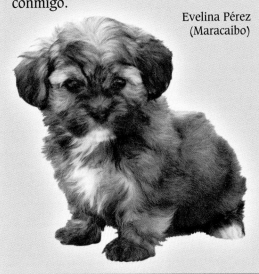

La mascota de la semana

Ésta es mi perrita. Se llama Reina y tiene ocho meses. Mi perrita es muy mimosa. Ella es muy juguetona pero a veces me muerde. También muerde mis zapatos. Voy al parque con ella todos los días. Le gusta mucho correr conmigo.

Evelina Pérez
(Maracaibo)

VOCABULARIO EXTRA

el caballo	*horse*
el conejo	*rabbit*
juguetón, juguetona	*playful*
la mascota	*pet*
mimoso/a	*affectionate*
muerde	*bites*
el pájaro	*bird*
el pez de colores	*goldfish*

☀ CLOSE

Divide the class into groups of three or four. Each group comes up with eight to ten questions about the families on page 235 and then answers them. Students peer-edit each other's work and then read the questions and answers aloud. Groups take turns asking each other questions.

☀ ASSESS

▸ Testing Program, pp. 91–92
   Quiz 6-1
   Audio CD 6, Tr. 19

▸ Grammar and Vocabulary Quizzes
   Quiz 6-1A or
   Alternative Quiz 6-1A

▸ Alternative Assessment Guide, p. 24

PERFORMANCE ASSESSMENT

Ask students to develop a conversation with a partner to present to the class. They pretend to be new acquaintances and ask each other about their families. They demonstrate interest in each other's family with their questions. Answers should include descriptions of the family members. Remind students that their answers may be about an imaginary family. For additional Performance Assessment ideas, see Situation Cards 6-1.

VIDEO INTEGRATION

Adelante LEVEL 1A

Video Program

Videocassette 2, 47:52–50:30

MOTIVATING ACTIVITY

Ask students to think about how often they see members of their extended families. Ask them how often they write or speak to their relatives on the phone. Are they close?

PRESENTATION

Show the video or read Valeria's speech bubble and then have students answer the questions in **¿Qué dijo?** Afterwards, have students describe their own (or an imaginary) family by reading through Valeria's speech bubble and replacing her information with theirs.

CULTURE NOTE

Point out that **tamales** are made from corn meal. The corn meal is ground into a paste (**masa**), spread onto corn husks, and filled with meat or other fillings. The husks are then rolled and steamed. **Tamales** are a favorite food especially on holidays or other special occasions.

ENCUENTRO CULTURAL

La importancia de la familia hispana

Valeria lives in San Antonio, Texas, although she has relatives all over the world. She keeps in touch with her relatives with letters and videotapes. And when she's with loved ones in San Antonio, she spends as much time with them as she can.

¡Hola! Me llamo Valeria. Para mí, la familia es muy importante. Ésta es mi abuela. También vive en San Antonio. Es muy cariñosa. Siempre cuenta historias de su pasado. Y ésta es mi hermana... Cuando hay una fiesta, ellas siempre preparan tamales juntas.

 ¿Qué dijo?

Valeria describes how she feels about her family and what they do together.

▶ "...Para mí, la familia **es muy importante**."

▶ "...siempre **cuenta historias** de su pasado."

▶ "Cuando hay una fiesta, ellas siempre **preparan tamales juntas**."

1. How does Valeria feel about her family?
Her family is very important.

2. What does Valeria's grandmother always do? tells stories

3. For special occasions, what traditional dish does Valeria's family prepare?
tamales

2 ¡Piénsalo! Answers on p. 227K

1. How many generations do you see in the painting?

2. What family relationships do you think are portrayed?

3. There are three main activities going on in this painting of a **tamalada**, or **tamal**-making party. In what order would the following steps be done?
   a. rolling up and folding the **tamales**
   b. filling the cornhusks
   c. preparing the cornhusks

Carmen Lomas Garza, **Tamalada,** 1987, Gouache on paper. 20″ x 27″.

3 ¿Y tú?

How would you describe your family? Answers will vary.

1. ¿Hay una persona en tu familia que es importante para ti? ¿Quién es?

2. ¿Por qué es especial esa persona?

3. ¿Qué te gusta hacer con tu familia? ¿Tienen ustedes algunas tradiciones especiales? Explica.

ENCUENTRO CULTURAL

doscientos cuarenta y tres **243**

BACKGROUND
Carmen Lomas Garza, born in Kingsville, Texas, later moved to San Francisco, California. Her art typically depicts recollections of family and friends from her childhood in South Texas. She often illustrates everyday activities or special family traditions such as the **Tamalada** shown here.

SUGGESTION
Have students look at the **Tamalada** and describe the family. Allow students to be creative in their answers.

ART LINK
Have students choose a family event and paint a mat drawing similar to the **Tamalada.** Students can present their work to the class by introducing and describing their family as well as the traditional family event they have depicted. Students will learn more expressions for describing family members in the **Segundo paso.**

VIDEO INTEGRATION

Adelante LEVEL 1A
Video Program
Videocassette 2, 39:06–39:34 OR
Videocassette 3, 58:01–58:29
(captioned version)

¡Ven conmigo! LEVEL 1
DVD Tutor, Disc 1

Bell work
Tell students there will be a family reunion with these people present: **madre, padre, hermanos, abuelos, tíos.** Have them write four sentences, each one describing a different family member with at least two adjectives.

SUGGESTION
16 Have students read these questions as advance organizers before showing the video.

SEGUNDO PASO

 Storytelling Book pp. 22, 24

WV3 FLORIDA-6

Describing people; discussing things a family does together

> Éstos son mis padres.
> Ellos son de Cuba. Les gusta mucho trabajar en el jardín.
> Mi mamá es muy buena cocinera. Alguna vez debes probar la barbacoa que ella prepara. ¡Es fenomenal!

16 El álbum de Raquel
Use the information that Raquel gives about her family to answer the following questions.

1. ¿Quiénes están en la foto? Los padres de Raquel.
2. ¿De dónde son ellos? Son de Cuba.
3. ¿Quién cocina *(cooks)* bien? La mamá de Raquel.
4. ¿Qué les gusta hacer a estas personas? Les gusta trabajar en el jardín.

ASÍ SE DICE   Describing people

PA p. 67 Act. 9

To ask for a description of someone, say:

Some responses might be:

¿**Cómo es** tu abuelo?

Él es alto y cariñoso.

¿**De qué color son sus ojos?**

Tiene los ojos verdes.
He has green eyes.

¿**De qué color es su pelo?**

Tiene canas.
He has gray hair.

17   ¿Ciencia o ficción?   Script and answers on p. 227E

Listen to the following descriptions of some fictional characters. Use **probable** or **improbable** to tell what you think of their appearances.

CD 6 Tr. 4

VOCABULARIO

La profesora Fajardo es muy lista. Es pelirroja *(redheaded)*, delgada *(thin)* y tiene los ojos azules.

PA p. 67 Act. 10

Los hijos de Julio son traviesos *(mischievous)*. Pepe es mayor *(older)* y Pedro es menor *(younger)*. Julio y sus hijos tienen pelo negro y los ojos de color café.

GV pp. 47–48 Acts. 5–7

6-B

Los abuelos son muy cariñosos. La abuela es guapa y un poco gorda *(a little overweight)*. El abuelo es viejo *(old)*. Tiene canas pero se ve joven *(he looks young)*.

☀ MOTIVATE

Ask students if they can think of occasions on which it is important to be able to describe someone's appearance. (to point out people in a crowd, to describe a new classmate)

☀ TEACH

PRESENTATION
ASÍ SE DICE

Post pictures from magazines or display Teaching Transparency 6-1. Use phrases from **Así se dice** to describe each person. Point out the use of the definite articles **el, la, los,** and **las** for parts of the body. Model pronunciation and ask students to identify classmates or celebrities who have eyes or hair of a certain color. (¿**Quién tiene los ojos azules? ¿Quién tiene el pelo negro?**)

VOCABULARIO

Have students repeat the captions after you. Then have students describe themselves to a partner. Remind them to make the adjective endings agree.

CHALLENGE

17 Ask students to make the improbable statements into probable ones.

18 ¿Cómo somos?

 With a partner, take turns asking and answering these questions.

MODELO ¿De qué color son tus ojos? Tengo los ojos azules.

1. ¿De qué color son tus ojos?
2. ¿De qué color es tu pelo?
3. ¿De qué color son los ojos de *(name)*?
4. ¿De qué color es el pelo de *(name)*?

VOCABULARIO EXTRA

pelo castaño *brown hair*
pelo rizado *curly hair*
pelo liso *straight hair*
pelo largo *long hair*
pelo corto *short hair*

19 ¿Cómo son tus amigos?

CD 6 Tr. 5 Listen as Rogelio describes some people and his pets to his Aunt Maki. For each item, write the name of the character or characters he is describing. Script and answers on p. 227E

Rebeca

Simón y Quique

Conchita y Gabriel

David

Maki

20 Los amigos de Rogelio

Choose one of Rogelio's friends from the drawings in Activity 19. Write three sentences describing him or her. Include hair and eye color, and say how old he or she is. You can also use words from the **Vocabulario** on page 245. Then write a description of another of Rogelio's friends.

21 Así son

María is telling you about her friends and neighbors. Complete her descriptions using the words below. Make sure to use the right form of the word!

1. Eduardo tiene catorce años. Su hermana tiene trece años. Su hermana es _____. menor
2. Amparo es una chica muy _____. Mide seis pies *(she's six feet tall)*. alta
3. Carlos es _____. Tiene seis años. joven
4. Manuel tiene quince años. Luisa tiene veinte. Luisa es _____. mayor
5. La señora Medina es muy _____ con los niños. cariñosa
6. Daniel es muy _____. Trabaja como modelo *(model)*. atractivo
7. El señor Villa tiene ochenta y cinco años. Él es _____. viejo

cariñoso/a   menor   joven   viejo/a

atractivo/a   mayor   alto/a

Nota cultural

p. 74 Act. 21

Spanish speakers often use special names when they're talking to someone they like a lot. You might use **Juanito** for your friend Juan, or **Rosita** for your friend Rosa. You could call your grandmother **abuelita** and your parents **mami** and **papi**. Other words adults often use to refer to people they care about are **mi cielo** or **mi vida** *(darling* or *dear)*. **Mi hijo/a** doesn't necessarily refer to an actual son or daughter, but to a young person the speaker is very fond of. What affectionate names have you heard people use in English?

Toma la pelota, mi vida.

Estoy lista, papi.

El papá de Cristina es muy cariñoso.

22 Adivina, adivinador

Work in a group of three or more. First choose a movie or TV show the whole group has seen. Take turns describing characters from the movie or show. Your partners must guess who you're describing.

SUGGESTION

22 Have students peer-edit each other's descriptions. Take them up and read them aloud. Have students guess as a class.

LANGUAGE NOTE

Point out that when **joven** becomes plural, it has an accent mark over the *o*. (**jóvenes**)

CULTURE NOTES

Many native speakers use the diminutive forms **abuelita** and **abuelito** when referring to their grandparents. They are similar to the English words *grandma* and *grandpa*.

The diminutive forms **hijito** and **hijita** are not only common for one's own children but for any young person thought of fondly.

ENGLISH LINK

Point out that English can in some instances form diminutives by adding *-y* or *-ette* to words. (doggy, kitty, kitchenette) Ask students if they can think of any other examples.

ART LINK
23 Have students draw a picture of themselves to go with the descriptions they write. You might want to post students' work throughout the class.

PRESENTATION
ASÍ SE DICE
On pairs of cards write infinitive verb phrases of things people do on weekends. (**salir, ir al parque, nadar, hacer un viaje,** etc.) Pass the cards out among students and have them "find their twin" by asking the question **¿Qué haces los fines de semana?** Once they have found their twin, ask each newly-formed pair **¿Qué hacen ustedes los fines de semana?** Use gestures to make sure it's clear to students that their answers should be in the **nosotros** form. Follow up with Activity 24 and Additional Listening Activity 6-3. Or, display Transparency 6-2 and have students describe what the families do together.

23 El anuario

Imagine that you're a member of the Spanish club. You've decided to have a page in your school yearbook with descriptions of all the club members. First, write a description of yourself using at least five sentences. Include what you look like and how old you are. Describe your personality. You can also use vocabulary from pages 245 and 246. Then write three sentences describing the club's sponsor.

VOCABULARIO EXTRA

egoísta   *selfish*

perezoso/a   *lazy*

trabajador/a   *hard-working*

What do you think these words mean?

agresivo/a   desorganizado/a
artístico/a   generoso/a
atlético/a   responsable
creativo/a   independiente
             tímido/a

p. 69
Act. 13

6-2

ASÍ SE DICE   Discussing things a family does together

To find out what a family does together, ask:

¿Qué hacen ustedes los fines de semana? *What do you do on weekends?*

Some responses might be:

Salimos juntos y **visitamos a** nuestros abuelos. **Casi siempre cenamos** con ellos los domingos. *We go out together and visit our grandparents. We almost always eat dinner with them on Sundays.*

¿Hacen ustedes **algo** durante el verano? *Do you do something in the summer?*

Sí. Siempre **hacemos un viaje.** *Yes. We always take a trip.*

24 Lupe y Víctor

Lupe is curious about her friend Víctor's family. Complete their conversation with the words from the word box.

LUPE   ¿Qué ___1___ ustedes los fines de semana?

VÍCTOR   Los fines de semana ___2___ juntos a pasear en la plaza. A veces, si tenemos dinero, ___3___ en un restaurante. Mi restaurante favorito sirve *(serves)* ___4___ mexicana. Casi siempre visitamos a mis tíos Elena y Juan los sábados por la tarde.

LUPE   ¿Y hacen ustedes ___5___ durante el verano?

VÍCTOR   Siempre ___6___ algo. A veces hacemos un ___7___ a las montañas o a la playa.   Answers on p. 227K

cenamos
hacen
comida
salimos
hacemos
viaje
algo

GRAMÁTICA The verbs **hacer** and **salir**

pp. 48–49
Acts. 8–9

Hacer *(to do, make)* and **salir** *(to go out)* are regular verbs in the present tense except in the **yo** form, which has an irregular **-go** ending.

(yo)	hag**o**	(nosotros) (nosotras)	hac**emos**
(tú)	hac**es**	(vosotros) (vosotras)	hac**éis**
(usted) (él) (ella)	hac**e**	(ustedes) (ellos) (ellas)	hac**en**
	sal**go**		sal**imos**
	sal**es**		sal**ís**
	sal**e**		sal**en**

25 Con la familia Script and answers on p. 227E

CD 6 Tr. 6

Listen as four friends discuss what they do with their families and friends. Match the description you hear with the correct photo.

PRESENTATION
GRAMÁTICA

Teach students the following rhyme:
**Salir y hacer
como tú puedes ver
en la forma de yo
terminan en -go.
En las otras personas
no hay que olvidar
que la conjugación
es muy regular.**

PRELISTENING

25 As a prelistening activity, have students list phrases or expressions they're likely to hear according to the pictures. As they listen, have them check the phrases off.

LANGUAGE NOTE

The verbs **ir** and **salir** are often followed by **a** plus a destination. Often, when an infinitive comes between the conjugated verb and the destination, the preposition **a** does not change if the speaker wants to stress motion toward that destination. (**Salimos a jugar al parque. Voy a estudiar a la biblioteca.**)

26 El verano

Look at the cartoon and answer the questions based on what you see and read.   Answers in side column

1. ¿Dónde están los chicos?
2. ¿Qué hacen?
3. ¿Dónde están los tiburones (sharks)? (Hint: **Mar** means sea.)

27 ¿Qué haces cuando sales? Answers will vary.

Contesta estas preguntas personales. Escribe oraciones completas.

MODELO   Casi siempre salgo al parque los fines de semana.

1. ¿Sales los fines de semana?
2. ¿Qué te gusta hacer cuando sales?
3. ¿Con quién o con quiénes sales?
4. ¿Qué te gusta hacer cuando sales con tu familia?
5. Si no sales, ¿qué haces?

GV
p. 49
Act. 10

NOTA GRAMATICAL

After most verbs, a "personal a" is used with nouns referring to people and pets. When referring to a place or thing, no "a" is used.

Visito **a** mis tíos en Guatemala todos los veranos. Cuando estoy con ellos, siempre visitamos las ruinas mayas.

28 Visitas

Complete the sentences that need the "personal **a.**" If the sentence doesn't need it, write "no personal **a**" on your paper.

1. Visitamos ===== nuestros primos tres veces por mes. a
2. Mario va a ver ===== la Exhibición de Arte con su hermana. no personal **a**
3. Llamo ===== mis abuelos todos los domingos. a
4. Voy a visitar ===== mis amigos en Colorado este verano. a
5. Paula quiere conocer ===== unos nuevos amigos este año. a
6. Miro ===== la televisión con mi familia por la noche. no personal **a**

29 ¿Con qué frecuencia?

Use the following questions to interview a partner about his or her family, or about an imaginary family. Switch roles and be prepared to report your findings to the class.

1. ¿Dónde vives? ¿Quiénes viven contigo?
2. ¿Sales con tu familia los fines de semana? ¿Adónde van ustedes y qué hacen?
3. ¿Con quién vas al centro comercial? ¿Cómo se llama el centro comercial?
4. ¿Con qué frecuencia visitas a (tus abuelos, tus primos...)?
5. ¿A tu familia le gusta pescar, acampar, bucear o hacer esquí acuático? ¿Qué les gusta hacer?

30 Los hermanos

Together with a partner, read the descriptions of **la hermana mayor, la "chica sándwich"** (middle child), and **el hermano menor.** Imagine that you're one of the three pictured and describe yourself to your partner. See if your partner can guess if you're the oldest, the youngest, or the middle child in the family.

TRES HERMANOS, TRES PERSONALIDADES

Retrato de "la mayor". Madura, responsable, trabajadora y organizada.

Retrato de "la chica sándwich". Es completamente diferente de sus hermanos.

Retrato de "el baby de la familia". Es simpático, alegre y divertido, pero nada responsable.

ADDITIONAL PRACTICE
29 Teach the words for street (**la calle**), avenue (**la avenida**), and boulevard (**el paseo**) so that students will be able to give their addresses when asked **¿Dónde vives?** Teach them to say the street name first and then the number.

☀ CLOSE

Use Teaching Transparency 6-2 to review descriptive adjectives and terms presented in the **paso.** Ask students questions and elicit appropriate answers with these terms.

☀ ASSESS

▸ Testing Program, pp. 93–94
 Quiz 6-2
 Audio CD 6, Tr. 20

▸ Grammar and Vocabulary Quizzes
 Quiz 6-2A or
 Alternative Quiz 6-2A

▸ Alternative Assessment Guide, p. 24

PERFORMANCE ASSESSMENT
Ask each student to develop a set of interview questions to find out about someone's family and what they like to do. Then ask them to interview someone in the class using their list of questions. Students should be sure to use questions and expressions from **Así se dice** on pages 245 and 248. For additional Performance Assessment ideas, see Situation Cards 6-2.

Énlaces

EL ARTE

La familia   The word "family" has different meanings for different people. **La familia extendida** (extended family) includes relatives such as grandparents, aunts and uncles, and cousins. When Spanish speakers talk about **mi familia**, they often include their extended family.

Look at the two portraits of families, one by Miguel Cabrera and the other by Joan Miró. Miguel Cabrera lived in Mexico in the 1700s. He is famous for his paintings of families. Joan Miró, born near Barcelona, Spain, in 1893, is famous for his playful drawings and paintings.

Answers on p. 227K

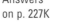 **La familia y el arte**

Work with a partner to answer these questions about the family portraits.

1. How many people are in each family?

2. Identify the family members.

3. Which portrait do you like the most and why?

2 **Un dibujo**

Draw a picture of your idea of family. Show your drawing to a classmate and explain it. How does your drawing compare to your classmate's?

Miguel Cabrera, *De Español y d'India, Mestisa,* 1763, 132 x 101 cm.
México, Colección Particular

Joan Miró, *La Familia,* 1924, Chalk on glass paper. 29 1/2" x 41", The Museum of Modern Art, New York

LA HISTORIA

Un árbol genealógico   Have you ever seen your own family tree? How many relatives can you think of in your family? Where do they go on your tree? Family trees can be drawn in many different ways. Gabriela's family tree goes from the top (the past) down the page to the present. Complete the family tree by figuring out the missing relatives. Copy the tree on your own paper to complete it.

La familia de Gabriela

3 ¿Cómo se llaman?   Answers on p. 227K

1. ¿Cómo se llaman los hermanos de Gabriela?
2. ¿Cómo se llaman sus abuelos paternos (los padres de su padre)?
3. ¿Cómo se llama la tía de Gabriela?

4 La familia de Gabriela   Answers on p. 227K

1. El hermano de Juan es Antonio. Escribe su nombre completo en tu copia del árbol genealógico.
2. El primo de Gabriela es Pablo. Escribe su nombre completo en tu copia del árbol genealógico.

5 ¡Te toca a ti!

Work with a partner to draw your own real family trees or imaginary ones. Come up with your own symbols for events like marriage, divorce, death, and other events that affect your family. Compare your trees with those of other classmates.

ENLACES

doscientos cincuenta y tres   253

ADDITIONAL PRACTICE
3 After finishing this activity, students answer the questions in Spanish as if they were taking a survey, substituting their names for Gabriela's name. For the second question, students may choose to write about **los abuelos maternos de** _____ (**los padres de su madre**) and for the third question they may talk about **el tío** if they wish.

TEACHER NOTE
5 Allow students to talk about and draw an imaginary family if they feel uncomfortable talking about and drawing their own family.

SLOWER PACE
5 Ask volunteers how many brothers and sisters they have. Have them write the real or imaginary names of their brothers and sisters. Then lead a brainstorming session in which students suggest symbols for marriage, divorce, death, and other events. Finally, draw your family tree (or an imaginary one) as a further example. Then have students work in pairs to make their own family trees.

CHALLENGE
5 Have students present their family trees to the class in Spanish.

VIDEO INTEGRATION

Adelante LEVEL 1A

Video Program
Videocassette 2, 40:58–41:06 OR
Videocassette 3, 59:53–60:01
(captioned version)

¡Ven conmigo! LEVEL 1
DVD Tutor, Disc 1

Bell work
On the board or on a transparency write the following scrambled expressions:
1. **ecahr nu jeavi**, 2. **tarivis a ols obeausl**, and 3. **rlias raap reocm**. Ask students to unscramble them to find three things they might do with their families. (1. **hacer un viaje**, 2. **visitar a los abuelos**, 3. **salir para comer**)

SUGGESTION
31 Show the video without sound and ask students to try to remember what's happening in the story at this point.

☀ MOTIVATE

Ask students to think of advice they might give to their family and friends. Ask them to share some of those things they already know how to say in Spanish.

TERCER PASO Storytelling Book pp. 23, 24

WV3 FLORIDA-6

Discussing problems and giving advice

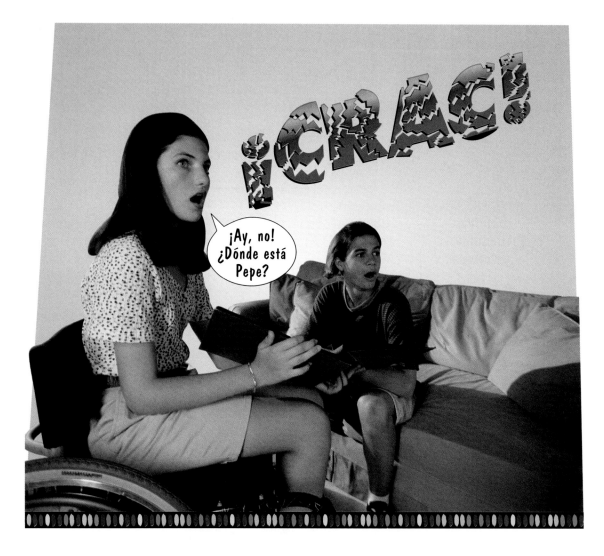

31 Pepe, el travieso
Answer these questions based on what you see in the photo.
1. What do you think happened in the photo? Pepe, the dog, broke something.
2. What does Raquel say to show she's surprised and upset? ¡Ay, no! ¿Dónde está Pepe?
3. What problem does she possibly have now? She might need to clean up the mess that the dog made.

ASÍ SE DICE Discussing problems and giving advice

PA pp. 70–71 Acts. 14–15

To discuss a problem, say:

Tengo un problema. El profesor **dice que** hablo **demasiado** en clase, **pero no es cierto. ¿Qué debo hacer?**
I have a problem. The teacher says that I talk too much in class, but it's not true. What should I do?

Your friend might answer:

Debes hablar **menos** en clase y escuchar más.
You should talk less in class and listen more.

NOTA GRAMATICAL

CD-ROM DISC 2

The verb **deber** *(should, ought to)* is a regular **-er** verb.

(yo)	deb**o**	(nosotros) (nosotras)	deb**emos**
(tú)	deb**es**	(vosotros) (vosotras)	deb**éis**
(usted)		(ustedes)	
(él)	deb**e**	(ellos)	deb**en**
(ella)		(ellas)	

GV p. 50 Acts. 11–12

32 El consejo

You love to give advice, even to yourself! Complete each sentence with the correct form of **deber**.

1. Mi hermano _____ hacer su tarea. debe
2. Yo _____ organizar mis cosas para el colegio. debo
3. Rita y Naomi _____ escuchar a la profesora. deben
4. Tú y yo _____ comer el desayuno antes de ir al colegio. debemos
5. Tú _____ practicar para la clase de piano. debes
6. Efraín y Saúl _____ cuidar a su hermana menor todos los miércoles por la tarde. deben

33 Los problemas de Mónica Script and answers on p. 227F

CD 6 Tr. 7

Listen as Mónica describes her family. Then match a photo below to each description you hear. One of her relatives isn't pictured. Who is it?

1. Mónica
2. su mamá
3. su hermana
4. su tía

a

b

c

※ TEACH

PRESENTATION
ASÍ SE DICE
Read the problem and question from column 1 and have a student reply with the advice in column 2. Repeat this two or three times. Then ask students to practice the new expressions in pairs, using a new problem and new advice.

NOTA GRAMATICAL
Explain **deber** in Spanish as follows: **El verbo *deber* es un verbo regular que termina en -er. Se usa con el infinitivo: Debemos hablar español en clase.** Have students list five things they should and shouldn't do to do well in school. They work in pairs to compare lists. Ask one student **¿Qué debes hacer para ser buen estudiante?** He or she should reply **(No) debo _____.** Then ask **¿Qué deben hacer ustedes?** to the other partner. He or she should answer with **Nosotros (no) debemos _____.**

PRELISTENING
33 As a prelistening activity, ask students what problems they see in the photos.

34 ¿Qué deben hacer?

Think about what you heard Mónica say about her family's problems in Activity 33. Match the columns to identify each person's problems. Then suggest a solution from the phrases below.

Persona
1. La mamá de Mónica
2. La hermana de Mónica
3. Mónica

Problema
a. estudia todo el tiempo
b. toca la guitarra muy mal
c. trabaja demasiado

3, b Debe practicar más.   1, c Debe descansar más.

2, a Debe salir con amigos a veces.

VOCABULARIO

p. 72 Act. 17

Los quehaceres domésticos   *Household chores*

p. 51 Acts. 13–15

6-C

 cortar el césped

 trabajar en el jardín

 hacer la cama

 limpiar la cocina

 pasar la aspiradora en la sala

 poner la mesa

 cuidar al gato

 planchar

35 El sábado · Script and answers on p. 227F

Today is Saturday and Luisa and her family have made some plans. First, read the list of activities below. Then, listen as they tell about their plans. Answer **sí** for every activity Luisa is going to do, and answer **no** for each activity she isn't going to do.

CD 6 Tr. 8

1. cuidar al gato
2. patinar en línea
3. hacer la cama
4. limpiar la cocina
5. cortar el césped
6. desayunar

NOTA GRAMATICAL

On page 249, you learned the verbs **hacer** and **salir**. The verb **poner** also has **–go** in the **yo** form. **Poner** means *to put, to place,* or *to set (a table).*

p. 52
Acts.
16–17

(yo)	pon**go**	(nosotros) (nosotras)	pon**emos**
(tú)	pon**es**	(vosotros) (vosotras)	pon**éis**
(usted) (él) (ella)	pon**e**	(ustedes) (ellos) (ellas)	pon**en**

Pongo la mesa todos los días. Mi hermanita nunca la **pone.**

36 ¿Dónde lo pongo?

A friend is staying with you for a few weeks and wants to know where you put all the stuff at your house. Complete the sentences with the correct form of **poner.** Answers in side column

1. Yo _____ mis libros en el escritorio en mi cuarto.
2. Papá _____ las zapatillas debajo de la cama.
3. Mi hermana y yo siempre _____ la ropa en el armario.
4. Martín y Daniel _____ sus libros en el estante.
5. Lola _____ el gato en el patio.
6. _____ mis lápices y cuadernos en mi mochila.

37 ¿Qué pasa aquí? · Answers on p. 227K

Get together with a partner. For each drawing, write two sentences. In the first sentence tell what the person should not be doing. In the second sentence tell what the person should be doing. Compare your sentences with your partner's.

MODELO   Pablo no debe poner la mesa en su cama.
               Debe poner la mesa en la cocina.

a. Pablo   b. Diana y Lola   c. Federico   d. Miguelito   e. Frida

TERCER PASO

doscientos cincuenta y siete **257**

CAPÍTULO 6

PRESENTATION

NOTA GRAMATICAL
Write the paradigms of **hacer** and **salir** side by side in vertical columns on the board. In a third column, add the forms of **poner** as you use them in sentences. **(En mi casa, nunca pongo la mesa. ¿Pones la mesa en tu casa?)** Model pronunciation and then elicit sentences with forms of **poner** from students.

AUDITORY LEARNERS

37 Do this as a listening activity with the following script. Have students match each photo with the correct sentence. Emphasize the italicized words.

1. No debe pasar aspiradora *en el césped.* (**c**)
2. No debe poner la mesa *en la cama.* (**a**)
3. Deben trabajar *en el jardín.* (**b**)
4. Debe *sacar* la basura. (**d**)
5. Debe cuidar *al gato.* (**e**)

Answers to Activity 36

1. pongo
2. pone
3. ponemos
4. ponen
5. pone
6. Pongo

ADDITIONAL PRACTICE
38 Have students assign chores to people in their house, according to what members of their family like to do. (**Mi hermano debe lavar los platos porque come mucho.**)

GAME
Tell students you are **el sabio** or **la sabia** *(the wise one)*. Offer to help them with an imaginary problem they have. Provide them with a suitable answer. After you have modeled this several times, have a student take your place as **el sabio** or **la sabia**.

CHALLENGE
39 Have students write their own letters to an advice columnist about a simple problem, real or imaginary. Students exchange letters and write responses offering each other advice.

38 ¡Todo bajo control!

You're assigning everyone a chore using phrases from the **Vocabulario** on page 256. Try to assign each person the chore he or she likes. Some people may have more than one job. Answers on p. 227K

MODELO   A mí me gusta tener el cuarto organizado.
Debo limpiar mi cuarto.

1. A ti y a tu hermana menor les gustan los animales.
2. A tus abuelitos les gustan las plantas.
3. A tu primo le gusta pasar el rato con tus hermanos menores.
4. A tu hermano mayor le gusta la comida.
5. A ti te gusta estar afuera *(outside)* y te gustan las máquinas *(machines)*.
6. A Ana y a ti les gusta tener la ropa bonita.

39 Querida Amalia

A Read this letter that was written to a newspaper advice columnist.

Querida Amalia,
Nosotros vivimos en una casa muy bonita, pero nunca se ve bien porque mis hermanitos no limpian la casa. Yo no tengo mucho tiempo libre. El problema es que mis padres dicen que yo nunca ayudo en casa. ¿Qué debo hacer?
Un cordial saludo de,
Una chica trabajadora

B Now help complete the letter with Amalia's advice. Use the words below. Each word will be used only once.

2 quehaceres
3 limpia
1 ayudar
4 cocina
5 trabajan
6 bonita

Querida Chica trabajadora,
¡Qué bueno que quieres ___1___!
Pregúntale a tu mamá por qué no divide los ___2___. Cada semana alguien ___3___ la sala, y todos los días otra persona limpia la ___4___ después de cenar. De esa forma ustedes ___5___ un poco, y tienen una casa limpia y ___6___.
Atentamente,
Amalia

40 Una encuesta

Take a survey of five classmates. Ask them what chores they do around the house. Using **dice que...**, write five sentences reporting what your classmates say. Be prepared to share your survey with the class.

41 En mi cuaderno

Write a description of two friends or family members from a book, movie, or TV series. Include their ages, where they live, and what they're like. Next, describe any problems they may have, such as household chores they don't like doing, or problems they have at home or at school. Finally, give them some advice about what to do. Write at least ten sentences in your journal.

Leonardo dice que lava los platos todos los días.

LETRA Y SONIDO

Script on p. 227F

CD 6
Trs. 9–13

A. The **r** in Spanish does not sound like the *r* in English. English does have a sound that is similar, however. It's the sound made by quickly touching the tip of the tongue to the ridge behind the upper teeth, as in bu*tt*er, ba*tt*er, la*dd*er.

1. The **r** is pronounced this way between vowels.

cariñoso   cara   moreno   favorito   pero

2. At the beginning of a word or after an **n** or **l**, the single **r** has a trilled or rolled sound. It is also usually trilled at the end of a word.

rojo   rubio   enrojecer   Enrique   alrededor

3. The double **r** in Spanish always has a trilled or rolled sound.

pelirrojo   perro   carro   correo

B. Dictado
Listen to a TV ad that features a famous athlete, Rafael Ramírez. Write what you hear.

C. Trabalenguas
La rata roe la ropa del rey de Roma.

VIDEO INTEGRATION

Adelante LEVEL 1A
Video Program
Videocassette 2, 50:31–52:08

¡Ven conmigo! LEVEL 1
DVD Tutor, Disc 1

TEACHER NOTES
- See *Video Guide* for activities related to the **Panorama cultural**.
- Remind students that cultural information may be included in the Quizzes and Chapter Test.
- The language of the people interviewed represents informal, unrehearsed speech. Occasionally, text has been edited for clarity.

MOTIVATING ACTIVITY
Ask students to think about the number of people in their family. Ask them if they have an opinion on how big a family should be. Ask students what sorts of things they enjoy doing with their families. Would they like to spend more or less time with them? Why? Would they like to spend more time with their grandparents if they could? Why or why not?

Panorama cultural

CD 6
Trs. 14–17

¿Cuántas personas hay en tu familia?

In this chapter, we asked some people about their families and what they do to help around the house.

Hay cuatro personas en la familia de Melisa. ¿Cuántos son en tu familia?

●Melisa
Santo Domingo de Heredia, Costa Rica
CD 6 Tr. 15

Somos cuatro. Mi mamá, mi papá, mi hermano y yo. [Mi hermano y yo] peleamos mucho a veces.

Pablo trabaja bastante en casa. ¿Y tú? ¿Qué haces en casa? ¿Tienes hermanos que ayudan?

●Pablo
Quito, Ecuador
CD 6 Tr. 16

En mi familia hay cinco personas. Yo lavo los platos, eh... limpio la cocina, arreglo mi cuarto y limpio mi baño.

En la familia de Éric hay siete personas.
¡Claro que hay mucho que hacer en casa!

● **Éric** CD 6 Tr. 17
Ponce,
Puerto Rico

Somos siete:
mis dos hermanas y tres
hermanos. Tengo un hermano
menor. Algunas veces tengo
que cuidarlo.

1 ¿Cuántos hermanos tiene Melisa? un hermano

2 ¿Se llevan bien Melisa y su hermano? ¿Cómo lo
sabes? *(How do you know?)* No. Pelean muchas veces.

3 ¿Cuántos son en la familia de Pablo? cinco

4 ¿Cuáles son tres de los quehaceres que hace Pablo?
Possible answers: Lava los platos, limpia el baño y limpia su cuarto.

5 ¿Cuántos hermanos mayores tiene Éric? dos hermanos

6 ¿Cómo ayuda Éric en casa? Cuida a su hermano menor.

Para pensar y hablar...

A. Of the three interviewees, whose family is most like your
own? Name two ways in which that interviewee's family is
like yours.

B. Pablo mentions several chores he does at home. With
a partner, talk about how you help out at home. Use
Spanish to describe the chores you do. Use the vocabulary on page 256.

Cuaderno para
hispanohablantes,
p. 29

PRESENTATION
After showing the video,
have students assume the
identity of one of the interviewees. Ask the question
¿Cuántos son en tu familia?
Have students answer
based on their new identity.
Encourage students to
answer without looking at
their books. Stress that the
fluency of the exchange is
more important than providing the exact information.

CRITICAL THINKING
Have students deduce the
meaning of **peleamos.** *(we
fight)* They should first be able
to identify it as a verb, then as
a verb in the **nosotros** form.

VAMOS A LEER

READING STRATEGY
Using pictures, titles, and sub-titles to determine the organization of a passage

MOTIVATING ACTIVITY
Have students skim the reading to find words they already know. (**parque, restaurante, frutas**)

⚜ PREREADING

 RE-ENTRY

A After students have skimmed for the answers to **¡A comenzar!**, review vocabulary by asking **¿Te gusta la comida china? ¿Te gustan los restaurantes chinos? ¿Te gusta probar comida nueva? ¿Les gusta bailar? ¿Dónde bailan ustedes?**

NATIVE SPEAKERS
Ask native speakers to discuss traditional customs that their family or friends observe. Ask them if they know how these traditions began.

LANGUAGE NOTE
The word **parador** comes from the verb **parar** (to stop).

🌐 CULTURE NOTE
Flamenco originated in 18th-century Spain in the southern region of **Andalucía**. Today, flamenco is very popular throughout the Spanish-speaking world and beyond.

Estrategia

Using context and cognates Sometimes you encounter words you haven't learned yet. Look at an unknown word to see if it looks like an English word. Also use the words surrounding the unknown word, or its context, to help you guess its meaning.

¡A comenzar!

A This reading is from the **Guía oficial de la Pequeña Habana**, a guide for tourists in Miami. Skim it to find out which of these items is not among the four suggestions.

- buying fruit
- watching a cultural dance
- ⊙ visiting museums
- playing dominoes
- eating Chinese-Cuban food

Al grano

B You've already studied two important ways to guess the meanings of words: using cognates and using context. Now you can combine these two skills to read more effectively.

Cognates. See if an unknown word looks like an English word. Does the English meaning make sense in context?

Context. Look at all the words before and after the word you don't know. Understanding the rest of the sentence will help you guess what the unknown word means.

C Your family needs help reading the guide. Listed here are the words they're having trouble with. The first two words in each item are cognates. You can guess the third word through context. Go back and be sure your guess makes sense with the rest of the sentence.

1. Your brother might like to try a game of dominoes. Help him with these words:
   cognates: **espectáculo, interrumpe**
   context: **cafetín** (a. caffeine b. game ⓒ café)
2. Help your mother with these words about the Chinese-Cuban restaurant:
   cognates: **tradiciones, numerosos**
   context: **probar** (a. break b. prepare ⓒ taste)
3. Your sister is trying to decide if she wants to watch a flamenco performance.
   cognates: **fabulosos, movimientos**
   context: **cuerpo** (a. handsome ⓑ body c. carpet)
4. You have decided to buy some fruit. Decide what these words mean:
   cognates: **variedades, coco**
   context: **paradores** (ⓐ roadside stands b. walls c. parades)

D Write a list in Spanish of four interesting things you can do where you live. Then discuss these activities with a partner.

La Pequeña Habana

VER UN BAILE FLAMENCO

El flamenco es una danza expresiva y emocionante. Es una celebración de la forma del cuerpo humano. Tradicional en España, el flamenco es un espectáculo que se presenta diariamente en fabulosos restaurantes de la Pequeña Habana, como el Málaga.

JUGAR DOMINÓ EN EL PARQUE DEL DOMINÓ

Éste es un espectáculo que no tiene igual en todos los Estados Unidos. Los hombres se reúnen alrededor de las mesas de dominó para jugar. Aquí los hombres (no hay mujeres) juegan casi sin hablar. Sólo se interrumpe el juego para ir al cafetín de al lado y comprarse un fuerte café cubano.

IR A UN RESTAURANTE CHINO-CUBANO Y PROBAR SUS PLATOS

Durante los años de 1800 a 1900, muchos chinos llegaron a Cuba como esclavos y combinaron su cultura con la cultura cubana. Todavía se mantienen las tradiciones de la cocina china en los numerosos restaurantes aquí en la Pequeña Habana.

COMPRAR DIFERENTES VARIEDADES DE FRUTAS

Abundan mangos, papayas, mameyes, cocos, plátanos, bananas, naranjas y toronjas en diferentes tiendas y paradores.

Cuaderno para hispanohablantes, pp. 26–28

☀ READING

B and **C** Have students do Activity B as individual work. If needed, this may be assigned as homework. Emphasize the importance of testing a word in context, even if the word is a cognate. Other words you may want your students to guess: **espectáculo, esclavos, diariamente.**

☀ POSTREADING

D If this task is challenging to some students, assign pairs so that one of each pair is able to help the other.

GROUP WORK

Have students construct a bulletin board about interesting things to do in your community. Decide on five locations. Then assign each one to a group. Each group prepares the Spanish description of a location and brings in photographs.

COMMUNITY LINK

Ask students to interview a local grocer to find out which fruits are grown in their area and which are imported.

The **Repaso** reviews and integrates all four skills and culture in preparation for the Chapter Test.

ADDITIONAL PRACTICE
Have students clip comic strips from the newspaper and cover the speech bubbles. Exchanging comics, students can then use Spanish to describe a problem and tell what should be done.

Answers to Activity 3
Answers will vary. Possible answers:

A **padrino** is a godfather and a **madrina** is a godmother.

Godparents provide love, support, and advice for their godchild.

Godparents are usually very close with the parents of their godchild and are often considered part of the family.

 REPASO

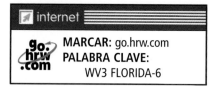

1 First read the statements about Marcos and his family. Then listen as Marcos describes his family. Match a family member with each numbered item. *Script and answers on p. 227F*

CD 6 Tr. 18

1. Es un poco gordo.
2. Debe trabajar menos.
3. Ella es inteligente.
4. Tiene un cuarto organizado.
5. Es músico (a musician).
6. Debe estudiar más.

2 Complete the following letter with words from the box. Make sure to use the correct form of the verbs.

1. prima
2. alta
3. hermanos
4. delgado
5. gato
6. vive
7. ayudamos
8. Tengo
9. viaje

viaje · vivir · primo/a · tener · delgado/a · ayudar · gato/a · hermanos/as · alto/a

¡Hola!

Me llamo Carolina. Soy tu __1__ . Tengo doce años. Soy morena y tengo los ojos de color café. Soy __2__ y un poco gorda. Tengo dos __3__ , Guillermo y Paco. Paco tiene catorce años y es muy __4__ . Guillermo tiene cinco años y es travieso pero cariñoso. Tenemos un __5__ . Se llama Nacho.

Mi familia __6__ en una casa grande. Todos __7__ a limpiar la casa. __8__ un cuarto muy bonito. ¿Y tú? ¿Cómo es tu casa? ¿Y tu familia? Siempre hacemos un __9__ durante el verano. ¡Algún día te visitamos!

Saludos,
Carolina

3 Work with a partner. What are a **padrino** and **madrina**? Explain two things about this relationship. *Answers in side column*

4 Your drama class is going to write a one-act comedy about a large family. Your task is to describe the cast of characters. Tell how many there are, where they live, their names, ages, and what each one looks like. Also say what each is like or what things each one likes.

MODELO El abuelo se llama Pablo. Tiene setenta y ocho años. Tiene canas y tiene los ojos de color café. Es muy inteligente. A él le gusta...

5 # Vamos a escribir

Answer your pen pal Carolina's letter. Write at least two paragraphs. In the first paragraph, describe your family and yourself. In the second paragraph, tell Carolina what you do with your family. You may write a third paragraph with anything else you want to say. Use an appropriate closing.

Estrategia

Writing a letter When writing a personal letter, always start with the date and then the salutation or greeting. Some salutations you might use include **Hola...**, **Querido/a....** Remember to indent the first line of each paragraph. Finally, write a closing such as **Saludos,** *(Greetings),* **Abrazos,** *(Hugs),* **Recuerdos,** *(Regards),* followed by a comma. Write your name directly under the closing.

> 3 de julio de _____
> Querida _____,
> _____
> _____
> _____
>
> Saludos,

6

 # SITUACIÓN

It's summer, and your pen pal Carolina has come from Miami to visit for a week. Introduce her to your family. Be sure to tell what activities your family does together. Ask Carolina about her family.

> Cuaderno para hispanohablantes, p. 29

PORTFOLIO

4 Oral You might have students work in groups to create a dialogue for their one-act comedy. They might then perform their work for the class and record it for their oral Portfolio. For Portfolio information, see *Alternative Assessment Guide,* p. 17.

5 Written Your students may wish to enclose their letter to Carolina as an addition to their Portfolio. For Portfolio suggestions, see *Assessment Guide,* p. 17.

This page is intended to help students prepare for the Chapter Test. It is designed for the students to work on their own initiative and consists of a brief checklist of the major points covered in the chapter. The students should be reminded that it is only a checklist and does not necessarily include everything that will appear on the Chapter Test.

Answers to Question 3

Answers will vary. Possible answers:

a. Su abuelo tiene canas. Es viejo y delgado y es muy cariñoso.

b. Su mamá tiene pelo negro y trabaja en el jardín.

c. Toño tiene pelo negro y ojos de color café. Es cómico.

d. Óscar es moreno. Tiene pelo negro y es travieso.

  A VER SI PUEDO...

WV3 FLORIDA-6

▼ **Can you describe a family?** p. 236

1 Can you tell Ramiro, a new student at your school. . .?   Answers will vary.

1. how many people there are in your family
2. how many brothers and sisters you have
3. what the names of your family members are
4. what they like to do in their free time

2 Can you complete each sentence with the correct family member?

1. La mamá de mi papá es mi ___abuela___.
2. El hijo de mi tía es mi ___primo___.
3. La hija de mis padres es mi ___hermana___.
4. El hermano de mi mamá es mi ___tío___.

▼ **Can you describe people?** p. 245

3 Describe these members of Florencia's family.   Answers in side column

a. su abuelo

b. su mamá

c. su hermano, Toño

d. su hermano, Óscar

▼ **Can you discuss things a family does together?** p. 248

4 Can you tell someone . . .?   Answers on p. 227K

1. how often your family has dinner together
2. who your family visits and how often you visit
3. where your family goes on outings

▼ **Can you discuss problems and give advice?** p. 255

5 Paula and her family need help solving these problems. What should each person do?   Answers on p. 227K

1. Her sister is disorganized and can't find any of her things.
2. Paula's brother works all the time and he's very tired.
3. It's six o'clock in the evening and everyone's hungry.

VOCABULARIO

PRIMER PASO

Describing a family

la abuela   *grandmother*
el abuelo   *grandfather*
los abuelos   *grandparents*
¿Cómo es tu familia?   *What is your family like?*
¿Cuántas personas hay en tu familia?   *How many people are there in your family?*
la esposa   *wife*
el esposo   *husband*
éstas   *these (feminine)*
éstos   *these (masc., masc. and fem.)*
la familia   *family*
el gato   *cat*
la hermana   *sister*
la hermanastra   *stepsister*
el hermanastro   *stepbrother*
el hermano   *brother*
los hermanos   *brothers, brothers and sisters*
la hija   *daughter*
el hijo   *son*
los hijos   *children*
la madrastra   *stepmother*
la madre/mamá   *mother/mom*
la media hermana   *half sister*
el medio hermano   *half brother*
mi/mis   *my*
nuestro/a   *our*
el padrastro   *stepfather*
el padre/papá   *father/dad*
los padres   *parents*
la prima   *female cousin*
el primo   *male cousin*
los primos   *cousins*
ser unido   *to be close-knit*
Somos cinco.   *There are five of us.*
su/sus   *his, her, their, your (formal)*
la tía   *aunt*
el tío   *uncle*
tu/tus   *your (familiar)*
unido/a   *close-knit*
vivir   *to live*
vuestro/a   *your (pl., Spain)*

SEGUNDO PASO

Describing people

azul   *blue*
cariñoso/a   *affectionate*
de color café   *brown*
¿De qué color es/son...?   *What color is/are . . .?*
delgado/a   *thin*
listo/a   *clever, smart (with **ser**)*
mayor   *older*
menor   *younger*
negro/a   *black*
los ojos   *eyes*
pelirrojo/a   *redheaded*
el pelo   *hair*
un poco gordo/a   *a little overweight*
Se ve joven.   *He/She looks young.*
Tiene canas.   *He/She has gray hair.*
Tiene los ojos verdes/azules.   *He/She has green/blue eyes.*
travieso/a   *mischievous*
verde   *green*
viejo/a   *old*

Discussing things a family does together

algo   *something*
casi siempre   *almost always*
cenar   *to eat dinner*
hacer un viaje   *to take a trip*

¿Qué hacen ustedes los fines de semana?   *What do you do on weekends?*
salir   *to go out, to leave*
visitar   *to visit*

TERCER PASO

Discussing problems and giving advice

cortar el césped   *to cut the grass*
cuidar al gato   *to take care of the cat*
deber   *should, ought to*
Debes...   *You should . . .*
demasiado   *too much*
dice que   *he/she says that*
hacer la cama   *to make the bed*
limpiar la cocina   *to clean the kitchen*
menos   *less*
No es cierto.   *It's not true.*
pasar la aspiradora   *to vacuum*
planchar   *to iron*
poner la mesa   *to set the table*
un problema   *a problem*
¿Qué debo hacer?   *What should I do?*
los quehaceres domésticos   *household chores*
la sala   *living room*
trabajar en el jardín   *to work in the garden*

GAME
El ritmo See pages 227I–227J for this game and others to review vocabulary.

CHAPTER 6 ASSESSMENT

▶ **Testing Program**
Chapter Test, pp. 97–104
Audio Compact Discs, CD 6, Trs. 22–23
Speaking Test, p. 114

▶ **Alternative Assessment Guide**
Performance Assessment, p. 24
Portfolio Assessment, p. 17
CD-ROM Assessment, p. 31

▶ **Interactive CD-ROM Tutor, Disc 2**

¡A hablar!
¡A escribir!

▶ **Standardized Assessment Tutor**
Chapter 6

▶ **One-Stop Planner, Disc 2**
Test Generator
Chapter 6

▶ **Final Exam**
Testing Program, pp. 125–136
Audio CD 6 Trs. 24–26

SUMMARY OF FUNCTIONS

Functions are probably best defined as the ways in which you use a language for particular purposes. When you find yourself in specific situations, such as in a restaurant, in a grocery store, or at a school, you'll want to communicate with those around you. In order to do that, you have to "function" in Spanish: you place an order, buy something, or talk about your class schedule.

Such language functions form the core of this book. They're easily identified by the boxes in each chapter labeled **Así se dice**. The functional phrases in these boxes are the building blocks you need to become a speaker of Spanish. All the other features in the chapter—the grammar, the vocabulary, even the culture notes—are there to support the functions you're learning.

Here is a list of the functions presented in this book and the Spanish expressions you'll need in order to communicate in a wide range of situations. Following each function is the chapter and page number where it was introduced.

SOCIALIZING

Saying hello   Ch. 1, p. 27

Buenos días.	Buenas noches.
Buenas tardes.	Hola.

Saying goodbye   Ch. 1, p. 27

Adiós.	Hasta luego.
Bueno, tengo clase.	Hasta mañana.
Chao.	Tengo que irme.

Introducing people and responding to an introduction   Ch. 1, p. 29

Me llamo...	Se llama...
Soy...	¡Mucho gusto!
¿Cómo te llamas?	Encantado/a.
Éste es mi amigo...	Igualmente.
Ésta es mi amiga...	

Asking how someone is and saying how you are   Ch. 1, p. 31

¿Cómo estás?	Estupendo/a.
¿Y tú?	Excelente.
¿Qué tal?	Regular.
Estoy (bastante) bien, gracias.	Más o menos.
	(Muy) mal.
Yo también.	¡Horrible!

EXCHANGING INFORMATION

Asking and saying how old someone is   Ch. 1, p. 35

¿Cuántos años tienes?	¿Cuántos años tiene?
Tengo ... años.	Tiene ... años.

Asking where someone is from and saying where you're from   Ch. 1, p. 38

¿De dónde eres?	¿De dónde es...?
Soy de...	Es de...

Talking about what you want and need   Ch. 2, p. 66

¿Qué quieres?	Necesito...
Quiero...	¿Qué necesita?
Quiere...	Ya tengo...
¿Qué necesitas?	Necesita...
¿Necesitas...?	

Saying what's in your room   Ch. 2, p. 76

¿Qué hay en tu cuarto?	Hay ... en su cuarto.
(No) tengo ... en mi cuarto.	¿Tienes...?
	¿Qué tiene ... en su cuarto?
¿Qué hay en el cuarto de...?	Tiene ... en su cuarto.

Talking about what you need and want to do   Ch. 2, p. 85

¿Qué necesitas hacer?	Quiero hacer...
Necesito...	No sé, pero no quiero...
¿Qué necesita hacer...?	
Necesita...	¿Qué quiere hacer...?
¿Qué quieres hacer?	Quiere...

Talking about classes and sequencing events   Ch. 3, p. 110

¿Qué clases tienes este semestre?	Primero tengo..., después... y luego...
Tengo...	¿Y cuándo tienes un día libre?
¿Qué clases tienes hoy?	Mañana por fin...

Telling time   Ch. 3, p. 112

¿Qué hora es?	Son las ... y cuarto.
Es la una.	Son las ... y media.
Es la una y cuarto.	¿Ya son las...?
Es la una y media.	Es tarde.
Son las...	

Telling at what time something happens
Ch. 3, p.119

¿A qué hora es...?	¡Es ahora!
(Es) a las ... de la tarde.	En punto.

Talking about being late or in a hurry
Ch. 3, p. 122

Estoy atrasado/a.	Tengo prisa.
Está atrasado/a.	¡Date prisa!

Describing people and things   Ch. 3, p. 125

¿Cómo es...?	¿Cómo son...?
Es...	Son...
No es...	No son...

Talking about what you and others do during free time   Ch. 4, p. 152

¿Qué haces después de clases?	¡Descanso!
Antes de regresar a casa...	En el tiempo libre practico la guitarra...

Telling where people and things are
Ch. 4, p. 161

¿Dónde estás?	No, no está aquí.
Estoy en...	Está en...
¿No está en...?	

Talking about where you and others go during free time   Ch. 4, p. 171

¿Adónde vas?	Va a...
Voy a...	Va al...
¿Adónde va...?	Va a la...

Discussing how often you do things
Ch. 5, p. 195

¿Con qué frecuencia...?	Durante la semana
Todos los días	A veces
Siempre	Muchas veces
Nunca	Sólo cuando...
¿Todavía...?	

Talking about what you do during a typical week   Ch. 5, p. 209

¿Qué haces típicamente durante el día?
¿Qué hace ... por la mañana?
¿Qué hacen ... por la tarde?
¿Qué hacen ... por la noche?

Giving today's date   Ch. 5, p. 213

¿Cuál es la fecha?	Hoy es el primero de...
¿Qué fecha es hoy?	Hoy es el ... de...
El cuatro de este mes hay...	

Talking about the weather   Ch. 5, p. 216

¿Qué tiempo hace?
Hace buen tiempo.
Hace muy mal tiempo hoy.

Describing a family   Ch. 6, p. 236

¿Cuántas personas hay en tu familia?	Somos cinco. Somos muy unidos.
¿Cómo es tu familia?	Tenemos...
Hay ... en mi familia.	

Describing people   Ch. 6, p. 245

¿Cómo es...?	¿De qué color es...?
Tiene...	¿De qué color son...?

Discussing things a family does together
Ch. 6, p. 248

¿Qué hacen ustedes los fines de semana?	Salimos ... y visitamos a...
¿Hacen ustedes algo durante el verano?	Hacemos un viaje juntos.

EXPRESSING ATTITUDES AND OPINIONS

Talking about what you like and don't like
Ch. 1, p. 43

¿Qué te gusta?	Me gusta (más)...
¿Te gusta...?	No me gusta...

Talking about things you like and explaining why   Ch. 3, p. 129

¿Te gustan...?	Sí, a ella le gustan mucho.
Sí, me gustan.	
¿Cuál es...?	¿Por qué?
¿A ella le gustan...?	Porque...

Talking about what you and others like to do   Ch. 4, p. 149

¿Qué te gusta hacer?	¿A quién le gusta...?
Me gusta...	A mí me gusta...
¿A él le gusta...?	Por eso, me gustan...
No, no le gusta...	
pero le gusta...	

Talking about what you and your friends like to do together   Ch. 5, p. 203

¿Qué les gusta hacer?	Especialmente durante las vacaciones.
¿Les gusta ... juntos?	
Nos gusta...	

Discussing problems and giving advice
Ch. 6, p. 255

¿Qué debo hacer?	Dicen que... demasiado pero no es cierto.
Tengo un problema.	
Debes ... más/menos.	

GRAMMAR SUMMARY

NOUNS AND ARTICLES

GENDER OF NOUNS

In Spanish, nouns (words that name a person, place, or thing) are grouped into two classes or genders: masculine and feminine. All nouns, both persons and objects, fall into one of these groups. Most nouns that end in **-o** are masculine, and most nouns that end in **-a, -ción, -tad,** and **-dad** are feminine.

MASCULINE NOUNS	FEMININE NOUNS
libro	casa
chico	universidad
cuaderno	situación
bolígrafo	mesa
vestido	libertad

FORMATION OF PLURAL NOUNS

Add **-s** to nouns that end in a vowel.		Add **-es** to nouns that end in a consonant.		With nouns that end in **-z**, the **-z** changes to **-c**.	
SINGULAR	PLURAL	SINGULAR	PLURAL	SINGULAR	PLURAL
libro	libro**s**	profesor	profesor**es**	vez	ve**ces**
casa	casa**s**	papel	pape**les**	lápiz	lápi**ces**

DEFINITE ARTICLES

There are words that signal the class of the noun. One of these is the definite article. In English there is one definite article: *the.* In Spanish, there are four: **el, la, los, las.**

SUMMARY OF DEFINITE ARTICLES

	MASCULINE	FEMININE
Singular	**el** chico	**la** chica
Plural	**los** chicos	**las** chicas

CONTRACTIONS

a	+	el	→	**al**
de	+	el	→	**del**

INDEFINITE ARTICLES

Another group of words that are used with nouns is the *indefinite article:* **un, una,** *(a or an)* and **unos, unas** *(some or a few)*.

SUMMARY OF INDEFINITE ARTICLES

	MASCULINE	FEMININE
Singular	**un** chico	**una** chica
Plural	**unos** chicos	**unas** chicas

SUBJECT PRONOUNS	DIRECT OBJECT PRONOUNS	INDIRECT OBJECT PRONOUNS	OBJECTS OF PREPOSITIONS
yo	me	me	mí (conmigo)
tú	te	te	ti (contigo)
él, ella, usted	lo, la	le	él, ella, usted
nosotros, nosotras	nos	nos	nosotros, nosotras
vosotros, vosotras	os	os	vosotros, vosotras
ellos, ellas, ustedes	los, las	les	ellos, ellas, ustedes

ADJECTIVES

Adjectives are words that describe nouns. The adjective must agree in gender (masculine or feminine) and number (singular or plural) with the noun it modifies. Adjectives that end in -**e** or a consonant only agree in number.

		MASCULINE	FEMININE
Adjectives that end in -**o**	Singular	chico alt**o**	chica alt**a**
	Plural	chicos alt**os**	chicas alt**as**
Adjectives that end in -**e**	Singular	chico inteligent**e**	chica inteligent**e**
	Plural	chicos inteligent**es**	chicas inteligent**es**
Adjectives that end in a consonant	Singular	examen difícil	clase difícil
	Plural	exámenes difícil**es**	clases difícil**es**

DEMONSTRATIVE ADJECTIVES

	MASCULINE	FEMININE
Singular	**este** chico	**esta** chica
Plural	**estos** chicos	**estas** chicas

	MASCULINE	FEMININE
Singular	**ese** chico	**esa** chica
Plural	**esos** chicos	**esas** chicas

When demonstratives are used as pronouns, they match the gender and number of the noun they replace and are written with an accent mark.

POSSESSIVE ADJECTIVES

These words also modify nouns and tell you *whose* object or person is being referred to (*my* car, *his* book, *her* mother).

SINGULAR		PLURAL	
MASCULINE	FEMININE	MASCULINE	FEMININE
mi libro	**mi** casa	**mis** libros	**mis** casas
tu libro	**tu** casa	**tus** libros	**tus** casas
su libro	**su** casa	**sus** libros	**sus** casas
nuestro libro	**nuestra** casa	**nuestros** libros	**nuestras** casas
vuestro libro	**vuestra** casa	**vuestros** libros	**vuestras** casas

AFFIRMATIVE AND NEGATIVE EXPRESSIONS

AFFIRMATIVE	NEGATIVE
algo alguien alguno (algún), -a o ... o siempre	nada nadie ninguno (ningún), -a ni ... ni nunca

INTERROGATIVE WORDS

¿Adónde? ¿Cómo? ¿Cuál(es)? ¿Cuándo?	¿Cuánto(a)? ¿Cuántos(as)? ¿De dónde? ¿Dónde?	¿Por qué? ¿Qué? ¿Quién(es)?

COMPARATIVES

Comparatives are used to compare people or things. With comparisons of inequality, the same structure is used with adjectives, adverbs or nouns. With comparisons of equality, **tan** is used with adjectives and adverbs, and **tanto/a/os/as** with nouns.

COMPARATIVE OF INEQUALITY

$$\left.\begin{array}{c}\textbf{más}\\[1em]\textbf{menos}\end{array}\right\} + \left\{\begin{array}{c}\text{adjective}\\\text{adverb}\\\text{noun}\end{array}\right\} \qquad \left.\begin{array}{c}\textbf{más}\\[1em]\textbf{menos}\end{array}\right\} + \textbf{de} + \text{number}$$

COMPARATIVE OF EQUALITY

tan + adjective or adverb + **como** **tanto/a/os/as** + noun + **como**

VERBS

REGULAR VERBS

In Spanish we use a formula to conjugate regular verbs. The endings change for each person, but the stem of the verb remains the same.

PRESENT TENSE OF REGULAR VERBS

INFINITIVE	PRESENT			
hablar	(yo) hablo (tú) hablas (él/ella/usted) habla		(nosotros/as) hablamos (vosotros/as) habláis (ellos/ellas/ustedes) hablan	
comer	(yo) como (tú) comes (él/ella/usted) come		(nosotros/as) comemos (vosotros/as) coméis (ellos/ellas/ustedes) comen	
escribir	(yo) escribo (tú) escribes (él/ella/usted) escribe		(nosotros/as) escribimos (vosotros/as) escribís (ellos/ellas/ustedes) escriben	

VERBS WITH IRREGULAR YO FORMS

hacer		poner		saber		salir		traer	
hago	hacemos	**pongo**	ponemos	**sé**	sabemos	**salgo**	salimos	**traigo**	traemos
haces	hacéis	pones	ponéis	sabes	sabéis	sales	salís	traes	traéis
hace	hacen	pone	ponen	sabe	saben	sale	salen	trae	traen

VERBS WITH IRREGULAR FORMS

ser		estar		ir	
soy	somos	estoy	estamos	voy	vamos
eres	sois	estás	estáis	vas	vais
es	son	está	están	va	van

PRESENT PROGRESSIVE

The present progressive in English is formed by using the verb *to be* plus the *-ing* form of another verb. In Spanish, the present progressive is formed by using the verb **estar** plus the **-ndo** form of another verb.

-**ar** verbs	-**er** and -**ir** verbs	For -**er** and -**ir** verbs with a stem that ends in a vowel, the -**iendo** changes to -**yendo**:
hablar → estoy habl**ando** trabajar → trabaj**ando**	comer → com**iendo** escribir → escrib**iendo**	leer → le**yendo**

STEM-CHANGING VERBS

In Spanish, some verbs have an irregular stem in the present tense. The final vowel of the stem changes from **e → ie** and **o → ue** in all forms except **nosotros** and **vosotros**.

e → ie		o → ue		u → ue	
preferir		**poder**		**jugar**	
pref**ie**ro	preferimos	p**ue**do	podemos	j**ue**go	jugamos
pref**ie**res	preferís	p**ue**des	podéis	j**ue**gas	jugáis
pref**ie**re	pref**ie**ren	p**ue**de	p**ue**den	j**ue**ga	j**ue**gan

The following is a list of some **e → ie** stem-changing verbs:	The following is a list of some **o → ue** stem-changing verbs:
empezar **pensar** **querer** **preferir**	**almorzar** **doler** **encontrar** **poder**

THE VERBS GUSTAR AND ENCANTAR

To express likes and dislikes, the verb **gustar** is used in Spanish. The verb **encantar** is used to talk about things you really like or love. The verb endings for **gustar** and **encantar** always agree with what is liked or loved. The indirect object pronouns always precede the verb forms.

gustar		encantar	
If one thing is liked:	If more than one thing is liked:	If one thing is really liked:	If more than one thing is really liked:
me te le } gusta nos les	me te le } gustan nos les	me te le } encanta nos les	me te le } encantan nos les

PRETERITE OF REGULAR VERBS

INFINITIVE	PRETERITE OF REGULAR VERBS		
hablar	(yo) hablé (tú) hablaste (él/ella) habló	(nosotros/as) hablamos (vosotros/as) hablasteis (ellos/ellas) hablaron	
comer	(yo) comí (tú) comiste (él/ella) comió	(nosotros/as) comimos (vosotros/as) comisteis (ellos/ellas) comieron	
escribir	(yo) escribí (tú) escribiste (él/ella) escribió	(nosotros/as) escribimos (vosotros/as) escribisteis (ellos/ellas) escribieron	

PRETERITE OF HACER, IR, SER, AND VER

hacer	ir	ser	ver
hice	fui	fui	vi
hiciste	fuiste	fuiste	viste
hizo	fue	fue	vio
hicimos	fuimos	fuimos	vimos
hicisteis	fuisteis	fuisteis	visteis
hicieron	fueron	fueron	vieron

ADDITIONAL VOCABULARY

Use this additional vocabulary to personalize activities. If you can't find a word you need here, try the Spanish-English and English-Spanish vocabulary sections beginning on page 277.

ANIMALES

el caballo   *horse*
el canguro   *kangaroo*
la cebra   *zebra*
el conejillo de Indias
   hamster
el delfín   *dolphin*
el elefante   *elephant*
la foca   *seal*
el gorila   *gorilla*
la jirafa   *giraffe*
el león   *lion*
el mono   *monkey*
el oso   *bear*
el pájaro   *bird*
el pingüino   *penguin*
el ratón   *mouse*
la serpiente   *snake*
el tigre   *tiger*

COMIDA   *(FOOD)*

el aguacate   *avocado*
el bróculi   *broccoli*
la carne asada   *roast beef*
la cereza   *cherry*
la chuleta de cerdo   *pork chop*
el champiñón   *mushroom*
las espinacas   *spinach*
los fideos   *noodles*
los mariscos   *shellfish*
la mayonesa   *mayonnaise*
el melón   *cantaloupe*
la mostaza   *mustard*
la pimienta   *pepper*
la sal   *salt*
el yogur   *yogurt*

COMPRAS   *(SHOPPING)*

el álbum   *album*
los aretes   *earrings*
la billetera   *wallet*
el collar   *necklace*
las flores   *flowers*

el juego de mesa   *(board) game*
las llaves   *keys*
el regalo   *present, gift*

DEPORTES

las artes marciales   *martial arts*
el atletismo   *track and field*
el boxeo   *boxing*
el ciclismo   *cycling*
la gimnasia   *gymnastics*
el levantamiento de pesas   *weightlifting*
patinar sobre hielo   *ice skating*

DIRECCIONES   *(GIVING DIRECTIONS)*

a la derecha de   *to the right of*
a la izquierda de   *to the left of*
en frente de   *in front of*
Dobla a la derecha.   *Turn right.*
Sigue derecho.   *Go straight.*

EN LA CASA

la alcoba   *(bed)room*
la alfombra   *rug; carpet*
el balcón   *balcony*
las cortinas   *curtains*
el cuarto de baño
   bathroom
el despertador   *alarm clock*
las escaleras   *stairs*
el espejo   *mirror*
el garaje   *garage*
la lavadora   *washing machine*
los muebles   *furniture*
el patio   *patio*
el refrigerador   *refrigerator*
la secadora   *(clothes) dryer*
el sillón   *easy chair*
el sofá   *couch*
el timbre   *doorbell*

EN LA CIUDAD   *(IN THE CITY)*

el aeropuerto   *airport*
la autopista   *highway, freeway*

la avenida *avenue*
la calle *street*
el banco *bank*
la barbería *barber shop*
el cuartel *police station*
la esquina *corner*
la farmacia *pharmacy*
el hospital *hospital*
la iglesia *church*
la mezquita *mosque*
la parada de autobuses
 bus stop
el pueblo *town*
el puente *bridge*
el rascacielos *skyscraper*
el salón de belleza *beauty salon*
el semáforo *traffic light*
el templo *temple*

MÚSICA

el bajo *bass*
la batería *drum set*
el clarinete *clarinet*
la guitarra eléctrica
 electric guitar
el oboe *oboe*
el saxofón *saxophone*
el sintetizador *synthesizer*
el tambor *drum*
el trombón *trombone*
la trompeta *trumpet*
la tuba *tuba*
la viola *viola*

NÚMEROS ORDINALES

primero/a *first*
segundo/a *second*
tercero/a *third*
cuarto/a *fourth*
quinto/a *fifth*
sexto/a *sixth*
séptimo/a *seventh*
octavo/a *eighth*
noveno/a *ninth*
décimo/a *tenth*

PALABRAS DESCRIPTIVAS

amistoso/a *friendly*
bien educado/a *polite*

llevar anteojos *to wear glasses*
las pecas *freckles*
el pelo liso *straight hair*
el pelo rizado *curly hair*
ser calvo/a *to be bald*
tener barba *to have a beard*
tener bigote *to have a moustache*

PASATIEMPOS (PASTIMES)

el anuario *yearbook*
la banda *band*
la canción *song*
coleccionar... *to collect . . .*
el coro *choir*
coser *to sew*
el drama *drama*
la fotografía *photography*
jugar a las cartas *to play cards*
jugar a las damas *to play checkers*
jugar al ajedrez *to play chess*
la orquesta *orchestra*

PROFESIONES

la abogada, el abogado *lawyer*
la agricultora, el agricultor *farmer*
la bombera, el bombero *firefighter*
la carpintera, el carpintero *carpenter*
la cartera, el cartero *mail carrier*
la enfermera, el enfermero *nurse*
el hombre de negocios *businessman*
la mujer de negocios *businesswoman*
la plomera, el plomero *plumber*
el policía *police officer*
la policía *police officer (fem.)*
la secretaria, el secretario *secretary*
la trabajadora, el trabajador *worker*

ROPA (CLOTHING)

los bluejeans *bluejeans*
las botas *boots*
la camisa *shirt*
la camiseta *T-shirt*
la chaqueta *jacket*
la falda *skirt*
los pantalones *pants*
las sandalias *sandals*
el suéter *sweater*
el traje de baño *bathing suit*
el vestido *dress*

SPANISH-ENGLISH VOCABULARY

This vocabulary includes almost all words in the textbook, both active (for production) and passive (for recognition only). Active words and phrases are practiced in the chapter and are listed on the **Vocabulario** page at the end of each chapter. You are expected to know and be able to use active vocabulary. An entry in **boldface** type indicates that the word or phrase is active. All other words are for recognition only. These are found in **De antemano**, in the **Pasos**, in realia (authentic Spanish-language documents), in **Enlaces, Panorama cultural, Encuentro cultural,** and **Vamos a leer,** and in the **Location Openers** (travelogue sections). Many words have more than one definition; the definitions given here correspond to the way the words are used in the book. Other meanings can be looked up in a standard dictionary.

Nouns are listed with definite article and plural form, when applicable. The numbers after each entry refer to the chapter where the word or phrase first appears or where it becomes an active vocabulary word. Vocabulary from the preliminary chapter is followed by the letter "P".

Although the **Real Academia** has deleted the letters **ch** and **ll** from the alphabet, many dictionaries still have separate entries for these letters. This end-of-book vocabulary follows the new rules, with **ch** and **ll** in the same sequence as in English.

Stem changes are indicated in parentheses after the verb: **poder (ue).**

a *to,* 4; *at,* 3
a comenzar *let's begin,* 1
a ellas *to them,* 5
a ellos *to them,* 5
a menudo *often,* 5
A mí me gusta + infinitive
  I (emphatic) *like to . . . ,* 4
¿A qué hora es ...? *At what
  time is . . .?,* 3
¿A quién le gusta...? *Who
  likes (to) . . .?,* 4
¿A ti qué te gusta hacer?
  What do you (emphatic) *like
  to do?,* 4
a todo color *in full color,* 2
a ustedes *to you,* 5
a veces *sometimes,* 5
a ver si puedo *let's see
  if I can,* 1
el abrazo *hug,* 1
abril (m.) *April,* 5
la abuela *grandmother,* 6
el abuelo *grandfather,* 6
los abuelos *grandparents,* 6
abundar *to abound,* 6
aburrido/a *boring,* 3; **No
  es aburrido/a.** *It's not
  boring.,* 3
acabemos *let's finish,* 5
acampar *to camp,* 5
el acceso *access,* 4
el acento *accent mark,* P
acompañar *to accompany,* 4
la actitud *attitude,* 3

la actividad *activity,* 4
el actor *actor* (male); mi actor
  favorito es *my favorite
  actor is,* P
la actriz *actress;* mi actriz
  favorita es *my favorite
  actress is,* P
acuático/a *aquatic, water*
  (adj.)
adelante *let's get started,* P
adiós *goodbye,* 1
adivinar *to guess,* 6;
  ¡Adivina, adivinador!
  Guess!, 6
¿adónde? *where (to)?,* 4;
  ¿Adónde vas? *Where are
  you going?,* 4
aeróbico/a *aerobic,* 5; **una
  clase de ejercicios aeróbicos**
  aerobics class, 5
agitar *to agitate, to stir
  up,* 3
agosto (m.) *August,* 5
agotar *to use up; to exhaust,* 3
agresivo/a *aggressive,* 6
la agricultura *agriculture,* 3
el agua (f.) *water,* 5
el águila *eagle,* P
la ahijada *godchild,* 6
el ahijado *godchild,* 6
ahora *now,* 1
el ajedrez *chess,* 5
el ají *chile pepper,* 3
al (a + el) *to the,* 4; al
  contrario *on the contrary,* 3;
  al grano *to the point,* 1; **al
  lado de** *next to, to one side*

of, beside, 4; el cafetín de al
  lado *the coffee shop
  around the corner,* 6
la alberca *swimming pool,* 4
el álbum *album,* 6
alegre *happy,* 6
el alfabeto *alphabet,* P
algo *something,* 6
alguno/a (masc. sing. algún)
  some, any; alguna parte
  someplace; alguna vez
  sometime, 6
allá *there,* 4
allí *there,* 4
el almacén *department
  store,* 5
el almuerzo *lunch,* 3
alquilar *to rent,* 5
alrededor de *around,* 6
alta mar: en alta mar *on the
  high seas,* 6
alto/a *tall,* 3
la alumna *student* (female), 3
el alumno *student* (male), 3
amarillo/a *yellow,* P
americano/a *American,* 1
la amiga *friend* (female), 1, 4;
  Ésta es mi amiga. *This is
  my* (female) *friend.,* 1
el amigo *friend* (male), 1, 4;
  amigo/a por correspondencia
  pen pal, P; **Éste es mi amigo.**
  This is my (male) *friend.,* 1;
  nuevos amigos *new
  friends,* 2; **pasar el rato con
  amigos** *to spend time with
  friends,* 4

la amistad *friendship*, 1
amplio/a *large*, 4
anaranjado/a *orange*, P
¡Ándale! *Hurry up!*, 3
los anfibios *amphibians*, 2
el ángulo *angle*, 3
el animal *animal*, 2
antes de *before*, 4
antipático/a *disagreeable*, 3
el año *year*, 5; **¿Cuántos años tiene?** *How old is (he/she)?*, 1; **¿Cuántos años tienes?** *How old are you* (familiar)*?*, 1; **Tengo ... años.** *I'm . . . years old.*, 1; **Tiene ... años.** *He/she is . . . years old.*, 1
el apartado postal *post office box*, 4
el apellido *last name*, 1
aquí *here*, 4
el árbol *tree*, 4; el árbol genealógico *family tree*, 6
la arboleda *grove (of trees)*, 4
el arco *bow;* Andean stringed musical instrument, 4
el armario *closet*, 2
la arquitecta *architect*, 3
el arquitecto *architect*, 3
arreglar *to arrange, to pick up (one's room)*, 6
el arroz *rice*, 6
el arte *art*, 3 (pl. las artes)
artístico/a *artistic*, 6
las arvejas *peas*, 1
asado/a *roasted*, 6
así *in this way, so, thus*, 6; así se dice *here's how you say it*, 1
la asistencia *attendance*, 3
asistir a *to attend*, 5
la aspiradora *vacuum cleaner;* **pasar la aspiradora** *to vacuum*, 6
atlético/a *athletic*, 6
el atletismo *track and field*, 4
atractivo/a *attractive*, 2
atrasado/a *late;* **Está atrasado/a.** *He/She is late.*, 3; **Estoy atrasado/a.** *I'm late.*, 3
el auditorio *auditorium*, 4
el autobús *bus*, 5; **tomar el autobús** *to take the bus*, 5
la avenida *avenue*, 4
las aventuras *adventures*, 1
las aves *birds*, 2
el avión *airplane* (pl. los aviones), 4
ayudar *to help;* **ayudar en casa** *to help at home*, 5
azul *blue*, 6

B

bailar *to dance*, 4
el baile *dance*, 3
bajo/a *short*, 3; *under*, 4
el baloncesto *basketball*, 1
el banco *bank*, 2
los banquetes *banquets*, 4
bañarse *to take a bath*, 5
las barajas *card games; decks of cards*, 3
la barbacoa *barbecue*, 6
el barco *boat, ship*, 5
el basquetbol *basketball*, 1
bastante *quite; pretty* (adv.), 1; **Estoy (bastante) bien, gracias.** *I'm (pretty) well, thanks.*, 1
la **basura** *garbage, trash;* **sacar la basura** *to take out the trash*, 4
el bautizo *baptism*, 1
beber *to drink*, 5
el béisbol *baseball*, 1
el beso *kiss*, 2
la biblioteca *library*, 4
la bicicleta *bicycle;* **montar en bicicleta** *to ride a bike*, 4; pasear en bicicleta *to ride a bicycle*, 3
bien *good; well*, 1; Está bien. *All right.*, 2; **Estoy (bastante) bien, gracias.** *I'm (pretty) well, thanks.*, 1
bienvenido/a *welcome*, P
la biología *biology*, 3
blanco/a *white*, P
el bolígrafo *ballpoint pen*, 2
el bolívar *unit of currency in Venezuela*, 2
bonito/a *pretty*, 3
borrar *to erase;* **goma de borrar** *eraser*, 2
botar *to throw (out)*, 4
el boxeo *boxing*, 4
Bs. abbreviation for *bolívares*, unit of Venezuelan currrency, 2
bucear *to scuba dive*, 5
Bueno... *Well . . .*, 1; **Bueno, tengo clase.** *Well, I have class (now).*, 1
bueno/a *good*, 3; **Buenos días.** *Good morning.*, 1; **Buenas noches.** *Good night.*, 1; **Buenas tardes.** *Good afternoon.*, 1
el burro *donkey*, P
buscar *to look for*, 5; busco *I'm looking for*, P

C

el caballo *horse*, 6
cada *each*, 2
el café *coffee;* **de color café** *brown*, 6
el cafecito *little cup of coffee*, 5
la cafetería *cafeteria*, 1
el cafetín *coffee shop*, 6
el caimán *alligator* (pl. los caimanes), 5
la caja *box*, 3
la calculadora *calculator*, 2; la calculadora gráfica *graphing calculator*, 2
el calendario *calendar*, P
la calificación *grade*, 3
el calor *heat;* **Hace calor.** *It's hot.*, 5; Hace un calor espantoso. *It's frightfully hot.*, 5
la cama *bed*, 2; **hacer la cama** *to make the bed*, 6
la cámara *camera*, 1
el cambio *change*, 4
caminar *to walk;* **caminar con el perro** *to walk the dog*, 4
la campana *bell*, 3
el campeón *champion* (f. la campeona), 4
las canas *gray hair*, 6; **Tiene canas.** *He/She has gray hair.*, 6
cantar *to sing*, 4
el cántaro *pitcher;* llover a cántaros *to rain cats and dogs*, 5
la capital *capital city*, 3
el capítulo *chapter*, 1
la cara *face*, 6
el Caribe *Caribbean Sea*, 1
el cariño *affection*, 2
cariñoso/a *affectionate*, 6
la carne; *meat;* la carne asada *roast beef*, 1
la carpeta *folder*, 2
el carro *car;* **lavar el carro** *to wash the car*, 4
la carta *letter*, 5; la carta de amor *love letter*, 5
el cartel *poster*, 2
la casa *house, home*, 4
casero/a *home-made*, 4
casi *almost*, 6; **casi siempre** *almost always*, 6
la casilla *post office box*, 4
caso: en caso de *in case of*, 1
castaño/a *brown, chestnut-colored*, 6
las castañuelas *castanets*, P
el castellano *Spanish language*, 2

el castillo *castle*, 1
la cátedra bolivariana *teachings about Bolívar*, 3
la categoría *category*, 1; categoría liviano *lightweight* (adj.), 4; categoría mediano *middleweight* (adj.), 4
catorce *fourteen*, 1
la cena *dinner*, 4; **preparar la cena** *to prepare dinner*, 4
cenar *to eat dinner*, 6
el centro *downtown*, 4
Centroamérica *Central America*, 1
el centro comercial *shopping mall*, 2
cerca de *near*, 4
el cerdo *pig*, 2
cero *zero*, 1
el césped *grass*, 6; **cortar el césped** *to cut the grass*, 6
el chaleco *vest*, P
la chamaca *girl*, 4
el chamaco *guy*, 4
Chao. *'Bye.*, 1
el charango *Andean stringed musical instrument*, 4
la charla *chat*, 1
la charrería *rodeo-like exhibition of horseback riding skills*, 3
la chava *girl*, 4
el chavo *guy*, 4
la chica *girl*, 5
el chico *boy*, 5
chino/a *Chinese*, 6
el chocolate *chocolate*, 1
el ciclismo *cycling*, P
cien, ciento *one hundred*, 2
las ciencias *science*, 3; ciencia ficción *science fiction*, 5; ciencias naturales *natural sciences*, 3; **ciencias sociales** *social studies*, 3
cierto *true*, 6; **No es cierto.** *It isn't true.*, 6
la cima *summit, top*, 4
cinco *five*, 1
cincuenta *fifty*, 2
el cine *movie theater*, 4
el cinturón *belt*, 5
la ciudad *city*, 4
el civismo *civics*, 3
el clarinete *clarinet*, 4
claro/a *light color*, P
la clase *class, classroom*, 1; **Bueno, tengo clase.** *Well, I have class* (now)., 1; **la clase de baile** *dance class*, 5; **la clase de inglés** *English class*, 1; **una clase de ejercicios aeróbicos** *aerobics class*, 5; ¿Qué

clases tienes? *What classes do you have?*, 3; **¿Qué haces después de clases?** *What do you do after school?*, 4
clásico/a *classical*, 1
el club campeón *champion (first-rank) club*, 4; club deportivo *sports club, gym*, 5
la cocina *kitchen*, 6; **limpiar la cocina** *to clean the kitchen*, 6
la cocinera *cook (female)*, 6
el cocinero *cook (male)*, 6
el coco *coconut*, 6
el cognado *cognate*, 1
el colegio *high school*, 2
la coliflor *cauliflower*, 1
el color *color*, 6; a todo color *in full color*, 2; **de color café** *brown*, 6; **¿De qué color es/son...?** *What color is/are . . .?*, 6; lápiz de color *colored pencil*, 2
la comadre *term used to express the relationship between mother and godmother*, 6
la comedia *comedy*, 3
comer *to eat*, 5
comercial: centro comercial *shopping mall*, 2
la cometa *kite*, 5
cómico/a *comical, funny*, 3
la comida *food; meal* (Mex.); *lunch;* **la comida mexicana/ italiana/ china** *Mexican/ Italian/Chinese food*, 1
el comienzo *beginning*, 1
como *like; as*
¿Cómo? *How?*, 1; **¿Cómo es...?** *What's . . . like?*, 3; **¿Cómo es tu familia?** *What's your family like?*, 6; **¿Cómo estás?** *How are you* (familiar)?, 1; ¿Cómo se escribe? *How do you write (spell) it?*, P; **¿Cómo son?** *What are . . . like?*, 3; **¿Cómo te llamas?** *What's your name?*, 1
el compadrazgo *relationship between parents and godparents of a child*, 6
el compadre *friend (male)*, 4; *term used to express the relationship between father and godfather*, 6
la compañera *friend, pal, companion (female)*, 3
el compañero *friend, pal, companion (male)*, 3; compañero/a de clase *classmate*, 3

la comparación *comparison*, 2
la competencia *competition*, 3
completamente *completely*, 6
la compra *purchase;* las compras *shopping*, 2
comprar *to buy*, 2; comprarse *to buy (for) oneself*, 6
comprender *to understand*, 1
compuesto/a *composed*, 2
la computación *computer science*, 3
la computadora *computer*, 2
común *common* (pl. comunes), P
con base en *based on*, 6
con *with*, 4; **con frecuencia** *often;* conmigo *with me*, 4; **contigo** *with you*, 4; **¿con qué frecuencia?** *How often?*, 5
el concierto *concert*, 3
el concurso *game; competition, contest*, 3
el conejo *rabbit*, 6
confirmar *to confirm*, 4
el conflicto *conflict*, 6
conmigo *with me*, 4
conocer a *to get to know (someone)*, 2; **conocer** *to be familiar or acquainted with*
los conocimientos *information; knowledge*, 2
el consejo *advice*, 6
la constitución *constitution*, 4
la construcción *construction*, 1
construido/a *built*, 4
contestar *to answer*, 1
contigo *with you*, 4
convertir *to convert*, 3
la cordillera *mountain range*, 1
el córdoba *unit of currency in Nicaragua*, 2
el coro *choir*, 3
corregir *to correct*, 3
el correo *post office*, 4
correr *to run*, 5
la correspondencia *mail*, 1
cortar *to cut*, 6; **cortar el césped** *to cut the grass*, 6
la cortesía *courtesy*, 1
corto/a *short* (to describe things), 6; pelo corto *short hair*, 6
la cosa *thing*, 2
creativo/a *creative*, 6
la cruz *cross* (pl. las cruces), 2
el cuaderno *notebook*, 2; en mi cuaderno *in my journal*, 1; cuaderno de rayas *lined notebook*, 2; cuaderno de cuadros *graph paper notebook*, 6

cual, cuales *which* (relative pronoun)
¿cuál? *which?*, 3; **¿Cuál es la fecha?** *What is today's date?*, 5; **¿Cuál es tu clase favorita?** *Which is your favorite class?*, 3
cuando *when*, 5; **sólo cuando** *only when*, 5
¿cuándo? *when?*, 3
¿cuánto/a? *how much?*, 2; **¿cuántos/ as?** *how many?*, 2; **¿Cuántas personas hay en tu familia?** *How many people are there in your family?*, 6; **¿Cuántos años tiene?** *How old is (he/she)?*, 1; **¿Cuántos años tienes?** *How old are you?*, 1; **¿Cuántos son en tu familia?** *How many (people) are in your family?*, 6
cuarenta *forty*, 2
cuarto *quarter, fourth*; **menos cuarto** *quarter to (the hour)*, 3; **y cuarto** *quarter past (the hour)*, 3
el cuarto *room*, 2
el cuate *friend*, 4
cuatro *four*, 1
cubano/a *Cuban*, 6
cubierto/a *covered*, 4
cuenta *he/she tells*, 6; cuéntame *tell me*, 1
el cuento *story*, 3; los cuentos de aventuras *adventure stories*, 5
el cuerpo *body*, 6
la cuestión *question*, 1
el cuestionario *questionnaire*, 6
cuidar *to take care of;* **cuidar al gato** *to take care of the cat*, 6; **cuidar a tu hermano/a** *to take care of your brother/sister*, 4
el cumpleaños *birthday*, 3
curioso/a *curious, strange*, 6

D

da *he/she gives*, 2; dale un click a... *click on . . .*, 4
los dados *dice*, 2
la danza *dance*, 3
¡Date prisa! *Hurry up!*, 3
los datos *facts, data*, P; datos personales *personal information*, 6
de antemano *beforehand*, 1
de *from*, 1; *of*, 2; el cafetín de al lado *the coffee shop around the corner*, 6; de

antemano *beforehand;*
de color café *brown*, 6;
¿De dónde eres? *Where are you* (familiar) *from?*, 1;
¿De dónde es? *Where is she/he from?*, 1; **de la mañana** *in the morning* (A.M.), 3; **de la noche** *in the evening* (P.M.), 3; **de la tarde** *in the afternoon* (P.M.), 3; **¿De qué color es/son?** *What color is/are?*, 6; ¿De qué se hace? *What is it made of?*, 4; de todo *all kinds of things*, 4; de vacaciones *on vacation*, 5; de vez en cuando *once in a while*, 5; de visita *visiting*, 3; de vuelta *returning*, 2; **del (de + el)** *of the, from the*, 3
debajo de *under, beneath*, 4
el debate *debate*, 1
deber *should, ought to*, 6; **Debes...** *You should . . .*, 6; **Qué debo hacer?** *What should I do?*, 6
decir *to say*, P; para decir *for speaking*, P
el dedo *finger; digit*, 2
del (de + el) *of the, from the*, 3
delgado/a *thin*, 6
demasiado *too much*, 6
los **deportes** *sports*, 1
el derecho *right*, 1
el desastre *disaster*, 2
desayunar *to eat breakfast*, 5
descansar *to rest*, 4; **descansar en el parque** *to rest in the park*, 4
el descanso *recess, break*, 3
la descripción *description*, 3
el descubrimiento *discovery*, 2
desde *since*, 3
desorganizado/a *disorganized*, 6
la despedida *farewell, goodbye, leave-taking*, 1
después *after*, 3; **después de** *after*, 4; **¿Qué haces después de clases?** *What do you do after school?*, 4
el destino *destination*, 3
determinar: sin determinar *undetermined*, 4
el **día** *day*, 4; **Buenos días.** *Good morning.*; día de santo *saint's day*, 1; cada ... días *every . . . days*, 5; día escolar *school day*, 3; **día libre** *day off*, 3; los días de semana *weekdays*, 4; los días de la semana *the days of*

the week, 5; **todos los días** *every day*, 5
diariamente *daily*, 6
dibujar *to draw*, 4
el dibujo *drawing*; dibujos animados *animated cartoons*, 2
el **diccionario** *dictionary*, 2
dice *he/she says*, 1
dice que *he/she says that*, 6
diciembre (m.) *December*, 5
el dictado *dictation*, 1
diecinueve *nineteen*, 1
dieciocho *eighteen*, 1
dieciséis *sixteen*, 1
diecisiete *seventeen*, 1
diez *ten*, 1
difícil *difficult*, 3
dijo *he/she said*, 2
el dineral *large sum of money*, 2
el dinero *money*, 2
el dinosaurio *dinosaur*, 2
la dirección *address*, 4
directo/a *direct*, 4
el director *principal (of a school)* (male), 3
la directora *principal (of a school)* (female), 3
el disco compacto *CD*, 2
el disgusto *distaste*, 1
la diversión *entertainment*, 5
divertido/a *fun, amusing*, 3
divorciado/a *divorced*, 6
doblado/a *dubbed* (film), 2
doce *twelve*, 1
el doctor *doctor* (male), 3
la doctora *doctor* (female), 3
documental *documentary*, 2
el **dólar** *dollar*, 2
doméstico/a *household;* **los quehaceres domésticos** *household chores*, 6
el domicilio *residence*, 1
el **domingo** *Sunday*, 4
el dominó *dominoes*, 6
don (title of respect for men), 1
donde *where;* **¿Adónde?** *Where (to)?*, 4; **¿De dónde eres?** *Where are you* (familiar) *from?*, 1; **¿De dónde es?** *Where is he/she from?*, 1; **¿Dónde?** *Where?*, 4; ¿Dónde te gustaría estudiar? *Where would you* (familiar) *like to study?*, 3
dos *two*, 1
la duración *length, duration*, 2
durante *during*, 5

E

la ecología *ecology*, 1
la edad *age*, 1

la edición *edition*, 5
el edificio *building*, 4
la educación *education*, 3; la educación artística *art education*, 3; **la educación física** *physical education*, 3; la educación tecnológica *shop (school subject)*, 3
educar *to educate*, 2
egoísta (m/f) *selfish*, 6
el ejercicio *exercise*, 5; **una clase de ejercicios aeróbicos** *aerobics class*, 5; **hacer ejercicio** *to exercise*, 5; hacer ejercicios aeróbicos *to do aerobics*, 5
el *the (sing.)*, 1; **Es el... de...** *It's the (date) of (month).*, 5
El... de este mes hay... *On the (date) of this month, there is/are . . .*, 5
él *he*, 2; **Él es...** *He is . . .*, 3
ella *she*, 2; **Ella es...** *She is . . .*, 3
ellas *they*, 3; **a ellas** *to them*, 5
ellos *they*, 3; **a ellos** *to them*, 5
Ellos/Ellas son... *They are . . .*, 3
emocionante *thrilling*, 6
empezar *to begin*; empiezan *they begin*, 3
en *in, on*, 3; *at*, 4; en alta mar *on the high seas*, 6; **en punto** *on the dot*, 3
Encantado/a. *Delighted to meet you.*, 1
la enciclopedia *encyclopedia*, 2
encima de *on top of*, 4
encontrar (ue) *to find*, 2
el encuentro *encounter, meeting*, 2
la encuesta *survey*, 1
enero (m.) *January*, 5
los enlaces *links, connections, ties*, 1
enrojecer *to turn red; to blush*, 6
la ensalada *salad*, 1
entonces *then*, 3
entrar *to go in, to enter*, 3
entre *among*, 6; entre clases *between classes*, 1
la entrevista *interview*, 1
¡Epa, 'mano! *What's up, brother?*, 1
eres *you (familiar) are*, 1
es *he/she/it is*, 1; **es de...** *he/she/it is from . . .*, 1;

Es el ... de ... *It's the (date) of (month).*, 5; **Es la una.** *It's one o'clock.*, 3
el esclavo *slave* (f. la esclava), 6
escolar *school* (adj.), 3; día escolar *school day*, 3
escondido/a *hidden*, 4
escribamos *let's write*, 3
escribir *to write*, 5
el escritorio *desk*, 2
escuchar *to listen*, 4; escuchar la radio *listen to the radio*, 4; **escuchar música** *to listen to music*, 4; para escuchar *for listening*, P
la escuela *school*, 3
eso *that (pron.)*, 5; **por eso** *that's why, for that reason*, 4
los espaguetis *spaghetti*, 1
espantoso/a *terrible*, 5; Hace un calor espantoso. *It's terribly hot.*, 5
España (f.) *Spain*, 1
el español *Spanish (language)*, 1
especial *special*, 3
especialmente *especially*, 5
el espectáculo *show; spectacle*, 6
la esposa *wife*, 6
el esposo *husband*, 6
esquiar *to ski*, 5
esta *this (adj.)*, 1; **estas** *these (adj.)*, 6
ésta *this (pron.)*; **Ésta es mi amiga.** *This is my friend (female).*, 1
el estacionamiento *parking*, 4
las estaciones *seasons*, 5
la estadística *statistic*, 2
el estado *state*, 4
estamos *we are*, P
las estampillas *stamps*, 4
el estante *bookcase*, 2
estar *to be*, 4; **¿Cómo estás?** *How are you?*, 1; **Está atrasado/a.** *He/She is late.*, 3; Está bien. *It's all right*; **Está lloviendo.** *It's raining.*, 5; Está lloviendo a cántaros *It's raining cats and dogs*, 5; **Está nevando.** *It's snowing.*, 5; **Está nublado.** *It's cloudy.*, 5; **Estoy atrasado/a.** *I'm late.*, 3; **Estoy (bastante) bien, gracias.** *I'm (pretty) well, thanks.*, 1
éstas *these (pron.)*, 6
este *this (adj.)*, 1; **El ... de este mes hay...** *On the (date) of this month, there is/are . . .*, 5

el este *east*, 1
éste *this (pron.)*; **Éste es mi amigo.** *This is my friend (male).*, 1
el estéreo *stereo*, 2
el estilo *style*, 1; el estilo personal *personal style*, 1
estos *these (adj.)*, 6
éstos *these (pron.)*, 6
estoy *I am*, 1; **Estoy atrasado/a.** *I'm late.*, 3; **Estoy (bastante) bien, gracias.** *I'm (pretty) well, thanks.*, 1
la estrategia *strategy*, 1
la estrella *star*, 1
estricto/a *strict*, 3
el estudiante *student* (male), 3
la estudiante *student* (female), 3
estudiar *to study*, 4
Estupendo/a. *Great./Marvelous.*, 1
la etiqueta *etiquette*, 1
Europa *Europe*, 1
la evaluación *grade; grading period*, 3
el examen *exam* (pl. **los exámenes**), 3
Excelente. *Great./Excellent.*, 1
la experiencia *experience*, 5

fabuloso/a *fabulous*, 6
fácil *easy*, 3
la falda *skirt*, 5
falso/a *false*, 1
la falta de asistencia *absence (from class)*, 3
la familia *family*, 6; familia extendida *extended family*, 6; familia extensa *extended family*, 6; familia nuclear *nuclear family, immediate family*, 6
familiar *family* (adj.), 6
favorito/a *favorite*, 3; **¿Cuál es tu clase favorita?** *Which is your favorite class?*, 3
febrero (m.) *February*, 5
la fecha *date*, 1
la fecha *date*, 5; **¿Cuál es la fecha?** *What is today's date?*, 5; **¿Qué fecha es hoy?** *What's today's date?*, 5
feliz *happy*, 5
femenil *women's* (adj.), 4
fenomenal *phenomenal*, 6
feo/a *ugly*, 3
la fiesta *party*, 3

filmado/a *filmed*, 2

la filosofía *philosophy*, 2

el fin *end*, 4; **el fin de semana** *weekend*, 4

la firma *signature*, 1

la física *physics*, 3

flamenco *flamenco (music, singing, dancing)*, 6

la flauta *flute*, 4

la forma *shape*, 6

la foto *photo*, 6

la fotonovela *illustrated story*, 1

el francés *French*, 3

la frase *sentence, phrase*, P

la frecuencia *frequency*, 5; **¿con qué frecuencia?** *how often?*, 5

la fresa *strawberry*, 4

fresco/a: Hace fresco. *It's cool (weather).*, 5

los frijoles *beans*, 6

frío *cold*, 5; **Hace frío.** *It's cold.*, 5; Hace un frío tremendo. *It's incredibly cold.*, 5

la fruta *fruit*, 1

la frutería *fruit store*, 2

fue *was*, 4; fue construido/a *was built*, 4

fuerte *strong*, 6

fundado/a *founded*, 2

el fútbol *soccer*, 1; **el fútbol norteamericano** *football*, 1

el futuro *future*, 2

la gaita *bagpipes*, 4

gallego/a *Galician*, 3

ganar *to win*, 3

ganas: tener ganas (de) *to feel like doing something*, 3

el gato *cat*, 6; **cuidar al gato** *to take care of the cat*, 6

general *general;* por lo general *in general*, 4

generoso/a *generous*, 6

¡Genial! *Great!*, 2

la gente *people*, 3

la geografía *geography*, 3

el gimnasio *gym*, 4

el gobierno *government*, 6

la goma de borrar *eraser*, 2

gordo/a *fat, overweight*, 6; **un poco gordo/a** *a little overweight*, 6

Gracias. *Thanks.*, 1; **Estoy (bastante) bien, gracias.** *I'm (pretty) well, thanks.*, 1

la gráfica *graphic*, 2

la gramática *grammar*, 1

grande *big*, 3

gris *gray*, P

el grupo *group*, 1

guapo/a *good-looking*, 3

la guerra *war*, 3

la guía *guide*, 2

el güiro *Andean percussive musical instrument*, 4

la guitarra *guitar*, 4

gustar *to like someone/something;* **A mí me gusta** + infinitive *I (emphatic) like to . . .*, 4; **¿A quién le gusta...?** *Who likes . . .?*, 4; **le gustan** *he/she likes*, 3; **les gusta** *they like*, 5; **Me gusta...** *I like . . .*, 1; **Me gusta más...** *I prefer . . .*, 1; **me gustan** *I like*, 3; **No me gusta...** *I don't like . . .*, 1; **nos gusta** *we like*, 5; **Nos gustan...** *We like . . .*, 5; **¿Qué te gusta?** *What do you (familiar) like?*, 1; **¿Qué te gusta hacer?** *What do you (familiar) like to do?*, 4; **Sí, me gusta.** *Yes, I like it.*, 1; **¿Te gusta...?** *Do you (familiar) like . . .?*, 1; **Te gustan...** *You (familiar) like . . .*, 3

gusto: Mucho gusto. *Nice to meet you.*, 1; gustos personales *personal likes*, 1

haber *to have (auxiliary verb)*, 4

hablando *speaking*, 2

hablar *to speak, to talk;* **hablar por teléfono** *to talk on the phone*, 4

hacer *to do, to make*, 2; **Hace buen tiempo.** *The weather is nice.*, 5; **Hace calor.** *It's hot.*, 5; **Hace fresco.** *It's cool.*, 5; **Hace frío.** *It's cold.*, 5; **Hace mal tiempo.** *The weather is bad.*, 5; **Hace (mucho) frío.** *It's (very) cold.*, 5; **Hace sol.** *It's sunny.*, 5; Hace un calor espantoso. *It's terribly hot.*, 5; Hace un frío tremendo. *It's incredibly cold.*, 5; Hace un tiempo precioso. *It's a beautiful day.*, 5; **Hace viento.** *It's windy.*, 5; **hacer ejercicio** *to exercise*, 5; **hacer la cama** *to make the bed*, 6; **hacer un viaje** *to take a trip*, 6; haga *do (command)*, 3; **¿Qué debo hacer?** *What should I do?*, 6; ¿Qué hacemos? *What shall we do?*, 4; **¿Qué hacen ustedes los fines de semana?** *What do you do on weekends?*, 6; **¿Qué tiempo hace?** *What's the weather like?*, 5

el hado *destiny, fate*, 2

haga *do (command)*, 3

la hamburguesa *hamburger*, 5

haría *he/she would do/make*, P

hasta *until;* **Hasta luego.** *See you later.*, 1; **Hasta mañana.** *See you tomorrow.*, 1

hay *there is, there are*, 2

el helado *ice cream*, 4; **tomar un helado** *to eat ice cream*, 4

el helicóptero *helicopter*, P

la herencia *heritage*, P

la hermana *sister*, 6; **la media hermana** *half sister*, 6

la hermanastra *stepsister*, 6

el hermanastro *stepbrother*, 6

el hermano *brother*, 6; **el medio hermano** *half brother*, 6

los hermanos *brothers, brothers and sisters*, 6

el héroe *hero*, 3

la hija *daughter*, 6

el hijo *son*, 6

los hijos *children*, 6

hispano/a *Hispanic*, P

hispanohablante *Spanish speaking*, P

la historia *history*, 3

¡Hola! *Hello!*, 1

el hombre *man*, 6

la hora *hour, time;* **¿A qué hora es...?** *At what time is . . .?*, 3; es hora de... *it's time to . . .*, 5; hora latina *Latin time*, 3; hora local *local time*, 3; **¿Qué hora es?** *What time is it?*, 3

el horario escolar *school schedule*, 3

Horrible. *Horrible.*, 1; ¡Qué horrible! *How terrible!*, 2

el hospital *hospital*, 3

hoy *today*, 3; **¿Cuál es la fecha hoy?** *What is today's date?*, 5; **Hoy es el... de...** *Today is the (date) of (month).*, 5;

¿Qué fecha es hoy? *What's today's date?*, 5
el huevo *egg*, 4
el humor *humor*, 1
el huracán *hurricane*, 5

el idioma *language*, 4
la iglesia *church*, 6
  igual *equal*, 6
  Igualmente. *Same here.*, 1
ilustrada *illustrated*, 2
la imagen *image* (pl. las imágenes), 4
  ¡Increíble! *Incredible!*, 2
independiente *independent*, 6
la industria extractiva *mining industry*, 3
infantil *for children*, 3
la ingeniera *engineer* (female), 3
el ingeniero *engineer* (male), 3
el inglés *English (language)*, 1; **la clase de inglés** *English class*, 1
ingresar *to enter*, 1
la instalación *installation, facility*, 1
el instituto *institute*, 3
el instrumento (musical) *instrument*, 4; **tocar un instrumento** *to play a musical instrument*, 4
inteligente *intelligent*, 3
interesante *interesting*, 3
interrumpirse *to be interrupted*, 6; interrumpe *interrupts*, 6
íntimo/a *intimate*, 1
intocable *untouchable*, 3
la intriga *intrigue*, 3
el invierno *winter*, 5
  ir *to go*, 2; **ir al centro comercial** *to go to the mall*, 2; ir de compras *to go shopping*, 4
la isla *island*, 2
  italiano/a *Italian*, 1; **la comida italiana** *Italian food*, 1

el jabón *soap*, P
el jardín *garden*, 6; **trabajar en el jardín** *to work in the garden*, 6
el jazz *jazz*, 1
el jefe *boss*, 3
  joven *young*, 6; **Se ve joven.** *He/She looks young.*, 6
el juego *game;* juego de ingenio

guessing game, 1; **el videojuego** *videogame*, 3
el jueves *Thursday*, 4
jugar (ue) *to play*, 4; jugar al tenis *to play tennis*, 4
el jugo *juice*, 5
  juguetón *playful* (f. juguetona), 6
  julio (m.) *July*, 5
  junio (m.) *June*, 5
juntamos: nos juntamos *we get together*, 4
juntos/as *together*, 5
la juventud *youth*, 3

el kilómetro *kilometer*, P

L

  la *the* (sing.), 1
el lado *side;* **al lado de** *next to*, 4; el cafetín de al lado *the coffee shop around the corner*, 6
el lago *lake*, 5
la lámpara *lamp*, 2
la lancha *launch, boat*, 5
el lápiz *pencil*, 2; lápiz de color *colored pencil*, 2
  largo/a *long*, 5
  las *the* (pl.), 3
el latín *Latin (language)*, 3
  lavar *to wash;* **lavar el carro** *to wash the car*, 4; **lavar la ropa** *to wash the clothes*, 4
las lecciones *lessons*, 5; tomar lecciones *to take lessons*, 5
  leer *to read*, 5
  legítimo/a *legitimate*, 1
  lejos *far;* **lejos de** *far from*, 4
el lempira unit of currency in Honduras, 2
  Les gusta + infinitive *They/You (plural) like to . . .*, 5
la letra *(alphabet) letter*, 1
el levantamiento de pesas *weightlifting*, 4
el libertador *liberator*, P
  libre *free*, 3; **día libre** *free day*, 3; **tiempo libre** *free time*, 4
la librería *bookstore*, 2
el libro *book*, 2
la licenciada woman with academic degree comparable to Bachelor of Arts, 3
el licenciado man with academic degree comparable to Bachelor of Arts, 3

limpiar *to clean*, 6; **limpiar la cocina** *to clean the kitchen*, 6
la línea *line*, 4
el lío *mess;* **¡Qué lío!** *What a mess!*, 3
liso/a *straight;* pelo liso *straight hair*, 6
la lista *list*, 2
  listo/a *clever, smart* (with **ser**), 6; *ready* (with **estar**), 2
la literatura *literature*, 3
la llamada *telephone call*, 3
  llamarse *to be named;* **¿Cómo te llamas?** *What's your* (familiar) *name?*, 1; **Me llamo...** *My name is . . .*, 1; **Se llama...** *His/Her name is . . .*, 1
la llanta *tire*, P
  llegué *I arrived*, 3
  llover (ue) *to rain;* 5; **Está lloviendo.** *It's raining.*, 5; Está lloviendo a cántaros. *It's raining cats and dogs.*, 5; **Llueve.** *It's raining.*, 5
lo más rápido posible *as quickly as possible*, 5; lo que pasó *what happened*, 4; lo bueno *what's good; the good thing*, 5
el lobo *wolf*, 4
  lograr *to achieve*, 4
  los *the* (pl.), 3
  ¿los conoces? *do you know them?*, P
las luces *lights*, 2
la lucha libre *wrestling*, 1
  luego *then, later*, 3; **Hasta luego.** *See you later.*, 1
el lunes *Monday*, 4
la lupa *magnifying glass*, 2
la luz *light*, 2

M

la madrastra *stepmother*, 6
la madre *mother*, 6
la madrileña *resident of Madrid* (female), 1
el madrileño *resident of Madrid* (male), 1
la madrina *godmother*, 6
maduro/a *mature*, 6
los maduros *ripe plantains*, 6
la maestra *teacher* (female), 3
el maestro *teacher* (male), 3
  mal *poorly; bad*, 1; No está mal. *It's not bad.*, 2
  malo/a *bad*, 3; **Hace maltiempo.** *The weather is bad.*, 5

la **mamá** *mom*, 6
el mamey *mamey* (fruit), 6
el mamífero *mammal*, 2
el mango *mango* (fruit), 3
'mano *friend* (short for 'hermano'), 4
mantener (ie) *to maintain*, 6; mantener correspondencia *to write letters back and forth*, 4
mantuvieron *they maintained*, 6
la **mañana** *morning*, 3; **de la mañana** *in the morning* (A.M.), 3; **por la mañana** *in the morning*, 5
mañana *tomorrow*, 3; **Hasta mañana.** *See you tomorrow.*, 1;
el mapa *map*, 1
la máquina del tiempo *time machine*, 2
el mar *sea*, 6; el Mar Mediterráneo *Mediterranean Sea*, 1
el marcador *marker*, 2
marrón *brown*, P
el **martes** *Tuesday*, 4
marzo (m.) *March*, 5
más *more*, 1; **Más o menos.** *So-so.*, 1; **Me gusta más...** *I prefer . . .*, 1
la máscara *mask*, P
la mascota *pet*, 6
las **matemáticas** *mathematics*, 3
la **materia** *subject*, 3
la matrícula *enrollment*, 3
mayo (m.) *May*, 5
mayor *older*, 6
mc *(to, for) me*, 1; me acuesto *I go to bed*, 3; **Me gusta...** *I like . . .*, 1; **Me gusta más...** *I prefer . . .*, 1; **me gustan...** *I like . . .*, 3; **Me llamo...** *My name is . . .*, 1; me meto *I go in*, 6; me pongo *Me pongo a estudiar.: I start studying.*, 3; me quedo con *I stay with*, 6
medio/a *half;* **media hermana** *half sister*, 6; **medio hermano** *half brother*, 6; **y media** *half past (the hour)*, 3
el mediodía *noon, midday*, 3
mejor *best; better*, 5
menor *younger*, 6
menos *less*, 6; **Más o menos.** *So-so.*, 1; **menos cuarto** *quarter to (the hour)*, 3
menudo/a *minute, small;* a menudo *often*, 5

el mercado *market*, 3
el mes *month*, 5; **El ... de este mes hay ...** *On the (date) of this month, there is/are . . .*, 5
la mesa *table*, 2; **poner la mesa** *to set the table*, 6
mestizo/a *of mixed Indian and European descent*, 6
meter *to put in*, 6; me meto *I go in*, 6
mi *my*, 2; **mis** *my*, 6
mí *me* (emphatic); **A mí me gusta** + infinitive *I* (emphatic) *like to . . .*, 4
el microscopio *microscope*, 2
el miedo *fear*, 6
el miércoles *Wednesday*, 4
la **milla** *mile*, 5; las millas por hora *miles per hour*, 5
mimoso/a *affectionate*, 6
el minuto *minute*, 2
mirar *to watch, to look at*, 4; mira *look*, 1; **mirar la televisión** *to watch television*, 4
mismo/a *same*, 3
el misterio *mystery*, 1
la **mochila** *book bag; backpack*, 2
el modelo *example, model*, 1
el modo *way, mode*, 2
la montaña *mountain*, 5
montar *to ride;* **montar en bicicleta** *to ride a bike*, 3
morado/a *purple*, P
moreno/a *dark-haired, dark-skinned*, 3
la moto *motorcycle*, 1
el motoesquí *jet-ski*, 5
el movimiento *movement*, 6
la muchacha *girl*, 3
el muchacho *boy*, 3
mucho *a lot*, 1
mucho/a *a lot (of)*, 2; **Mucho gusto.** *Nice to meet you.*, 1
muchos/as *many, a lot of*, 2; **muchas veces** *often*, 5
muerde *bites*, 6
la mujer *woman*, 6
el mundo *world*, P
municipal *municipal, city* (adj.), 4
el mural *mural*
el museo *museum*, 3
la **música** *music*, 1; escuchar música *to listen to music*, 4; **la música clásica/pop/rock** *classical/pop/rock music*, 1; **la música de...** *music by . . .*, 1

muy *very*, 1; **muy bien** *very well*, 1; **(muy) mal.** *(very) bad*, 1

nada *nothing*, 5
nadar *to swim*, 4
nadie *nobody*, 5
el náhuatl *Nahuatl* (language), 4
la naranja *orange*, 6
la **natación** *swimming*, 1
necesitar *to need*, 2; **necesita** *he/she needs*, 2; **necesitas** *you* (familiar) *need*, 2; **necesito** *I need*, 2
negro/a *black*, 6
nevar (ie) *to snow;* **Está nevando.** *It's snowing.*, 5; **Nieva.** *It's snowing.*, 5
ni *nor*, 6; ni... ni... *neither... nor . . .*, 6
la niña *child* (female), 2
el niño *child* (male), 2
los niños *children*, 2
el nivel *level*, 4
no *no*, 1; **¿no?** *isn't it?*, 3; **No es aburrido/a.** *It's not boring.*, 3; **No es cierto.** *It isn't true.*, 6; **No me gusta...** *I don't like . . .*, 1; **No sé.** *I don't know.*, 2; **No te preocupes.** *Don't worry.*, 3
la **noche** *night;* **Buenas noches.** *Good night.*, 1; **de la noche** *in the evening* (P.M.), 3; **por la noche** *at night*, 5
el nombre *name*, P; nombre completo *full name*, 6; nombres comunes *common names*, P
normal *normal*, 5
normalmente *normally*, 2
el norte *north*, 1
norteamericano/a *of or from the U.S.*, 1
nos *we, us*, 5; **Nos gusta** + infinitive *We like to . . .*, 5; nos juntamos *we get together*, 4
nosotros/as *we*, 4; **nosotros/as** *us* (after preposition), 5
las noticias *news*, 5
notificar *to notify*, 1
la **novela** *novel*, 3
noventa *ninety*, 2
noviembre (m.) *November*, 5
nublado/a *cloudy*, 5; **Está nublado.** *It's cloudy.*, 5
nuestro/a *our*, 6

nueve *nine,* 1
nuevo/a *new,* 3; **nuevos amigos** *new friends,* 2
el número *number,* 1; el número secreto *secret number,* 1
numeroso *numerous,* 6
nunca *never, not ever,* 5

o *or;* **Más o menos.** *So-so.,* 1
o ... o *either . . . or*
el oceanario *oceanography institute,* 2
el océano *ocean,* 5; océano Atlántico *Atlantic Ocean,* P; océano Índico *Indian Ocean,* P; océano Pacífico *Pacific Ocean,* P
ochenta *eighty,* 2
ocho *eight,* 1
octubre (m.) *October,* 5
el oeste *west,* 1
la oficina *office,* 4
oír *to hear, to listen to,* 4; ¡Oye! *Listen!,* 3
los ojos *eyes,* 6; **Tiene ojos verdes/azules.** *He/She has green/blue eyes.,* 6
la ola *wave,* 5
olímpico/a *Olympic,* 5
once *eleven,* 1
operar *to operate,* 5
la oración *sentence,* 6
el orden *order (sequence),* 6
las órdenes *orders;* a sus órdenes *at your service,* 5
organizado/a *organized,* 6
organizar *to organize,* 2
el orgullo *pride,* 3
el oro *gold,* 4
oscuro/a *dark,* P
el oso *bear,* P
el otoño *fall,* 5
otro/a *other; another,* 4
¡Oye! *Listen!,* 3

el padrastro *stepfather,* 6
el padre *father,* 6
los padres *parents,* 6
el padrino *godfather,* 6; los padrinos *godparents,* 1
la página *page,* 4
el país *country,* 4
el palacio de gobierno *town hall,* 4
la papa *potato,* 5; **las papas fritas** *french fries,* 5
el papá *dad,* 6
la papaya *papaya* (fruit), 2

el papel *paper,* 2
el par *pair,* 5
para *for, to,* 4; **para +** infinitive *in order to,* 4
el parador *roadside stand,* 6
el pariente *relative,* 6
el parking *parking lot; parking garage* (Spain), 4
el parque *park,* 4; **descansar en el parque** *to rest in the park,* 4
participar *to participate,* 5
el partido de... *game of . . .* (sport), 3
el pasado *past,* 6
el pasaje *fare; passage,* 3; *passageway,* 4
pasar *to pass; to spend (time),* 4; **pasar el rato con amigos** *to spend time with friends,* 4; **pasar la aspiradora** *to vacuum,* 6
el pasatiempo *hobby, pastime,* 1
el paseo *walk, stroll;* 4
el paso *step,* 1
pasó *happened;* lo que pasó *what happened,* 4
pata: ¡Hola, pata! *Hey, man!* (slang: Peru), 4
patinar en línea *to in-line skate,* 6
la pecera *fishbowl,* 2
los peces *fish* (sing. el pez), 2
la película *movie, film,* 4; **ver una película** *to see a film,* 4
pelirrojo/a *redheaded,* 6
el pelo *hair,* 6
la pelota *ball,* 6
pequeño/a *small,* 3
la pérdida *loss,* 1
perezoso/a *lazy,* 6
el periódico *newspaper,* 5
el permiso *permission, permit,* P
pero *but,* 1
el perro *dog,* 4
personal *personal,* 2; anuncios personales *personal ads,* 4; estilo personal *personal style,* 2
la personalidad *personality,* 1
pesado/a *heavy,* 2; ¡Qué pesado/a! *How annoying!,* 2
pescar *to fish,* 5
¡Pésimo! *Terrible!,* 2
el peso *unit of currency in Mexico (and other countries),* 2
el pez *fish* (los peces), 2; el pez de colores *goldfish,* 6
el piano *piano,* 4
¡Piénsalo! *Think about it!,* 2
el pincel *paintbrush,* 2

pintar *to paint,* 4
la pintura *paint,* 2; *painting,* 4
la piña *pineapple,* 2
los Pirineos *Pyrenees (Mountains),* 1
la piscina *swimming pool,* 4
el piso *apartment,* 2
la pizza *pizza,* 1
la pizzería *pizzeria,* 2
la placa *license plate,* P
planchar *to iron,* 6
el planeta *planet,* 5
la planta *plant,* 2
la plata *silver,* 4
el plátano *banana,* 6
el platero *silversmith* (f. la platera), 4
el plato *dish,* 6; lavar los platos *to wash the dishes,* 6
la playa *beach,* 5; **por la playa** *along the beach,* 5
la plaza *town square,* 4
la pluma *ballpoint pen,* 2
poco *a little,* 6; un poco de todo *a little bit of everything,* 4; **un poco gordo/a** *a little overweight,* 6; pocas veces *not very often,* 5
el poema *poem,* 5
policíaco/a *police* (adj.), *detective* (adj.), 3
el pollo asado *roasted chicken,* 6
poner *to put, to place,* 2; Me pongo a estudiar. *I start studying.,* 3; **poner la mesa** *to set the table,* 6
por *at,* 3; *by,* 5; *in; around,* 4; **por eso** *that's why, for that reason,* 4; por favor *please,* P; **por fin** *at last,* 3; **por la mañana** *in the morning,* 5; **por la noche** *at night, in the evening,* 5; **por la playa** *along the beach,* 5; **por la tarde** *in the afternoon,* 5; por lo general *in general,* 4; **por teléfono** *on the phone,* 4
¿Por qué? *Why?,* 3; **¿Por qué no...?** *Why don't . . .?,* 3
porque *because,* 3
la portada *cover* (of a book or magazine), 2
posible *possible,* 5
practicar *to practice,* 4; **practicar deportes** *to play sports,* 4
el precio *price,* 4
precioso/a *beautiful; really nice,* 5; Hace un tiempo precioso. *It's a beautiful day.,* 5
la pregunta *question,* 3

preliminar   *preliminary,* P

el Premio Nóbel   *Nobel Prize,* 3

preocuparse   *to worry;* **No te preocupes.**   *Don't worry.,* 3

preparar   *to prepare,* 4

preparatorio/a   *preparatory,* 3

presentable   *presentable, well dressed,* 6

presentar   *to introduce,* 1

la prima   *cousin* (female), 6

la primavera   *spring,* 5

primero/a   *first,* 3; **el primero**   *the first (of the month),* 5

el **primo**   *cousin* (male), 6

los primos   *cousins,* 6

la princesa   *princess,* 4

la prisa   *haste;* ¡**Date prisa!**   *Hurry up!,* 3; **Tengo prisa.**   *I'm in a hurry.,* 3

el prisionero *prisoner* (f. la prisionera), 3

probar (ue)   *to try, to taste,* 6

el **problema**   *problem,* 6

el **profesor**   *teacher* (male), 3

la **profesora**   *teacher* (female), 3

el programa   *program,* 3; el programa de televisión   *television program,* 3

el pronóstico del tiempo   *weather report,* 5

el protagonista   *protagonist, main character,* 2

próximo/a   *next,* 5

la prueba contra reloj   *time trial,* 4

la psicopedagogía   *educational psychology,* 3

ptas.   abbreviation of **pesetas,** currency of Spain, 2

pueden   *(they) can,* 2

puedo   *I can,* 2

la puerta   *door,* 2

pues   *well . . .,* 2

punto: **en punto**   *on the dot,* 3

el pupitre   *student desk,* 2

que   *that, which, who,* 4; **Dice que...**   *He/she says that . . .,* 6

¿**Qué?**   *What?;* ¿**Qué clases tienes?**   *What classes do you* (familiar) *have?,* 3; ¿**Qué fecha es hoy?**   *What's today's date?,* 5; ¿Qué hacemos?   *What shall we do?,* 4; ¿Qué hacen?   *What are they doing?,* 4; ¿**Qué haces después de clases?**   *What do you*

(familiar) *do after school?,* 4; ¿**Qué hay?**   *What's up?,* 1; ¿**Qué hay en...?**   *What's in . . .?,* 2; ¿**Qué hora es?**   *What time is it?,* 3; ¡Qué horrible!   *How terrible!,* 2; ¿Qué hubo?   *What's up?,* 1; ¡Qué lío!   *What a mess!,* 3; ¿Qué onda?   *What's up?,* 1; ¡Qué padre!   *How cool!,* 2; ¿Qué pasa?   *What's happening?,* 1; ¡Qué pesado/a!   *How annoying!,* 2; ¿**Qué tal?**   *How's it going?,* 1; ¿**Qué te gusta hacer?**   *What do you* (familiar) *like to do?,* 4; ¿**Qué te gusta?**   *What do you* (familiar) *like?,* 1; ¿**Qué tiempo hace?**   *What's the weather like?,* 5

los quehaceres domésticos   *household chores,* 6

querer (ie)   *to want,* 2

querido/a   *dear,* 6

el quetzal   *Guatemalan bird, Guatemalan currency,* P

¿**quién?**   *who?,* 4; ¿**quiénes?**   *who?* (plural), 5

Quiere...   *He/She wants . . .,* 2; quiere decir   *means,* 4; **Quieres...**   *You* (familiar) *want . . .,* 2; **Quiero...**   *I want . . .,* 2

la química   *chemistry,* 3

quince   *fifteen,* 1

la radio   *radio,* 2

rápido/a   *quick, fast, quickly,* 5

el raspado   *snowcone,* 4

real   *royal,* 1

recibir   *to receive,* 5

el recorrido   *tour,* 4

el recuerdo   *souvenir, remembrance,* 1

el refresco   *soft drink,* 4; **tomar un refresco**   *to drink a soft drink,* 4

el regalo   *present,* 4

la regla   *ruler,* 2

regresar   *to return, to go back, to come back,* 4

Regular.   *Okay.,* 1

la reina   *queen,* P

la religión   *religion,* 3

el reloj   *clock, watch,* 2

remar   *to row,* 4

el remo   *paddle, oar,* 5

el repaso   *review,* 1

el reportaje   *report,* 5

los reptiles   *reptiles,* 2

respondes   *you answer,* 1

responsable   *responsible,* 6

la respuesta   *answer, response,* 2

el restaurante   *restaurant,* 4

el retrato   *portrait,* 6

la reunión   *meeting, reunion,* 6

reunirse   *to gather, to meet,* 6

la revista   *magazine,* 2

el rey   *king,* 6

el río   *river,* 5

el ritmo   *rhythm,* 5

roer   *to gnaw,* 6

rojo/a   *red,* P

romántico/a   *romantic,* 4

la ropa   *clothing,* 2; **lavar la ropa**   *to wash the clothes,* 4

rosado/a   *pink,* P

rubio/a   *blond(e),* 3

el **sábado**   *Saturday,* 4

saber   *to know (information);* **No sé.** *I don't know.,* 2; **Sé.** *I know.,* 2; No saben.   *They don't know.,* 6

¿sabías?   *did you know?,* P

el sabor   *taste,* 4

el sacapuntas   *pencil sharpener,* 2

sacar   *to take out,* 4; **sacar la basura**   *to take out the trash,* 4; sacar buenas/malas notas   *to get good/bad grades*

la sala   *living room,* 6; la sala de clase   *classroom,* 4

salgo   *I go out,* 5

salir   *to go out, to leave,* 6

el salón   *hall,* 4

saludar   *to greet,* 3

el saludo   *greeting,* 1

salvar   *to save,* 2

el salvavidas   *life jacket,* P

la sandía   *watermelon,* 2

el sándwich   *sandwich,* 5

santo/a   *saint,* 1

Se llama...   *Her/His/Your name is . . .,* 1

Se ve joven.   *He/She looks young.,* 6

sé   *I know,* 2; **No sé.**   *I don't know.,* 2

el secreto   *secret,* 1

seguidamente   *immediately afterward,* 5

segundo/a   *second,* 1

seis   *six,* 1

el semáforo   *traffic signal,* 5

la semana   *week,* 4; los días de semana   *weekdays;* 4;

los días de la semana *the days of the week,* 5; **fin de semana** *weekend,* 4

el semestre *semester,* 3

señor *sir, Mister,* 1; **el señor** *the (gentle)man*

señora *ma'am, Mrs.,* 1; **la señora** *the woman, the lady*

señorita *miss,* 1; **la señorita** *the young girl; the lady*

el sentido *sense, faculty of sensation,* 5

septiembre (m.) *September,* 5

ser *to be,* 1; **¿Cómo es?** *What's he/she/it like?,* 3; **¿Cómo son?** *What are they like?,* 3; **¿De dónde eres?** *Where are you* (familiar) *from?,* 1; **Es de...** *He/She is from . . .,* 1; **Es la una.** *It's one o'clock,* 3; **No es cierto.** *It isn't true.,* 6; **ser unido(s)** *to be close-knit,* 6; **somos** *we are,* 3; **Son las...** *It's . . . o'clock.,* 3; **soy** *I am,* 1; **Soy de...** *I'm from . . .,* 1

serio/a *serious,* 5

el servicio *service,* 1

sesenta *sixty,* 2

la sesión *session,* 4

setenta *seventy,* 2

si *if,* 4

sí *yes,* 1

la sicología *psychology,* 1

siempre *always,* 5; **casi siempre** *almost always,* 6

siento *I regret;* lo siento *I'm sorry,* 1

la siesta *nap; afternoon rest,* 3

siete *seven,* 1

el siglo *century,* 4

siguiente *following*

la silla *chair,* 2

simpático/a *nice,* 3

sin *without,* 3; sin determinar, *undetermined;* 4

la situación *situation,* 1

sobre *about, on,* 5

el socio *member, associate* (f. la socia), 1

la sociología *sociology,* 1

el sol *sun,* 5; **Hace sol.** *It's sunny.,* 5

sólo *only,* 5; **sólo cuando** *only when,* 5

el sombrero *hat*

somos *we are,* 3; **somos cinco** *there are five of us,* 6

son *(they) are,* 3; **¿Cómo son...?** *What are . . . like?,* 3; **Son las...** *It's . . . o'clock.,* 3

el sonido *sound,* 1

la sopa *soup,* 1

soy *I am,* 1; **Soy de...** *I'm from . . .,* 1

Sta. abbreviation of **santa** *(saint),* 1

Sto. abbreviation of **santo** *(saint),* 1

su(s) *his, her,* 2; *their, your (formal),* 6

el suéter *sweater,* 5

la sugerencia *suggestion,* 2

el supermercado *supermarket,* 4

el sur *south,* 1

tal: ¿Qué tal? *How's it going?,* 1

el taller *shop, workshop,* 1

la tamalada *party to make tamales, a Mexican dish,* 6

el tamaño *size,* 5

también *too, also,* 1; **Yo también.** *Me too.,* 1

las tapas *hors d'oeuvres* (Spain), 1

la taquilla *ticket office,* 4

tarde *late,* 3; **Es tarde.** *It's late.,* 3

la tarde *afternoon,* 3; **Buenas tardes.** *Good afternoon.,* 1; **de la tarde** *in the afternoon* (P.M.), 3; **por la tarde** *in the afternoon,* 5

la tarea *homework,* 1

la tarjeta *card;* **tarjeta postal** *postcard,* 5

te *(to, for) you,* 1; **No te preocupes.** *Don't worry.,* 3; **¿Te acuerdas?** *Do you remember?,* 5; **¿Te gusta...?** *Do you like . . .?,* 1; **te gustan** *you like,* 3; te presento a... *I'd like you to meet,* 1; te toca a ti *It's your turn.,* 2

el teatro *theater,* 1

la tecnología *technology,* 1

tecnológico/a *technological,* 3

la tele *TV,* 3

el teléfono *telephone,* 4; **por teléfono** *on the phone,* 4

la telenovela *soap opera,* 3

la televisión *television,* 4; el programa de televisión *television program,* 3; **mirar la televisión** *to watch television,* 4

el televisor *television set,* 2

tenemos *we have,* 3

tener (ie) *to have,* 2; **Bueno, tengo clase.** *Well, I have class.,* 1; **¿Cuántos años tiene?** *How old is (he/she)?,* 1; **¿Cuántos años tienes?** *How old are you* (familiar)*?,* 1; **tengo** *I have,* 2; **Tengo ... años.** *I'm . . . years old.,* 1; **Tengo prisa.** *I'm in a hurry.,* 3; **Tengo que irme.** *I have to go.,* 1; **tiene** *he/she has,* 2; **Tiene ... años.** *He/She is . . . years old.,* 1; **Tiene canas.** *He/She has gray hair.,* 6; **Tiene ojos verdes/azules.** *He/She has green/blue eyes.,* 6; **tienes** *you* (familiar) *have,* 2

el tenis *tennis,* 1; **las zapatillas de tenis** *tennis shoes* (Spain), 1

tercero/a *third,* 1

terminar *to end, to finish,* 5

la terraza *balcony,* 4

el terror *terror,* 2

ti *you* (emphatic); **¿A ti qué te gusta hacer?** *What do you* (emphatic) *like to do?,* 6

la tía *aunt,* 6

el tiburón *shark,* 6

el tiempo *weather, time,* 5; **(en) el tiempo libre** *(during) free time,* 4; **Hace buen tiempo.** *The weather is nice.,* 5; **Hace mal tiempo.** *The weather is bad.,* 5; Hace un tiempo precioso. *It's a beautiful day.,* 5; pronóstico del tiempo *weather report,* 5; **¿Qué tiempo hace?** *What's the weather like?,* 5

la tienda *store,* 4

tiene *he/she has,* 2; **Tiene ... años.** *He/She is . . . years old.,* 1; **Tiene canas.** *He/She has gray hair.,* 6

tienes *you* (familiar) *have,* 2

la tierra *Earth,* 2

las tijeras *scissors,* 2

la tilde *tilde,* (diacritical mark over the letter ñ), 1

tímido/a *shy,* 6

el tío *uncle,* 6

típicamente *typically,* 5

típico/a *typical, characteristic,* P

el tipo *type, kind*

las tiras cómicas *comics,* 5

el tocador de discos compactos *CD player,* 2
tocar *to touch, to play;* **tocar un instrumento** *to play an instrument,* 4
todavía *still, yet,* 5
todo/a *all, every,* 5; todo el mundo *everyone, everybody,* 4; todo el tiempo *all the time,* 5; **todos los días** *every day,* 5
tomar *to drink, to take,* 4; **tomar el autobús** *to take the bus,* 5
el tomo *volume, tome,* 2
la toronja *grapefruit,* 6
la tortilla *omelet* (Spain), 1; *corn cake* (Mexico)
los tostones *fried green plantains,* 6
trabajador/a *hard-working,* 6
trabajar *to work,* 4; **trabajar en el jardín** *to work in the garden,* 6
el **trabajo** *work, job,* 4
el trabalenguas *tongue twister,* 2
tradicional *traditional,* 6
las tradiciones *traditions,* 6
transportado/a *transported,* 2
el transporte *transportation,* 1
travieso/a *mischievous,* 6
trece *thirteen,* 1
treinta *thirty,* 1
tremendo/a *tremendous, incredible,* 5; ¡Hace un frío tremendo! *It's incredibly cold!,* 5
tres *three,* 1
el trivia *trivia,* 1
tú *you* (familiar), 1
tu(s) *your (familiar),* 2
el tubo *tube,* 4
tuvo *he/she had,* 4

un *a, an,* 2; **un poco gordo/a** *a little overweight,* 6
una *a, an,* 2
la una *one,* 3; **Es la una.** *It's one o'clock.,* 3
único/a *only, unique,* 1
unido/a *close-knit,* 6
el uniforme *school uniform,* 2
uno *one,* 1
unos/as *some, a few,* 2
usar *to use,* 5
usted *you,* 4
ustedes *you* (pl.), 4; **a ustedes** *to you,* 5

útil *useful,* P
la utilización *use,* 1
la uva *grape,* 4

va *he/she goes,* 5
las **vacaciones** *vacation,* 5
el vals *waltz,* 4
vamos a... *let's...;* vamos a escribir *let's write,* 3; vamos a leer *let's read,* 1; **¡Vamos!** *Let's go!, we go,* 3
las variedades *varieties; variety section* (of a magazine or newspaper), 6
varios/varias *various, several,* 3
varonil *men's* (adj.), 4
vas *you* (familiar) *go;* **¿Adónde vas?** *Where are you going?,* 4
las veces *times* (sing. **vez**); **a veces** *sometimes,* 5; **muchas veces** *often,* 5
veinte *twenty,* 1
el velero *sailboat,* 5
la velocidad *velocity, speed,* 5
venezolano/a *of or from Venezuela,* 2
vengo de *I come from,* 1
la **ventana** *window,* 2
ver *to see,* 4; **ver una película** *to see a movie,* 4
el **verano** *summer,* 5
¿verdad? *don't you?, right?,* 3
verde *green,* 6
el vertebrado *vertebrate,* 2
la **vez** *time, turn, occasion, occurrence;* de vez en cuando *once in a while,* 5; **a veces** *sometimes,* 5; **muchas veces** *often,* 5; tres veces por semana *three times a week,* 5; una vez *once,* 5
el **viaje** *trip,* 6; **hacer un viaje** *to take a trip,* 6
el video *video,* 1
la videocasetera *VCR,* 2
el **videojuego** *videogame,* 3
viejo/a *old,* 6
viene de *comes from,* 4
el **viento** *wind,* 5; **Hace (mucho) viento.** *It's (very) windy.,* 5
el **viernes** *Friday,* 4
el violín *violin,* 4
visitar *to visit,* 6
las visitas *visitors,* 6

vivir *to live,* 6
vivo *I live,* 1
vivo/a *alive,* 6
el vocabulario *vocabulary; glossary,* 1
volar cometas *to fly kites,* 5
el **voleibol** *volleyball,* 1
vosotros/as *you* (familiar plural), 4
votar *to vote,* 4
voy *I go* (from **ir**), 3
el vuelo *flight,* 3
vuestro/a *your* (pl., Spain), 6

y *and,* 1; **y cuarto** *quarter past (the hour),* 3; **y media** *half past (the hour),* 3; **¿Y tú?** *And you* (familiar)?, 1
ya *already,* 2
el yate *yacht,* P
yo *I,* 1; **Yo también.** *Me too.,* 1

la zapatería *shoe store,* 4
las **zapatillas de tenis** *tennis shoes* (Spain), 2
el **zapato** *shoe,* 3
el zócalo *main square* (Mex.), 4

ENGLISH-SPANISH VOCABULARY

This vocabulary includes all of the words presented in the **Vocabulario** sections of the chapters. These words are considered active—you are expected to know them and be able to use them. The number after each entry refers to the chapter in which the word first became an active part of your vocabulary.

Longer phrases are listed under the English word you would be most likely to look up. If a Spanish verb is stem-changing, the change is indicated in parentheses after the verb: *querer(ie)*. To be sure you are using the Spanish word in the correct context, refer to the chapters in which they appear.

A

a/an   *un, una,* 2
aerobics   *los ejercicios aeróbicos,* 5
a few   *unos, unas,* 2
affectionate   *cariñoso/a,* 6
after   *después,* 3; *después de,* 4
afternoon   *la tarde,* 3; **in the afternoon**   *de la tarde,* 3; *por la tarde,* 5
afterward   *después,* 3
a little   *un poco,* 6
all   *todo/a, todos/as,* 5
a lot   *mucho,* 1
a lot of; a lot   *mucho/a, muchos/as,* 2
almost   *casi,* 6; **almost always** *casi siempre,* 6
along   *por,* 5; **along the beach** *por la playa,* 5
already   *ya,* 2
always   *siempre,* 5
American   *americano/a,* 1; *norteamericano,* 1; **American football**   *el fútbol norteamericano,* 1
amusing   *divertido/a,* 3
and   *y,* 1; **And you?**   *¿Y tú?,* 1
April   *abril,* 5
art   *el arte,* 3; *las artes* (pl.)
at   *a, por,* 3; **at last**   *por fin,* 3; **at night**   *por la noche,* 5; **At what time . . .?**   *¿A qué hora...?,* 3
attend, to   *asistir a,* 5
August   *agosto,* 5
aunt   *la tía,* 6
autumn   *el otoño,* 5

B

backpack   *la mochila,* 2
bad   *malo/a,* 3
ballpoint pen   *el bolígrafo,* 2
baseball   *el béisbol,* 1
basketball   *el baloncesto,* 1; *el basquetbol,* 3
be, to   *ser,* 1; *estar,* 4;

to be in a hurry   *tener prisa,* 3
beach   *la playa,* 5
because   *porque,* 3
bed   *la cama,* 2
before   *antes de,* 4
belt   *el cinturón*
beneath   *debajo de,* 4
bicycle   *la bicicleta,* 4
big   *grande,* 3
black   *negro/a,* 6
blond   *rubio/a,* 3
blue   *azul,* 6
book   *el libro,* 2
book bag   *la mochila,* 2
bookstore   *la librería,* 2
boring   *aburrido/a,* 3
boy   *el chico,* 5
break   *el descanso,* 3
brother   *el hermano,* 6; **brothers and sisters**   *los hermanos,* 6
brown   *de color café,* 6
bus   *el autobús,* 5
but   *pero,* 1
buy, to   *comprar,* 2
by   *por,* 5
'bye   *chao,* 1

C

cafeteria   *la cafetería,* 1
calculator   *la calculadora,* 2
camp, to   *acampar,* 5
car   *el carro,* 4
cat   *el gato,* 6; **to take care of the cat**   *cuidar al gato,* 6
chair   *la silla,* 2
children   *los hijos,* 6
Chinese food   *la comida china,* 1
chocolate   *el chocolate,* 1
chores   *los quehaceres domésticos,* 6
class   *la clase,* 1
classical music   *la música clásica,* 1
classmate   *el compañero* (male)/ *la compañera* (female) *de clase,* 3
clean, to   *limpiar,* 6; **clean the**

kitchen, to   *limpiar la cocina,* 6
clever   *listo/a,* 6
clock   *el reloj,* 2
close-knit   *unido/a,* 6
closet   *el armario,* 2
clothing   *la ropa,* 2
cloudy   *nublado,* 5; **It's cloudy.** *Está nublado.,* 5
cold   *frío;* **It's cold.**   *Hace frío.,* 5
color   *el color,* 6
Come along!   *¡Ven conmigo!,* P
comical   *cómico/a,* 3
comics   *las tiras cómicas,* 5
companion   *el compañero* (male), *la compañera* (female), 3
computer science   *la computación,* 3
concert   *el concierto,* 3
cousin   *el primo* (male), *la prima* (female), 6
cut, to   *cortar,* 6; **to cut the grass**   *cortar el césped,* 6

D

dad   *el papá,* 6
dance   *el baile,* 3
dance, to   *bailar,* 4
dark-haired   *moreno/a,* 3
dark-skinned   *moreno/a,* 3
daughter   *la hija,* 6
day   *el día,* 4; **every day**   *todos los días,* 5; **a day off**   *un día libre,* 3
December   *diciembre,* 5
delighted   *encantado/a,* 1
desk   *el escritorio,* 2
dictionary   *el diccionario,* 2
difficult   *difícil,* 3
dinner   *la cena,* 4
disagreeable   *antipático/a,* 3
do, to   *hacer,* 2
dog   *el perro,* 4; **to walk the dog** *caminar con el perro,* 4
dollar   *el dólar,* 2
door   *la puerta,* 2
downtown   *el centro,* 4
draw, to   *dibujar,* 4

drink, to *tomar*, 4; *beber*, 5
during *durante*, 5

E

easy *fácil*, 3
eat, to *comer*, 5; **to eat breakfast** *desayunar*, 5; **to eat dinner** *cenar*, 6
education *la educación*, 3; **physical education** *la educación física*, 3
eight *ocho*, 1
eighteen *dieciocho*, 1
eighty *ochenta*, 2
eleven *once*, 1
end *el fin*, 4
English class *la clase de inglés*, 1
eraser *la goma de borrar*, 2
especially *especialmente*, 5
evening *la noche*, 5; **in the evening** (P.M.) *de la noche*, 3
every *todo/a, todos/as*; **every day** *todos los días*, 5
exam *el examen*, 3
excellent *excelente*, 1
exercise *el ejercicio*, 5; **to exercise** *hacer ejercicio*, 5
eyes *los ojos*, 6

F

fall *el otoño*, 5
family *la familia*, 6
fantastic *fantástico/a*, 3
far *lejos*, 4; **far from** *lejos de*, 4
father *el padre*, 6
favorite *favorito/a*, 3
February *febrero*, 5
few, a *unos/as*, 2
fifteen *quince*, 1
fifty *cincuenta*, 2
find, to *encontrar (ue)*, 2
first *primero/a*, 2
fish, to *pescar*, 5
five *cinco*, 1
folder *la carpeta*, 2
food *la comida*, 6; **Chinese food** *la comida china*, 1; **Italian food** *la comida italiana*, 1; **Mexican food** *la comida mexicana*, 1
football *el fútbol norteamericano*, 1
forty *cuarenta*, 2
four *cuatro*, 1
fourteen *catorce*, 1
free time *el tiempo libre*, 4
French *el francés*, 3
french fries *las papas fritas*, 5
Friday *el viernes*, 4
friend *el amigo* (male), *la amiga* (female), 1; *el compañero* (male),

la compañera (female), 3
from *de*, 1
fruit *la fruta*, 1
fun *divertido/a*, 3
funny *cómico/a*, 3

G

game of . . . (sport) *el partido de...*, 3
garden *el jardín*, 6
geography *la geografía*, 3
get to know someone, to *conocer a*, 2
girl *la chica*, 5
go, to *ir*, 2; **to go out** *salir*, 6; **to go to the mall** *ir al centro comercial*, 2
good *bueno/a*, 3; **Good afternoon.** *Buenas tardes.*, 1; **Good evening.** *Buenas noches.*, 1; **Good morning.** *Buenos días.*, 1; **Good night.** *Buenas noches.*, 1
Goodbye. *Adiós.*, 1
good-looking *guapo/a*, 3
grandfather *el abuelo*, 6
grandmother *la abuela*, 6
grandparents *los abuelos*, 6
grass *el césped*, 6
gray hair *las canas*, 6
great *excelente*, 1; *estupendo*, 1
green *verde*, 6
guitar *la guitarra*, 4
gym *el gimnasio*, 4

H

hair *el pelo*, 6 **He/She has gray hair.** *Tiene canas.*, 6
half brother *el medio hermano*, 6
half past (the hour) *y media*, 3
half sister *la media hermana*, 6
hamburger *la hamburguesa*, 5
have, to *tener (ie)*, 2; **to have breakfast** *desayunar*, 5; **to have to go** *tener que irse*, 1
he *él*, 2
heat *el calor*, 5
Hello! *¡Hola!*, 1
help at home, to *ayudar en casa*, 5
her *su(s)*, 2
here *aquí*, 4
high school *el colegio*, 2
his *su(s)*, 2
home *la casa*, 4; **at home** *en casa*, 4
homework *la tarea*, 1
horrible *horrible*, 1
hot, to be *hacer calor*, 4
hour *la hora*, 3
house *la casa*, 4

how? *¿cómo?*, 1; **How are you?** *¿Cómo estás?* (familiar), 1
how many? *¿cuántos?, ¿cuántas?*, 2
how much? *¿cuánto/a?*, 2
how often? *¿con qué frecuencia?*, 5
How old are you? *¿Cuántos años tienes?* (familiar), 1
How's it going? *¿Qué tal?*, 1
hundred *cien, ciento*, 2
hurry *la prisa*; **Hurry up!** *¡Date prisa!*, 3; **I'm in a hurry.** *Tengo prisa.*, 3
husband *el esposo*, 6

I

I *yo*, 1
in *en, por*, 5; **in order to** *para + infinitive*, 4; **in the afternoon** (P.M.) *de la tarde*, 3; *por la tarde*, 5; **in the evening** (P.M.) *de la noche*, 3; *por la noche*, 5; **in the morning** (A.M.) *de la mañana*, 3; *por la mañana*, 5
intelligent *inteligente*, 3
interesting *interesante*, 3
iron, to *planchar*, 6
isn't it? *¿no?*, 3
Italian food *la comida italiana*, 1
It's cold. *Hace frío.*, 5
It's cool. *Hace fresco.*, 5
It's hot. *Hace calor.*, 5
It's raining. *Está lloviendo.*, 5; *Llueve.*, 5
It's snowing. *Está nevando.*, 5; *Nieva.*, 5
It's sunny. *Hace sol.*, 5
It's windy. *Hace viento.*, 5

J

January *enero*, 5
jazz *el jazz*, 1
job *el trabajo*, 4
juice *el jugo*, 5
July *julio*, 5
June *junio*, 5

K

kitchen *la cocina*, 6
know, to *saber*, 2; *conocer*, 2

L

lamp *la lámpara*, 2
late *atrasado/a*, 3; **to be late** *estar atrasado/a*, 3
later *más tarde*, 7
leave, to *salir*, 6

less *menos*, 6
letter *la carta*, 5
library *la biblioteca*, 4
like, to *gustar*, 1
likewise *igualmente*, 1
listen, to *escuchar*, 4; to listen to music *escuchar música*, 4
little, a *un poco*, 6
live, to *vivir*, 6
living room *la sala*, 6
lot, a *mucho*, 1
lunch *el almuerzo*, 3

ma'am *señora*, 1
magazine *la revista*, 2
make the bed, to *hacer la cama*, 6
mall *el centro comercial*, 2; to go to the mall *ir al centro comercial*, 2
many *muchos/as*, 2
March *marzo*, 5
mathematics *las matemáticas*, 3
May *mayo*, 5
me too *yo también*, 1
Mexican food *la comida mexicana*, 1
mile *la milla*, 5
mischievous *travieso/a*, 6
miss *señorita*, 1
mister *señor*, 1
Monday *el lunes*, 4
money *el dinero*, 2
month *el mes*, 5
more *más*, 1
morning *la mañana*, 5; in the morning (A.M.) *de la mañana*, 3; *por la mañana*, 5
mother/mom *la madre/mamá*, 6
movie *la película*, 4
movie theater *el cine*, 4
Mr. *señor*, 1
Mrs. *señora*, 1
music *la música*, 1; classical music *la música clásica*, 1; music by . . . *la música de...*, 1; pop music *la música pop*, 1; rock music *la música rock*, 1
my *mi*, 2; *mis*, 6

named, to be *llamarse*, 1; My name is . . . *Me llamo...*, 1
near *cerca de*, 4
need, to *necesitar*, 2
never *nunca*, 5
new *nuevo/a*, 3; new friends *los nuevos amigos*, 2
newspaper *el periódico*, 5

next to *al lado de*, 4
nice *simpático/a*, 3
Nice to meet you. *Mucho gusto.*, 1
night *la noche*, 1; at night *por la noche*, 5; Good night. *Buenas noches.*, 1
nine *nueve*, 1
nineteen *diecinueve*, 1
ninety *noventa*, 2
no *no*, 1
nobody *nadie*, 5
nor *ni*, 6
not *no*, 1
notebook *el cuaderno*, 2
nothing *nada*, 5
novel *la novela*, 3
November *noviembre*, 5
now *ahora*, 3
number *el número*, P

October *octubre*, 5
of *de*, 2
often *muchas veces*, 5
okay *regular*, 1
old *viejo/a*, 6; older *mayor*, 6
on *en*, 3; on the dot *en punto*, 3; on top of *encima de*, 4
one *uno*, 1
only *sólo*, 5
organize, to *organizar*, 2
ought to, should *deber*, 6
our *nuestro/a*, 6
overweight *gordo/a*; (a little) overweight *un poco gordo/a*, 6

paint, to *pintar*, 4
pal *el compañero* (male), *la compañera* (female), 3
paper *el papel*, 2
parents *los padres*, 6
park *el parque*, 4
party *la fiesta*, 3
pencil *el lápiz*, 2; (pl. *los lápices*)
physical education *la educación física*, 3
piano *el piano*, 4
pizza *la pizza*, 1
pizzeria *la pizzería*, 2
play an instrument, to *tocar un instrumento*, 4
pop music *la música pop*, 1
postcards *las tarjetas postales*, 5
poster *el cartel*, 2
post office *el correo*, 4
potato *la papa*, 5
practice, to *practicar*, 4
prepare, to *preparar*, 4
pretty *bonito/a*, 3

problem *el problema*, 6
put, to *poner*, 2

quarter to (the hour) *menos cuarto*, 3
quite *bastante*, 6

radio *la radio*, 2
read, to *leer*, 5
receive, to *recibir*, 5; to receive letters *recibir cartas*, 5
recess *el descanso*, 3
redheaded *pelirrojo/a*, 6
rest, to *descansar*, 4; to rest in the park *descansar en el parque*, 4
restaurant *el restaurante*, 4
return, to *regresar*, 4
ride, to *montar*, 4; to ride a bike *montar en bicicleta*, 4
right? *¿verdad?*, 3
rock music *la música rock*, 1
room *el cuarto*, 2
ruler *la regla*, 2
run, to *correr*, 5

salad *la ensalada*, 1
Same here. *Igualmente.*, 1
sandwich *el sándwich*, 5
Saturday *el sábado*, 4
say, to *decir*, 6
science *las ciencias*, 3
scuba dive, to *bucear*, 5
seasons *las estaciones*, 5
See you later. *Hasta luego.*, 1
See you tomorrow. *Hasta mañana.*, 1
semester *el semestre*, 3
September *septiembre*, 5
set the table, to *poner la mesa*, 6
seven *siete*, 1
seventeen *diecisiete*, 1
seventy *setenta*, 2
she *ella*, 2
shopping mall *el centro comercial*, 2
short *bajo/a*, 3
should *deber*, 6
sing, to *cantar*, 4
sir *señor*, 1
sister *la hermana*, 6
six *seis*, 1
sixteen *dieciséis*, 1
sixty *sesenta*, 2
ski, to *esquiar*, 5
small *pequeño/a*, 3

smart   *listo/a,* 6
snow   *la nieve,* 5; **It's snowing.**
   Nieva., 5
soccer   *el fútbol,* 1
social studies   *las ciencias*
   sociales, 3
soft drink   *el refresco,* 4
some   *unos/as,* 2
something   *algo,* 6
sometimes   *a veces,* 5
son   *el hijo,* 6
so-so   *más o menos,* 1
Spanish   *el español,* 1
speak, to   *hablar,* 4
spend time with friends, to
   pasar el rato con amigos, 4
sports   *los deportes,* 1
spring   *la primavera,* 5
stepbrother   *el hermanastro,* 6
stepfather   *el padrastro,* 6
stepmother   *la madrastra,* 6
stepsister   *la hermanastra,* 6
still   *todavía,* 5
store   *la tienda,* 4
strict   *estricto/a,* 3
study, to   *estudiar,* 4
subject   *la materia,* 3
summer   *el verano,* 5
Sunday   *el domingo,* 4
supermarket   *el supermercado,* 4
swim, to   *nadar,* 4
swimming   *la natación,* 1
swimming pool   *la piscina,* 4

table   *la mesa,* 2
take, to   *tomar,* 4
take a trip, to   *hacer un viaje,* 6
take care of, to   *cuidar,* 4; **to take**
   care of your brother/sister
   cuidar a tu hermano/a, 4
take out the garbage, to   *sacar*
   la basura, 4
take the bus, to   *tomar el*
   autobús, 5
talk, to   *hablar,* 4; **to talk on the**
   phone   *hablar por teléfono,* 4
tall   *alto/a,* 3
teacher   *el profesor* (male),
   la profesora (female), 3
telephone   *el teléfono,* 4
television   *la televisión,* 4
television set   *el televisor,* 2
tell, to   *decir,* 6
ten   *diez,* 1
tennis   *el tenis,* 1; **tennis shoes**
   (Spain) *las zapatillas de tenis,* 2
Thanks.   *Gracias.,* 1
that   *que,* 4
that's why   *por eso,* 4
the   *el, la,* 1; *los, las,* 3

their   *su(s),* 6
then   *luego,* 3
there   *allá,* 4
there is, there are   *hay,* 2
these   *éstas, éstos,* 6
they   *ellas, ellos,* 3
thin   *delgado/a,* 6
thing   *la cosa,* 2
thirteen   *trece,* 1
thirty   *treinta,* 1
this   *ésta, éste,* 1
three   *tres,* 1
Thursday   *el jueves,* 4
time   *la hora,* 3; **to spend time**
   with friends   *pasar el rato con*
   amigos, 4
to   *a,* 4; **to the**   *al (a + el), a la,* 4
today   *hoy,* 3
together   *juntos/as,* 5
tomorrow   *mañana,* 3
too   *también,* 1
too much   *demasiado/a,* 6
trash   *la basura,* 4
Tuesday   *el martes,* 4
twelve   *doce,* 1
twenty   *veinte,* 1
two   *dos,* 1
typically   *típicamente,* 5

ugly   *feo/a,* 3
uncle   *el tío,* 6
under   *debajo de,* 4

vacation   *las vacaciones,* 5
vacuum cleaner   *la aspiradora,* 6
vacuum, to   *pasar la aspiradora,* 6
very   *muy,* 1; **very bad**   *muy*
   mal, 1; **very well**   *muy bien,* 1
videogame   *el videojuego,* 3
visit, to   *visitar,* 6
volleyball   *el voleibol,* 1

walk, to   *caminar,* 4; **to walk the**
   dog   *caminar con el perro,* 4
want, to   *querer (ie),* 2
wash, to   *lavar,* 4
watch   *el reloj,* 2
watch, to   *mirar,* 4; **to watch TV**
   mirar la televisión, 4
water   *el agua,* 5
we   *nosotros/as,* 4
weather   *el tiempo,* 5; **The**
   weather is bad.   *Hace mal*
   tiempo., 5; **The weather is**
   nice.   *Hace buen tiempo.,* 5
Wednesday   *el miércoles,* 4

week   *la semana,* 4
weekend   *el fin de semana,* 4
Well . . .   *Bueno...,* 2
what?   *¿cuál?,* 3; *¿qué?,* 3
What are . . . like?   *¿Cómo son...?,* 3
What color is . . . ?   *¿De qué*
   color es...?, 6
What do you like?   *¿Qué te*
   gusta? (familiar), 1
What do you like to do?   *¿Qué*
   te gusta hacer? (familiar), 4
What is today's date?   *¿Cuál es*
   la fecha?, 5
What's . . . like?   *¿Cómo es...?,* 3
What's the weather like?   *¿Qué*
   tiempo hace?, 5
What's your name?   *¿Cómo te*
   llamas? (familiar), 1
What time is it?   *¿Qué hora es?,* 3
when   *cuando,* 5
when?   *¿cuándo?,* 3
where   *donde,* 1
where?   *¿dónde?,* 4; **Where are**
   you from?   *¿De dónde eres?,* 1
where (to)?   *¿adónde?,* 4
which   *que,* 4
which?   *¿cuál?,* 3; *¿qué?,* 1
who   *que,* 4
who?   *¿quién?,* 4; *¿quiénes?,* 5;
   Who likes . . . ?   *¿A quién le*
   gusta...?, 4
why?   *¿por qué?,* 3
wife   *la esposa,* 6
window   *la ventana,* 2
winter   *el invierno,* 5
wish, to   *querer (ie),* 2
with   *con,* 4; **with me**   *conmigo,* 4;
   with you   *contigo* (familiar), 4
work   *el trabajo,* 4
work, to   *trabajar,* 4; **to work in the**
   garden   *trabajar en el jardín,* 6
worry, to   *preocuparse,* 3; **Don't**
   worry!   *¡No te preocupes!,* 3
write, to   *escribir,* 5

year   *el año,* 5
yes   *sí,* 1
yet   *todavía,* 5; **not yet**   *todavía*
   no, 5
you   *tú, vosotros/as* (familiar), 4
you   *usted, ustedes* (formal), 4
young   *joven,* 6; **He/She looks**
   young.   *Se ve joven.,* 6
younger   *menor,* 6
your   (familiar) *tu,* 2; *tus,* 6;
   (formal) *su,* 2; *sus,* 6

Z

zero   *cero,* 1

GRAMMAR INDEX

Page numbers in boldface type refer to **Gramática** and **Nota gramatical** presentations. Other page numbers refer to grammar structures presented in the **Así se dice, Nota cultural, Vocabulario,** and **¿Te acuerdas?** sections.

a: see prepositions
accent marks: 7, **30**
adjectives: agreement—masculine and feminine **78, 127;** agreement—singular and plural **78, 127,** 271; demonstrative adjectives—all forms 271; possessive adjectives 76; all forms **237, 271**
adverbs: adverbs of frequency—**siempre, sólo cuando, nunca, todavía, todos los días, muchas veces** 195; **una vez, de vez en cuando, todo el tiempo, cada día, a menudo** 209; adverbs of sequence—**primero, después, por fin** 110; adverbs of time—**por la mañana, por la tarde, por la noche** 209
affirmative expressions: **algo, alguien, alguno (algún), alguna, o ... o, siempre** 272
al: contraction of **a + el** 163, 270
-ando: see present participle
-ar verbs: see verbs
articles: see definite articles, indefinite articles

commands: 122, 125
comparisons: with adjectives using **más ... que, menos ... que, tan ... como** 272; all comparatives, including **tanto/a/os/as ... como** 272
con: see prepositions
conjunctions: **pero** 43, 152, 255; **y** 29, 76, 85, 149; **o** 31, 203; **porque** 129; subordinating conjunction: see **que**
conmigo, contigo: 155
contractions: see **al** and **del**
cuánto: agreement with nouns **78,** 236

dates (calendar): **213**
days of the week: **174**
de: 121; used with color 245; see also prepositions
deber: all present tense forms **255**
definite articles: **el, la 46,** 270; **los, las 109,** 270
del: contraction of **de + el 121,** 270
demonstrative adjectives: all forms 271
demonstrative pronouns: see pronouns
diminutives: 247
direct object pronouns: see pronouns
doler: all present tense forms 273
durante: see prepositions

e → ie stem-changing verbs: 273
el: see definite articles

empezar: 273
en: see prepositions
encantar: all present tense forms 274
-er verbs: see verbs
estar: 31, 161, **162,** 273

frequency: adverbs of—**siempre, sólo cuando, nunca, todavía, todos los días, muchas veces** 195; **una vez, de vez en cuando, todo el tiempo, cada día, a menudo** 209

gender of nouns: 270
giving the date: **213**
gustar: to express likes and dislikes 43, 129, 149, 203; all present tense forms 274

hacer: 85, 248; all present tense forms **249,** 273; **hacer** with weather 216, 217; preterite 274
hay: 76, 236

-iendo: see present participle
imperatives: see commands
indefinite articles: **un, una 66, 68,** 270; **unos, unas 68,** 270
indirect object pronouns: see pronouns
infinitives: **86**
informal commands: see commands
interrogatives: see question words
-ir verbs: see verbs
ir: all forms **172,** 273; preterite 274
irregular verbs: see verbs

jugar: all present tense forms 273

la: see definite articles, see pronouns
las, los: see definite articles
le, les: see pronouns, indirect object
lo, la: see pronouns, direct object

más ... que: see comparisons
me: see pronouns, indirect object

GRAMMAR INDEX

CREDITS

PHOTOGRAPHY

Abbreviations used: (t) top, (b) bottom, (c) center, (l) left, (r) right, (i) inset, (bkgd) background. All other locations are noted as "other".

All pre-Columbian symbols by EclectiCollections/HRW.

All photos by Marty Granger/Edge Video Productions/HRW except:

FRONT COVER: (bl), Townsend P. Dickinson/Comstock; (br), Dallas and John Heaton/Westlight; (bkgd), © Robert Fried; (c), Joe Viesti/Viesti Associates, Inc.

TABLE OF CONTENTS: Page vii (r), Andrea Booher/Tony Stone Images; viii (tl), Sam Dudgeon/HRW Photo; ix (tr), David Phillips/HRW Photo; (br), Christine Galida/HRW Photo; xi (br), Sam Dudgeon/HRW Photo; xii (tr), David Young-Wolff/PhotoEdit; (br), Sam Dudgeon/HRW Photo; xiii (tr), Bachmann/ProFiles West, Inc.; (bl), Daniel J. Schaefer; xv (tr), S. Howell/Gamma Liaison; xvi (bl), Linc Cornell/Stock Boston, Inc.

PRELIMINARY CHAPTER: Page 2 (cl), Superstock; (bl), Index Stock Photography; 3 (br), Sam Dudgeon/HRW Photo; 4 (tr), AP/Wide World Photos; (cl), Culver Pictures, Inc.; (cr), HRW/File Photo; (bl), Bettmann Archive; 5 (tl), Bettmann Archive; (cl), Viacom/Shooting Star; (cr), S. Howell/Gamma Liaison; (br), Simon Bruty/Allsport USA/PNI; 8 (other), (a), Digitalimagery®; (other), (b, ch, d, e, f, g, j, l, ll), Sam Dudgeon/HRW Photo; (other), (c), © 2003 PhotoDisc, Inc./HRW; (other), (h), Corbis Images; (other), (i), Animals Animals; (other), (k), © 2003 PhotoDisc, Inc./HRW; 9 (other), (m, n, ñ, p, s, t, u, v, x), Sam Dudgeon/HRW Photo; (other), (o), © 2003 PhotoDisc, Inc./HRW; (other), (q), Michael Fogden/Animals Animals; (other), (r), C. Prescott-Allen/Animals Animals; (other), (rr), Robert Maier/Animals Animals; (other), (w), Michelle Bridwell/Frontera Fotos; (other), (y), Superstock; (other), (z), Bob Pizaro/Comstock; 10 (tr); 11 (tr); 14 (t), Michelle Bridwell/Frontera Fotos.

LOCATION OPENER - SPAIN: Page 16–17 (bkgd), Macduff Everton; 18 (tr), Danilo Boschung/Leo de Wys; (c), David R. Frazier Photolibrary; (br), Zoom/Vandystadt/Allsport USA; 19 (tl), David R. Frazier Photolibrary (bc).

CHAPTER ONE: Page 20–21 (bkgd), Scott Van Osdol/HRW Photo; 21 (bl), Bill Bachmann/Photo Network/PNI; 28 (br), Christine Galida/HRW Photo; 32 (cr), John Langford/HRW Photo; 35 (b); 36 (other), (0, 2, 3, 4, 5, 6, 7, 8), Sam Dudgeon/HRW Photo; (other), (1, 9), Mavournea Hay/Frontera Fotos; (other), (10) Laurie O'Meara/Frontera Fotos; 39 (tr), John Lei/Stock Boston, Inc.; 43 (cl), Nathan Bilow/Allsport/PNI; (c), Roy Morsch/The Stock Market; (cr), Scarborough/Shooting Star; (bl), Superstock; (br), Peter Van Steen/HRW Photo; 46 (bl), David R. Frazier Photolibrary; (cr), Leif Skoogfors/Woodfin Camp; (br), Aaron Haupt/David R. Frazier Photolibrary; 47 (all), Sam Dudgeon/HRW Photo; 48 (tr), AP/Wide World Photos/Daniel Maurer; 55 (br), John Langford/HRW Photo; 57 (br), Aaron Haupt/David R. Frazier Photolibrary.

CHAPTER TWO: Page 58–59 (bkgd), Scott Van Osdol/HRW Photo; 59 (bl), John Langford/HRW Photo; 61 (tr), (other), (clock, 10:00, clock, 10:30) Sam Dudgeon/HRW Photo; 62 (tl), Michelle Bridwell/Frontera Fotos; (cr),

Sam Dudgeon/HRW Photo; 64 (cr), Michelle Bridwell/Frontera Fotos; 70 (all), M. L. Miller/Edge Video Productions/HRW; 71 (all), Christine Galida/HRW Photo; 72 (t), Michelle Bridwell/Frontera Fotos; 77 (c), John Langford/HRW Photo; 78 (tr); 79 (cl), (cr), Michelle Bridwell/Frontera Fotos; 80 (tl), (cr), (cl), (tr), Sam Dudgeon/HRW Photo; (bc), David Phillips/HRW Photo; (i), Stock Editions/HRW Photo; (br), John Langford/HRW Photo; (bl), Image Copyright © 2003 PhotoDisc, Inc./HRW; 84 (tl), Michelle Bridwell/Frontera Fotos; (tr), Sam Dudgeon/HRW Photo; 86 (tl), (tr), (cl), (cr), Michelle Bridwell/Frontera Fotos; 88 (all), © European Communities; 91 (bl), Stock Editions/HRW Photo; 91 (br), (cl), (cr); 92 (cl), Image Copyright © 2003 PhotoDisc, Inc./HRW; 94 (all), Michelle Bridwell/Frontera Fotos; 95 (c), John Langford/HRW Photo.

LOCATION OPENER - MEXICO: Page 98–99 (bkgd), Tony Stone Images; 100 (tr), Marie Ueda/Leo de Wys; (br), Jorge Nuñez/Latin Focus; 101 (tl), Tony Freeman/PhotoEdit; (b), Melinda Berge/Bruce Coleman, Inc.

CHAPTER THREE: Page 102–103 (bkgd), Scott Van Osdol/HRW Photo; 102 (b), Jeff Greenberg/PhotoEdit; 104 (br); 108 (cr), Michelle Bridwell/Frontera Fotos; 112 (all), Peter Van Steen/HRW Photo; 114 (cl), © Robert Fried; (c), Robert Brenner/PhotoEdit; (cr), Michelle Bridwell/Frontera Fotos; (bl), (br), Christine Galida/HRW Photo; (bc), Michelle Bridwell/PhotoEdit; 115 (tr), Robert Brenner/PhotoEdit; 119 (cl), Michelle Bridwell/HRW Photo; (c), David Phillips/HRW Photo/HBJ; (cr), Russel Dian/HRW Photo; 120 (tl), (tc), (tr), (cl), Sam Dudgeon/HRW Photo; (c), Michelle Bridwell/HRW Photo; (cr), Image Copyright © 2003 PhotoDisc, Inc./HRW; 128 (c), Michelle Bridwell/Frontera Fotos; 131 (i), Sam Dudgeon/HRW Photo; 135 (br), Stuart Cohen/Comstock; 136–137 (b); 137 (all), Image Copyright © 2003 PhotoDisc, Inc./HRW; 140 (t), Peter Van Steen/HRW Photo; (other), (Yolanda) Michelle Bridwell/Frontera Fotos; (other), (Gabriela) Kent Vinyard/ProFiles West, Inc.; 141 (tr), Image Copyright © 2003 PhotoDisc., Inc./HRW; (c), Sam Dudgeon/HRW Photo.

CHAPTER FOUR: Page 142–143 (bkgd), Scott Van Osdol/HRW Photo; 142 (c), David Young-Wolff/PhotoEdit; 153 (tl), Robert Brenner/PhotoEdit; (tc), Lawrence Migdale/Stock Boston, Inc.; (tr), (cl), (cr), Michelle Bridwell/Frontera Fotos; 154 (tl), Chip & Rosa María de la Cueva Peterson; (tc), Index Stock Photography; (tr), (cr), Michelle Bridwell/Frontera Fotos; (cl), Bob Daemmrich; (other), (refresco, helado), Peter Van Steen/HRW Photo; 155 (cr), Sam Dudgeon/HRW Photo; 157 (tr), Ron Davis/Shooting Star; (br), Richard Hutchings/HRW Photo; 158 (t), Michelle Bridwell/Frontera Fotos; 174 (cr), Melanie Carr/Zephyr Pictures; 176 (tl), Paul Rodriguez/Latin Focus; (tr), Sam Dudgeon/HRW Photo; (cl), Latin Focus; (cr), Suzanne Murphy-Larronde; (br), David Simson/Stock Boston, Inc.; 177 (tl), AP Photo/Beth A. Keiser; (tc), AFP/CORBIS; (cl), AP Photo/Amy Sancetta; 178 (cl), Image Copyright © 2003 PhotoDisc, Inc./HRW.

LOCATION OPENER - FLORIDA: Page 184–185 (bkgd), Jim Schwabel/Southern Stock/PNI; 186 (tr), Tony Arruza; (b), Steve Ferry/P & F Communications; 187

(tl), Steve Ferry/P & F Communications; (cr), Latin Focus; (bl), David Phillips/HRW Photo.

CHAPTER FIVE: Page 188–189 (bkgd), Scott Van Osdol/HRW Photo; 189 (tr), Lisa Davis/HRW Photo; (bl), David Young-Wolff/PhotoEdit; 190 (all); 191 (all); 192 (all); 193 (bc); 194 (tl), M. L. Miller/Edge Video Productions/HRW; 196 (br), David R. Frazier Photolibrary; 197 (bl), (bc); 203 (all); 204 (all); 208 (tl), (tr), (cl), (c), Michelle Bridwell/Frontera Fotos; (tc), HRW/File Photo; (br), Stuart Cohen/Comstock; (cr), Sam Dudgeon/HRW Photo; 211 (c), David R. Frazier Photolibrary; 215 (tr), Steve Ferry/P & F Communications; 216 (other), (frío) Randy O'Rourke/The Stock Market; (other), (fresco) Leon Duque/Duque Múnera y Cia; (other), (nieva) Linc Cornell/Stock Boston, Inc.; (other), (llueve) Mary Kate Denny/PhotoEdit; (other), (viento) Michelle Bridwell/Frontera Fotos; (other), (calor) Peter Van Steen/HRW Photo; (other), (nublado) Weston Kemp/Bentley-Kemp Corp.; 220 (br), Robert Frerck/ Odyssey Productions; 221 (tr), Jack Kurtz/Impact Visuals/PNI; (bl), Index Stock Photography; 222 (cl), Image Copyright © 2003 PhotoDisc, Inc./HRW; 223 (t), Michelle Bridwell/Frontera Fotos; (br), (tr), Comstock; (b), David R. Frazier Photolibrary; 224 (tr), Superstock; (cl), David Young-Wolff/PhotoEdit; (c), Susan Van Etten/PhotoEdit; (cr), Michelle Bridwell/Frontera Fotos; 226 (all), Michelle Bridwell/Frontera Fotos.

CHAPTER SIX: Page 228–229 (bkgd), Scott Van Osdol/HRW Photo; 228 (c), Sam Dudgeon/HRW Photo; 235 (tl), (tr), Michelle Bridwell/Frontera Fotos; (cl), Bachmann/ProFiles West, Inc.; (cr), David Young-Wolff/ PhotoEdit; 237 (cr), Daniel J. Schaefer; 239 (br), Nik Wheeler/Westlight; 241 (bl), Image Copyright © 2003 PhotoDisc, Inc./HRW; 242 (t), Michelle Bridwell/ Frontera Fotos; 244 (br), Image Copyright © 2003 PhotoDisc, Inc./HRW; 245 (bl), (cr), M. L. Miller/Edge Video Productions/HRW; 249 (cl), (bl), Michelle Bridwell/Frontera Fotos; (cr), HRW/File Photo; (br), Robert Frerck/Woodfin Camp; 250 (c), *Billiken Almanaque 1997,* December 30, 1996, p. 34. Reprinted by permission of Editorial Atlántida S.A.; 251 (all), Sam Dudgeon/HRW Photo; 255 (all), Michelle Bridwell/HRW Photo; 265 (tr), John Langford/HRW Photo; 266 (all), Natasha Lane/HRW Photo.

ACKNOWLEDGMENTS

For text acknowledgments, see page ii.

ILLUSTRATIONS AND CARTOGRAPHY

Abbreviated as follows: (t) top; (b) bottom; (l) left; (r) right; (c) center. All art, unless otherwise noted, by Holt, Rinehart & Winston.

FRONT MATTER: Page viii, Elizabeth Brandt; xiii, Fian Arroyo/Dick Washington; xvii, MapQuest.com; xviii-xix, MapQuest.com; xx, MapQuest.com; xxi, MapQuest.com; xxii, MapQuest.com; xxiii, MapQuest.com.

PRELIMINARY CHAPTER: Page xxiv-1, MapQuest.com; 3, MapQuest.com; 4-5, Annette Cable/Claire Jett & Associates; 12, Deborah Haley Melmon/Sharon Morris Associates; 13 (tc), Boston Graphics; 13 (c), Eva Vagretti Cockrille; 15, Precision Graphics.

CHAPTER ONE: Page 17, MapQuest.com; 25, Boston Graphics; 27 (tl), Precision Graphics; 27 (br), Boston Graphics; 28, Edson Campos; 30, Boston Graphics; 31, Precision Graphics; 37, Manuel García/Richard Salzman; 40, MapQuest.com; 44, Eldon Doty/Pat Hackett; 45, Eldon Doty/Pat Hackett; 49, Fian Arroyo/Dick Washington; 50, Boston Graphics; 52, Eldon Doty/Pat Hackett; 55 (c), Boston Graphics; 57 (cr), Precision Graphics.

CHAPTER TWO: Page 65, Elizabeth Brandt; 66, Elizabeth Brandt; 67, Mauro Mistiano; 75, Antonio Castro/Cornell & McCarthy; 76, Boston Graphics; 79, Eldon Doty/Pat Hackett; 82, MapQuest.com; 85, Eldon Doty/Pat Hackett; 87, Elizabeth Brandt; 96, Eva Vagretti Cockrille; 97, Elizabeth Brandt.

CHAPTER THREE: Page 99, MapQuest.com; 109 (br), Boston Graphics; 109 (t), Deborah Haley Melmon/ Sharon Morris Associates; 113 (c), Michael Morrow; 116, MapQuest.com; 121, Holly Copper; 123, Meryl Henderson; 125, Elizabeth Brandt; 126, Holly Cooper; 129, Michael Morrow; 130, Holly Copper; 134, Precision Graphics; 135 (t), Michael Morrow; 138, Deborah Haley Melmon/Sharon Morris Associates; 141, Deborah Haley Melmon/Sharon Morris Associates.

CHAPTER FOUR: Page 146, Eva Vagretti Cockrille; 149, Edson Campos; 151, Ignacio Gomez/Carol Chislovsky Design, Inc.; 156, Boston Graphics; 159, Elizabeth Brandt; 161 (c), Ignacio Gomez/Carol Chislovsky Design, Inc.; 161 (b), Lori Osiecki; 163, Eva Vagretti Cockrille; 164 (t), Manuel García/Richard Salzman; 164 (b), Deborah Haley Melmon/Sharon Morris Associates; 167, Ignacio Gomez/Carol Chislovsky Design, Inc.; 168, MapQuest.com; 177, Michael Morrow; 181, Bethann Thornburgh/Lindgren & Smith; 182, Edson Campos; 183, Edson Campos.

CHAPTER FIVE: Page 185, MapQuest.com; 194, Edson Campos; 198 (tl), Edson Campos; 198 (br), Boston Graphics; 199, Edson Campos; 200, MapQuest.com; 204, Deborah Haley Melmon/Sharon Morris Associates; 206, Meryl Henderson; 209, Edson Campos; 212, Fian Arroyo/Dick Washington; 213, Edson Campos; 214, Bethann Thornburgh/Lindgren & Smith; 217, Precision Graphics; 218, Fian Arroyo/Dick Washington; 224, Precision Graphics; 225, Boston Graphics; 227, Edson Campos.

CHAPTER SIX: Page 236, Edson Campos; 238, Lori Osiecki; 241 (bl) Nishi Kumar; 241 (br), Fian Arroyo/ Dick Washington; 246, Meryl Henderson; 256, Ignacio Gomez/Carol Chislovsky Design; 257, Fian Arroyo/Dick Washington; 260, MapQuest.com; 267 (tc), Meryl Henderson; 267 (br), Ignacio Gomez/Carol Chislovsky Design, Inc.

BACK MATTER: Page 275 (tl, cl), Fian Arroyo/Dick Washington; 275 (bl), Elizabeth Brandt; 275 (cr), Eva Vagretti Cockrille; 276 (tl), Lori Osiecki; 276 (cl), Lori Osiecki; 276 (tr), Edson Campos; 276 (cr), Meryl Henderson; 276 (br), Elizabeth Brandt.